S0-CKW-764

FIVE HUNDRED
DELINQUENT WOMEN

by

SHELDON AND ELEANOR T. GLUECK

With an Introduction by
ROSCOE POUND

19 34

NEW YORK · ALFRED · A · KNOPF

364.973
G567fi

COPYRIGHT 1934 BY ALFRED A. KNOPF, INC.

All rights reserved. No part of this book may be reproduced in any form without permission in writing from the publisher, except by a reviewer who may quote brief passages in a review to be printed in a magazine or newspaper.

FIRST EDITION

MANUFACTURED IN THE UNITED STATES
OF AMERICA

53232

TO

JESSIE D. HODDER

Who, in a lifetime of devoted service, transmuted a prison into a reformatory and in the process builded herself into the hearts and minds of many erstwhile delinquent women

INTRODUCTION

BY ROSCOE POUND

Few things are more difficult than to turn a current of human thought out of a channel in which it had first begun to flow. Men began to think seriously about the treatment of offenders in a rationalist and humanitarian era. It was an era in which the rational was taken to be the real, and hence men felt that they need not trouble themselves to do more than exert their reasons upon social and political and legal problems. It was confidently assumed that what reason pointed out as what ought to be would maintain itself in action in government and in law by virtue of its inherent reasonableness. Maine has pointed out in another connection that " there was always a close association between the law of nature and humanity." The ideal law, based on reason, was always humane. So it was in the present connection. Reason revolted from the crudities and barbarities of a régime of punitive justice substituted for organized and orderly public vengeance. The humanitarian ideas of the eighteenth century gave direction to this revolt, and dictated our classical theories of crime and of penal treatment. At the end of the nineteenth century, and in the present century, came social utilitarianism, a movement to direct penal treatment consciously toward social ends, and later the movement for individualization of penal treatment, a phase of a general movement for individualization in every direction of governmental and legal activity. Unhappily, these movements found men thinking in the channels of rationalism and humanitarianism, in which the stream of thought had first flowed. In consequence we have had a rationalist and humanitarian social utilitarianism and a rationalist and humanitarian individualization which have contributed to make our most modern devices in penal treatment much less effective than we had confidently hoped. If the criminal and penal science of the latter part of the nineteenth century and of the first decade of the twentieth century were positivist, theirs was a rationalist and humanitarian positivism.

It was unfortunate, also, that social utilitarianism and a movement for individualization in penal treatment took form before psychology, psychiatry, sociology, and organized social work had so far developed as to afford a better basis for traditional rationalism. All social utilitarianism has been affected (or infected) by the presupposition that social advantage is something given, or at least is something which reason may discover by a mere scrutiny of the phenomena of social life as the observer looks about him. Social utilitarian criminal and penal science have been particularly affected because there was no other criterion of the social effects of penal legislation and administration and of modes of penal treatment available except reasoning as to what rationally must be. Much of this reasoning was affected by humanitarian ideas which went along with rationalism. Today psychologist and psychiatrist and sociologist and social worker may tell us much of what we may and may not hope to achieve and much of the difficulties to be reckoned with and the factors which make for good or bad results. But the institutions had been set up or had taken form without such help.

Nor must we overlook two other circumstances which have affected the working of the agencies of penal treatment which Americans were pioneers in setting up. One of these is the rapid growth of large metropolitan areas in the present century, and the consequent unforeseen burden upon reformatory institutions. When our institutions were formative, crime and criminal were largely local. It was possible to appraise the work of a reformatory because the man who went in and the man who came out were known or to be known in the locality of the crime and were easily observed by those interested instead of being lost in a land of great distances and manifold and inexpensive means of transportation. Again, the agencies of reformation and of individualized penal treatment call for developed personal, developed administrative methods, and scientific administrative technique. But administration is the weak point in our polity. We are traditionally suspicious of it, and we have been having to learn how to administer at the very time when the burden upon penal administration had become well-nigh overwhelming.

Of late there has been much popular dissatisfaction with the institutions of individualized penal treatment from which we expected so much a generation ago. There is danger that unless the causes of unsatisfactory operation are made clear, unless it is brought home to the public that the fault is not inherent in these institutions nor in their aims and purposes, general irritation at the ineffectiveness of our system of punitive justice will lead to the undoing of much of the progress made in the past two generations and a return to methods even more futile than those men are now criticizing.

Professor and Mrs. Glueck, in a series of books of which the present volume is the third, have been showing us how things actually work in penal administration, not simply by way of criticism, but more especially in order to lead us to perceive why they work as they do, and how they are to be made to work better. For example, it is enlightening to have revealed to us what reformatory institutions have to contend with. Bad inheritance, bad bringing up, bad economic and physical and psychological conditions have unfitted many who are turned into a world organized on a basis of competitive struggle to find places for themselves. Reformation in such cases is an undoing of the results of a long process. It is nothing less than a remaking of one "whom the world made crooked." We have much more here than what rationalism saw — one who having the choice of right and wrong chose to go wrong and was to be taught to go right. We have much more than what social utilitarianism has seen — a conscious directing of penal treatment to a social end of rehabilitating certain human assets of society. Very likely we must not expect to achieve any notable percentage of success with the material which this study reveals. Certainly we must marvel if any success is achieved when the average time in the reformatory is but a year and a half. Yet the lesson of this study and of two which have preceded it is not at all that we are to despair of our reformatory institutions. Rather we must learn what to expect of them and what not, whom to send to them, and how to administer them. We must not think of them as penal panaceas, but rather as wise creations of American inventive genius to be used intelligently as part of a scientifically organized and scientifically administered system of individualized treatment of offenders.

Toward these ends Professor and Mrs. Glueck give us an insight into the factors in the reformations which have been achieved. When we see the part played respectively by native and acquired endowment, by provision of suitable individualized treatment, and by chance circumstances after the return to the community, we are on the way to commit more intelligently, to administer more scientifically, and to follow up the penal treatment on a surer basis.

What is most promising, however, this study confirms what had seemed to be shown by the prior studies: namely, that it is possible to determine the form of penal treatment most likely to prove efficacious in an individual case, and hence to do with a reasonable degree of objectivity and certainty of result what had been done for the most part blunderingly or perfunctorily. Judicial discretion in sentences did not excite much criticism when the local judge sentenced the local offender in the small town or rural community of our formative era. With the rise of statutory offences involving much divergence of opinion as to their intrinsic seriousness, its defects in action became apparent. But the system of hard and fast prescribed punishments proved to have quite as serious defects, and neither wide discretion nor hard and fast prescribed penal treatment proved equal to the task imposed by large criminal dockets and offenders unknown to judge or prosecutor, often passing through the courts of many successive jurisdictions, none of which had knowledge of or access to the others' records, and with insufficient means of obtaining any adequate picture of the individual offender with whom the tribunal or magistrate was dealing. Rule-of-thumb methods applied perfunctorily, or else drastic or lax sentences, according to the personality or mood of the judge, or the public temper of the moment, and like methods on the part of administrative agencies whose discretion was substituted in whole or in part for that of the judge, brought discredit on all administrative individualization. Yet there must be such individualization, for we are dealing with human beings and human conduct.

Professor and Mrs. Glueck are showing us that we may do what the rationalist and humanitarian penal science sought to do, if not for all cases, yet for more than enough to make the effort worth while, and that we may hope for as high a proportion of success in our endeavour, by scientifically demonstrated formulas and tested conceptions, as we are able to reach in any of the practical activities of life.

It remains to say that the present study is the first of a series projected under the auspices of the Institute of Criminal Law of the Harvard Law School.

ROSCOE POUND

Harvard Law School
7th June 1934

PREFACE

It is always pleasant to write a preface. Therein one reviews the generous assistance of friends and colleagues without whose encouragement the task of writing a book would have been much more difficult and the work itself much less inspired.

In dedicating this work to Mrs. Jessie D. Hodder, the late superintendent of the Massachusetts Reformatory for Women, the authors do so with a feeling of sincere admiration for her as a pioneer in the institutional treatment of delinquent women. It is their deep regret that Mrs. Hodder, because of her long illness and untimely death, was not able to participate as much as they had hoped in the planning and execution of this research. It was through her insistence that some evaluation of her years of effort was undertaken, to be carried out along lines similar to the authors' investigation into the careers of ex-inmates of the Massachusetts Reformatory for Men.[1]

This is the first volume to be published in the series which the members of the Institute of Criminal Law of the Harvard Law School hope to contribute in the fields of criminal law and criminology. We wish to thank Professor Francis B. Sayre, who recently resigned his Directorship of the Institute to become Assistant Secretary of State, and Dean Roscoe Pound, for their encouragement to research of this nature.

Funds for the present work were provided by the Bureau of Social Hygiene at the request of the Institute of Criminal Law. We take this opportunity to thank Mr. Lawrence B. Dunham and the members of the staff of the Bureau of Social Hygiene for their generosity, their unfailing confidence in the enterprise, and the spirit of friendliness which has characterized our association with them during the four years in which this work has been in process.

We are indebted to Dr. A. Warren Stearns, formerly Commissioner of Correction of Massachusetts, for granting permission to utilize the case records on which this work is based.

We owe a debt of gratitude not only to Mrs. Hodder but to the members of her staff at the Women's Reformatory, who have cheerfully lent us every assistance, particularly Miss Barbara W. Sanborn, Mrs. Tess L. McKernon, and Miss Florence B. Lathrop. If not for the exceptionally thorough case-history work of Miss Sanborn at the Reformatory during the years when the women studied in this research were in that institution, our task would have been much more burdensome than it turned out to be.

[1] *500 Criminal Careers*. New York: Alfred A. Knopf; 1930.

xi

Our thanks are due also to the officers of the Massachusetts Parole Department for their willing co-operation.

We are ever grateful to the Department of Correction, to the Board of Probation of Massachusetts, the Finger Print Bureau of the Department of Public Safety, the Massachusetts Department of Mental Diseases, the Massachusetts Department of Public Welfare, and the Boston Social Service Exchange, for their continuous assistance in our researches. In Appendix A, " Method of this Research," is a full account of the agencies and individuals who contributed materials to this study. To the hundreds of public and private social agencies, to police departments, probation bureaus, courts, and individuals throughout Massachusetts and in other parts of the country, without whose unflagging assistance certain of the materials of this study could not possibly have been gathered, we owe much. Although they must remain unnamed, we take this opportunity to acknowledge our obligation to them.

Our thanks are due to Professor Ernest A. Hooton of the Department of Anthropology of Harvard University, and his staff, to whom we have learned to go for sound advice on statistical problems, and to Professor Edmund M. Morgan for making constructive criticism of the last chapter of the book.

To our valued friend Dr. Richard C. Cabot, who has followed our work with such interest and who has given us unbroken encouragement and much valuable criticism, we cannot be too grateful. To him, to Miss Barbara Sanborn and Mr. Frank Loveland, Jr., as well as to the members of our staff, all of whom have read portions of this work, we are indebted for constructive suggestions.

Of the five hundred former inmates of the Reformatory and the members of their families who so generously responded to our personal and written inquiries we can only say that they rarely failed to comprehend the reason for our investigations and to treat us with genuine courtesy. The layman cannot possibly realize what this means. Here are many hundreds of persons upon whom we had no official claim and most of whom were eager to cut off any connection with their past, who none the less were made to understand, by our two very skilful field investigators, the meaning of a scientific endeavour.

And, lastly, to the members of our staff, Mr. Samuel C. Lawrence and Mrs. Mildred P. Cunningham, both of whom have been associated with us since we began our follow-up studies in 1925, and as always gave untiringly of themselves to the intricate task of field investigation as well as to other phases of the research; and to the three secretaries who at one stage or another participated so intelligently and enthusiastically in the work, Mrs. Helen Boyd, Mrs. Miriam B. Sachs, and Mrs. Laura Reitmayer; and to Mrs. Edith Miller, who gave us much time as a volunteer in the statistical computations, our deepest appreciation is due. Their unselfish collaboration and loyalty are not the least of the compensations we derived from the enterprise.

Sheldon and Eleanor Glueck

Harvard Law School
July 1934

CONTENTS

INTRODUCTION BY ROSCOE POUND

PREFACE

PART ONE. THE GRIST OF THE MILL

CHAPTER I. INTRODUCTION

Introductory. — Professional study and classification of offenders. — Improvement in the health of inmates. — Improvement of the Reformatory's industrial program. — Improvement of the educational program. — Provision of adequate equipment. — Need for extending the indeterminate sentence. — Conclusion

CHAPTER II. A GALLERY OF WOMEN

Marie — a victim of circumstance. — Alice — a professional criminal. — Grace — the black sheep. — Florence — a drug addict. — Annie — an adulteress. — Fleur — a professional prostitute. — Margaret — a " stubborn child." — Angelina — a psychotic. — Minnie — " everybody's woman." — Dora — a chronic drunkard. — Louisa — a murderess

CHAPTER III. FAMILY BACKGROUND OF DELINQUENT WOMEN

CHAPTER IV. CHILDHOOD AND ADOLESCENCE OF DELINQUENT WOMEN

CHAPTER V. SEXUAL AND MARITAL LIFE

page 92

CHAPTER VI. LEGAL ENTANGLEMENTS

CHAPTER IX. A GALLERY OF WOMEN (continued)

CHAPTER X. IN THE REFORMATORY

CHAPTER XI. ON PAROLE

CHAPTER XII. AFTER EXPIRATION OF SENTENCE

CHAPTER XIII. AFTER EXPIRATION OF SENTENCE
(continued)

CHAPTER XIV. BEHAVIOUR TRENDS

PART THREE. AN AUDIT OF THE SITUATION

CHAPTER XV. EFFECT OF REFORMATORY EXPERIENCE

CHAPTER XVI. OTHER REFORMATIVE INFLUENCES

CHAPTER XVII. PREDICTING RECIDIVISM AND APPROPRIATE TREATMENT

CHAPTER XVIII. SUMMARY, CONCLUSIONS, AND RECOMMENDATIONS

APPENDICES
APPENDIX A. METHOD OF THIS RESEARCH

PART ONE

THE GRIST OF THE MILL

CHAPTER I

INTRODUCTION

1. Status of Knowledge about Delinquent Women

No students of crime have been as prolific in their writings as the American. The books, pamphlets, and periodicals from their hands have run into the thousands, and a major fraction of these contributions has been made during the past decade. Yet in all this welter of literature on crime and punishment there are few publications that give a detailed description of the characteristics and background of delinquent women, or trace their careers both before and after they have been subjected to the penal restraints and corrective blandishments of a society eager "to do something about this crime problem," yet halting and confused in its policies and practices.[1]

There has long been a need for a detailed survey of the background and traits of delinquent and criminal women, of the peno-correctional treatment to which such offenders are subjected, and of the practical results of such treatment in terms of reform or recidivism. There has also been a genuine need for a searching inquiry into the response of various classes of offenders to the different types of peno-correctional treatment actually provided by society.

In this book we have attempted to meet some of these needs.

2. The Size of the Problem

It is generally known that women delinquents form only a fraction of all offenders, whether imprisonments, convictions, arrests, or crimes reported to the police are used as an index of criminality. The total number of admissions to state and federal prisons and reformatories in the Census Area during 1930 (the latest report available at the present writing) was 78,866, of which only

---

[1] Particular attention should be directed to the studies of Anne T. Bingham: "Determinants of Sex Delinquency in Adolescent Girls," *Journal of Criminal Law and Criminology*, Vol. XIII (1923), pp. 494 et seq.; Mabel R. Fernald, Mary H. S. Hayes, and Almena Dawley: *A Study of Women Delinquents in New York State*, Bureau of Social Hygiene, 1920; Mabel A. Elliott: *Correctional Education and the Delinquent Girl — A Follow-up Study of One Hundred and Ten Sleighton Farm Girls*, Harrisburg, Pennsylvania, 1928 (in which the "field material" was gathered by a "house mother" and "parole officer" of the institution whose product was investigated). For a bibliography on the general subject of American reformatories for women, see *Reformatories for Women in the United States*, by Eugenia C. Lekkerkerker, Groningen, 1931.

3,522 (4.5%) were females.[2] Of course this number, and probably also this proportion, is much lower than the actual number and proportion of female offenders committed to various jails and houses of correction. From the nature of their offences, as well as their sex, female offenders are disproportionately committed to short-term institutions instead of to prisons and reformatories. That the number of women incarcerated for crimes is not a negligible one is shown by the fact, for example, that in 1930 in Massachusetts alone, 609 women were sentenced to jails and houses of correction, in addition to the women sentenced to the Reformatory. When the number of women offenders disposed of by commitment to girls' training schools, fines, probation, and other methods is added, the extent of officially recognized female criminality, though well below that of male, begins to assume serious proportions.

The problem is not merely one of institutional treatment, however. In 1930, for example, 3,150 women were *released* from penal and correctional institutions reporting to the Census.[3] Of this number, 1,142 (36.3%) were discharged on expiration of sentence, 1,538 (48.8%) were paroled, 19 (.6%) were released as the result of pardon, and 451 (14.3%) were otherwise released.[4] Hence the important problem of parole methods, as well as of institutional treatment, is involved in any consideration of female criminality.

Despite the fact that there are substantially fewer female than male offenders in penal and correctional institutions and under parole oversight, they bulk large in any statement of the weighty problems of social policy and social engineering dealt with by penologists. The more progressive correctional institutions for women have served as experiment stations in testing various correctional practices which many penal institutions for men might, with appropriate modification, profitably take over.[5] However, not all of the institutions for women offenders are of this nature. In some penal institutions, correctional farms, and training schools both male and female prisoners are housed and varying degrees of classification are applied to them. There are some separate correctional and reformatory institutions for women which, regardless of their names, are essentially prisons in both spirit and régime.[6]

[2] *Prisoners in State and Federal Prisons and Reformatories 1929 and 1930*, U. S. Department of Commerce, Bureau of the Census, p. 2.

[3] This total excludes 118 women who died before release as well as those who escaped.

[4] *Prisoners*, etc., op. cit., p. 38. " Otherwise released " includes " released by order of court, commutation of sentence, furlough, payment of fine, by being turned over to Federal officials for deportation or to other State authorities to serve sentences for other offenses, and other methods of discharge." — Ibid.

[5] " These reformatories represent a marked advance in methods of caring for women prisoners. From many of them, particularly those of Massachusetts, New York, New Jersey, Pennsylvania, Connecticut and the Federal Reformatory, the institutions for men can learn valuable lessons." — P. W. Garrett and A. H. MacCormick: *Handbook of American Prisons and Reformatories* (1929), p. xxxiii.

[6] For a list of correctional institutions for women, see *State and National Correctional Institutions of the United States and Canada,* compiled by American Prison Association, 125 East 15th Street, New York, 1933. See also Lekkerkerker, op. cit.

3. What We Ought to Know about Delinquent Women

Who are delinquent women? From what soil do they spring? What are their physical, mental, and social characteristics? What are they like in childhood, in adolescence, and in adulthood? What occupations do they embark upon? Are they steady and reliable workers, or the reverse? What about their sexual experiences? Do they make good wives and mothers? How do they respond to the régime of a reformatory? How do they behave while under parole supervision in the community? How do their careers develop after official restraint has been removed? What proportion of them reform and settle down to at least a law-abiding, if not a constructive life? Is it possible to predict what will happen to various types of delinquents as a result of different forms of treatment? These are some of the major questions we have set ourselves to answer in this study of five hundred delinquent women sentenced by the Massachusetts courts to the Reformatory for Women and released sufficiently long ago to permit of a reliable check-up of their post-institutional experiences.[7]

4. Traditional Attacks on the Crime Problem

The early proponents of reformatories, of the indeterminate sentence, of parole, probation, and other penologic reforms which have had so considerable a vogue in the American scene knew little about the human beings for whose " reform " they were urging these departures in traditional punitive methods. They were swept along on that current of noble humanitarianism that can be traced to the Rousseaus, the Voltaires, the Montesquieus and the Beccarias of the latter part of the eighteenth and early nineteenth centuries. Their knowledge of the characteristics of criminals and of the results of punishment was little less impressionistic and sketchy than that of the speculative masters from whom they drew their inspiration. To be sure, the American reformers of penal practices were also influenced by the work of the Italian criminalist Lombroso, who was the first to make a systematic study of prisoners from an anthropologic point of view. But this element of questionable scientific research at the basis of their reforms was undergoing criticism at the very time when the American reformers were agitating for correctional-educative institutions instead of prisons and for the indeterminate sentence and parole instead of fixed sentences.

Serious students of the crime problem can today no longer be satisfied with unsupported views or guesses as to the traits and background of criminals or with merely wishful thinking about the efficacy of correctional instruments. They are beginning to demand much more solid, systematic, and pertinent scientific research than has hitherto underlain criminal procedure, punitive and correctional institutions and practices. While they believe that an ethics of punishment (or of correction) is one of the needs of a rational program for coping

[7] See Appendix A, " Method of this Research," for details regarding selection of cases.

with crime, they also insist that scientific knowledge of human psychology and response to various forms of control, as well as of the social culture-medium of conduct and misconduct, is indispensable to an effective penology. The modern program for coping with crime can no longer be spun from outworn superstitions regarding human nature, or from guesses as to the efficiency of various types of punishment, or from rationalizations of the revenge motif so deeply rooted in man's attitude to man. A new partnership between ethics and science is called for, and both parties must adhere as fully, honestly, and accurately as possible to the terms of the agreement.

The scientific partner to this modern attack upon crime cannot shirk the tremendous tasks that lie before him, tasks which, to be sure, can be attacked with but imperfect tools,[8] but which must nevertheless be coped with. He must systematically and as accurately as possible explore the problems of the make-up of offenders of different types and of the efficacy of various forms of prisons, reformatories, and such other correctional devices as parole and the indeterminate sentence.

We know of no practitioner in the field of penology who was more eager to subject her work to a critical audit than the late Mrs. Jessie D. Hodder, for some two decades the superintendent of the Massachusetts Reformatory for Women. A woman of sympathetic insight into the foibles of humanity, a person ever in search for the gold in the dross of the distorted and diseased women who for many years formed an unbroken procession in and out of her Reformatory, she was eager for an impartial appraisal of the efforts of herself and her staff on behalf of their charges.[9] In her 1922 report Mrs. Hodder called for a frank exploration of the work of the Reformatory. How many correctional administrators, even today, are as eager to have their efforts put to the test of so searching an audit as Mrs. Hodder proposed in the following remarkable passage?

"In 1927 the Reformatory will be fifty years old, and 12,000 women will have passed through its doors. What has become of them, their children, their grandchildren? Was the experience here but an episode on life's way overcome later by stronger currents? Was the sentence here a 'knockout blow,' killing faith in self and thereby casting the individual on the social and economic scrap heap of life? How many took the experience lightheartedly and why? Because of a gay temperament; because they were cynical at being cast here when their rich companions were freed with a fine? In how many were the conduct manifestations which brought them here premonitory indications of insanity?

"Has the Reformatory done better for women prisoners or worse under its varying policies, and under which? For instance, during the period of short sentences or under the indeterminate sentence; and during the latter has the period in which the sentence was misinterpreted and parole arbitrarily fixed

8 See Jerome Michael and Mortimer J. Adler: *Crime, Law and Social Science*, New York, 1933.
9 See, for example, *Annual Report of the Commissioner of Correction, 1929*, p. 54.

at the minimum been better or worse for the subsequent welfare of the inmates than the present method, which waits, encourages, urges development before release, and is fearless to do what it believes is best for the individual woman? Can such factors be estimated? Have the varying industrial policies had any effect on the development of the inmates? We have passed from contract system to piece price and to state use. Under none have we given the inmates a wage. Which policy offers the best approach for trade training and good wage earning on release? Have we considered these points in establishing our equipment? Can the Reformatory look itself in the face and say that it has honestly sought *first,* last and all the time, the greatest good of the inmates? Has it at any time lost its ideals in the belief that prisoners should make reparation, not only by loss of liberty but by 'hard labor'; that is, by industrial drudgery? Is the defence of its industrial policy sound? Can a reformatory have a sound developmental policy in view of its isolation from community life? How long should a reformatory cling conservatively to its brick and mortar alone as reform equipment? Should confinement within the institution be the only tool given a superintendent to use? Can a reformatory be projected into the community, and the neighborhood used as part of the equipment? In how far has fear of the prisoner held us from blazing the trail toward new methods and a new attitude? Is the prisoner herself ready to grasp new methods? Has something happened in the world that is making for closer kinship of which prisoners too are aware? Have the old methods of silence and fear given way before this holier impulse of kinship? Might different educational methods have prevented misconduct in many cases? Should any one be sent to a penal institution until every other known method of intelligent effort has been tried? Should the prison, being the most expensive institution of state government, be the least used? Has the moment come to break in on our persistent use of the prison as the *only* place to treat all offenders against the law? Shall we scrutinize law and its relation to conduct disorders and revamp the present relationship between the two? What manner of woman has been committed to the Reformatory for Women during these forty-five years? From what social, what economic strata did she come? How many who have been sent here were not criminals but problems of social maladjustment? Has the court process continued the same too long? How often has the court sentenced to a jail for the convenience of the sheriff's wife without regard to the needs of the woman? Is the development of the prisoner always the first consideration of the sentencing forces?

"We need honest answers to all of these questions." [10]

That questions such as these must be faced honestly, scientifically, and fearlessly there can be no doubt. To obtain reliable answers to all of them and the many others involved, however, would require the efforts of many trained investigators over a good many years. Unfortunately, Mrs. Hodder and her staff were too constantly occupied with the daily tasks of the Reformatory to make

[10] *Annual Report of the Commissioner of Correction, year ending November 30, 1922,* pp. 54-5.

any headway in utilizing the great stores of case-history materials developed in the institution for an audit of its effectiveness and a possible reorientation of its policies. This book reflects the beginning of such an attempt, though it deals with only part of the many significant queries of the preceding quotation.

5. Aims of the Women's Reformatory Movement

We are concerned in this study with the treatment of delinquent women in the Massachusetts Reformatory and their response to such treatment. It will therefore be helpful, at the outset, to describe the development and changing aims of the women's reformatory movement in general before turning to a consideration of the goals and philosophy of the Massachusetts institution in particular.

The latter part of the nineteenth century witnessed the growth of a great interest in improving the methods of coping with criminals. The various penologic experiments of certain English and Irish reformers, of which the chief features were the stressing of the educational-rehabilitative aim side by side with the vindictive-deterrent, the use of such devices as the "mark system," the passing of prisoners through several grades of lessening control on their road to complete freedom, the employment of some form of official supervision of ex-prisoners in the community for a brief time after their discharge from the institution, the indeterminate sentence, the payment of prison wages, the improvement of the penal régime proper by the introduction of educational programs, medical examinations, and the like [11] — these came to be more or less integrated in a few American jurisdictions as a basis for new correctional institutions of the Elmira Reformatory type. At the same time more immediate needs, like the classification of the conglomerate populace of penal institutions along primary lines of sex, age, and prior criminal record, also engaged the attention of American penal reformers in the last quarter of the past century.

As part of this latter movement, though not unaffected by the general wave of revolution in the underlying principles of penology, the states of Indiana and Massachusetts established so-called reformatories for women, the one in 1873, the other in 1877. An accurate account of the motivations behind these establishments is to be found in a report of Mrs. Hodder, who, though writing considerably after the event, correctly reconstructed the ideas that the founders had in mind:

> "The reformatory was founded in order that women law breakers need not be sent to jails or houses of correction, but might be treated in an institution whose entire purpose should be their development. The problem was not complex as its founders saw it: sin was the cause of crime and conversion the cure; there should be industrial training, school work and medical care

[11] For a brief analysis of these features, see S. and E. T. Glueck: *500 Criminal Careers*, Chapter II. See also E. Lekkerkerker, op. cit., Chapter V.

as assistance to the central purpose of religious conversion. These women, its founders argued, divide themselves into two groups: those who have sinned and are or may become sorry, and those who have sinned and prefer to continue to sin or have become hardened." [12]

Thus the chief aim was to remove women from prisons and jails, where association with men was not uncommon. The conception of the Massachusetts establishment as primarily a prison, a place for the chastisement of sinfulness on the part of vicious and deliberate wrongdoers, was embalmed in the original name of the institution: " Reformatory Prison for Women." Not until 1911, shortly after Mrs. Hodder took office, was the word " prison " stricken from the name, marking the advent of a régime with quite a different orientation.[13]

As more thought and discussion came to be devoted to penologic problems, the major aims and practices of the women's reformatories were modified in a direction today conceded to have marked a definite improvement over prior conditions.[14] In the Massachusetts Reformatory, despite the early recognition of the general lines of reform,[15] the major impetus to the transformation of the prison into an institution with reformative aims, based on a scientific as well as humanitarian approach, came from Mrs. Hodder, superintendent of the Reformatory from 1911 until her demise in 1931.[16] The history of this evolution is the story of the perseverance and vision of Mrs. Hodder, as the following account will demonstrate.

[12] *Third Annual Report of the Bureau of Prisons of Massachusetts, for the year 1918*, p. 63.

[13] Commenting on this change, which heralded the new régime, Mrs. Hodder said: " Those who saw their [the inmates'] joyous handclapping and heard the sobs that followed when the change was announced were convinced that the spirit which dictated it was none in advance of the thought of the women themselves. They too were wondering why they and theirs should forever bear the stain of prison and prisoners, and why the men implicated with them get a shorter sentence in a minor correctional institution, and why the people who make bad liquor and those who flaunt it in their faces should go free as respectable citizens while they are branded." — *Eleventh Annual Report of the Board of Prison Commissioners of Massachusetts for the year 1911*, p. 49.

[14] For the number of reformatories for women in the United States, their programs, etc., see E. Lekkerkerker, op. cit.

[15] In the 1928 report Mrs. Hodder enumerates the many constructive recommendations made by her predecessors as far back as the very beginning of the Reformatory: " The commissioners early recommended changes in existing laws to prevent the sentencing to the reformatory of the weakminded, the aged, and the nervously unstable, who were unsuited for reformatory training, and made it impossible to do proper work for those who needed it." Not only the removal of irreformable types from the institution, but classification of inmates within the Reformatory was recommended by the early superintendents. The " grade system," which, with modifications, is still in force, was instituted by the second superintendent as a means of internal classification on the basis of behaviour. An early law made possible the transfer of some of the " old rounders," the definitely insane, and those suffering from certain diseases to other institutions, though the extent of transfer was dependent on available facilities. The practice of placing out certain inmates of the Reformatory on indenture was resumed under an 1879 law, anticipating the institution of parole in 1903. Even research was spoken of as desirable in 1880, but was not started until Mrs. Hodder took office in 1911. — *Annual Report of the Commissioner of Correction, year ending November 30, 1928*, pp. 58–9.

[16] Mrs. Hodder was succeeded by Dr. Miriam Van Waters.

6. *The Aims of the Massachusetts Reformatory*

Introductory. A statement of Mrs. Hodder's program upon taking office will show with what a modern chart and compass she embarked on her voyage. Her first report (1911) contained her objectives, which may be summarized as follows:

1. That the Reformatory should be conceived of and equipped as a " clearinghouse as well as a penal institution ";
2. That the inmates should be studied " under a medical and psychological expert with investigation of heredity, environment, etc., together with psychoanalysis," [17] in addition to their routine activities in the institution.
3. That the progress of the women during parole should be studied with a view to " working out that provision of the indeterminate sentence."
4. That " careful and detailed records of each division " of the foregoing study should be maintained.[18]
5. That the training in the institution should embrace " vital needs," chief among which are physical upbuilding, " training for service in the home to which they may, sooner or later, return, and recreation."
6. That certain fundamental improvements in the physical establishment of the Reformatory should be brought about, among them the transformation of an old cell-block into a modern gymnasium, and the provision of cottages " with no walls." [19]

It will be seen that for the year 1911 these suggestions were well in the direction of progress. Some of them, such as the introduction of case histories, were instituted immediately; others she again and again urged upon a not too receptive legislature. We shall consider the story of her struggle for higher standards under the major topics of (a) professional examination and classification of types of offenders, (b) improvement of the health of the inmates, (c) improvement of the Reformatory's industrial program, (d) improvement of its educational program, (e) provision of adequate housing and equipment, (f) the need for extending the indeterminate sentence.

Professional study and classification of offenders. From the very beginning Mrs. Hodder recognized the need of medical, psychiatric, psychologic, and social examinations of each woman committed to her institution, and the keeping

[17] Mrs. Hodder, writing in 1911, probably meant the study of personality traits over a period sufficient to give more than purely surface descriptions, instead of psychoanalysis in the technical sense.

[18] It should be pointed out that these recommendations were originally motivated by the fact that the legislature had just established a department for " defective delinquents " to be housed at the Reformatory for Women. Though they referred essentially to such special type of offenders, it soon became evident that the recommendations as to a clearing-house and its technical equipment were applicable to all the inmates of the Reformatory and, later, to all women convicted in the courts.

[19] *Eleventh Annual Report of the Board of Prison Commissioners of Massachusetts, for the year 1911*, pp. 51–3.

of careful records of such investigations. In the 1913 report she stressed the need of developing the records, " making them valuable for the treatment of the women in the institution, for the general study of the criminal woman, and for the use of the Board of Parole, when release is being considered," by basing them on " investigations and studies of the social, hereditary, environmental and economic causes which may have led to a woman's break with society." [20]

In the 1914 report the superintendent presented a tentative classification of some of the inmates into three groups, based on a case-record system which she had previously recommended for noting the results of examinations by a well-known psychiatrist: [21] " Mental defectives of pronounced types without aberrational tendencies (undoubted defective delinquents); aberrational mental types with or without mental defect, who are very unstable and include the psychopathic group, often thought of as ' defective delinquents '; the recidivist group, who do not belong in either of the preceding classes but have proven their inability to live in society." [22] She conceived of the nature of a reformative institution in the following terms:

" We believe that the reformatory of to-day should be a laboratory of criminalistics. Having taken that step within the last two years in the direction of mental, physical and sociological studies, we need to be able to extend this research by testing given groups and their reactions under more nearly normal conditions of living, industry and education." [23]

This frequent call for the *testing* of various forms of treatment under differing situations is something that one rarely meets with among correctional workers.

In the 1915 report the relation of an intelligent system of classification to the problem of discipline is vividly illustrated:

" During the last winter a committee of the Legislature visited the reformatory after a psychopathic-epileptic inmate, a girl of twenty, had practically demolished a room, — furniture broken to bits, windowpanes shattered, plaster gouged out, door panels in kindling wood.

" The gentlemen of the committee were shown the room and then the girl, lying on the floor of a punishment room, unwilling to speak, scarcely nodding yes or no to questions. The committee recognized that there was something wrong about a system which housed reform types with abnormal types; something wrong with a system whose only alternative was punishment for a woman who demolished a room either because of an epileptic seizure, an hysterical attack, or hyperstimulation in a life unsuited to her overwrought nervous temperament; *i.e.,* a woman not essentially vicious, perhaps, or insane, but too unstable nervously to bear the strain of living at a pace set for normal people.

[20] *Thirteenth Anuual Report,* etc., p. 55.

[21] Dr. Edith R. Spaulding.

[22] *Fourteenth Annual Report,* etc., p. 43. Most of the remaining inmates are presumably fitted for reformatory treatment.   [23] Ibid., p. 45.

" Together with this actual practical illustration of the incompatibility of nervously and mentally unstable types living in the same building with normals, charts were shown which demonstrated that the prison plan of building is no longer suited to reform work for women.

" Reform institutions are no longer dealing only with the people who commit crimes because they are bad or vicious. There are stronger underlying causes than defiance of law and order." [24]

In support of her general argument the superintendent presented a table based on the mental classification of 500 women, in which 16% of them are found to be morons or imbeciles, many of the morons also being abnormal according to a psychiatric classification.[25] She gave it as her reasoned opinion that " psychopathic women are overstimulated by the normal, and so react to the detriment of both "; hence " no fair test of either can be made while they are kept together." The feeble-minded woman, if she " is inhibited by normal people and becomes their drudge . . . should be given her place in the sun, i.e., an institution within her focus, where she may contribute her mite." [26] Mrs. Hodder went so far as to experiment with the segregation of psychopathic women under special conditions in a separate part of the institution, but without making progress.[27]

Returning to the attack in the 1916 report, Mrs. Hodder again stresses the importance of special study and treatment of psychopathic inmates, among which are many who today might be diagnosed as psychoneurotic. " Our experience during the year . . . has strengthened our belief that the only hope in regard to women prisoners of this type is that a method of treatment may be worked out which shall define whether they are insane, whether they are normal but undisciplined, whether they belong in a custodial group as yet undefined." [28] It should be mentioned that, despite a number of interesting researches, insufficient progress has as yet been made in the surer definition and more effective treatment of this type of offender. It is a common complaint among correctional

[24] *Fifteenth Annual Report*, etc., pp. 51-2.

[25] Ibid., p. 52.

[26] Ibid., p. 54.

[27] " During the past year, in an effort to study the psychopathic women by themselves and to alleviate somewhat our own situation, we converted a small third-story set of rooms into a ' cottage.' The plan was to give these women gardening, housework, industrial training, school and play. The ' cottage ' was equipped so that baths and packs could be given. One of our psychopathic women, who had been in an insane hospital, became a helper. She was creative in making the rooms homelike and cheery. There were never more than five or six women at a time in the ' cottage,' and a nurse was in charge with two normal inmates as assistants. The plan failed. We believe it failed for much the same reason that these women fail in their community life, and also because separation could not be complete enough in any part of our building with its excellent acoustic properties. These women are egotistical and self-centered. Instead of keeping their nerves in the proper place as sources of energy and big purpose they wear them on the surface for every human quiver to bruise and sting. They boil up like a kettle of sugar and are over before they can be saved. They *will* occupy the center of the stage. Unhappily, with us they can always have an audience, awestruck often, and often imitative." — Ibid., pp. 52-3.

[28] *First Annual Report of the Bureau of Prisons of Massachusetts, for the year 1916*, p. 66.

administrators that psychopaths " bedevil the administration," interfering with educational, industrial, and other activities and requiring special disciplinary handling, which is all too ineffective.

That Mrs. Hodder saw beyond the merely local problems presented by certain classes of her inmates, to an important question of social policy in general, is indicated by the following passage from this same report: " Whatever the ulti- mate findings as to disposition may be, it is obvious that only by working out a method of treatment can society free itself from the sin of handling probably sick prisoners on a punishment basis." [29] This argument flows from ethical and humanitarian motives, and the more practical point might be added that indis- criminate handling of all sorts and conditions of offenders by one mechanically administered device or a few such devices is extremely wasteful and socially dangerous.

In her 1917 report the superintendent again stressed the need of classification of offenders before they are committed. She referred to the fact that of 240 women committed to the Reformatory in the past year only 106 (44.2%) were of the " type that reformatories were originally meant for, that is women of workable mentality, to be taken in morally sick and returned to the community morally well," the balance being either psychopathic or of defective mentality.[30] She related this finding to an analysis of the disciplinary records made two years previously, " when the institution seemed to be going through a conduct crisis," which proved that the " nervously unstable women form our disciplinary problem, that is, the women who do not legitimately belong to a reformatory population." [31] Of a total of 707 women admitted during the three years 1915-17, 113 (16%) were found to be psychopathic, and 17 (1.8%) epileptic; 374 (52.9%) belonged to the " defective delinquent or segregable group." [32]

Reviewing pertinent extracts from the reports of her predecessors, Mrs. Hodder, in her 1918 report, summarized the basic problem of classification and specialized treatment for different classes in the words of the superintendents who preceded her in office:

> " These superintendents speak of 'illiteracy,' 'inability to study,' 'vicious,' 'contaminating,' 'discharged from insane hospital and committed here,' 'not insane but willful,' 'irresponsible,' 'degenerate,' 'bordering on insanity,' — they do not use the terms feeble-minded, hysterical, psychopathic, epileptic, moron, borderline, because these terms were not known in prison work in their day. It is not difficult, however, to match up the description they give with the terms we use and to realize that the prison population offered the same complexities then as now." [33]

The problem of primary classification of various types of offenders is again the major concern in the 1919 report. Referring to the activities of the psycholo-

---

[29] Ibid. [30] *Second Annual Report of the Bureau of Prisons, for the year 1917*, p. 72.
[31] Ibid., pp. 72-3. [32] Ibid., p. 73. [33] *Third Annual Report, for the year 1918*, p. 65.

gist, Mrs. Hodder indicated that 48% of the inmates were found to be " intellectually defective," the majority of them of moron grade; and that 15% were found to be of " neurotic, inferior or psychopathic constitution." [34] She pointed out, however, that though so high a percentage of the inmates " must be classed as defectives on the intellectual side, only a relatively small percentage of them could be segregated on the basis of that defect alone. Neither is it true that the more defective are the less socially competent. The social histories of these girls show that under more favorable circumstances many of the dullest of the group might have made good in the community." [35]

In the 1920 report the superintendent indicated the relationship of classification to the type of treatment called for in the case of various types of offenders. The " old rounder," whose class had long formed a large fraction of the inmates, not being as a rule reformable, can be handled in a routine way: " She needs a place to rest from the ardors of summer hotel work and the autumnal cafés." The young offender, on the other hand, " is an adventuress in life; having started at the wrong end she will not turn back easily. She must be convinced. She wants expression — wants to stamp her ego on the universe." To her, " penance is boresome, to be good deadly dull. One girl says, ' I've been on the street four months — best business I know,' as she hands in a roll of $403. Stealing, says a young shoplifter, is the most thrilling thing. ' I'm crazy about it! ' A young homosexual takes herself seriously, and is sure that her interpretation of life is for every one." [36]

Again, Mrs. Hodder urged that it be kept in mind that the existing method of caring for delinquent women " is but a makeshift — that the population is a group of totally unrelated units bound together only by the common tie of acknowledged failure.[37] No one can treat stealing, fornication, adultery, murder, etc. The treatment should be based on the causes which have led a person to steal, commit adultery, murder, etc." [38]

We have already quoted the searching queries put by Mrs. Hodder in her 1922 report, calling for a thoroughgoing audit of the results of treatment and for a re-examination of the aims and methods of reformatories. In that report she made the following bold assertion, based on much experience:

> " Believing that the present penal system is all wrong we believe that research such as here planned, is the only means by which the system can be shaken to its foundations. Classification of prisoners on the basis of the type to which they belong is the keynote of the new penology, and is the next step which will give us a new and better prison system. True classification will take place after conviction and before commitment, so that the right person

---

[34] *Fourth Annual Report of the Bureau of Prisons, for the year 1919*, p. 63.
[35] Ibid., p. 64. Compare our findings and inferences, Chapter IX.
[36] Ibid., p. 69.
[37] The extent to which this is a correct appraisal will be inferred from Chapters II–VIII.
[38] Ibid., pp. 69–70.

can be sent to the right institution, namely, that one equipped to treat his basic defect with the maximum hope of cure." [39]

In line with the trend of progressive thought, she recommended the establishment of a clearing-house as a possible adjunct to the court:

"Let us approach the problem of the evil doer as science approaches its work, namely in the laboratory which would act as a clearing house as well. It could be under the court, or a new department of research might be established, to which every individual found guilty should be sent by the court for study and diagnosis, after which they would return to the court with the laboratory findings and recommendations, and thus the judge would only send to the penal and correctional institutions normal prisoners." [40]

Other types would be committed to appropriate specialized custodial and curative institutions.

In the 1923 report the superintendent claimed that in the past five years the Reformatory had "a more nearly reformable population, than at any other time during its history; *i.e.*, more young women whose adolescence and slow mental and moral growth have thrown them out of tune with the social and economic machinery of life." [41] She called for the publication of the results of the institution's analysis of thousands of case histories, and gave a descriptive analysis of recent admissions, concluding that defective home training plays a considerable role in their lives. The study "also by inference shows serious gaps in school life and training, and the need of the public schools to analyze their failures as a basis of modification of their policies toward backward, or forward, unruly children." [42]

In the 1925 report Mrs. Hodder asked for a resident psychologist to analyse the more complex personalities in the inmate population, particularly the more intelligent, psychopathic women, and for the services of a vocational expert "who can estimate what process it is, if any, which will bring this group to an interest in carrying its own share of the work of life." [43] She again urged the need of research into the histories of the women who had been inmates of the Reformatory (some thirteen thousand), in order to estimate the "worth of its service, and help us to outline the work it is to undertake in the years ahead." [44] This call for intensive research with a view to checking up on treatment and to improving practices is repeated in the 1926 report. [45]

The 1927 report is remarkable as giving some insight into the methods developed by the Reformatory, and the relationship of individualization to classi-

[39] *Annual Report, etc., 1922,* p. 54.
[40] Ibid., p. 57.
[41] *Annual Report of the Commissioner of Correction, year ending November 30, 1923,* p. 45.
[42] Ibid., p. 46.
[43] *Annual Report of the Commissioner of Correction, year ending November 30, 1925,* pp. 42–3.
[44] Ibid., p. 43.
[45] *Annual Report of the Commissioner of Correction, year ending November 30, 1926,* p. 42.

fication. The literature of penology in recent years is full of references to the magic term, " individualization of treatment." But what content has been poured into that phrase? In the 1927 report Mrs. Hodder gives a few illustrations, in response to a request made to her by a judge, who had " said it would help him in his talks with parents of our girls if we told . . . something of our scheme of treatment. The social significance of this request is remarkable." [46] And in truth it is so, when one considers that most judges have hardly taken the trouble even to visit, much less study, the penal and correctional institutions to which they daily commit offenders.

The superintendent begins with the underlying principles of modern reformative efforts: that they are " educational, based on a psychiatric knowledge of each inmate," and personal, keeping in view " the development of the individual." " The old thought that punishment will ' teach them a lesson ' is obsolete; instead we look upon each woman as a new and interesting problem which we must make every effort to understand and to solve." [47] Then follow a number of illustrations so important as reflecting the process of rehabilitation and obstacles in its way as to deserve extended quotation:

> " If we learn that her mother deserted her and her little sister when she was a baby; that she has been in an academy most of her life; has been eager to know her mother and suspicious of ' Aunt Jennie,' her father's housekeeper; and we note that she is not only jealous but has recently been seeing her mother secretly, who ' looks like me and is neither pretty nor ugly,' and who equally hates ' Aunt Jennie,' though the court *did* give the daughters to the father in granting the divorce, we have a clue to work on." [48]

> " When search shows the father to be a kindly person, a plodder, respected and devoted to his children, but bewildered by this youngest willful spitfire gone wild with a ' gang ' of her own age, 19, bent on imitating the gangs of toughs they read of in the papers, we have another clue to her problems. She boasts of her temper and what she might do under provocation. Her mother is living in immorality; the eldest sister has been as steady as the father and is happily married. A two-year indeterminate sentence on a charge of being an idle and disorderly person, with parole possibilities at eleven months, is the time allotted us to turn the trick and send her back to the community cured; back to the community which has in no way changed its ideals nor its standards, and to a family situation both ugly and ambiguous. . . . This girl we saw at our Christmas Masque moved to tears before the Christchild, absorbed and overwhelmed by the beauty of the scene in the manger. Her appreciation was one key to her soul; another was in her letter home telling of the educational advantages here and her determination to accept them to the full and to forget what she was here for." [49]

[46] *Annual Report of the Commissioner of Correction, year ending November 30, 1927*, p. 48.
[47] Ibid.   [49] Ibid.
[48] Ibid.

"A brilliant girl who lost caste in her group through a stupid marriage drifted and got into trouble. Her intelligence was so outstanding and her interest in learning so keen, that we focused on that and opened to her all the educational avenues of the university extension service, and the result has been remarkable." [50]

"I think of a girl of brilliant mentality, hypersexed, and unhappy because her family were foreigners. An inferiority complex based on ancestry can be countered by showing the historic significance of the race and its accomplishments, and how grateful America is for the beauty and racial richness every candidate for citizenship brings to her shores. In this way are aroused fundamental loyalties, those priceless stabilizers of human conduct. Given our present lack of understanding of sex we can suggest no career to a hypersexed individual that will not intensify her inferiority complexes; and though we tried education, we did not feel we succeeded with this girl who needed long supervision and friendship. Adolescence sees other uses, and questions sincerity when we offer it house work at $7 a week as a substitute. How can honest living be made more tempting than fast living, is the question! This is the problem that baffles, and we wonder if it is solved when shortly after release marriage announcements come in!" [51]

"A young girl of the street marries a young widower with one child. She has no standards of home making or care of children, and his mother's efforts to help add to her sense of inferiority. He drifts toward his mother and she toward the street. They are no longer compatible; yet, he has been tender toward her here, proud of her progress, tells with naive joy of the pretty clothes his mother is making for her. When she scorns them he tells her his mother is the best dressmaker in town, and does not understand when she prefers to buy ready-made clothes! She is to leave us soon. Failure faces them because he is not weaned from his mother, and she is not big enough to accept this defeat and live an ideal life without him. We have given her an excellent training in household arts and sewing, which she has learned, pathetically enough, in order to make clothes for his child. The value of the training lay in its adaptation to her home.

"In this, as in so many cases with our young women, we need a longer period than the two-year indeterminate sentence gives, because they need a new outlook on life and to establish new mechanisms to meet it. We hate to give them up and see the inevitable failure, but where the legal control is lacking we are helpless. Sometime the real indeterminate sentence will be passed and then the training will be adapted to a plan of graduation and diploma." [52]

Interspersed with these summaries of different types of personality and conduct problems met with in the Reformatory are flashes of Mrs. Hodder's credo and technique:

[50] Ibid.   [51] Ibid.   [52] Ibid., p. 50.

"Our approach . . . is first to gather all the facts, to study the girl's personality, her learning ability, and to search for the things she cares for deeply and the loyalties which thrill her heart." [53]

" There is no single trick which will make a bad person good, but helping a bewildered person to see straight goes a long way toward helping in the choice of a constructive course of conduct.

" The particular crime for which a person is committed is not important; it might have been any other, given the slipshod condition of her character. Building character is our job — a slow process and not easy to do after . . . years of bad habits. If you discover, however, that the individual is a slow-growing person, still a child in vision, emotions and understanding, education and helpful talks may open lines of thinking." [54]

" Our task is easy when the needs of the person are striking and clear. The community is organized for the development of the individual and we use its resources. Our difficulties come when a girl does not know herself and we are slow in finding a clue to her." [55]

These examples illustrate the fact that primary classification of offenders by the courts is not sufficient; in addition, classification within the Reformatory is necessary, and must be based on a thoroughgoing study of the individual case and a comparison of it with similar cases treated in the past.

Mrs. Hodder's unflagging interest in matters of classification and the fitting of treatment to the make-up and needs of various types of offenders is again reflected in the 1928 report. Speaking of the necessity of giving the institution reasonably reformable human beings, she complained that the Reformatory " carried a dead load of 42% feebleminded women who can never be reformed, who are heavy breeders, and who should be leading a life normal for them, in an institution for 'feebleminded women of child bearing age.'" [56] She stressed anew the need of knowing the facts about offenders and the results of their treatment, before planning for the future: " What development should the reformatory take in its next fifty years? In order to answer such a question fairly, the reformatory should know the results of its first fifty years' work: 12,593 women have gone through its doors. We need to know what has become of them; whether they took up life in an honest fashion, before we can gauge whether or not we are pursuing the right methods." [57]

The 1928 report concludes with the prediction that the future will see the establishment of a " receiving and clearing-house, where all prisoners will be studied first, and diagnosed before commitment; this clearing-house will be under a board of experts in medicine, psychiatry, psychology, penology and education, and not under the Department of Correction. The judge will re-

[53] Ibid., p. 48.   [54] Ibid., pp. 48–9.   [55] Ibid., p. 49.
[56] *Annual Report of the Commissioner of Correction, year ending November 30, 1928,* p. 59.
[57] Ibid.

mand the prisoner to this board for diagnosis. After a decision is reached as to the treatment needed, the court will order the person to the institution indicated." [58]

Again in the 1929 report is the call sounded for adequate original classification of offenders, so that the various types might be sent to appropriate institutions. Mrs. Hodder points out that the courts are as a rule not equipped with psychiatrists or others qualified to classify offenders before their distribution to the different curative, correctional, or punitive establishments; hence the Reformatory continues to receive all sorts and conditions of women, many of them utterly unsuited to its régime and interfering with its effectiveness in the proper cases. She speaks with enthusiasm of the prospective research into the results of reformatory treatment.[59] She again urges that the Reformatory be utilized as a clearing-house or " laboratory, not under the Department of Correction, to which those found guilty could be remanded for diagnosis and disposition. It is an unintelligent outlook that the mistakes of the last fifty years should be carried on into the next." [60]

The battle for original classification of offenders was resumed in the 1930 report. Mrs. Hodder earnestly urged the commitment elsewhere of types of offenders for whom the Reformatory has little to offer, leaving it free to concentrate upon the more promising women:

> " For instance, the Reformatory for Women, with which I have been familiar for twenty years, has carried during that period an average case load of 25% feebleminded women of the gentle type who are breeders, with 5% incorrigible feebleminded, and with about 3% disturbed psychopathic women. We believe very little good, if any, has been done for these women by their confinement here, and much harm has come to the community on their return. We further believe that their presence here has impeded work for the more nearly normal inmates. To effect real classification within the Reformatory is not possible. Classification is more than grading for school purposes; it aims at separation to prevent moral and spiritual contamination; it aims to build up an atmosphere of ideals and fitness for association with a view to growth of character." [61]

Speaking of the possible results of scientific primary classification of offenders, she insisted that " the uneducable group referred to as forming 33% of our population should have permanent custodial care. Given such care and removed from the community which is as great a menace to them as they are to it, they could be made happy and successful in a little community institution of their own. Devoted to arts and crafts, horticulture, and small industries, their lives could be ideal." [62]

[58] Ibid., p. 59.   [59] The present study.
[60] *Annual Report of the Commissioner of Correction, year ending November 30, 1929*, p. 54.
[61] *Annual Report of the Commissioner of Correction, year ending November 30, 1930*, p. 66.
[62] Ibid., p. 67. " Do not let us deceive ourselves into believing that the community in which

Once more she urged that the Reformatory should be used as a clearing-house and laboratory " to which every one found guilty is remanded for study, and after diagnosis, each is committed to the institution best equipped to treat her needs." [63]

This analysis of Mrs. Hodder's views and recommendations shows her to have been constantly alert to the changing thought in the field of penal theory and practice. She insisted from the first upon intelligent primary and secondary classification of offenders on the basis of thorough and comprehensive investigations into their individual careers. And she urged the incorporation into the system of criminal justice of a clearing-house adequately staffed and equipped to distribute offenders more in accordance with reality than at present.

Improvement in the health of inmates. Turning now to Mrs. Hodder's struggle to improve the health of her charges, we find her in 1913 urging the appointment of an oculist and a dentist and insisting upon tests and treatment for venereal diseases.[64] These fundamental needs have gradually been met. Again and again she requested the legislature to make provision for a gymnasium both for health and for educative purposes. In the 1920 report, particularly, the importance of meeting the need of corrective gymnastics is emphasized.[65] The 1926 report records the activities of a specially trained director of physical education appointed when, after much urging, an old cell-block was transformed into a well-equipped gymnasium:

> " The custom of the department has been to require two hours a week in supervised exercise of some description for every inmate who is found, upon examination (medical, physical and orthopedic) to be able to undertake the work. Every woman must be examined before taking part in any of the department work, and it is suggested that each individual be re-examined every six or nine months in order to keep a record of any changes in her condition, whether for better or for worse. Every woman who has taken any work in the department should be re-examined before she leaves the institution, either on parole or expiration. I would suggest that a study of comparison be made yearly from these records in order to ascertain the effects that the work is having on the physical condition of the women." [66]

Improvement of the Reformatory's industrial program. One of the greatest difficulties with which a reformative institution is faced is the question of an effective balance between the income-producing and the vocational-training aspects of its industrial activities. From the beginning Mrs. Hodder was in-

---

we live is the only place where happiness is possible. The wear and tear of sinning and reforming is a great strain; one or the other should be taken out of the life of an irresponsible person." — Ibid.

[63] Ibid.   [64] *Thirteenth Annual Report*, etc., p. 53.   [65] Op. cit., p. 69.

[66] *Annual Report of the Commissioner of Correction, year ending November 30, 1926*, p. 51. About a fourth of the inmates were found physically unfit to do any gymnasium work.

clined to stress the Reformatory's role as a builder of character over and above its task of adding to the state's treasury through excessive industrial activity. In the 1913 report she stated her purpose " to develop vocational training for the women, making of our industries trade-training classes with commercial factory standards in speed and efficiency," but not neglecting classes in the domestic arts.[67] She long sought to get the authorities to consent to her devoting only half-days to the productive industries, so that the balance of the time might be used for educative and recreational work. She insisted that intensive activity in the industries for half a day would not materially reduce the amount of productivity, since added stimulus would be given to the work by the realization of the inmates that a substantial part of their time would be spent in activities for self-improvement. The plan would have the dual advantage of training the inmates to work at the standards of speed and efficiency they would meet in jobs on the outside and releasing time for the educative and character-building program. In the 1929 report she spoke enthusiastically of the results of this experiment, which was finally permitted. It was demonstrated that " one half day stiff industrial work and one half day academic education, is not only feasible but creates a more stimulating day. Greater industrial and educational effort is immediately noticeable among the inmates. . . . The terrible curse of the prison is the poison of serving time. Time is too precious to be ' served ' — it must be ' used,' every minute of it, to some worthy end, a lesson offenders against the law need to learn. Since industrial output is as high with one half day used for gymnasium and other educational activities, it leaves the evening free to prepare lessons for the next day, and to do personal reading." [68]

Improvement of the educational program. A chief aim of the superintendent of the Reformatory for Women was to integrate the various activities which had an educational aspect. On a number of occasions she presented her educational philosophy and program. Thus the 1919 report contains the following plan of education and therapy, based on a survey of the mentality of the inmates:

" Industries (including farm industries), taught in the beginning from the educator's point of view, educational occupation, therapeutic occupation, school subjects, gymnaso-therapy, hydrotherapy, psychotherapy, sociotherapy, — the attempt to straighten out family and similar problems that may be causing unrest or unhappiness. At the Reformatory this is provided for in the Research Department. Recreation, apart from that obtained in educational and therapeutic occupations and in the gymnasium. Discipline." [69]

Again, in the 1923 report Mrs. Hodder alluded to the complexity of the educational program, particularly in the all too artificial setting of a correctional

[67] Op. cit., p. 53.
[68] *Annual Report of the Commissioner of Correction, year ending November 30, 1929*, p. 55.
[69] *Fourth Annual Report of the Bureau of Prisons, for the year 1919*, p. 65.

institution. Recognizing the tendency of a reformatory to become routinized, she speaks of the staff's efforts " toward making the life of the inmates more complex, thus throwing greater responsibility upon each woman. . . . Life offers no compromise to routine — it calls for quick decisions, clean purposes and the traveling of devious and crooked ways in a straight, effective manner. How can a Reformatory, pledged to industrial output, food production, household routine and with a constant eye to education and character development, accomplish this for each woman? At best we can but approximate it by crowding as many new situations as possible into each day and telling the women our purpose in so doing — taking them in on the scheme." [70]

Sound insight into educational psychology is shown in Mrs. Hodder's analysis of the educative approach necessary to deal with adults in an institution where industry must be made educative as well as lucrative:

" If one were to begin with their education where they left off in school they would refuse it, but to swing them ahead into a sound educational enthusiasm catches their imagination and often holds them for continuous and constructive work. The Reformatory for Women is pledged to an industrial policy; under the state use system it has the needle industries, so important as training for women; the manufacture of flags, state, federal and municipal; and a stocking industry. The educational value of these industries under the state use system is obvious when one considers that more than 250 kinds of garments are made in the needle industry alone. There is no mass production, but there is detailed training. Pupils will take history, geography, economics, and incidentally their old enemies — grammar, spelling and arithmetic — from this background when it could not be gotten over to them in any other way." [71]

The 1928 report contains the superintendent's conception of the duties of a reformatory as related to the educational process:

" A reformatory must do for its patients everything a hospital does, but it must go further; it must teach the patient a trade or other means of earning a livelihood; it must encourage her to study and supplement her education. Further, it must drill her in principles of morals and ethics, to the end that she may grow spiritually and build her character as a true working force. No one of these points can be neglected in reformatory work; each is a part of the other, the strengthening and renewing of a broken life." [72]

That Mrs. Hodder took a broader view of the test of reformatory work, a view envisaged in her educational aims and program, is apparent from the following quotation from the 1928 report:

" The reformatory is judged on its reform of the girl, not on her restoration to health, as are state hospitals, but on whether or not she leads a good life.

[70] *Annual Report of the Commissioner of Correction, year ending November 30, 1923,* p. 47.
[71] *Annual Report of the Commissioner of Correction, year ending November 30, 1925,* p. 42.
[72] *Annual Report of the Commissioner of Correction, year ending November 30, 1928,* p. 59.

Leading a good life once one has the habit of leading a bad one, involves a revision of one's attitude toward life. In helping a person to do this we look to the elimination of removable handicaps, — ill health, ignorance, inability to earn a living, as important first steps. A reformatory's duty then is greater than any other form of state control, or indeed, any school." [73]

These are not merely pious wishes or unattainable ideals. From the first the superintendent sought to put them into practice through the employment of a specially qualified director of education. As far back as 1915 she urged the need of strengthening the educational program and asked for a trained " educator who would study the correlation of . . . industrial and trade training material with the academic work and the varied student body, and develop for us a well-defined school plan." [74] In 1918 she renewed her request for a supervisor of schools to co-ordinate the various occupational opportunities with academic work " and build up a curriculum which might hold the most restless girl." [75] In the 1926 report she spoke of the progress of the educational program with the aid of normal-school graduates and looked forward " to the time when it will be a part of the required course of future teachers to serve as teachers in reformatories and schools for the feebleminded." [76] The long-sought co-ordination of the industrial and academic activities into a realistic educational program was finally launched in 1925, and some progress has been made in this difficult task.[77]

Provision of adequate equipment. To give expression to these various aspirations and activities which the superintendent of the Reformatory was so eager to realize in practice required certain facilities which were non-existent when she took office. Her reports are filled with requests for basic physical equipment necessary to implement her program. Thus in the beginning (1913) she expressed her conviction that a new reformatory institution should be established to facilitate the carrying-out of a truly forward-looking program. She wisely pointed out that " it does not need to be a monumental structure, or series of structures, nor a sudden growth, but can develop cottage by cottage, according to well-laid plans . . . out of the present institution in its capacity of State laboratory for the study of women offenders." [78] She indicated the value of such a scheme as a basis for classifying different types of inmates. Again, in the 1914 report she alludes to the overcrowding at the Reformatory and, after considering alternative remedies (enlargement of the existing buildings, transfer of the surplus population to jails and houses of correction, construction of a new reformatory, or the development of the existing institution " as an experiment station for the study of various types of offenders "), concludes that the fourth

[73] Ibid.
[74] *Fifteenth Annual Report*, etc., p. 54.
[75] *Third Annual Report*, etc., p. 68.
[76] *Annual Report of the Commissioner of Correction, year ending November 30, 1926*, p. 43.
[77] See p. 123.
[78] *Thirteenth Annual Report*, etc., p. 55.

alternative is the desirable one. " The second is an obviously retrogressive step, the first not worth considering, and the third impracticable, because no one knows whom to put into the new institution; *i.e.,* type classification not being as yet established, the population of a new institution, given the present (1914) state of our knowledge of criminal women, would be as conglomerate as the population of the present one." [79]

Her recommendations for appropriate facilities to cope with the problems presented by the Reformatory's clientele, presented in detail in the 1914 report, are important enough to quote at some length:

> " As a solution of the problems here presented, and in the line of the logi-cal development of our work, we earnestly urge that there be started this year, on the land belonging to the Reformatory for Women, three separate village colonies for the study of the women committed to this institution, who belong in either of the foregoing groups. These colonies should be far enough apart so that their homogeneity could be preserved and the individual group tested by itself.
>
> " The buildings should be inexpensive frame construction. These village colonies should be known as outposts of the Reformatory for Women, and as its classification stations for research in criminalistics.
>
> " These colonies should receive their inmates from the Reformatory for Women alone, and then only after careful study has been made showing that a given line of treatment and training is needed.
>
> " A large part of the interest in working up such colonies would be to see what kind of a community life would make these women self-respecting and self-supporting.
>
> " With the simple defective delinquents it might be a form of education and industry found so effective with the feeble-minded.
>
> " With the recidivist and psychopath the problem would be more complex. In the latter colony a hydrotherapeutic equipment would be necessary to help the violent women. Both groups would need regular academic work.
>
> " One gets suggestions as to possible occupations by glancing through the Auditor's report. There it will be found that State institutions buy eggs, but-ter, cheese, poultry, ham, bacon, veal, salt pork, canned fruits and vegetables.
>
> " These can all be produced on farm colonies and by women. We believe that by combining such work with State-use industries a well-selected choice of interests would be available with which to carry out the proposed experi-ments." [80]

Here we see the exercise of constructive imagination in grappling realistically with a complex problem. Unfortunately, Mrs. Hodder's suggestions for special-ized colonies and equipment for the different classes of offenders never material-ized, though they were urged on several occasions.[81] In the 1918 report, par-

[79] *Fourteenth Annual Report,* etc., pp. 42–3.　　　[80] Ibid., pp. 45–6.
[81] See particularly the reports of 1916 (pp. 66–7) and 1917 (p. 72), which refer to the defeat

ticularly, a strong plea is made for the furnishing of adequate housing and other facilities to take account of the different types of offenders and the need for experimenting with various methods of treating them. Referring to the newly-developing concept of " defective delinquent," [82] Mrs. Hodder points to the inadequacy of the existing plant to deal with the psychopathic and feeble-minded women embraced by this classification. She again recommends the establishment of special quarters removed from the main buildings, so that the psychopathic women will not disturb the others. Enumerating many structural defects in the existing plant, the superintendent asks for such necessities as a " pavilion camp " on a separate piece of land, for housing the normal inmates, and another especially equipped for coping with the feeble-minded. In the 1929 report she again strongly urges the establishment of experimental cottages " to try other methods with the young women," this time, however, those of " super-normal I. Q.," as well as those " who show qualities which offer outstanding experimental material." [83]

Although Mrs. Hodder never succeeded in obtaining her cottage reformatory, she did make considerable progress in transforming a building that originally was poorly constructed for its purpose into one in which there are a number of modern facilities. In the 1918 report she asked for equipment to transform the hospital annex into a " receiving and detention ward with sound-proof rooms and hydrotherapeutic sections . . . to be equipped with an elevator," the addition of forty beds to the hospital, enlargement of the operating and gynæcological rooms, and the remodelling of other parts of the structure to make them more appropriate for the special cases and problems involved. While not all the changes called for were made, the hospital facilities were greatly improved (owing to a fire in 1919) until today they rank among the better institutions of this character.

---

of a legislative bill for " a cottage in which the psychopathic women committed to the reformatory might be given proper treatment," and whereby a method would be worked out " which should help define the policy of the Commonwealth toward these women." See also the 1918 report (pp. 66–7), etc. We understand that a special house for mothers and infants, and another for young offenders, are at last about to be built (January 1934).

[82] " The term has come to mean delinquents who are nervously as well as mentally defective, and in the minds of many it even means those whose social adjustments are persistently defective even when the mental or nervous defect is not marked enough to seem a causative factor in crime. The defective delinquent group includes criminals who range in mentality from feeble-minded to normal with one or more nervous phenomena, such as hysteria, neurosis, epilepsy, psychopathic constitution. The term has really come to include every criminal who proves herself to be non-reformable. It is a custodial proposition. It means the beginning of the classification of prisoners according to type. It should be kept vividly in mind that each type of defective delinquent is as distinct from the other as the defective delinquent is distinct from the normal. The problem is *the* most important one in the field of work with women prisoners." — Ibid. The extension of the term " defective delinquent " to include such a great variety of personality and behaviour types has resulted in the development of institutions for defective delinquents into catch-alls, presenting further problems of diagnosis and classification.

[83] *Annual Report of the Commissioner of Correction, year ending November 30, 1929,* p. 53.

The 1916 report contains an account of the establishment of the library:

" We wanted not only books but space to see books; and their companions, light, soft tones and pictures. The space was available, but crude and unfinished. A group of inmates, under the capable leadership of a long-sentence woman, lathed and plastered the walls and ceiling, putting on the metal beading in a truly professional manner. Later the walls and woodwork were painted also by one of the women. With this splendid start we shall soon complete the project and have a homelike room where love of books and beauty can be absorbed." [84]

Visitors to the Reformatory will see that the superintendent's enthusiasm was justified.

In 1919 a home for the staff was established, apart from the Reformatory. But the structural improvement that the superintendent regarded as the greatest triumph was the transformation, after many years of effort on her part, of a cell-block symbolic of the old régime into a modernly equipped, well-lighted gymnasium. This pleasant place is of great practical value not only for corrective and recreational gymnastics, but for singing, the production of plays, and like activities. Speaking of the transformation, Mrs. Hodder in her 1924 report, showed how much it meant:

" The old Grade III cell block . . . had forty-five cells in three tiers looking toward the north; no sunshine ever reached it and it had not one quality which meant health, self-respect or hope. We have watched it being torn down with a *Te Deum* in our hearts! " [85]

Not only did Mrs. Hodder tirelessly seek the improvement of the existing structure, if not its replacement by a new one, but with much foresight she again and again warned against allowing private industry to encroach upon the lands of the Reformatory. " A farm, a garden, outdoor work, freedom beyond the walls, are basic principles of reform work established forty years ago and proven sound ever since." [86] In the 1930 report she strongly called for protection against encroachment of commercial airports on the land of the Reformatory. " This plan ruins the Reformatory which is an educational institution. It needs peace and quiet for its work and must be protected from the idly curious." [87]

Need for extending the indeterminate sentence. As a basic prerequisite to

[84] *First Annual Report of the Bureau of Prisons of Massachusetts, for the year 1916*, p. 68.

[85] *Annual Report of the Commissioner of Correction, year ending November 30, 1924*, p. 43. " It is symbolic of the new penology that discipline through repression and punishment should give way to discipline through education and expression; that discipline which robbed of self-respect should go down before discipline which builds self-respect through control consciously acquired." — Ibid.

[86] Ibid., p. 44.

[87] *Annual Report of the Commissioner of Correction, year ending November 30, 1930*, p. 66.

rehabilitative efforts that give any promise of permanency, either a wholly indeterminate sentence or one allowing a much wider zone of incarceration for
certain types of offenders is beginning to be called for. This need was early
recognized by the superintendent. Pointing out in 1914 that in a study of 400 of
the inmates 196 (49%) were found to fall into the mentally defective, aberrational, or markedly recidivist groups, she called for an extension of the indeterminate sentence " from 1 to 14 years on all sentences now under five years,"
this to be " safeguarded by flexible parole rules." She insisted that " a short indeterminate sentence does not meet the needs of the treatment of women
offenders. . . . Early parole is unwise for groups like these, both because of
their power for danger in the community, and because of the expense involved
in repeated arrests and convictions. They need greater protection than unrestrained freedom offers." [88] In the 1930 report she again pointed out the un-
desirability of committing women for periods too brief to do much good: " We
have these young people for far too short a period at best. They come to us
after seventeen years or longer of mistakes and bad training; we have them but
an average of fourteen months. It is far too brief a period in which to undo
the old and plant the new, even if we had them under the best classification
and the most ideal surroundings." [89] That more time needs to be devoted to the
education and training of offenders than many of them receive under the
existing régime will be brought out elsewhere in this book.[90]

Conclusion. Even this brief and incomplete sketch of the growth of the Massachusetts institution for female offenders has shown that many years of effort,
much constructive imagination, and a good deal of faith in the reformability of
delinquent women have gone into the difficult task of transforming a prison into
a reformatory.[91]

The régime of the Massachusetts Reformatory for Women as it was when
our five hundred offenders were under its care is described in Chapter VIII.
Before showing the mill in action we ought to look at the grist, however. And
a proper first step in this direction is to make the acquaintance of a number of
the women whose vicissitudes included an enforced sojourn in the Reformatory. Such is the object of the next chapter.

[88] *Fourteenth Annual Report,* etc., pp. 44, 46.
[89] *Annual Report of the Commissioner of Correction, year ending November 30, 1930,* p. 66.
[90] See pp. 188 et seq.
[91] This is not meant to be an exhaustive statement of Mrs. Hodder's efforts to build up the
Reformatory for Women in Massachusetts. It would take one volume at least to do this adequately.

CHAPTER II

A GALLERY OF WOMEN

1. Introductory

Who are these delinquent women whose paths converged into the Reformatory? How do they differ from each other? Is it possible to classify them into types on the basis of some reasonable set of principles? What are the problems presented by women offenders against the law? How have the various social institutions dealt with them, and to what extent have they succeeded? Questions such as these can best be answered by a statistical analysis of the entire group of five hundred delinquent women whose make-up and vicissitudes concern us.[1] But by way of introduction, we need a more intimate picture of the clientele of the Reformatory than can be painted by the broad brush-strokes of mass statistics. Let us, therefore, make the acquaintance of some of them before considering the background and characteristics of the group as a whole.[2]

2. Types of Delinquent Women

Marie — a victim of circumstance. Marie's commitment to the Reformatory for Women at the age of eighteen has proved to be a fortunate circumstance for her. She is the daughter of German parents who have been in America about twenty years and are naturalized citizens. Her father is a Protestant and her mother a Catholic, and this difference in religion has been the cause of much friction in the home. All of the seven children, with the exception of the youngest one, were baptized in the Catholic Church, but Marie's father, not being a church-goer himself, refused to allow any of the youngsters to attend.

Marie's father is a mechanical draftsman with a high-school education. He has had a steady position with a large firm in New York City and has earned about forty dollars weekly, of which he has given only enough to his wife for bare necessities, keeping the remainder for clothes, trips to the seaside, a motor boat, and a motor cycle. He has been not only selfish, but cruel, and has often beaten his wife into subjection to his will. His actions have caused her and the children, Marie particularly, to dislike and fear him. His mother was insane,

---

[1] See Appendix A, *Method of this Research*, p. 336, where the selection of cases for this study is described.

[2] Names, places and other identifying data have of course been disguised.

and his father deserted her many years ago, migrated to America, and has lived with another woman, who is known as his wife and who Marie always thought was her real grandmother.

Marie's mother has never worked outside of her home. Her relatives, several of whom are in America, are respectable small shop-owners. They always disapproved of Marie's father, because of his being somewhat of a drinker, though never intoxicated, and because of his severity with his family. Marie's mother, on the other hand, a frail, ailing person, has been quite lenient with the children.

Throughout Marie's childhood and early adolescence the family of nine lived in a five-room tenement in an open urban neighbourhood. There was some overcrowding in the home, and the children were not encouraged to entertain their friends there.

Marie entered school at the age of six, graduating at fourteen. She was promoted regularly through the grades and at no time misbehaved. She went on to high school, and after she completed the first year, her father encouraged her to prepare herself for clerical work. She registered for a commercial course and remained for almost a year before finally running away from home.

Marie enjoyed music, and her parents allowed her to take piano lessons. She was very fond of dancing and eager to attend dances with her friends, but her father did not permit this. Without his knowledge Marie's mother gave her consent, and before long Marie was winning prizes in dancing contests, truanting occasionally from her classes at the business school to go to shows and dances. As Marie's father would punish her severely for staying out late nights and was suspicious of all her young friends, she occasionally did not return home at all.

The other children did not give their parents any particular trouble, but Marie expressed her resentment of her father's attitude by frequent quarrels with him. Fuel was added to the fire by his attempt to convert her to Protestantism. Because Marie was preparing for her first communion, he was extremely harsh with her. He scolded her so often and so loudly that the family were requested to move because of disturbing the neighbours. Following one such quarrel with her father when she was fifteen years old, Marie disappeared from home. Two months later her father located her in Connecticut and brought her home. The S. P. C. C., which had been called on by the parents to assist in finding Marie, now made every effort to reconcile Marie and her father. For a month or so the situation improved, but as her father again became most abusive, the girl ran away to an aunt in New Jersey. Her father again found her and in a few days brought her home. The agent of the S. P. C. C. learned from Marie's mother that conditions were no better at home and several times asked Marie to call at the office for a talk. As the girl did not do so, he referred the case to the probation officer of the Children's Court and to the Big Sister

Organization, but before they had any opportunity to take action, Marie again disappeared from home, and her family heard nothing more of her until her subsequent arrest and commitment to the Women's Reformatory.

On leaving home, Marie took the first position she could find, as a domestic in a family near by, where she earned four dollars weekly in addition to her board and room. After working for two months, she went to the home of her paternal grandmother, with whom her parents had never been on friendly terms, and found work in a factory. As her grandmother did not wish Marie to use her own surname, the girl adopted an alias, which she used from then until her marriage, some eight months later. Her grandmother insisted that Marie should help with the housework evenings, so the girl, who longed for recreation after the day's work at the factory, decided to leave. Through a newspaper advertisement she secured a position as companion to a well-to-do lady who was about to go to her summer home in New England, stopping on her way in a mill town in Massachusetts. Marie accompanied her and on her first evening in the mill city went alone to a moving-picture show, where she sat beside a young man who later addressed her and to whom she was attracted. As he seemed very agreeable, she met him again the following evening and he very quickly persuaded her to accompany him to Rhode Island on the promise of marriage. The girl knew nothing whatsoever about him except that he was an Italian, about twenty-three years of age. Not until she was arrested with him some months later did she learn that he had a long criminal record for theft and white slavery, that he had been in prison for violation of the white-slave Act, and that when he met Marie he was closely affiliated with a gang of procurers and was also receiving stolen goods.

She claimed later that he threatened to shoot her if she did not comply with his request to engage in prostitution. He immediately began to bring men to her, demanding a dollar from each of them before permitting them to have relations with her. Marie very quickly contracted gonorrhœa and syphilis and became quite ill. He cared for her during this time and expressed affection for her, always promising marriage as soon as they "settled down." Before long, Marie's lover took her to a small manufacturing town in Massachusetts where he had relatives and accomplices. Before settling in their own quarters, they lived for a short time with a friend of his who proved to be one of his accomplices in white slaving and thieving.

In the new home Marie's lover purchased a small fruit-store, which she helped tend. It later developed that he used this store merely as a cloak to his activities in selling stolen goods. When they had lived together for four months, he suddenly announced that they were to be married. They went through the ceremony, but on the following day Marie and her husband were arrested, he on a charge of breaking and entering, and she on a charge of being implicated with him.

For several weeks previously, the police had been closely watching the Italian quarter, as there had been much fighting and disturbance there, which had culminated, on the day of Marie's marriage, in the shooting of a police officer. Marie's husband and two other men, all of whom were strangers in the town, were strongly suspected of commercializing women, and the police found cards which he had circulated among prospective patrons inviting them to come to his home. The police decided to enter the dwelling of one of the white-slave suspects, but though finding the alleged " mother " of one of the men " dressed up to kill " and the tenement illuminated, they did not get sufficient evidence to bring a charge. Although they watched the homes of all three men, they did not see anyone going in or out.

Finally, on the morning following the marriage of Marie and her lover, the police discovered that a wealthy home in the neighbourhood had been looted. They strongly suspected the white-slave ring, searched one of the houses of the trio, and discovered many valuables, curios, and silver. They arrested several suspects, among them Marie and her husband, whose rooms they searched, discovering that Marie had in her possession the keys to the house which had been robbed and various small articles which were easily identified by the owner. On her husband's person they found some stolen articles and a bill of lading for stolen property consigned from the fruit-store to a brother in a near-by city. Marie claimed absolute innocence of any knowledge of the robbery and has stuck to her story, consistently denying any part in it. But there seems to be no doubt that she was preparing to help her husband to " make his get-away " at the moment that the police arrived on the scene.

When it was revealed during the trial that her husband had for years been a white-slaver, Marie was genuinely astonished and created quite a scene in court, evidencing great emotionalism and affection for him. The police carried on an extended investigation and were able to track down several young men who had had relations with Marie in her home after paying the fee demanded by her lover. All of these men claimed to have contracted venereal disease from her. The police were certain that the only reason why Marie's lover had married her was that he knew the police were on his trail and feared arrest as a white-slaver.

Although Marie denied that she had any relatives, her father unexpectedly appeared, having learned through the newspapers of her arrest. At first she refused to recognize him, but the Chief of Police, who was very much interested in helping her and who himself did not believe that she was implicated in the robbery, persuaded her to see him. He reported later that the girl's father " just seemed heart-broken about Marie." Her father expressed the hope that Marie would be held in an institution for the remainder of her minority and that she would not return to her husband after her release.

Marie's husband was sentenced to the State Prison and she was given a five-year indeterminate sentence to the Women's Reformatory for "breaking and entering." Marie was then seventeen years old.[3]

* * *

Alice — a professional criminal. At the age of eighteen, Alice is already a shoplifter of considerable note. She is a charming girl with auburn hair and wide blue eyes, has an assumed air of good breeding which cloaks an underlying coarseness, is a ready and interesting talker, a "born leader," and a young person whose calm, open expression belies an emotionalism which manifests itself on the slightest provocation.

Who is this girl who is expending her abundant energy in criminalistic activities rather than in socially wholesome ways? Alice is the youngest of five children of Canadian parentage. On the paternal side there is a history of alcoholism and thievery, and among the maternal relatives, of over-sexuality. Alice's father has been something of a drinker, but has worked steadily. Because he has been generally irritable and unsympathetic and on occasion abusive, his wife and children have feared him and early learned to hide their difficulties from him. Alice's mother is well-intentioned, rather easy-going, ignorant, and fond of her children, but has not known how to imbue them with wholesome ideals and standards of conduct.

Little Alice was a most attractive child and, being the youngest of the family, was much pampered by her parents and her brothers and sisters, some of whom were years older than she. Alice's father, a stone-mason, normally earning about four and a half dollars a day, though not able to provide luxuries for his family, has nevertheless usually managed to give them decent comforts. The family were well settled in a not too crowded lower-middle-class residential neighbourhood, in a nine-room flat. Alice's mother spent her time in housekeeping, occasionally taking in a few lodgers to ease the family finances. She experienced little difficulty in rearing her children except for young Alice, who from babyhood was so different from the others that "I could hardly believe that this was my child." She offers as a possible explanation for Alice's difficulties the fact that her husband was unusually abusive during her pregnancy.

Almost from babyhood Alice began to lie and steal. She was also a persistent bed-wetter. At first her thieving propensities were rather overlooked by her family who were charmed by her "cuteness" and believed that she would outgrow these habits. Even as a little girl Alice was very much of a tomboy, indulging enthusiastically in athletics and rough games and not enjoying passive amusements. In the public school which she entered at the age of five, she was most troublesome and very much of a "sneak." When she was only in the third grade, at the age of eight, she was discovered one day by the police on a wagon with an old man and a girl much older than herself. She had had

[3] Marie's story is continued on p. 142.

no sexual connection with him, but admitted that she and the man had improperly handled each other and that she had received money from him.

Almost from the beginning of her schooldays a monitor was sent with her to the toilet because she was wont to write filthy expressions on the walls of the basement. On several occasions the principal of the school was on the verge of expelling her, but did not do so in consideration of her youth. The girl was bright and alert, but never could concentrate on her studies. She was regarded by her teachers as a vicious influence on the children of the neighbourhood, because she would incite them to steal and entertained them with tales of her exploits.

Alice's mother, who was fully aware of the girl's doings, made some effort to remonstrate with her, but was never able to keep her in check. She dared not tell her husband of Alice's goings on, because he would vent his anger at the girl's misdeeds on her mother. At eight Alice was already stealing considerably from grocery and candy shops and on several occasions took articles of clothing from stores. Her mother and even neighbours accepted the things which she and a little companion stole, thus lending acquiescence to her exploits. When store-proprietors sought to report Alice to the police, her mother invariably made private settlements with them.

When Alice was twelve years old, she began to play truant, ostensibly to take care of some children of whom she was very fond. She did not have any unusual interest in boys at this time, but, at the instigation of playmates, had sexual relations several times in a public park not far from her home. When she was not quite thirteen, she was arrested with another girl for larceny of candy. This case was placed on file, however, and although Alice continued to steal, her mother was always inclined to excuse her and to make good the thefts, not reporting them to Alice's father if she could possibly avoid doing so.

While Alice was still attending school, she was caught with another girl by the proprietor of a hardware store from whom they had stolen a wad of money which was lying on the counter near the cash-register. The girls were traced to their homes. Alice's father made restitution, severely reprimanded her, and threatened to take her to court if she did not mend her ways. A few months later, with this same girl, Alice stole handkerchiefs, lace collars, and other small articles, having already learned how to secrete them skilfully in her garments. She had for some time adopted the practice of wearing long, ample skirts in which she could hide her loot. On this occasion she was not taken to court because her parents were well known in the neighbourhood, and the storekeeper did not wish to press the charge.

One day, Alice and her girl companion were caught in a department store in the act of stealing a hat. Even though both girls were only fourteen years old, they already had worked out their schemes for " getting away with the goods."

Alice's companion took a hat from the counter and slipped it into a paper bag. The plan was that Alice should then take the hat to the floorwalker and tell him that her mother had purchased it and wished to return it. The store detectives had been watching the girls, however, and as soon as Alice approached the floorwalker, she and her companion were taken into custody. The girls were arrested and appeared in the juvenile court. The judge placed Alice on probation, allowing her to remain at home with the understanding that her mother would report to him if she stole again.

Thinking to curb Alice's desire to steal, her father gave her plenty of pocket money and anything in reason that she asked for. Within two months, nevertheless, she was haled into another court to answer to a charge of assault and battery on two little children with whom she had got into a street brawl. The judge continued the case for a week. Meanwhile the officer who had arrested the girl reported after investigation that she had recently stolen some money from a dentist. It was learned that the dentist had already reported his loss to Alice's mother, and, as usual, she had settled with him privately.

Shortly after this incident Alice was continued on probation by the juvenile court in whose custody she had been since her first arrest some months before, and the court asked a children's society to supervise her. The executive of this society felt at this time that

> "Alice is perhaps a coarse-grained girl, has a very strong physique and an almost adult face, has never broken down before and only gave way a little after trial today . . . looks to me as if nobody had coped with her successfully up to date. . . . It seems to me quite likely that she could be influenced if somebody with a little extra skill could take hold of her. Think may be there are some girls who can go to a reform school and be improved but it seems as if Alice would be put into the toughest classes and would deteriorate if placed in a reform school. It seems as if change of environment has never been tried. She has been kept right in the place where it was evident that she could not succeed. . . . Seems to be not so much a case of early immoral development but possibly of precocious physical development. No one has taught her how to handle her abnormal understanding, cleverness, energy, etc. Therefore it seems to me that it would be a mistake if the organized forces of moral recuperation in the community life would send the girl to a reform school."

The judge, who was inclined to consider the recommendation of the children's society, asked them to place Alice in a foster-home. The social worker of the society who made the arrangements for placing her, and who supervised her quite constantly throughout the next few years, was an especially capable, kindly young woman with a great fund of common sense, patience, and understanding. She first placed Alice in a temporary boarding-home until she could make more permanent arrangements for her. Alice wept bitterly and begged to return home, insisting it would break her heart if she could not see her sister's baby of whom she was very fond.

It is characteristic of Alice that during the next few years, when she was moved from one boarding-home to another because she had not given satisfaction or because she stole, or carried on with boys, she had frequent emotional outbursts, quickly recovering from them, however, and forgetting the reason for their provocation. From her first foster-home she wrote to the social worker who had her in charge: " I know I am now a new girl. I would not take a match or a pin any more than I would cut my right arm off." However, it was not long before Alice was making free with stationery and postcards and was fighting with the daughter of the family. She did try to behave herself, but resented the restrictions put upon her about going to the stores whenever she wanted to and having to show all her correspondence to her foster-mother. When Alice had been in this home only a month, her foster-mother reported: " She is untruthful, untrustworthy, and a great responsibility," and said that she was friendly with a male neighbour of disreputable character who was secretly receiving her mail for her.

After she had been in the foster-home for some six weeks, Alice one evening ran away to her sister, having been given money for this by the above-mentioned neighbour. When she was found by the social worker, she asserted that she had run away because the foster-home was filthy and that she could not stand it any longer. (It was later found that this was true.) Although Alice protested violently, she was again placed in a temporary home pending a more permanent arrangement. The judge of the juvenile court meanwhile decided to give her another chance in a foster-home rather than commit her to a correctional school.

A home was found for her on a farm where she could help with the chores and take care of a little girl, of whom she grew to be very fond and to whom she was most devoted. During the eleven months that Alice was with this family, the social worker, who visited her often, noted that the girl seemed to have lost nearly every trace of her hardness and brazenness, and that she seemed to enjoy the farm work and made herself useful in every way possible. " I do not feel like the same Alice at all," she wrote. " I feel as if I had carried a lode all my life time and these six months that I have been away from home, I have left that lode."

Alice was making every effort to behave herself in order that her probation might be terminated and she be allowed to return home. But after eight months her foster-mother began to report that the girl was saucy and untruthful, and very free with small articles belonging to the family; that she worked splendidly when she wanted to, but of late was becoming slipshod, restless, and uneasy, making every excuse to visit neighbours whom the foster-mother considered disreputable.

Alice, who from earliest childhood had been a persistent bed-wetter until she was nine or ten years old, was now, at the age of fifteen, reverting to this habit. Her foster-mother was so annoyed at Alice's uncleanliness that she refused to keep her any longer. So the girl was permitted to return to her parents for a brief period, pending further arrangements. She would very much have preferred to remain at home, but was soon placed on a farm, where she received a dollar a week to look after the children. She soon began to write enthusiastic letters to the social worker, asking her for some materials for a party dress, as she had recently met a very reputable young fellow at church and wanted to go to a dance with him. Her foster-mother at this time noted that " the girl is very easily excited by the presence of anyone of the opposite sex; she is very free in her manner toward men." After consulting the judge, the social worker decided that it would be best to allow Alice to receive visits from the young man, on the theory that " with a girl so mature as Alice and with her strong sex tendencies, it is much safer to allow her to enjoy men's society in a legitimate way under supervision than to try to prevent her from having boy friends." Alice was much exhilarated over the attentions she was receiving from this most reputable young gentleman and wrote: " I shall act just as Alice knows how to and act like a lady as I have learned if you act like a lady both young ladies and young men think a great deal of you."

Alice's new foster-family grew to be very fond of her, even though she was something of a care. She was most devoted to their children and the foster-parents always felt that they could trust her to take care of them during their absence. When the second summer of her stay was approaching, Alice begged to be allowed to return home for a visit. In view of the fact that her foster-mother found that, because of Alice's carelessness, she could not use her for anything on the farm such as berry-picking and gardening, the social worker determined that it would be well to remove the girl from this home.

After spending a few days with her family, Alice was again placed in the country. She ran away after only a day, however, and two days later returned to the home of her parents after seeing a cheap vaudeville performance in the company of a man whom she had picked up. The next day she was brought to the juvenile court by her mother and sisters, who insisted that she had been harshly treated by being moved about so much from one home to another. Alice asserted that she would not behave herself from now on if she had to go to another home. The judge talked the matter over with her family and they finally consented that she be again placed out; not, however, until he had given her a suspended sentence to a correctional school. Alice on hearing of this decision made a wild scene and pleaded to be sent directly to the institution. But, as usual, she soon recovered her spirits and promised to behave herself. The next day, however, while awaiting placement, Alice disappeared from home with a girl of bad reputation with whom she had been going about a good deal for the last few days. The girls were found hanging about cheap restaurants and cabarets patronized by sailors and prostitutes. They had attired themselves in tawdry, tough-looking clothes and were found chatting with some very dissipated youths. Both girls were brought back to the juvenile court, Alice's companion being released, as she claimed to be seventeen years of age.

On the next day Alice was placed in a temporary home. The same night she made her escape by jumping from a window. The children's society, when notified of this, recommended to the judge that Alice be committed at once to the correctional school. She was located the next day in her own home and claimed that she had just married and was going to join her husband. This story she fabricated, expecting on account of it to be released from supervision. It was true that she had fallen in with a young fellow who was a member of a vaude-ville troupe and whom she had met seven or eight times between placements. She claimed that he had promised to marry her, but had recently gone off to New York. In order to gain time to trace this man, the social worker placed Alice temporarily in a home before carrying out the plan to send her to the correctional school. Alice meanwhile made one or two attempts to run away. After a month it was decided to commit her to the correctional school, as the man in question could not be found.

Although she was at first tractable in the institution, where she impressed the authorities as being bright and alert, Alice would steal whenever an oppor-tunity offered itself. She soon became a most pernicious influence, rallying the worst girls about herself. The institution officials reported:

"She submitted cheerfully to any means of discipline which might be devised, continually used vile and profane language and missed no oppor-tunity of attracting in an indecent manner the attention of any man who chanced to be about the place. She boasted too that she never meant to turn her hand to any honest work once she was out of the institution."

She tried in every way possible to have herself transferred to the cottage for incorrigibles: "They are game and no squealers." She repeatedly created a rumpus and finally gained her wish to be transferred to this cottage, imme-diately expressing penitence and resolving to turn over a new leaf. It was not long, however, before she was organizing a plot to escape. She most cleverly secured the necessary tools and assistance from outside and almost succeeded in outwitting the officers.

After she had been in the correctional school six months, it was decided to transfer her to the Reformatory for Women. (This is not the particular incar-ceration which we are studying.) Again she expressed regret for her misconduct and made numerous good resolutions, all of which she soon broke. In the Re-formatory she was as unmanageable as in the correctional school. She was found to be of "dull mentality, an unstable adolescent, and of precocious physical de-velopment without enough outlet for her abnormal energy."

Alice remained in the Reformatory for almost a year and was then retransferred to the care of the correctional school under parole. She was permitted to return home, but after she had been there for hardly a month, her mother complained that she was staying out late nights and was saucy and stubborn. She had secured a job as a stock clerk in a shoe store, but was shortly discharged for lack of interest. Her mother was under the impression that Alice was working, when in reality she was hanging about the moving-picture shows.

Alice was now seventeen years old and was going about with a man much older than herself, with whom her family believed she was committing immoralities. She worked very irregularly, was often discharged, and would hang about cheap dance-halls and restaurants in the company of disreputable girls. Every now and then during her parole period she would express her determination to improve her conduct, but always her promises were shortlived.

Meanwhile Alice's parents built an attractive small house in a pleasant town about twenty miles distant from the city, hoping that if the girl settled in another locality, it would bring more wholesome interests into her life and separate her once for all from her vicious haunts and companions. But after she remained with them fairly quietly for a few weeks, Alice ran away from home and went off to the city, where she soon fell in with an old friend, the same girl with whom she was arrested just prior to her commitment to the correctional school. She became intimate at this time, also, with a young Italian who paid her expenses and with whom she lived for about a month.

Alice and her girl friend began to steal from all the large department stores, and Alice boasted that she got away with a great deal because she was " acquainted with store detectives." She was by this time an expert shoplifter (her technique she claims she perfected through knowledge gained at the correctional school), and her girl friend was a pickpocket. Between them, they had secreted about nine hundred dollars' worth of goods in their room. One day while they were on a marauding expedition, Alice was caught in the act of stealing a pair of ear-rings. Her arrest followed, and after due investigation it was ascertained that the girls had stolen shoes, dresses, rings, shirts, coats, hats, waists, underwear, and the like, to the value of about five hundred dollars. Alice was represented by counsel and pleaded guilty to a charge of larceny, for which she received a five-year indeterminate sentence to the Women's Reformatory. She was then eighteen years of age, remarkably pretty and disarmingly charming, already having the reputation among the police of being a very clever shoplifter. She was suspected also of being the leader of a gang, to whom she had been selling for ridiculously small sums much of the finery which she had stolen.[4]

* * *

Grace — the black sheep. Grace is the sixth of seven children of Scotch Presbyterian parentage. Her father is a stone-mason and contractor who has

[4] The story of Alice is continued on p. 147.

been in business for himself for many years, an industrious person of excellent habits, thoroughly respected by his neighbours of a suburban community in which he has lived with his family for many years. The family occupied a six-room house which Grace's father owned, very cozy, with a small flower-garden and back yard. The father has a keen sense of responsibility for his children. Grace's mother died of " shock " when the girl was but four years of age, leaving her husband and a brood of seven children to get along as best they might without maternal oversight. The oldest sister, then ten years of age, became the nominal housekeeper for the family. As she continued her education through high school, the children had very little care. Despite this they all bore a very creditable reputation and developed into normally wholesome young men and women with the exception of Grace and one of her brothers who early became a drinker and was turned out of the home by his Scotch Presbyterian father.

Before the birth of Grace her mother had had three miscarriages, followed by an operation in which one of her ovaries was removed. Grace's father was told by the doctors that his wife could bear no more children. The birth of Grace followed within a year, however. Grace was a normal full-term baby, whose delivery was natural. She was very puny and delicate, and her development was slower than that of the other children of the family. She had no serious illnesses, however. Her father first noticed that she was mentally retarded when she could not learn even the simplest verses in Sunday school. In the public schools she showed herself to be of poor ability and was pushed through the grades by her teachers until she attained the sixth grade at the age of fourteen. Her behaviour in school was good, however, and she was very regular in her attendance. Because of her retardation, it was considered advisable to transfer her to a pre-vocational school where she might learn to do handiwork.

The only outstanding characteristic of her grade-school days as recalled by her teachers seems to have been " nervousness." Her father remembers, however, that Grace always enjoyed playing with children much younger than herself, and that she had always been " hard to manage." Grace herself says she always felt that she was the " odd member of the family," that her brothers and sisters treated her more or less as an outcast, and, as she was the youngest girl in the family they made her do most of the housework and refused to take her about with them. This resulted in a good deal of sulking and wailing on Grace's part about the indifference of her sisters to her. During these episodes her father usually sided with her.

When Grace was sixteen years old, just at the time that she had matured sexually (menstruation began at that time), she was allowed to leave school, as she had no inclination to pursue her education further and no ambition other than to keep house. Grace went to work in a shoe factory and was found to be a steady, honest worker, of good ability. When she left this job to take one in another factory it was only because she had the opportunity to earn more. She soon began to show marked tendencies toward sexual promiscuity, however.

Her first sex experience was with a fellow-employee at the factory. At about this time Grace began to seek amusements away from her own home. She became a frequenter of skating-rinks, dance-halls, and movie shows in the company of any man who invited her. Though the girl had no particular charm, men approached her in the street, perhaps sensing her suggestibility and sexual responsiveness. Grace does not admit that she ever loved any man or that she enjoyed sexual intercourse or the romance of love-making, but says that she longed for a gaiety and freedom which she found she could secure by giving herself to any man for the asking. Because the moral standards of her family were high, the girl resorted to deceit at every turn in order to continue to indulge herself in the kind of recreational outlets which attracted her.

At a skating-rink Grace met a young sailor who called on her several times at her home. As he made a good appearance, her father approved of her companionship with him. Very shortly thereafter the girl became pregnant. She would not admit until many months later that her sailor friend might not be the father after all, as she had been associating promiscuously with others; at the time, Grace accused the sailor of being responsible. Her family insisted that she leave her employment in the factory where she had worked steadily for eight months, and for two months thereafter she acted as housekeeper for her father, who then arranged that she be sent to the Florence Crittenton Home for delivery. Soon after the birth of the child, a girl, Grace at her father's urging took out a warrant against the alleged father of the child on the charge of bastardy. He was given the choice of a jail sentence or marriage with her and chose the latter. So the couple were married. They have not seen each other since.

It was later ascertained that her husband was considered a good-for-nothing even by his own parents and that another girl in New York City also had a " claim on him " as she had become pregnant by him. He was forced, nevertheless, to allot thirty dollars a month to the support of Grace's child, which he did with a fair degree of regularity.

While Grace was at the Crittenton Home, she made the acquaintance of a girl who was also later sent to the Reformatory and with whom Grace's association continued for many years, much to her detriment. This girl, Edith, had been running around promiscuously with sailors and had become pregnant during one of her many escapades. The two girls named their babies after each other.

Grace and her baby returned to her father's home and for a small wage she kept house for him. It was only a short time before Grace again began staying out late nights and permitted herself to be picked up here and there by men. Her father now sought the aid of one of the local societies for the care of girls who undertook to supervise her. Soon thereafter Grace disappeared from the house, taking with her a hundred dollars of the allotment sent by her husband for the support of her child. This she proceeded to spend during the next four weeks in the company of her girl friend Edith, who had persuaded Grace to live with her at a very disreputable hotel. Her father instituted a search for her, and she was finally located by the police and arrested on a warrant taken out by him on a charge of " abandonment of child." During this brief period away from home, Grace admitted, she had indiscriminate relations with many men to whom she was introduced by her pal, Edith. They had a month of such promiscuous living and tawdry gaiety before they were finally apprehended.

Grace was given a suspended sentence and allowed to return home on bail provided by her father, in order that she might be taken to the Psychopathic Hospital for examination by the agent of the girls' society. Here she was diagnosed as a " constitutional psychopathic inferior " with a mental age of eleven years, ten months, and it was recommended that she be closely supervised. It was also discovered, through an examination at the general hospital where she was taken by the agent of the girls' society, that she was again pregnant and needed treatment for venereal disease, so that when her case came before the court for final disposition, the girls' society reported to the judge that they could not supervise her in family life. Consequently, Grace was sentenced to the Reformatory for Women.

The girls' society, which by this time knew Grace quite well, said of her: " She has no real sense that she has done wrong in living a promiscuous sex life. . . . She is not particularly the aggressor in sex approach to men but is of a peculiarity and temperament that yields very easily. This high suggestibility is apparently obvious to certain types of men who meet her, as she has been approached on the street when the society visitor was with her."

During the brief time that Grace had lived at home with her father, he had intercepted several letters containing indecent language, improper suggestions, and even indecent photographs. When he remonstrated with her, she professed penitence, wept easily, or assumed an attitude of defiance. Both her father and the agent of the girls' society hoped that it might be possible to have Grace committed to a school for the feeble-minded if observation of her at the Women's Reformatory indicated that this was necessary. The society meanwhile placed her baby in a boarding-home, and Grace, at the age of nineteen, was admitted to the Reformatory on a two-year indeterminate sentence for " abandonment of child." [5]

* * *

Florence — a drug addict. Florence's parents were very much devoted to her. Until she was nine years old, she was an only child. A sister born at this time died when Florence was eighteen; another sister, born when Florence was already twenty-three, died four years later. Florence's father long had charge of a livery stable, and as he was quite steadily employed, the family was never in want. He comes of wholesome Yankee stock whose people have for generations

[5] The story of Grace is continued on p. 152.

been prosperous farmers. Except for the death of his father of senile psychosis, there is no history of mental disease in his family. On her mother's side there was much tuberculosis, a tendency to which Florence's mother inherited.

Florence's early childhood was wholesome in every way. She attended church, took music and elocution lessons, and attended school regularly, leaving at the end of her first year in high school, at the age of fifteen, because of ill health. She was at this time in a highly nervous condition, and the family physician, fearing that she might develop St. Vitus's dance, urged her removal from school. Thereafter she lived at home, helping her mother with the housekeeping and the care of the younger sister. Occasionally she took a position as a cash-girl, but it was not until she was eighteen years old that she really began to work steadily. She was a very attractive, jovial girl and made many friends among the best families in the community.

At about this time Florence's mother began to fail in health. Her physician considered her highly neurotic — a person who very much enjoyed illness. Though not actually bedridden, she demanded a great deal of attention from her family. Shortly after the onset of her illness she began to take morphine in moderation upon prescription of her physician, to relieve pain. This was the beginning of a slight addiction to drugs, to which Florence was a witness. The mother had to be watched very closely, as she would occasionally become almost unbalanced. She would call for the doctor on the slightest provocation, and this tendency was also noted in Florence by her father, who claimed that " she was always a great hand to go to a doctor if she had any kind of a pain anywhere."

When Florence was eighteen, she was employed as a sales-girl in a small department store, the manager of which, the son of the owner, soon began to pay her considerable attention. As he was Jewish, and both young people realized that there would be great opposition to their marriage, they had to exercise the utmost care that their interest in each other should not become apparent to their families. During the three years in which they kept company, their relations were entirely honourable, and Florence's fiancé had the utmost respect and affection for her. When Florence was twenty-one, the couple were married secretly and did not establish their own home. She continued to live with her parents and held her position in the store. Her husband often visited in her parents' home, and the couple soon confided to them the news of their marriage, but did not reveal it to his parents.

Although the actual circumstances under which Florence began to use drugs are somewhat clouded, it seems quite clear that some two or three years after her marriage, following an abortion, as a result of which she suffered some complications and much pain, she took morphine, remembering that her mother had been greatly relieved by it. She very quickly became habituated. She was then twenty-four years old. Florence has since continued the use of the drug by mouth in combination with atropin, varying the morphine with alcohol when she could not secure the former. Florence's husband, out of affection and pity for her, gave her every assistance in securing the drug.

When Florence had been married some six years, her mother died. By this time, Florence had become weary of her husband, and she took this occasion to leave her home, in Maine, and go to a small city in Massachusetts, not far from Boston, where the family had lived for a few years during her early childhood. There she met a young fellow with whom she very quickly became infatuated. Though not yet divorced from her husband, against whom she entered suit on the grounds of desertion, she went through a marriage ceremony with this man, returning with him to her home town and resuming work in her husband's store, managing somehow to keep from husband number two the fact of her previous marriage. Florence was now twenty-seven years old.

After some months the couple returned to Massachusetts, and upon the insistence of her second husband's relatives she was sent to a private hospital for a drug " cure." He remained faithful to her during this time, but as the cure was not at all effective and she had to be returned for further treatment, he became impatient and disappeared before she was discharged. They had lived together for some five years, and as he supported her well, Florence had not worked since their return to Massachusetts.

Now at the age of thirty-two, finding herself without means of support, Florence sought a position in a state hospital as an attendant, which she readily secured. From this time on for several years she worked sporadically in hospitals for the mentally ill, being frequently discharged on suspicion of drug addiction. Meanwhile, she communicated often with her first husband, from whom she was now legally divorced. He sent her small sums of money and even packages of drugs by mail or express until the Harrison law went into effect.

While Florence was working in a hospital, she fell in love with a Jewish fellow-employee, who was at least ten years younger than herself. Florence did not inform him of the existence of husband number one nor of her illegal marriage to a second man. Until they were married, her affianced was not aware that Florence was a drug addict. When they had been married for only a month, she had to be committed to a state hospital for treatment not only for morphinism, but for alcoholic hallucinosis. Florence had fallen into the habit of taking alcohol as a substitute for morphine, and as her resistance to alcohol was very low, she would quickly develop hallucinations, alternating between periods of great excitement and depression. She was very much attached to her new spouse and was shocked by his desertion into a determination to try every possible drug cure. She was now thirty-eight years old.

During all these years Florence's father had remained most loyal and devoted to her and had sent her money for " cures." Between treatments she continued to work in state hospitals, frequently stealing drugs. She was finally discharged on suspicion of being an addict and was one day caught in a drug store writing an illegal prescription. She had recently resorted to stealing prescription blanks from physicians and forging their names to them. She would go to all lengths to secure the drug, and when she did not succeed, would use alcohol, paregoric, " Arnold's Balsam," and numerous so-called " cholera cures."

The judge who sentenced Florence to the Women's Reformatory realized that she was a confirmed addict, and though it was not his primary intention to send her to a penal institution, he felt that treatment there might be effective and was worth trying. So Florence at the age of thirty-nine, was given a two-year indeterminate sentence for " writing illegal prescriptions." [6]

*   *   *

Annie — an adulteress. When Annie was fourteen years old, she came to America from Ireland with a girl friend. She attended a convent, which she left in the sixth grade, at the age of thirteen. Annie was the eldest of thirteen children, of whom six had died. Her father was a cattle-trader, and the family was one of respectability. Her parents somewhat reluctantly gave their consent to her leaving home and paid her passage to America. She has never had to send money to them, so that she has been able to keep her earnings entirely for her own uses. A brother followed Annie to America a few years after her arrival.

When she arrived in this country, she went directly to Massachusetts and lived for five months with relatives of the girl who had accompanied her on the trip across. Then, having got her bearings, she took a position as a domestic, which she held for three years, until the family of her employer was broken up by death. She was very regular in her religious duties in the Catholic Church, and the few friends that she made were girls of her own age whose interests were wholesome. Annie went with them to movies and dances, but never was wild or indulged in immorality.

When Annie lost her first position, she went to board with a girl acquaintance and found a job in a shoe-factory where she was able to earn from seven to nine dollars weekly on piece work. When this factory shut down, she secured work in another shoe-factory. Here she became acquainted with the overseer, a man some twenty-five years her senior, wholesome, steady, but very unattractive in appearance. Six months after they met, when Annie was nineteen, the couple were married, but not in the Church, as her fiancé was a Protestant.

She continued to work in the factory after her marriage, much preferring this to idleness. She was a very neat housekeeper and in no way neglected her home. As she was so much younger than her husband, her interests were quite different from his. He made no objection to her going to dances and entertainments, but rarely accompanied her.

The difference in religious faith between herself and her husband was the

[6] The story of Florence is continued on p. 157.

cause of some friction, particularly after the birth of their little daughter. After a few years Annie's husband came to realize that his wife did not love him. He had the first inkling of this when she wept bitterly upon hearing of the death of a man who lived not far away and for whom she then admitted a deep affection. Soon thereafter Annie became much infatuated with a young man of about her own age who worked in a factory near by and whom she had met in a friend's home. Although he was a drinker and would sometimes become " silly drunk," he was never abusive. Annie began to go out with him. When her husband sensed that his wife loved this man, he told her that she might go to him, and if after a little while she wanted to return home, she might do so. Otherwise he thought a separation advisable.

Annie thereupon left her husband and her little girl, who was not quite four years old, and went to live in a boarding-house where her lover was also rooming. Although they were together constantly, she asserts that for two years after she left home she and her lover had no illicit sexual relations. Annie continued to work in factories, earning enough to support herself, and did not expect any assistance from her husband, whom she very rarely saw during the five years which preceded her arrest for adultery. Her husband, realizing that she did not intend to return to him, took a housekeeper for the child and has been getting along as best he can ever since. He did not divorce Annie, but told her she was free to secure a divorce if she wished. She made no move in this direction, however, because her lover, like her husband, was a Protestant. He did not want to adopt Catholicism, and Annie was determined that if she married again, it should be in the Church. Up to the time of her arrest no divorce proceedings had been instituted.

For the two years preceding her arrest Annie lived steadily with her lover and was known to neighbours as his wife. Finally, the couple were arrested on a charge of adultery, complaint having been made by a neighbour that the couple, although they were not married, were living together. Several weeks before the arrest a child had been born to Annie. Her lover, who was frank to acknowledge his paternity, paid for her confinement and supported her and the child for two months, after which the arrest took place.

Annie pleaded guilty to a charge of adultery and received a five-year indeterminate sentence to the Women's Reformatory. Her two-months-old baby was admitted with her. Her lover was committed to a House of Correction for one year, also for adultery.[7]

*   *   *

Fleur — a professional prostitute. Fleur is one of two living children of French-Canadian parents, both of whom are illiterate and speak very little English. On her father's side there is much insanity, mental deficiency, and alcoholism. Fleur's mother was notoriously immoral before her marriage. The parents set-

[7] The story of Annie is continued on p. 161.

tled in a factory town and have both been mill-hands. From her earliest child-hood the family have lived in crowded quarters, bare, dirty, and disorderly, and Fleur has seen squalor of the worst sort. When she was but four years old, her parents were so poverty-stricken that it was necessary to place the child in an orphanage in order that she might be sufficiently fed and clothed. She was kept there for only a few months and was then returned home. When Fleur was five years old, her parents separated because her father was jealous of the attentions his wife was giving to and receiving from other men. He settled himself in a small shack within a short distance of his family. The mother took up with another man and by him gave birth to an illegitimate child, which soon died.

Both Fleur and her little sister were from their earliest years eyewitnesses of the sexual immoralities of their mother, who moved about very frequently both to avoid payment of rent and because of the many complaints of neighbours about her drinking, disorderliness, and illicit affairs with men. The two little girls were frequently stolen by their father under whose roof they were again witnesses of drinking and immoral acts. And so they spent their childhood, being bandied about between their parents. It is little wonder, then, that both the children began a promiscuous sex life very early. As the mother was a mill-hand and away from home most of the day, the two girls had to shift for themselves without any supervision. They early took to drinking beer and to smoking, and Fleur could very easily " handle a cigar."

Fleur was seduced at the age of eleven by the same man who was the father of her mother's illegitimate child. She was no more than twelve when she and her sister began to frequent cellars in the neighbourhood for the purpose of having immoral relations with men and boys. She began to truant from school shortly after her first sexual experience and had for some years already mani-fested a most ungovernable temper. " She seems almost insane and then gets over it," said her mother. Finally neighbours of the family reported to the priest that Fleur was becoming most unmanageable and loose in her ways, and he arranged for her admittance to a House of the Good Shepherd. She was in the third grade at school at this time and did not continue her education further.

She stayed at the House of the Good Shepherd for nine months. There she proved herself to be most disobedient and violent. She was restrained by the use of strait-jackets on twelve occasions during her stay. As the Sisters feared that the girl might throw herself from a window, they finally decided, for her own safety, not to keep her any longer and sent her to a psychopathic hospital for observation. There she was given a thorough examination and was found to be very well developed and well nourished and in excellent physical condition. She remained under observation for ten days and during this brief period was al-lowed to work on the ward, washing dishes and sweeping. Though a bit noisy and talkative, she was agreeable and had no fits of anger. She was diagnosed as " feeble-minded, but not insane."

Fleur was then returned to her mother, and her conduct was somewhat improved for a few weeks, but she soon began chasing about in the streets. She herself admits that she supported herself largely by prostitution, even though her mother was not aware of this, as Fleur was careful to get home not later than eleven at night.

The girl had frequent outbursts, when she would throw furniture about and strike her sister and even assaulted fellow-employees of the mill. She worked very irregularly and was soon discharged for " fooling " and for " having liquor on her breath."

Then she began to stay out late nights, attending picture shows and frequenting road-houses, sometimes even staying away from home all night. Twice she ran away from home with a girl chum. When she was only fourteen, she contracted gonorrhœa. Her mother again complained that she could not control the girl, and arrangements were made, with the aid of one of the local agencies, to admit Fleur to a home for wayward girls. Here she again proved unmanageable. As a result of this she was taken to court by her mother on a charge of " stubbornness " and was given a sentence, at the age of fifteen, to a correctional school for girls. Her case was appealed and she was placed on probation, but after six months she was again arrested for stubbornness. The girl herself admitted that she had been running around with various men and boys and that she had been doing more streetwalking during her probation period than formerly. Though she had appealed her sentence to the superior court, she agreed to withdraw her appeal and was continued on probation, promising to secure employment and behave herself. She soon ran away from home, however, and when her case was once more heard, she was committed to the correctional school. She made a dreadful scene in the court-room, refusing to bid her mother good-bye and shouting that she hated her.

In this institution Fleur was profane, saucy, ugly, and completely unmanageable. She had frequent outbursts of temper for no apparent cause, absolutely refused to work, and when reprimanded would stick pins and needles into her hands and arms, apparently enjoying the trouble that she was causing by these assaults upon herself. She was found to be a most pernicious influence among the other girls, inciting them to misconduct at every turn and almost succeeding in staging an escape with two other girls.

After six months she was transferred to the Reformatory for Women (this is not the particular sentence we are studying) in the hope that she would be more amenable to the routine there. But she continued to be troublesome and childish, teasing and annoying other inmates and involving herself and others in petty disturbances. She had to be transferred from one kind of work to another and always found the hours too long or the job too tedious; she could not concentrate on any one task for long. She was frequently reprimanded for insolence and kept in isolation. On one occasion, when asked by a matron to put a basin outside of her door, she replied " I'll put it out when I get ready."

On recommendation of the superintendent of the Reformatory and by court order, Fleur was removed and committed to a school for the feeble-minded. For the few days that she was kept there, she was a great trouble-maker. While walking about the grounds, she passed a girl whom she had known previously, and without apparent provocation attacked her. She had several outbursts of temper and was considered " mentally irresponsible " during these periods.

After one week she was discharged and committed to a mental hospital, where she remained for five months. For a brief time she evinced a feeling of shame at her misconduct and insisted that " when people are good " to her, she does not cause any trouble. But after her second day there she became excited, threatening the noisy patients with injury if they disturbed her during the night. She was very desultory about her work, often refusing to work at all, and soon revealed her sullenness, impudence, and profanity. It was often found necessary to give her hydrotherapeutic treatments in order to quiet her. The hospital psychiatrist commented on her at this time:

> " The patient's reaction to her environment throughout her stay at this hospital has been very changeable. At times she is good-natured, most agreeable, and apparently very desirous of cooperating. She is extremely susceptible to any disturbance which occurs on the ward, and without any warning, changes from a good-natured mood to one in which she is resistive, noisy, profane, and at times assaultive. She is never satisfied for more than a short time with any type of employment, frequently necessitating change of work. She is somewhat unstable emotionally, very talkative as a rule, at times boastful, and frequently precipitates trouble among other patients."

Fleur's own commentaries about her conduct are worth quoting. In speaking of her behaviour while at the correctional school, she told the doctors at the hospital:

> " I didn't behave myself, I used to sing all the time and whistle in my room, but other girls told me to do it. They punished me by putting handcuffs on me, and gave me bread and water and locked me into a room. Finally, they said I was too noisy, they didn't want me to stay, so they put me over at Sherborn [Reformatory for Women]. I was there seven months; I didn't behave myself there either; there you are not supposed to talk at the table, and because I did, I got locked in my room and got bread and water for three days. Sometimes I got locked down in the dungeon. They left me there for two weeks and gave me bread and water. There are two kinds of dungeons, — a dark dungeon and a light dungeon. I was in the dark dungeon at eight different times for periods of a few days at each time. There you have no bed — just a board with bread and water to eat. At Sherborn they said I was too bad, and claimed that I was insane because I put needles and pins in my hands. . . .

I wanted to show off, and put them in; they used to hurt bad. From Sherborn I went to —— [school for the feeble-minded]. I stayed there about a week; I got into a fight with a girl because I was going around with another one, and while we were out to walk, she struck me and so I hit her back, so they sent me here."

It was noted during Fleur's stay at the hospital that she was neat in her appearance, particularly as to her clothing, and that she showed a great fondness for ribbons and other ornamentation.

After five months Fleur was transferred to the Y — State Hospital by order of the Massachusetts Commission on Mental Diseases, as " not improved." There she was again much disturbed, frequently requiring restraint; she was exceedingly destructive, breaking glass and furniture and during her sick periods mutilating herself. Although apparently there was some question that Fleur might be suffering from *dementia præcox,* this diagnosis was not confirmed, because of the " findings of mental sub-normality, with no evidence of deteriorative processes," and " by absence of any evidences suggestive of hallucinations or delusions." The possibility that she was suffering from a manic-depressive psychosis was considered, but was also ruled out because of " absence of true periodicity during outbreaks, absence of true retardation or flight of ideas." Psychopathy was also ruled out " by the positive findings of feeble-mindedness, as shown by the psychological tests."

Fleur had been at the Y — State Hospital for twenty months, when she finally made her escape with the assistance of one of the hospital attendants, a Syrian with a long court record, whom she married three days later. The couple went to her mother's home, where they lived for about a year, separating with the encouragement of Fleur's mother because she found that the husband already had a wife in Syria. The hospital attendants either made no attempt or were unable to find her. During their year together her husband encouraged Fleur in prostitution, bringing men to her in her own home and insisting on sharing with her the profits of this illicit traffic. He was most abusive, drank a great deal, and was frequently arrested.

While Fleur was still living with her husband, she became pregnant by another man and gave birth to an illegitimate child, which very shortly died. When she and her husband separated, she lived, off and on, with her mother and her sister, who was now married. Perhaps by reason of her bleached-blonde attractiveness, her fair features and blue eyes, and her sensual build, she soon preempted the role of " Queen of the Jitneys," collecting easy money from the jitney runners who took girls to questionable road-houses not far from the city.

Because of these activities, Fleur was being carefully watched by the police, who called her as a witness in a jitney case and finally arrested her after she had defaulted in this case. Two months after this she was arrested for " common night walking " and for " violating the true name law." The first charge was dismissed and the second was nol-prossed. Some six months later she was again arrested for " common night walking " and given a two-year indeterminate sentence to the Reformatory for Women, on the commitment which we are now studying. Fleur was then twenty years of age.[8]

*   *   *

Margaret — a " stubborn child." Margaret at seventeen is a well-poised girl of dark complexion and with glossy black hair, who has a bright alert expression, at times pert and impudent. She is the fourth of eight living children of an Italian father and an American-born, English-Irish mother. Her father, who has earned his living as a barber, comes of an intelligent, city-bred family, his father having been a court interpreter. Though an alcoholic, Margaret's father is an industrious and well-meaning man. He has been an extremely rigid disciplinarian of his children from their earliest childhood and has never spared the rod in forcing compliance with his standards of conduct. " What he says is law," according to her mother who is an extremely nervous and very ignorant woman. She had been brought up in an orphanage. Two of Margaret's sisters are, like herself, almost entirely illiterate, and one of them is at present confined in a mental hospital; three of her brothers are alcoholic and at least one of them is feeble-minded.

As the father barely managed to eke out a living for his rapidly growing family, there were no luxuries for the children. There was always enough food, however, no undue crowding of sleeping-quarters, and no need to ask for assistance from relatives or social agencies.

From earliest childhood Margaret has resented parental authority, and her father, despite his zealous attempt to control the girl, could not subject her to his will even by the frequent use of the strap. Margaret never felt any great regard for her father and his relatives. As the mother puts it, " They are Italians, and my children don't care to associate with them, so we don't go near them." Margaret's brothers and sisters never got quite so much out of hand as she did, although later on some of the boys of the family, rather than tolerate the parental sharpness of temper and stringent control, left home and enlisted in the Navy.

Soon after Margaret entered school, she began to manifest to her teachers a complete defiance of authority. She was very wilful, impudent, and inattentive and " was one who would take the bit in her mouth and not care for her mother or anyone." She was considered bright enough, getting along particularly well with her arithmetic and grammar, and her teachers always felt that she could make good progress if she would only put her mind to it.

Shortly after Margaret had entered the eighth grade, at the age of fourteen, she was expelled from school because of impudence. Her parents, much disturbed over this, arranged for her admission to a parochial school, where, how-

[8] The story of Fleur is continued on p. 162.

ever, her behaviour was no better. "She gave more trouble than any pupil we ever had. She was one whom we had to watch all the time. She would associate always with girls inclined to be wayward and did not put her mind on her studies at all." As Margaret was found to be quite unmanageable in the parochial school, her parents decided to withdraw her. In an effort to keep her contented they bought a cheap piano, but the girl refused to practise. Possibly because of ill health, her mother was often irritable and nervous with Margaret and the other children, which did not contribute to the girl's happiness.

For some time Margaret had been manifesting a great desire for pretty clothes and was continually demanding them from her mother, who, however, was unable to gratify the girl's desire. This was a constant source of friction between them. After Margaret had been at home for about a year helping a little with the housework, she insisted on going to work in an automobile-factory. As her parents were in very straitened circumstances at this time, they reluctantly consented, demanding, however, that she turn over her pay envelope to them, from which they gave her an allowance of twenty-five cents a week. Margaret felt that this was altogether too little for her needs. Her parents bought the necessary clothes for her out of her meagre earnings, but were never able to satisfy her taste for "high-toned" things. "It wasn't so much spending money as it was clothes," says her mother.

After Margaret had worked in her first position for three months, she had a severe quarrel with her parents about being too restricted and not being able to go out of the house unless she was accompanied by some member of the family. As a result of this quarrel she made an attempt at suicide by taking sulpho-naphthol. When she had recovered, her parents became stricter than ever with her and would not allow her to return to work for some months. But when she finally took a job again, they permitted her to keep her earnings.

The girl now entered a shoe-factory as a packer, remained there on a weekly wage for about three months, and was then placed on piece work. Through this arrangement she actually worked only a day or two a week, though she gave her parents the impression that she was constantly on the job. In reality she had fallen in with several boys and girls — fellow-employees — with whom she began going off afternoons for a good time. When her parents discovered what Margaret was doing, they tried to cut her off from her friends and secured a position for her in a shoe-factory where her brother was working, so that he might keep an eye on her. Here she remained for a few months and when she was transferred to piece work, again began going off afternoons without her parents' knowledge. She was by this time seventeen years old.

Margaret was always looking forward to the time when she would be eighteen years of age and her parents could have no more legal control over her. "I'll be eighteen soon. Then you'll see what I'll do." One day when Margaret's mother got wind of one of the girl's intended escapades, she severely reprimanded her.

As a result of this Margaret ran off in a tantrum to the home of a sister-in-law and, encouraged by her, spent the next two days away from home (as it later turned out, in the home of two respectable maiden ladies who had formerly been neighbours of the family). Margaret's parents then determined to take out a complaint against her as a " stubborn child," so that she might be placed under the supervision of a probation officer or sent to some institution for a brief period to be disciplined. They felt this was absolutely necessary to save the girl from herself and to prevent her from disgracing them. They were certain that she had never indulged in illicit sex relations, but sensed that she might be on the verge of such conduct and wanted to protect her in the only way they knew how. So Margaret was haled into court. When offered probation, she refused, preferring to be sent to an institution so that she could get away from home.

Thus when Margaret was not quite eighteen, she was committed to the Women's Reformatory on a two-year indeterminate sentence on the charge of being a " stubborn child." [9]

*   *   *

Angelina — a psychotic. Angelina's parents are Portuguese who had been in America only two years when the girl was born. Upon their arrival from Portugal, they settled in a coastal village in Massachusetts, among relatives who were mostly fisher-folk. The parents are illiterate and hardly speak English. Angelina's father, a barber by trade, is a meek little man, anxious to provide for his family; but though he has worked steadily and hard, he has been able to earn only about seventeen dollars weekly.

When Angelina was but a year old, her mother died, leaving five children, of whom she was the youngest. A year later her father remarried, the stepmother being also Portuguese. The family then moved to a large city, where they settled in a poor tenement district overrun with small shops. Although their home was crowded, the three-family house boasted a small back-yard, in which Angelina and her brothers and sisters were wont to play. The little girl was rarely allowed leisure hours, as her stepmother insisted that she and an older sister help with the housework.

Angelina's stepmother was very insistent that all the youngsters attend church regularly, and Angelina was confirmed when she was thirteen. Of the six children born of her father's second marriage, two were epileptics. Most of Angelina's brothers and sisters were, like herself, mentally retarded and also very much neglected physically. One of Angelina's brothers was arrested for larceny, and a sister ran away from home. Other than this there has been no serious delinquency in the family.

As Angelina was frail and small for her age, she was not sent to school until she was eight years old. She was very shy and nervous as a child, a bed-wetter,

[9] The story of Margaret is continued on p. 164.

and on occasion would waken from sleep shouting and crying. This annoyed her stepmother to such an extent that she developed a hostility to Angelina, which expressed itself in frequent scoldings and in a demand that the child do more than her share of the housework. For the first few years of her schooling, Angelina was in public school, but was then sent to a parochial school, leaving in the sixth grade at the age of fifteen. Although she was backward in her studies, she was quiet and not particularly noticed by her teachers. On several occasions the school nurse had to take her in hand because she had " nits in her hair," which was very long and thick and of which the little girl was very proud.

Angelina very early showed a love for pretty clothes and a pride in her appearance which, however, was confined only to her outward clothing. From childhood she was inclined to adorn herself. On one occasion she stole a gay scarf from a neighbour to make into a shirtwaist, and she would often beg her parents for little trinkets, which, however, they were not able to give her.

When Angelina left school, she found a job in a five- and ten-cent store with the help of an older brother, of whom she was very fond because he always " took my part." After about three months she was laid off, and as she did not seem to be able to find other work at this time, her parents allowed her to remain at home. Despite her stepmother's objections, Angelina began going about to dance-halls and, in order to escape punishment, lied about her doings.

After Angelina had been helping at home with the housework for about a year, she found a job as a chocolate-dipper. In the factory she very soon fell in with several immoral girls, from whom she learned to pick up men. Though she went about only with men whom she " liked and not for money," one young fellow gave her inexpensive clothes and trinkets, which she dared not show her parents, but which she joyously exhibited to her girl friends. When this young fellow induced her to be his " steady " on promise of marriage, she had immoral relations with him often from the time she was sixteen years old. Only because it was physically impossible (a fact later revealed in the Reformatory) did she escape pregnancy.

About this time Angelina cut off her heavy hair, telling a fantastic tale about having been kidnapped and having her hair cut off by her abductor, from whom she succeeded in escaping. Not long after this she dyed her hair a flaming red, took to high-heeled shoes, bright-coloured bérets, and tawdry dresses. Her parents were inclined to think that she was " queer " and did not know what to make of her, nor did they know how to handle her fast-developing lack of control of her bladder and her bowels.

Finally, when Angelina was seventeen, she ran away from home. On the next day her father had her arrested on a charge of being a " stubborn child." She was placed on probation and was taken by her father to a girl's protectory, where she was kept for only two weeks, as she proved unmanageable and was unclean about her person. When she returned home, Angelina began to run around again. Although she did not actually prostitute, she allowed men to pick her up, give her a meal in a cheap restaurant, or take her to a dance. Angelina's stepmother grew very impatient with her, and her meek little father rarely interfered with the discipline of the girl. Not long after, Angelina again ran away from home, and as she was drifting about wondering what she would do next, she was picked up by a young Italian who offered her a bed in his home. He lived in the basement of an apartment-house, of which his father was janitor. Angelina stayed with this boy for two weeks, having illicit relations with him and with his brother. It was later revealed that these young fellows often brought girls there for disorderly purposes. When Angelina was found, she was arrested upon her father's complaint. She was asked by the judge whether she preferred to return home or go to the Reformatory and shouted: "I would rather go there because I don't dare face my stepmother again. . . . People that haven't got a stepmother think it's fun, but they don't know what it is." So she was given a two-year indeterminate sentence on the charge of being a "stubborn child." At this time she was eighteen years of age.

A few days after her commitment Angelina had to appear in court on a writ of habeas corpus at the trial of the Italian youth with whom she had been living just prior to her arrest. Though she testified against him, she yelled and screamed and begged that no harm be done him, as she expected to marry him on her release. She claimed later that he had promised marriage to her "if anything happened." Her pleas did not prevent his sentence to jail.[10]

*   *   *

Minnie — "everybody's woman." On the maternal side Minnie is a descendant of a degenerate, run-down, Yankee family, notoriously feeble-minded, numerous members of which have been supported by the public welfare department of their town for three generations. Minnie's maternal great-grandfather was a full-blooded Indian. The second wife of her maternal grandfather was formerly an inmate of the Reformatory for Women. The women of the family on the mother's side have the reputation of "liking the fellows — it seems to run in our family."

Minnie is the oldest of three children. Both her parents were born in Massachusetts. Her father was a wood-chopper who earned a very scanty living for his family. A hard drinker, he was very unkind to his wife and children when intoxicated. It was often necessary for the mother to take the children away from home for short periods, to stay with relatives during his drinking spells. Although Minnie's mother kept house for the family and very rarely worked out, she was a very poor disciplinarian, very nervous, and entirely incapable of controlling the girl.

During Minnie's early years the family moved about a great deal in rural

[10] The story of Angelina is continued on p. 168.

communities and small towns, because of the occupation of the father. This meant that she was transferred from school to school. Despite the fact that she stammered somewhat, bit her nails, and was very stubborn, she does not seem to have been singled out in her school years for any particular attention.

When Minnie was twelve years old, her father died, leaving the mother with three daughters to support, and Minnie was sent to her grandmother's temporarily. At this time her mother applied for assistance to the S. P. C. C. in placing Minnie in a boarding-home; she herself was about to remarry and her prospective husband did not wish to have the girl in their home, as she was " incorrigible, stubborn, lazy, impudent, and profane." Minnie's mother had already made several attempts to place her as a domestic, but the girl remained in the situations secured for her for only short periods. In desperation, her mother thought it might be well if the girl were sent to a correctional school, since she was beginning to fall in with bad companions. The situation was complicated by the fact that Minnie's mother had now married again and she and the girl's step-father were living in the home of the husband's father, who refused to allow Minnie to remain under his roof any longer. There were no relatives who were willing to board her, so the mother continued her attempts to place Minnie as a domestic.

While the S. P. C. C. was determining what to do with Minnie, her mother, who was growing very nervous and irritable because of her continued inability to control the girl in any way, made application to the Department of Public Welfare and also to a children's home to take Minnie off her hands. Meanwhile the girl decided that she did not wish to attend school any longer and left at the age of fourteen, having reached only the sixth grade. The S. P. C. C. at this point placed the girl in a near-by family, and the mother, encouraged by this action, withdrew her request of the other two organizations to act in the case. When Minnie had been in the foster-home for two months, her mother, against the wishes of the S. P. C. C., removed her and soon arranged a marriage for her with the feeble-minded son of feeble-minded parents who lived in the neighbour-hood. He was several years older than Minnie. As the girl was only fourteen, her mother falsified her age on the marriage certificate and got her " safely married," being much relieved to have the girl off her hands.

As the earning capacity of Minnie's husband was very low, the young couple who had taken a small house, were forced to move for non-payment of rent. Throughout the first winter Minnie's husband was able to earn only twenty-five dollars. For a short time the two lived with the husband's father and then moved from shack to shack on various farms where Minnie's husband was able to pick up a little work. Then they built a shack of their own on the pasture grounds of his father's farm. Minnie's mother found that she soon had to come to the assistance of the couple if they were not actually to lack even the bare necessaries of life.

Some ten months after marriage Minnie gave birth to a boy. When the child was only seven months old, complaints were received by the S. P. C. C. that this child was being grossly neglected and that Minnie was having immoral relations with a cousin of her husband's. Minnie meanwhile was boasting that her husband was not the father of her child, and frankly told a number of persons that she hated her husband and had not wanted to marry him. She soon got into the habit of staying out late nights and having " a hell of a time " with two of her husband's cousins.

She made no effort to keep her miserable little home in any kind of trim. The place, which was tiny, was always in great confusion. The girl had made some attempt to keep her first home clean and neat, but gave up when they were forced to live in shacks. Dishes were left unwashed for days. The furniture was shabby, and food scarce. Minnie was becoming very impatient of this situation and was eager to find work.

When her first baby was ten months old, Minnie again became pregnant. She expressed the desire to have the state assume the care of the coming child and would have been willing to let almost anyone take guardianship of her first baby. Even her mother-in-law admitted that not only was the girl incompetent to bring up children, but that Minnie's husband was unable to care for his family. As the home situation was becoming entirely unbearable, the S. P. C. C. arranged for Minnie and her child to board out, and work was obtained for her husband so that he could support his wife and child until her confinement. When the second child was to be born, Minnie went to the home of her mother-in-law, and her husband joined her there. Very soon after, the couple were turned out and went to live with an aunt of Minnie's husband.

Meanwhile Minnie continued to be very free with men, even in her husband's presence. When the second child was not quite two years old, she left home and went to work in a restaurant frequented by college boys, boarding her younger child in the vicinity. The older boy was left in the care of her husband's parents. There was no help forthcoming from her mother who was also in very difficult circumstances and living in a shack. Though Minnie soon rejoined her husband, she was constantly running about with other men, claiming that her husband knew all about her actions and didn't care what she did. Meanwhile their younger boy was still being boarded out and the older child was with Minnie's mother-in-law, who had refused to harbour the younger one because she felt quite certain that her son was not its father.

A few months later, Minnie and her husband again separated, Minnie going to her mother's home with her younger boy and continuing to work here and there as a domestic and in restaurants. Although her husband was not contributing to the support of the child, Minnie had no grounds against him for non-support, as she had refused to live with him. He had been contributing to the support of the older boy but was now unable to do even this.

It soon became apparent that Minnie was badly neglecting her child, and the S. P. C. C. brought her, her mother, and her husband to court on a " neglect " charge. As it was found that none of the three was able to contribute to the youngster's support, he was adjudged " neglected " and committed to the care of the state. Minnie did not return to her husband, and her mother did not wish to have her at home, either, because she considered her a deleterious influence on her young sisters. So Minnie was turned out on her own resources, entirely free of the responsibility of caring for her two children and with no further ties to her husband.

Five months later she gave birth to a third boy. Her expenses at the hospital were paid by the town. Minnie returned to her mother's home for after-care, the town paying her a small amount for nursing the girl. Minnie did not assume any responsibility for this third child and made no effort to breast-feed or care for it in any way. The agent of the S. P. C. C. finally brought a complaint against Minnie for neglect of her third child and against her husband for non-support of his wife. The couple were arrested and taken to court. The complaint against her husband was dismissed, as the judge decided that he was not competent or able to support his wife and child. But upon testimony of the local town clerk, a landlady, a police officer, a physician, and several others, more than sufficient evidence was presented for a charge of adultery against Minnie. It was even revealed that the alleged father of Minnie's third child had made a bet with some of the neighbourhood bums that he could have intercourse with Minnie under a street light, and that he had won his bet, the act taking place behind a bowling-alley while the gang watched from outside the window.

Thus, at the age of twenty, Minnie, the mother of three children, at least two of whom were illegitimate, was committed for adultery to the Women's Reformatory, and an order was issued that the youngest child, then only one month old, should accompany her.[11]

* * *

Dora — a chronic drunkard. Dora is the third of seven children. From the age of four until she was fourteen she attended a convent school in Canada, always paying particular attention to her religious duties. The family lived very comfortably on a farm, two children sharing a room, and later each having his own room. Dora was a healthy tomboy; she enjoyed bicycling, swimming, and other outdoor sports. She played a great deal with her three brothers and their friends, whose company she very much enjoyed. She " never thought to do anything wrong with boys, — treated them all just like brothers."

Dora's father was born in France; her mother was a French-Canadian. Both parents had a high-school education. From her father, who was a voracious reader, Dora acquired her love of books, particularly the classics. While she was

[11] The story of Minnie is continued on p. 172.

still in school, she was reading Shakspere, Voltaire, Hugo, and other famous writers. Dora's maternal grandfather was a well-to-do lawyer in Canada. Most of her mother's people had established themselves in the professions, in the public service, or as merchants. One of Dora's brothers subsequently became a publisher of a French newspaper. All of her six brothers and sisters, now grown to mature manhood and womanhood, are highly respected citizens of their communities. Dora is the only one who has given her family grave concern.

When Dora was fourteen, the wheat crop failed on her father's farm and her parents decided to sell the place and migrate to Massachusetts. So the girl left the convent school and went to work in a mill as a spinner. She held her first job for a year and then, hearing of a more remunerative opening, changed to another mill. She was an efficient worker and able to earn from twelve to twenty-two dollars weekly. She kept her second job, during the seasonal periods of employment, for many years and soon joined the mill-workers' union.

When Dora was eighteen years old she became deeply infatuated with a young police officer who was already married and had several children. She carried on a secret affair with him for six years. It was during this time that she had her first taste of gin, offered her by her lover. A local priest and the chief of police, knowing of her affair with this man and becoming very much concerned for them both, begged them to break the alliance. After a severe quarrel Dora decided not to see her lover again. She was now twenty-four years old. Very shortly after breaking with her lover she was arrested for drunkenness and for being idle and disorderly. From this time on, Dora has been in and out of jail many times because of drinking.

In the company of several other girls and two men, she began to travel about among the mill cities of New England, "following the wages," going from town to town wherever there was a possibility of better pay. Occasionally she would return to the home of her parents and take up her work at the local mill, where she was always reinstated. Most of her earnings, when she was not on a spree, Dora would send to her parents:

> "When I don't drink, I spend my money in a very good way, — help the poor, give it to my mother, dress up nice, save a little, too. When I am drinking, I spend it for booze or lend it to somebody. Might as well say good bye to it, — it's never returned."

During her periods of drunkenness, Dora would not communicate with her family, as she did not want them to feel the disgrace of her conduct.

Shortly after the termination of her love-affair Dora took up with another man, who has since been " like a brother " to her and has helped her out of many difficulties. Speaking of her alcoholic habit, Dora said: " I was wild and I go what you'd call crazy-like. Sometimes I stopped for six or seven months and go right. Immorality don't bother me much. It's liquor and going out. Of course sometimes, if you're full of liquor and feel like raising the Devil you'll do it." Though Dora was occasionally immoral, it was always with men whom she knew. She had no particularly strong sex urge, but when very drunk would yield to her friends.

When Dora was twenty-nine years old, she was again arrested for being " idle and disorderly " and was sentenced to the Reformatory for Women (this is not the particular sentence we are studying), where she remained for nine months. After her release, although she was many times found drunk by the police, they rarely took her into custody. It was not until nine years later that she was again arrested. On this occasion she was released. Four months thereafter she was apprehended for " lewd and lascivious cohabitation " and was given a sentence of five months in jail. She was arrested several more times for drunkenness, but it was not until two and a half years later that she was once more sent to jail, this time for four months. Six months after her release, when Dora was forty-two years old, she was arrested in the company of two strange men from whom she had got some " moonshine," and was committed to the Reformatory for Women on a two-year indeterminate sentence for " common night walking." [12]

* * *

Louisa — a murderess. Louisa's childhood was spent among the vine-clad hills of a tiny village in a sunny province of northern Italy. Her parents managed by grape-growing to make a living for their three children, a son and two daughters, of whom Louisa was the youngest. The father and brother spent the winters in near-by France as farm-hands in order to meet the tax payments on their little property.

Louisa's parents had been born and bred in the village in which the little girl spent her childhood. They came of wholesome peasant stock, people whose ancestors were of sound reputation and were known in their community for honest dealing. The parents were devoted to their children, and although they were always on the border of poverty, the youngsters had no realization of the financial plight of their parents until a casual remark of her mother's, when Louisa was about eight years of age, about the difficulty of meeting the tax payments, set the little girl to thinking how she could make the family fortune.

The leisure hours of the children were spent climbing among the hills, picking grapes, blackberries, and peaches, and wading in streams under the bright Italian sky. The family's social life was among the local peasantry and mainly centred in the church. Little Louisa loved the colourful religious ceremonies. When she was six years old, she attended a near-by convent school, where she was taught by the Sisters. When she reached the highest grade in the school, at the age of eleven, she insisted on starting her vocational training. Though her parents were loath to part from her, the little girl was so determined that they finally agreed

[12] The story of Dora is continued on p. 177.

she should serve as an apprentice to a cousin of her mother's who was a dress-maker in a neighbouring city. Here Louisa lived for seven months, when she grew so homesick that she was sent back to her parents.

Though she was not yet twelve, Louisa shortly decided that she really did not want to spend the rest of her life on the farm. Relatives found a position for her as a domestic. In her first place she remained for nine months and then went to the family of a French physician, where she remained for over a year as cook and general housemaid. She then worked for some months as a lady's maid, and for two years as a cook, changing jobs only to increase her earning capacity. During these years Louisa was in very close touch with her parents and visited them often. She sent them a large part of her earnings, as her father was ill and in great straits.

When Louisa was fifteen years old, her brother emigrated to America, return-ing several years later with a considerable amount of savings and glowing ac-counts of the opportunities there. He built a small house in the village of his birth for himself and his wife and took his parents to live with him. Louisa was now more determined than ever to help in their support because her sister-in-law resented their presence in her home. After much persuasion she won her parents' consent to go to America, and as an old friend of the family was about to mi-grate with a group of his townspeople, her parents agreed that she should ac-company them.

Louisa was now twenty-two years old, an olive-skinned, eager, vivacious girl with large dark eyes and heavy black hair, full of ambition to keep her parents in comfort. Before she left home, she paid up all their small debts and left a small sum of money with her brother for their use. When she arrived in America, she had fifteen dollars. With her friends she went directly to a small manufac-turing town where some of them had relatives. With their help she shortly se-cured a job in a mill, where she was able to earn eight to nine dollars weekly on piece work. She lived first with one of the girls with whom she had travelled to America, but as soon as she had got her bearings, moved into the home of a French family where she was able to live more economically, sending to her parents whatever money she could save — at times as much as fifty dollars.

When Louisa had been in America a few months, she met, through the family with whom she lived, a French-Canadian boy of sixteen who was also working in the mills. After some six months of casual acquaintance he avowed his love for her. He visited her regularly at her boarding-house, often taking her to the movies and for walks. Louisa's Italian friends were indignant at her association with a " Canuck " and in every way possible attempted to prevent her engage-ment to him, trying to make her believe that he was a " good-for-nothing loafer." Meanwhile, on promise of marriage, Louisa permitted sex relations. One of her Italian friends wrote Louisa's mother of her affair with this boy, putting the girl in a rather bad light, and her mother promptly urged Louisa not to delay marriage. When the couple had been acquainted for about a year, the boy introduced her to his parents and she was a frequent visitor in their home, although they were not enthusiastic about having an Italian daughter-in-law and felt that their boy was much too young to marry. He himself constantly put off talk of marriage, but upon Louisa's insistence finally gained the consent of his parents to the marriage, this being necessary as he was only seventeen years old at the time. The wedding was set for the coming Easter.

Until two months before the time for their marriage Louisa believed that her fiancé was loyal to her. Then some of her friends told her that he was visiting another girl. When she questioned him about this, he assured her that he still loved her and that the accusations were entirely false. Her suspicions were aroused, however, and she began to watch him very closely. She learned the identity of his new sweetheart and for several evenings watched her house until she saw her lover approaching. Meanwhile one of his friends who had noticed her lurking in the neighbourhood warned the boy before he reached there and he immediately turned on his heel. He went to Louisa's room and, not finding her there, did not await her return but left a message that he had been there. When he called on the next night, he remonstrated with her for being so suspicious of him.

For the next three weeks Louisa and her fiancé saw each other often, but quarrelled repeatedly because Louisa accused him of unfaithfulness. More fuel was added to the fire when Louisa, on returning home one evening, found her lover and another Frenchman, both half intoxicated. Her lover's companion was impatient to get away and wanted the boy to accompany him. Angered by his refusal to do so, the man blurted out to Louisa that her lover " was through " with her and was going with another girl. Louisa's resentment and jealousy were unbounded. She turned on her lover, who, as before, denied any infidelity. Without his knowledge, Louisa had secreted a revolver in the pocket of her sweater. This she had kept in her bedroom for some three weeks, ever since she first had suspicions of his unfaithfulness. The two went out for a walk, and a bitter quarrel ensued, in which she again accused him of going with another girl. He shouted that if she continued to watch his every move, he would " slap her." Louisa became thoroughly infuriated at this and quickly pulled out her revolver and shot him five times, then turning the weapon on herself. As there were no bullets left, however, she was not able to carry out her intent. She immediately gave herself up to the police and was jailed, tried, and held for eleven months before sentence was finally imposed.

Immediately there was much interest in her case, not only among the Italians of the community, but among many other citizens. Louisa had worked for almost three years in the local mill — her only place of employment since coming to America — and her reputation was of the best. She was known as a sober, attractive girl, deeply devoted to her family in Italy. Only a few weeks before the shooting she had sent them a hundred dollars. Immediately petitions were circulated for leniency, and several people offered to forward money to her parents so that they might not know of her plight.

While Louisa was in jail awaiting trial, she wrote frequently to her mother, without giving any hint of the tragedy which had befallen her. When her mother finally became suspicious and wrote to a friend to inquire whether her daughter was having some difficulty, Louisa learned of this and wrote her mother telling her the truth, imploring her not to feel too harshly toward her. Her mother's reply to this letter gave Louisa the courage which she needed to go through the long months of waiting in jail:

> "God forgive my little Louisa. I pray for you morning and night. In my heart I know you cannot do wrong, and your mother is many times more your mother in your hour of sorrow."

Not only Louisa's mother and her relatives, but many friends in Italy wrote to comfort the girl. Even the French physician for whom Louisa had worked as a girl wrote an offer of assistance. Louisa's friends felt that in killing her lover she had done what any self-respecting girl would do under the circumstances and Louisa soon became a heroine in her own eyes, coming to believe that she had performed a public service in ridding the community of an undesirable person.

Louisa was represented by counsel who made an eloquent plea for her at the trial. The charge originally against her was murder in the first degree, but finally, after much pressure on the district attorney by the lawyer and the local citizenry, he agreed to accept a plea of manslaughter, and Louisa was sentenced to five years and six months in the Women's Reformatory.[18]

3. Conclusion

In these sketches of a few of our delinquent women, we have traced their careers to the point of their commitment to the Reformatory, reserving for Chapter IX the resumption of their biographies beyond this particular crisis in their lives. But it is evident from even this portion of their life-stories that these women exemplify practically all the major problems of individual and social pathology. The psychiatrist and psychoanalyst will readily discern in them unsolved problems of neuroticism; the educator will recognize instances of faulty training; the eugenist will seize upon the evidences of tainted inheritance; the social reformer will point to the inequities and iniquities of the existing economic order. Like the famous blind men of the fable, each of whom gave his philosophy of the make-up of the elephant by feeling but a part of his structure, every specialist in the field of individual and social pathology who expresses a specialized opinion

[18] The story of Louisa is continued on p. 182.

on the causes and significance of careers such as these will be partly right and partly wrong. Case histories are impressionistic; though they suggest hypotheses, they supply no reliable estimate of the extent and ramifications of the problems involved in delinquency. The statistical method brings us nearer to such a goal.

Let us, therefore, turn to a description of the lives of the entire group of our five hundred *misérables*.

CHAPTER III

FAMILY BACKGROUND OF DELINQUENT WOMEN

1. Introductory

Having made the acquaintance of some typical inmates of the Massachusetts Reformatory for Women, let us now regard our five hundred offenders as a group, to see what traits characterize them and in what soil they were reared. The next five chapters are devoted to a detailed examination of the family background of our women, their childhood and adolescence, their marital and sex ventures, their entanglements with the law, and their activities within a year of commitment to the Reformatory.[1]

2. Parental Nativity, Citizenship, and Religion

Nativity of parents. Were the parents of our girls mostly Americans, or foreigners? Forty per cent of the fathers were born in the United States and the remaining sixty per cent were born either in Canada or in various parts of Europe, 13.6% of them all coming from French Canada and 8.5% from English Canada; almost 7% from Great Britain, 12.6% from Ireland, and the remainder from Italy, Portugal, Poland, Lithuania, Russia, and Finland, with a few from other European countries (Appendix D, Table 2–7).[1a] A considerably lower proportion of the fathers of our girls are of native birth than of the general male population of Massachusetts, where the native-born population in 1920 was 56.6% as compared to 39.8% for our group.[2]

It was found that 41.5% of the mothers of our girls were born in the United States, and that the remaining 58.5% are distributed in about the same way as the fathers in respect to place of birth (Appendix D, Table 2–8). As with the fathers,

[1] To be of the utmost value, the statistical description of any special class of the population, such as women prisoners, must be supplemented by comparisons with the *general* population. It is one of the vexing obstacles to sociologic and psychologic research, however, that reliable data respecting the general population are often not available. Wherever comparable statistics exist, they have been utilized in the chapters that follow.

[1a] These references to the detailed tables in Appendix D are inserted for the benefit of students and others who may wish quickly to consult them. The general reader is asked to ignore them.

[2] Percentage derived from the *Abstract of the Fourteenth Census of the United States* (1924), p. 21. The comparative data used throughout are as a rule facts regarding the situation in 1920, this being the census date nearest to the year when the highest proportion of our women entered the Reformatory.

a much higher proportion of the general female population in 1920 than of the mothers of our girls were born in the United States — 58.6% as compared to 41.5%.[3] In other words, there is a disproportionately high incidence of foreign birth among the parents of our delinquent women.

Because of the possibility of conflict of standards between foreign-born parents and native-born children, it is important to know for how many years each of the parents of our girls had been in the United States up to the time of the commitment of their daughters to the Reformatory. In 51% of the cases one or both parents had lived in America throughout their lives; in 33% one parent had resided here for sixteen years or more; in 2.7% of the cases for eleven to fifteen years; in 21.1% for six to ten years; in .8% for five years or less; and in 10.3% neither parent had ever been in the United States (Appendix D, Table 2–10a). Thus a substantial proportion of the parents of our girls had not lived in America at all or had been in the country for too brief a period to make an adequate adaptation to new-world ideals and customs. Some evidence of conflict of cultures may be gleaned from the fact that in 7.8% of the homes only a foreign language was spoken; in 14.9% some foreign language was spoken almost exclusively, although the parents knew English (Appendix D, Table 2–24b). These facts will be further taken into account in discussing the relationship of the nativity of the offenders themselves to that of their parents.[4]

Citizenship of parents. Did the foreign-born fathers of our girls become citizens of the United States or have they remained aliens? Of the 179 foreign-born fathers about whom this fact was ascertainable, 37.4% were naturalized citizens; 4.5% had their first papers; while the large proportion of 58.1% were aliens (Appendix D, Table 2–10b). In the foreign-born male population of Massachusetts in 1920 a slightly higher proportion were naturalized citizens — 44.3% as compared to 37.4%; 15.7% had their first papers; and 40% were aliens.[5]

Religion of parents. Of the 464 cases in which the religion of the parents of our girls was ascertainable, both parents were found to be Catholic in 54.5%; Protestant in 34.7%; Hebrew in 2.2%. In 8.4% of the cases, one parent was Catholic and the other Protestant; and in .2% one parent was Catholic or Protestant and the other Hebrew (Appendix D, Table 2–9).[6]

3. Socio-Economic Status of Families

Education of parents. Do our girls spring from families which have had good educational advantages? Are they the daughters of college or even high-school

[3] Percentages derived from the *Abstract of the Fourteenth Census of the United States* (1924), p. 21.

[4] See pp. 74–5.

[5] Percentages derived from the *Fourteenth Census of the United States, State Compendium, Massachusetts* (1924), p. 21.

[6] See p. 75 for comparison of religion of offenders with religious distribution of the general population of Massachusetts.

graduates? In 77.3% of the cases both parents had not attended school or were either entirely illiterate or could barely read and write; in 10.6% of the cases one parent had attended grammar school; in 7.4% more, both parents had attended common school; in 3.9% one parent went to high school; in .4% (two cases) both parents; while in but .4% of the cases did even one parent attend college. In no instances did both parents have a college education (Appendix D, Table 2–11). Certainly the educational achievement of the parents of our girls is far below that of the general population, of whom but 5.9% of those twenty-one years old and over in 1920 were illiterate as compared to 34.8% of the parents of our women.[7]

Occupation of parents. The meagre schooling of the parents of our delinquent girls is suggestive of low occupational status. Thus, only five of the fathers (1.1% of the known total) were professional men; 1.7% were engaged in clerical work; 25.6% were occupied in skilled trades of one kind or another (as carpenters, machinists, plumbers, and the like); 19.9% were factory hands; 27.3% day labourers; 10% farmers; 3.4% small shopkeepers or contractors; 7% porters, waiters, janitors, watchmen (Appendix D, Table 2–12). In the general male population of Massachusetts in 1920, 4.6% were engaged in the professions and 20.1% in clerical occupations, while in our group 1.1% were in the professions and 1.7% in clerical occupations.[8] Clearly, then, the occupational status of the fathers of our girls is far below that of the general population.

Did the fathers of our girls provide steadily for their families, thereby ensuring to them security of income, no matter how small it might be? Did they work continuously or were they frequently unemployed? Only 56.7% of the fathers were " regular " workers; 18.4% were " fairly regular " workers; and 24.9% were irregularly employed (Appendix D, Table 2–14a). By " regular " employment is meant almost continuous work, very few breaks in employment, and these not due to any fault of the worker. The " fairly regular " worker is one who has some periods of unemployment, due essentially to his own fault, but who also has certain periods of continuous work. The " irregular " worker is one who has frequent stretches of unemployment, due to loafing, laziness, excessive drinking, and other such undesirable conduct.

To what extent did the mothers of our girls supplement the family income by gainful employment? Almost half (44.3%) of the mothers [9] remained housewives throughout the childhood and adolescence of our girls; 55.7% of them worked to supplement the family income. In 1910 in Massachusetts, 11.6% of all married women were gainfully employed, which proportion contrasts greatly

---

[7] *Fourteenth Census of the United States, State Compendium, Massachusetts* (1924), p. 20.

[8] Percentages based on figures derived from the *Fourteenth Census of the United States, State Compendium, Massachusetts* (1924), pp. 62–5.

[9] If the mother was removed from the home by either death, desertion, separation, or divorce before the offender was five years old, this refers to the usual occupation of the stepmother or foster-mother.

with the 55.7% of mothers of our girls gainfully employed.[10] Of those mothers who worked to add to the family income, 35.1% were factory hands; 33.2% were engaged as domestics, usually living at home, but sometimes also living out; 6.9% worked on farms; 12.4%, though not going out of their homes to work, brought their work (laundry, sewing, and the like) into the home; 2.7% ran lodging-houses or stores; and the remaining 9.7% were engaged in various occupations such as practical nursing, clerical work, vaudeville (Appendix D, Table 2–13). Over half the women (54.1%) worked steadily, which means that they were almost continuously away from home; 21.9% worked fairly regularly; and 24% worked sporadically (Appendix D, Table 2–14b).

Economic condition. In view of the large proportion of mothers of our girls who helped to supplement the family income, we are not surprised to find that only 8.7% of the families were in " comfortable " economic circumstances during the childhood and adolescence of the girls,[11] which signifies that they had resources sufficient to maintain themselves for at least four months in case of the unemployment of the bread-winners; 78% were in " marginal " circumstances; that is, were living on daily earnings and saving little or nothing. Temporary aid from either public or private sources might have been resorted to occasionally in order to tide over a critical situation, but with this small assistance the family was able to manage its economic problem. The remaining 13.3% of these families were " dependent " during the childhood and adolescence of our girls, which means that they were receiving aid continuously from public funds or from private social agencies (Appendix D, Table 2–34a).

Social agency contacts. Another indication of the low socio-economic status of our families is afforded by the extent to which they were dealt with by social service agencies. The high proportion of 76.6% of these families were known professionally to social agencies at one time or another prior to the commitment of the daughters to the Reformatory. At least 697 agencies had contacts with these families. Of this group of families (representing 359 households about which the facts were known), 24.2% were dealt with by one welfare agency, 24.2% by two, 15% by three, 9.2% by four, 7% by five, 5.9% by six, 14.5% by seven or more, the mean number of organizations concerned with the social welfare of these families being 3.65 ± .07 (Appendix D, Table 2–38).

The rendering of assistance to a family by a social agency does not necessarily imply giving them financial relief. The social services given to 49.6% of the families had to do with the physical or mental health of one or more of its members; the service rendered to 67.6% of the families dealt with problems relating to child welfare; 10.4% with correctional problems; 9% with provisions for recreational

---

[10] *Fifteenth Census of the United States, Population Bulletin " Families," Massachusetts* (1933), p. 23; *Occupation Statistics, Massachusetts* (1932), p. 70.

[11] Where the economic condition was not the same throughout childhood and adolescence, the lower economic status was tabulated.

expression. Half (53.4%) of the families, however, were given financial relief in one form or another, even though only occasionally (Appendix D, Table 2-39).[12]

How old were our girls at the first contact of a social service agency with their families? Of the 353 girls whose families were dealt with by welfare organizations and whose age at that time was definitely known, 18.4% were five years or younger, 13.6% were six to ten years old, 21.8% were between eleven and fifteen years of age, 27.2% were between sixteen and twenty, and 19% were twenty-one years or older (Appendix D, Table 2-37). The mean age of the girls at the time of the first contact of a social agency with their families was 14.5 years, ± .29.

Home and neighbourhood conditions. It may readily be inferred that our girls did not grow up in homes which afforded them many of the comforts or even the necessities of life. In fact during their childhood,[13] only 24% of the girls lived in homes the physical condition of which might be termed " good," in that they contained adequate space for wholesome living (not more than two people, excluding an infant, to a bedroom), were light, clean, and well ventilated, and had at least the minimum of furniture needed for comfort; 44.3% of them spent their childhood in " poor " homes which were overcrowded, filthy, scantily and shabbily furnished, and not infrequently even lacking ventilation and light. Almost a third (31.7%) of our girls grew up in homes that might be considered " fair," in that they had some features of the good home and some features of the poor one (Appendix D, Table 2-28a). Nor was there much change in the physical character of the homes of our girls during adolescence, only 24.1% being good, 31.5% fair, and the high proportion of 44.4% poor (Appendix D, Table 2-28b). Unattractive, overcrowded homes are well known to have an expulsive effect, the children seeking adventure in the streets.[14] Hence it becomes important to know the neighbourhood setting of these households.

The neighbourhoods in which our girls lived must be considered in relation to the constructive and destructive influences which pervaded them. A neighbourhood whose influences are " good " is one in which there are no street gangs and no centres of vice or crime within a radius of two square blocks in the city or a mile in the open country, and where there are opportunities for constructive

---

[12] The social services of health agencies as they are here construed include hospital and clinic care, either free or for a very small fee, supervision by a hospital social service department or a department of health; and for problems relating to mental health they include free hospital or out-patient treatment, and treatment in schools for the feeble-minded. The services rendered by relief and family welfare agencies include relief or any service that has to do with problems of family adjustment, such as domestic relations, and unemployment. The social services rendered in relation to child or adolescent welfare have to do with problems which relate specifically to the protection of children and adolescents, such as, provision for proper supervision, for nourishment, for clothing, for schooling. Correctional agencies deal specifically with the problems of delinquency.

[13] " Childhood " as used throughout this study means the period up to fourteen years; and " adolescence " from fourteen to twenty-one years.

[14] See, for example, the case of Marie, pp. 28 et seq.

recreation such as public playgrounds, settlements, school or community centres, within easy walking distance. A " fair neighbourhood " is one in which there are no street gangs and no centres of vice or crime, but also no opportunities for wholesome recreation near at hand. A " poor " neighbourhood is one in which there are corner gangs, bootlegging " joints," houses of ill fame, and similar centres of vice or crime, regardless of whether facilities for wholesome recreation exist or not. On this basis 17.6% of our girls resided, during their childhood, in neighbourhoods in which the influences were good; 49.7% in neighbourhoods in which the influences were fair; and 32.7% in neighbourhoods in which they were poor (Appendix D, Table 2–29b). In the adolescent years there was an increase in the proportion of girls living in neighbourhoods in which the influences were poor — 44.3% as compared to 32.7% (Appendix D, Table 2–30a). As indicated later, this increase is partly explained by the fact that some of our girls left home in early adolescence or before and established themselves in even worse neighbourhoods than their families had lived in.

During childhood 20.5% of the homes of our girls were located in what might be termed partly residential urban areas; that is, in business, factory, or lodging-house districts; 13.6% were in urban residential districts, meaning areas of tenements or private houses used mainly as permanent residences and not to house transients and from which business and factory areas are more than two blocks distant; 25% more lived in urban areas the nature of which could not be reliably determined; 6.7% of the homes were in outlying residential areas, or suburban districts in which there are mainly private houses, with considerable open space about them; and 34.2% lived in towns having a population of less than five thousand or in the country (Appendix D, Table 2–25). The only change in the neighbourhood setting of the homes of our girls during their adolescence is that a smaller proportion of them resided in rural districts or in small towns — 34.2% as compared with 21.8% during childhood (Appendix D, Table 2–26). This does not necessarily mean, however, that the families of our girls moved to urban districts, but rather, as will be seen later, that the girls themselves left their homes very early and drifted to the cities. As the general rural and small-town population of Massachusetts during the childhood and adolescence of our girls was 12.4%,[15] it will be seen that a far greater proportion of them lived in rural and small-town areas during their childhood and adolescence than did the general population.

4. Mental Characteristics

Little of a conclusive nature is yet known about the heredity of mental disease or its relation to criminality; or of the effect of low mentality of parents on the mental make-up and criminal conduct of their offspring. The high incidence of

[15] Percentages derived from *Abstract of the Fourteenth Census of the United States* (1923), p. 9, figures for the year 1910.

mental disease and defect among parents, siblings, and the immediate blood relations of our girls must be noted, however. In at least 58.6% of the families mental disease or marked " peculiarity," [16] or mental defect, or both, were present. Because such information is difficult to obtain, we are inclined to the belief that in some of the 41.4% of families in which neither mental disease nor defect has been noted, such conditions were actually present (Appendix D, Table 2–21). Reliable data as to the incidence of mental disease or defect in the general population (those not in hospitals or institutions as well as the others) are unfortunately not available.

5. The Pattern and Quality of Family Life

Size of families.[17] Turning now to the internal life of the families of our girls, let us consider first the size of the households. In but 3.1% of the families was there only one child (our girl). In 4.7% of the families there were two children, in 10.5% three, in 21.2% four or five, in 22% six or seven, in 17.9% eight or nine, and in 20.6% ten or more children. The mean number of children per family was 6.43 ± .08 (Appendix D, Table 2–18). If the parents are included, there is an average of 8.43 persons per family, which is twice the size of the average family in the general population of Massachusetts (4.4 persons).[18]

Conjugal relations of parents. Congenial relationships between parents are more likely to provide a wholesome atmosphere for growing children than the bickerings and hatreds of marital infelicity. What was the relationship of the parents of our girls to each other? [19] What example of marital felicity might our girls have absorbed? In 48.4% of the cases the conjugal relations of their parents were " good," which means that the spouses were compatible and there was no undue quarrelling between them; in 24.2% the conjugal relations were only " fair," in that there was gross incompatibility manifested by much quarrelling and lack of affection. In 27.4% of the cases the conjugal relations of the parents were " poor," which means that their incompatibility resulted in the desertion of one or both parents, in separation, or divorce (Appendix D, Table 2–23b). To over half of our girls, therefore, an example of marital infelicity was given.

Broken or poorly supervised homes. Recent criminological literature has frequently alluded to the high incidence, among delinquents, of households which have been broken by death, desertion, separation or divorce of the parents.[20] In

---

[16] As used here this includes " nervousness," psychoneuroticism, epilepsy, sufficiently marked to have been noted by those in authority.

[17] This refers to children born alive and includes step- and half-siblings.

[18] Abstract of the Fourteenth Census of the United States (1920), p. 459.

[19] This refers to own parents if both were living; if one or both were not living, it refers to their last known relationship, unless one parent died before the girl was five years old, in which event it refers to the relationship of one own parent to a step-parent or the relationship between foster-parents.

[20] See J. C. Colcord: Broken Homes (1919); E. J. Cooley: Probation and Delinquency (1927), pp. 87 et seq.; S. and E. T. Glueck: 500 Criminal Careers (1930); C. Shaw and H. D. McKay:

58.4% of the families of our girls there was such a break in the home before the girls had reached the age of twenty-one. And 31.8% more of the households, though not actually dissolved, were manifestly unfit for the wholesome rearing of children, because of the prolonged absence of one or both parents, or their incompatibility and constant quarrelling, or because the mother was gainfully employed and did not provide for the oversight of the children, or because the parents were extremely lax in their discipline. Only 9.8% of our girls were reared in homes which neither were broken during their childhood or adolescence, nor were for other reasons inadequate (Appendix D, Table 2–22).

The proportion of broken homes is much higher in our group of families than in the general population. In a recent study of Chicago families [21] it was found that slightly fewer than one seventh of the families in that city are broken by death, desertion, divorce, or separation. This gives us some general conception of the extent to which the families of delinquent women differ from those of the general population in this particular regard.

The significance of the factor of broken homes may be further inferred from the fact that 19.2% of our entire group of girls lost their mothers in childhood, and 6.9% more during adolescence; 18.2% of the whole group lost their fathers during childhood, and 9.8% more during adolescence. In 20.3% of all the cases the parents of the offender were separated or divorced during the childhood of the girls; and in 2.3% more, during their adolescence (Appendix D, Table 2–15).[22] In the 296 cases in which the homes of the girls were broken at any time before their commitment to the Reformatory, 47.6% were under seven years old when the first break in the home occurred, 16.2% were between seven and ten, 17.2% between eleven and fourteen years, 12.9% between fifteen and eighteen years, and 6.2% were nineteen or over. The mean age at which a break first occurred in these homes because of death, desertion, separation, or divorce of the parents was 9.06 years ± .21.

During at least half their childhood 68.7% of our girls lived with both their parents; 12.6% made their homes for the most part with one parent; and 9.1% with one parent and a step-parent. Eight per cent of them lived more than half their childhood either with relatives or with foster-parents, and 1.2% spent more than half their childhood in institutions (Appendix D, Table 2–31). Three fourths (76.7%) of our girls did not have step- or foster-parents at any time prior to their commitment to the Reformatory; 15.6% had step-parents; 7.7% had

"Social Factors in Juvenile Delinquency," *National Commission on Law Observance and Enforcement, Report on the Causes of Crime*, Vol. II, pp. 262 et seq.; S. and E. T. Glueck: *One Thousand Juvenile Delinquents* (1934), pp. 75–7, 91–2.

[21] M. Day: *A Study of Unpublished Census Data* (University of Chicago Press, 1932), p. 9.

[22] In 10% of all the cases the mothers of our girls remarried during the childhood of the offenders, and in 2.7% more they remarried during the adolescence of the girls; in 7.1% of all the cases, the fathers of our girls remarried during the girls' childhood, and in 1.3% more cases the fathers remarried during the adolescence of the girls.

foster-parents (Appendix D, Table 2–17a). The presence in the home not only of step- or foster-parents but of step- or half-siblings must be considered as a factor likely to contribute to psychological maladjustments in childhood. In 78.5% of the cases our girls did not have step- or half-siblings; 16.8% had half-siblings; 2.9% had step-siblings; and 1.8% had step- and half-siblings (Appendix D, Table 2–17b).

Parental discipline in childhood. It has already been inferred that a large proportion of the homes of our girls were inadequate to the wholesome rearing of children, either because they were very early disrupted or were otherwise unsuitable. As further evidence of their inadequacy we may consider the nature of the disciplinary practices of the parents. These might be deemed " good " in 8.2% of the cases, since there was consistent and firm control by both parents; not so strict, however, as to arouse an attitude of fear or hatred in the children. In 27.5% of the cases the discipline was at best only " fair," in that it was erratic, sometimes being firm, sometimes very lax; or inconsistent, in that one parent was very strict, the other very lenient. In the high proportion of 64.3% of the cases the disciplinary practices of both parents were " poor," in that they were either utterly neglectful in supervising their children or were so rigid in their control as to arouse strong resentment in them [23] (Appendix D, Table 2–35). In the larger proportion of these cases discipline was lax rather than rigid.

Moral standards.[24] The moral standards of the homes of our girls during their childhood might be considered " good " in 20.9% of the cases, " fair " in 30.9%, " poor " in 48.2% (Appendix D, Table 2–36a). As here used, " good " indicates thrift, temperance, wholesome ideals, conventional sex morality, and no delinquency among the members of the household (except for slight automobile offences or violation of licence laws). " Fair " is applied to homes in which there is an absence of thrift and wholesome ideals, but no delinquency. Homes of " poor " moral standards are those in which there is delinquency, or where antisocial conduct is lightly regarded or positively encouraged. During adolescence 55.1% of our girls lived in homes of poor moral standards, as compared to 48.2% during childhood (Appendix D, Table 2–36b).

Delinquency and criminality. What example of socially acceptable conduct did the parents and other close relatives of our girls set them? In the high proportion of 80.7% of the cases there was delinquency and criminality among the members of the family (excluding our girl), as follows: In 45.5% of all the families the parents or siblings had actually been arrested; in 31%, although arrests had not occurred, the antisocial conduct of parents or siblings was of such nature as to lay them open to arrest; and in 4.2% more of the cases, although there was no delinquency in the immediate family, near relatives with whom the girl was in

---

[23] See the case of Margaret, pp. 50 et seq.

[24] This refers to the moral atmosphere of the homes in which the offender lived. If she happened to be living alone, the standards of her immediate environment were considered.

frequent contact, or members of her foster-family, were known delinquents. Thus in but 19.3% of the families was there no delinquent conduct among the members of the families of our girls (Appendix D, Table 2–23a). Do we wonder that in such a milieu our girls early became delinquent?

6. Conclusion

It is not necessary to commit ourselves to any special theory of crime-causation in order to conclude from the foregoing analysis that our women offenders were most unfortunate in their biologic, social, and economic background. From a soil so unfavourable we can scarcely expect a hardy fruit.

In the succeeding four chapters we examine into the characteristics of the girls themselves.

CHAPTER IV

CHILDHOOD AND ADOLESCENCE OF DELINQUENT WOMEN

1. Introductory

Having described the family setting in which our five hundred girls spent their childhood and at least a part of their adolescence, we now turn to a consideration of the characteristics of the girls themselves. Who are they? To what environmental experiences were they subjected? How did they spend their leisure hours? With whom did they associate? What antisocial habits did they acquire? What was the nature of their employment? These are some of the many questions which naturally suggest themselves in an inquiry into their careers.

2. Colour, Nativity, Citizenship, Religion

Colour and nativity. In colour 93.6% of our girls are white, 5.2% are Negroes, and 1.2% are Indian or other (census designation) (Appendix D, Table 1–1b). This is a slightly lower proportion of whites and a higher proportion of Negroes than is found in the general population of Massachusetts, in which the white population in 1920 was 98.7%, the Negro 1.2%.[1]

Three fourths (75.7%) of our girls are native-born, 52.6% having been born in Massachusetts and 23.1% in other places in the United States; and 24.3% are foreign-born (Appendix D, Table 1–2b). Of the general female population of Massachusetts in 1920 (excluding the small number of Negroes, etc.), 71.9% were native-born, 27.1% foreign.[2] Of the foreigners among our girls, 13.2% were born in French Canada, 24.8% in English Canada, 11.6% in Russia or Finland, 10.8% in Ireland, 10.8% in Poland or Lithuania, 9.9% in Great Britain, 7.4% in Italy, 4.1% in Portugal or the Atlantic islands, and 7.4% in other foreign countries (Appendix D, Table 1–3).

In view of the possible conflict of cultures and traditions between native-born children and foreign-born (or mixed native and foreign-born) parents, the relationship of the nativity of our girls to that of their parents becomes significant. In 23.7% of the cases both the girl and her parents are foreign-born; in

---

[1] *Fourteenth Census of the United States, Massachusetts State Compendium* (1924), p. 18.
[2] Ibid,

31.3% they are all native-born; in 26.8% the girl is native-born and her parents foreign-born; in 17.8% the girl is native-born and one of the parents is native, the other foreign-born (Appendix D, Table 2-24a). In the general female population of Massachusetts in 1920 there was a somewhat higher proportion of foreign-born women of foreign parentage — 28% as compared with 23.7% in our group; and an essentially similar incidence of native-born of native parentage — 32.4% and 31.3%. Contrary to the usual findings,[3] there is a somewhat higher proportion of native-born girls both of whose parents are foreigners, in the delinquent group than in the general population — 26.8% as compared with 28.7%; but there is a substantially lower proportion of native-born women of mixed parentage (one parent foreign-born, one native-born) — 17.8% as compared with 10.9% in the general population. This suggests the hypothesis, subject to further research, that it is not so much a difference between the nativity of parents and their children that tends to create family friction and delinquency, as it is the difference in nativity of the parents themselves.

Were our foreign-born girls in the United States for any appreciable time prior to their admission to the Reformatory? A third (33.2%) had been in this country for eighteen years or longer, 23.6% for fourteen to seventeen years, 13% for ten to thirteen years, 16.3% for six to nine years, 6.5% for four to five years, 4.1% for two to three years, and 3.3% for less than two years. Thus it will be seen that by far the largest proportion of them have been in America for ten years or more (Appendix D, Table 1-6).

Citizenship and religion. Of those who are foreign-born and whose citizenship is known, eight (13.6%) are citizens by naturalization; one (1.7%) has her first papers; ten (16.9%) became citizens by marriage to citizens; and forty (67.8%) are aliens (Appendix D, Table 1-5).

What are the religious affiliations of our girls? Catholics are preponderant, comprising, as they do, 58.7% of the total; 39.3% are Protestants; and 2% are Hebrews. In the general population of Massachusetts there is presumably a somewhat higher proportion of Catholics than is found in our group (66.4%), a considerably lower proportion of Protestants (25.2%), and a higher proportion of Hebrews (6.7%) (Appendix D, Table 1-4b).[4]

---

[3] See E. H. Sutherland: *Criminology*, p. 101; S. and E. T. Glueck: *500 Criminal Careers*, pp. 118–19; and C. R. Shaw and H. D. McKay: "Social Factors in Juvenile Delinquency," *National Commission on Law Observance and Enforcement, Report on the Causes of Crime*, Vol. II, Chapter i.

[4] American Volume of the *World Survey*, prepared by the InterChurch World Movement (1920), pp. 206–7. The estimate given here cannot be considered absolutely reliable, particularly in respect to the Protestants, owing to the difference in methods of counting. The Catholic and Jewish estimates of religious affiliations are supposedly the equivalent of the whole Catholic or Jewish population; but the Protestant estimate is based on "confirmed membership" and those actually received as members.

3. Developmental Physical Condition [5]

In looking into the health of our girls we have taken account only of chronic physical conditions, or such handicaps as might partially or totally have incapacitated them for vocational adjustment or for normal recreational activity. Much thought has been given by certain psychologists and psychiatrists to the relationship between " organ inferiority " and deviations of personality, and it is for this reason that we are taking account of any serious incapacities. From this point of view, 65.7% of our girls had no serious physical condition or handicap during childhood or adolescence; while 34.3% did have such conditions, which included convulsions or " fits " (diagnosis not definite), fainting spells, epilepsy, violent and frequent headaches, and dizziness; such handicaps as deafness, markedly defective vision, deformity, or paralysis of a limb; and such seriously disadvantageous diseases as tuberculosis, asthma, rheumatism, and heart affections (Appendix D, Table 1–15).

4. Environmental Experiences

Earliest abnormal environmental experiences. We already know that a very large number of the homes in which our girls spent their childhood and adolescence were broken by the death, desertion, separation, or divorce of their parents. Four fifths of our girls who left the parental roof did so for reasons other than the disruption of the home, however. Only 11.1% of our girls suffered no breach with their home ties at any time prior to their commitment to the Reformatory. In the 88.9% of cases in which such a breach occurred it resulted in the girls' running away from home, going to live with relatives or foster-parents, being placed in non-penal or correctional institutions, moving about so excessively as not to establish any community ties, or migrating from a foreign country to the United States (Appendix D, Table 1–11).

How old were our girls at the time when these unusual experiences first occurred? A fourth of them (25.3%) were under seven years of age; 13.4% were between seven and ten; 17.1% between eleven and fourteen; 30.8% between fifteen and eighteen; and 13.4% were nineteen years or older, the mean age of the group at the time being 12.46 years ± .19 (Appendix D, Table 1–12). More than half of those girls who left the parental roof when they were under fifteen did so as a result of the break-up of the household, while almost half the girls who were between fifteen and eighteen years of age when they first left home, and two fifths of those nineteen or older, actually ran away.

It is of interest to determine the circumstances of or reasons for this first breach with the family. In 12.5% of the cases it was due to the death of one or both parents; in 4.6% to the separation, desertion, or divorce of the parents; in .7%

---

[5] This information was obtained from social agencies and institutional physicians. Such conditions as defective vision and the like had to be designated by them as existing to a marked degree, before being included as defects.

to the illness of a parent. In 12.5% of instances it was due to the fact that the girl was neglected or her home was for others reasons unsuitable so that the State or a private social agency had to intervene to protect her. In 15.7% of the cases it was due to the girl's own delinquency, as a result of which she was placed in a foster-home or committed to a correctional institution. In 6% of the cases the girl left home to go to work; in 17.1% she quarrelled with the family and ran away. And in 23% of instances the girl migrated to the United States (Appendix D, Table 1–13).[6]

Changes in household. In how many different households had our girls lived during the years prior to their commitment to the Reformatory?[7] In 14.5% of the cases they resided in the same household throughout; 20.2% of the girls had lived in two different households; 24.5% of them in three different households; 8.3% in four; and 32.5% in five or more (Appendix D, Table 2–32).

Mobility. Too frequent moving obviously interferes with the striking of roots in any one community, with making friends there, with participating in communal activities — in a word, becoming a stable and responsible local citizen. Excessive mobility is not, as will be seen, necessarily confined to those who later become delinquents and criminals, but is a common phenomenon of modern American urban life that obviously carries certain socially undesirable consequences in its wake. For the present purpose we have defined " excessive mobility " as moving about within a city from one neighbourhood to another more than once a year, or from city to city on the average of once in two years. With this as the basis of classification, no less than 66.2% of our girls moved about excessively (Appendix D, Table 1–10a). Although this proportion may appear to be high, it should be compared with the 64% of total changes of residence recorded in the city directory of Boston for 1921.[8] Of those girls who moved about excessively, 15.7% moved within one city; and 84.3% moved from city to city or came from a foreign country to the United States, this latter necessarily involving a complete uprooting of community ties (Appendix D, Table 1–10b). Even of those girls who did not leave the homes of their parents, 34% moved about so much with their families as not to become rooted in any one community. But the greatest amount of mobility (65.7%) occurred among those girls who left home.

Foster-home and institutional experiences. Over a fourth (29.1%) of our girls

[6] See also Appendix D, Tables 1–26, 1–27.

[7] If the girl lived for a time with her parents and then went off to work, living by herself, this is considered one change in household; if she then married and lived with her husband, this is considered two changes of household; if she left her husband to go to a lover, this is three changes in household; if she left the lover to return to her parental home, this is four changes, etc. A case in which the girl was living with her parents and married, and her husband joined her in this home, is not considered a change in household. See Appendix C, " Definition of Terms," *Household Stability.*

[8] This figure includes new names added in 1921, those crossed off as presumably having moved to other cities, and changes of address from one part of the city to another. The publishers state that such changes vary from 64% to 69% from year to year. These figures, then, give a rough estimate of the mobility of the population of Boston.

lived with foster-parents at one time or another prior to their commitment to the Reformatory. They had been placed in boarding-homes by the State or by private agencies or were sent by their parents to relatives, because their own homes had either been broken up or were for other reasons inadequate. Of the girls who were placed in foster-homes, 11.6% lived with their foster-parents for less than six months; 4.7% for six months to a year; 13.9% for one to two years; 5.4% for two to three years; 7% for three to four years; and 57.4% for more than four years (Appendix D, Table 1–69). The mean period of time which these girls spent in foster-homes was 33.28 months ± .88.

Over half our girls (54.7%) had been in penal or non-penal institutions at one time or another prior to their commitment to the Reformatory. About a tenth (8.1%) of all the girls had spent some time in correctional institutions for juveniles; 11.7% had been in orphanages; 1.2% (6 girls) in schools for the feeble-minded; 31.8% in a House of the Good Shepherd, almshouses, maternity homes, and similar protective homes for girls; 24% in institutions for adult offenders; 7.7% in hospitals for the mentally diseased, mostly for short periods of observation; and 4.8% were at one time or another, for considerable periods, in hospitals for chronic diseases to receive treatment for rheumatism, tuberculosis, heart disease (Appendix D, Table 2–6). These figures are not mutually exclusive, some girls having been in two or more types of institutions.

How many such institutional experiences did these girls have? Two fifths (42.4%) had had only one institutional experience, 18.9% had two, 12.1% three, 8% four, 6.1% five, 4.5% six or seven, and 8% eight or more, the mean number of institutional experiences among these girls being 2.71 ± .09 (Appendix D, Table 1–66).

Whether the time spent by the girls in institutions prior to their commitment to the Reformatory was sufficiently long to bring about a permanent change in their careers may be inferred from the fact that 23.5% of these girls had spent less than six months in institutions of one kind or another; 17.8% six months to a year; 20.5% one to two years; 10.8% two to three years; 7.7% three to four years; and 19.7% four years or more. The mean length of time spent in penal and non-penal institutions by the girls prior to their commitment to the Reformatory was 21.58 months ± .61 (Appendix D, Table 1–67).

5. Education

Illiteracy. Only 4.5% of our girls had not attended school at all, but 2% more, though having attended for a short time, were practically illiterate, making a total of 6.5% of illiterates among them (Appendix D, Table 1–36a). This is higher than the proportion of illiteracy in the general female population of Massachusetts in 1920, ten years of age and over, which was 4.9%.[9]

---

[9] *Fourteenth Census of the United States, Massachusetts Compendium, Population* (1924), p. 20.

Kind of schools attended. Of the 95.5% of the girls who had any formal education, 59.4% attended public schools in this country, 9% parochial schools, and only .4% (two girls) went to private schools; 17.2% attended both the public and parochial schools; 2% received their schooling in orphanages; 2.2% attended both the public schools and schools in orphanages or other institutions; 9% attended schools in foreign countries (Appendix D, Table 1–35).

Extent of schooling. The type of school attended is not so significant as the amount of schooling actually acquired. It should be mentioned that the mean age of our group on entrance to school was 5.8 years ± .04 (Appendix D, Table 1–36b). Hence it cannot be said that the inadequate schooling of our girls is essentially due to the fact that they were kept out of school until they were well advanced in years. Yet the high proportion of 21.9% of our girls had only six years or less of schooling; 15.8% had seven years; 22.3% eight years; 21.7% nine years; and 18.3% ten years or more. The mean number of years of schooling of our girls was only 6.34 years ± .07 (Appendix D, Table 1–37).

From this it may be anticipated that they had progressed relatively little through the grades or in high school and college. In fact, 35.8% (this includes 2.5% who were in special or ungraded classes) did not pass beyond the fifth grade; 16.8% the sixth grade; 17.5% the seventh; 21.7% the eighth. Only 8.2% attended high school, and of these all but 1% (four girls) never completed the course, while not a single one of the girls matriculated in a college (Appendix D, Table 1–39).

Compared to an average age of 5.8 years (± .04) on entrance, our girls left school permanently at a mean age of 14.5 years (± .04). This finding must be qualified, for not all of the girls attended school regularly. If by " regular attendance " is meant only occasional absence due to illness, and by " irregular attendance " absences so frequent as to interfere with the continuity of study — say an average of one absence weekly because of either illness, truanting, helping at home, or the like — then only 40.7% of our girls attended school regularly, and 59.3% attended irregularly (Appendix D, Table 1–42b).

Scholarship; retardation. How did these girls respond to instruction? Only 11.8% had at one time or another been rated by teachers as above the average in scholarship, 27.7% as average; and the high proportion of 60.5% were poor students (Appendix D, Table 1–42a). This should be borne in mind when the mental characteristics of the group are described.[10] The scholarly attainment of our delinquent girls is much lower than that of Boston school girls whose scholarship was excellent in 12.7% of cases, average or passable in at least 77.0%, and poor in only 10.3% as compared to 60.5% of our group.[11]

How much were our girls retarded in school? The word " retardation," as

---

[10] Pp. 192–3.

[11] Percentages compiled from figures given in *Boston School Document No. 12* (1925), pp. 102, 106, Tables LVI and LX. Figures for all of Massachusetts were not available.

used here, does not necessarily imply mental deficiency. It has to do rather with deviation from the norm at which certain grades are attained. In judging this, the scale applied in the Boston public schools for age-grade attainment was used.[12] This revealed that only 10.4% of our girls were not retarded in school; 10.7% were one year behind grade, 23.8% two years, 24.7% three years, and 30.4% four years or more, making the high total of 89.6% who were retarded one or more years. Even when we omit those who were retarded for only one year, we still have the considerable proportion of 78.9% who were two years or more behind grade for their age (Appendix D, Table 1–41). This is a very much higher proportion than the retardation of girls in the Massachusetts schools in 1926, of whom 8.7% were retarded one or more years, 61% were in the normal grade for their age, and 30.3% were one or more years advanced in school.[13]

Correlation between the school retardation of our group and their intelligence level suggests that, while mental deficiency partly explains it, retardation is partially due to other causes. For instance, while 43% of the girls retarded two or more years were feeble-minded, 15.5% were of normal intelligence.

Reasons for leaving school. The reasons why our girls left school may be summarized as follows: 51.7% left on economic grounds; that is, usually, because the circumstances of the family necessitated that they go to work or that they help with the housework at home; 8.2% left primarily because they or their families felt they were unable to make any further progress; fifteen girls (3.7%) left because of physical disability.[14] A tenth of the group (9.5%) left school mainly because they were not interested in pursuing their education any further; seven girls (1.8%) were expelled from school for misbehaviour of one kind or another; 5.2% left when they were committed to correctional institutions or placed in welfare homes, such as the House of the Good Shepherd; 5.7% gave as their reason for leaving school graduation from grade school; and in 14.2% of the cases various other reasons for leaving were given, such as dislike of the teacher, or that the school was too far away from home (Appendix D, Table 1–38). A lower proportion of Boston schoolgirls leave grade school for economic reasons — 34.7% as compared with 51.7% of our girls — and also a lower proportion because of dissatisfaction with school — 3.8% as compared with 9.5% in our group. It is striking, however, that 18% of Boston schoolgirls left grade school because of physical disability, as compared with 3.7% of our girls.[15] The difference in proportion is probably explained by the fact that our girls left school so much earlier than the girls of the general population and therefore in ad-

---

[12] See Appendix C, "Definition of Terms," *Retardation in School,* for age-grade scale.

[13] *Massachusetts Department of Education Bulletin,* "An Age-Grade Study in Massachusetts" (1927).

[14] Of these, five were forced to leave because they were pregnant, and the others because they had some condition, such as tuberculosis or rheumatism, which needed hospitalization.

[15] Percentages based on figures in *Boston School Document No. 12* (1925), Table XXXIV, opposite p. 70, and Table XXXIX, p. 77.

vance of the development of any physical disabilities sufficient to warrant their leaving school.

6. Industrial History

First employment. As so many of our girls left school when they were still very young, they were wholly unprepared to earn a livelihood. Only 5.7% of them took vocational courses such as secretarial, millinery, or dressmaking, after the completion of their formal schooling. It is to be noted, however, that 48.6% of them had expressed some definite vocational ambition at one time or another during their childhood or adolescence. Thus 15.8% had expressed a wish to become nurses, 4% to be teachers, 5.4% nuns, 7.1% clerks, book-keepers, or stenographers, 4.8% to go on the stage, 5.7% to be dressmakers or milliners [16] (Appendix D, Table 1–17). To what extent these ambitions were actually fulfilled we shall see shortly.

Because of the early age at which our girls left school, we are not surprised to find that they entered gainful employment almost equally early, the mean age being 14.9 years ± .06 (Appendix D, Table 1–44). The proportion of 14.2% began to work before they were fourteen. This is striking, especially in view of the important step recently taken to abolish child labour throughout the country. Over a third (37.4%) were fourteen years of age when they entered gainful employment, 33.6% were fifteen or sixteen, 8.4% were seventeen or eighteen, and 6.4% were nineteen years or older.

For the purposes of this study the classification of occupations utilized by Mabel R. Fernald and others in their book: *A Study of Women Delinquents in New York State* [17] was adapted in order that the findings of the two researches might be comparable. " Domestic service " applies to those working at general housework or as nurse-girls, waitresses, ladies' maids, cooks, or housekeepers in private homes, where room and board are in addition to wage. " Factory workers " include women working in a factory where there is a group of employees. " Laundry workers " are also included in this category, as the general conditions of work are similar to those in factories. " Home work " applies to women who earn their living while remaining in their own homes and who, for the most part, work alone. This applies to dressmakers, lodging-house keepers, janitresses, and those who bring work home from the factory. " Restaurant and hotel workers " include waitresses in restaurants and hotels and laundry workers in hotels. " Workers in stores " include saleswomen, cash-girls, messengers, errand-girls, demonstrators, milliners. By " clerical work " is meant book-keeping,

---

[16] The statements of vocational ambitions were secured from the girls themselves upon their admission to the Reformatory when they were questioned about their earlier interests and desires. These statements were, where possible, confirmed by parents or others who had been in close touch with the girls.

[17] New York: Century Company; 1920.

cashiering, secretarial, and other office work. " Day work " applies to those engaged in any kind of domestic service but not living in their place of employment, or to women who clean offices and factories.

Because of the moral hazards involved, the importance of a proper choice of the first occupation which a young girl enters cannot be over-estimated. On the basis of the above classification, it was found that the high proportion of 53.4% of our girls went into factories, or worked in laundries where the general conditions of employment are similar to those in factories; 22.5% entered domestic service; 8.9% did various kinds of domestic work by the day — cleaning, cooking, laundry work — but lived at home; 4.9% took jobs in stores, usually as errand- or sales-girls; 4.4% went to work in restaurants, hotels, or rooming-houses, as waitresses or chambermaids; 2.9% did various kinds of clerical work in business offices; 1.5% were engaged in gainful occupations in their own homes, such as sewing for factories or dressmakers; and the remaining 1.5%, a miscellaneous group, became vaudeville performers or took jobs as hospital attendants, or as ward maids (Appendix D, Table 1–45).

It has already been pointed out that a substantial proportion of our girls left school in order to supplement the family income. What remuneration did they receive in their first occupations? A wage of five dollars or less per week was paid to 39.7% of the girls; 51% received six to ten dollars, 8.9% eleven to fifteen dollars, and .4% (one girl) from sixteen to twenty dollars (Appendix D, Table 1–46). The mean earnings of the group in their first job were $6.50 ± .13.

How long did the girls remain in their first place of employment? Although the number of cases in which this point was unascertainable is uncommonly large (201), the findings are nevertheless significant. The analysis shows that 19% of the girls remained in their first jobs for less than a month, 31.3% from one to three months, 16.8% from four to nine months, 23.5% from one to two years, 6.6% three to four years, and 2.8% five years and over (Appendix D, Table 1–47). The younger girls held their jobs longer than those who were older when they began to work. This is partially explainable on the ground that those who were older upon entering employment are on the whole the girls who were more retarded in school and therefore whose adjustment was more difficult.

Usual employment. Even though our girls did not remain in their first jobs for very long, did they later pursue the same type of work? Did it become their usual occupation? By " usual occupation " is meant the one which was engaged in for most of the time or the one to which the girl returned the most frequently or, in the small number of cases in which different types of occupations were engaged in for about the same length of time, the one which required the most skill. Comparison between the first job and the usual occupation of our girls shows a considerable decrease in domestic service (from 22.5% as a first occupation to 13.4% as the usual one); a slight decrease in factory work (from 53.4% to 47.7%); a slight increase in restaurant and hotel work (from 4.4% to 6.5%);

a decrease in clerical occupations (from 2.9% to 1.7%); the movement of 10% of the group from outside pursuits into housekeeping; and entry into illegitimate occupations on the part of 8.4% of the girls (Appendix D, Table 1–49).

The average weekly earnings of our girls, though remaining low, nevertheless increased over the wage which they received in their first jobs. Thus, 1.9% still earned less than five dollars, 44.9% were able to earn from five to ten dollars a week, 40.8% from ten to fifteen dollars, 11.1% from fifteen to twenty dollars, and only 1.3% twenty dollars or more. The mean weekly wage of the entire group advanced from $6.50 ± .13 to $11.25 ± .14 (Appendix D, Table 1–5). The mean of the *highest* earnings achieved by the group at any one time was still greater — $15.45 ± .22 (Appendix D, Table 1–52).

How steadily did these girls work? By "regular employment" is meant almost continuous work, with not more than an average of two months of unemployment a year. By "fairly regular" work is meant unemployment in excess of two months a year, but compensated by periods of sustained work. The "irregular worker" is one who has frequent or long protracted periods of unemployment and no periods of sustained work. Three per cent (fifteen) of our girls never entered gainful employment. Of those who did, however, 7.5% were regular workers, 32.8% were fairly regular workers, and 59.7% were irregular workers. The longest time that our girls held a job was less than three months in 15.2% of the cases, three to six months in 13.7%, six months to a year in 21%, one to two years in 18.1%, two to three years in 14.4%, three years or longer in 17.6%, the mean for the group being 19.42 months ± .72 (Appendix D, Table 1–50).

From the fact that such a large proportion of our girls were only fairly regular or irregular workers, we are not surprised to find that to a very great extent their work habits were "poor" or at best only "fair." The girl whose work habits may be regarded as "good" is one who is reliable and industrious, has capacity for the work, and is an asset to her employer. The girl with "fair" work habits is one who has the capacity to be a good worker, but whose employment is interrupted by drinking, drug addiction, prostitution, and like vices; this term also describes the girl who makes considerable effort in her job, but is inefficient. The "poor" worker is one who, by her unreliability, laziness, or dishonesty is a liability to her employer. The term also includes those girls engaged in illegitimate employment. On the basis of such classification, the work habits of 16.2% of our girls were good, of 55.4% fair, and of 28.4% poor (Appendix D, Table 1–57b). More specifically, 75.2% of the girls were usually discharged for inefficiency, lack of dependability, drunkenness, or dishonesty, or left jobs because of laziness, restlessness, or desire for excessive leisure time (Appendix D, Table 1–53).

Summary of industrial adjustment. In order to make a composite summary of the employment history of our girls, we judged them, case by case, on the basis of their steadiness of employment and their work habits. Thus, if a girl is rated an " industrial success," it means that her work habits were good and that she was a regular worker. This class comprises only 2.9% of the group. A girl was rated a " partial success " if her work habits were good and she was a fairly regular or irregular worker; or if her work habits were fair or poor and she was a regular worker. In this category were 38.8% of our girls. A girl was rated an " industrial failure " if her work habits were poor and she was a fairly regular or irregular worker; or if she was engaged in illicit occupations to the exclusion of any, or almost any, legitimate work. The high proportion of 58.3% of our girls had to be placed in this last group (Appendix D, Table 1–43a).

7. Recreations

Constructive interests. The point need hardly be laboured that the more numerous the opportunities for wholesome utilization of leisure, the less the likelihood of indulgence in vice and delinquency. It therefore is important to know how many of our five hundred girls, at any time prior to their commitment to the Reformatory, belonged to any clubs or organizations in which their leisure time was constructively supervised. How many had any wholesome interests, such as music or gardening; or any hobbies which absorbed their playtime; or took any courses to further themselves vocationally? It is disquieting to find that only 19.7% of these girls had any such constructive recreations or interests at any time prior to their commitment to the Reformatory (Appendix D, Table 1–18a).

Church attendance. Church attendance, particularly on the part of children and adolescents, can have much value, not only in contributing to a character-building process, but in affording, through parish activities, a wholesome recreational outlet. Analysis shows that 55.4% of our girls attended church regularly during their childhood, 38.7% attended only occasionally, and 5.9% did not attend at all (Appendix D, Table 1–20a). During their adolescence there was a considerable falling off in church attendance, 24.1% of the group attending regularly, 62.8% occasionally, and 13.1% not at all. Probably the many unwholesome interests which developed in the lives of these girls during the adolescent years have much to do with the falling off in their church attendance (Appendix D, Table 1–20b).

Correlation of the religion of the girls with the regularity of their church attendance shows that those who were of the Catholic faith attended church more regularly than the Protestants during childhood, 65.3% of them attending regularly, 31.8% irregularly, and only 2.9% not at all; while only 44% of the Protestants attended church regularly, 48.8% irregularly, and 7.2% not at all. During adolescence there was a greater falling off in church attendance among the Protestants than among the Catholics — 33.3% of the Catholic girls attending church regularly, 60.1% irregularly, 6.6% not at all; while 11.6% of the Protestants attended church regularly during their adolescent years, 68.3% occasionally, and 20.1% not at all.[18]

Companionships and haunts. How many of our girls played about during childhood with boys and girls with whom association might lead to delinquency? How many associated with children whose influence, though not necessarily wholesome, was not harmful? At least 26.1% of our girls ran about in childhood with youngsters whose influence might be considered harmful. Actually the proportion is probably higher. This information was not easy to secure and we have no assurance that the data are complete (Appendix D, Table 1–18b). During adolescence there was a marked increase in unwholesome companionships, 87% of the girls associating with young people whose influence could be none other than detrimental to them. These included streetwalkers, " drunks," " pick-ups," bootleggers, persons known to the police as idlers, and like shady companions (Appendix D, Table 1–18c).

What were the play locales of our girls in childhood and adolescence? Did they attend community centres, supervised playgrounds, settlements? During childhood 23.9% of our girls played in alleyways, hung about the streets, frequented the movies, or idled around factories or army camps and other places entirely unsuitable to the recreational needs of children (Appendix D, Table 1–19b). During adolescence there enter into the picture cheap cafés and restaurants, houses of ill fame, pool-rooms, commercialized dance-halls and skating-rinks, disreputable hotels, and cabarets, no less than 81.1% of the girls frequenting such places (Appendix D, Table 1–21). The effect of these recreational outlets on the lives of our girls during their formative and impressionable years can well be imagined, though it cannot be precisely gauged.

8. Bad Habits and Early Misconduct

Harmful habits. Only 30.9% of our girls did not manifest during childhood any bad habits which might lead to conflict with the law, such as truancy, stubbornness, excessive lying, immorality, stealing, drinking. The remaining 69.1% had one or more such habits, sufficiently marked to have been noted and remembered by parents, social workers, teachers. At least 25.6% of the girls bunked out, ran away, or truanted at one time or another before they were fourteen years old; 38.6% were what might be termed " stubborn children," in that they continually defied their parents or other authorities; at least 11.5% of them were persistent liars; at least 23.9% indulged in illicit sex habits. At least 14.1% of our girls stole during their childhood; 1.7% (six girls) were, as children, addicted to drink (Appendix D, Table 1–21).

[18] Figures for the attendance of the Jewish women are not given because the numbers are so small.

As might well be expected, there was an increase of such harmful habits among our girls during their adolescence. In this critical period of their lives, only 5.3% of them had no bad habits. There was more running away and truancy during this time (a rise from 25.6% to 42.2%), and a very great increase in illicit sex habits (from 23.9% to 86.9%) and in drunkenness (from 1.7% to 25.4%). During the adolescent years also 2.6% of the girls developed the drug habit (Appendix D, Table 1–22).

Age at first misbehaviour manifestations. Criminologists are coming more and more to believe that delinquency has its roots in very early childhood. In our cases this conviction is borne out by the fact that at least eleven (2.3%) of our five hundred girls were under seven years of age when the first signs of delinquency became manifest in the form of truancy, stubbornness, stealing, or other such misbehaviour; 2.9% were seven or eight years of age, 4.9% were nine or ten years old, 9.9% were eleven or twelve, 20.5% were thirteen or fourteen, 22.8% were fifteen or sixteen, 17.1% were seventeen or eighteen, and 19.6% were nineteen or older (Appendix D, Table 1–25).

We have already pointed out that broken homes were of frequent occurrence in this group. The significance of this factor is increased by the finding that there exists some relationship between broken homes and early delinquency. Thus, while only 15.2% of the girls whose homes were not broken became delinquent at the age of twelve or less, the higher proportion of 23.1% of those whose homes were broken became delinquent so early.

9. Conclusion

The picture we have sketched is one of physical and mental handicap, broken and inadequate homes, early uprooting of family ties, abnormal environmental experiences, limited educational achievement, necessity for early self-support, poor industrial adjustment, hazardous recreations and habits, unwholesome companionships and haunts, and, most significant of all, early signs of such antisocial traits of character and behaviour as are commonly designated delinquent or criminal.

With the sinister background of these girls, and their personal defects, the task of society's institutions for coping with them may properly be regarded as herculean. Moreover, not only those agencies specially set up to deal with delinquency and criminality are involved, but practically all social institutions — the State and community, the home, the school, the recreational agencies, religious organizations, welfare agencies, and the general economic order as well as the standard of civilization which we pride ourselves upon having achieved. For it must be obvious from the description of the childhood and adolescent careers of our girls that by the time they fell into the hands of police, courts, and correctional institutions, they were in many respects finished products, the failures of all our socialized efforts. This significant fact must be borne in mind in assigning praise or blame to the Reformatory and the parole system which were compelled to deal with these women and their problems after other social institutions had obviously made a botch of the task.

CHAPTER V

SEXUAL AND MARITAL LIFE

1. Introductory

In a very large proportion of cases the occasion for the arrest, conviction, and imprisonment of our girls was the commission of a sex offence which society deems sufficiently serious and harmful to label " criminal " and to punish. Hence it becomes especially important for us to analyse the sex behaviour and marital life of our women. Such analysis is patently necessary, regardless of our views on the soundness and fairness of the laws governing the social control of the sex impulse.

2. Illicit Sex Life

Sex activity before marriage. Reliable estimates of the sexual unconventionality of the general female population in the socio-economic class of our women are not available. However, in a recent questionnaire study of the sex life of a thousand women of whom seven tenths were college graduates, it was recorded that 71 of the thousand had, by their own admission, indulged in sexual relations prior to marriage.[1] In our group, 254 of the women were married prior to commitment to the Reformatory, and of this number the high proportion of 74.1% are known to have indulged in illicit sex practices before marriage. Although an accurate comparison is not possible, it is safe to say that this is certainly a higher proportion of illicit sexual indulgence before marriage than in the general population.

Definition of illicit sex life. Of great significance is the nature of the illicit sex life of our women, married as well as single. For the purposes of this study, we have adopted some of the definitions of illicit sex activity from Abraham Flexner's well-known work *Prostitution in Europe,*[2] modifying them where necessary and adding some of our own, based on intensive study of our case histories.

The following categories were arrived at: (1) professional prostitute; (2) occasional prostitute; (3) one-man prostitute; (4) promiscuous adulteress; (5) one-man adulteress; (6) promiscuous-unattached; (7) unconventional; (8) doubtful.

[1] Katharine Bement Davis: *Factors in the Sex Life of Twenty-Two Hundred Women* (New York, 1929), Table A, pp. xviii, 19.

[2] New York: Century Company; 1914.

1. *Professional prostitute* refers to the woman who earns her livelihood entirely by prostitution and has no legitimate employment. She has sex relations habitually and promiscuously for money or other mercenary considerations.

2. The *occasional prostitute* is the woman who alternately emerges from and relapses into promiscuous prostitution between periods of legitimate employment or carries on prostitution without interrupting her legitimate occupation.

3. The term *one-man prostitute* is applied to the woman of the " mistress " type who gives her favours to one man only, for a period of time, in return for money or other mercenary considerations.

4. The *promiscuous adulteress* is the woman who, though living under the same roof with her husband, indulges in sex relations with other men.

5. The woman who lives with her husband for at least part of the time is categorized as *adulterous with one man* if she is having an illicit alliance which is not based primarily on mercenary considerations.

6. An unmarried woman, or one who is widowed, separated, or divorced before the beginning of the particular period during which her sexual immorality is being judged is considered *promiscuous-unattached* if she has sex relations with several men during this period, either because of a strong sex urge, or desire for excitement, adventure, or affection, there being no barter involved in the relationship.

7. A woman who enters into an informal union with one man which serves as a substitute for marriage, or who has sex relationships with her fiancé before marriage, is termed *unconventional* in her sex life.

8. In view of the fact that it is not always possible to estimate the character of the sex life of a woman, particularly if she has not made herself a public nuisance and is unknown to the police, the category *doubtful* has been used to include those girls who are not prostitutes, adulterous, or very promiscuous, but are probably unconventional or slightly promiscuous in their sex relationships, the suspicion of such conduct being based on rumour and hearsay sufficient to raise a question about their sex morality, but not substantiated by positive proof.

Incidence of sexual immorality. In sorting the cases, a girl who had indulged in several forms of sex activity was classified but once. For this purpose the different types of sexual activity were ranged according to their presumed relative social harmfulness, prostitution taking precedence over adultery, promiscuous adultery over the promiscuous sex indulgence of unattached women, and the like. There may, of course, be some difference of opinion as to the relative social harmfulness of these various types of illicit sex indulgence.

Prior to commitment to the Reformatory, 7.1% of our girls were known to be professional prostitutes, 42% were occasional prostitutes, 3% were one-man prostitutes; 6.6% were promiscuously adulterous; 6.6% committed adultery with one man; 22% were promiscuous; 8.6% were unconventional in their sex life. The sex relationships of 2.3% were " doubtful." And only 1.8% of all our girls can definitely be said not to have been sexually immoral at any time prior to their commitment to the Reformatory (Appendix D, Table 1–34).

Age at which illicit sex life began. Nor does the high incidence of illicit sex activity among our women tell the whole story. Of the girls who had illicit sexual relationships prior to commitment to the Reformatory, 2% had the first such experience between the tender years of five and nine; the amazingly high proportion of 18.5% had their first illicit sexual adventure when they were between ten and fourteen years old; 57.2% when they were between fifteen and eighteen years; and 22.3% when they were nineteen or older. The mean age of our girls when they had their first illicit sex experience was 17.02 years ± .13 (Appendix D, Table 1–28).

The full significance of these facts may be inferred from the following associated findings: (1) A close relationship was found to exist between the age at the first illicit sex experience and the onset of other delinquent conduct, such as truancy, running away from home, lying, stealing. For instance, of 92 girls who had illicit sex experiences at the age of fourteen or under, 90 first showed other misbehaviour manifestations at such an early age. (2) So also a close association was found between the age at which the earliest abnormal environmental experiences occurred (such as foster-home placements and the like) and the time when the first illicit sex indulgence began. For example, 27.8% of 223 cases in which the earliest abnormal environmental experiences occurred when the girls were fourteen or younger entered upon illicit sexual relations at so early an age; and of 124 girls whose earliest abnormal environmental experiences occurred when they were between the ages of fifteen and eighteen, the high proportion of 74.2% also began their illicit sex adventures during these years. So also, of 47 girls who were subjected to abnormal environmental experiences at the age of nineteen or over, 61.7% first had illicit sexual relations at this time. (3) Related to these findings is the existence of a definite correlation between the age when our girls left the parental roof and the age at which their illicit sex affairs began. Thus, of 167 girls who first left home when they were fourteen or younger, 33.5% also began their illicit sex practices at this early age; of 157 girls who left home when they were between fifteen and eighteen years old, 75.8% also had their first illicit sex adventures during this age-span; of 67 girls who were nineteen or older when they left the parental roof, 55.2% had their first illicit sex experience during these years.

It is impossible to determine, merely by correlation, which factor is cause and which effect. All that can be said is that the evidence clearly points to the practically simultaneous occurrence of the phenomena of sex delinquency and the onset of various other misbehaviour manifestations; and of sex delinquency with unstabilizing environmental experiences. Careful analysis of individual careers sometimes indicates the order of precedence of these phenomena; but even such analysis does not permit of too ready generalization regarding women offenders as a whole. That these various factors are somehow related, however, seems a rational assumption.

Duration of sexual irregularity. Only 8.1% of our girls had been sexually irregular for less than a year prior to their commitment to the Reformatory, 11.5% had indulged in illicit sex practices for one or two years, 22% for two or three years, 18.1% for four or five, 18.3% for six to ten; and the considerable proportion of 22% had been sexually delinquent for ten or more years. The mean length of time that our girls had been sexually irregular prior to their commitment to the Reformatory was 53.78 months ± 1.41 (Appendix D, Table 1–33).

Sexual maturation. Study of the relationship between the age at which the illicit sex activities of the girls began and the age at which menstruation was established may give some indication of the extent to which their early sex indulgence is associated with early sexual maturity or with hypersexuality. Menstruation among girls of the general population, usually begins at fourteen years.[3] In our group the mean is 13.94 years ± .06, but 18.9% of the girls were twelve years old or younger when menstruation was established. Two fifths (45%) of them were thirteen or fourteen, 31% were fifteen or sixteen, 5.1% were seventeen or older (Appendix D, Table 1–16a). In relating the age at which menstruation was established to the age at which illicit sexual indulgence began we find that some illicit intercourse occurred before the onset of menstruation. For instance, of 124 girls who began to menstruate when they were between fifteen and eighteen years of age, 15 had had sex relations prior to that time. But in the largest proportion of cases sex activity did not occur until shortly after the onset of menstruation.

With whom illicit sex life began. In the Davis study already referred to, half of the 71 women who had had sex intercourse prior to marriage, had their first and only sex relations with their fiancés; only 15% of our girls, on the other hand, had their first sexual experience with a fiancé. In 32.3% of all our cases the first illicit sex venture was with a man whom the girl had known well for some time, but to whom she was not engaged. In 20.2% sexual intercourse first occurred with a casual acquaintance, someone whom the girl knew by sight, such as a delivery man, storekeeper, and the like. In 4.8% of the cases it took place with a fellow-employee, in 5.5% with a schoolmate, in 16.5% with a " pick-up." In .6% (two cases) the girls first had illicit intercourse with their own fathers, in 2.1% (seven cases) with a step- or foster-father, in 3% (ten girls) with some other relative (Appendix D, Table 1–29). The high proportion of 30.5% of the girls who had their first illicit sex adventure with a pick-up, a casual acquaintance, a schoolmate, or a fellow-employee were only fourteen years or younger at the time; while only 10.3% of those whose first illicit sex experience was with a fiancé or a friend of long standing were so young. Of those girls whose first illicit sexual connection was with their fathers, stepfathers, foster-

---

[3] William P. Graves: *Gynecology,* third edition (1923), p. 18.

fathers, or other male relatives, the high proportion of 73.7% were but fourteen years or younger at the time.

The notion seems to be quite prevalent that girls are physically forced into their first illicit sexual experience. By their own admission, however, not more than 20.5% of our girls were raped, four fifths of the group entering upon their first illicit sex adventure voluntarily (Appendix D, Table 1–30a); however, of those girls who had their first sex experience with their fathers or other relatives, 83.3% were raped on this occasion; in the cases in which the first sexual intercourse was with a fiancé or friend, only 9.5% were raped. Where the girls first had intercourse with a pick-up or chance acquaintance, 23.3% suffered rape.

Prostitution. In the foregoing analysis we have discussed the various deviations from normal sex conduct. Now let us consider the group of 243 women (60.6% of the entire number about whom this fact was known) who indulged in prostitution in one form or another prior to commitment; that is, who bartered their sexual services for money or other mercenary consideration. Of these, 4.1% were fourteen years old or younger when they first began the practice, 18.5% were fifteen or sixteen, 30.2% were seventeen or eighteen, 19.8% nineteen or twenty, 27.4% twenty-one or older, the mean age at which these girls began to prostitute being 18.76 years ± .13 (Appendix D, Table 1–31). How soon after the first illicit sex experience did our girls enter upon the practice of prostitution? Of those who began their illicit sex ventures when they were eighteen or younger, 65.3% also became prostitutes within this age-span; and of those who first entered into illicit sexual relationships when they were nineteen years or older, all became prostitutes during these years.

For how long a period of time did these girls engage in prostitution prior to their commitment to the Reformatory? About a fourth (27.3%) of them had been prostituting themselves for less than a year, 21.7% for one to two years, 20% of them for two or three years, 8.3% for four or five, 6.5% for six or seven, 6.5% for eight or nine, and 9.7% for ten years or longer, the mean time during which they practised prostitution prior to commitment to the Reformatory being 45.38 months ± 2.02 (Appendix D, Table 1–32). Hence the practice of prostitution was of long standing in this group.

Illegitimate pregnancies; venereal disease. Knowledge of contraception was apparently not prevalent among our girls, nor did they protect themselves against venereal disease. The appallingly high proportion of 54.4% had illegitimate pregnancies at one time or another prior to their commitment to the Reformatory, not all of which resulted in the birth of children, however (Appendix D, Table 1–30b). But 35.5% of the girls actually gave birth to illegitimate children — that is, children conceived out of wedlock, whose mothers did not marry before the birth of the child. Of the 249 women who had children, 29.3% had legitimate children only, 22.5% had some legitimate and some illegitimate children, and 48.2% had only illegitimate children (Appendix D, Table 2–20b).

That our girls did not protect themselves from venereal disease is obvious from the fact that at least 67.8% of them had contracted either gonorrhœa or syphilis or both at one time or another before they were twenty-one years of age (Appendix D, Table 1–14). That they did not possess the knowledge (or intelligence) requisite to such protection may readily be inferred.

3. Marital History

Introductory. With so large an experience in illicit sexuality among them, what kind of wives did our girls make? Did they marry very early or often? How did they become acquainted with their husbands? Did they assume their marital responsibilities? Were they conscientious housekeepers? How long did their marriages endure?

Age at first marriage. About half (48.8%) of our girls did not marry at any time prior to their commitment to the Reformatory, 43.4% of them married once, 6.2% twice, and 1.6% three times (Appendix D, Table 2–41a). How old were they when they married? The mean age at which they entered upon matrimony was 19.49 ± .18. An eighth (12.3%) of these girls were between twelve and fifteen years old on the occasion of their first marriage, 37.9% were between sixteen and eighteen, 26.5% between nineteen and twenty-one, 11.9% between twenty-two and twenty-four, and 11.4% were twenty-five years and older (Appendix D, Table 2–42). On the whole, they married earlier than the girls in the general population of Massachusetts, of whom but .4% married when they were not yet sixteen years old, as compared with 12.3% of our girls who married at this early age. Only 11.2% of the girls in the general population marry when they are not yet nineteen years old, while half of our girls married so young.[4] It can be readily inferred that they were hardly well prepared or mature enough to assume the duties and responsibilities of marriage. It does not surprise us, therefore, that their marital ventures usually went on the rocks.

Number of marriages. The 254 of our five hundred girls who were married experienced 301 marriages. How long did these marriages last? To what extent were they " forced "? How did the girls meet their future husbands? How long did they know them before marriage? To what extent did they and their mates assume their marital responsibilities? Were our girls competent homemakers? Why were the marriages terminated? These and similar questions require answer if we are to judge the marital careers of our women.

Manner of meeting husbands. We consider first the question of how our girls met the men whom they married. In 39.8% of the cases, they met their future husbands in the conventional way — through parents, relatives, or friends. In 29% their future husbands were casual acquaintances, such as neighbouring

---

[4] Figures based on *Commonwealth of Massachusetts, Seventy-Fourth Annual Report on Births, Marriages, and Deaths, for 1915,* pp. 54–5.

storekeepers or delivery men; and 31.2% of the husbands were " pick-ups " with whom the girls scraped an acquaintance in the street or in restaurants (Appendix D, Table 2–H65).

This casualness in the choice of a mate is reflected by the fact that the average length of time our girls were acquainted with their prospective husbands was only 7.62 months ± .25. In 13.6% of the cases the girls knew their husbands for less than one month prior to marriage, in 14% for one to two months, in 8.4% for three to four months, in 8.9% for five to six months, in 3.2% for seven to ten months, in 16.4% for about a year, and in 26.6% for over a year (Appendix D, Table 2–H66).

Reliable information about the courtship practices of people of the socio-economic class from which our women come is not available. But whether they resemble the practices of our women or not, it may legitimately be inferred that the casual and irresponsible entry upon matrimony which characterizes our group can hardly lead and actually did not lead to enduring and socially desirable unions. One evidence of this is the fact that 34.1% of all the marriages were " forced," in that they were urged and arranged by a priest, a judge, or the parents, because the girl had cohabited with her fiancé or was pregnant (Appendix D, Table 2–H64). The sponsors of such marriages apparently had little regard for anything except the desire to put a religious or legal sanction upon an unconventional union, thereby hoping to transform a bad situation into a good one. The subsequent life of these couples proves that too often judge and clergyman only bound together those who might better have been permanently separated.

Assumption of marital responsibilities. One evidence of this fact is that only a very small proportion of our married women assumed their marital responsibilities — that is, did not neglect or desert their husbands or their children, were not unfaithful, were not abusive, performed their household duties and contributed to the support of the family when such assistance was needed. By this standard, in only 16.2% of all the marriages did the girls assume their marital responsibilities, while in 83.8% they neglected them (Appendix D, Table 2–H68). Only 26.4% of the husbands assumed their marital responsibilities, and 73.6% did not (Appendix D, Table 2–H69). In fact, in only 13 of the 301 marriages did both husband and wife assume their marital responsibilities.

Of the 155 marriages which were " blessed " with children, the attitude of their mothers toward them might be considered " good " in only 14.2% of the cases, " fair " in 36.1%, and " poor " in the high proportion of 49.7%. " Good " indicates that they were fond of their children and took care of them; " fair " means either that they were casual in their affection for their children or, though fond of them, were neglectful; " poor " means that they gave their children no supervision and no affection or were positively abusive to them (Appendix D, Table 2–44b).

Homemaking practices. Training in homemaking is relatively new in the curricula of high schools and is seldom offered in the grade schools. It may be inferred with some assurance, therefore, that very few if any of our girls received training in homemaking prior to their commitment to the Reformatory except what they may have acquired during incarceration in peno-correctional institutions or absorbed from their mothers, so many of whom, as we have seen, were illiterate or barely educated. Because our girls left school so early and married so young, it does not surprise us that only 8% of them were "good" homemakers; 44.7% were "fair" homemakers, and 47.3% "poor" homemakers (Appendix D, Table 2–H70). The "good" homemaker is one who is systematic, economical, clean, and neat in household management. The "poor" homemaker is one who is wasteful, indifferent, careless. The "fair" homemaker is one who has some of the qualities of the good homemaker, but is at times wasteful, indifferent, or careless in housekeeping. It is common experience that a badly kept, slovenly home militates against the happiness of the household.

Marital relationships. We have indicated the probability that marriages contracted as carelessly as these could hardly be enduring. This inference is rendered conclusive by the fact that the conjugal relations of the couples were "poor" in the high proportion of 81.7% of all the marriages, which means that the spouses separated occasionally or permanently, or one or the other mate deserted. The conjugal relations were deemed "fair" in 10% of the marriages, as no open breach occurred, but there was gross incompatibility. In only 8.3% of the marriages could the conjugal relations be regarded as "good," by which is meant that the couple lived together harmoniously (Appendix D, Table 2–H67). The further extent of the instability of the marital relationships of our women is shown by the fact that 76.4% of all the marriages were broken by desertion, separation, or divorce [5] (Appendix D, Table 2–H73); while in a study of Chicago families it was found that only 2.5% of marriages in the general population of Chicago were thus terminated.[6]

In only 15.3% of the cases were the couple still living together at the time of the wife's commitment to the Reformatory. The destined instability of the marital state is strikingly shown by the finding that the average length of time that all these marriages lasted was 35.9 months ± 1.4 (Appendix D, Table 2–H63), 19.5% of the marriages being disrupted after less than six months, 11.9% after six to twelve months, 7.3% after one to two years, 8% after two to three years, 7.3% after four to five years, 7.6% after five to seven years; while only 16.8% of the marriages endured for more than seven years, though even these were sporadically or permanently disrupted before the wife was committed to the Reformatory.

By considering a "successful" marriage as one in which the couple live to-

[5] Nine per cent more were broken by death.
[6] Based on figures from M. Day: *A Study of Unpublished Census Data* (1932), p. 9.

gether continuously and husband and wife both assume their marital responsibilities, only two (.7%) of the 301 marriages were successful. The "fairly successful" marriage is one where only the husband or the wife assumes marital responsibilities, and of these there were 16.4%. The "unsuccessful" marriage is one which culminates in separation and in which both husband and wife neglect their marital responsibilities when living together. Of these, the proportion in our group was no less than 82.9% (Appendix D, Table 2–H62).

Reasons for failure of marriages. The reasons for the failure of marriages can only be inferred, many of them being of a subtle, unmeasurable, and imponderable nature and therefore not lending themselves to statistical presentation. They more readily permit of the descriptive method of the case histories in Chapters II and IX. Certain facts, however, afford a legitimate basis for inference as to the reason for the incompatibility of the spouses and the weaknesses of the marital relations. For instance, only 34.7% of the husbands were regular workers; 16.6% worked fairly steadily, and the high proportion of 48.7% worked irregularly (Appendix D, Table 2–H78). From this one may infer that economic difficulties were involved in the marital vicissitudes, particularly in view of the fact that only in 7.5% of the marriages was the economic status of the husband better than that of the girls' parents. In 71.6% of the cases the economic status of the women was the same as before marriage, and in 20.9% it was actually lower, so that few of the women had improved their economic condition by matrimony (Appendix D, Table 2–H72).

The unwholesomeness of the men to whom our girls were married no doubt also has much to do with the failure of these marriages. As many as 41.5% of the husbands had official criminal records (exclusive of the offence of drunkenness), 6.8% more were arrested for drunkenness, 32.5% though known to be delinquent or criminal, had somehow escaped the toils of the law, and only 19.2% of the husbands were decent and well-behaved (Appendix D, Table 2–H81).

The presence of third persons in a household is a notoriously disrupting factor in marital life. Only 48.2% of our women lived alone with their husbands; in the remainder of the cases the couple either lived with parents-in-law or other relatives or had boarders or lodgers (Appendix D, Table 2–H71). Further contributing to their marital infelicity was the profound ignorance of our girls, which is reflected in their low educational achievement and their low mentality, their emotional immaturity, their craving for adventure, their extreme youthfulness, and their general irresponsibility.[7]

4. Conclusion

From the foregoing analysis it is clear that a major problem involved in the delinquency and criminality of our girls is their lack of control of the sex impulse.

[7] See prior chapters.

Illicit sex practices were extremely common among them, began surprisingly early, and carried in their train disease, illegitimacy, and unhappy matrimony.

Obviously, therefore, the Reformatory has to cope with deep-rooted impulses and attitudes of long standing. The temporary or permanent cure of sexual diseases is a personal and social service of considerable value; but the intelligent and wholesome management of the sex impulse is the hard lesson that the Reformatory must attempt to teach these girls, because other constituted agencies have obviously failed in the task. It is not merely a matter of the teaching of new standards of sex morality, however. The unsuccessful marital ventures of these women are partially intertwined with our entire civilization, both material and moral. They did not live in a vacuum before their commitment to the Reformatory, nor did they return to one upon their discharge. To an unmeasurable degree they are the products of forces not only beyond their own control, but beyond the control of the Reformatory and the parole system which attempted to cope with the problems reflected in their unwholesome lives.

Whether it is possible, by existing methods, to achieve more than a very modest success in the difficult enterprise of rehabilitating these women is a question which may be partly answered later, in the light of the facts regarding their careers after they left the Reformatory.

CHAPTER VI

LEGAL ENTANGLEMENTS

1. Introductory

It is an open question whether such unconventional behaviour as adultery and fornication should be coped with at all by means of the criminal law. Experience with prohibition has rendered commonplace that which some sociologists and historians of the law have long known: namely, that certain forms of human conduct cannot be effectively controlled through the instrumentality of punitive laws, and that behind the purely legal sanction there must stand a sufficiently powerful and pervasive social sanction (religion, custom, and the like) to give effectiveness to the control of conduct through law.

In the matter of sex offences it is well known that public opinion brings about the enforcement of some laws and not of others; and that in certain communities public opinion is emotionally charged against one type of act to which in others it may be more or less indifferent. Rape is punishable with the death penalty in certain states of the Union, and with a few years' imprisonment, or even probation, in others. Certainly in the more populous and sophisticated states adultery is of small importance so far as actual arrest, prosecution, conviction, and imprisonment are concerned, judging by the high number of cases in which divorces are granted on the ground of adultery and the small number of actual prosecutions for adultery. Fornication is an offence that has shrunk to insignificance in certain large cities, where the police, more or less supported by public opinion, wink at such acts of human frailty. And even in more strait-laced communities one hardly ever hears of a person of favourable socio-economic standing being arrested for such an offence. It is only people of the class from which our women come who are arrested for such acts, and the number of arrests varies with the community. In Massachusetts the police seem to be uncommonly active in respect to minor sex offences.

Bearing these considerations in mind, let us examine the criminal records of our five hundred girls.

2. Conflicts with the Law

Number of arrests. To what extent were these girls caught up in the machinery of the law prior to their commitment to the Reformatory? Only 33.1% of them had not been arrested at any time prior to the arrest which resulted in their sentence to the Reformatory; 20.1% had been arrested once, 15.7% twice, 14.3% three or four times, 7.6% five or six, 9.2% seven or more times. The mean number of arrests of those who had actually been taken into custody prior to the apprehension which resulted in sentence to the Reformatory was 3.66 ± .12 (Appendix D, Table 2–2). It is clear that arrest was not a novel experience for two thirds of our girls.

Frequency of arrests. How frequently were these girls arrested? Of those arrested more than once prior to commitment, 17.8% had been apprehended once in less than three months, 20.6% once in three to five months, 19.6% in six to eight months, 12.3% in nine to eleven months, 12.3% in twelve to seventeen months, 5.5% in eighteen to twenty-three months, and 11.9% once in two or more years (Appendix D, Table 1–63). The average frequency of arrests of those taken into custody more than a single time was once in 10.06 months ± .33.[1] It is of course impossible to say how frequently these girls actually deserved to be arrested for violation of existing laws.

Age at first arrest.[2] How old were our girls when they first ran afoul of the law? Of the entire group, 7.9% were under fifteen, 11.9% were fifteen or sixteen, 22.5% were seventeen or eighteen, 16% were nineteen or twenty, 18.2% twenty-one to twenty-four, 23.5% twenty-five or older. The mean age at which they were first arrested was 20.9 years ± .16 (Appendix D, Table 1–61).

Number of convictions. We find that 5.1% of those arrested had never been convicted, 36.6% had been convicted once, 22.5% twice, 16.9% three or four times, 10.8% five to seven times, and 8.1% eight or more times. The mean number of convictions of the girls who had been arrested at one time or another prior to the arrest which resulted in their commitment to the Reformatory was 2.64 ± .08 (Appendix D, Table 2–3).

First offence for which arrested. The first arrest in 1.8% of the cases was for offences against the person, such as assault and battery; 7.6% of the girls were first apprehended for committing adultery, 5.8% for " common night-walking," 5.2% for fornication, 1% (five girls) for keeping a house of ill fame or sharing in the proceeds of prostitution, 18% for being " lewd and lascivious," this group making a total of 37.6% of the entire number who were first taken into custody for an offence involving chastity. The first arrest of 20.2% of the girls was on a charge of being a " stubborn child," which in some instances meant running away from home or truancy or waywardness or disobedience to parents or im-

---

[1] Frequency of arrests prior to commitment to the Reformatory was calculated as follows: From the time of the first arrest to the date of the arrest for the offence on which the girl was committed to the Reformatory was subtracted the total time spent in penal or non-penal institutions. The remaining period was divided by the number of arrests which occurred during this period, not including the arrest for which the girl was committed to the Reformatory on the sentence which we are studying.

[2] This includes the age at time of arrest which was followed by commitment to the Reformatory on the sentence we are studying if this happened to be the first arrest.

morality. In 16.2% of the cases the first arrest was for an offence against the public health, safety, or policy, such as being idle and disorderly, violating licence laws, violating the true-name law, and the like. The first arrest in 12.4% of the cases involved the commission of property crimes, such as larceny, burglary, and robbery. The first arrest of 9% of the girls was for drunkenness, of .4% (two girls) for violating the drug laws, and of 2.4% for offences against the family, usually neglect of children (Appendix D, Table 2–1).

All offences for which arrested. Of the 333 girls who were arrested prior to their commitment to the Reformatory, 6.6% were at one time or another apprehended for offences against the person, 51.9% for offences against chastity, 3.6% for offences against family and children, 30% for offences against public health, safety, and policy, 29.7% for drunkenness, 1.5% for violation of the drug law, 23.7% for offences against property rights, and 27% for stubbornness (Appendix D, Table 2–5).

These 333 girls were arrested 1,261 times. Of all the 1,261 arrests, 35.1% were for drunkenness (including, in a few instances, keeping and exposing liquor and illegal sale of liquor); 23.9% were for offences against chastity of which the largest number were for common night walking; 14.4% were for offences against property rights (mostly larceny and including a few cases of extortion, forgery and uttering, shoplifting, possessing stolen property, arson); 11% were for offences against the public health, safety, and policy (largely for being idle and disorderly or disturbing the peace); 9.1% for stubbornness, running away, waywardness, or truancy; 3.4% for violation of probation or for default or for escape; 6% (eight arrests) for offences involving violation of the drug law, such as possessing drugs or being present where drugs are sold; 1.1% were for offences against the family and children (non-support or neglect of children); and 1.4% for offences against the person, such as assault with intent to rob, manslaughter, assault with dangerous weapon (Appendix D, Table 1–H71).

All dispositions. Of the 333 girls who were arrested prior to their commitment to the Reformatory, 70.9% had been placed on probation at one time or another, 45.6% had been committed to penal or correctional institutions, and 3.3% more were at one time or another committed to jail for failure to pay a fine; 17.1% had been fined following one or more arrests; the charges against 23.7% of the girls were filed; 7.8% (in custody for drunkenness) had been released by the probation officer without formal court appearance; 2.1% had cases nol-prossed by the prosecutor; and 26.7% were at one time or another found not guilty and were released (Appendix D, Table 2–4). Considering now the dispositions of all the arrests, 34.6% of the total resulted in probation, 28.4% in commitment to peno-correctional institutions, 11.9% in the filing of the cases, 6.1% in fines or restitution, 4% in release by the probation officer, 9.7% in a finding of not guilty, .6% (eight arrests) in nol prossing, .16% (two arrests) in a finding of " no bill," 1.7% in commitment for non-payment of fine, and 2.8% in various other dispositions (Appendix D, Table 1–H72). Thus our girls had practically run the gamut of treatment prescribed by society for wrongdoers.

Probation experiences. Of the 238 girls who had experienced probation, 63% (or 30.2% of all the 500 girls) had been placed on probation once, 19.3% twice, 8.8% three times, and 8.9% four or more times, the mean being 1.74 ± .06 (Appendix D, Table 1–70).

Penal experiences. Of the 149 women who had been committed to some peno-correctional institution prior to their sentence to the Reformatory, 48.3% (or 14.5% of all the women) served one sentence, 22.8% two, 12.8% three or four, and 16.1% five or more. The mean number of commitments to penal institutions of those who were committed was 2.68 ± .13 (Appendix D, Table 1–68). The length of time actually served in peno-correctional institutions by these girls was less than six months in 26.5% of the cases, six to twelve months in 18.4%, twelve to eighteen months in 12.2%, eighteen to twenty-four months in 9.5%, twenty-four to thirty months in 13%, thirty to forty-eight months in 12.2%, and more than forty-eight months in 8.2%, the average being 19.94 months ± .85 (Appendix D, Table 1–65).

When the girls were first committed to penal or correctional institutions (including the Reformatory on the sentence which we are studying if this happens to be the first commitment), 4.9% were under fifteen years of age, 7.3% were fifteen or sixteen, 21.5% were seventeen or eighteen, 16.9% were nineteen or twenty, 18.9% were between twenty-one and twenty-four, 11% were between twenty-five and twenty-eight, and 19.5% were twenty-nine or over. The mean age at the time of first commitment was 21.98 years ± .16.

Summary of criminal conduct. The foregoing details regarding the delinquent and criminal conduct of our girls may now be viewed from a somewhat different angle. First of all, it should be stressed that only 1% (five) of our girls were never arrested and had never misbehaved in any way that might bring them into conflict with the law, prior to the occasion of the arrest which resulted in their commitment to the Reformatory (Appendix D, Table 1–60b). Of the 99% of girls who were delinquents, 66.4% either had actually been arrested at one time or another, or there were warrants out for their arrest; and 33.6% more, though not having come to the official attention of the police, misconducted themselves in such manner (drank, stole, neglected their families, and the like) as to have been subjected to arrest had they come to official notice (Appendix D, Table 1–60a). The fact that 52.5% of our girls used aliases at one time or another prior to their commitment to the Reformatory indicates that they were well schooled in the tactics of evading detection (Appendix D, Table 1–1a). This may partially account for the finding that a third of them, although actually delinquent, had never been arrested.

In determining the particular kind of offence which each of our girls committed most frequently, we considered not only those offences for which they had been arrested, but any misbehaviour for which they might have been arrested. For this purpose the " predominant offence " is the one which occurred oftenest in the particular case. Where it was not possible to distinguish the predominance of two or three types of offences they were recorded as of equal weight. With the exception of the five girls who could be categorized as non-offenders prior to commitment to the Reformatory, the predominant offence committed by 56.1% of the girls was sexual immorality in one form or another; stealing in 4.7% of the cases; drunkenness in 3.9%; drug addiction in .8% (four cases); avoidance of family responsibility in .8% (four cases); stubbornness and disobedience in 4.1%; a combination of immorality and stealing in 9.2%, of immorality and drunkenness in 15.7%, of immorality and drug addiction in .8% (four cases), of immorality and two or three other types of offences in 3.9% (Appendix D, Table 1–64). Clearly, violations of society's official rules regulating the expression of the sexual impulse predominate in our group; but other forms of misbehaviour are also numerous.

3. Conclusion

In the preceding chapter we determined that these women who were committed to the Reformatory were in large measure experienced in various forms of illicit sex behaviour. In this chapter we see that other forms of delinquency also played a major role in their careers, and that a goodly proportion of the girls had received (apparently without much success) various forms of peno-correctional treatment long before their entrance to the Reformatory. These findings therefore confirm the conclusion already reached that the attitudes, traits, and habits of women offenders of this type are deep-rooted and that the problems presented by them are not exclusively those of sex immorality. A recognition that the illicit sex life of women delinquents is intertwined with many other conduct deviations is important to any program for their correctional treatment.

CHAPTER VII

STATUS WITHIN A YEAR OF COMMITMENT

1. Introductory

In a prior chapter we dealt with the activities and experiences of our five hundred girls during their childhood and adolescence. It is our purpose here to describe them as they were within a year of their commitment to the Reformatory. This is necessitated by the fact that many of them were more or less beyond the adolescent years when they were committed, their average age being 24.7 years ± .23; two fifths (41.2%) of them were twenty years or younger, 22.6% were between twenty-one and twenty-five years old, 16.4% between twenty-six and thirty, 14.8% between thirty-one and forty, 5% between forty-one and sixty (Appendix D, Table 1–2a). Early post-adolescence presents its peculiar problems; hence it should be of value to describe the status of our women at this time in their careers, comparing it where feasible with their previous behaviour. Moreover, a description of the women within a short period before their entrance into the Reformatory should help us the better to understand the more immediate problems with which the institution officials were faced in receiving them as inmates.

2. Marital and Family Relations

Household. With whom were our women residing when arrested for the offence which resulted in their commitment to the Reformatory? Almost a third (29.7%) of them were living with one or both parents; 6% were living with brothers, sisters, or other relatives, 8.8% with a husband, 2% with grown-up children, 13.7% with a lover, 5.2% in the homes of employers, usually as domestics; 22.3% were living alone, and 12.3% were living with friends or acquaintances (Appendix D, Table 1–8).

Marital status. Were these women wives and mothers at the time of their commitment to the Reformatory? Almost a half (48.8%) of them were single, 8.8% were living with their husbands, 36.6% were separated but had not been divorced, and 2.4% were widows (Appendix D, Table 2–40). Over half of them (54.4%) did not have any children, legitimate or illegitimate, 21.9% had one child, 10.5% had two children, 5.8% had three, 3% had four, and 4.4% had five or more children, the mean number of children being 2.87 ± .09 (Appendix D, Table 2–20a).

A correlation between the marital status of our women and the legitimacy of their children indicates that 41% of those having illegitimate children were single and 59% of them were married.

Marital relations. How many of these women were enjoying happy marital relations within a year of commitment? Their conjugal relations were " good " in only 7.8% of the cases, in that husband and wife were compatible; " fair " in 11.5%, as there was gross incompatibility between husband and wife, although no open breach had occurred. In the high proportion of 80.7% of the cases the conjugal relations were " poor," in that the couple had actually separated, or had been divorced (Appendix D, Table 2–43a).

Only 15.1% of the married women were assuming their marital responsibilities within a year of commitment to the Reformatory, in the sense that they were not sexually unfaithful, did not neglect or abuse their husbands and children, and were contributing to their support when the need arose. The high proportion of 84.9% of the women neglected their marital responsibilities, however. (Appendix D, Table 2–43b). In not one instance had both the husband and wife been assuming their marital responsibilities within a year of commitment; so that from this point of view not one of the marriages could be considered " successful." In 15.7% of the cases, the marriages could be deemed " fairly successful," in that the husband and wife were living together, but one or both of them were not assuming their marital responsibilities. In the high proportion of 84.3% of the cases the marriages must be considered " failures," in that both husband and wife did not fulfil their marital obligations.

Only 6.8% of the married women were good homemakers, systematic, economical, clean, and neat; 47.7% were poor homemakers, wasteful, indifferent, careless; 45.5% were fair homemakers, in that they had some of the qualifications of the competent homemaker and yet were poor homemakers.

These facts are important as indicating a specific problem of education which the Reformatory had to face in training these women in the homemaking arts. (Appendix D, Table 2–44a).

Family relations. Let us now gauge the strength of the family ties of our women within a year of their commitment to the Reformatory. Several situations are embraced in a consideration of family relationships: (a) If the women were single or had been separated, divorced, or widowed for more than the year prior to commitment, had no children, and lived with their parents, their family relationships were designated " successful " provided they considered the parental home more than merely a place to eat and sleep in. (b) If they did not live at home during this year, but maintained a contact with their parents or closest relatives, their family relationships were also deemed " successful." (c) If any of these women had children, and their relations with them were good or fair,[1] they too were considered successful in their family relationships. (d) Finally, if

---

[1] For definition, see Appendix C, *Attitude toward Children.*

the women were married and living with their husbands at the beginning of the year prior to their commitment to the Reformatory and their marital relationships were good or fair,[2] they were included among those whose family relationships were deemed successful. If the women did not meet one or another of the above standards, they were considered "failures" in their family relationships.

On this basis 12.6% of our women might be considered successful in their family relationships, and the high proportion of 87.4% of them failures. Thus we see that within a year of their commitment to the Reformatory the family ties of a large proportion of our women were not strong (Appendix D, Table 2–34c). Whether weak family relationships are a cause or an effect of delinquent careers cannot be vouchsafed. The fact remains, nevertheless, that in assuming the task of rehabilitating these women the Reformatory had to cope with individuals whose familial attachments were far from strong and who were indifferent to the major responsibilities of marriage, family, and children.

3. Environmental Circumstances

Physical aspects of the home. The homes of only 11.1% of our women might be considered " good " within a year of their commitment to the Reformatory, in that their living quarters were not overcrowded (not more than two people, excluding an infant, to a bedroom), were well lighted and ventilated, clean and comfortable to the extent of having furniture for minimum needs. The homes of 65.7% of our women were " poor," in that they were overcrowded, dirty, or shabbily furnished; and 21.9% of the homes might be considered " fair," in that they had at least one feature of a good home, but one or more features of a poor home (Appendix D, Table 2–29a).

A comparison of the home conditions of the group during childhood and adolescence and within a year of commitment to the Reformatory shows that a much larger proportion of our women lived in poor homes within a year of commitment than during childhood or adolescence (66.6% : 43.8% : 43.6%).[3] This is no doubt explainable by the fact that many of them had long departed from the parental roof and were shifting for themselves in rooming-houses.

Neighbourhood conditions. Within a year of commitment to the Reformatory 75% of our women made their homes in partly residential urban districts — lodging-house, business, or factory areas; 15.7% lived in residential districts (including suburbs); 7.4% in towns with a population of five thousand or less, or in the open country; and 1.9% lived for part of the time in urban and part of the time in rural districts (Appendix D, Table 2–27). A larger proportion of our women resided in urban neighbourhoods within a year of commitment than

---

[2] For definition, see Appendix C, *Marital Relationships.*

[3] Comparisons of this kind indicate the value of a separate analysis of the status of offenders within a year of commitment.

during childhood or adolescence — 64.9% in childhood, 81% in adolescence, and 92.4% within a year of commitment.

In only 5.9% of the cases were the homes of the women within a year of commitment located in neighbourhoods in which the influences might be considered " good," by which is meant that there were no street gangs and no centres of vice or crime within a radius of two square blocks in urban districts or one mile in the country, and there were opportunities for wholesome recreation within easy walking distance. In 23.2% of the cases the neighbourhood influences were only " fair," since there were no such opportunities for wholesome recreation. In 69.3% of the cases the neighbourhood influences were " poor," as there were corner gangs or centres of vice or crime within the radius mentioned. (Appendix D, Table 2–30b).

During this time a much larger proportion of our women were living in neighbourhoods in which the influences were poor than during their childhood and adolescence. In childhood 32.3% had lived in poor neighbourhoods; during their adolescent years 43%; and within a year of commitment to the Reformatory 70.4%.

Moral standards of the home. The moral standards of the households in which our women lived within a year of their commitment were " good " in only 10.4% of the cases. Good moral standards are reflected by wholesome ideals, and no delinquency (except for slight motor-vehicle misdemeanours or violation of licence laws) among the members of the household. In 14.9% of the cases the moral standards of the household might be considered " fair," in that although there was no delinquency, there was an absence of wholesome ideals. The high proportion of 74.7% of our women lived in households the moral standards of which were poor, as there was alcoholism, immorality, or other delinquency among the members (Appendix D, Table 2–36c).

A much larger proportion of our women lived, within a year of commitment, in households in which the moral standards were poor than during childhood and adolescence — 48.1% during childhood, 55.1% during adolescence, and 74.7% within a year of commitment.

The foregoing findings suggest that a major aim of the parole authorities should be to find homes for these women in which both the physical conditions and moral standards are more wholesome than they were in the past. No matter how intelligently and devotedly the Reformatory authorities may cope with the problems presented by delinquents placed in their charge, their efforts are largely wasted if the women return to the kinds of homes and neighbourhoods in which they were living at the time of admission to the institution. The extent to which the parole agents actually met this need is revealed in Chapter XI.

4. Industrial Experiences

Time since last employed. At the time of the arrest which resulted in the sentence of our women to the Reformatory, 71.6% were idle (this includes 3.6% who did not work at any time prior to commitment); 4.8% were doing their own housework, and 23.6% were gainfully employed (Appendix D, Table 1–55b). It should be pointed out that most of our women were arrested at a period when there was no markedly high unemployment. Of those who were idle at the time of the arrest, 49% were last employed less than three months prior to commitment, 16.2% within three to five months of commitment, 14.9% within six months to a year, 13.6% within one to three years, and 6.3% were last employed three or more years prior to commitment (Appendix D, Table 1–56).

Nature of last occupation. A fifth (19.4%) of our women were last employed in domestic service prior to their commitment to the Reformatory, 44.4% had last worked in factories, 14.2% in restaurants or hotels, 10.3% had done char work and similar jobs by the day, living at home, however; 3.4% worked in stores as sales-girls and the like, 2.1% were engaged in clerical work in offices, and 4.6% were in various other occupations (Appendix D, Table 1–54).

5. Economic Situation

Last earnings. In the occupation in which they were last engaged prior to commitment to the Reformatory, the mean weekly earnings were $11.30 ± .17, 3.8% of the women earning five dollars or less a week, 44.8% six to ten dollars, 35.8% eleven to fifteen dollars, 12.8% sixteen to twenty dollars, and 2.8% twenty-one to twenty-five dollars (Appendix D, Table 1–55a).

Economic condition. As many of our women were married, the joint situation of husband and wife was considered in determining economic status if they lived together at any time within a year of commitment. In the case of women who were single, widowed, separated, or divorced, their personal economic status was considered. Only 6.7% of our women were in " comfortable " economic circumstances within a year of their commitment, which means that they had sufficient resources for maintenance for at least four months in case of loss of earning capacity of themselves, or of their husbands if they were married and living with them. Three fourths (78.4%) of the group were in " marginal " economic circumstances — that is, living on daily earnings, but saving little or nothing — and 14.9% were " dependent " — that is, continually receiving aid from social agencies or relatives (Appendix D, Table 2–34b). There was no improvement in the economic condition of our women within a year of their commitment to the Reformatory as compared with their circumstances during childhood and adolescence. They had not, on the whole, improved their economic condition either by marriage or by self-support. At the time of their sentence to the Reformatory only 14.1% of the women (or their husbands if they were living with them) had any savings, and these were small, rarely amounting to over a hundred dollars (Appendix D, Table 1–58). Obviously the saving habit was not prevalent even among the women who had earned more than an average wage.

Economic responsibility. In determining economic responsibility the following were considered as having met their economic obligations: (a) Single women who had no dependents (parents or children) and supported themselves or at least made earnest effort to do so (unless ill or otherwise incapacitated), even if by illegitimate means; or married women who had been separated, widowed, or divorced more than a year prior to their commitment to the Reformatory and who had no dependents, or, having dependents, aided them or made every effort to do so. (b) Women living with a husband or a lover who, when the bread-winner was incapacitated or unable to support them, contributed toward, or made every reasonable effort to aid in, the support of the family. Those women who did not achieve the above standard are deemed to have failed to meet their economic responsibilities.[4]

According to the above standard of judgment, the surprisingly high proportion of 83.8% of our women showed a disposition to meet their economic responsibilities at one time or another within a year of their commitment to the Reformatory, at least 10.9% of them, however, by illegitimate means. A tenth (9.5%) of the women failed to meet their economic responsibilities. In 6.2% of the cases self-support was not necessary since these women were being adequately supported by a husband or lover and did not have to work outside the home; and .5% of the women (two women) were unable to assume their economic responsibilities because of chronic illness (Appendix D, Table 1–43b).

The inclination of our women to meet their economic obligations toward those near to them is one of the few bright spots in their entire activity during the year prior to their commitment. It indicates a valuable trait of character that both the Reformatory and the parole agents might seize upon as a basis for reconstructing the attitudes and behaviour of their charges. The extent to which they did so is indicated in subsequent chapters.

6. Recreations and Habits

Use of leisure. Only four of our women (.8%) could be said to have used their leisure " constructively " within a year of their commitment to the Reformatory, in the sense that they were members of well-supervised recreational groups, such as the Young Women's Christian Association, or were utilizing their spare time to further themselves educationally or vocationally, and had no bad habits

---

[4] Self-support was not considered necessary in cases in which women were being supported at least in marginal economic circumstances by a husband or a lover or were receiving compensation funds or insurance money sufficient to keep them in marginal circumstances.

(such as stealing, lying, drunkenness, and the like). Six women (1.2%) may be said to have made " negative " use of their leisure time within a year prior to commitment, in that they were at least not engaged in harmful activities, although not using their leisure constructively. They had no pronounced bad habits, however, with the possible exception of sex relations with a fiancé. The high proportion of 98% of our women used their leisure time "harmfully"; that is, they associated with disreputable persons, or drank excessively, or gambled, or frequented houses of ill fame and other questionable resorts (Appendix D, Table 1–16b).

From data such as these social planners can begin to envisage the crucial problems affecting the utilization of the large amount of spare time that our machine age is releasing.

Church attendance. Only 13.5% of our women attended church regularly within a year of their commitment to the Reformatory; 50% of them attended irregularly, and 36.5% did not go to church at all (Appendix D, Table 1–20c). This represents an increase in the proportion not attending church, only 5.9% of the girls not having been church-goers during childhood, 13.1% during adolescence, and 36.5% within a year of commitment. A falling off in attention to church duties had taken place from 55.4% during childhood to 24% during adolescence and to 13.5% within a year of the commitment of these women to the Reformatory.

Companions and haunts. Almost all (97.3%) of our women were associating with streetwalkers, pickpockets, drunks, pick-ups, idlers, bootleggers, drug-pedlars, and other such disreputable companions within the year of their commitment (Appendix D, Table 1–18d). There was a rise in such associations from 26.1% during childhood to 87.3% during adolescence and to 97.3% within a year of commitment.

The high proportion of 89.8% of the women were habitués of very unwholesome places of recreation, such as cheap cafés, houses of ill fame, and other hangouts of the idle and degenerate. During childhood 23.9% of the girls had idled about such resorts, and during adolescence 81.1%.

These findings indicate what a veritable revolution is necessary in the attitudes and practices of these women before any truly penetrating and enduring influence upon their delinquent conduct can be exerted. To attempt to cope merely with the single phenomenon of sex delinquency or other *unlawful* behaviour is to be doomed to failure. Such misconduct is but one blossom of a plant bearing many vicious blooms and deeply rooted in a sickly soil. The extent to which this was recognized and dealt with by the Reformatory and the parole authorities is indicated in subsequent chapters.

Misbehaviour manifestations. Only two of the women (.4%) evinced no harmful habits or behaviour within a year of commitment to the Reformatory. Fully 94% indulged in illicit heterosexual habits, and 2.8% more in other sex habits.

At least 41.5% of the women drank to excess within a year of commitment, and at least 4.8% were addicted to drugs. At least 20.6% were stealing during this year, at least 5.6% were persistently lying, and at least 31.4% (this refers mainly to the younger girls in the group) were " stubborn," in that they were very disobedient or ran away from home frequently or truanted from school (Appendix D, Table 1–23). There was a marked increase in the proportion of women manifesting conduct difficulties during the year prior to commitment than during childhood and adolescence, the proportion rising from 69% during childhood to 94.7% during adolescence and to 99.6% within a year of commitment.

Obviously, then, the Reformatory and the parole system were called upon to undertake a colossal task of redirecting the leisure-time habits and activities of these women into more wholesome channels. Whether their efforts met with success will be seen presently.

7. Conclusion

The foregoing analysis clearly demonstrates that, up to the time of their sentence to the Reformatory, the condition and behaviour of our women had been growing steadily worse. This is reflected in their weaker family relationships, their poorer environmental circumstances, their increasing unemployment, their lower economic condition, their more unwholesome use of leisure, their flagging attention to church duties, and their poorer habits. The fact that they had gained considerable momentum on the downward path obviously rendered the tasks of the Reformatory and the parole system all the more difficult.

We have observed our straggling army of *misérables* in their corrupt and corrupting adventures and misadventures which have brought them, finally, to the portals of the Reformatory. Let us, in the next chapter, enter the institution and examine its program and its facilities for coping with the manifold problems of delinquent women, not ignoring the parole system, which comes into action after the Reformatory has done its work.

PART TWO

THE MILL AND ITS PRODUCT

CHAPTER VIII

THE MASSACHUSETTS REFORMATORY FOR WOMEN AND THE PAROLE SYSTEM[1]

1. Introductory

What is the régime to which our five hundred women were subjected? In Chapter I we have already described something of the philosophy which permeated the institution during the superintendency of Mrs. Jessie Hodder, under whose supervision our women came. We have had some insight into the purposes behind the program of this institution and into its goals. In this chapter we try further to catch the spirit of the Reformatory and to describe in some detail the régime to which our five hundred women were subjected. It must be remembered in this connection that they were sentenced to the Reformatory between the years 1914 and 1924. A number of significant changes have been made in the régime since 1924, of some of which we shall take account. But these transformations do not directly concern us, since our women did not experience them. They are of importance, however, as an evidence of the long-time aims of the superintendent.[2]

It is not easy to describe the spirit of an institution. In the first place, an objective account of a peno-correctional institution and its régime is very likely to give an impression of static routine. But the Reformatory régime was in many respects dynamic. Both from our personal contacts with Mrs. Hodder and from the evidence of her professional friends, as well as of the women whose careers concern us, we are markedly impressed with the sincerity and devotion that permeated her work at the Reformatory. Some attempt in addition to that already made in Chapter I is here made to describe these intangibles and imponderables that are so all-important in an institution which undertakes to rehabilitate offenders against the law. The reader will perhaps gain some further conception of them in the latter part of this chapter and in Chapter X, where we present extracts of letters written by Mrs. Hodder to inmates and their letters to her.

[1] In gathering the facts for this chapter we have been assisted by Miss Barbara Sanborn and Mr. Frank Loveland, Jr.

[2] It is not our purpose to describe any of the changes which have occurred in the régime of the Reformatory since the incumbency of the new superintendent, Dr. Miriam Van Waters, who took office in 1932. This description pertains therefore to the institution as it was under the superintendency of Mrs. Hodder.

A second difficulty in describing the institution arises from the nature of researches such as this one: namely, that they involve the relating of present results to past efforts.

2. Plant and Equipment

Introductory. Prison architecture may be regarded as frozen prison policy. It is its peculiar characteristic that structure is very likely to canalize and dictate function. Given an antiquated institution with its typical long and gloomy corridors, stone cells, and barred windows, even the most enlightened and inventive of prison administrators will find it difficult to avoid a routinized, lock-step régime. Occasionally, however, a correctional worker appears on the scene who is able to shake off the shackles of architecture, and such a one was the late Mrs. Hodder. This is best symbolized by her years of effort, finally crowned with success, to transform a dungeon-like block of cells into an attractive, light, and airy gymnasium.[3] But let us, after these introductory remarks, examine the institution and its régime.

Location and buildings. The Massachusetts Reformatory lies on the outskirts of Framingham, a small industrial town about twenty-five miles from Boston. Situated in a hilly wooded section, its locale is very well suited to its purposes. Some two hundred acres of land are under cultivation, and the hundred and twenty-five additional acres of wood surrounding the buildings permit of protection against the encroachment of the city. Transportation service is good, the water-supply adequate.

The plant, however, is in many respects archaic. Begun in 1874, it was one of the first in the country designed especially as a reformatory for women. Unlike many a modern institution, it is a " congregate type " of prison. It is three storeys high, of brick construction. From a main corridor branch two pairs of wings used for housing the inmates, for the industries, and for dining-quarters; and an odd wing comprising the hospital and receiving-ward. The superintendent's residence connects with the main corridor. Instead of bars there are mesh screens on the windows. Around one section of the Reformatory grounds is an eight-foot wooden fence topped with barbed wire, which encloses a yard partly devoted to gardens and partly to a sports field. There are dairy buildings and poultry sheds not far from the main building. The quarantine section, of five rooms and nurses' room and bath, is separated from the remainder of the building by a corridor with a door at each end.[4]

Mrs. Hodder exercised considerable ingenuity in transforming this antiquated structure into a building more suited to the requirements of modern correctional work. Thus, originally the institution had, in addition to its small rooms, several large dormitory rooms and a three-tier cell-block. The large rooms are now each

---

[3] See Chapter I, pp. 23 et seq.
[4] The fire hazard was greatly reduced in 1925 by installation of a sprinkler system.

equipped with table, chairs, and piano and used as sitting-rooms for the inmates. The cell-block was transformed into a gymnasium and assembly hall.

The hospital and physician's and the dentist's rooms are modernly equipped and well lighted. There is an enclosed porch for convalescents and an open-air porch for tubercular patients. There are several adequately equipped class-rooms, an attractive library, and two sewing-rooms.

The rooms of the inmates vary somewhat in size, the smallest being nine and a half by six feet, and ten feet high, others being larger. As to light, ventilation, and heat, especially the latter, the facilities of the institution might be more adequate. The room windows face outside and are of good size and so orientated that sunshine penetrates during part of the day. In addition to the windows there are air vents. Steam radiators in the adjacent corridors keep the rooms moderately warm. The rooms are fairly well equipped, each being furnished with a steel bed with good spring and fair bedding, a chair, and a wash-stand. Each room has a mirror, water-glass, enamel wash-basin and pitcher, and (a survival from the older régime) a toilet bucket. In addition, each " first-grade " [5] inmate has a writing-table and a rug. Rooms are as a rule profusely decorated with pictures cut by inmates from magazines. There is a toilet-room with large wash-basins at the end of each corridor, where hot and cold water are available and buckets are cleansed. A large bathing-room in the basement contains a dozen bathtubs. Showers were once used but were given up, for some reason, by an earlier superintendent.[6] Each inmate receives towels, soap, tooth-brush and powder, combs, and toilet paper.

From this brief description it will be seen that, despite its age, the physical plant of the Reformatory has been modified to render more easy a constructive régime.

3. Reception and Placement

Quarantine. Upon entrance to the Reformatory the new prisoner is turned over to the receiving officer, who enters identifying data in the records and then takes the inmate to a specially equipped room where her clothes and other possessions are taken and a record made of them. These articles are disinfected, laundered, and stored, to be returned to the offender on her release. The inmate is next required to bathe, great precaution being taken to prevent the introduction of vermin into the institution. She is then furnished clothing to wear during her stay in the isolation ward. Before assignment to her room, she is given a preliminary medical examination to detect any infectious condition, particularly venereal infection.

She is then assigned to her room in the quarantine ward (" probation corri-

---

[5] For meaning of this see p. 124.

[6] Considering the physical condition of many of the women, it would seem that showers would be much more sanitary than tubs.

dor ") adjacent to the hospital, where she remains for three weeks. During this period she is given a medical, dental, psychometric, and psychiatric examination; her finger-prints and photograph are secured for identification purposes; she is interviewed by the institution social worker; and, after a few days, is given some sewing to do or assigned to cleaning the rooms and like unskilled work. The privilege of the isolation-ward dining-room is not given until after she has had a physical examination; and she is not permitted access to other parts of the building until the physician has certified that she may be transferred.

Contact with family. Upon entering the isolation ward the inmate is given a copy of the rules of the institution, and soon thereafter her family are, by letter, made acquainted with the rules about writing and visiting the inmate and making gifts to her. At this time the superintendent appeals to the family of the inmate for co-operation, in the following words:

> " The Reformatory for Women is one of the correctional institutions maintained by the Commonwealth of Massachusetts. It is equipped with an excellent hospital; every medical need is provided for. In case of serious illness the family will be notified and allowed to see the patient. The institution is visited regularly by clergymen of the different denominations, so that every spiritual incentive is given to each inmate. The school of letters and trades' departments offer academic and industrial opportunities. Regular use of the library is encouraged, which affords inspiration through its books and current magazines.
>
> The purpose of the institution is training and development of each individual committed to its care. She must respect authority and the rights of others, and must observe the rules for good management here as in any other walk in life. A co-operative spirit and desire to do well will prevent irksomeness in obedience to regulations. Each inmate may be helped or hindered in her development by the attitude of her family. I trust we may have your full co-operation."

In cases presenting particular difficulties, some representative of the family is usually seen in person as soon as possible.

Preliminary staff conference. At the end of the three weeks of isolation the case of the new inmate is taken up in a staff conference. By this time the social worker has interviewed her and obtained her story, which embraces an analysis of her family background and personal factors, including such factors as health, education, home conditions, employment, record of delinquencies, attitude, interests, and capacities.[7] A report of her physical, intellectual, and emotional condition is also given at this time by the resident physician. Through the staff discussion, the superintendent, deputy, head of the schools, physician, and social

---

[7] Our investigation indicates that a high proportion of the information found in the case histories of the Reformatory for Women has been verified and is reliable, a praiseworthy condition when compared to that of the ordinary reformatory or prison. See Appendix A, " Method of this Research," pp. 337–8.

workers become familiar with the offender's social background, her physical and mental capacities, and her general attitude. Some of this information is of course subject to later modification, but it is sufficient at this stage for assignment of the new-comer to a room and to employment and for outlining a probably beneficial educational course.[8]

When the new inmate is ready for transfer from isolation to regular living-quarters, she is interviewed by the deputy superintendent, who is charged with placing inmates in industry and in living-quarters and with maintaining the routine discipline of the institution. She explains to the new-comer the regulations, privileges, and obligations and tries to dispel any doubts in the inmate's mind as to what is expected of her, and to win her confidence and co-operation. The inmate is then assigned to a room in the living-quarters of the " second grade " (west wing) or, if she was admitted with a child, to the " Mothers' Corridor," and to employment, largely on the basis of the information revealed in the staff meeting and also the needs of the institution itself.

4. Health and Medical Supervision

Food. The Reformatory officials proceed on the theory that a healthy body is a good basis for building a healthy mind and a wholesome outlook upon life. Hence every effort is made to keep the inmates physically fit. The diet is varied and wholesome, and the dietician watches the waste to determine the likes and dislikes of the women. The kitchen is well equipped and spotlessly clean. Food is served to inmates in three separate dining-rooms, depending on their " grades." [9] Special diets are prepared in the hospital kitchen when prescribed by the physician.

Clothing. Clothing is kept clean. When the new-comer is about to leave the isolation ward for the " second grade," she is given two blue gingham dresses, two new sets of undergarments and stockings, and a dark blue sweater. Upon promotion to the " first grade " she receives two new dresses of striped gingham and a white dress for Sundays. The psychologic effect of winning the right to wear the white dress is of greater significance than the layman is prone to think. The women are of course expected to keep their clothes in repair.

Medical facilities and practices. In addition to the woman resident physician, the institution has a visiting surgeon who comes weekly or oftener, a dentist who spends two days a week at the Reformatory, and a part-time eye, ear, and nose specialist.

---

[8] We did not, however, find any record of this detailed plan in the case-history folders, or any written check-up of the progress or modification of the plan of treatment. Summaries of the staff discussions have been provided in more recent years, beginning about 1926. During the time our women were in the institution, cards were kept giving brief synopses of the cases, including some suggestions for training, education, and the like.

[9] See pp. 23 et seq.

One of the most constructive avenues of effort in the institution is attention to the health of the inmates. The physical examination is thorough, particularly as regards venereal infections; women needing surgical attention are so advised, and the state bears the expense of all operations. Glasses, general dental work, and like needs are also supplied. Most important of all, considering the make-up of the women admitted to the Reformatory, is the elaborate treatment of venereal diseases.[10] If the statistical year 1928-9 may be taken as typical, the number of inmates " having gonorrhea is approximately 5 to 2 of those having syphilis, although . . . 16.58 per cent are suffering from both diseases. Standard, intensive treatment is given, varying somewhat according to the general health of the individual and her tolerance of the drugs used. Careful observation and several successive negative laboratory reports are required before these patients are eligible for parole. Some are held even beyond the expiration of their sentences if they are considered in an infectious condition.[11] The babies of syphilitic mothers are also examined when necessary." [12] Tests are made within a day or two of admission of a woman to the institution, and if positive reactions are found, treatment is begun immediately. No inmate under treatment for venereal disease is allowed to work in the kitchen or dining-room, and those who may be in an infectious state are detained in the isolation ward.

The physician makes the rounds of the building each morning, and the patient is given treatment in the clinic, the hospital, or her own room. Tubercular patients are kept in isolation in a special section of the hospital. Drug addicts are entirely cut off from drugs on admission, and in serious cases hospital treatment with special diet is given. Expectant mothers are transferred to the State Infirmary, not far from the institution, remaining there until about a month after delivery.

The presence of babies under two years of age presents a special health problem.[13] In 1928-9, for example, a total of 72 babies was cared for. During the day,

[10] See pp. 191 et seq. During the statistical year 1928-9, 187 women were admitted to the Reformatory, of whom 40 (21.4%) showed positive Wassermanns and 40 (21.4%) positive " smears "; 92 (49.2%) " gave a history of previous treatment, or presented clinical evidence of gonorrhea even in the presence of a negative laboratory report. All of these women were immediately placed on treatments." — *Annual Report of the Commission of Correction, Year Ending Nov. 30, 1929, Physician's Report,* p. 64.

[11] Sec. 121, Chap. 111, of the General Laws of Massachusetts provides that a person in penal institutions " afflicted with syphilis, gonorrhœa or pulmonary tuberculosis " shall be placed under medical treatment and isolated if necessary, and if, " in the opinion of the attending physician of the institution or of such physician as the authorities may consult, his discharge would be dangerous to the public health, he shall be placed under medical treatment and care . . . in the institution where he has been confined until, in the opinion of the attending physician, the said symptoms have disappeared and his discharge will not endanger public health." It is questionable whether this provision is always followed in the case of male prisoners, but it has been scrupulously observed at the Reformatory for Women.

[12] *Physician's Report,* p. 64.

[13] Children of mothers committed to the Reformatory may be kept in the institution with their mothers, placed with relatives, or placed under charge of the Division of Child Guardianship of the State Department of Public Welfare, depending upon the circumstances of the individual case.

children are kept in the nursery while their mothers are at work; in the evening and at night they may be with them. Sometimes a child must be taken away from its psychopathic or feeble-minded mother. The rooms in the " Mothers' Corridor " are each furnished with a child's crib and a small tub in addition to the regular bed. Each child's food is individually prescribed for it and prepared in the special diet kitchen near the nursery.

Physical exercise. The value of physical exercise is stressed in the Reformatory for Women. But not until 1926, after most of our women had already left the Reformatory, was a full-time director of physical education engaged and the gymnasium which replaced the cell-block equipped with appropriate apparatus.[14] Each inmate not excused by the physician devotes at least an hour on two afternoons a week to systematic physical training, and there are classes in the correction of posture and foot defects. Other exercises, appropriate to the different types of women, such as basketball, are provided. In summer months the women participate in various games on the sports field. Occasionally teams from near-by colleges compete with the inmate teams. Employment on the farm and " berry-picking expeditions " are other sources of wholesome outdoor exercises.

5. Institutional Régime

Daily program. Mechanical routine is the keynote of most penal institutions. In the Reformatory for Women it is kept to the minimum necessary where many people are living together. Between the hours of 6.30 a.m. and 7.00 a.m. the women dress and enter calls for the doctor or for interviews with other officials. Breakfast is at 7.00 and work begins at 7.30. Inmates are required to work steadily and intensively until 11.45, when they have fifteen minutes to prepare for lunch. From 12.30 until 1.00 p.m. the inmates are permitted to lounge in the living-rooms or on the " campus." The industries run until 4.40, and inmates spend the time not devoted to class work in the industrial rooms. But a majority of the women use the afternoons for various classes or physical-culture exercises. Recreation lasts until 5.30, and supper is from 5.30 to 6.00. The remainder of the evening is spent in various ways, depending upon the day of the week, the grade in which the inmate belongs, whether she is attending an evening class, and the like. On one evening a week the inmate is required to go to the bathroom for a tub bath, one evening may be spent in the library, Friday evenings are usually given over to talks or entertainments, and many women spend part of several evenings rehearsing for plays or other exercises. This general routine is of course broken by various other activities in the different grades, such as the Friday afternoon visits of clergymen, the weekly meeting of the inmate-government unit,[15] treatment for venereal and other conditions, and like matters.

[14] Prior to 1926 there was no organized physical-culture work, a need long felt by Mrs. Hodder; but there were sporadic efforts to organize classes in physical education when teachers could be obtained during vacation periods from the regular schools.

[15] See pp. 125 et seq.

Saturday afternoons are devoted to physical education and various inmate "stunts," and part of the evenings to "fancy sewing" which the women do for themselves or for sale on their own account. On Sunday mornings from 8.30 to 10.00 the women are free, and their rooms are inspected by the councillors of the student-government unit; from 10.00 to 11.00 they are in the chapel; from 11.00 to 12.30 those in good standing congregate in the different sitting-rooms, the others remaining in their own rooms. Dinner is from 1.00 to 1.30, and thereafter until 3.00 the women are again in their rooms. Mass is attended by both Catholics and Protestants at 7.00 in the morning, and Protestant services, also for all the inmates, are held at 3.00 in the afternoon.[16] From 4.00 until 5.00 the women are in their rooms, this being the "quiet hour."

Industries and vocational training. Opportunities for occupational training available to the inmates of the Reformatory are the following: (*1*) *Industries,* which embrace garment-making (various processes in the manufacture of shirts and similar articles by the operation of single-needle and double-needle power sewing-machines and buttonhole machines), flag-making (not only power-machine operations, but stencilling and painting of flags for public use), manufacture of stockings (in which the different processes in this industry are taught), canning (a seasonal occupation, involving training in the canning of vegetables and fruit). (*2*) *Farm work,* including gardening, dairying, and the raising of poultry. (*3*) *General housekeeping and administrative activities* of the institution, such as cleaning, collecting, and sorting clothes and linens, laundry work, kitchen activities, dining-room work, storeroom tasks, duties connected with receiving and discharging inmates, rug-weaving and repairing (to which kitchen, dining-room, and other helpers are assigned when not occupied with their regular tasks), hand-sewing (largely on infants' garments), care of gymnasium, library, and chapel, office work, inmate assistance in teaching. (*4*) *Hospital work,* including simple nursing activities, aiding the dentist, assisting in the diet kitchen and the day nursery. (*5*) *Work outside the institution on indenture,* usually consisting of employment in a near-by hospital on such tasks as are performed by ward maids, kitchen helpers, and laundresses. Details and definitions of these various occupations offered the inmates of the Reformatory are given in Appendix C, "Definition of Terms," *Vocational Experiences at Women's Reformatory.*

It should be pointed out that, increasingly, the institutional authorities have made an effort to correlate the industries and occupations of the Reformatory with vocational training and with the teaching of the theoretical background of the occupations. For instance, in connection with the work in the shirt room interest is stimulated through the study of the manufacture of textiles from raw materials; the flag-room activities are given greater significance by study of the

---

[16] There is of course no attempt to do any proselytizing; the chief object of having the inmates attend the services of the different denominations is to break down prejudices against any sect.

symbolic meaning and history of the state and national flags. Referring to the course of study mapped out for laundry workers, the supervisor of schools gave as its objectives: " to increase efficiency through interest and understanding of the processes; to see laundry as a cooperative industry; and to develop skill in caring for clothing."

The process of integrating practical institutional tasks with theoretical study is not an easy one, since the state's demand for profits from the industries is not always consistent with the aim of giving the inmate a well-rounded conception of an occupation and fitting her for an independent economic and domestic life on the outside. While the highest total production can be secured by keeping each woman at a single operation for as long a time as possible, the vocational-guidance aim dictates the need of practice in as many operations as can be learned thoroughly within the period of service. During the latter part of Mrs. Hodder's incumbency particularly, the emphasis was placed on the principle of training, conscious effort being made to advance the worker to more complicated operations as soon as she had mastered the simple ones.

Education. The educational activities of the Reformatory have undergone many vicissitudes, depending on the philosophy of the various superintendents, on the funds available for teaching, or on the insistence of different political régimes that the industries should primarily be a source of profits to the state treasury. Though a few classes in simple school-work were established at the beginning (1878), limitations of time, the smallness of the schoolroom, and the lack of trained teachers prevented the development of any considerable educational program. As far back as 1913 Mrs. Hodder called for a complete reorientation of the educational efforts of the institution and their integration with the industrial activities:

" Our educational work is being extended to take in all the women and not alone the illiterates and foreign-born, as in the past, and so we need more school rooms. In order to interest a group of women so varied in age, we shall have to use not only the academic work but the industries, and the agricultural opportunities, including the greenhouses, as laboratory material. The purpose is to develop vocational training classes with commercial factory standards in speed and efficiency. Along with this must of course go classes in domestic training, cooking, hand sewing, mending and millinery." [17]

Later (1915) she asked for a trained supervisor to organize and head a new department of education, pointing to the need of a system which would take into account differences in individual make-up and equipment:

" We have normal pupils, grammar to high school grades, as well as foreign, illiterate, feeble-minded and nervously unstable pupils. We have a shirt factory — a miscellaneous garment factory where fifty different kinds of gar-

[17] *Thirteenth Annual Report of the Board of Prison Commissioners*, p. 53.

ments are manufactured; a laundry with machine and hand work training, dressmaking, millinery, hand sewing, mending, dairy, poultry work and gardening. We need an educator who would study the correlation of the industrial and trade training with the academic work and the varied student body and develop for us a well-defined school plan." [18]

In more recent years the central problem of education has been attacked in a serious fashion. In 1919, when a new home was built for the officers, several of the rooms formerly occupied by them in the main building were converted into schoolrooms. Educational advantages were thrown open to all inmates, and physical education was made compulsory except for the women excused by the physician. Definite progress has been made in correlating industrial training with academic work and in adapting both to the needs and limitations of the individual inmate. But this is only the beginning. Considering the large incidence of defective women (both intellectually and emotionally [19]) and the drastic un-learning process that most of the new inmates must undergo — the sloughing off of antisocial attitudes and habits, and the substitution of wholesome view-points and energy-outlets — education in such an institution must consist in much more than academic-industrial training; it must include the best con-tributed by modern educational art and applied psychology to the reconditioning, socializing, and training of the women for a self-sustaining and law-abiding career outside the Reformatory.

Recognizing this fact, Mrs. Hodder, during the last years of her incumbency, made a sincere attempt to employ as officers in the institution only women with training and qualifications as teachers. A department of education was organized under a supervisor with graduate training in educational courses at a recognized university. Six or eight part-time trained teachers were appointed. The super-visor began to interview each prisoner soon after her admission and to outline a program of education suited to her needs and based upon consideration of her prior educational and economic history, mental capacity, interests, and vocational aptitudes.

The new-comer is gradually fitted into her educational program, being first entered in the appropriate industrial field. Classes are held during four hours on five afternoons a week, instead of the meagre half hour or less allowed earlier in the history of the institution. This necessitates taking the inmates away from their industrial activities — a procedure which, when first suggested by Mrs. Hodder, was severely questioned and even condemned. But despite the many hours taken from industry, production showed a continuous

[18] *Fifteenth Annual Report of the Board of Prison Commissioners,* p. 54.

[19] See pp. 192–3. Of the 170 women examined during the statistical year 1928–9, 29% were diag-nosed as feeble-minded. Of the population in the Reformatory on January 1, 1928, about a tenth were found by the institutional physician to be psychopathic. In progressive school systems no such incidence of abnormality is found in the regular class-rooms, special classes being devoted to such problem students.

increase, and the women were benefited not only by improved education but by the requirement that during the work hours their speed and accuracy of performance should be increased to a point where they might successfully compete with free labour after release.

In addition to the hours spent in the class-rooms, students in classes requiring outside preparation are allowed study periods during afternoons, studying being done in the library under supervision of a teacher. The curriculum is not so detailed as that found in the public schools. It does not include as separate subjects history, arithmetic, civics, and the like, the purpose being to teach these particular disciplines only incidentally to more general problems, thereby retaining the interest of the student. For example, some American history, as well as geography, is taught in the reading courses, and on every legal holiday appropriate exercises are arranged which interpret the historical background suggested by the holiday. Again, citizenship is taught to some extent by membership in the inmate government organization, which conducts its business in a formal manner. There are also discussions of current events, in connection with which various illustrative materials are used.

Courses of study have been planned which tend to interweave the academic and industrial training. In the laundry, for example, the course includes a description of the operations, machinery, qualifications required for such work outside the Reformatory, opportunities for work in this trade in the community, remuneration, and the like, and such technical matters as the history of laundry work, study of fabrics, removal of stains, discussion of soaps, starches, blueing and bleaching, equipment of home and commercial laundries, first aid in the laundry, and the like.[20]

Social and recreational activities. All the facilities of the Reformatory have a more or less "socializing" influence. But certain activities are deliberately organized to bring about a conception of social responsibility, through a constructive use of leisure. These include the library, entertainments, music, games, talks, publications, and various organizations within the institution.

The library is a very attractive room, equipped to accommodate sixty readers at one time. The collection consists of some six or seven thousand volumes, a third of which are fiction, and is added to yearly. The books are chosen by a trained librarian. Good novels, biography, and travel books are emphasized. About a dozen standard periodicals, largely women's magazines, are on file, and several copies of a conservative newspaper are distributed to the various divisions of the institution. The number of books allowed differs with the grade

[20] During 1929–30 the superintendent of schools was engaged in an elaborate plan of analysis of each industry with a view to correlating the work and study in the manner illustrated above. Special classes in stenography, cooking (a long-felt need), and other subjects have been established in recent years.

While fifteen or twenty years ago only a small fraction of the inmates attended classes (and then only for an inconsiderable time), in 1928–9 no less than 83% of the inmates attended classes.

which the inmate has achieved in the institutional classification scheme. The library is open on two evenings a week, and many inmates can be seen reading in and outside the library during their spare time.

Numerous plays, tableaux, concerts, and occasional light operas are given by the inmates or by casts composed of inmates and officers, on the theory that wholesome ways of self-expression should be encouraged for as many of the inmates as possible. Costumes are made by those who participate, and with the exception that an officer directs, productions are wholly the work of the inmates. Each summer there is a circus day, and throughout the year there are several vaudeville " stunts," each working unit (laundry, sewing-room, etc.) devising these.[21] On Christmas Eve appropriate productions are given, which may enlist the co-operation of as many as a fourth to a third of the population. Rehearsals occupy a good deal of the spare time of the inmates, such activity being encouraged as a substitute for idleness and gossip.

While the institution does not have the familiar inmate publication, one of the three " grades " in which the women are classified edits a small paper, copies of which are distributed among all. This gives the news of the institution and contains articles describing various kinds of employment and the like.

Another important constructive organization is the inmate-government division, composed of women of the first grade.

6. Grade System and Inmate Participation

Grades and privileges. The inmates of the Reformatory are divided into three grades. Upon entering the second grade from quarantine, the new-comer is eligible to advancement to the first grade after five months of satisfactory behaviour or may be demoted to the third grade by way of punishment. Membership in the second grade means, in general, fewer privileges and less responsibility than in the first grade, while membership in the third grade entails loss of certain privileges. Thus, members of the first grade may write two letters twice a month, those of the second grade one a month, while those of the third grade are denied the privilege of letter-writing.[22] Occasional special need of their being allowed more frequent correspondence is of course met.

[21] Reactions of the inmate audiences to these entertainments illustrate the comparative freedom of expression evident in the relationship between staff and inmate population. A joke on a member of the staff or on the Reformatory, if coming naturally, is followed by good-natured laughter, applause, and whispered comments which show a good spirit that indubitably is a better reformative atmosphere than the suspicion and repression found in many penal institutions.

[22] Other privileges of the student-government division not enjoyed by the other inmates are: to have a voice in the " town meeting," to be heard before the council, to wear a blue and white dress distinguishing them from members of the other grades, and to wear a white dress on Sundays (a privilege highly esteemed by the women), to have the room door unlocked until eight at night (the doors of second graders being locked as soon as they return to their rooms in the evening), to use the living-room during free time, to use the more attractive first-grade dining-room with its special advantages of conversation and of sitting at small tables with only a few other women, each table presided over by an inmate " hostess."

Grade promotions. An inmate is not automatically transferred to the first grade after the five-month probation period, although the great majority of them are. The policy of the institution is that before promotion a woman must give evidence of being able to accept responsibility, of improvement in conduct and attitude, of some effort to overcome undesirable personality traits, and the like.

While in the second grade, the women attend weekly discussions conducted by one of the teachers, in which the elements making for responsible citizenship are discussed. The organization of the first grade or " student-government division," with its attendant duties, rights, and privileges, is explained to them. They are deemed to be " junior citizens " of the institution, who must be trained in the principles of citizenship before they can become full-fledged participants in the activities of the first grade. Papers are prepared by the inmates on such subjects as " Loyalty," " Truth," and the like. While one may question the extent to which " the good life " can be taught by mere precept, the earnest effort of the institution officials to afford the inmates opportunities for doing so cannot be denied.

At the expiration of the probationary service in the second grade, the inmate appears before the assistant superintendent, who considers her institutional record from the point of view of her conduct and effort at work. If the assistant, taking into account the natural and acquired handicaps of the woman, thinks she has made reasonable progress and is capable of assuming the responsibilities of the student-government division, the inmate is promoted; if not, her case is put off to the following month for consideration.

Student-government division. Upon promotion to the first grade the inmate may apply for membership in the student-government division, to which she must be elected by a vote of its members. Though not required to join, practically all first-graders apply for citizenship.[23] The purpose of the inmate-government unit, as stated in its constitution, is " to raise the standard of living by helping and encouraging each member to develop a high sense of responsibility and duty — to the individual herself, to her community and to society. It shall be the duty of every citizen (1) to keep the pledge, (2) to observe neatness and cleanliness in the care of her clothes and person, (3) to care for her room, (4) to report misdemeanors and irregularities to the Council, and (5) to contribute to the welfare of the Self-Government Division."

There are several sections of the inmate-participation plan, each being patterned on forms of local government, with its mayor and council. Each council consists of a mayor, a clerk, a house steward, a clothes steward, and a health

[23] Upon formal admission to the division, the " citizen " takes the following pledge: " I do solemnly undertake to be loyal to this institution and to the self-government division; to obey the rules of the institution and of my division, especially to refrain from profanity and harsh speaking; and to be helpful to as many people as I can, as often as I can, in as many ways as I can. This I promise to do to the best of my knowledge and ability."

steward representing the inmates, and the superintendent or assistant as well as the regular institutional officer of the division, representing the staff. Inmate officers are elected for three months, and nominations must be approved by the superintendent or assistant, thus ensuring control over elected personnel.[24] No action or ruling of the " town meeting," which is held once a month and of which all citizens of the self-government division are members, is binding until approved by the superintendent or her assistant.

Despite a controlled democracy, there is still room in this miniature government for practice in the duties and responsibilities of citizenship. The council hears and judges cases of infringement of rules by inmate citizens, or any other irregularity whose occurrence is deemed inimical to the best interests of the student-government division or the institution. In addition, each inmate officer has important duties and responsibilities. Thus, the mayor calls meetings, has charge of the conduct of the division in the absence of the regular officer (matron), makes out the daily clinic lists, lists for conferences, names of citizens who desire to see the superintendent or other staff officers. The inmate house steward has charge of the condition of the household, directs, inspects, and approves the cleaning work of the house crew, reports to the council the names of citizens who are negligent in the care of their rooms.[25] The inmate clothes steward has charge of the clothing and bed linen, of the incoming and outgoing laundry, and of the distribution of supplies. She also supervises the mending, and reports to the council all members who are lax in the care of their clothes. The inmate health steward has charge of the bath schedule and reports to the council the names of citizens who fail to conform to bathing-regulations. In addition, she has such duties as distributing the newspapers and taking weekly orders for fruit, individual knitting supplies, and the like. It will be seen that the inmate officials of the self-government division are given very valuable training in the assumption and execution of responsibilities. They, in fact, conduct a considerable portion of the régime.

But what of the large majority of the inmate citizens? While they are less active and responsible participants, they too receive some benefit in the way of

---

[24] A major weakness brought out by experience with inmate self-government schemes in various male institutions is that unscrupulous, selfish inmates sooner or later get into power, and, unless the head of the institution holds the reins firmly, they may bedevil the administration of the institution and may even plot escapes or riots. Hence, after the first flush of enthusiasm that accompanied the familiar Mutual Welfare League established under the patronage of Osborne at Auburn and Sing Sing, the trend has been away from complete " prison democracy " to some form of inmate *participation,* which, of course, means official control.

[25] Psychologically, this device of inmate self-government is of the utmost importance. It neutralizes the familiar attitude of prisoners toward one of their number who " squeals " and thereby actually and symbolically aligns himself with the authorities against his fellow-prisoners. By making the reporting of offences a *corporate* responsibility, assigned *openly* to one of their number, the element of talebearing is counteracted if not eliminated. At the same time, most of the inmates are more or less unwittingly taken over into the camp of the prison administrators, becoming part of a common community.

new and useful experiences. Each of the three sections of the self-government division has weekly evening meetings of one hour. One of these is the " town meeting," at which the business of the division is transacted; the other meetings are devoted to discussion of current events, religious subjects, and morals and to music.[26]

While an inmate is given increasing responsibility as her attitude and conduct improves, supervision by officers is a predominant factor at every stage and in every department of the process. One gets the very definite impression that not the smallest feature of the institutional régime is out of the hands of the authorities, despite the existence of inmate participation.

7. Discipline and Morale

Rules. Unlike most penal institutions, with their mechanically administered punishments and rules, the Reformatory has taken the more difficult disciplinary path of individualizing punishment and of developing an institutional morale that acts as a greater disciplinary force than a multiplicity of strictly enforced rules. The first path makes for institutional robots; the second gives the possibility of true internal improvement of the inmates. Outward conformity to rules, based solely on fear of punishment, is not likely to " carry over " into the life of freedom for which the prisoner is supposedly being prepared. It is not to be implied that punishment and rules are unknown in the Reformatory, but a study of the history of the institution illustrates a slow but steady progress in the elimination of restrictions upon the individual and a substitution therefor of self-government and group responsibility. When Mrs. Hodder entered office, in 1911, she found existing innumerable regulations restraining individual initiative and action; and although a rational basis for their persistence could not be found and the origin of some was unknown, this had only served to invest them with greater sacredness. The erosive effect of numerous, petty, irksome, and apparently unreasonable rules upon the morale of inmates is well known. Interviews with former inmates of penal institutions frequently divulge the useless suffering entailed by irksome rules and the resentment thereby engendered.

Twenty years ago it was a rule that a woman prisoner was not allowed to look

[26] The following is some evidence of the spirit that prevails and its value in maintaining discipline and morale:

" One of our women escaped this summer. Most of the inmates were deeply disturbed, as they felt her doing so a slur on their efforts in upholding a high standard of citizenship throughout the Reformatory. A self-appointed committee waited upon the Assistant Superintendent, Mrs. McKernon, expressing indignation, and asking if they might appoint a committee of their group to investigate and report ' on so grave a breach of the Reformatory spirit.' They chose ten citizens for their committee, who planned the procedure, scheduled meetings and summoned those suspected of aiding and abetting. One witness who undertook to swear and show gay toughness was dismissed with dignity, and told she would be heard when she apologized to the committee, and showed the spirit and manners of a citizen of the Reformatory." — *Annual Report of the Commissioner of Correction, year ending November 30, 1929*, p. 54.

out of her window; neither could she open her window more than three inches, and then only from the top. Violations incurred prompt punishment. Evidently these old rules had been adopted for the purpose of keeping the inmates from staring at passers-by. This is now accomplished through a more general education that involves an appeal to the self-respect of the individual and her sense of responsibility. Also, in the past it was a strict rule that second-grade inmates while walking down the corridor must hold their hands behind their backs; first-grade women must walk with the right arm at the side, the left over the chest. Also, when an inmate met an officer in a corridor, she was required to face the wall until the officer had passed. Again, inmates were punished if caught ironing their dresses. Irksome, militaristic rules of this type were abolished and as many " don'ts " as possible eliminated from the routine. In this way, reasoned Mrs. Hodder, there was an opportunity to develop a sense of responsibility in the inmates, and habits of self-control. The dire consequences which old-time officers always predicted when the slightest change was made in institutional routine of course failed to materialize.

Individualization of punishments. At the time that our women passed through the Reformatory, there were few if any rules to which concomitant punishments were inevitably attached. Each instance of misbehaviour was treated on its own merits, and the offending individual according to her needs. When a regulation was violated by an inmate, she was sent to the assistant superintendent, who has charge of discipline and punishment. The inmate told her story, and if the offence was not serious or when serious, if the official thought that by reasoning with the inmate a change could be produced in her conduct, she was allowed to return to her work. The conscious attempt was made to have the offender view her misdeed from a rational, adult standpoint and explain the reason for its occurrence.[27]

Deprivation of privileges; solitary confinements. If the inmate cannot be reached through an appeal to reason and self-respect, she may be deprived of some or all privileges or be confined to her own or another room. Deprivation of privileges includes demotion in grade with loss of attendant rights, substitution of distasteful work for the Saturday afternoon recreation period, loss of educational privileges and substitution of labour, loss of weekly store privileges (purchase of fruit, toilet articles, books, materials for " fancy-work " sewing, and, on holidays, candy), loss of letter-writing or visiting privileges, these last being rarely curtailed, since their deprivation works a hardship more destructive than helpful. Reinstatement in a grade can be earned in the same way that original promotion is obtained, and there is no established term during which an inmate must remain in the grade to which demoted. Demotion to the third grade is so

[27] Naturally, however, the motivation for misconduct is not always clear either to the authorities or the inmate, and patent reasons may not be the true ones. Hence it would be an improvement if a well-trained psychiatrist or psychiatric social worker participated in the disciplinary process to supplement the long experience of the assistant superintendent.

infrequently used that it has a great effect when employed. As a rule there are only three or four inmates in the third grade.

In addition to the punishments above enumerated, confinement in solitary rooms of varying degrees of discomfort is used. If an inmate is confined to her own room, she is given state sewing to do, not being allowed private sewing or reading or any of the privileges of the institution. Her meals are taken to her. More serious confinement is that in a room of the receiving ward. This type of room is more plainly furnished and has a solid door. Still more serious is assignment to rooms having no bedsteads or chairs, but only a pallet of boards, raised a few inches from the floor, on which the mattress and bedding are laid. The windows of these rooms are such that when the outer solid door is closed, the room is in semi-darkness. The lowest grade of solitary room, which has been used very rarely, is the single room of wood and cement in the basement — the " dungeon." It is several feet from the nearest wall which has a window opening on the court and is equipped with two iron-barred doors and solid wooden doors which, if closed, make the room completely dark.[28]

8. Case Work, Individualization, Classification

Case histories. The Reformatory for Women early took the lead, not only in Massachusetts, but in the United States, in the study of the individual prisoner, in the construction of carefully prepared case histories, and in the attempt to do social " case work." The information secured at the Reformatory is well organized and substantially reliable. It has three possible uses: (1) it is employed in directing intelligently the efforts of the institution to improve the individual offender, (2) it is utilized by the Board of Parole in determining whom to release and when, as well as by the parole agents in learning some of the problems of the parolee; (3) the information available in the case records of the Reformatory may be used as raw material for the scientific study of female delinquency. Until very recently, the work done has been limited almost entirely to the first two fields. The present volume is an illustration of some of the work of a research nature that can be done by supplementing the institution's case-history material with independent field investigations.[29]

The machinery for obtaining sociologic information about the individual offender was set up by Mrs. Hodder in 1912, and perfected and carried out by her research assistant, Miss Barbara Sanborn, funds for its operation being

[28] These doors are not now used, since dark solitary confinement has been prohibited.

[29] The far-sightedness of Mrs. Hodder is shown in the following statement from her 1925 report: " Government, it seems to us, has three duties to prisoners as well as to other wards of the state. 1. It should protect society from them. 2. It should educate and train them, *i.e.,* cure them. 3. It should study them, *i.e.,* use them as laboratory material for the benefit of mankind, as a preventive measure. Society already provides for the first two functions, it is harder to persuade it to spend money for the third, which is the only hope of prevention." — *Annual Report of the Commissioner of Correction, 1925,* p. 43.

originally secured by economizing in other departments. The careful study of the individual and her specific problems was considered of sufficient importance to warrant the creation of a " research " department, with its own offices and director, two special workers, and several clerks and stenographers. This department secures the pre-institutional social history of the individual, co-ordinates the data from the various other departments of the institution bearing on the individual offender, and prepares the " calendar," a convenient summary of the case history, for the parole board.

The basis for each case history is the inmate's " own story." She is seen by the social worker in her private office some time during the three weeks' isolation period and after the various medical examinations have been made. The inmate's account of her personal history is guided by questions which begin with early childhood and include the influences and make-up of the home, her own characteristics, education, and religious training, her health, ambitions, employment history, recreation, and companions during childhood and adolescence, and phases of her adult life. Special consideration is given the history of her delinquencies, and an attempt is made to learn something of the causative factors by analysis of the inmate's earlier offences and childhood delinquencies. An attempt is also made to have the inmate herself analyse the possible causes of her delinquencies. Her attitude toward various aspects of her past, present, and future and toward her family is learned and generally quoted in the report in her own words. A summary is made of her vocational capacities, and her preferences as to special training are discovered.

During the course of the interview the name of the family physician is learned, and also of the public institutions in which the inmate and members of her family have been. The social worker gains many impressions during the interview that are of use in helping to interpret and evaluate the data given. At this stage much of the information thus obtained has not yet been verified by correspondence and field investigation.

Use of case-histories. The information obtained from the inmate, divided into the main headings of Addresses, Family History, and Personal History, with appropriate detailed headings, is presented for discussion at the staff conference after the inmate has been in the institution two or three weeks. The social worker presents to the conference her summary of the individual's social background and history; the physician reports on her physical, intellectual, and emotional characteristics; others who may have had contact with the new inmate report the nature of their contacts and the impressions gained of the individual. A stenographic record is usually kept of staff discussions.

Though no specific plan of treatment is formulated in conference, each officer is expected to plan her future contacts with the inmate on the basis of the information exchanged during the staff meeting.

Verification of data. After the first staff conference the research department makes a field investigation on Massachusetts cases, and social workers in other states are called upon to make a field study of the cases of women coming from other states. These investigations and the correspondence sent out by the research department are for the purpose of verifying the information obtained from the inmate herself. Well-known sources of social data (for example, the records of the Massachusetts Board of Probation and Boston Social Service Exchange) are consulted as a matter of routine. The comprehensive nature of the information thus gathered is indicated by the fact that the case folder for each inmate contains the following items: copy of the mittimus, reports of inmate's own detailed story of her career, of the outside investigation (information derived from members of the family, other relatives, employers, clergymen, social workers, the family physician, school principals, hospitals, overseers of the poor, probation and police officers, Board of Probation, offices which verify births, marriages, deaths), reports of information secured from members of the inmate's family during visits to the Reformatory, of happenings in the Reformatory [30] (promotions, demotions, conduct, changes of work, miscellaneous reports of development), staff-conference notes, copies of letters sent by the inmate, information received in letters to the inmate, summary of the psychometric examination, summary of the whole case prepared for the parole board, and data regarding the parole board's action in the case.

It was planned by Mrs. Hodder that the complete, verified report in each case should be reconsidered by the staff at a conference to be held after three months, with a review of the institutional history of the inmate up to that time. But pressure of other work prevented such a systematic review of all cases, though the research-department workers from time to time brought up cases in which new data were secured as well as those involving problems which should be considered by the entire staff.

Final staff conference. About a month before an inmate is eligible for parole consideration, her case is again taken up in staff conference. The purpose of this is to review the offender's entire history in order to place the essential data in convenient summarized form before the parole board and to recommend appropriate disposition of the case. At this conference the case record, together with the history of the inmate within the institution, is presented by the director of the research department, and the heads of all departments discuss the progress of the inmate in their respective fields. The physician has just previously given the inmate another physical examination and now advises whether she is fit to be returned to free life; the assistant superintendent discusses both the attitude and the institutional behaviour of the woman and the status of her vocational training and economic fitness; the educational director reports on her

---

[30] In addition to obtaining reports from the heads of the various departments on the progress of the individual inmate, the research department censors the correspondence, thereby obtaining certain information, and light on the true attitudes of the individual.

progress in schooling. Her relations to her family, as well as the opportunity for proper placement if she is granted parole, are discussed. If the staff agrees that parole at this time would be for the best interests of the individual and society, her parole is recommended and — something unusual in correctional work — is generally accompanied by a suggested plan of treatment of the parolee. A written summary of the case-history is presented to the parole board a week before its session, enabling the members of the board to familiarize themselves thoroughly with the history of each candidate for parole.

If the applicant is granted parole, the agent who is to supervise her attends a special conference in which the history of the case and plans for the future are discussed, and the inmate is interviewed.

Classification. Although a substantial fraction of the inmates are coloured, it has not been found necessary to separate them from the white women; neither has it been deemed advisable to separate the inmates into groups according to age or offence or recidivism. Except for the isolation of new-comers, practically the sole basis of classification is the grade system. Nevertheless, certain patent cautions are observed. Thus, it has been recognized that to place several emotionally unstable (psychopathic) women together in the first grade, where they are given a good deal of freedom, is inadvisable, inasmuch as minor disturbances would quickly assume large proportions. Again, rather than group together all the homosexual women (of whom there are relatively few), as is customarily done, an effort is made to place each one with a small group of inmates who are known to be uncommonly stable and of sound moral stamina.[31]

Mrs. Hodder fully recognized the defects inherent in the congregate type of institution and in several ways succeeded in bringing about a grouping of inmates for which the small-cottage type of correctional institution was evolved. Thus, in the first-grade dining-room she established small, homelike tables with six women at each, of which one was the inmate hostess. Again, group loyalty, effort, and healthy competition were engendered in the Saturday afternoon " stunts," in which industrial and other social groups co-operated. So, also, each corridor was designed to be a " home unit," having its own sitting-room in which the women living in the rooms adjacent to the corridor assembled.

Clearly, then, the aim of Mrs. Hodder and her staff was to treat the women as individuals, each of whom had special problems as well as those common to all, and to classify them for various enterprises into more or less congenial groups on the basis, essentially, of capacity for assuming responsibility. She of course long recognized the need of special facilities for such extreme types as certain psychopathic and low-grade feeble-minded women, for whom the régime was not intended, since they needlessly complicated many a situation and rendered it difficult to train women of a more normal make-up. Until adequate facilities are provided for the transfer to other institutions of women

[31] The two cottages on the grounds of the Reformatory, recently provided for, should be of considerable aid in allowing experimentation in the field of classification and wholesome, homelike living.

of extreme intellectual or emotional deviation, the earnest work of the Reformatory will continue to be unfairly handicapped.

9. Special Efforts at Rehabilitation

Introductory. We pointed out at the beginning of this chapter how difficult it is to fix and describe the spirit of an institution such as a reformatory, and particularly of the persons in charge. One way of gaining light on this important aspect of a reformatory régime is to turn to the recorded testimony of those who have lived in the institution as prisoners. Unfortunately, however, the staff of the Massachusetts Reformatory for Women did not make it a practice to keep a diary record of the more intimate, personal treatment which was accorded the inmates, particularly in its subtle aspects involving the interplay of personalities. A number of case records do disclose, particularly in the correspondence between the inmates and Mrs. Hodder, the nature of the efforts expended by the staff in attempting to understand and meet the particular problems of each inmate.

It may be said in general that toward practically all its charges the Reformatory adopted a protective, maternal attitude. This is revealed in the meticulous care with which such personal matters were attended to as the collection of moneys due inmates from former employers or the claiming of clothing or baggage belonging to them. Much time was spent in unravelling legal entanglements having to do with separation, divorce, support accruing from a husband, the search for relatives of the inmates, the reuniting of inmates with their husbands, and like significant services.

On what basis an offender was singled out for a special kind of treatment can only be inferred, however, since the records are not always clear on this point. It would appear, on the whole, that those women who seemed more promising than others, or superior to the type usually sent to the Reformatory, or those whose problems were very pressing were given the advantage of more intimate personal attention than the others. This is partially reflected in the fact that some women, especially the younger offenders or those to whom the Superintendent was greatly attracted (see the cases of Margaret, pp. 164 et seq., and Louisa, pp. 182 et seq.) were placed at general housework in her home so that they might be more protected from the baneful influences of free intermingling with all kinds of offenders, and so that the Superintendent might, by frequent talks, give them a more personal guidance. Some twenty-five of our women lived at one time or another during their stay at the Reformatory in the Superintendent's home or that of some other officer. This does not mean, of course, that only these women had the advantage of an intimate kind of supervision. Other officers of the Reformatory as well as Mrs. Hodder herself gave to many of the inmates the benefit of frequent personal contacts in an effort to imbue them with new outlooks on life and more decent standards of behaviour.

This intensive and individual approach to the problems of the inmates is also reflected in the transfer of certain women to other institutions because it was felt that the treatment which would be there accorded them was more appropriate to their particular needs than anything which the Reformatory, as then organized, could offer (see p. 189, on Transfers to other Institutions). It is further reflected in the fact that some of our women were released on parole before the usual time (see pp. 189 et seq., on Parole from Reformatory), either because the staff felt that they did not need institutional treatment or that a longer period on parole would be of greater advantage than incarceration, as it would provide an easier transition from imprisonment to complete freedom. In relation to parole, also, just before the release of an inmate the Reformatory officials would sometimes make suggestions to the parole officers regarding the specific problems and needs of an offender (see Chapter XI, p. 208, section on Recommendations made by Reformatory Staff). The fact that certain of our women were placed on indenture (see below) is also proof of the individualized approach to the problems of the inmates.

Illustrations. A few examples will serve to illustrate more pointedly the protective attitude of the institution, the deep personal interest of Mrs. Hodder in the welfare of her charges, and the faith that animated her:

(1) In this case, after making an intensive investigation into the character of a fiancé by whom one of the inmates was pregnant on admission, and being thoroughly satisfied that he was a wholesome enough young fellow and able to support the girl, Mrs. Hodder encouraged their marriage [32] and even made every effort to bring it about before the birth of the child. But as this could not be arranged because the child's father was in the Navy and stationed on the Pacific coast, Mrs. Hodder later guided the parents through the intricacies of legitimatizing the birth. After getting permission from the parole board for the girl to go to California, Mrs. Hodder secured the co-operation of social workers there in receiving her and her child and arranging the details of her marriage, even to providing a trousseau and a wedding bouquet. She went so far as to take the precaution of communicating with Travelers' Aid Societies along the railroad route, requesting them to keep an eye on the girl and see that the baby was given proper food.

(2) In another case in which Mrs. Hodder felt that the girl " really does represent the top notch of the kind of girls we get here," she managed, after much difficulty, to reunite the offender with her mother, from whom she had been separated since early childhood. Because the offender was immature, she arranged that the mother should adopt her daughter's two illegitimate children, who to this day believe that the offender is their sister. The mother, who was discovered in a distant city, was encouraged to make a visit to the Reformatory to see her daughter. After this visit she wrote to the girl:

[32] This is far different from the " marriage at any price " attitude described elsewhere.

" My dear little daughter — How happy I was today to see you, but how sorry I felt to see your tears, the first in all the years that you have been my baby.

" I could not rest until I had written a little message of love to you my dear.

" I called Mrs. W— on the phone this evening and I have an appointment with her at nine o'clock on Friday morning and I am praying hard to take my two little babies home with me and love them for you till you come, and I will be waiting with open arms to take *you* into our home, yours and mine. I have waited twenty-four years, and my heart has been so heavy dear, you will never understand. I am praying for the months to fly by; be a good little girl, and remember I am waiting for you and so patiently too. M— dear, do you realize how much Mrs. Hodder has done for us, just stop and think how much it meant to me to take my little girl in my arms today and to have you call me ' mother.'

" Just a little of the longing for years and years. I'll be so happy when the day arrives that I am to take you home. We will live our lives all over, and together just as it had been intended.

" Mrs. Hodder said I might see you again before going home and I appreciate that so much.

" M—, always be nice and kind to her. Mrs. Hodder is so good. You look just the same to me today, as when I saw you so many years ago. I will not write any more now, and just say good night and keep on saying to yourself my ' Mother ' loves me and needs me at home. Lovingly, Mother."

(3) Another girl, who had proved to be extremely delicate, though her condition was not definitely diagnosed at the Reformatory, was kept by Mrs. Hodder at her home and given extra food and nourishment. Shortly after she was released on parole, it was discovered that she had tuberculosis and she was transferred to a sanatorium, where she died after a few months. When Mrs. Hodder learned of her illness, she wrote continually to the girl, keeping her informed of events at the Reformatory and in every way showing her little kindnesses. Here is an illustration:

" Members of our big family here have been very fortunate this year in escaping any serious illnesses. We were quarantined for a time so that there might be no danger of admitting any sickness. We are all looking forward longingly to the time when we shall be able to get out of doors again. All winter we have been having recreation Saturday afternoons, some of the girls going to the Chapel for games, others to the Library to read and others to the Sewing Rooms to sew. We have been very fortunate in having a series of interesting lectures about once a week, so that although the winter has been long and hard, there have been a few compensations. . . ."

And at another time: " We had a very delightful Fourth as usual, and last week our girls played the Dennison girls' baseball team and our girls won with a score of 20 to 13."

(4) Another girl, who was bright, attractive, and talented but very unstable, Mrs. Hodder apparently felt might respond to strong reprimand for her treat-

ment of her husband. This proved effective, as we see by a letter which the inmate wrote to her mother:

" She certainly laid it on — I s'pose I deserved it all — and more — but as for his being a poor pitiful broken man — he was that before I ever met him — and he had had his troubles before I ever gave him any. I can stand just so much — didn't I feel like retaliating — I s'pose I ought not to have written all this — but it hurt so — coming from her — she said I ought not to think so much of getting home as of saving my soul — I wonder if she knows what's in my heart or how much I'v suffered in every way — *I have got hopes* — I do want to live — and *I'm going to live*. Mrs. Hodder is such a big noble woman — and can be so kind — and wonderful. I wish you could hear her pray — a little word from her — of encouragement, or kindness, is as good as medicine — she feels that I have been made so much of at home — that I have pitied myself so much — that a little hardness in here hasn't hurt me any — that it has been like a surgeon's knife — cut to heal — and it is so. I have always been too fond of praise and I'm getting bravely over it — I'm glad to say — along with other silly traits — and I'm bigger and braver and stronger in every way by coming here. So its really worked — she had many years of experience with all kind's of women and knows just what she's doing — If the day ever comes that she will say to me — ' Pauline I think you are ready to go out into society — I have Faith in you ' — I shall be the happiest and proudest woman on earth — I guess.
" There were a few things I felt like saying to her when we were talking — a cowardly feeling of trying to defend myself — to excuse myself — but she would have had only a feeling of contempt for me and I would have been very sorry after."

(5) Mrs. Hodder was so convinced of the potentialities of another inmate, believing that she was very much the distorted product of a miserable environment who, with careful attention, might be brought back to wholesome living, that she asked the parole board to parole the girl into her care. Then, in order to keep her within sight and guide her development, she arranged that the girl's grandmother, who was most sympathetic and desirous of doing everything possible for her grand-daughter, come to live at the Reformatory for a few months to teach rug-making in return for board and maintenance:
" This will give you the opportunity to live here with your grand-daughter, who would have a room adjoining yours and who would work in one of the factories in Framingham. She is to be released from the institution on July 23rd, and I should like you to arrange to come on that date so that in making her application for work in Framingham she may give as a reason for living here the fact that you will be employed here.
" My suggestion would be that you keep your home just as it is for the present giving this plan say a month's trial."
In a somewhat earlier letter to the grandmother she had written:
" It seems to me that every word in your letter takes me back years ago

to my own grandmother, whose writing very much resembled yours, and I assure you that it is with no difficulty at all that I put myself by your side in thinking of M—.

" She is a dear girl who has unusual possibilities. Unhappily she has seen the wrong side too much and she has seen the practicabilities of the wrong side, — the fact that to a frail girl it offers gayety and financial help. I think the problem that we must work out for M— is the problem of proper placing.

" I have had one or two talks with her, — not very long ones, — since I have your letter, but talks sufficiently real and fundamental to make me believe that she is trying and that she is searching for a way out, — a way that will bring her help and will make it possible for her to go to you on visits at least with a clean record.

" I do not know just when we shall come to the point where we believe she had better be tried in the community, but it must be soon, otherwise she will not have had an opportunity for us to watch her and help her on parole."

(6) A girl who was particularly unmanageable and troublesome, having violent psychotic episodes, but never diagnosed as " insane," Mrs. Hodder was interested in the idea of having subjected to glandular treatment, thinking that some of her difficulty might be due to disturbed endocrine balance. In this connection she wrote to an eminent physician asking him to do some experimental treatment of the girl, but the arrangements were apparently never completed:

" I think she wants to be good. If I believed in witches I should say she was possessed of the devil. I do not think it is a wilfull devil; I think it is an involuntary devil. I think she has no control. She is not stupid. She is not well informed because she has never been able to sit still long enough to gather information. There is so much good in her best moments that I wonder whether through experimentation of the kind in which you are interested you might make the whole of herself usable to her. Is it worth while for us to make use of the material in this institution for that kind of research? Reformatories all over the United States are at their wits ends about this class of prisoner. No one knows what to do with them either inside or outside of the institution. If it could be found to be due partly or largely to abnormal gland secretions and a norm established for these women, it would be the biggest thing that had happened to penology."

(7) When Mrs. Hodder learned that another inmate, with a severe venereal infection, had been sleeping for some years with a son now twelve years old, she immediately communicated with his guardians, after gaining the mother's consent, and urged them to take the boy to a public health clinic in order to determine whether or not he had been infected by his mother. An infection was discovered and he was treated over a period of many months.

(8) Instead of encouraging another girl to place her illegitimate child in the care of the state (the child having reached the age of two and therefore being

no longer eligible for care at the Reformatory), Mrs. Hodder cast about among the girl's relatives to see if there was not someone who would take the young-ster. In writing to this relative, the girl's maternal aunt, Mrs. Hodder pointed out that:

" C— is really very fond of her child and we feel that it is the biggest influence for good in her life. For that reason I asked her if there was any one in her family who would be interested to take the child and have it grow up under good conditions, letting C— see it from time to time, and letting the child be a guide to her life. She mentioned you and I offered to write to you. C— feels very unhappy over what she has done, and there is a big hope for her and for her future if she will hold on to the child and what it means in her life. There is no hope for her if she destroys her love for the child."

These cases — and many other instances might be cited — illustrate, as do some of the case-histories summarized in Chapters II and IX, that within the general framework of individualization and classification Mrs. Hodder made considerable effort to humanize the practices of the institution. Despite this fact, the criticisms levelled by ex-inmates against the Reformatory cannot be completely overlooked. There is a feeling on the part of some of them that the institution staff " played favourites," meaning, of course, that some of the in-mates received more attention than others. Many of our women would have liked to communicate freely with certain members of the staff after release, but said they were not encouraged to do this except in rare instances, and expressed regret that such interest as the officials may have had in them apparently ceased as soon as they left the Reformatory. This criticism should be considered in the light of the fact that it is hardly the province of the Reformatory officials, as the correctional system is at present organized, to keep in touch with inmates after they have been released. That some sort of a liaison between a reformatory and its ex-inmates is desirable is another matter.

Even with the relatively small population of the Reformatory, the staff naturally could not give as much time and attention to all the inmates as they did to some. Limitation of time and facilities dictates that the greatest emphasis should be given to the most promising cases, a policy that seems to have been followed by Mrs. Hodder. In the enforcement of such a practice, however, there is always danger that certain inmates will develop jealousies and grudges.

10. Indenture of Prisoners

One of the most interesting experiments in correctional work undertaken anywhere was begun by Mrs. Hodder in October 1918. Under an old law [33] which permits the prison authorities, with the consent of the woman serving

---

[33] Chap. 229, Sec. 3, 1879, and Chap. 151, Secs. 2–4, 1880, now embraced, with modifications, in Chap. 127, Secs. 85–6, *General Laws of Massachusetts.*

a sentence, to "contract to have her employed in domestic service for such term, not exceeding her term of imprisonment, and upon such conditions as they consider proper with reference to her welfare and reformation," Mrs. Hodder experimented with allowing certain Reformatory inmates to work at a near-by hospital. Up to January 1931, a total of some fifty women had been thus indentured, earning considerable sums of money.[34] The wages of indentured women are held in a bank at interest under trusteeship. All but one or two of the women thus working independently outside of the institution carried out their side of the bargain without running away. Mrs. Hodder considered the advantages of the indenture system to be as follows:

"It offers the tool by which to hold the prisoner as society demands, and it offers the prison warden the tool with which to teach the prisoner to know and to understand the value of the community and how to share in its growth for good. No prison or reformatory can do that, because the groups are too big, the isolation too complete, the atmosphere too abnormal." [35]

While Mrs. Hodder's experiment was limited to hospital work, the practice could easily be extended to other forms of activity.[36] A serious defect in the experiment was "the lack of organized use of the non-working hours." To meet this, Mrs. Hodder suggested the rental of a small house or apartment where a group of the women might keep house under the training and supervision of one or two of the better workers of the Reformatory.

Unfortunately, the indenture system was not applied on any considerable scale,[37] and only a few of the women studied in this book had the benefit of it. But no description of the Massachusetts Reformatory for Women under the régime of Mrs. Hodder could be complete without mention of the indenture system introduced (or rediscovered) by her.

[34] "They have not cost the state one penny. They earn the same wages that other workers do in like work. They have their time off during the day and their day off a week as do other workers. . . . One woman went to night school in the town last winter and earned a diploma; another, an old rounder, finished out her sentence and earned a set of teeth; a third, who was with us for manslaughter, is to be deported and is earning a few hundred dollars to take home to her peasant mother." — J. D. Hodder: "Indenture of Prisoners: An Experiment," *Journal of Criminal Law and Criminology*, Vol. XI (May 1920–February 1921), p. 30.

[35] Ibid., p. 32.

[36] "The same principle would apply in placing a group of girls who hate housework, and there are such, to work in a factory . . . in the same town. . . . I should like to experiment with one other group than these two described, *i.e.*, a housework group on the eight-hour system. I should like to see if housework, with proper hours, wages and conditions cannot be made a dignified profession, honorable for any one to take up." — Ibid.

[37] We understand that the present superintendent, Dr. Miriam Van Waters, is considerably expanding the indenture experiment.

11. Parole

Preparation of data for the parole board. The gathering of sociological and medical data, the preparation of the systematic parole summary, and the staff conference preceding the hearing on parole have already been described. Details as to the history of parole and the organization and functions of the Massachusetts Board of Parole are set forth in a prior publication.[38] Here we need only advert to the chief features of parole in Massachusetts.

Theory. The ideas behind the practice of releasing prisoners after they have served a fraction of their sentences in an institution, and of supervising them in the community, have been well summarized in a report of the Prison Association of New York:

" 1. That the prisoner ordinarily arrives at a period of his imprisonment when further incarceration will be of less service to him and to the state as a reformative measure than a like period passed in liberty under parole supervision.

" 2. That in the determination of the proper time at which to admit the prisoner to parole an exhaustive and painstaking study will be made of the individual case, in order that both the right of society to be protected, and the right of the prisoner to rehabilitate himself, may be preserved.

" 3. That the supervision of prisoners while on parole shall be conducted thoroughly, and with efficiency and sympathy." [39]

Paroling authority and practices. The parole body in Massachusetts is a board of three members, one of whom is a deputy commissioner of correction appointed by the commissioner, another is a full-time appointee, the third a part-time appointee, of the governor. Though the board is supposed to be a unit of the Department of Correction, it is in actual practice almost an independent body. Permits to be at liberty on parole may be granted by the board " to prisoners in the penal institutions of the commonwealth or transferred therefrom to jails or houses of correction." [40] The prisoner appears before the board at stated intervals in accordance with a time-schedule based partly upon statutory prescription and partly upon the rules of the parole board, which are occasionally revised.[41] The board meets at the Reformatory about once a month to consider the cases of inmates eligible for a hearing. A list of these, together with the " calendar " of case summaries already described, is forwarded to the board by the superintendent of the institution. Study of the operations of the parole board has convinced us that the board has devoted its best energies to the work of the Reformatory for Women, the intelligence of Mrs. Hodder and the careful case summaries evidently being largely responsible for this.

[38] *500 Criminal Careers*, pp. 46 et seq.

[39] *Prison Progress in 1916, Being the Seventy-second Annual Report of the Prison Association of New York*, p. 72.

[40] *General Laws*, Chap. 127, Sec. 128.

[41] See pp. 189 et seq. for the time when the women studied in this book were released on parole.

Rules and conditions. Certain rules are published by the board and given to the new inmates, which indicate the factors that " count toward a parole," among them the conduct of the prisoner while in the Reformatory, her attitude toward relatives and friends, whether employment is obtainable on the outside, be-haviour on previous parole, seriousness of her offence, prior criminal record, ability " to tell the exact truth " when questioned by board members, freedom from venereal disease. Certain conditions of parole must be " faithfully ob-served " by the parolee, among them to be industrious, to avoid bad associations, to abstain from intoxicants and illicit sex behaviour, to report to the supervising authorities once a week for the first month of parole and once a month there-after, and the like.

Supervision. The parole agents visit the Reformatory shortly before the inmate is to be released on parole [42] and confer with the institution authorities regarding her. The agent may consult the case-history, particularly the suggestions made by the institution staff for the extra-mural oversight of the parolee. In general the duties of the parole agent are to visit parolees at least monthly, to help them ob-tain employment, to put them in touch with needed medical and social agencies, and to make reports on the progress of supervision. " If the parolee violates her parole by indiscreet conduct or by being found guilty in court of a felony or misdemeanor, it is the duty of the agent to get all the facts of the story from the police and other sources, and write them up for the Board of Parole. These facts are carefully considered by the Board of Parole to determine whether or not the parolee should be returned for violation of her parole." [43] The work of the agents is under the general supervision of the deputy commissioner of correction who is a member of the Board of Parole. He looks over their reports [44] of the conduct and activities of the parolees and may make suggestions to them.

12. Conclusion

From the foregoing description of the Massachusetts Reformatory for Women and the parole system it will be seen that there are a good many constructive elements in the régime. How these practices have influenced the lives of our five hundred women, the degree of success and failure of these women in the chief enterprises of life after leaving the Reformatory, the extent to which their ad-justments can be attributed to the Reformatory and to parole oversight or to other influences — these are some of the questions we must later set ourselves to answer.

[42] At the time our women were in the Reformatory, parole agents operated out of the central parole office in the Department of Correction. We understand that since December 1, 1933 they have been transferred to the Reformatory in order to effect a better liaison between institutional and parole oversight.

[43] Letter from deputy commissioner.

[44] Until recently these reports have consisted of " parole slips " more or less routinely filled out and filed in the folders; today a record of supervision is kept that is a continuation of the original case-history and is more accessible and helpful.

CHAPTER IX

A GALLERY OF WOMEN (*continued*)

1. Introductory

In Chapter II we left several women at the gateway to the Reformatory. Let us now accompany them into the institution, out again on parole, and over a period of five or more years beyond the completion of their sentences, noting their response to the pressures and demands and responsibilities of life.

2. In the Reformatory and after Release

Marie.[1] When Marie entered the Reformatory, she insisted that neither she nor her husband was guilty of the charges made against them and that they had both been convicted on circumstantial evidence. She professed the deepest affection for him and the determination to remain true to him even though he was serving a long sentence in state prison. Marie felt very bitter toward her father, but had a most affectionate regard for her mother.

Physical examination disclosed that she had gonorrhœa and signs of primary syphilis. She was found to be of normal mentality and, when placed at work as a machine-operator in the shirt room, proved herself very efficient and capable. Her conduct in the institution was in every way beyond reproach. The superintendent of the Reformatory became very much interested in Marie, feeling that she was more sinned against than sinning, and Marie developed a great affection and respect for her.

In the early months of her incarceration Marie received many pleading letters from her husband begging forgiveness for implicating her in his crimes and asking her to write to him frequently. At first Marie responded, insisting that she loved him and would be loyal. The Reformatory officials attempted to make her see that her continued devotion to a man who had tried to wreck her life could lead only to further suffering. It was not more than four or five months after her admission that Marie came to realize that she must break with her husband and forgive her father for his sternness toward her, as he had been acting only in her best interests. She therefore began to write to him, and her parents were overjoyed to know that she was eager to come back to them.

Her father, at this time, wrote to the superintendent of the Reformatory:

[1] Continued from p. 32.

" I know that I am not the only father in trouble on account of girls going into the world unaware of the many dangers and pitfalls but I realize that your behavior towards them must bring a large number back to us. Thanking you for all you do and have done
Yours most respectfully . . ."

Marie, in asking for parole, wrote a note to the superintendent in which she revealed much insight into the reasons for her delinquency:

" But I'm no criminal. I never knew anything about such things and I'm not perfect or else I would never have ran away from home there's where I made my mistake, and I had a pretty lot of handicaps and also a great deal of advantages in my life which perhaps some women here have never had. My father sent me thro' Public School and after that to high school but I only stayed one year there, and then he was very good to me but I didn't know it then, and he sent me to a Business College where I only stayed 3 mo. when I ran away from home, in fact that isn't the first time I ran away. I didn't like my home because my father didn't make it comfortable for us kids and I truly believe if I had a better home and could bring my girl friends, who went to school with me, home I would never have ran away in the first place."

After serving fourteen months in the Reformatory Marie was paroled and was placed in charge of her father, who came from New York to escort her home. Meanwhile the parole agent was in constant communication with her and asked a social agency in New York to keep an eye on her and assist her in any way possible. Marie lived with her parents for five months and soon found a job as a clerk in a department store. She turned over her wages to her father, who gave her a small amount of spending-money. For a few months the whole situation was agreeable enough. Marie's mother was overjoyed to have her back and felt certain that the girl would never run away from home again.

It was not long, however, before Marie asked permission of the parole agent to take a job as a domestic in order to live away from home. She wished to save money to provide a better home for her mother and the younger children. Her father was inclined to remind her of her arrest and the circumstances preceding it, and Marie, not wanting to be strained to the point of actually running away again, asked permission to board away from home.

The parole agent in Massachusetts and the social worker in New York finally decided that Marie should be placed in an infants' hospital on Long Island where she would have a six-months training course as a nursemaid and ten dollars monthly. In order to be accepted she had to take a physical examination and was found to be free of venereal disease. Marie was delighted with the opportunity given her for training and plunged into her work with tremendous enthusiasm, writing frequently to the parole agent and to the superintendent of the Reformatory about her good fortune:

> "I wish to thank you for the letters you wrote to me for I assure you they helped me a great deal. I get so excited and worried sometimes and just a few words of encouragement helps such a great deal."

They, in turn, wrote often to her so that she was made to feel that she had friends on whom she could depend for advice and encouragement.

When Marie completed her training course, she was placed by the superintendent of nurses in an excellent position where she had the care of a child. As Marie had revealed a strong maternal feeling, it found a satisfying outlet in this work. But she was distressed over the fact that she had not revealed her Reformatory record to the superintendent of nurses. She was assured by the parole agent, however, that she need have no misgivings in this regard:

> "I hope you will always keep in touch with her. You need not feel in the least guilty in not telling her everything concerning the past. She knows and loves you for what you are."

During the three years that Marie was on parole, she reported regularly to the parole agent and continued to write many long and affectionate letters to her and to the superintendent of the Reformatory expressing the deepest gratitude for their willingness to stand by her in securing an annulment of her marriage. While Marie was still in the Reformatory, it had been suggested to her by the superintendent that she could perhaps have her marriage annulled. After she had been on parole for only a few months, she wished to go forward with the proceedings and was referred by the parole authorities to a legal-aid bureau, which prepared to represent her. Both the Reformatory and parole officials offered her every assistance in securing the annulment, as they were convinced that it was the better part of wisdom:

> "I hardly know what to do with myself I am overjoyed at the thought of all you people who are so desirous of helping me in my need. All these many months I have been wondering how I would go through it all alone I dreaded it so, you can hardly understand." (This refers to securing an annulment.)

Marie was a steady worker. In one position she remained for fifteen months, leaving only because she had an opportunity to earn more in another place. Between jobs she visited her family, never staying more than a day or two, because she could not reconcile herself to her father's selfishness and nagging. When her father decided to move to California with the family and asked Marie to accompany them, she refused because she sensed that he would continue to remind her of her past.

When Marie had been on parole for almost three years, she finally secured the annulment of her marriage and shortly after that expressed to her parole agent the wish that her parole might soon be over:

> "I can hardly wait to hear . . . my day of freedom. . . . My time will be up then. . . . I consider you all as my redeemers you snatched me from a terrible predicament and . . . if you only knew how I loathe the common man and woman . . . my soul longs for higher ideals I don't think I ever was a criminal just a victim of environment those with whom I fell in with directed my life to a great extent."

So the parole agent arranged that Marie should not have to make regular reports for the remainder of her sentence, of which still almost a year remained: "She has been one of our greatest successes and deserves every encouragement."

Two months later Marie confided by letter to the parole agent, to whom she wrote as a friend, that for the past two years she had been acquainted with a young man whom she had come to love dearly and that when he asked her to marry him, she felt that she must tell him of her past:

> "It was hard beyond all description for me to do this but my conscience would not let me rest. I felt guilty keeping it from him and I loved him and did not want to deceive him. I was deeply repaid for this course of action for he extended to me only the deepest sympathy . . . we will bury the past and only live in the present."

The parole agent wrote most encouragingly to Marie at this time as did the superintendent of the Reformatory.

During their engagement Marie and her fiancé made definite plans for their future. He was a steamfitter earning an excellent salary, but as he had to travel about a good deal in connection with his work and did not like to leave Marie alone, they had decided to postpone marriage until he could find work which did not necessitate his being away from home. They shortly heard about an opening for a couple on an estate on which was a small cottage for their own use, and they decided to take this opening until something more suitable presented itself. They were determined to save as much as possible toward the building of their own little home.

Marie had introduced her fiancé to her mother's relatives, who thoroughly approved of him, and a few months before the expiration of her parole period, the couple were married. Marie described in glowing terms to her parole agent the simple ceremony in a Catholic church, followed by a wedding supper at the home of her aunt:

> "It was all so sweet and the memory of it is something that will linger with us all forever. After that we went off on a little ten day trip — and now both of us are doing our share to contribute to the fund we are trying to raise to

build our own little cottage. . . . We are so supremely happy just being with one another God is indeed infinitely good that out of chaos he has created such wonderful peace and happiness as mine is. . . . I want to say that what happened to me in Massachusetts was the only way out of a very stubborn little girl's way of thinking. . . . I am extremely happy to know that my full term has expired and altho there was nothing very unpleasant attached to those 3 years and 10 months still the thought was ever in my mind that I was under some one's care and not altogether as other people are, but it is all over now and gone the way everything and everyone of us must eventually pass on into eternity."

Marie and her husband worked on the estate for a few months until he was able to establish himself in a small business. They rented a little apartment, into the furnishing of which Marie threw her whole heart and soul. She continued to write to the parole agent, whom she considered to be her dearest friend, and confided to her that she was very anxious to have a child: "Oftimes I think it is but God's wisdom that withholds the gratification of that one wish of mine but it is so hard to bear."

The young couple made many friends in the little suburban community in which they lived, and enjoyed the respect of their neighbours. Marie kept in touch with her family in California, and her husband made it possible for her to visit them for a summer. She was very happy to find that their situation was considerably improved and that her father, who was now in the real-estate business and making a decent living, was no longer nervous and irritable and was treating his family with very much greater regard than before.

Marie and her husband continued to save money toward the building of their own home and purchased a small lot of land on which they planned to raise a bungalow.

Some two and a half years after they had been married, when Marie had medical assurance that it would not be possible for her to have a child, she and her husband decided to adopt a baby boy:

"He is so darling. He is two years, eleven months old and the dearest, prettiest child I have ever seen. He is so good and both of us love him so."

At about this time, her husband was offered the position of plumber on a large estate, and the little family moved into a bungalow provided by his employer. Marie's neatness and ability as a homemaker was the cause of much friendly comment among friends and neighbours and her mother's relatives, who visited her often and with whom she kept in close touch.

Some four years after the adoption of the little boy, Marie developed a large goitre, which greatly devitalized her and two years after the growth began, it was necessary to have it removed. This left her in a much weakened condition and hastened a nervous collapse. Her husband urged her to go to California to visit her family, and after she had been there for two and a half months, she returned home somewhat improved. Her nervous condition soon reappeared, however, and Marie went into a severe depression during which period she twice made attempts at suicide. On the advice of physicians, she was committed to a hospital for mental diseases. She very shortly contracted pneumonia and died. Her husband, who was deeply affected by her death, wrote to the superintendent of the Reformatory at this time:

" It breaks my heart to think I should be separated from One I so dearly loved. We were very happy together. . . . She was the most thoughtful and loving person . . . God love her. . . . She told me of her past life before we were married and it was never mentioned in the ten years of our happy married life. . . . We adopted a little boy about seven years ago. Now he is the only comfort I have. . . . And speaking for my dear wife you do wonderful work and there are some that appreciate your great efforts."

The diagnosis made of Marie's condition when she entered the hospital was " neuro-syphilis — general paralysis, — cerebral type." [2] Marie was thirty-two years of age at the time of her death. There can be no doubt that she contracted syphilis while she was prostituting for her first husband, who was a white-slaver.

* * *

Alice.[3] When Alice was admitted to the Reformatory, she readily acknowledged delight in the excitement of the life which she had been leading, and said that her fingers " itched " to take things. She seemed determined at the outset, however, to make a better record at the Reformatory than she had done on her previous commitment and was sure she could do so if she really wanted do. She expressed a liking for heavy physical work in which she might utilize all of her abundant energy. Mental examination showed her to be of dull-normal intellect, and the examiner recorded that " deception and plausibility is the foundation of her mental make-up . . . a leader . . . a good actress, capable of intense friendships with women . . . has great ambitions toward high standing among criminals." Medical examination revealed gonorrhœa, but her physical condition was otherwise excellent.

Alice was placed at work in the kitchen, where she proved to be an incessant talker and very disorderly. During the nineteen months that she spent in the Reformatory she had to be isolated on several occasions for using vile

---

[2] Marie was found to have primary syphilis on admission to the Reformatory, for which condition she was treated. Before her release blood tests were found to be negative. It now becomes apparent, however, that the condition persisted even though tests did not reveal its presence. This is due to the imperfection of tests as applied years ago, compared to the more modern procedures and techniques for discovering the presence of syphilis.

[3] Continued from p. 38.

language and for disobedience. For two months she was allowed to work in the shirt room, but as she set such a bad example to the other girls, it was decided to put her on the job of plastering walls, at which task she was practically isolated. She "worked like a horse" and behaved very well, but as soon as this job was finished, she again became restless and unmanageable. The superintendent of the Reformatory made every effort to gain Alice's confidence and to help her overcome her difficulties.

When she had been in the institution for about a year, Alice seemed a little more amenable to the good influences about her, and at this time she wrote her mother:

"I am going to try and forget the past and start a new book. . . . If there is the least bit of good in me, I will break my neck to show her [the superintendent] I can be good but just imagine the fight I am up against. I have had a long time to think, some days I have not been out of my cell at all and some days the matron would come in and let me work for ten or fifteen minutes and perhaps I would not appreciate it . . . and as for you, Ma, you are never out of my mind. . . . She [the superintendent] read one of your letters today and said her heart just fairly ached for you but Ma don't worry over me but think that this time might be the makings of me . . . from your heartbroken daughter."

However, Alice's good resolutions went their usual way. When she was again under punishment for smoking a cigar which she had rolled out of a piece of heavy khaki, she insisted on making an apology for her conduct to all the inmates, saying that she wanted to humiliate herself and cut out her old life and wanted them to help her; that she was disgusted with the way she was behaving. The superintendent continued her efforts to understand and direct Alice, so that the girl one day asked, "Why do you care for me so much? Why don't you let me go to the devil?" "Because your face doesn't yet match up with your soul," replied the superintendent.

When Alice was paroled, she agreed it was best she be placed as a domestic. A position was found for her by the parole agent, where she remained only a few hours and then ran off home. She quickly rejoined her old gang, but, being so well known to store detectives, was constantly under suspicion even when on a legitimate shopping tour with her mother or sisters. Six weeks after her release on parole, she was arrested on a charge of shoplifting and was returned to the Reformatory. She spent a large part of her two months' stay in the institution in a punishment cell, because she was constantly encouraging other inmates to disorderliness and was even on occasion stealing. There was some hint at this time that pressure was brought for her release. Her family had engaged a lawyer for her when she was first committed, and he made frequent appeals on her behalf, to very little avail, however, as the superintendent of the Reformatory rarely allowed him to see Alice alone.

When Alice was paroled the second time, she went directly to the home of her sister, frequently visiting her parents. For about three months she behaved quietly enough. She shortly made the acquaintance of a young railroad brakeman who was earning about twenty dollars a week. He was a steady worker and presumably of good reputation, although she knew nothing of his family. After living with him illicitly for a few months, she married him without the permission of the parole agent. The parole agent and the Reformatory officials had good reasons to believe that Alice was continuing her old activities, as other girls committed to the Reformatory were reporting that Alice had trained them to steal and that she was the acknowledged leader of a gang of shoplifters. They therefore had her apprehended when one day, on the insistence of her husband, she took him out to visit the Reformatory.

On readmission Alice was placed at work plastering, at which occupation she had been successfully engaged on a prior occasion. It was reported that she " is a capable young worker when so inclined." Her sister, her husband, and her lawyer visited her several times with a view to expediting her release. When she was questioned by the Board of Parole, Alice confessed that not only had she continued to shoplift, but that her husband had been arrested for shoplifting, in which she had involved him soon after they were married. Alice was no more tractable during this third period in the institution than she had been before. She had often to be reprimanded for insolence and disorderliness and even made an attempt to escape. Finally, after sixteen months, she was once more paroled, returning to her mother's home, but soon rejoining her husband.

During a period of almost two years before she was again apprehended, Alice continued her shoplifting activities, left her husband, lived with other men in expensive suites which they provided for her, was always clothed most elaborately in stolen finery, yet for a long time managed to allay the suspicions of the parole agent. Finally she was again arrested on a charge of shoplifting and instead of being returned to the Reformatory was transferred to a house of correction where she was to serve the remainder of her sentence. Meanwhile there were warrants out for her arrest in several other states.

Alice was now twenty-four years of age and was generally referred to by the police as a " thief de luxe." She had committed larcenies totalling many thousands of dollars and had the reputation of being one of the ablest women thieves of the East. At the time of her arraignment she was wearing a two-hundred-dollar dress and the price tags had not yet been removed from her hand-made underclothing. She frankly told her parole officer that she was not going " to work the stores any more but the big buildings."

When, after two years, Alice had finally completed her sentence, she was determined to " get some place in this world this time." For a brief space she returned to the home of her parents, but only to get her bearings. She soon took up her residence in the city in a region which is notorious for housing well-to-do professional prostitutes and gamblers. She quickly resumed her old connections, surrounding herself with several clever girl shoplifters and male accomplices. Alice made a few short trips through the East to establish connections with crooks in other cities who could dispose of her stolen goods. She was most skilful in evading the police. She frankly boasted that she had paid for police " protection "; that she has sold expensive stolen garments for ridiculously low prices to city and state officials; that she was always able to secure political assistance when she was " in a jam." Alice has kept in touch with her family, often supplying them and their neighbours with expensive clothing. One of her sisters and a brother have become associated with her in the shoplifting business.

Some sixteen months after her release Alice was haled into court for violating an auto law, for which she paid a five-dollar fine. Shortly after this she was arrested for larceny. The case was continued for a few days and she defaulted. Some days later the default was removed and she then received a sentence to the Reformatory for Women, which she appealed. While the appeal was pending, she was charged with adultery with a man with whom she was arrested in a notorious hang-out for thieves. Alice was well represented by counsel and was placed on probation. She went to live with her parents for a short time and was encouraged by them to establish herself in a small millinery business. She hired a store, from which she was soon requested to move, however, because her landlord suspected that she was using the place as a hang-out for thieves and as a cloak for her shoplifting activities.

Meanwhile Alice had secured a divorce from her husband on the charge of " cruel and abusive treatment and neglect to provide," and the case was uncontested. She asserts that while she was serving sentence, her husband had consoled himself with another woman, and that she therefore felt entirely justified in seeking a divorce.

Alice's closest pal, whose name she has borrowed on occasion, was a notorious underworld character who aided and abetted her in her activities. Nine months after her last-mentioned arrest Alice was again apprehended, this time for concealing leased property. She was sentenced to one month in jail, but appealed, and the case was filed. Again she was represented by counsel. The charge against her was that she had purchased household goods on which she was making payments gradually and that she had transferred them to someone else without notifying the company which sold her the goods. At this time Alice still had her " millinery business," which she was later forced to give up because the police were watching her for proof that what seemed to be a legitimate place of business was in reality a meeting-place for crooks. Alice meanwhile had been maintaining an apartment from which she was directing her shoplifting activities. Within a few months detectives hired by several department stores precipitated a raid upon her apartment and found Alice with several other women and several men, all of whom were well known to the police. They were all arrested, but only Alice and her principal male accomplice were brought to trial. About four thousand dollars' worth of goods was found. The two pleaded guilty and she was sentenced to serve two years in the House of Correction.

Alice was described at this time as being "dogmatic in manner, cunning and resourceful in avoiding answers to unwelcome questions. Has a violent temper . . . glories in her ability to cover her tracks." During the trial it became apparent that a young man, presumably of very good repute and occupying a steady and well-paying position, was very much interested in her and said that he intended to marry her on her release. Alice's accomplice, who felt that he had some claim on her, was very threatening to her alleged fiancé, and Alice appeared to be somewhat frightened that he might do him harm. She was greatly relieved when he was given a long sentence.

During her incarceration Alice was examined by a psychiatrist,[4] who reported:

"No psychosis, no neurosis, of average intelligence. Rather peculiar mental make-up and is elated and exalted and feels that she is much better than other people. . . .

"She has always taken the easiest way of obtaining her living and has formed habits which at the present time are ingrained. Repeated sentences have had no effect on her conduct, and it would seem unlikely that her present sentence would be otherwise. She is fundamentally unamenable to correction and would best classify in an institution for psychopathic delinquents for an indefinite period."

During her two years in jail Alice was frequently visited by her mother, her sister, and her fiancé, whom she was looking forward to marrying upon her release. The officers of the jail asserted that she was the worst inmate they had ever had and that she was a very peculiar person. "One day she would be as nice a prisoner as one could ask for and the next day she was the other way and she was the other way most of the time. As to her future prospects of social and moral rehabilitation, she is far beyond that."

When Alice was released from jail, she was already thirty-one years old. She returned to the home of her parents, remaining there only long enough to get her bearings, and went off to marry her fiancé. She has never been able to produce her marriage certificate, nor has our investigation revealed any verification of this marriage. Alice's "husband" presented her with a very expensive automobile, and the couple lived in considerable luxury, soon purchasing their own house in a very respectable suburb — a good-sized house, which they

4 In 1924 a Division for the Mental Examination of Persons Accused of Crime was established in the Massachusetts Department of Mental Diseases.

furnished luxuriously. They kept a maid and wore expensive clothes, and Alice even sported several prize chow dogs.

For about a year and a half there seemed to be no particular suspicion directed against either Alice or her husband, but again when shoplifters became unusually active among the department stores, police began to keep a close watch and one day caught several women with numerous bundles entering a fine automobile in front of a large store. Upon questioning them they discovered that the car was the property of Alice's husband. This led to the revelation that Alice had been continuing her illegitimate activities and that in the attic of her house was a " nigger pool " lay-out which netted her and her husband and their accomplices about fifteen hundred dollars a week. Alice's trial created much scandal, and great attention in the newspapers, because shortly before her case was to appear before the Grand Jury several court attachés were found dining in her house. It was strongly suspected that she had much influence among politicians and would receive a minimum sentence for her offence. No matter how high her bail, she was always able to secure a bondsman. Although Alice pleaded not guilty to a complaint of larceny, conspiracy to steal, and receiving stolen property, she subsequently, on advice of counsel, changed her plea to guilty and was given a two-year sentence to jail, where she is at present.

Alice is now thirty-five years of age, a crafty, thoroughly experienced criminal, skilled in her business and well acquainted with the abuse of legal machinery for her protection. Through all these years she has been able to impose her will on those about her. She has had the devotion not only of several men, but also of women. To her " friends " she has quite generally been loyal and is known in the underworld as a " square shooter." She can usually be depended upon to fulfil her obligations, and will come to the protection of a friend even at the risk of personal embarrassment.

Further outlook for Alice is not encouraging. She is still a very handsome woman, said by the police to be one of the prettiest defendants that they have ever known, and although she has lost the disarmingly candid expression of her adolescence, she still has a coarse charm which will no doubt continue to attract many people to her.

*　　*　　*

Grace.[5] When Grace came to the Reformatory, she was very quiet and agreeable, though very much puzzled as to why she had been committed. She was very frank about her misdoings, however, and not at all ashamed of them. She professed very little affection for either her child or her sisters and brothers, but expressed a fondness for her father, to whom she wanted to return on release. " I just got in with the wrong crowd. I did wrong and I have to be

[5] Continued from p. 41.

punished." She stated that she would like to secure a divorce from her husband in order that she might marry a chance acquaintance whom she had met previous to her Reformatory sentence and from whom she received several affectionate letters which she was not permitted to read. When asked what kind of work she would like to do in the Reformatory, she replied: "I like most anything that is interesting."

A week after her admittance she had a miscarriage, being delivered of a two month's fœtus. When she had sufficiently recovered, she was placed as a machine-operator in the shirt room, at which assignment she worked fairly dependably for a year. She had to be reprimanded for occasional insolence and talking out of turn and was sometimes heedless. When she had been at the Reformatory for nineteen months, it was found necessary to perform an operation upon her for bilateral salpingitis, which made child-bearing impossible.

For about another year Grace worked as a general helper in the receiving and packing room of the institution, where she was found to be a willing enough worker, but inefficient. Meanwhile her father married a kindly and motherly woman who was very willing to have Grace return home. The father, however, felt that because of the girl's easy infatuation for men, her adjustment was doubtful. For this reason he was not at all eager that she should be released, and urged her to take every opportunity for development while she was in the Reformatory. Meanwhile Grace's child was returned from a boarding-home to the home of her father because Grace's husband had ceased sending money for its care.

As Grace's father strenuously objected to her parole, she remained in the Reformatory for the full twenty-four months of her sentence. She, of course, was eager to be released and wrote to the superintendent a few months after admission:

"I try very hard to be good it is pretty hard in one way an of course If I never had the baby I would not worry but I have her to think of. . . . I no my father will feel bad when he heres I never got parroled but would like to show him I can do good. I never had a chance to do right for my sister always found fault an now that I am here they are glad if I did not have the baby I would not care for I do not want to go home an be a burden to my father as he has enough to bear now."

The Reformatory officials felt that during her stay in the institution Grace had not developed any dependability though she was quiet and agreeable. She took little interest in her work and showed no planfulness. It was felt by the staff there that she needed constant supervision.

When Grace was released from the Reformatory, at the age of twenty-one, she went to a position as a domestic which had been secured for her by one of the parole officers. The position was offered her merely as a courtesy to the institution officials, because it is not the practice of the parole department to find positions for girls who have not been paroled. The family to whom she went knew that she had been in the Reformatory and were willing to make allowances for her, but were forced to discharge her after six weeks because she was keeping such late hours and running around with questionable companions. She returned almost immediately to her promiscuous sex habits and to her search for gaiety and adventure. After being discharged from her first position, she went back to her father's home for a brief period, spending the following summer in doing hotel work at various New England resorts. During the fall of that year she drifted about in the South End of Boston in the company of her friend Edith, returning home at Christmas time with a sailor whose family lived not far away from hers and whom she had picked up in a dance-hall. Shortly afterwards she disappeared from home and again drifted around Boston, living with Edith for about three months and carrying on in the same old way.

Finally, some fourteen months after her release from the Reformatory, Grace was arrested for fornication with the sailor who had visited her at her home at Christmas time, in a raid on a disorderly house where sailors and others were permitted to come with girls and where professional prostitutes brought the men whom they picked up. She was found guilty, and it was the feeling of the probation officer who had been asked to make an investigation of her case that she should properly be returned to the Reformatory. But the judge instead gave her a suspended sentence of three months in jail, placed her on probation, and warned her that association with Edith would constitute a violation for which sentence would be enforced.

Grace was instructed to return to her home, but it was soon found that she had gone to live with the co-defendant's mother, who had previously invited her to her house and did not know that Grace had been arrested with her son.

Upon the insistence of the probation officer Grace returned home. She was treated with much consideration by her stepmother; her father, sisters, and brothers were very strict with her as usual, feeling that Grace, though outwardly behaving herself, was only awaiting the end of her probation period to go off again to her former associates. Her family obviously did not trust her, but her stepmother succeeded in gaining the girl's confidence to the extent that if Grace was planning to go out for an evening or to be away for several days, she would tell her so. Under the stepmother's kindly influence the girl was also beginning to take a little more interest in her child, Edith, who was six years old at this time.

Upon the occasion of her recent arrest Grace was found to have syphilis. Treatment was advised and she was very regular in her attendance at the clinic. As the clinic was held evenings, she used it as an excuse to spend a day away from home. It was strongly suspected that she was again associating with her former companions.

During the early part of her probation Grace helped her stepmother with the housework, but was very erratic about this, sometimes doing a thorough day's work of cleaning, washing, and ironing and at other times being extremely lax. She was urged by her family to seek a position in order that she might help to support her child, and found a place at a local laundry where she was able to earn fourteen dollars a week, of which she paid her father ten dollars for board. At about this time Grace began to receive visits from a respectable man several years older than herself who knew about her marriage and showed a great interest in her little daughter. Grace sought advice from the probation officer about securing a divorce, and the officer assisted her in starting the necessary proceedings. But Grace's interest in her new admirer soon petered out, and she became enamoured of a young Scotchman who called frequently. Though her father approved of him, he did not encourage the association, and it can only be suspected that because Grace had syphilis, he did not feel that she had the right to marry anyone at the time.

Meanwhile Grace, who had been working steadily at the laundry, was promoted, now receiving seventeen dollars a week. She was becoming a little neglectful of her child, however, and allowing her father and sisters to assume more of the burden and was also beginning to keep late hours.

While she was still on probation, she began to receive communications from a brother of the man with whom she had been arrested. In a confidential moment she told her stepmother that this man promised to get an apartment for her in Norfolk, Virginia, and bring sailors to her for sexual intercourse. By arrangement they were to divide the proceeds. The co-defendant himself was also writing to Grace at this time, urging her to give up drinking. Grace confided to the clinic physician that she drank a little, but never to the point of intoxication. The probation officer warned her to have no more correspondence with either the co-defendant or his brother.

Grace's probation period, which had been continued from time to time because she needed further treatment for syphilis, was finally ended after two years. Although the family thought that she would leave home again as soon as supervision was over, she remained and continued to work in the laundry, contributing quite steadily to the support of her child. She did, however, revert to promiscuous sexual relations with men. When she was asked by the agent of the Girls' Society, which had through all these years continued oversight of her child, why she behaved as she did, she replied, " I am not bad. I am just natural." Though she did not bring any particular scandal on her family during these years, she continued to go about in the company of young men who encouraged illicit relations. Her oldest sister told our investigator that the family, despite all their attempts, never succeeded in influencing Grace very much, as she did not like their kind of life. She had no interest in church-going and could find no recreational outlets in normally accepted ways.

Finally, when Grace was twenty-eight, she met a man eleven years older than herself whom she married after a year's acquaintance (seven years after her release from the Reformatory). Her husband, also a Protestant, has had a common school education and is a steady worker, of good reputation. Though he knows about Grace's Reformatory commitment, he has no knowledge of her subsequent delinquencies. They met through a common friend at whose house he was calling when Grace was also there. Shortly after their engagement he was transferred to New York State in connection with his work. When he settled himself there properly, he sent for her and they were married. She travelled about with him for a time, and then they settled in New Jersey. A short time ago, because of the financial depression, they decided to move back to Massachusetts and settle near her family. They have had no children. He is a sober, industrious fellow who apparently understands her and with whom she finds happiness.

Grace lives in a very attractive three-room apartment in a modern house very near the home of her father. It is comfortably furnished and there is plenty of light and air. The home shows signs of being well cared for. In the early days of their marriage, Grace's husband was getting as much as fifty dollars a week, but has recently, on account of the depression, been thrown out of employment. However, Grace has contributed very substantially to the support of herself and her husband, for after returning from a few months' stay in New York State and New Jersey, where her husband's work took them, she was given back her old position in the laundry. Her husband is at present working a little, and between them they make sufficient to provide for their own needs and for Grace's daughter.

Grace and her father and sisters are on very friendly terms. Now that Grace is safely married to a respectable man and is living a conventional life, her relatives approve of her. Grace attends the Presbyterian church on occasion and even goes to entertainments given there. She no longer has such a fondness for dances and rarely goes anywhere except in the company of her husband.

At the present writing, Grace's child, who is fourteen years old and has been in a foster-home since the death of Grace's stepmother, is beginning to show sexual problems very similar to those of her mother. She is, however, brighter. The Girls' Society which is still supervising the situation is watching her carefully. The social workers feel that it is well for Grace not to play too prominent a role in the life of her daughter, as she is inclined to encourage her to dress in a very "flapperish way" and to show off her charms rather pointedly to her boy and girl friends.

Whether Grace's adaptation to marriage and a conventional form of social life is permanent remains to be seen. She is now (1933) thirty-three years old and has been married for four years.

* * *

Florence.[6] When Florence was admitted to the Reformatory, she was found to be in very poor physical condition as the result of drug addiction. She was very thin and wan, almost hysterical, very talkative. She soon revealed a "neurasthenoid temperament" and great emotional instability. Mental examination showed her to be of average intelligence. She was placed at work as a helper in the dining-room, where she proved efficient, faithful, and dependable. As all drugs were withdrawn, she suffered some discomfort, but seemed to be able to overcome this by throwing herself with vigour into her work.

After fifteen months in the Reformatory she was paroled and secured a position as an attendant in a small private sanatorium. For about two months Florence worked there very efficiently and enthusiastically. She acted as companion and nurse to a suicidal patient who was in a highly depressed state. It was Florence's task to watch her closely and to accompany her on walks and look after her wants. Florence's only complaint at this time was that she was not working hard enough and did not feel that she deserved the good salary she was receiving.

It was only a short time before Florence discovered how she might easily secure the drug she craved. As she was dressed in a nurse's uniform, she was able, during walks with her patient, to purchase from drug stores in the neighbourhood quantities of "Arnold's Balsam" and other drug-containing preparations, without arousing the suspicions of the pharmacists. She even began at this time to use a hypodermic needle. Not until she was found, on one of her days off, by her father in his home, in a semi-conscious condition did the parole authorities realize that she was again using drugs. A considerable quantity of morphine tablets was found in her room at the sanatorium. Her father took her back there and she was put to bed. When she had recovered sufficiently from her " spree," she was returned to the Reformatory on revocation of parole.

On readmission to the Reformatory, Florence was confused, incoherent, and noisy. For some time it was necessary to isolate her in the hospital. Although during her previous stay in the institution she had been most amenable in her conduct, she was now excitable and uncontrollable, even manifesting delusions of persecution by some members of the Reformatory staff. Her father visited her frequently and expressed the hope that she would be held to the

6 Continued from p. 44.

end of her sentence and then permanently committed to a state hospital. He felt that this was the only solution of her problem and was thoroughly convinced that there was no cure for her.

Florence made numerous efforts to gain an early release, demanding from her father in the most petulant manner the services of a lawyer, which, however, he absolutely refused. He was sincerely attached to the girl and concerned about her welfare and was ready to do everything possible for her. He could not offer to take her into his home, however, as he merely rented a room and there were no facilities for a guest. Meanwhile Florence's third husband had instituted divorce proceedings.

Florence served the remainder of her two year indeterminate sentence in the institution and was released after nine months. The Reformatory officials felt at this time that she should have permanent custodial care. She was now forty-one years old. Despite her father's inability to care for her, she went to live with him and made no effort to find employment. She had a small legacy of several hundred dollars which had been left her by a relative and on which she now drew for support. Before long she communicated with her first husband in Maine, from whom she had many years previously been divorced, and he, through sheer kindness and pity for her, frequently sent her ten or fifteen dollars. She immediately began to seek drugs, insisting that she did not take morphine, but confined herself to paraldehyde and paregoric. Her father says that she would sleep all day and stay out all night and that she was very clever in obtaining drugs.

Florence shortly drifted back to Maine around the summer resorts and into the city where her first husband lived and where she had spent the greater part of her young womanhood. She was soon picked up there as a dope addict, but was released, and, becoming restless, returned to Massachusetts, where she was picked up by the police and sent to a hospital for observation. From there she was discharged as " not insane."

Florence's father at this time again expressed the hope that she would be permanently committed, as she was utterly hopeless and was constantly forging permits for drugs. But somehow or other she was not committed. Again she drifted to Maine, begging her way, rooming in cheap lodging-houses, avoiding payment of rent, always having a plausible hard-luck story about having lost her money or being an heiress and waiting for her legacy to arrive, or being very ill and needing care. In Maine she was again picked up by the police and sent for safekeeping to the state hospital, where she was held only a few months. Here she was diagnosed as a " constitutional psychopathic inferior."

Once more Florence returned to her father's home and was soon asking aid of a welfare agency, even though she was now regularly receiving money from her first husband. Again she was arrested for drug addiction, sent to a hospital for observation, diagnosed as " not insane," and committed to the state farm, where she remained for three months. The psychiatrists at the hospital who had studied her case before felt at this time that Florence was definitely a " psychopathic personality."

After each release from jail or hospital Florence would drift back and forth between Maine and Massachusetts, usually to towns where she had acquaintances or relatives to whom she might go for aid. Again she was arrested in Maine and committed to the state hospital for a few days, was released, and a few days later was arrested for larceny of a watch. Florence made it a practice to go to private homes, ring the door-bell, pretend sudden illness, and ask permission to rest for a while. Once having gained entry to the house, she would try to persuade her involuntary hosts to keep her for several days. On such occasions she would often steal small articles, which she would pawn in order to obtain drugs. The police frequently had to be called to evict her. When Florence rented a room in a private house or a lodging-house, she would remain until she was asked to leave.

One day she was found on the street in a dazed condition and taken to a hospital, where she was held for a day and found to be suffering from acute alcoholism. She was not a steady drinker, but took alcohol and water when she could not obtain morphine. Soon thereafter she was sent to a hospital in another city where she had been begging among friends, was kept for two days, and was then discharged to a state hospital on a ten-day commitment. Soon after release from the hospital she was again arrested and sent to the state farm, where she remained for five months and was then transferred to another state hospital for treatment and care, being discharged after two months there.

Again her father pleaded that she be kept permanently in an institution, as he felt that she was a menace to the community and was entirely incapable of earning her own living. A month after her release from the hospital she was again picked up by the police and sent for ten days' observation to a hospital where she had previously been on two occasions. She was again diagnosed as " not insane." Once more she drifted to Maine and within the next two months was picked up three times by the police, held a few days in jail for safekeeping, and on the third occasion sent to a city farm. Then she went back into Massachusetts again, begging her way, telling pitiful stories of need, stealing small articles here and there in order to have money for drugs; then back again to Maine, where she was picked up by the police once for larceny, once for vagrancy, and a third time for drug addiction and again sent to the state hospital. Released after a few months, she was again arrested for larceny, this time of a typewriter. It had become her habit, in order to obtain money for drugs, to hire typewriters and pawn them.

During one of her begging expeditions in Massachusetts, Florence was referred to the charities by a local minister of whom she had asked aid. It happened that her father's sister was at this time an agent of this organization, and, realizing Florence's condition, she wished to have her permanently committed. She was not able to bring this about, as Florence quickly disappeared.

Within two months Florence was again picked up in Maine, and at this time it was alleged by the police that she was enlisting the services of young girls to obtain paregoric from drug stores for her and even paying taxi-drivers to help her procure morphine. The police were inclined to be lenient with her because of her mental and physical condition, so that when she was arrested for larceny, she was usually placed on probation. In addition to the arrests already mentioned, her record discloses several arrests for being idle and disorderly, for violating probation, for vagrancy, and for larceny, and one for defrauding an innkeeper. She was several times more sent to state hospitals for brief periods for treatment. She also made numerous overtures to social agencies for financial assistance in both Maine and Massachusetts, being usually given a few dollars for temporary relief and requested to return in a day or two, pending investigation, so that some plan might be made for her, but she did not do so. She sometimes wrote to the Reformatory and parole officials for assistance and on one occasion found her way to the summer home of a member of the Reformatory staff.

Since her release from the Reformatory ten years ago Florence has been arrested twenty-one times; has been sent to mental hospitals for observation on five occasions, each time being diagnosed as "not insane"; has been twice committed for treatment; has been in jail three times on very short sentences; and has been dealt with by six different social agencies, each of which gave her temporary relief. Although on almost each occasion that she was in jail or in a hospital she was examined for venereal disease, it was not until very recently that she was found to have gonorrhœa. If she has had illicit sexual relations, it has been only to obtain money for drugs, as there is no indication whatsoever that Florence has any marked tendency toward immorality. Her sex adventures, such as they may be, and her stealing are secondary to her addiction to drugs and serve only as a means of obtaining money to purchase them. In 1933 Florence is fifty-three years old. She has drifted from pillar to post, a nervous wreck of a woman, on an endless quest to satisfy her strong craving, a drag on her relatives, her acquaintances, and the communities into which she has wandered. As she is "not insane," however, the law makes no provision to keep her in permanent custody. Commenting upon the situation, the superintendent of one of the state hospitals writes:

> "The hospital fulfills its duty by caring for the patient when mentally disturbed, and after all evidences of a psychosis have disappeared and the patient appears healthy and well, he should be released, even though the tendency to submerge long-standing disharmonies of personality by the use of drugs continues to persist."

*   *   *

Annie.[7] When Annie was admitted to the Reformatory, she was in a highly emotional state, greatly upset over having been committed to an institution of this type. " If I could have the man I love, I would be happy. I do love him, I don't care whatever happens, we both love each other and idolize each other. I am sorry I have done what I done."

Mental examination showed Annie to be of fair general ability, but her " concentration difficult and she is easily confused." She was found to have gonorrhœa, contracted probably from her lover, since there is no suspicion against her husband, who is known in the community as a " good clean man."

Because she had some rheumatism, Annie could not do heavy work in the institution and was allowed to help in the nursery with the children and to care for the officers' bedrooms. She was always capable, agreeable, and obliging in every way. " One of the best helpers we have ever had." She was devoted to her baby and it was her plan upon leaving the institution to secure a divorce and marry her lover if he was willing; if not, to find a position as a domestic where she could keep her baby with her.

She did not communicate at all with her husband during the fourteen months that she was in the Reformatory, but wrote once to her daughter (now a girl of ten), a very emotional letter in which she begged the child's forgiveness for having disgraced her and her father and asked that she write and tell her all about herself. The letter was not sent, as the Reformatory officials pointed out to Annie that it would not be very wise to send such a communication to a little girl, to which she agreed.

When Annie was paroled, she was placed at housework with her baby. Here she remained for eight months and proved to be most satisfactory to her employer. Her lover, who after his release from the House of Correction was again working in the factory where he had been employed for many years, called to see her frequently, and Annie's employer was favourably impressed with him because it was obvious that he meant to assume his responsibilities toward Annie and their child. When her employer decided that she could get along without a maid, the parole agent found her another position in domestic service, where she remained for nine months. One day she disappeared with her baby, and the parole officer was not able to find any trace of her.

Meanwhile Annie had rejoined her lover, who had left his place of employment a few weeks previously and gone to New York, sending for her as soon as he found work. They have lived together ever since as man and wife and she has been entirely out of touch with her husband and her first child. There has never been a divorce between herself and her husband, although the relatives of Annie's lover appear to believe that the couple are legally married. Annie has not worked outside of her home since rejoining her lover. Until the recent

[7] Continued from p. 45.

financial depression he has worked steadily and made a comfortable home for her and their little girl. There have been no other children.

Annie and her husband have been regarded in the community as respectable married people who are very happy together. Recently, because of unemployment and the illness of her " husband," it has been necessary for the couple to go to Canada to live with relatives of his, who know nothing about Annie's prior marriage and her sentence to the Reformatory and were not informed because " they are conservative people and would be deeply shocked."

Annie has grown very stout of late years and rarely goes out of the house except to attend church. She has become extremely religious. She spends most of her free time in religious services and church work in a Protestant church, having entirely given up her Catholicism. She is now (1933) forty-six years old. Recently her oldest daughter, who has lived during all these years with her father (Annie's first husband) and has been deeply devoted to him, has married. On the occasion of her marriage she wished to notify her mother, but did not succeed in locating her. Annie has no interest whatsoever in this daughter or in her first husband and has in all these years not once communicated with them. The reason may be that, as she left Massachusetts without notifying her parole agent, she has a notion that she is still a fugitive from justice.

*   *   *

Fleur.[8] When Fleur was admitted to the Reformatory, she feigned hallucinations; she said she was very much frightened and heard voices talking to her, and that she could hear her husband shouting and calling her names. She soon quieted down, however, and when asked about this a few hours later, said that she knew nothing about it. She evinced her usual periods of excitement and unmanageableness; and the superintendent, who had felt on the occasion of Fleur's previous stay that nothing could be accomplished for her in the Reformatory, arranged for her transfer to a house of correction. Within a month and a half of the expiration of her two-year indeterminate sentence Fleur was released on parole.

She told the parole agent that she would like to find a good home where she could earn a little money and be self-respecting, and that she would like to be placed in a position away from her home city, where she was so notorious. The parole agent found a place for her as a domestic in a fine home with a lady who promised to keep a watchful eye on the girl. Fleur told her employer repeatedly on that first day how happy she was at the opportunity to work. She seemed to take hold very nicely and her employer was very much pleased. After two days, however, the girl left the house, presumably only to do an errand, and failed to return.

She was shortly arrested for violation of parole and was returned to the house

[8] Continued from p. 50.

of correction to complete her sentence. After a month and a half she was released to her mother, who had agreed to give her a home. Fleur's mother, whose legal husband had died about two years previously, was as usual living with another man, ostensibly as his housekeeper. When Fleur returned home, her mother expected her to find work and turn over her earnings. The girl promised to do this, but almost immediately left home. She returned to her old haunts and her old companions and within a few months was married to a young fellow of very unsavoury reputation. In her marriage application she stated that she had been divorced. Her mother, however, says that Fleur's husband died of tuberculosis. No record of either a divorce between Fleur and her first husband or of his death can be found.

Fleur and her new husband settled in a small bungalow owned by her husband's father, at a cheap, crowded summer resort. They lived there for two years, and during this time caused much annoyance to their neighbours to whom it was obvious that Fleur was allowing all kinds of men to come to her home to buy liquor, to drink, and to have illicit relations with her. Her husband was aware of her goings on and aided and abetted her in all her activities. She and her husband proved to be such nuisances that the neighbours made complaint to the police department, which gained the co-operation of the bank that held the mortgage on their little property, and the bank foreclosed, ostensibly on the ground that they were in arrears on their payments.

During the five-year period following the expiration of her sentence Fleur has been arrested fourteen times — twice for illegal sale of liquor, twice for keeping and exposing liquor, once for illegally manufacturing liquor, four times for drunkenness, three times for disturbing the peace, once for assault and battery, and once for violating a city ordinance. For these arrests she was fined eight times, the fines ranging from ten to seventy-five dollars; she received one sentence of three months to the house of correction; on one occasion her case was filed. It was generally known to the police that when Fleur was to be arrested, it was necessary to send at least two officers after her, because she was such a fighter and so hard to handle. During this same period her husband was arrested once for adultery, once for disturbing the peace, once for assault and battery, and once for unlawful sale of liquor. On all four occasions he was fined, one fine amounting to a hundred dollars, and in addition he served one month in the house of correction.

Fleur's most intimate chum is a notorious prostitute; and Fleur's sister, although married, is living much the same life as Fleur, but is not so temperamental and boisterous. Fleur has been drinking considerably, and during three years following the end of the five-year post-parole period she has been arrested sixteen times more for drunkenness, and once for disturbing the peace. Three of these cases were filed; twice she was fined; six times she was given suspended sentences to the house of correction; and on six occasions she was committed to the house of correction for short sentences, ranging from ten to thirty days in length. She has recently separated from her husband and is going her own way, rarely seeing even her relatives. Her mother is extremely hostile to her and does not even care to know the girl's whereabouts. Fleur is now (1933) twenty-nine years old. She has had syphilis for some years and is not receiving any treatment for it.

*   *   *

Margaret.[9] Mental examination at the Reformatory revealed that Margaret was of " border-line intelligence." Her physical condition was found to be excellent and she had no venereal disease. The Reformatory officials felt that the girl needed a great deal of personal direction and intensive supervision. For this reason she was placed at work in the superintendent's home, where she had pretty constant oversight and could be kept away from more hardened offenders.

Margaret's parents soon began to relent their harshness in having had her committed to a penal institution and came often to visit her. At first she refused to see them, feeling that her difficulties were entirely due to them; but soon she began to realize that they had done what they thought was best for her.

Margaret behaved well enough in the Reformatory, realizing that early parole was a reward of good behaviour. At the end of four months she was released and returned to her parents, who expressed a desire to do everything possible to make her happy. They purchased an outfit of clothes for her at an expenditure of about sixty dollars, which they expected her to pay back to them in small sums out of her weekly earnings. Margaret went to work in a box-factory where she had been previously employed, and, out of her nine dollars weekly earnings, had to give five dollars to her parents for her board. She soon began to feel that this was much too exorbitant a sum and expressed to the parole agent her wish to keep her wages entirely to herself and spend them as she liked. The parole agent had much difficulty in reasoning with her about this, and Margaret continued to complain and find fault. For some three months she worked steadily enough, and except for her dissatisfaction at having to give a large part of her earnings to her parents, she behaved herself well.

Soon, however, she began to stay out late and on one occasion remained away from home for two nights, returning only to demand her clothes, which her mother refused to give her. The girl left in a huff, saying she was going to board elsewhere, and her parents soon discovered that she was staying next door with a married woman of poor reputation who entertained soldiers and coloured men. The parole agent insisted that Margaret return home. This she finally did, but she continued to be defiant to her parents.

On one occasion not long after, Margaret's father struck her for being impudent to him. On the following day her parents refused to speak to her, locked

[9] Continued from p. 52.

up her clothes, and obliged her to get her own meals. The next evening Margaret went to a party, and her parents decided to call for her. Much to their amazement, they discovered that the " party " was in a disorderly house. When Margaret saw her parents she rushed out into the street and was chased by her father, who did not, however, succeed in catching her. The girl hid herself in the neighbourhood until she thought she could enter her home unnoticed. When she tried to do so, however, she found the door barred against her and had to spend the night with a neighbouring family. Meanwhile Margaret's parents, greatly enraged at her conduct, rushed to the police station and demanded the arrest of their daughter. The police refused to act, telling the mother that she must report Margaret to the parole agent, as the girl was still under supervision. So on the next day Margaret was taken into custody by the agent. Her parole was revoked and she was returned to the Reformatory to complete her sentence.

On this second admission to the Reformatory, Margaret was very much subdued and not nearly so flippant as before. She honestly insisted that she did not understand why she had been returned, as she had not been immoral. She was placed in the laundry to work. Occasionally she had to be reprimanded for impudence and once for causing a disturbance in the dining-room. On this occasion Margaret was very defiant, claiming that the officer in charge had lied about her conduct. She acknowledged later that the officer was right, however. Margaret was taken back to the superintendent's house to work.

After six months, when the question of her parole arose and her parents once more insisted on her release, Margaret wrote to the superintendent:

" My mother was here to see me Tuesday and she wants me to go back home again. She said she was going to the State house and see what could be done about getting me out. I told her it would do no good and that I didn't want to go home.

" I told her I had learned how to work and I would like to go and work for myself before I came home.

" So, I want to ask you to give me a chance to be indentured at the hospital for a while to earn something for myself."

And the superintendent determined that Margaret should not be returned to her family:

" I am absolutely opposed to her release at present, and I do not want to be held responsible for any such step as that. It is not Reformatory work — this jacking them in and out. The child will never succeed with her family, and if she develops properly here, I shall probably give her a chance later on indenture."

Margaret was placed on indenture in a hospital, which meant that she received maintenance and a small salary, helping in the hospital kitchen and serving as a ward maid. Meanwhile the girl's parents continued to demand her release and the superintendent of the Reformatory tried to make them understand that this was against the girl's best interests:

" As you know, the Board of Parole did not see fit to release Margaret again on parole, she having returned home once and failed and having been returned here. An opportunity came for me to place her in a position of trust outside the institution upon indenture. I am watching Margaret's progress there very closely. I believe that she is doing well. In order for this plan to be successful, however, it is altogether important that she have every bit of encouragement and no discouragement. In your letter, you show dissatisfaction at having her placed out in this way, apparently preferring that she remain in the institution. I am withholding your letter, but I wish that you would write to her again in a different tone and give her all the encouragement you can. I hope that she will make good in the position which she now holds and that it may not be necessary for me to return her here. You can help a great deal, or you can hinder this plan. I hope you will choose to help."

Margaret remained on indenture for seven months, up to the expiration of her sentence. She was very happy, working steadily and conscientiously until the time of her release.

Meanwhile her parents had moved to a suburb in order that Margaret might come to a new neighbourhood, away from the influences of her former companions. During the short time that she made her home with her parents, she did not work regularly. When she had been at home for a month, her parents decided to wash their hands of her, as she was staying out late nights. " She would not be bossed by me or her mother. We advised her what was right but it did no good. She was out late nights with her gang and as she would not be guided by me or her mother, I told her she had better take the air."

Margaret then went to her brother and sister-in-law, who lived in an inferior, three-family house in an unkempt neighbourhood in which the racial elements were very much mixed — a business and factory area not far from an elevated station. As this was in the region of Margaret's early exploits, she soon found her old companions. Former neighbours of the family treated her cordially, sympathizing with her as a victim of her parents' harsh discipline and lack of tact. Margaret soon secured a position in a shoe factory and worked quite steadily, paying her sister-in-law for her board and between jobs helping with the housework.

As the living-quarters were cramped and there were four young children in the family, Margaret was not able to entertain her friends in her brother's home, and such meagre recreational outlets as her brother and sister-in-law could supply were not sufficient for an active, pleasure-loving girl. So Margaret was usually away from home evenings. Her relatives did not attempt to control her as her parents had done, so she was happy enough with them.

At a party in the home of a friend, Margaret became acquainted with a young American of Irish extraction who lived in a near-by city and was working in a pool-room. Both his parents had been city employees for many years — his father a labourer, and his mother a matron in a police station. The young man had been born and bred in the community and was well known as reputable and steady. Margaret began going about with him, and a year after they met, and almost two years after Margaret's sentence from the Reformatory had expired (1923), they were married. Margaret's father, whom she did not consult, greatly opposed her marrying an Irishman. At the time of her marriage Margaret was six months pregnant.

She and her husband set up their own little home and Margaret's husband has continued to the present time (1933) to work in the pool-room, the reputation of which is at least not bad. He earns as much as fifty dollars a week on occasion. Margaret has not worked since her marriage. The couple have two little boys, to whom they are devoted, and Margaret's sister-in-law feels that the training in housework which she received at the Reformatory and her nursing experience on indenture have helped her tremendously in caring for them. The little family has moved several times, always to a better neighbourhood and a larger home. They are now occupying half of a two-family house in a suburban neighbourhood within walking-distance of her husband's work. There is a pleasant yard and a comfortable porch. Margaret and her husband are very congenial, enjoying the radio and movies together and occasionally attending a dance or going to a cabaret.

Margaret keeps in touch with her brothers and sisters, but very seldom sees her parents. She still feels that her earlier difficulties were due entirely to their strictness and to her Italian father's old-fashioned notions about how a girl should be brought up. Margaret believes that her commitment to the Reformatory was unjust and that even her parents had no idea of sending her to a penal institution. Although she has suffered no discrimination because of it, and told her husband all about the experience before they were married, she has been occasionally embarrassed by meeting former inmates of the institution who have tried to seek her out. However, she recalls with gratitude the superintendent, who did everything possible to protect her from the pernicious influences of more hardened offenders and who, throughout the years, continued to send a card at Christmas. Margaret has written to her occasionally, but not so often as she would like, being somewhat fearful that the superintendent would discover that she was pregnant at the time of her marriage.

At thirty-three Margaret is happily settled as wife and mother. The wish expressed to her parents some years ago, when she would often say: " I'll be eighteen soon; then you'll see what I will do," has been fulfilled in a manner acceptable to society.

* * *

Angelina.[10] Upon admission to the Reformatory, Angelina was very much frightened, became hysterical, and insisted that her father had told her that rats would bite her and that she would be whipped. She was boastful of her sex adventures in a childish " smarty " sort of way and particularly delighted that she was " attractive to the fellows." She expressed no affection for either her father or her stepmother and showed attachment only to the one brother who, she says, always took her part when she was in trouble. " I would never go home no matter how much I would have to work. If my brother lived home I would go." Very soon after her admission, the Reformatory officials realized that Angelina would be very difficult to handle. She was allowed to work in the garden, but it was not possible to keep her there very long. She was excitable and irritable, would attack the other inmates and was so filthy about her person that she had to be kept in isolation most of the time. Mental examination revealed her to be feeble-minded, and the Reformatory physician thought that she might be developing a psychosis. However, the state alienist who was called in to examine her about six months after her admission reported that " while she has been more or less depressed this depression does not seem to be a pathological one, but rather the reaction of one mentally deficient and unable to appreciate the reason for her present confinement. I find no evidence of insanity."

Many times Angelina was placed in solitary confinement or kept in an annex of the institution and isolated from other inmates. She would often refuse to eat or to bathe herself and was on many occasions extremely noisy, always demanding attention and insisting that she be allowed to go home. When her parents or brothers called to see her, however, she would pay very little attention to them, and on the occasion of one such visit she entered the room waving her arms about and insisting that in a dream which she had had on the previous night she had seen a man at her window whom she recognized as her father, but he was dressed like a priest. While she was telling this story, she would keep turning to look behind her as though startled and expecting someone to come into the room. She asked her father to stand up and placed herself close in front of him, saying that she could see his tongue when he talked; then several times she asked him if he could move his legs. Toward the end of the interview she dropped listlessly back into a chair, saying that her father's face looked dark. She refused to go near him again and insisted that he was not her father after all. He, in great distress, pointed to his head to imply that she was crazy.

Angelina had not been in the Reformatory very long when the young man appeared on the scene with whom she had been having illicit relations since she was sixteen years old, claiming that he was her sweetheart and wanting to marry her. Her father, who felt that this might be a way out of her difficulty, asked the officers to release her so that she might marry this boy and settle down.

[10] Continued from p. 54.

This request was of course not acceded to, and it was explained to him that in her present condition she had no right to marry anyone.

On several occasions Angelina threatened to kill herself, but would repeatedly say that she was sorry and wanted God to forgive her. The Reformatory physician was convinced that she was a psychotic and should be transferred to a state hospital. In due course, after she had been in the Reformatory for nine months, she was brought before the parole board for a hearing. They deferred her release, as they agreed with the officials of the Reformatory that she needed custodial care. When Angelina had been in the Reformatory for a year, the superintendent asked another one of the state psychiatrists to come down to examine her. Though he agreed as to her feeble-mindedness, and recommended commitment to a state school for feeble-minded, he expressed the opinion that she was not psychotic.

For some months Angelina had been isolated in the annex and could rarely be made to do any sort of work. At times she was listless, at times excited and hallucinatory, more and more inclined to be alone and to talk to imaginary people. The content of her thought was mostly concerning home affairs and very erotic in character. She was often sexually excited and would frequently masturbate. Whenever she soiled herself, she would refuse to clean up the mess and always shouted: " Let the dirty niggers do it." Her bed-wetting and unsanitary habits kept several officers busy, and she was under the constant supervision of the resident physician. On occasion, when she was very much hallucinated, she would insist that one of the male helpers about the institution was her father. At times she would be heard talking to herself in a most disconnected manner:

" My brother Jerry is my stepbrother. He don't have to and he won't do it. . . . He said your brother is the only one that . . . and I tried to have me change it but I wouldn't change it."

Or:

" Your shape is bad enough; it may be was the worst. . . . Instead of giving your brother, because he squeals on you . . . to buy cigarettes with and tobacco . . . yes they kick about it, they spit on it, they put it in their pocket, and their pockets will be dirty. And then they go and spit it in the street, won't they? A bite of tobacco. . . ."

Many times Angelina tried to attack members of the institution staff and would have to be handcuffed. Twice she got hold of a pair of scissors and cut off her hair. Finally, after she had been in the Reformatory for nineteen months and had become more excitable and hallucinatory than ever, one of the state psychiatrists was sent for again and this time agreed that " she shows by her talk and actions that she is hallucinated; denies the identity of her own father, is destructive and violent, scratching and biting her attendants; is very untidy, soils her bed and scatters excretions over the room. I believe this patient is insane and needs care and treatment in a hospital."

By order of the district court, Angelina was removed from the Reformatory to a state hospital. There she was troublesome, difficult to take care of, and untidy; she masturbated incessantly. Though her state of excitement shortly died down, she continued to be unmanageable. After being in the hospital for a few months, she improved slightly, refrained from sex abuse, and became more careful about her appearance. She even manifested some eagerness to keep herself occupied. At just about the time when the hospital authorities were preparing to return her to the Reformatory, they were notified that her sentence had expired. A few weeks later, upon the insistence of her family, she was allowed out on a visit.

Angelina immediately took up with her sweetheart (the young man who had visited her in the Reformatory), resuming sexual relations with him — in his own home, with the full knowledge of his mother. Within a few months she became pregnant (her physical defect having been corrected in the Reformatory) and went to a hospital clinic, demanding a statement to this effect. When her parents and her lover realized her condition, the marriage was immediately consummated.

By her own admission Angelina was promiscuous sexually after leaving the state hospital, and though she at first insisted that her husband was the father of her child, she later admitted her uncertainty of this. At no time after her release was she reinfected with venereal disease, however.

After marrying, Angelina went to live in the home of her husband's mother. She behaved so peculiarly that shortly before the approach of her confinement, her husband, on the pretence that she needed hospital care, took her to a hospital for mental diseases, where she was examined and immediately returned to the state hospital, from which she had still been "out on visit." Very shortly she had to be transferred to the state infirmary for the delivery of her child, a girl, and was then, by order of the Massachusetts Department of Mental Diseases, returned to the state hospital. Here she remained for nine months and was again allowed to go "on visit" to her parents, but entirely against advice. "Should she have to be returned, this may be done within one year of that date without further legal formalities."

Meanwhile Angelina's husband had sought annulment of his marriage to her, on the ground of "false and fraudulent representations," basing his plea on the fact that Angelina's mental condition was not known to him at the time of their marriage. Angelina later claimed that he knew all about this as he had corresponded with her while she was at the state hospital. The annulment was granted, however, and the child was placed in the custody of Angelina's father. Her husband was required to contribute a small amount toward the baby's support.

Angelina returned to the home of her parents, and as she was very fearful of being recommitted to a mental hospital, she tried hard to restrain her desire for sexual intercourse and did not run about the streets. Her parents and brothers and sisters watched her more closely than in the past.

When Angelina's baby was two years old, the child died of pneumonia. Angelina was not very greatly concerned over her loss. She worked here and there in factories, not causing any particular trouble to her employers. She renewed an acquaintance with a war " buddy " of her former husband's, a young Italian widower with a small child, who was receiving one hundred dollars monthly compensation for a serious cardiac condition and gassing. Angelina's family approved of her marrying him, but her father first took the precaution of informing the young man of Angelina's Reformatory and hospital commitment. Two years after the annulment of her first marriage the couple were married. They went to live in the home of her husband's parents, but soon set up housekeeping for themselves. Angelina's second husband had as a boy been an inmate of a school for the feeble-minded. Prior to their marriage he already had a considerable court record for gaming, trespassing, adultery, and violating the auto laws. All of his brothers and sisters were delinquents, one brother being a notorious thief.

Angelina and her husband were not long married before they began to quarrel bitterly, particularly during the periods of Angelina's pregnancies, of which there were three, one resulting in miscarriage. At these times she would go to her parents for protection, but would soon return to her husband. Although refraining from abuse, he would give her very little money for food. Despite the fact that they had a hundred dollars monthly to live on, their children were under-nourished. Angelina's husband spent most of his money for the upkeep of a small automobile.

Not long ago neighbours made a complaint to the S. P. C. C. that Angelina and her husband were beating their children and quarrelling continually. Although Angelina feared that she might be returned to the state hospital if she took her husband to court on a charge of non-support or assault and battery, she was finally persuaded by a neighbour to do so. All her husband's relatives were arrayed against her and insisted that she was " crazy." The judge placed her husband on probation. On the way home in their auto after the court hearing, Angelina, claiming that her husband threatened to kill her, jumped out of the moving car and had to be taken to a hospital for treatment for a slight concussion.

When Angelina was shortly thereafter interviewed by our field investigator, she was found to be still very frail, much worried about being recommitted to the state hospital, very childish in her manner, and pathologically frank about sex matters. She has a real affection for her own two children, who are most attractive brown-eyed boys, and tries hard to be kind to her young stepson because "I know what it is to have a stepmother." Her relations with her step-mother, incidentally, have been much pleasanter of late years. Angelina lives in a small brick house, the property of her husband's mother, at a cheap sea-side resort. There is a small garden, and lately Angelina has started to raise chickens here. She is a neat housekeeper, but knows nothing about budgeting and dietetics. Recently a local agency has stepped in to help her in this regard. Her young stepson is mentally retarded and will soon be committed to a school for the feeble-minded. Her own two children, who are one and two years old respectively, have not yet revealed any marked backwardness.

Since Angelina returned from the hospital following the accident, her fa-vourite brother has been living with her. She feels that things are much better for her since he has been there, as he protects her from her husband, who has somewhat restrained his attitude of violence toward her. Angelina is now twenty-eight years old. Her family admit that she is still somewhat nervous and excitable and a "little weak-minded," but say that she does not show any such evidence of psychosis as she did previously. Whether she will have further psychotic episodes remains to be seen.

*   *   *

Minnie.[11] Mental examination at the Reformatory revealed that Minnie is feeble-minded. Her general physical condition was found to be poor and she was infected with gonorrhœa. Her clothes and person were filthy. She was ex-tremely nervous, her speech was disconnected, and she insisted that she was not guilty of wrongdoing. She denied ever having had intercourse with any man except her own husband. She was found to have very little liking or ability for housework or sewing. She considered it "too nerve-racking" and would not "waste" her time making clothes for herself or her child, because "you can buy them." She was placed at work in the shirt room of the institution, where she remained for nineteen months, and also did general cleaning for part of each day. On the whole her conduct in the Reformatory was good. She seemed quite amenable to the institution routine although she was occasionally inclined to meddlesomeness. Minnie's case was considered three times by the Board of Parole before parole was finally granted, as it was necessary to hold her for treat-ment for venereal disease.

After being in the Reformatory for nineteen months she was released on parole to serve the remainder of her five-year indeterminate sentence. Minnie's mother, who had made frequent appeals for her release, was willing to have the girl live with her. Despite the protests of the S. P. C. C., which had known Minnie and her family for several years, the parole agent permitted her to re-turn with her child to her mother's home, as "her mother is her best friend and will help her." She found a job in a paper-mill, where she received eight dollars

<hr>

[11] Continued from p. 57.

a week, of which she gave her mother a few dollars toward the support of herself and the baby. She was soon complaining to the parole agent that she was not earning enough, however, and that she did not want to keep the baby with her. Her mother and stepfather grew impatient with her and resented the burden of looking after her child. Her mother admitted to the parole agent that Minnie was unable to care for " that child, poor little fellow. I feel sorry for him, but I can't do anything."

When Minnie had been at home for three months, her stepfather made an urgent request of the parole agent that she be removed from his home:

> " She acts worse than we ever saw her before. She has been out in the yard fooling with a married man for more than one hour today and swearing so you could hear her a block away. When she is working she tells about walking from and to work with some man. She will laugh and talk with any man that will speak to her. Her mother is nearly sick because she acts so and from the extra work for Minnie and the baby. I want you to take Minnie and the baby from here as I will not have them in my house."

The parole agent therefore removed Minnie from her parents' home and placed her in the laundry of a hospital, where she received her room and maintenance. Here she was under the supervision of a kindly, intelligent woman who had had special experience in handling feeble-minded girls. The baby meanwhile was placed out in a boarding-home, but Minnie soon got behind in the weekly payments for his board. She remained for five months in her job at the hospital; then she fell ill and had to leave. Those under whom she worked were convinced that she had no affection or feeling of responsibility for her child, and regarded her as entirely unfit to bring him up.

Several local and state agencies now made every effort to see that the baby was properly cared for. The parole agent, however, hesitated to have the baby taken away from Minnie and therefore did not encourage any efforts to bring a charge of " neglect of child " against her.

When Minnie recovered from her illness, she went to work in a mill for about a week, then for a month as a waitress in a restaurant. The parole agent then secured a position for her as a waitress and kitchen-maid in a large sanatorium, where she had a room and maintenance in addition to pay.

Meanwhile it was only through the efforts of the several agencies interested in Minnie's child that the foster-mother who was caring for him did not sue Minnie for board due. The parole agent then made arrangements with Minnie's employer to make out all checks for her monthly, in payment of her debts. It was not long, however, before Minnie began to resent this arrangement and wished to handle her own money.

After working in the kitchen of the sanatorium for a short while, Minnie expressed a desire to be a ward maid. The superintendent made the comment, however, that " she is in every way unsuited to such work. She is extremely noisy and destructive as well as morally unfit to associate with the patients. Even as she is situated at present, she will get the men aside, and her conduct in that respect is most trying."

After holding this job for about a year, Minnie began to chafe under the supervision and watchfulness of her employers and wanted to go to a near-by city to live. Permission to do so was not granted her by the parole agent. But Minnie found opportunity, in going back and forth to visit her boy, to become acquainted with a youth of twenty-one, a widower with one child, who offered her marriage if she secured a divorce. Although the marriage did not materialize, the parole agent assisted Minnie to institute divorce proceedings.

Shortly before Minnie's parole period was to expire, the children's society which had been supervising Minnie's boy expressed regret that the child should be allowed to return to the care of his feeble-minded mother. The boy had greatly improved during the last year or two and was found to be of normal mentality for his age. The organization stated that one of its directors would be glad to be appointed legal guardian of the child. The parole agent, however, did not accede, as Minnie " will be free and her boy is absolutely her own property. No association has a particle of right to take out guardianship papers . . . she is the mistress of herself and her child . . . it would not be the right thing at this time to try to take X away from his mother. If she proves herself incompetent after she is free, that is another matter . . . she must have her chance first."

As Minnie had been working steadily for almost three years in one place and had been paying the child's board regularly, the parole agent felt that she should be allowed to keep the boy until it was definitely proved that she was unfit to care for him; and so she gave Minnie permission to return once more to the home of her parents, who were now living in Maine and were receiving aid from the charities there.

At the expiration of her five-year indeterminate sentence Minnie was twenty-five years old, and her boy was five. When Minnie had been at home for only a few months, her family became very impatient with her. She was erratic, insistent in her demands, and continually had the family in a turmoil. As they encouraged her departure, Minnie took her boy and returned to Massachusetts, placing the child to board near by and supporting herself as best she could. Having been granted a divorce, she shortly married, after a brief acquaintance, a man eight years her senior, whom she had " picked up " — a steady worker, who was able to support her. As Minnie did not have to work after marrying and her boy was being boarded out, she had plenty of time on her hands. While her husband was away, she entertained men in her home and one day induced the seventeen-year-old son of the woman with whom she was boarding her boy, to have illicit relations with her. The boy told the story to his mother, who brought him back to Minnie's house and forced him to repeat it in the presence of Minnie's husband. The latter decided not to make any criminal complaint against her, but as " apparently one man was not enough for her," he thought it best that they separate.

So Minnie took her boy and went to the home of her mother, who had since returned from Maine. (This was at about the end of the five-year post-parole period.) Although Minnie's stepfather was at this time working steadily, her family refused to support her and she was forced to take whatever jobs she could find. Having had some little experience as a ward maid, Minnie registered with several nurses' agencies and had no difficulty in securing positions as a practical nurse, but kept the jobs for only very short periods, frequently returning to the parental roof.

During one year of her longer periods of unemployment Minnie's family requested a local society to assist them in getting rid of the girl, as she was a most disturbing influence in their home. The social worker, who described Minnie as " slight, unkempt, dishevelled, vulgar and common," suggested that she return to her husband. But Minnie absolutely refused to go back to " that good-for-nothing man." So the society helped Minnie place her boy out to board and urged her to find another position. She worked in a hospital for about six weeks, and then both she and the boy again returned to the parental home because Minnie did not pay his board regularly. As the home was over-crowded, Minnie and her son slept together, although he was already eleven years old. Her sister complained to the social worker that Minnie was allowing undesirable men to come to their home in spite of her stepfather's threats to turn her out. The society, in an effort to determine a further course of action, wrote to the superintendent of the Reformatory who replied that in her opinion Minnie should be committed to a school for the feeble-minded. Minnie's mother wholly approved this idea, as she was greatly discouraged at trying to do anything more for the girl. When the family took her to church, for example, Minnie would spend her time trying to pick up men there. But before any further plans could be made, Minnie disappeared from home taking her boy with her. The social agency, after much effort to trace her, " closed the case."

Meanwhile Minnie returned to the town in which she had lived with her second husband. As she was not able to find regular employment, she " lived on friends " for a few months until she " picked up " a carpenter who offered her a ride on his truck. This casual meeting very quickly ripened into friend-ship and " love," and the man, who was some ten years older than Minnie, offered her financial help so that she might board out her boy. Minnie soon took up her residence with this man, ostensibly to keep house for him. Although she greatly wished to secure a divorce from her second husband, she did not dare to start proceedings, because of her questionable reputation. She lived with the carpenter for four years, until the death of her second husband, when the couple were finally able to marry.

Minnie had boarded her son out until some two years after she had taken up with her lover. Then she took her boy to live with her, because she was warned by the local constable that she would be less liable to arrest if she had a third person living under her roof while housekeeping for a bachelor. The boy soon began to complain of the treatment he was being accorded by his mother and her lover. As a result of their hostility he finally threatened to kill his mother's lover. When a neighbour complained to the S.P.C.C. that the boy was being cruelly beaten, this organization decided that it would be well to have Minnie make a complaint against the boy as a " stubborn child " for his own protection, after which he was placed on probation and sent to a farm. He soon returned home, however, and again there was much quarrelling and insubordination, with the result that the boy was taken in charge by the town authorities, who decided to give him into the permanent custody of the State. He was placed in a family and has not lived with his mother since.

Minnie is thus relieved of all responsibility for any of her offspring. She is married to her lover and is living in a little bungalow which her husband built at the edge of the woods in a semi-rural district where there are mostly single houses at considerable distances apart. The four rooms are well furnished and give a very comfortable and homelike appearance. Everything is clean and well cared for. Our investigator who saw her and her third husband described her as being

> " short, heavy, with dark hair, of florid complexion, a plump face, gray eyes, walks with a limp, is rather attractive in appearance, apparently has a good deal of what is called sex appeal, is quick-witted, impulsive, extremely emotional, explosively excitable; flies into a passion with little cause, raises her voice and shouts, waves her arms in meaningless gestures, seems to exhaust herself, and then, having passed through this storm, becomes quite calm. Shows a many-sided interest in many things, is very imaginative, and seems almost unconsciously to mix truth and falsehood. Is extremely profane when excited, and uses profanity for emphasis even when not excited, uses words quite naturally that border on the obscene, but her profanity seems to be so ingrained in her that she almost seems unconscious of using it; does not show it off but apparently can't express herself otherwise. In fact, she seems so much like her mother, whom investigator has met, that investigator thinks that her emotionalism is a heritage."

Although in the past Minnie has never saved any money, she now takes pride in helping her husband to put by a little. As he is an excellent carpenter and earns good wages, they have been able to save several hundred dollars each year. Minnie is not on friendly terms with her family over any long period of time. Although she and her husband quarrel somewhat, they seem to be sticking to each other. At least she has lived with him for a longer period than with any other man, and since meeting him has not been carrying on with other men. She is extremely hostile to all the social agencies who have tried for so many years to watch over her and her children and almost exhausts her supply of profanity in talking of them. She is now (1933) thirty-five years of age. Is the passage of time solving the problem of Minnie? What will she do next?

* * *

Dora.[12] Examination at the Reformatory revealed that Dora was in good physical condition, but suffering from gonorrhœa and syphilis. She was found to be only slightly below normal mentally, but somewhat deteriorated from chronic alcoholism. Dora took her incarceration philosophically:

> " When a person can't see things right they have to what you call stop you and let you think. When you defy laws and when you defy God, you have to be put somewhere for they are your masters."

She very soon developed a strong loyalty to the superintendent of the Reformatory, who was greatly impressed with Dora's interest in fine literature and her determination not to allow her family to suffer for her misdeeds. When, a few months after her commitment, Dora's mother learned of her incarceration, she wrote feelingly:

> " For me you are always my child of olden days whose regard was dear, whose looks were dear, and who was bright, and for whom I felt grateful to God when I saw you coming from the convent with the rosette of honor you had won by your work and your good conduct. . . . What terrible day was that when you left us, your dear companions, when you were so happy . . . but . . . for drunkenness you would have been an accomplished daughter, pious, charitable . . . but alas! my God, what distressing passion to take you where you are and to render my life a complete failure . . . your afflicted mother. . . ."

Although Dora worked well at times, particularly when she was allowed to help on the institution farm, she did not get along with most of the officers, as she resented taking orders. She utilized any occasion which presented itself to tell the other inmates not to obey the matrons: " Don't you listen to what they tell you."

Dora early revealed the religious trend in her nature, and gave testimony to the gift of the superintendent of the Reformatory in stirring the emotions of certain inmates:

> " We have had a wonderful holy day at Christmas here by the direction of our Superintendent; O, things were grandiose. . . . O, if I could only write on this poor piece of paper what is in me. What is the use? Let it be buried

[12] Continued from p. 59.

deep in my head where only One can read and judge. Mother I have received a picture at New Year Evening of our superintendent at chapel, giving us in her lecture which I call ' The Vision of the Future,' the understanding of the soul. Working with the Golden Key of Humanity. Yes, standing up dressed in purple, the picture of Christ Mother . . . you too, dear mother are another ' vision of a Saint.' God bless you both. I pray for you. I am very happy. Write soon."

When Dora appeared before the Board of Parole, she spoke very thoughtfully of the changed conditions in the Reformatory since her last sentence there, thirteen years previously, pointing out how much pleasanter things were now for the inmates. The board members were quite impressed with her.

Although Dora at first expressed a desire to be placed at work not far from the Reformatory, so that she might keep in touch with the superintendent, she shortly decided to live with a married sister whose home was near her mother's. Before being paroled she was warned by the superintendent to check her desire for drink and was reminded to guard her quick temper. Dora realized how difficult it would be to put this advice into practice:

"Well the thing is I am going home. If they throw that in my face and I lose my temper, it will be the same thing over again, its hard to face all those people. . . ."

Dora found a job in a mill as a spinner, for which she received twenty-nine dollars weekly. She worked steadily for two months, and even after a long day at the mill would help her sister in the evening with the housework and the care of the children. On Mother's Day, which occurred a month after her release, Dora sent a bouquet of red roses to the superintendent of the Reformatory with deep expressions of affection for her.

Two months after her release Dora chanced to meet an old pal who invited her to come to her house. They drank together and Dora was soon intoxicated. She returned to her sister's house the next day " paralyzed drunk " and was refused admittance. She then went to her mother and told her: " I break my parole." Her mother urged her to stay with her, but Dora went off to rejoin her old friends and after some two or three weeks of carousing with them, she was picked up by a police officer and turned over to the parole agent. On her way back to the Reformatory, Dora confided to the agent that the superintendent of the Reformatory was the only person in the world that she trusted, " because I love her like a mother and she has been awfully good to me."

When she was readmitted to the Reformatory, Dora expressed a wish to remain until the end of her sentence. She was most apologetic for her misconduct and explained that once having started to drink, she realized that she had broken her parole and was so discouraged that she did not care what happened to her, so she kept on drinking. During this second period in the Reformatory,

Dora's conduct improved somewhat. Regarding her problems she had many discussions in French with the superintendent, for whom her affection and loyalty continued to grow.

In five months Dora's sentence expired. As she was in good physical condition, and her conduct did not warrant her further detention, she was released. This time she went to the home of her mother.

Dora was now forty-five years old. The agent of a society for aiding discharged prisoners tried to secure a job for her in a mill in a small town where she had not previously lived. Because of the business depression (1924), no opening could be found and Dora was advised to return to her mother's home. She went about looking for work and day after day met with no success. After two or three weeks of this she became very much discouraged and again began to drink. Speaking of Dora's relapse, her mother said:

> "When I saw my daughter Dora come, I was very happy over her return but hope of seeing her abandon her black passion has waned. Why should she be here and again find her old friends?"

Dora quickly used up her small savings, but did not seek aid from her family. Two months after her release she was picked up by the police for drinking and was again sentenced to the Reformatory on a charge of being "idle and disorderly." She appeared relieved at her recommitment, feeling that in the Reformatory she would be protected. There was no evidence of any venereal re-infection, and Dora absolutely denied any sexual immorality during her two months of freedom, but added that male friends might have taken advantage of her while she was drunk.

She was placed at work in the laundry. During her incarceration of two years she had often to be reprimanded for disobedience and on several occasions had to be isolated from the other inmates. Dora was irritable and excitable, insolent, and defiant of the officers. She did her work well enough when left alone, but resented taking instructions. After a few months she was permitted to work in the flag room and on the farm. But she was of the kind who cannot remain at one type of work for very long. After the novelty of it had worn off, she would become very critical of the matrons, grouchy, and insolent. The other inmates were afraid of her. Because she was so unpleasant in the dining-room, she was made to eat by herself most of the time. Many of the officers asked not to have her in their group as she was so hard to manage. The superintendent and one or two of her assistants were the only ones to whom Dora responded. She continued to worship the superintendent and was happy to remain in the institution as long as the law would allow.

Dora was released at the expiration of her two-year sentence. She was now forty-seven years old. A position was secured for her (by the agent of the same society which had aided her previously) as a ward maid in a hospital in a small residential community far enough away from her old friends so that she could not visit them. At this time she wrote to the superintendent of the Reformatory:

> "O how sweet to feel free once more and to be able to offer God sincere repentance. . . . Madam, God will answer my prayer. He hears it and will give me strength. . . . I like my work. I help the cook who is perfection in her work. I do my best to be helpful. . . . I'm reading 'The Brazen Peacock' by H. Bedford Jones."

And again a month later she wrote the superintendent:

> "In the holy church, among the strange throng, my thought will be going out to you; or, rather you are always in my thought, God and you, always always. . . . Write me . . . do not forget me. . . . I need you; I love to hear from you."

After she had held this job for three months, Dora felt a longing to return to the home of her sister, to whose children she was very much devoted. She found a job in the mills and for a few months worked quite steadily, often visiting her mother and doing little kindnesses for her. When Dora had lived with her sister for about eight months, her periodic desire for liquor came upon her and she went off with her old friends. She was shortly arrested for drunkenness and again committed to the Reformatory on a two-year indeterminate sentence on a charge of being "idle and disorderly." She was again found to be free of venereal disease. After being held in the Reformatory for three weeks, she was transferred to a house of correction, as the Reformatory officials felt that they could do nothing more for Dora and that she created too much disturbance among the other inmates. It was with great reluctance that she left the Reformatory which she had grown to consider her haven of refuge.

Not long after this, Dora's mother died, and the superintendent of the Reformatory now became a real mother-substitute and was dearer than ever to Dora. At her mother's death she wrote the superintendent:

> "She is happy now no more suffering for the poor old sad heart that I have break so often. I love her more in Death for she will pray for me as you do dear Old Friend. . . ."

Hardly a month passed by without a letter of deep affection from Dora to the superintendent. She took every occasion which presented itself — Easter, Christmas, Mother's Day, St. Valentine's Day — to send a word of greeting, a poem, a postcard. Dora's letters reflected a deep religious zeal and devotion to the Catholic Church:

> "My thoughts were with you that beautiful day [Mother's Day]. Also for my lost one. I had the happiness to receive the holy communion in joy and sorrow."

And the superintendent of the Reformatory wrote frequently to Dora in response to her letters from the House of Correction:

"I am very much touched by your constant tokens of affection. Please do not think that one of them is lost on me. I got your cards and your wonderful letter. I do hope that God will give you help and will give you an opportunity to serve him; that you will have strength to serve him as your dear mother would wish you to do. I am sure that it seems long and tedious waiting your turn, but if you will listen each day and get God's message which I am sure he is trying to give you, and to make you strong for the future, the time will soon go by.

"With every good wish and my very sincere affection, believe me always your friend."

Dora soon developed a loyalty to the sheriff of the house of correction and his family and was grateful to be allowed to work in their home. After she had served twenty months of her sentence, she was released on parole. Shortly before this she had written to the superintendent of the Reformatory:

"O, How I long to be free again to try once more to be good. Don't you think that I have pay dearly enough for the foolishness of life. . . . I am sorry to waste my life for nothing. God knows best. I do not ask for nothing some day it will come."

But five days after Dora was released, she was again arrested for drunkenness, and her parole to the house of correction was revoked. Again she placed her trust in the future:

"I am planning to leave this country when the time comes for my release. . . . I don't see why that I stay in the city where temptations always get the best of me. I'll never lose hope; soon I'll be free again and try again in a different way."

The superintendent of the Reformatory wrote to Dora at this time:

"It would be a great blessing to me to know that you had made up your mind to step on these evil things that drag you down each time. It is not fair that a person who is so fine as you are should be so cruel to herself."

After serving three months, to the expiration of her sentence, Dora was released and went to her sister's home. A few days later she was again arrested for drunkenness, but this time the case was filed. She worked here and there in the mills, always keeping away from her family when she was drinking. Three months later she was again arrested for drunkenness and was sentenced for four months to the house of correction on a charge of being "idle and disorderly." Dora now wrote apologetically to the superintendent of the Reformatory, "If we go back it's our own fault." And again shortly thereafter:

"Let me tell you that while there is a God above, I shall always have hope. He want me in this place what can I do only to submit to His will."

After serving five months of this sentence Dora was again released and went to her sister's home. Within a month she was once more arrested for being "idle and disorderly" and on this occasion was committed for two years to the state farm. Again she was found to be entirely free of venereal disease.

It was during this commitment that the superintendent of the Reformatory passed away. Dora was deeply moved by her loss and wrote to the assistant superintendent of the Reformatory:

"Deep from my heart accept my most sincere regrets in that great loss of our beloved superintendent. May the soul of the faithful departed rest in peace. . . . We will cherish and love her memory in Death."

While Dora was at the state farm, she continued to write often to the assistant superintendent, still sending little tokens in memory of her departed friend. Dora is now (1933) fifty-four years old, haggard, wistful, hopeless about overcoming her desire for alcohol, and finding it hard to understand why "God has failed" her in her wish to overcome the habit. She claims she has never married because she would never want to bring tragedy to a husband or to the children that she might bear. She has a deep affection for her sisters and brothers, with whom she communicates only when she is not drinking. She does not write to them when she is in a penal institution, as she does not wish to bring them disgrace. Dora says that when she was in the Reformatory, she felt "near to God," and that if she could have her way, she would prefer to serve all her sentences there.[13]

*   *   *

Louisa.[14] There is no doubt that on her admission to the Reformatory, Louisa showed considerable remorse over the shooting of her fiancé, but she insisted that life would have been unbearable for her had her lover lived and married another woman. She was greatly ashamed to find herself actually in a penal institution, but this was partly counteracted by the glamour attaching to her trial for murder, and the attention she was receiving from the Italian community.

Except for gonorrhœa, which Louisa had contracted from her lover, she was in excellent physical condition, of normal mentality, bright, quick, intelligent, but somewhat conceited and vain. For many months she worked faithfully in the superintendent's house, doing general domestic work. The superintendent

---

[13] Since the last writing we have learned that soon after Dora was released from the state farm she gave herself up to the police, begging to be sentenced to the Reformatory so she might die there. She has developed a serious heart-lesion and wants the feeling of protection which the institution has always afforded her. She was given a two-year indeterminate sentence for drunkenness and is now at the Reformatory.

[14] Continued from p. 62.

felt that Louisa should be protected from the insidious influences of more hardened offenders and so kept a close watch on her. Gradually the girl's amiability began to wane and it was quite apparent to some members of the Reformatory staff that she was suspicious that those about her did not have her best welfare at heart. " She is inclined to attach a personal meaning to little incidents which in themselves are of almost no importance. . . ." " She has occasional periods of moodiness when she is quite unreasonable, disinterested, and does not do her work well. . . ." " She loves devotedly and hates absolutely."

While Louisa was at the Reformatory, she was visited by an Italian priest who had taken much interest in her during the trial; by the matron of the jail where she was held before the trial; and by the only relative whom she had in this country, a male cousin, who lived in New York and who gave her every assistance and much sympathy. Some of her friends even instituted a movement to gain a pardon for her, and Louisa was very resentful that this was not granted. She soon regained her equanimity, however, and determined to behave herself in such a way as to merit early parole.

When she had been in the Reformatory for twenty-seven months she was placed on " indenture " [15] at a near-by hospital where she received maintenance and a small salary. She was put in charge of the hospital dining-room and worked very steadily and satisfactorily for seven months, until she was released on parole, after having served almost three years of her five-and-a-half-year sentence.

Although it had been Louisa's wish to return to Italy and start a small dressmaking establishment there, she decided not to do so, as her parents had both recently died. Just after Louisa's release on parole, the superintendent of the Reformatory wrote the immigration authorities to inquire whether " deportation of an alien who has committed murder, not in self-defense, but through jealousy, is required." To this the immigration authorities replied that the " committing of crimes involving moral turpitude formerly related to crimes committed prior to entry. The new law of February 5, 1917, provides that any alien may be arrested and deported if he is sentenced to imprisonment for a term of one year or more because of conviction in this country of a crime involving moral turpitude; limitation — that the crime shall have been committed within five years after entry; deportation shall not occur until termination of imprisonment."

Although Louisa's case fell within this ruling, no action was ever taken in the matter. Louisa had already been paroled to the cousin who had expressed such an interest in her and who, with his bride, had visited her at the Reformatory, offering her a home with them. Permission had been granted by the parole authorities for Louisa to join these relatives in New York, and she lived with them for eight months. She reported regularly by letter to the parole agent and never made a move without asking permission. In the early part of her parole

15 For meaning of " indenture " see p. 138 et seq.

period she worked for a very brief time in a restaurant and then in the office of a physician, helping to receive patients and making out bills. She earned fourteen dollars a week, but remained for only four months, because she had an opportunity to earn more in a factory. After some months of this her cousin found a still more remunerative position for her as a waitress in a restaurant.

At about this time Louisa, with the permission of the parole agent, moved from her cousin's home because she did not like the neighbourhood in which they lived and because the home was crowded. They had three small rooms and Louisa had to sleep in the dining-room. The girl was constantly eager to advance herself, and at the suggestion of the parole officer, to whom she wrote often, she took a six-months' course given by the Salvation Army for training in nursing and dietetics, and also improved her English by attending night school. She had for some time fostered an ambition to be a nurse. As Louisa did not have to be at work until noon, she spent her mornings practising the piano.

During her parole period she wrote to the superintendent of the Reformatory:

" Well now I want to thank you very much for all that you have done for me and are still doing.

" If you are interested in my letters I will write again and tell you all my plans and dreams to become a nurse . . . kindest regards to your own dear self from one of your girls that thinks a lot of you of whom she is very
" Gratefully yours — "

While Louisa was working as a waitress she met a young Mexican of good family who had been sent to New York three years previously to attend college. His father had given him an allowance and was, throughout these years, under the impression that the boy was studying, but in reality he had been going about with a gay crowd of young men in New York having a good time. When relatives of the boy notified the father of his son's antics, the father withdrew his allowance, and the boy was forced to take any kind of work he could get. Thus, at the age of twenty, he drifted into the restaurant where Louisa was working, and secured a job as counterman.

A friendship soon sprang up between the two, which resulted in an engagement. After a few months Louisa asked permission of the parole agent to marry him. She had yet three months to serve before the expiration of her parole. She explained to the agent that she had told her fiancé about her Reformatory sentence, but not that she was still on parole. Permission to marry was granted her, and after a brief honeymoon the couple returned to their work in the restaurant, where together they earned forty dollars a week, she as a cashier, and he as a counterman.

After her parole expired, Louisa continued to work in the restaurant. Before her marriage she had saved up six hundred dollars, and she and her husband took a small furnished apartment. She sent to Italy for her one sister, who has since lived with her. When Louisa had been married for almost a year, her first child was born. Since then Louisa has devoted herself to her home affairs. She wrote at this time to her parole agent:

"My heart is full of gratitude for every one that worked to send me to New York because it is to them I owe my happiness now."

Two years after the birth of the first child another child was born and the little family moved to a six-room apartment in a good residential district for which they have been paying eighty dollars a month rent. Financial aid has been forthcoming from the husband's family, so they have always been comfortable. They have been living in the same place for eight years.

Louisa has been a faithful attendant at a dietetic clinic and has been giving her two children very intelligent care. She has never regretted her marriage, as her husband has been very kind to her and they have been happy together. She is only sorry that her husband does not have so much ambition as she would like. He has never been able to advance himself because of his interrupted education, and still works as a counterman. His relatives, whom they have visited occasionally in Mexico, are genteel and cultured people and have been most kind to her. She is sure that if they knew of her past, they would entirely disown their son for marrying her. She was rather disturbed about being interviewed so many years after her trouble. She says that no one in New York, except her cousin and his wife and her husband and sister, knows anything about her Reformatory sentence, and she is determined that this chapter of her life shall remain closed.

Louisa confessed to our investigator that she had really married her husband to " spite " another fellow, a young Italian with whom she had been going about for two years (there is no indication that the parole agent knew of the affair), who accused her of jealousy and told her that she would probably never marry because of her jealous disposition.

3. Conclusion

From these glimpses into the experiences of a sample of our women in the Reformatory, on parole and later, we have obtained some impressions of the manifold and puzzling problems presented by the entire group of five hundred women. We have also gained some conception of the manner and extent of the institution's influence upon them. But these are impressions. We need to know how typical are the careers of these few women whom we have described. We need a more comprehensive picture; hence a statistical analysis of the experiences of the five hundred women while in the Reformatory, on parole and after.

In the next few chapters we follow them therefore into the Reformatory, out on parole, and during a five-year period after the expiration of their sentences to the Reformatory.

1. Introductory

Having in prior chapters described the Reformatory and parole system as well as the background and characteristics of our five hundred delinquent women, let us in this chapter turn our attention to the response of the group to the Reformatory régime. Several preliminary matters should, however, be first considered.

2. Facts Regarding Commitment

Year of commitment. The modal year of commitment of the women to the Reformatory was 1919, 2.2% having entered in 1915 or earlier, 5.4% in 1916, 11.2% in 1917, 12.4% in 1918, 18.2% in 1919, 14.6% in 1920, 16% in 1921, 16.2% in 1922 and 3.8% in 1923. (Appendix D, Table 2–56.)

Offence and sentence. Four of our women (.8%) were committed to the Reformatory for offences against the person, of which three were for manslaughter and one was for assault and battery. A total of 54% of the entire group was sentenced to the Reformatory for offences involving the sex impulse, 12.6% of the five hundred women having been sentenced for adultery, 6.8% for "common night walking," 4.4% for fornication, 1% (five women) for keeping houses of ill fame, 24.4% for being "lewd and lascivious," and 4.8% for other sex offences. Seventeen (3.4%) of the women entered the institution on a charge of neglect of family or children; 23.8% for offences against the public health, safety, or morals — mainly for being "idle and disorderly," an offence that often involves sexual immorality; 6.6% were committed for drunkenness, and .2% (one woman) for possessing drugs. Only 11.2% were sentenced for offences against property rights, such as larceny, robbery, burglary, concealing leased property, and the like (Appendix D, Table 1–9).[1]

---

[1] As indicative of the typicality of this group of 500 women offenders in relation to the entire population of the Massachusetts Reformatory for the years 1915 to 1925, when 1,668 women were admitted (omitting 123 who were committed for stubbornness), 1.7% were committed for offences against the person, 48.9% for offences against chastity, 3.2% for offences against the family and children, 20.3% for offences against the public health and policy, 15.6% for drunkenness, and 10.3% for offences against property.

As indicative of the differences in crimes committed by male and female offenders, it is pertinent to note here that of 24,002 admissions to the Men's Reformatory of Massachusetts between the years

Previous chapters have already revealed how deep-seated are the antisocial habits of our group of women, and have suggested that to effect any changes in their habits and attitudes would doubtless require much time. In the light of this the length of the sentences imposed upon the women becomes important. A one-year indeterminate sentence was imposed on 8.2% of the women, a two-year indeterminate sentence on 53.6%, a four-year indeterminate sentence on 1% (five women), a five-year indeterminate sentence on 34%, and .8% (four women) were given definite sentences ranging from less than three to ten years (Appendix D, Table 2–45). The term of the sentence and the time actually spent in the Reformatory are not synonymous, however, as will be seen below.

Some three fourths of the women (78.6%) were committed to the Reformatory by direct sentence; 17.4% were on probation or suspended sentence to the institution, the sentence having been put into effect because they violated the conditions of probation. Eleven (2.2%) of the women were transferred to the Reformatory from the Lancaster Industrial School, .8% (four women) from a jail or house of correction, and 1% (five women) from penal institutions in other states (Appendix D, Table 2–57b).

Age at commitment. At the time of their commitment to the Reformatory 41.2% of the women were twenty years old or younger, 22.6% were between twenty-one and twenty-five, 16.4% between twenty-six and thirty, 14.8% between thirty-one and forty, and 5% between forty-one and sixty (Appendix D, Table 1–2a). As an indication of the long standing of the problem which the Reformatory had to face in rehabilitating these women, it is worth noting that in only 6.3% of the cases had less than a year elapsed between the onset of delinquency and the commitment of the women to the Reformatory; in 12.2% of the cases one to two years had elapsed, in 19.8% three to four years, in 18.8% five to six years, in 16.2% seven to ten years, in 14.9% eleven to fourteen years, and in 11.6% fifteen years or more. Thus almost two thirds of our women (61.5%) had been delinquents for five or more years before the Reformatory was called upon to apply its remedial program to their problems. While it is true that because of age limitations the Reformatory could not legally have accepted many of these offenders when their delinquencies first became manifest, the fact remains that even of 174 women who were first delinquent when they were seventeen or older, 63 (36.2%) were not given Reformatory treatment until they were thirty-one years of age or older. The difficulty of modifying long-standing habits and attitudes in women of this age can readily be appreciated.

Admission with children. A women's reformatory has a problem which a men's institution does not have to face: namely, the presence of the children of

---

1885 and 1931, .5% were for rape, 1.7% were for sex offences, and 97.8% were for other types of offences (property crimes, drunkenness, vagrancy, assault, etc.).

inmates. Thirty-two (6.4%) of our women were admitted to the Reformatory with a child,[2] and 11.4% more (fifty-seven women) were pregnant on admission (Appendix D, Table 2–57a).

Previous Reformatory commitments. Nine tenths (92%) of our women had never been in the Reformatory before; 7% had served one sentence in the Reformatory prior to this commitment, .4% (two women) two sentences, .6% (three women) three sentences (Appendix D, Table 2–46b). Of the forty women who had previously been in the Reformatory, three of them had served less than six months, thirteen had been in the institution for six to twelve months, nine for one or two years, twelve for two to three years, and three for three years or longer (Appendix D, Table 2–47). Obviously their antisocial behaviour had not been permanently affected by their previous stay in the Reformatory.

3. Length of Reformatory Experience

Need for an adequate period of incarceration. Aside from the possible deterrent effect of punishment, the rational measure of institutional incarceration should be the length of time required to bring about a substantial improvement in the inmate's equipment for legitimate activity in free society. This period of course varies with the needs of the individual case; but a certain minimum is necessary in all instances, determined roughly by the length of time required to cure venereal disease, to improve attitudes and habits, to teach occupational skills which will enable the offender to compete with free labour after release, and like considerations. Superintendents of reformatories hardly know what this general minimum should be; few have thought of the matter. We may legitimately infer, in view of the incidence of venereal disease in our group, their long-standing antisocial attitudes and behaviour, their less than mediocre industrial achievements, and their limited intelligence, that an incarceration of less than two years, and certainly of less than one year, would on the whole prove of little value, if not wasteful.

Time in the Reformatory. How long did our women actually remain in the Reformatory?[3] In 5% of the cases they were held in the Reformatory for less than three months, in 4.8% for three to nine months, in 14% for nine to twelve months, in 18.8% for twelve to fifteen months, in 13.4% for fifteen to eighteen months, in 20.6% for eighteen to twenty-four months, in 17.8% for twenty-four to thirty-six months, and in 5.6% for three years or longer. The average length of time which our women spent in the Reformatory on the sentence we are concerned with was 18.5 months ± .26 (Appendix D, Table 2–49).

[2] Under the law the child must be below two years of age.

[3] This excludes any time spent in other institutions by transfer either to or from the Reformatory except brief periods in hospital for confinement or other illness, or time on indenture. It embraces, however, the time spent in the Reformatory by reason of revocation of parole or on " in-between " sentences.

A correlation between the length of the sentences imposed on these women and the actual time which they spent in the Reformatory indicates that of the 170 women who received indeterminate sentences of five years, 21.8% actually served from fifteen to eighteen months in the Reformatory, 20% from twelve to fifteen months, and 20% less than twelve months. Of the 268 women who received two-year indeterminate sentences, almost half (45.5%) served eighteen months or less in the Reformatory; 6.7% served less than three months. It will be seen from these illustrations that the action of the courts in imposing indeterminate sentences gives little indication of what portion of such sentences will actually be spent in the Reformatory.

Transfers to other institutions. Modern penology requires great flexibility in the institutional régime so that prisoners requiring various types of treatment may be freely transferred from one institution to another. Of our women, 75.4% were at no time transferred to any other institution after they had begun serving sentence in the Reformatory; and 11.4% more, though temporarily transferred to a hospital for confinement, operation, or other treatment, were very shortly returned to the Reformatory. Eighteen women (3.6%) were transferred to another penal institution and not returned to the Reformatory,[4] four (.8%) were transferred to a school for the feeble-minded and not returned to the Reformatory, twelve (2.4%) were transferred to a hospital for mental disease and not returned, and two women (.4%) were sent to a hospital for the treatment of chronic physical conditions and were not returned to the Reformatory. Nine women (1.8%), though transferred to penal institutions, were returned to the Reformatory, and twenty-one women (4.2%) were placed on indenture and not returned to the institution (Appendix D, Table 2–58).[5] One of the chief problems presented to the Reformatory staff is the difficulty of transfers to institutions for the feeble-minded and the mentally ill.

Parole from the Reformatory. The cases of 5.8% of our women were not brought up for parole at all. Twenty-nine per cent were paroled when their cases were presented to the parole board for the first time, 42% were held over in the Reformatory after one appearance before the board of parole, 15.2% after two, 6.8% after three, and 1.8% (six women) after four or five appearances before the board (Appendix D, Table 2–H89). In 60.6% of the cases the reasons for holding a woman in the Reformatory was the fact that her physical condition (usually venereal infection) did not yet warrant release. In 16.5% of the cases the women were held over because the institution authorities felt (and succeeded in convincing the parole board) that these inmates were of the custodial type (usually feeble-minded, with difficulties of temperament and behaviour) and should therefore not be allowed to return to the community

---

[4] Mrs. Hodder agitated for a law making it possible to transfer girls from the Reformatory to the Girls Industrial School. Girls under seventeen sometimes had falsified their ages, and as Mrs. Hodder felt strongly that they should be at the Industrial School, she transferred them when possible.

[5] See cases of Margaret, pp. 164–8; Angelina, pp. 168–72; Fleur, pp. 162–4; Louisa, pp. 182–6.

sooner than absolutely necessary. Such cases always present a vexing problem to the serious-minded reformatory official. Mrs. Hodder frequently spoke of this problem. It was her opinion that such women, if not permanently quarantined from society, should at least be kept in custody and under close supervision until they had passed the child-bearing period. Under existing laws, practices, and institutional limitations the best she could do was to postpone their release into free society as long as possible.[6] In 8.3% of the cases, our women were held over in the Reformatory because the officials felt that they would benefit by more training in control of emotions or that some personality defect might well be modified further. In 8.3% of instances the women were denied parole because of serious misconduct; in 3.1% pending arrangements in the community, as for marriage, for deportation, and the like (Appendix D, Table 2–H83).

Three fourths (75.4%) of all our women were ultimately paroled from the Reformatory, 15.8% served their full sentences within the institution, 4.6% were transferred to some other institution and remained there at least to the expiration of the Reformatory sentence; nine women (1.8%) died in the Reformatory, 1.8% were paroled from other institutions to which they had been transferred from the Reformatory, and three women (.6%) remained on indenture to the expiration of their sentences (Appendix D, Table 2–59b).[7]

For how long a time were our women held in the Reformatory before they were released on parole?[8] The mean period of time spent in the Reformatory up to the first parole of the women who were released on parole was 15.5 months ± .19. A few women (1.6%) were first paroled from the institution after they had been there only four months or less,[9] 3.6% after five to eight months, 31.1% after nine to twelve months, 23.1% after thirteen to sixteen months, 19.4% after seventeen to twenty months, 15.3% after twenty-one to twenty-four months, and 5.9% after twenty-five months or more.

Under the rules of the parole authority (which are evidently not always strictly adhered to), the earliest possible release on parole of a woman serving a one-year indeterminate sentence is after eight months. Of our women who received one-year indeterminate sentences, 63.5% served their full sentence in

---

[6] See cases of Angelina, pp. 168–72; Fleur, pp. 162–4; Florence, pp. 157–61.

[7] The conduct of the inmates in the institution is obviously taken into account in passing upon applications for parole. The incidence of various types of misconduct indulged in by our women while at the Reformatory is discussed below (pp. 193–4). Here it might be mentioned that the institutional behaviour of the women who were not granted parole was considerably worse than of those who were, the conduct of 24.4% of the 78 women who served their full sentences being poor as compared to 16.6% of the 377 women who were released on parole.

[8] This refers to *first* release on parole and is different from the total time spent by the women in the Reformatory, because a substantial proportion of them served several periods, having had their parole permits revoked for violation of conditions.

[9] For a time *fornication* was interpreted under an old law which provided that women so charged must not be held for more than three months. This partially accounts for the fact that some women were released early.

the institution, 2.4% were released after serving from five to eight months (none at eight months), 34.1% after serving nine, ten, or eleven months. Supposedly the earliest possible release of inmates serving a two-year indeterminate sentence is after eleven months. Of our women who had such sentences, 24.6% were not granted parole, 3.4% were paroled after serving less than eight months, 22% after serving nine to twelve months (2.5% at eleven months), 14.2% after thirteen to sixteen months, 17.5% after seventeen to twenty months, and 17.9% after serving twenty-one, twenty-two, or twenty-three months. The earliest release on parole of those serving five-year indeterminate sentences is supposedly after fourteen months in the Reformatory. Of the women who received five-year indeterminate sentences, 10.6% were not paroled at all, 4.5% were released on parole after they had served eight months or less, 24.7% after nine to twelve months, 27% after thirteen to sixteen months (8.4% at fourteen months), 16.5% after twenty-one months or longer.

From the above analysis it will be seen that an appreciable proportion of our women were released from the Reformatory after serving less than the minimal periods set by the parole board itself. This is largely attributable to the fact that the Reformatory officials convinced the board that good reasons existed for modifying the general rule in individual cases.[10]

Returns to the Reformatory. Serious violations of parole conditions, or convictions for new crimes, supposedly result in the return of parolees to the Reformatory. But the extent to which parolees are actually sent back to the institution depends not only upon their misbehaviour during parole but upon the intensity of parole supervision. In our group 89.8% of the 377 women who were paroled directly from the Reformatory were not returned to the institution either by revocation of parole or on " in-between " sentences, forty-two (12.9%) of the women were returned once during the period of the sentence, seven women (2.1%) were returned twice; and two (.6%) were returned three times [11] (Appendix D, Table 2–46a).

4. Physical and Mental Condition

Physical condition. It is the practice of the Reformatory physician to examine all inmates shortly after commitment. The examinations disclosed that 44.9% of our women were in " good " physical condition on admission (that is, they had no physical disorders except perhaps venereal disease of an uncomplicated nature); 43.1% were found to be in only " fair " physical condition, which means that they had some minor physical disorder; 12% of them were found to be in " poor " physical condition, in that they had a serious ailment, such as arthritis or diabetes. Only 21.5% of the women were found to be free of syphilis and gonorrhœa; 6.9% of the entire group had syphilis; 45.4% had

[10] See the case of Margaret, pp. 164–8.
[11] See the cases of Florence, pp. 157–61; Dora, pp. 177–83; Alice, pp. 147–53.

gonorrhœa; 25.4% had both gonorrhœa and syphilis (Appendix D, Table 2–50a). Clearly, a major task of the Reformatory is to cure inmates of venereal diseases and to warn them of the dangers of such infections in the future.

Any operative conditions deemed necessary as a result of venereal infection or for any other reasons are given surgical treatment (with the consent of the patient's family), the women sometimes being cared for in the institution's hospital. Of our women thirty-two were operated on during the term of their sentence — the operations including salpingectomies, oophorectomies, various abdominal operations and removal of ovarian cysts and many other conditions likely to be found in women whose sexual life has been so loose. Of the women who underwent operations, at least seventeen were left sterile as a result of these surgical procedures.[12] This is important in the light of its effect on reducing illegitimate pregnancies after release.[13]

When our women were released from the Reformatory, the physical condition of 45.4% of them was good; of 43.3% it could be considered improved, of 9.5% it was the same as on admission (either poor or fair), and only in 1.8% of instances could it be considered worse (Appendix D, Table 2–51). There was a gain in weight on the part of 83.9% of the women (Appendix D, Table 2–H82).

Mental condition. A standard psychometric examination was given each woman shortly after admission. These examinations revealed that 21.8% were of normal mentality; 28% were of " dull normal " mentality, which means that they had intelligence quotients from 81 to 90; 16.1% were of borderline mentality, their intelligence quotients ranging from 71 to 80; the high proportion of 33.8% might be designated feeble-minded, their intelligence quotients ranging from 61 to 70; and 2.3% of them were classified as imbeciles [14] (Appendix D, Table 2–51a). Mental examination further showed that ten of the women (2%) had definite psychoses, and that twelve more (2.4%) might be

---

[12] In addition some women became sterile as a result of venereal infection, but we do not know how many.

[13] See p. 232.

[14] There have been gradual improvements in intelligence tests since the time when the women embraced in this research were examined. But making ample allowance for this fact, the high incidence of defective intelligence still remains; and if our women be gauged by social incapability as well as psychologically, the findings throughout this research show that a large proportion of them would fall under the following well-known definitions of the British Royal Commission on the Care and Control of the Feebleminded:

" *Feeble-minded* are persons who may be capable of earning a living under favourable circumstances, but are incapable from mental defect existing from birth or from an early age: (a) of competing on equal terms with their normal fellows; or (b) of managing themselves and their affairs with ordinary prudence.

" *Imbeciles* are persons who are capable of guarding themselves from common physical dangers, but who are incapable of earning their own living by reason of mental defects existing from birth or from an early age."

It would be interesting to compare the incidence of mental deficiency as determined by modern tests with the findings respecting the five hundred women included in this research.

developing a psychotic condition of one kind or another;[15] that fifty-six of the women (11.2%) were psychopaths; twenty-one (4.2%) were either epileptics or had epileptic characteristics; thirteen (2.6%) had the stigma of alcoholic deterioration; ten (2%) showed definite signs of drug addiction; two (.4%) were diagnosed as congenital syphilitics; twelve (2.4%) were diagnosed as psychoneurotics or neurasthenics; and 39.8% of the women, though not having any of the conditions above mentioned, were either very unstable emotionally or extremely sensitive, seclusive, unsocial, stubborn, egocentric, grudging, or showed other neurotic trends. Only 33% of all the women were not found to be psychotics, psychopaths, epileptics, alcoholics, drug addicts, psychoneurotics, neurasthenics, or extremely unstable emotionally or to have marked neurotic trends (Appendix D, Table 2–52). Emotional instability was definitely noted in 49.6% of all the cases (Appendix D, Table 2–60a). There is no doubt that this is an understatement of the proportion of our women who had poor emotional control. Even this estimate, however, is sufficiently high to indicate the problem which the Reformatory faced in having to treat these women, especially in view of the limited knowledge yet available regarding the training of the emotions. Here is a vast field for experimentation.

But 6.6% of all our women were of normal intelligence and at the same time had no emotional imbalance or abnormalities. In only this small group of cases can the usual educational methods meet with success. It can readily be seen, therefore, to what extent a reformatory is called upon to devise special methods for dealing with " difficult " and " abnormal " personalities.

5. Conduct and Discipline in the Reformatory

Months in the second grade. Under the system of promotions used at the Reformatory, an inmate is placed in the " second grade " on admission. Here she normally remains for five months and is then, if her conduct is satisfactory, admitted to the rank of " first grade " and usually to the privileges of the student-government division. The adjustment made by the women to life in the Reformatory is indicated by the fact that 81.8% of them were promoted to the first grade at the end of five months of incarceration; while 11.6% were held in the second grade for over five months; and 6.6% were in the second grade for less than five months, having been either transferred to some other institution or granted early release (mostly the former), and this because of unmanageableness[16] in the Reformatory (Appendix D, Table 2–61).

Nature of misconduct. The behaviour of 49% of our women was " good " in the Reformatory, which means that they abided by all the rules of the institution; 31.9% of the women occasionally violated minor regulations, by " fooling," talking out of order, shirking, not making their beds properly, and the

---

[15] For definitions see Appendix C, *Mental Condition.*
[16] See the cases of Fleur, pp. 162–4; Margaret, pp. 164–8.

like; 19.1% either broke minor rules frequently, or committed serious offences, such as rebelling against authority, violence against the person, stealing, attempting to escape, fighting, and the like (Appendix D, Table 2–54b). It is the inmate of this latter type who creates the great disciplinary and educational problems of the reform institution, and considerable experimentation must precede any sound program of coping with them.

A total of 51% of our women broke one or another of the rules of the Reformatory. Specifically, 37.8% of them violated regulations which indicate lack of self-control (inattention, laughing, talking out of turn, or " fooling "); 34.2% manifested rebellion against authority, stubbornness, defiance, or insolence, attempted to escape, and committed other offences; 7.5% stole, destroyed, or injured property; 2.9% had to be severely reprimanded for personal disorderliness, such as not making their beds, not taking care of their clothing, or not dressing themselves properly; 2.9% committed offences of violence against the person, such as fighting, quarrelling, assault; 2.5% attempted or actually committed sex offences (usually perversions) of one kind or another (Appendix D, Table 2–55).

There was an improvement in their conduct, however, 63.3% of the women behaving better toward the end of their Reformatory experience. No improvement in conduct occurred in 35.2% of the cases, and the behaviour of 1.5% of the women was decidedly worse [17] (Appendix D, Table 2–61b).

Punishment by isolation. It was the practice of the Reformatory when our women were there to send to the office an inmate who misbehaved. If she continued " unreasonable," she might be asked to remain there several hours, or for the day, or required to go to her own room. If her misconduct did not cease, she might be sent to a work room where she remained alone. If she was violent or destructive, however, she was placed in a solitary punishment cell, the length of time she spent there being dependent upon her response to this type of punishment.[18] The high proportion of 31.2% of all our women were isolated from the other inmates at one time or another (even though for a very short time) while serving sentence (Appendix D, Table 2–H86).[19] Of 295 periods of isolation experienced by 156 of our women who were thus punished, only 2 (.7%) were spent in the office, 58 (19.6%) were spent in a solitary work room, 189 (64.1%) in the inmate's own room, and 34 (15.6%) in the punishment cells, sometimes called " dungeons " (Appendix D, Table 2–H87). The behaviour precipitating such punishment was in 58.3% of the instances the commission of offences against authority, in 29.8% offences indicating lack of self-control, in 3.7% offences against property, in 3% offences against the person, in 2.4% offences reflecting personal disorderliness, in 1.4% sex offences, and in 1.4% miscellaneous offences (Appendix D, Table 2–H86).

[17] See the case of Angelina, pp. 168–72.
[18] See the case of Fleur, pp. 162–4.
[19] Information secured from the Reformatory by letter, December 18, 1929.

Relation of conduct in the Reformatory to other factors. What circumstances, if any, tended to modify or explain the adjustment of our women to the routine of the institution? Did the intelligence of the women make any appreciable difference in their conduct? Or the fact that some of them had previously been subjected to an institutional régime? Or that the delinquency of some was of longer standing than of others?

On the whole there was very little difference in the conduct of the more and less intelligent among our women, as they all behaved in about the same manner, with but a slight preponderance toward good behaviour on the part of those of normal mentality. Though it might seem reasonable to assume that those who had previously been in institutions would be better behaved as a result of the experience, the fact is, however, that a slightly higher proportion of those who had never previously been in penal institutions conducted themselves better in the Reformatory than those who had been. The women whose delinquency was not of long standing, however, behaved better than the others in the Reformatory. We also find that those who were fifteen years old or over when they first became delinquent conducted themselves better in the institution than those who were fourteen or younger when they began their delinquencies. This would seem to indicate that early rooted delinquency becomes persistent and cannot be so readily checked even under reformatory control.

A substantially higher proportion of the women who were twenty-one years of age or older when they were committed behaved well in the Reformatory than of those who were under twenty-one; yet the women who were thirty-one years or older when sentenced conducted themselves better than those who were between twenty-one and thirty years of age. This may be due to the fact that the maturity of older inmates helps them to realize that conformity to the rules of an institution makes for less friction and earlier parole, while the greater exuberance of the adolescent years makes conformity to an institutional régime much more difficult.

Those of our women who were committed for offences against the person or for neglect of family or for drunkenness (especially the last two) were the best-behaved in the Reformatory. Those who were committed for property crimes were the worst-behaved; those who were committed for offences against chastity or against the public health, safety, and policy (many of which were probably also for sex offences), ranged midway between the best- and the worst-behaved. Those who might be considered primarily " stubborn " children were, as would be expected, the least amenable to institutional routine, while those who committed sex offences in conjunction with other offences such as stealing or drunkenness, though not quite so unmanageable as this latter group, nevertheless behaved almost as badly.[20]

20 See the case of Alice, pp. 147–53.

6. Vocational Training

Introductory. The great importance of vocational training for women of this kind is indicated by the fact that at the time of the arrest which resulted in their commitment to the Reformatory, 76% of the group were idle.[21] How did the Reformatory cope with this problem?

Homemaking capacities. As a basis for a vocational training program, the correctional authorities must ascertain the capacities of new inmates. When a woman is admitted to the Reformatory, she is questioned as to her experiences in housekeeping and homemaking. Because this information is secured from the inmates themselves and is not always verified, it may not be entirely reliable. It certainly reflects, however, the general experiences of our group of women. By their own statement 65.6% of them knew something about cooking, 68.6% of them had had some experience in laundering clothes, 67.8% in sewing, 36.8% in waiting on table, 32.2% in doing chamber work, and 6.2% in general housework; 40.8% of the women said that they knew how to embroider, 37.6% to knit, 34.8% to crochet. As to artistic achievements, 16.4% of them said they could sing, and 11.8% that they could play the piano or some other musical instrument (Appendix D, Table 2–H90).

On admission to the Reformatory the new inmate is asked her preference as to vocational training. Of the 165 cases in which this information was stated in the records, we find that the training desired by 56.4% of the women was actually given them in the Reformatory, in 43.6% of the cases the desired training was not given.[22] In view of the fact, however, that in such a large proportion of instances it was unknown whether the training requested by our women was given or not, conclusions on this point must be tentative (Appendix D, Table 2–60c).

Nature of vocational opportunities. The vocational experiences which our women had in the Reformatory were many and varied. A third of them (31.4%) had one occupational experience, an equal proportion (31.8%) two, 18.1% three, 10.9% four, and 5% five or more.[23] The mean number of occupational experiences of the women was 2.19 ± .04 (Appendix D, Table 2–53). Of all the women, 42% did general cleaning at one time or another while they were in the Reformatory,[24] 2.5% worked in the clothes room, where the collecting, mending, sorting, and distribution of clothing takes place, 23.4% in the laundry, 2.1%

---

[21] The lowest incidence of idleness was among the women arrested for offences against the person and those against the family and children; the highest among those arrested for offences against the public health, safety, and policy and those taken into custody for various sexual offences.

[22] We are informed by a former officer in the Reformatory that many of the women have but a vague vocational preference based upon some such slight stimulus as having seen some of the inmates in the attractive uniform of a nurse, for example.

[23] Because of illness, transfer, or early release, 2.8% of our women did not work at all in the Reformatory.

[24] For description of occupations, see Appendix C, " Definition of Terms," *Vocational Experiences.*

in the receiving-room, where they helped inmates to clean up and dress,[25] 2.1% in the office of the institution running errands, 2.9% in the store-rooms, where there were numerous miscellaneous duties, such as filling orders for supplies, meat-cutting, handling freight, etc.; 14.5% of the women had the experience of working on the farm (weeding, hoeing, transplanting, berry-picking); 12.4%, usually those admitted with children or those who were pregnant on admission, were assigned to work in the day nursery, where they had the care of the babies, mended clothing, prepared food; 8.7%, usually the women who expressed a desire to be nurses, were placed at work in the hospital of the institution, where they performed such simple tasks as bathing patients, taking their temperatures, and bringing their trays; 21.5% were placed at work in the kitchen of the Reformatory, where they assisted in cooking, preparing vegetables, cleaning meats, and washing utensils; 14.3% of the women were assigned to waiting on table, setting tables, cleaning silver, and other small duties having to do with the care of the dining-room; 10.8% were assigned to the sewing class, where they did hand sewing, largely on babies' garments; 34.6% were placed at work in the shirt room, where they learned how to operate single- and double-needle sewing and buttonhole power machines, in the various processes having to do with the making of shirts and other garments for state use; 9.7% of the women learned the various processes having to do with the manufacture of stockings, 11.2% with the making of flags; and 4.3% were placed on indenture in a near-by hospital, where they worked usually as ward maids, helpers in the kitchen, or laundresses (Appendix D, Table 2–H84). We shall see later to what extent they utilized the training which they received.

Extent of occupational training. By far the largest proportion of our women were given sufficient experience in the various occupations to which they were assigned to learn at least the rudiments of the work.[26] Of the women placed at work in the dining-room, 81.1% were there long enough to learn how to set and wait upon table.[27] Most of the women assigned to the clothes room [28] were there long enough to become familiar with its duties. Of those assigned to the laundry, 72.9% were there long enough to learn how to do even " fancy ironing," for which three months of experience is considered necessary. Of those placed at work in the store-room, 90.9% were there for a month or longer, which is the minimum deemed necessary to learn the various duties of filling orders, han-

[25] Women assigned here were usually themselves shiftless and untidy who, it was felt, would profit from the experience.

[26] Miss Lathrop of the staff of the Reformatory very kindly prepared a statement for us regarding the minimum length of time which would be considered necessary to learn the rudiments of each occupation at least sufficiently well for carrying on the particular work after release. It is obvious, of course, that the learning capacity of the women varied and was limited by their mentality. This was taken into account, however, by Miss Lathrop in preparing the statement.

[27] About two months is requisite. All the occupational experiences with the exception of general cleaning, kitchen work, and work in the stocking-room could be estimated quite definitely.

[28] Two weeks is sufficient to learn the work.

dling freight, etc. Three fourths of those assigned to the receiving-room of the institution were there long enough to learn the work. Two thirds (64.3%) of those given experience in the sewing-room were there for a month or longer, which is the minimum time necessary to learn the simple sewing taught there. Nine tenths (91.6%) of the women placed in the shirt room, and 91.7% of those assigned to the flag room, were there long enough to learn the rudiments of shirt- or flag-making, for which one month is considered the minimum required. All of the women assigned to work in the office of the institution, and 80.9% of those assigned to work in the nursery, were there long enough to become familiar with the various aspects of this work. In such work two weeks of experience is considered necessary. Three fourths (73.7%) of the women assigned to the hospital, and 66.7% of those allowed to work on the farm, were on the job two months or more, the minimum deemed necessary for learning the work; while 94.4% of those who were indentured remained at least one month, which is the minimum necessary to acquire the rudiments of this work.[29]

Vocational ability in the Reformatory. According to the judgment of the Reformatory officials, 38.1% of our women were " good " workers in the institution; that is, they were reliable, industrious, and capable and did not require much supervision; 54.6% were " fair " workers, in that though they made great effort and showed willingness to work, they were ineffective unless constantly watched; 7.3% were " poor " workers, being unreliable, lazy, dishonest, and needing constant supervision (Appendix D, Table 2–54a).

7. Conclusion

The materials of this chapter have revealed that:

1. Our women were committed to the Reformatory primarily for sex offences; they largely received two-year and five-year indeterminate sentences. Two thirds of them were younger than twenty-six at time of sentence, and relatively few were advanced in age. Nine tenths of them had never been in the Reformatory before. Almost a fifth of the group either were admitted with children or were pregnant on admission. The average length of time which they spent in the Reformatory was a year and a half (including periods of revocation), but a fourth of the women were there for less than a year; and the average time to their first release on parole was 15.5 months after commitment. Transfers to other institutions (aside from temporary transfers for medical reasons) were relatively few. Release on parole of two thirds of the group was postponed by the parole board, the usual reason for postponement being venereal infection,

---

[29] In keeping inmates in a job assignment sufficiently long to learn its rudiments, the Women's Reformatory makes a better showing than the Men's Reformatory, in which only 56% of the inmates whom we studied were occupied sufficiently long in a vocation to learn at least enough about it to be able to compete in the open labour market (S. and E. T. Glueck, op. cit., p. 161). But this may be due partially to the differences in vocations in the two institutions.

misconduct, and the need for further training of one sort or another. An appreciable proportion of the inmates were released before the time usually set by
the parole authorities; and nine tenths of those paroled were not returned to the
Reformatory for violation of parole.

2. Regarding the mental and physical condition of the women, four fifths of
them were venereally diseased at the time of admission, and many were otherwise in poor health. Many were of inferior intelligence, some were feeble-
minded, and many were emotionally unbalanced.

3. With respect to their behaviour in the Reformatory, many of the women
adjusted themselves to the régime with difficulty, over half breaking the rules
of the institution and a third having to be placed in isolation at various times.
An improvement in the conduct of a large majority of the inmates, however,
was noted after they had been in the Reformatory for several months.

4. Regarding the vocational training of the women in the Reformatory, some
of them were at one time or another placed at general cleaning (two fifths of the
group), garment-making (a third), laundry work (a fourth), kitchen work (a
fifth), dining-room work (a seventh), and farm work (a seventh); and on the
whole the women were kept in the various occupations for a period sufficient
to learn the rudiments. Less than two fifths of them were capable, efficient
workers in the Reformatory, most of them requiring constant supervision.

These findings reinforce our earlier impressions of the mental, physical, and
industrial inadequacy of the inmates of the Reformatory and indicate that the
institutional authorities had difficult problems of discipline and vocation to cope
with, which, on the whole, they seem to have met quite satisfactorily. How last-
ing the results of their efforts were we shall see in the next three chapters.

CHAPTER XI

ON PAROLE

1. Introductory

We have described the activities of our five hundred delinquents as children, as adolescents, and as inmates of the Reformatory. In order to appreciate what the institution accomplished for them, and the nature and proportion of the task facing the parole authorities who continued the treatment begun in the institution we must now describe our women as parolees.[1]

Three hundred and seventy-seven of our five hundred women served a part of their sentence to the Reformatory under parole supervision. The theoretical parole period, however (that is, the time from the date of release on parole to the official date of its termination by revocation or by expiration of sentence), was not always very long. Thus, the theoretical length of parole of 4.2% of the women was one month or less; 9% were on parole from one to three months, 12.2% from three to six months, 18.1% from six to twelve months, 16.7% from one to two years, 6.6% from two to three years, 22.6% from three to four years, and 10.6% for four years and over. The mean length of the theoretical parole period of the 377 women who were placed on parole was 22.82 months ± .63 (Appendix D, Table 3–1).

---

[1] In addition to describing the condition of our delinquent women during parole from the Reformatory, this chapter is devoted to a series of comparisons between their status prior to their admission to the Reformatory and their status during parole. However, inasmuch as the data concerning parole have been gleaned almost entirely from the meagre records kept by the parole officers, we are unable to follow through certain features which were taken into account in the history of the women prior to their commitment to the Reformatory.

The parole officers did not necessarily note such facts, for example, as the conjugal relations of the parolees, their competence as home-makers, their attitude toward their marital responsibilities and toward their children, the extent of their savings, and the like. When the research was originally planned, it was hoped that it would be possible to compare the behaviour and characteristics of our women prior to their commitment to the Reformatory and during parole. As the limitations of the data contained in the parole records became apparent, however, it was necessary to eliminate certain factors from consideration.

It should be pointed out that in analysing parole data, if an offender was on parole for less than three months, we made no attempt to gauge the stability of her household, her industrial adjustment, her economic responsibility, her steadiness of employment, her work habits, her longest period of employment, or her family relationships. The period was obviously too short.

2. First Home on Parole

With whom parolees resided. It should be recalled that at the time of their commitment to the Reformatory, 29.7% of our women were living with their parents, 8% with relatives (including married children), 8.8% with husbands, 5.2% with employers, 13.7% with lovers, 22.3% alone, and 12.3% with friends or acquaintances (Appendix D, Table 1–8). The parole officers were inclined to urge their charges to live under the parental roof or with relatives if such homes were decent, or with their husbands if a reunion was desirable. Or they placed the women as domestics in homes offering a protected environment. Thus, 36.9% of the women went to live in their parental homes as soon as they were paroled, 11.3% went to live with relatives, usually married sisters, 12.7% joined their husbands, to whom they had in some cases been reconciled while at the Reformatory, 35.3% went to the homes of employers as domestic servants, and 1.9% more went to live with friends who were particularly interested in their welfare. Only 1.9% of the parolees were permitted to live alone, as compared with 22.3% who were living by themselves at the time of commitment [2] (Appendix D, Table 3–6).

Length of time in first home. How long did our women remain in the households to which they went when paroled? A third of the women (36.9%) did not leave their first parole homes at all during the parole period, 15.6% remained there for one month or less, 20.1% for one to three months, 12.5% for three to six months, 9% for six to twelve months, 4.3% for one to two years, and 1.6% for two years or longer. The mean length of time during which the parolees remained in the first home was 6.08 months ± .26 (Appendix D, Table 2–34). Of those who left this household before the end of parole, the reason for their departure may be laid at the door of the parolees themselves in 50.9% of the cases, as they disappeared, or were arrested, quarrelled with members of the household, or otherwise disturbed the even tenor of the home, while 49.1% of the parolees left the household for reasons which do not discredit them, such as marriage, the desire to be nearer a place of employment, or to care for a sick relative, and the like (Appendix D, Table 3–35).

Character of first home and neighbourhood. Almost a third (31%) of the homes to which the parolees went (largely homes approved by the parole department) were in urban districts,[3] which were partly residential in character; 51% of them were in either urban or suburban residential neighbourhoods; and 18% were in small towns or in the open countryside (Appendix D, Table 3–3).

---

[2] In comparing the status of the women during parole with their status as to certain factors prior to commitment we would have utilized the same 377 cases had it not been for the fact that the comparisons between the 377 parolees and the entire 500 women involved in the study gave essentially the same results. We preferred, therefore, for the sake of ease in later comparisons between the pre-Reformatory, parole, and post-parole period, to retain the total of 500.

[3] For definition, see Appendix C, *Neighbourhood Type.*

One way of gauging the quality of parole work is to see whether the parole officers made an effort to place their charges in a more wholesome environment than they lived in just prior to their commitment to the Reformatory. It is obvious that the parole agents deliberately planned to remove their charges from crowded urban areas if possible, since there is a marked decrease in residence in such areas immediately after release on parole as compared with the year prior to commitment — from 75% to 31%. Furthermore, the agents were fully aware of the need of establishing the parolees in decent neighbourhoods. There is a striking improvement in the neighbourhood influences [4] surrounding the homes to which the women were allowed to go on parole over those of the homes in which they were living within a year of commitment. The neighbourhood influences were good in 49.7% of the cases as compared to 6.2% within a year of commitment; fair in 27.8%; and poor in 22.5% as compared with 70.2% within a year of commitment (Appendix D, Table 3–4).

There was also a marked improvement in the physical condition of the homes [5] to which the women were permitted to go on parole as compared to their homes within a year of commitment. Thus, the physical condition of the homes was good in the high proportion of 66.7% of the cases, while only 11.1% of the women had lived in such homes in the year before commitment; 19.3% of these first homes on parole might be considered fair; and 14% were poor in their physical conveniences in contrast to 67% within a year of commitment of the women (Appendix D, Table 3–5a).

Not only did the parole agents make great effort to place their charges in surroundings that were at least physically wholesome, but they were also fully alive to their responsibility of not approving residence in homes in which the moral standards [6] were not decent. The moral standards of these first homes on parole were good in the considerable proportion of 63.3% of the cases, as compared with only 10.4% of the homes in which the women had lived during the year prior to their commitment to the Reformatory. This improvement can be partially accounted for by the fact that the parole officers placed 35.3% of the parolees in private homes as domestics or in hospitals as ward maids. The moral standards of 18% of these first homes on parole were fair; in 18.7% they were poor, as compared with 74.7% within a year of commitment (Appendix D, Table 3–5b).

Household stability and mobility. Of those of our women who left the first household to which they went on parole (and who were on parole for more than three months), 28.3% lived in two different households during the parole period, 11.7% in three, 60% in four or more (Appendix D, Table 3–7). The average (mean) number of households in which these women lived during the parole period was 2.89 ± .09.

[4] For definition, see Appendix C, *Neighbourhood Influences.*
[5] Ibid., *Home — Physical.*
[6] Ibid., *Moral Standards of Home.*

Because of the variations in the length of the parole period and the pre-commitment period it is not possible to make any comparison of household stability in these two periods, but we can compare the mobility of the group. There was a slight decrease in moving from city to city during the parole period, but more moving within a city than formerly, 14.7% of the women making frequent changes of residence within one city during parole and 41.1% moving from city to city, while 44.2% did not move excessively (Appendix D, Table 3–2b).

It should be remembered that a parolee is expected to secure permission from her parole officer if she wishes to change her place of residence, although of course some parolees violate this rule. In the light of such a regulation, the fact that there was as much mobility [7] during parole as before commitment shows us that many parolees evidently did not ask permission to move, since it is not the policy of the parole agents to encourage much mobility.

3. First Job on Parole

How secured. It is generally requisite that an inmate of the Reformatory about to be released on parole have a definite job to which to go unless she is to do housework for her family or, for some legitimate reason, does not have to work. It is the responsibility of the parole agent to see that the offender has a place of employment which the agent herself has secured or which she has approved. Of all the parolees, 74.2% went to work directly after their release on parole. The jobs had been secured for them by the parole agents in 52.8% of these cases; in 30.8% by the parolees themselves; in 12.3% by some member of the family; and in 4.1% by various other people — an officer of the Reformatory, a former employer, a social worker (Appendix D, Table 3–12).

Nature of first job. Over half the parolees (57%) who went to work immediately after release on parole entered domestic service, the largest proportion of them living in the homes of their employers, but 7.6% living at home and going out to work by the day; 27.5% of the women went into factories, 3.7% took jobs as waitresses, or as chambermaids in hotels, 2.6% went into clerical positions in offices, 1.5% took jobs in stores, usually as sales-girls, 6.2% became ward maids or attendants in hospitals, and 1.5% did mending or washing in their own homes (Appendix D, Table 3–11). The bias of the parole agents in favour of domestic work for parolees is again obvious from the fact that they were themselves largely instrumental in securing such positions for their charges and left the obtaining of other types of employment, such as factory, restaurant, hotel, store, and office work, to the parolees or their families.

The requirement that a parolee have a job to which to go on her release from the Reformatory, though observed in letter is not necessarily carried out in spirit,

---

[7] For definition, see Appendix C, *Mobility.*

as only 18.2% of our women held these first jobs throughout the parole period. Of those who did not keep their first positions throughout parole, 31.1% held them for less than one month, 20.5% for one to two months, 20% for two to four months, 9.8% for four to six months, 12.6% for six to twelve months, and only 6% for a year or longer (Appendix D, Table 3-13). Of course, early abandonment of the first job was not always the fault of the parolee. Nevertheless, of those who left these first places of employment, the high proportion of 42.7% did so because of drunkenness, incompetence, or arrest; while 57.3% left because of illness, marriage, the seasonality of the job, and like reasons (Appendix D, Table 3-14).

4. Parole Supervision

Actual length of supervision.[8] Although, theoretically, the parole period extends from the date of release of the offender on parole to the official date of expiration of the sentence, actually many of our women were not under the direct supervision of a parole agent for this length of time, because they were granted permission to leave the state and not required to make reports to the agent, or were deported, or were committed to a state hospital or a penal institution during parole, and therefore, according to the rules of the parole department of Massachusetts, were no longer under parole supervision. In such cases the oversight afforded by parole may be referred to as "incomplete" or "broken." In 53.6% of the cases, the parolees were under supervision of a parole agent throughout the parole period. In 5% of the cases the actual time of parole supervision was one month less than the theoretical, in 5.8% it was one to two months less, in 4.5% three to four months, in 3.2% five to six months, in 3.5% seven to eight months, in 3.2% nine to twelve months, in 6.6% one to two years, and in 14.6% two or more years. The average difference between the two periods in those instances in which there was a difference was 15.7 months ± .55 (Appendix D, Table 3-27).

Reasons for broken supervision. If an offender disappeared during parole, or was excused from reporting by virtue of good behaviour, or had been granted permission to leave the state, she was of course technically under supervision, but the parole oversight was "broken." In 47.4% of the cases in which the parole agents did not personally supervise the parolees throughout the parole period, the reason was that the parolees were given permission to leave the state; in

---

[8] In calculating the actual number of months during which a parolee was under supervision we subtracted from the period extending from the date of parole to the date of expiration of the sentence the number of months during which the parolee was out of the state or in a foreign land by permission. We also deducted from this period any time during which the parolee was in the Reformatory by revocation of her parole or by reason of a new sentence imposed while she was on parole. We also subtracted any length of time during which she was in a hospital for mental diseases or in a penal institution (except when such incarceration was unknown to the parole officer). If a woman died during her parole period, the actual length of parole supervision was calculated to the date of her death.

41.1% of the cases broken oversight was due to the temporary or permanent disappearance of the parolees, in 6.3% to their being excused from further reporting, in 2.9% to their commitment to penal or non-penal institutions, and in 1.7% to their death before the end of the parole period (Appendix D, Table 3–28).

Far fewer of the women who were supervised continuously by the parole agents were delinquent or were suspected of misconduct during parole than those whose supervision was broken or incomplete (50.3% as compared to 85.9%), which indicates that uninterrupted oversight brings practical results in keeping parolees out of trouble.[9]

Parole agents. Two parole agents had the supervision of our women during their parole period. One agent had in charge 44.2% of them, the other 38.1%.[10] In 7.2% of the cases both agents supervised the same woman at one time or another during the parole period, and in 3.2% of the cases some other person, such as a member of the Reformatory staff or a parole or probation officer in another state, undertook the supervision of the parolees; in 7.3% of the cases, our women, though not under the direct oversight of one or another of the parole agents, were required to report to them regularly by letter (Appendix D, Table 3–2a).

Contacts of agents with parolees. One way of gauging the intensity of parole supervision is to determine the frequency of the contacts between parole agent and parolee. Naturally, it is particularly important that the oversight of a parolee should begin as soon as possible after her discharge from the Reformatory, since it is during the transitional period between the artificial and protected life within an institution and the unrestrained and undirected life of freedom that there is the greatest danger of recidivism.

Agents are requested by the parole department to visit parolees or their families, or others immediately concerned in their welfare, within a week or two after release of the prisoners on parole. Making all due allowance for delays resulting from pressure of work, we find that in only 46.9% of the instances did less than one month elapse before the parole agent made the first contact with the case; in 18.5% of the cases one to two months had gone by, in 13.9% two to four months, in 5.6% anywhere from four months to over a year. In 15.1% of the cases the parole agent did not make any contact whatsoever with the parolee or her family or any other person directly concerned in her welfare (Appendix D, Table 3–26). An average of 2.32 months ± .08 elapsed between the release of our women on parole and the first contact by the agents with them or their families. The parolees themselves were not always seen on the occasion of the first field

---

[9] A small part of the high association between continuity of supervision and non-delinquency during parole is attributable to the fact that the broken supervision in some cases was caused by the parolee's misconduct.

[10] The average monthly case load of the parole officers, as determined by their work in the year 1922, was as follows: One officer had the supervision on the average of 98 cases per month, and the other officer of 76 cases per month. In the year 1923 one officer had 111 parolees under her supervision monthly, and the other officer had 58 parolees. Obviously this is a considerable case load. (Information supplied by the parole department of the Massachusetts Department of Correction.)

visit made by the parole agents. In fact, in only 43% of all the cases did less than one month elapse before the first contact was made with the parolee herself; [11] in 16.6% one to two months passed, in 14.4% two to four months, in 4.3% four to eight months, and in 3.5% eight months or longer; in 18.2% of the cases no contact whatsoever was established by the parole officer with the parolee either by visit or by letter (Appendix D, Table 3–32). The mean length of time which elapsed between the release of our women on parole and the first contact with them directly by the parole agents was 2.56 months ± .13.

Obviously this reveals a serious weakness in the functioning of the parole system. Even though the parole agent sees the prospective parolee in the Reformatory once or twice before her discharge and immediately upon release (at the train) for policing-purposes, the fact that direct personal oversight is not in effect until two or more months later may have serious consequences. This conclusion is partially borne out by the fact that among the cases in which the first contact with the parolee was made less than a month after release from the Reformatory, there was a somewhat higher proportion of non-delinquents during parole than among those with whom personal contact was deferred (39.7% : 33%).

Frequency of visits by parole agents. In accordance with the policy of the Massachusetts parole department, the parole agent is expected to visit the parolee or her family on the average of once a month throughout the parole period unless the parolee is out of the state or in an institution. In fact, however, one contact a month was made in only 31.4% of the cases in which the parolees or their families were actually visited; in 33.3% of the cases visits were made once in one to two months, in 23.6% once in two to four months, in 7% once in four to eight months, and in 4.7% once in eight months or more (Appendix D, Table 3–30). The average frequency of visits to the parolees, their relatives, employers, or others directly concerned in their welfare was once in 2.8 months ± .10. The parolees themselves were not seen oftener than on the average of once in 3.9 months ± .13; only 18.1% were seen once a month, 27.5% once in one to two months, 29.1% once in two to four months, 11.7% once in four to six months, 6.5% once in six months to a year, and 7.1% once a year or less often (Appendix D, Table 3–29). That more intensive oversight by the agents tends to keep parolees on the straight and narrow path is seen in the fact that of those cases whom the agents visited as often as once a month, 50% were non-delinquent during parole; where the agents visited once in over one to two months, 38.6% of the parolees were non-delinquent; where visits were as frequent as once in two to six months, 33.9% of the parolees were non-delinquent; and where visits were made as rarely as once in six months, or not at all, only 20.5% of the parolees were non-delinquent during parole. Whether this relationship between intensity of parole supervision and good behaviour during parole is due chiefly

---

[11] This excludes meeting a woman at the train on the occasion of her release.

to the constructive nature of the oversight or to the deterrent effect of parole, or perhaps to other influences is hard to say.

In the course of 3,740 personal visits made throughout the parole period by the two agents, the parolees themselves were seen in 65.3%; [12] in 13.5% relatives were seen; in 3.1%, although neither the parolees nor their relatives were seen, employers were interviewed; in 15.1% other interested persons, such as social workers, ministers, friends (Appendix D, Table 3–H41).

Reports by parolee to agent. Parolees are required to report once a month to their parole officers either in writing or by a call on the officer, unless they are excused from so doing by reason of good behaviour. Three fourths (74.5%) of our women reported thus regularly; 9.7% reported once in over one to two months, 5.4% once in two to four months, 3.7% once in four to eight months, 3.5% once in eight months or more; 1.1% did not report at all, 2.1% were not required to report (Appendix D, Table 3–33). The average frequency with which our parolees reported to their parole agents was once in 2.16 months ± .08. Here again it is found that the frequency of contact between the agent and the parolee bears some relationship to her conduct, those parolees reporting more frequently having been less delinquent during parole than the others. Thus, of those who reported as often as once a month, 43.2% were non-delinquents; while of those who did not report to the agent oftener than once in over one to two months, only 18.8% were non-delinquents; and of those who reported once every two months or less frequently, only 4.8% were not delinquent during parole. Failure to report regularly is of course reflective of a parolee's negligence or indifference, or of a desire to keep her whereabouts a secret from the agent so that she can go her way untrammelled. Hence failure to report should be examined into by parole agents without delay.

Special efforts of the parole agents. The efforts made by the parole officers to rehabilitate our women took the form, in large measure, of letters of advice and encouragement to them. The parole agents also rendered considerable personal assistance in helping their charges to make domestic adjustments, to change their living-arrangements, to secure divorces, to provide for their children, to save money, to adapt themselves to particular jobs, or to straighten out misunderstandings with employers. Occasionally they enlisted the co-operation of social agencies. Sometimes they stimulated an interest in the parolees for further education or for care of their health. Occasionally the parole officers arranged for wholesome recreational outlets for certain of their charges. In 42.4% of all the cases constructive efforts of this kind were actually made by the parole officers (Appendix D, Table 3–H39). While they exerted more than a mere routine oversight, however, we are conscious of an abundant need for more intensive case work in the large majority of instances.

[12] This does not mean that employers, relatives, and others were not seen at the same time the parolees were visited.

Recommendations made by the Reformatory staff. One of the great weaknesses of peno-correctional practice is the lack of integration between the various branches of what ought to be a unified service. Not infrequently, for example, the parole authorities undertake the supervision of a woman to the point where the Reformatory officials leave off, yet do not make any co-ordinated effort to carry out the suggestions of the Reformatory staff. The latter, having observed and treated the offender over a considerable period, are often able to offer valuable suggestions to the parole agents. For some time it has been the practice of the Massachusetts Reformatory authorities to hold a conference with the parole agents shortly before the release of a woman on parole, at which time they briefly discuss the characteristics of the prospective parolee and what might best be done for her. There is no compulsion about these meetings. They merely reflect the need long felt by the Reformatory for relating its efforts to those of the parole department in the best interests of the offenders. The initiative toward such a co-ordinated approach came from the Reformatory.[12a]

In view of the fact that such meetings have not been held regularly, because of pressure of other work in the Reformatory, or not always recorded, owing to meagreness of stenographic service, it was not possible for us to secure information on all the cases. But of 97 recommendations made by the members of the Reformatory staff to the parole agents, 52 were carried out by the agents, and 45 were not put into effect. These recommendations had to do with placement of parolees as domestics, with permitting them to return to the parental home, with modifying some aspect of the home situation, with providing educational opportunities or helping a woman to make a vocational adjustment, with permitting a woman to return to her husband, with attention to her health, or with the need of especially careful supervision. For example, the Reformatory staff advised that one woman should not be allowed to return to her parents if she could be suitably placed elsewhere. Acting on this suggestion, the parole agent secured a position for the parolee as a " forelady " in a factory and found a boarding-place for her in a good family. The Reformatory staff recommended to another agent that the parolee be placed at housework. In view of the fact, however, that she expressed a marked preference for factory work, the parole officer found a job for her in a factory. The Reformatory staff recommended that another parolee should not be permitted to join her syphilitic husband, in which the parole officer acquiesced. In another instance the Reformatory officials advised that the woman should not be allowed to return to her parents unless the home situation be somewhat modified. The parole officer allowed her charge to return home, apparently intending to keep close watch on the family situation; but before she had any opportunity to take action, the parolee disappeared (Appendix D, Table 2–H85).

[12a] Since the above was written, parole agents operate out of the Reformatory instead of from the office of the Board of Parole, which is far removed from the institution. This should make for greater co-ordination between the activities of the Reformatory and parole.

Obviously a greater unity between the Reformatory and parole authorities, and also more individualized oversight on the part of the parole agents, are goals well worth striving for.

Revocation of parole. If a parolee is known to violate the conditions of her parole,[13] her permit to be at liberty is revoked. This happened in 20.7% of our cases (Appendix D, Table 3–25a). It does not follow, however, that all the parolees whose licence to be at liberty was rescinded were returned to the Reformatory. In reality only 13.8% of those whose parole permits were withdrawn were returned to the Reformatory. This is due to the fact that revocation of parole often took place after a parolee had disappeared. Of a total of 113 revocations only 65 were followed by return to the Reformatory (Appendix D, Table 3–40).

Delinquency. It is often claimed that from 70% to 90% of parolees are non-delinquent during parole.[14] Such optimistic reports of successful parole work when made by officials are likely to be based on cursory investigations or on mere impressions. Unwarranted claims are a serious obstacle to the building of a science of penology, and have already been disproved in several investigations.[15] In the present research it was found that of 256 women whose conduct was definitely known, 45% were not delinquent[16] during parole; 23% were actually arrested;[17] 32%, though grossly misbehaving, were not arrested (Appendix D, Table 3–25b).

As reflecting the casualness of parole oversight, it should be mentioned that the misbehaviour of 14.3% of all the parolees was entirely unknown to the parole officers even though these parolees lived in Massachusetts throughout parole. In 14.1% more of the cases, the bad conduct of the parolees was completely unknown to the parole officers because the women were living out of the state and had few if any contacts with the parole agents; and 3.4% more of the women had disappeared and the parole officers had no information regarding their misconduct (Appendix D, Table 3–25b).[18]

Despite the substantial proportion of delinquent parolees, it is obvious that some falling off in delinquency had occurred as compared to the year prior to commitment, when 99% of the women were delinquent.

We find that the conduct of our women during their stay in the Reformatory was roughly predictive of their behaviour during parole, as 60.5% of those who

---

[13] See p. 141 for parole rules.

[14] See S. and E. T. Glueck, op. cit., pp. 4–7, for illustrations of these claims.

[15] Ibid.

[16] For definition, see Appendix C, *Delinquency.*

[17] Eighteen arrests resulted in sentence to penal institutions other than the Reformatory; three to the Reformatory.

[18] The basis of the above analysis is the record kept by the parole agents. The incompleteness of this is shown by the fact that through such investigation as we ourselves were able to make of the conduct of the women during parole, we found that 32 women whose behaviour was not known to the parole officers were actually delinquents. Nine of them had been arrested in Massachusetts, seven in other states; and sixteen others had so misbehaved as to have been exposed to arrest had their misconduct come to the attention of the police (Appendix D, Table 3–H38).

were not delinquent during parole had also behaved well in the Reformatory, while only 38.6% of those who were delinquent on parole were well behaved in the Reformatory. This finding will interest those officials who conceive that their responsibility to offenders and society ceases with the completion of parole, since it justifies their stressing of good conduct in the institution as a requisite to release on parole. But it is hoped that such a short-sighted view of the task of Reformatory and parole officials will not long endure. The aim of a Reformatory should not be limited to the making of good inmates or success-ful candidates for parole, but good citizens; and the aim of a parole system should not be confined to the making of satisfactory parolees, but rehabilitated individuals. The high predictive value of institutional conduct so far as success-ful *parole* behaviour is concerned is to be expected; prisoners realize that by behaving well in the institution they have a better chance of early release on parole, and parolees realize that by conforming outwardly to parole regulations they avoid recommitment to the institution. But neither of these lines of conduct affords a complete and true test of the actual criminalistic tendencies of the ex-prisoner; these crop out after both incarceration and parole oversight have been replaced by complete freedom and self-governance. That is why in this and other studies the objective of the prediction tables we have developed is not con-duct on parole, but conduct during a five-year period beyond parole, which we take to be a sufficient span within which the behaviour tendencies of an ex-prisoner are likely to manifest themselves.[19]

5. Industrial History and Economic Responsibility

Occupational experiences. Of all the women who worked during parole, 46.5% were engaged as domestics at one time or another during this period; 39.2% worked as factory hands, 11% in restaurants or hotels, 13.7% did general house-work or cleaning by the day, 5.2% worked in stores, 4.4% were at one time or another engaged in clerical occupations, 9% worked as ward maids or practical nurses, 3.8% were gainfully employed in their own homes as dressmakers, janitresses, lodging-house keepers, 30.8% of all the women kept house for all or most of the parole period for either husbands or relatives, and 4.1% of them were at one time or another during parole earning a livelihood in some illegiti-mate occupation such as bootlegging, selling drugs, or receiving stolen goods (Appendix D, Table 3–36).

The type of work in which our parolees were engaged longest during the parole period, or to which they returned most often, was domestic service in 30.6% of the cases, factory work in 28%, restaurant and hotel work in 3.3%, work in stores in 1.2%, clerical work in 2.1%, housework by the day in 4.8%, as ward maids or hospital attendants in 5.6%, keeping lodging-houses in .6%,

---

[19] See Chapter XVII, and *500 Criminal Careers,* Chapter XVIII.

doing their own housework in 21.7%, illegitimate occupations in 2.1% (Appendix D, Table 3–17). In contrasting this with the usual occupation engaged in by the women prior to their sentence to the Reformatory, we find a marked increase in domestic service and a decrease in factory work. This is to be explained by the encouragement given the parolees by the agents to seek positions as domestics rather than as factory workers because of the more protected environment offered by the former.

Highest wages. During parole the highest weekly earnings of our women were less than five dollars in 2.2% of the cases, five to ten dollars in 36%, ten to fifteen in 40%, fifteen to twenty in 17.4%, and twenty to thirty in 4.4% (Appendix D, Table 3–15). The average of the highest weekly earnings during parole was only $12.35 ± .19, some three dollars less than the highest average weekly wage in the period prior to commitment to the Reformatory. This may partially be accounted for by the lower wage-scale of certain of the post-war years.

Steadiness of employment.[20] Despite the lower earnings, there was greater steadiness of employment among our women during parole. Thus, 37.5% of the women who were employed for more than three months of the parole period worked regularly, as compared to 7.5% who were steadily employed prior to commitment to the Reformatory. During parole, 38.5% were fairly steadily employed; while only 24% were irregular workers as compared to 59.7% previously (Appendix D, Table 3–18a). This greater continuity of employment during parole is partially attributable to the training which the women received in the Reformatory, partly also to their greater maturity, and partly to the pressure exerted by the parole agents, as parolees are not allowed to change jobs without permission.

Work habits.[21] Not only a greater regularity of employment but also an improvement in work habits was manifest during parole, 26.5% of the women being good workers as compared to 16.2% prior to commitment. The work habits of 52.6% of the parolees were fair, of 20.9% poor (Appendix D, Table 3–18b).

Of the women who worked, 43.1% usually left their places of employment through their own fault, such as inefficiency, dishonesty, drunkenness. Despite the seemingly high proportion of such cases, this nevertheless represents a great improvement over the years prior to commitment, when 83.8% of our women generally lost their jobs through their own fault (Appendix D, Table 3–19a).

Industrial success.[22] There clearly was a greater industrial adjustment on the part of our women while on parole than before their commitment. The proportion of industrial success was 22.7% as compared to 2.9% in the prior period; 54.6% of the parolees might be considered partially successful in their industrial

[20] For definition, see Appendix C, *Steadiness of Employment.*
[21] Ibid., *Work Habits.*
[22] Ibid., *Industrial History.*

adjustments as compared to 38.8% within a year prior to commitment, and only 22.7% of the group failed to make an adequate occupational adjustment during parole as compared to 58.3% prior to commitment (Appendix D, Table 3–10a).

The degree to which the occupational adaptations of the women were due to the training they received in the Reformatory is difficult to gauge. Of the parolees whose industrial habits in the institution were regarded by the Reformatory officials as good, 37.2% also had good work habits during parole, while 12.8% had poor work habits; of those who were considered poor workers in the Reformatory, not a single one had good work habits during parole, and the high proportion of 71.4% were poor workers. Clearly, then, there is a marked association between habits of industry in the Reformatory and during parole, which seems to indicate that the capacities of the women (as reflected in their work habits), more than the training which they received in the Reformatory, play the decisive role in their occupational adaptations. This surmise is supported indirectly by the finding that the high proportion of 77.6% of the parolees did not follow during parole the occupation in which they had been engaged while in the Reformatory (Appendix D, Table 3–16b). This last finding should indicate to the authorities that the occupations taught in the Reformatory need modification to take account of the vocational opportunities for ex-prisoners.

Economic condition and responsibility. Only 3.1% of the parolees were in comfortable economic circumstances during parole; 93.5% were in marginal circumstances, and 3.4% were economically dependent [23] (Appendix D, Table 3–21b). That there was a greater economic security in the group than before, however, is evident from the fact that during the parole period a larger proportion of women were in marginal circumstances (93.5% as compared to 78.4%), and fewer were dependent (3.4% as compared to 14.9%), than within a year of commitment.

This increased economic security is partly due to reduction in the need to be self-supporting, as during parole 29.8% of the women were married and did not have to supplement the husband's income, or, though not supported by a husband, did housework for relatives in return for room and keep. Of those women who had to engage in gainful employment during parole, 39.2% needed to support only themselves, as they had no dependents; 49.2% were married and had to aid in the support of their husbands and children; 5.8% had dependents outside of their immediate families to whose support they contributed; while 5.8% of the women, though having dependents, did not help to support them (Appendix D, Table 3–21a). By and large, over nine tenths (93.3%) of the parolees met their economic responsibilities [24] (Appendix D, Table 3–10b), a slightly greater proportion than within a year of commitment, when 89.8% were meeting their economic responsibilities.

[23] For definition, see Appendix C, *Economic Condition.*
[24] Ibid., *Economic Responsibility.*

6. Family Relationships

Marital status. At the beginning of parole, 47.2% of the women who were released were single, 14.5% were married and soon rejoined their husbands, 29.2%, though married, had for some time been separated from their husbands, 6.2% were divorced, and 2.9% were widows (Appendix D, Table 3-8a). By the end of parole only 36.4% of the parolees were still unmarried, 26.3% were married and living with their husbands, 27.5% were separated, 6.6% were divorced, and 2.6% were widows (Appendix D, Table 3-8b).

With whom resident at end of parole. Of those who were not living with a husband at the end of the parole period, 31.8% were residing in their parental homes; 9% were living with relatives or foster parents, 24.1% in the homes of employers, usually as domestic servants, seven women were rooming alone, one woman was living with a lover, two women were residing with friends, five were in institutions other than the Reformatory, and thirty were serving a new sentence in the Reformatory. Five more had died during parole, and the whereabouts of fifty women was unknown to the parole officer (Appendix D, Table 3-37). A far lower proportion of women were living in the homes of employers as domestic servants at the end of the parole period than at its beginning. This is partly due to marriage, but more to the fact that the confinement necessitated by such work was distasteful to some women, who soon drifted away, even disappearing altogether.

Success of family relationships.[25] The family relationships of our women improved markedly during parole, 59.6% then maintaining family ties as compared to 12.6% within a year of commitment (Appendix D, Table 3-19b). To what extent the re-establishment of family bonds can be credited to the efforts of the parole agents can only be surmised, as the supervision records are not sufficiently reflective of the work actually done.

7. Recreations and Habits

Use of leisure. During parole 9.2% of the parolees belonged to clubs or organizations in which their leisure time was wholesomely absorbed, such as the Young Women's Christian Association; or they had some constructive interest, such as music, choir singing, and the like. From the fact that 90.8% of them did not have any such interests, however, it may be inferred that the parole officers did not make sufficient effort to direct the leisure time of their charges into constructive channels (Appendix D, Table 3-20b). That they evidently did try to repress any harmful use of leisure, however, we infer from the fact that at least two fifths (42.3%) of the parolees did not engage in harmful activities, though not having any constructive outlets or pronounced bad habits; while only half the

---

[25] For definition, see Appendix C, *Family Relationships.*

parolees (51%) spent their leisure hours in unwholesome activities, or had pronounced bad habits or disreputable companions. This finding should, however, be considered in the light of the fact that within a year of commitment 98% of the women had used their spare time harmfully (Appendix D, Table 3–20b).

Since many of our women had never learned how to use their leisure in wholesome ways and many of them were oversexed, they particularly needed sublimative emotional and æsthetic outlets. But our findings lead to the two disturbing conclusions that there is little carry-over into free life of the recreational interests which the Reformatory attempts to develop in the inmates, and that the efforts put forth by the parole agents to supply decent recreational outlets for their charges are most inadequate.

Companionships. Despite the watchfulness of the parole agents, at least 44.2% of the parolees had disreputable companions, association with whom was likely to lead to delinquency, such as streetwalkers, "pick-ups," drunks, idlers, bootleggers. Nevertheless an improvement is manifest over the situation that existed within a year of the women's commitment, when the high proportion of 97.3% had harmful companionships (Appendix D, Table 3–24a).

Habits. Any analysis of the vicious habits of our women during parole is necessarily limited by the very nature and extent of parole itself; the parole agents, on whose supervision reports we had largely to rely for the information, did not always have knowledge of the habits of their charges. They knew definitely, however, that at least 47.1% of the women were engaging in illicit sex practices of one type or another during parole (Appendix D, Table 3–23). In all, 53.5% of the parolees were known to have bad habits — illicit sexuality, stealing, drink, or drug addiction. At least 13.9% stole while on parole, 20.2% drank to excess, and 2% were victims of the drug habit (Appendix D, Table 3–22). Because our picture of the illicit sex practices and other vicious habits of the parolees is so incomplete, no attempt is made to compare the incidence of such practices during parole and prior to commitment. We can infer, however, that there was some falling off during parole in illicit sex practices and perhaps in other bad habits, which may largely have been due to the deterrent effect of parole supervision.

Church attendance. In view of the fact that in more than half the cases the regularity of church attendance during parole is unknown, we cannot draw any definite conclusions regarding attention to religious duties. However, in the 119 cases in which the information was available, we find that 40.3% of the parolees attended church regularly, 58% attended irregularly, and 1.7% did not attend at all. Within a year of commitment to the Reformatory, only 13.5% of the women had attended church regularly, while 36.5% did not attend at all (Appendix D, Table 3–24b).

8. Conclusion

The meagreness of the records kept by the parole agents regarding the activities of their charges is a reflection of the weaknesses of parole as customarily practised. Adequate case histories, which should include detailed diaries of the supervision process, are indispensable to effective parole. As to some phases of the parole life of our women, however, sufficient information was obtainable on which to base conclusions.

From the findings we see that there was some, and often a marked, improvement in our women during parole. This is reflected in better environmental conditions, in stronger family ties, in better work habits, in greater assumption of economic responsibilities, in less harmful use of leisure, in improved habits, in better companionships, in greater attention to church duties, and so on. That this improvement is partly due to the fact of parole itself may be inferred from the findings that the parolees whose supervision was unbroken were to a greater extent non-delinquent during parole than the group whose oversight was for one reason or another interrupted; and also from the fact, revealed in Chapter XV, that some women responded well to parole, but recidivated after the expiration of sentence. Therefore more intensive and extensive parole oversight is much to be desired.

While the parole agents made some effort to rehabilitate their charges, as is shown particularly in their placing of many of the women in better homes and neighbourhoods than they had lived in before commitment, there was much room for constructive case work with the parolees and their families, especially in the matter of domestic relations and the wholesome use of leisure.

It is obvious that too much time elapses between the release of the women on parole and the first contact of the parole agents with them or their families. This shortcoming is greatly to be decried, because early contact with our women resulted in lessened delinquency during parole. The average frequency of visits of the parole agents should be greater, as we see that those of our women who were more frequently visited were in lesser proportion delinquent.

Since the object of reformative efforts should be the more or less permanent rehabilitation of offenders, rather than merely their good behaviour while under parole supervision, it is necessary to study the conduct of our women after oversight had been completely removed. In several succeeding chapters, therefore, significant findings are presented as to the careers of these women for a reasonable time following the expiration of their sentences.

CHAPTER XII

AFTER EXPIRATION OF SENTENCE

1. Introductory

Significance of post-sentence period. Of greater significance even than the status of parolees is the behaviour of ex-prisoners after the expiration of sentence, when they are no longer under legal restraint. During parole ex-inmates of a correctional institution are, after all, still under official control, and they would still have to serve portions of the uncompleted sentence behind lock and bars were they to violate the conditions of parole. Unquestionably, the knowledge that, without a new trial, they are subject to return to prison for violation of parole operates as a deterrent influence on many " graduates " of correctional institutions. The true gauge of the efficacy of the social equipment for coping with criminality comes only after all official restraint has been removed and the ex-prisoner is left to his own devices. A realistic system of criminal justice must aim to bring about more than a temporary deflection from criminal activity.

Did our women improve or retrogress after the expiration of sentence? It is to this crucial question that we turn our attention in this and the next chapter. In the analysis, comparisons are made, as a rule, between the status of the women prior to their commitment to the Reformatory and during a five-year period following the expiration of sentence.[1] Where possible, a comparison with their status during parole is also made.

Time span. The post-sentence period as we have defined it embraces five years from the date of the expiration of the sentence of our women to the Reformatory. It therefore applies to the entire group of women — the fraction who served their full sentence in the Reformatory as well as those who served part of their sentence on parole. For the sake of brevity, however, we shall sometimes refer to it as the " post-parole " period. In 18.4% of the cases the five-year period which we are studying extends to the year 1926, in 27.6% to 1927, in 28.6% to 1928, and in 25.4% to 1929 (Appendix D, Table 4-1).

Interviews with ex-prisoners. In the course of the research 44.6% of the ex-prisoners were personally interviewed by our investigators; of 35.4% more, although the women themselves were not seen, near relatives such as parents or siblings or husbands were interviewed. In 4.6% of the cases neither the offender

---

[1] Owing to the nature of certain factors this span is sometimes compared with the last year preceding commitment of the women to the Reformatory.

nor her relatives could be seen, but other persons who knew them well, such as social workers, police, employers, ministers, were interviewed. In but 15.4% of the cases were no interviews carried on, the information about the women being secured from the already recorded data of social agencies, courts, institutions, and the like (Appendix D, Table 4–H58).[2]

Age at end of post-parole period. At the end of the five-year period the average age of the women was 32.6 years ± .24, 15.7% of them being between twenty-one and twenty-five years of age, 35.5% between twenty-six and thirty, 18.5% between thirty-one and thirty-five, 14.7% between thirty-six and forty, 8.1% between forty-one and forty-five, 4.8% between forty-six and fifty, and 2.7% fifty-one years or older (Appendix D, Table 4–2).

Whereabouts at end of five-year period. At the end of the post-parole period a total of 34, or 6.8%, of our five hundred women were deceased.[3] Twenty-four (4.8%) of the women were in penal institutions, 19 of them being in institutions in Massachusetts and 5 in other states. Twenty-seven (5.4%) of the women were in non-penal institutions. Of these, 13 were in schools for the feeble-minded, 12 in hospitals for the mentally diseased, and 1 in a hospital for chronic physical diseases. It is to be remembered that a total of 18 women were in institutions throughout the five-year period. Ninety-six women (19.2%) were resident in Boston or vicinity at the end of the post-parole period, 141 (28.2%) were living in other cities in Massachusetts, 124 (24.8%) were living in other states.[4] Thirteen women (2.6%) were living in foreign countries at the end of the five-year period.[5] Four women (.8%) were fugitives from justice. Eight of the women (1.6%) were, at the end of the five-year period, drifting about the country. The whereabouts of 8 more (1.6%), though not definitely known at the end of the period, was known for part of the time; and the whereabouts of only 21 (4.2%) of the entire five hundred women was completely unknown throughout the five-year period (Appendix D, Table 4–H59). If we consider the location of our women at the end of the five-year period in the light of the fact that only 1% of them had never lived in Massachusetts prior to their commitment to the

[2] Appendix A, " Method of This Research," contains a detailed description of the way in which the field investigations were carried on.

[3] The causes of death were as follows: tuberculosis, 7; pneumonia, 5 (with contributing causes in 2 cases); Hodgkins disease and pneumonia, 1; influenza and pneumonia, 2; bronchitis and acute dilation of heart, 1; cardiovascular renal disease, 1; nephritis, 2; syphilis, 1; cerebral hæmorrhage, 2; cancer, 2; alcoholism, 2; accident, 3; suicide, 1; poisoning (probably suicide), 1; operation for intestinal obstruction, 1; diphtheria, 1; erysipelas (with contributing causes), 1.

[4] Of these, 22 women were in Connecticut, 8 in New Hampshire, 10 in Rhode Island, 8 in Maine, 1 in Vermont, 37 in New York, 10 in Pennsylvania, 1 in Delaware, 1 in Maryland, 8 in New Jersey, 1 in the District of Columbia, 3 in Ohio, 1 in Illinois, 1 in Missouri, 1 in Michigan, 1 in Wisconsin, 1 in West Virginia, 1 in North Carolina, 1 in South Carolina, 5 in California, 1 in Arizona, and 1 in Washington.

[5] Of these, two women were in England, one in Germany, one in Lithuania, one in Portugal, one in Poland, three in Canada, one in Prince Edward Island, one in Nova Scotia, and one in the Azores.

Reformatory, and that only 8% more had lived in the state for less than two years, we see how widely they have scattered since release (Appendix D, Table 1–7).

With whom resident. Of those women whose whereabouts was known, 9.6% were living with one or both parents at the end of the five-year period, 2.6% were living with sisters or brothers or other relatives, 45.1% with their husbands, 8.9% with lovers, 2.4% with married children, 6.3% in homes of employers, 13.1% were living alone, and 12% were in institutions (Appendix D, Table 4–3). Comparing these facts with the prior situation, we see that a far lower proportion of our women were now living in their parental homes or residing with siblings or other relatives than at the time of their commitment to the Reformatory. Slightly fewer women were now living alone or making their homes with lovers. On the other hand a far greater proportion of them were living with their husbands. The proportion of women residing with married children or living in the homes of employers is about the same at the end of the post-parole period as at the time of commitment (Appendix E, Table 8).

2. Environmental Circumstances

Length of time in community. For what part of the sixty-month post-parole period were our women free agents in the community? Sixteen of them were dead and therefore excluded from any further consideration. Eighteen more did not live in the community at all during the five-year period, as they were in institutions of one kind or another throughout the period. Seven women were at liberty in the community for less than a year, 11 for one to two years, 13 for two to three years, 28 for three to four years, 43 for four to five years, and 324 (70.4% of the total of 460 about whom this information was known) throughout the five-year period, except possibly for very brief stays in hospitals. The mean number of months during which our women lived in the community (of those who were in the community at all) in the five-year post-parole period is 40.94 months ± 1.02 (Appendix D, Table 4–8).

Institutional experiences. A fourth (25.4%) of all our women were in penal or non-penal institutions at one time or another during the post-parole period, as compared to 54.7% who had been in institutions at any time prior to commitment to the Reformatory (Appendix E, Table 7). Of the 134 institutional experiences which they had during the post-parole period, 17 (12.7%) were commitments to schools for the feeble-minded, 12 (9%) were to a House of the Good Shepherd, 19 (14.2%) were commitments to hospitals for mental diseases, 9 (6.7%) to hospitals for chronic physical diseases, and 76 (56.7%) to penal institutions [6] (Appendix D, Table 4–9).

[6] From this point on are excluded from consideration the sixteen women who died before the beginning of the five-year follow-up period (ten died in the Reformatory, and six during parole), the eighteen who were in institutions throughout the five-year period, three who died very shortly

Mobility. About half the group (52.8%) moved so much during the post-parole period as not to take root in any one community (Appendix D, Table 4–12b). Of those who changed residence so often, 45.2% moved excessively (that is, more than once a year) within one city, and 54.8% moved from one city to another on an average of once in two years (Appendix D, Table 4–13).[7] In comparing the extent of mobility prior to commitment, during parole, and within the post-parole period, we find that moving about has gradually lessened, from 66.2% prior to commitment to 55.8% during parole and 52.8% during the post-parole period (Appendix E, Table 5). This is reflective of a growing stability in our women and may partially be explained by their advancing years and partially, perhaps, by their marital adjustments.[8] Even of those who did move excessively, however, more changed residence within one city, and fewer moved from city to city (Appendix E, Table 6).

Household stability. Over a fourth (28.8%) of our women resided in only one household during the time they were at liberty in the community in the post-parole period; 19% of them resided in two different households, 12.7% in three, 39.5% in four or more (Appendix D, Table 4–16).[9] There were more changes of household during the post-parole period than prior to commitment, despite the fact that the women did not move about quite so much as before. The mean number of changes in household during the post-parole period was 3.19 ± .08 as compared to 1.87 ± .04 prior to commitment, and 2.89 ± .09 during parole (Appendix E, Table 9). This can be accounted for by the fact that the women were now older and had been busy setting up their independent households.

Home and neighbourhood conditions. During the post-parole period a fourth (24.9%) of the women lived in homes in which the physical conditions were for all or most of the period good,[10] 44.1% lived in fair homes, and 31% in poor homes (Appendix D, Table 4–10). The home conditions of our women had greatly improved, far fewer now living in poor homes than within a year of commitment — 31% as compared to 67%. Almost twice the proportion of women now lived in good and fair homes (Appendix E, Table 1).[11]

Throughout the post-parole period, or for such portions of it as they were in the community, 47.1% of the women resided in urban areas, partly residential in character; 25.6% of them lived either in residential urban districts or in residential suburbs, 8.2% in towns of under five thousand population or in rural

---

after the beginning of the five-year period, and one who was sent into an institution very shortly after the beginning of the period.

[7] For definitions, see Appendix C, *Mobility*.

[8] See pp. 221 et seq.

[9] For definition, see Appendix C, *Household Stability*.

[10] Ibid., *Home — Physical*.

[11] As to certain factors it was not possible to make comparisons with the parole period. See footnote 1, p. 200.

districts. A fifth (19.1%) more of the women made their homes for part of the time in cities and part of the time in the country, shifting about so much from one kind of neighbourhood to another that it was not possible to classify their residence specifically [12] (Appendix D, Table 4-11). During the post-parole period there was a falling off in permanent residence in urban areas, and more moving back and forth from country to city (Appendix E, Table 2).

During all or most of the time that they were in the community in the five-year period, 24.9% of the women resided in neighbourhoods in which the influences might be considered good,[13] 44.1% in fair neighbourhoods, and 31% in neighbourhoods in which the influences were decidedly harmful (Appendix D, Table 4-12a). As in home conditions, so we see a decided improvement in neighbourhood influences, a greater proportion of the women living in good neighbourhoods during the post-parole period than within a year of commitment (24.9% : 6.2%), more in fair neighbourhoods (44.% : 23.6%), and far fewer in neighbourhoods in which the influences were poor (31.% : 70.2%) (Appendix E, Table 3). The neighbourhood influences surrounding the first place of residence on parole were good in twice the proportion of cases as during the post-parole period; but this can be accounted for by the fact that the parolees had been largely placed by the parole agents, who naturally exercised care in establishing their charges in neighbourhoods where the influences were not harmful.

Moral standards of the home. During the post-parole period 25.6% of our women resided in households in which the moral standards were always or in the main good,[14] 26.2% in homes in which they might be considered fair, and the substantial proportion of 48.2% in households in which the moral standards were generally poor (Appendix D, Table 4-14a).[15] Nevertheless, a far greater proportion of our women now lived in homes in which the moral standards were good than within the year prior to their commitment (25.6% : 10.4%); and many fewer lived in homes of poor moral standards (48.2% : 74.9%). (Appendix E, Table 4).

Summary of environmental conditions. Let us now summarize the environmental circumstances of our women during the post-parole period as reflected by home conditions, neighbourhood influences, and the moral standards of the households in which they resided. In only 11.6% of the cases could the environmental conditions be considered *wholesome,* in that the physical aspects of the home, the neighbourhood influences, and the moral standards were all good. In 48.6% of the cases, the environmental conditions might be deemed *negative,* in that the home, the neighbourhood influences, and moral standards were at least

---

[12] For definition, see Appendix C, *Neighbourhood Type.*

[13] Ibid., *Neighbourhood Influences.*

[14] Ibid., *Moral Standards.*

[15] In 134 of the cases the poor moral standards of the household were the result of the delinquency of husbands (Appendix D, Table 4-20b).

not entirely bad.[16] In 39.8% of the cases the environmental circumstances were *poor* during the post-parole period, in that the home, the neighbourhood, and the moral standards of the household were unwholesome [17] (Appendix D, Table 4–15).

3. Marital Status and Family Relationships

Introductory. As we want particularly to compare the marriages which occurred prior to the commitment of the women to the Reformatory with those which took place after their release, we have included for consideration all the marriages which occurred during parole as well as during the five-year post-parole period. One would like to know whether any changes took place in the attitude of the women toward marriage since their Reformatory experience, whether they were more careful in their selection of a mate, whether there was as high a proportion of " forced " marriages after release as before commitment, whether the conjugal relationships in the newer marriages were any happier than those of the marriages made prior to commitment.

Number of marriages. Between the time that our women were released on parole and the end of the five-year post-parole period, 233 marriages took place. Two of these were marriages of Negroes and whites (Appendix D, Table 4–H66). About half the women (49.4%) married at one time or another between release from the Reformatory and the end of the five-year post-parole period, 94.5% of whom married once during this time, 5% twice, and .5% three times (Appendix D, Table 4–4).

Marital status. At the time of their commitment to the Reformatory, 48.8% of the women were single, 8.9% were married and living with their husbands, 36.7% were separated, 3.2% were divorced, and 2.4% were widows [18] (Appendix E, Table 10). Of 451 women who were alive at the beginning of the five-year post-parole period and whose marital condition was known, 39.9% were single, 21.7% were married and living with their husbands, 30.2% were separated, 5.5% were divorced, and 2.7% were widows (Appendix D, Table 4–H93). By the end of the five-year period only 16.2% of the women were single, 43.5% were married and living with their husbands, 28.5% were separated, 8% were divorced, and 3.8% were widowed. Thus we see that while, as the years passed, there were naturally fewer unmarried women, the incidence of separation and divorce remained about the same as before. This further confirms the instability of the marital relationship in the lives of women of the type with whom we are concerned in this study.

Courtship practices. Were there any appreciable differences between the pre-

[16] They were all fair; or two of them were fair and one was good or poor; or one was good and two were poor; or one was good, one fair, and one poor.

[17] Or at least two of them were poor.

[18] If a woman died during the five-year post-parole period, but before the end of it, her marital status at the time of her death was tabulated.

commitment and post-parole periods in the manner in which our women met the men whom they married? Of the marriages occurring after release from the Reformatory, 33.8% resulted from "pick-up" meetings, 39% from casual acquaintanceships, and 27.2% from proper introductions by parents, relatives, or friends [19] (Appendix D, Table 4–H63). There was a slightly higher proportion of "pick-up" marriages after release than before commitment (33.8% : 31.2%), a considerably higher proportion of marriages resulting from casual acquaintance (39% : 29%), and proportionately fewer marriages following introduction of the couple by parents, relatives, or friends (27.2% : 39.8%) (Appendix E, Table 21). This, although at first blush surprising, is readily explained on the ground that our women had long discarded the protection of home and parents and were making contacts more on their own initiative.

In 9.6% of all these marriages an acquaintance of less than three months preceded marriage, in 30.7% three to six months, in 16.5% seven to twelve months, and in 43.2% over a year. The mean number of months elapsing between acquaintance and marriage was 10.22 ± .28 (Appendix D, Table 4–H64). Although the meeting of couples was more casual than before, they "kept company" longer than formerly, 43.2% of the marriages after release from the Reformatory being consummated after an acquaintance of over twelve months, as compared to 26.6% of the marriages which took place before (Appendix E, Table 22). And it is to be noted that only 24.1% of these marriages were "forced," as compared to 34.1% of those which took place previous to commitment.[20] Greater age and experience of course has something to do with this situation.

Conjugal relations and marital responsibility. Among all the women who were married after release and who lived with their husbands at any time during the five-year post-parole period, the conjugal relations of 40.3% were good, of 24% fair, of 35.7% poor [21] (Appendix D, Table 4–H71). This is a marked improvement in marital compatibility, the conjugal relations in 40.3% of the subsequent marriages being good as compared with but 8.3% of the marriages which had been entered into previous to commitment [22] (Appendix D, Table 4–H71; Appendix E, Table 25). Correlative with greater felicity in the marital relationship is a greater assumption of marital responsibilities [23] (Appendix D, Table 4–H72; Appendix E, Table 28). There was also manifest a greater assumption of their responsibilities on the part of husbands with whom marriage was contracted after release from the Reformatory than before commitment (62.1% : 26.4%) (Appendix D, Table 4–H73; Appendix E, Table 26). This may be partly ex-

[19] For definition, see Appendix C, *Manner of Meeting Husband.*

[20] Ibid., *Marital — Forced Marriages* (Appendix D, Table 4–H62; Appendix E, Table 23).

[21] Ibid., *Conjugal Relations.*

[22] Ibid., *Conjugal Relations.*

[23] Ibid., *Attitude to Marital Responsibility.* In arriving at the above figures we have excluded from consideration the marital relationships of those women who were separated or divorced from their husbands prior to the beginning of the five-year post-parole period.

plained by the fact that during the post-parole period there was greater employ-ment of the husbands, three quarters of them (74.5%) being at least fairly regularly employed [24] (Appendix D, Table 4–H70).

The fact that in 59.9% of all the marriages which occurred subsequent to re-lease of the women from the Reformatory the couples were still living together at the end of the five-year period, while in only 15.4% of the marriages which took place before were they living together at the time that the wives were committed to the Reformatory, is also indicative of the greater stability in marital relation-ships. As to the duration of the marriages that occurred after release and that were terminated, 4.4% of them were dissolved in less than six months, 6.2% after six to twelve months, 3.5% after twelve to eighteen months, 3.5% after eighteen to twenty-four months, 5.7% after two to three years; 4.9% lasted three to four years, 8.4% four years or longer, while in 3.5% of the marriages the couples separated off and on. The average duration of marriages contracted and terminated after release was 31.7 months ± 1.94 (Appendix D, Table 4–H61), this being about the same as for marriages disrupted before commitment (35.9 months ± 1.4) (Appendix E, Table 24). Of the marriages that were entered upon after release and which were broken up (88 in all), 87.5% were terminated by desertion, separation, or divorce and 12.5% by death (Appendix D, Table 4–H65). A similar proportion of the marriages terminated prior to commitment came to an end in the same way (Appendix E, Table 27).

An important constituent of marital felicity is the skill of wives in home-making.[25] In 49.2% of all the marriages which occurred subsequent to release, the wives were good homemakers, in 37.6% they were fair, in 13.2% poor (Ap-pendix D, Table 4–H74; see also 4–19a). A much higher proportion of the women who married after release were competent homemakers than were those who married before commitment to the Reformatory (49.2%:8%) (Ap-pendix E, Table 26.)

It is obvious, therefore, that marital adjustment was far greater after release from the Reformatory than prior to commitment. Half of all the marriages which were entered upon after release can be deemed successful, in that not only did the couples live together continuously, but both assumed their marital re-sponsibilities [26] (Appendix D, Table 4–H75); while only 17.1% of all the mar-riages which took place before the commitment of the women to the Reforma-tory could be considered successful (Appendix E, Table 30).

Relation to children. In 47.8% of all the cases of women who had any living children (legitimate or illegitimate, including stepchildren), their attitude to-ward them during the post-parole period was good, in that they were very fond of their children and took excellent care of them; or, in instances in which the children were for various reasons not living with the mother, she nevertheless

[24] For definition, see Appendix C, *Industrial Stability.*
[25] Ibid., *Competence as Homemaker.*
[26] Ibid., *Marital History Judgment.*

maintained contact with them to the extent possible within the limits of the particular situation. In 21.9% of the cases the attitude of the women to their children was only " fair," in that they either were indifferent toward them or, though fond of them, neglected them because of drink, absorption in a lover, or like reasons; or, if the children were not living with them, the women, although not showing any particular interest, at least kept in touch with them. In 30.3% of the cases the attitude of the women toward their children was definitely " poor," in that they gave them no supervision or affection or were actually abusive to them, or, if the children were not living with their mothers, they were entirely out of touch with them (Appendix D, Table 4–20a). Many more of the women had close ties to their offspring during the post-parole period than prior to commitment (47.8% : 14.2%) (Appendix E, Table 11). This is particularly encouraging because it suggests that a wholesome and constructive attitude toward children can be engendered by a reformatory. It should be borne in mind, however, that some of this improvement in attitude is no doubt due to increasing maturity and greater stability in marital relationships.

Relation to relatives. During the post-parole period 53.9% of our women were in frequent touch with their parents or with their brothers and sisters if their parents were not living. In 21.2% of the cases, the women were in contact with their nearest relatives only when they themselves were in need of assistance. In 24.9% of the cases they scarcely maintained any communication with their parents or siblings (Appendix D, Table 4–17a).

Summary of family relationships. Considering, now, in summary the family relationships of our women — that is, their attitude toward husband and children if they were married and living with their husbands at any time during the five-year post-parole period, or to their parents or other near relatives if they were single or had been separated, divorced, or widowed before the beginning of the five-year post-parole period — 43.3% of our women maintained good family relationships, and 56.7% did not (Appendix D, Table 4–14b).[27] The family relations of our women were nevertheless very much better during the post-parole period than prior to commitment, when only 12.6% of them could be deemed successful in their relationship to their families.[28]

4. Industrial History

Usual occupation. During the post-parole period the usual occupation of 9.9% of our women was at domestic service; 22.3% of them were engaged in factory work, 10.2% in work in restaurants or hotels, 2.9% worked in stores, 8.2% did housework by the day, but lived at home, 22.5% were usually occupied

---

[27] For definition, see Appendix C, *Family Relationships.*

[28] During the parole period, however, a greater proportion of the parolees maintained good family relations (59.6%), which is of course due to the vigilance of the parole officers (Appendix E, Table 12).

in their own housekeeping affairs, 3.4% were idle most of the time, and 14.8% were usually engaged in some illegitimate employment (Appendix D, Table 4–33).[29]

There was less employment in domestic service during the post-parole period than prior to commitment or during parole. In the parole period there had been a great increase in the proportion of women engaged in domestic service, because the parole agents were very much inclined to place the women in such work. During the post-parole period, also, fewer women worked in factories than previously. This falling off had already manifested itself during parole and can be accounted for by the fact that marriage diverted quite a few of our women from gainful employment to their own housekeeping. A slightly greater proportion of women now worked as waitresses, however, or were chambermaids, or were employed in stores, or did housework by the day; and slightly more women made their livelihood in illegitimate ways during the post-parole period than before (Appendix E, Table 31).

Only 16.8% of the women actually utilized the occupational training which they received in the Reformatory, either directly, by engaging in the same occupation, or indirectly, by utilizing in some other work the technique acquired in the institution (Appendix D, Table 4–38a). This is a slight decrease from the proportion of women who, during parole, in any way utilized the occupation in which they had been engaged in the Reformatory (Appendix E, Table 36). Although complete information is not available as to why our women did not apply the skills which they had acquired in the institution, sufficient is at hand to conclude that the methods of work in competitive industry are different from those taught in the Reformatory. In some instances there was no opportunity for a particular type of work in the community in which a woman happened to reside, and in most cases she preferred some other type of employment (Appendix D, Table 4–H79).

Earnings. The average weekly earnings of our women in legitimate occupations during the post-parole period were less than five dollars a week in 2.9% of the cases, five to ten dollars in 22.4%, ten to fifteen in 51.8%, fifteen to twenty in 15.9%, and twenty to thirty in 7% (Appendix D, Table 4–35). The average earnings during the post-parole period were $13.10 a week ± .23, an increase over the average of $11.25 ± .14 earned by the women prior to commitment (Appendix E, Table 34).

The highest salary received by our women during the post-parole period was nine dollars or less in 7% of the cases, ten to fifteen dollars in 23.7%, fifteen to twenty in 37.2%, twenty to twenty-five in 17.3%, and twenty-five or more in 14.8% (Appendix D, Table 4–36). The mean for the group of women gainfully employed was $18.95 ± .37, which is more by several dollars than their highest

---

[29] For definition, see Appendix C, *Usual Occupation.* One third of all our women were at one time or another engaged in an illegitimate occupation during the post-parole period, regardless of whether they were usually engaged in it or not (Appendix D, Table 4–38b).

earnings prior to commitment and during parole, when they averaged $15.45 ± .22 and $12.35 ± .19 respectively (Appendix E, Table 33).

Steadiness of employment. During the five-year period 18.2% of those women who were gainfully employed worked regularly,[30] 31.8% fairly regularly, and 50% irregularly. In this latter group are included 22.3% who earned a livelihood mostly in illegitimate occupations (Appendix D, Table 4–34a). Prior to commitment 7.5% of the women had worked steadily; during parole, 37.5%; and during the post-parole period, 18.2% (Appendix E, Table 37). Hence a slightly greater proportion of our women were regular workers during the post-parole period. The fact that even a greater proportion had been steady workers during parole is probably due to the vigilance of the parole officers and to a realization by their charges that they had to adhere to the rules of parole in order to avoid being returned to the Reformatory.

The longest time which our women held a job during the post-parole period was two months or less in 17.8% of the cases, three to six months in 11.6%, six months to a year in 20.2%, one to two years in 15.5%, two to three in 16.3%, three to four in 10.1%, and four or five in 8.5% (Appendix D, Table 4–37). The average was 20.02 months ± 1.03, indicating but a slight improvement over the situation prior to commitment, when the longest period that the women held their jobs averaged 19.4 months ± .72 (Appendix E, Table 32).

Work habits. The work habits of our women during the post-parole period might be considered good [31] in 25.4% of the cases, fair in 33%, and poor in 41.6%. In this latter group are included the women who were usually employed in illegitimate occupations (Appendix D, Table 4–34b). There was during the post-parole period a slight improvement in the work habits of our women over the time prior to commitment, when only 16.2% had good work habits. The gains made during the parole period in improved habits of work were held during the post-parole period (Appendix E, Table 38). Two fifths (41.4%) of the women usually left or were discharged from post-parole jobs for their own fault — because they were inefficient, dishonest, addicted to drink, and the like (Appendix D, Table 4–39). Far more women terminated their employment in similar manner prior to commitment, however, when 83.8% lost their jobs for such reasons. The greater stability of employment established during parole was maintained throughout the post-parole period (Appendix E, Table 35).

Summary of industrial adjustment.[32] If we gauge the adjustment which our women made in industrial life during the post-parole period by a composite of their steadiness of employment and their work habits, we see that 18.6% of the women made a satisfactory adaptation — that is, were steady workers and had

---

[30] For definition, see Appendix C, *Steadiness of Employment.* In the case of women who had to work for only a part of the post-parole period — e.g., until they married — their steadiness of employment up to that time is considered.

[31] Ibid., *Work Habits.*

[32] Ibid., *Industrial History Judgment.*

good work habits — 32% were only fairly successful, as they worked irregularly or at best with only fair regularity, though they had good work habits, or they worked regularly, but their work habits were only fair or poor; while 49.4% of the women were industrial liabilities, as they had poor work habits and were irregularly employed, or at best employed with only fair regularity, or they engaged in illicit occupations to the exclusion of any or all legitimate employment (Appendix D, Table 4–32). There was a marked increase in the proportion of women who successfully adjusted themselves in industry, from 2.9% prior to commitment to 18.6% after expiration of sentence (Appendix E, Table 39).

As might well be expected, the women who were employed steadily also had good work habits. Thus, of those whose work habits were good, 53.7% were regularly employed and only 4.5% were irregular workers; of those having fair work habits, 16.7% were steadily employed and 19% irregularly; of those whose work habits were poor, not one was found to be regularly or even fairly regularly employed.

To what extent the habits of industry and the training acquired in the Reformatory contributed to the industrial adjustment of the women may be partially inferred from the fact that there is some association between the work habits of the women in the Reformatory and during the post-parole period. Thus, 28.7% of those who were deemed good workers in the institution proved successful industrially later, as did 13.4% of those who had there worked fairly well; while only 5% of those who were poor workers in the Reformatory succeeded later. Further, in relating the number of occupational experiences the women had in the Reformatory to their later industrial adjustment, it is found that those who experienced only one or two changes of occupation were to a greater extent successful industrially than those who experienced three or more shifts. This may be somewhat explained by the possibility that in the Reformatory those inmates who are capable workers are only occasionally shifted from one type of occupation to another, while those not making good vocational adaptations are shifted about in the hope that their particular niche may be discovered. But of the women who later used the techniques which they learned in the institution, a somewhat greater proportion made a satisfactory industrial adjustment than did the others (25% : 17.2%).

On the whole it must be concluded that the improvement in the industrial life of the women was not chiefly due to their Reformatory experience, but should rather be credited to their generally increasing stability.

5. Economic Condition and Economic Responsibility

Economic condition. During the five-year post-parole period 13.6% of our women were in comfortable economic circumstances,[38] 80.1% in marginal con-

[38] For definition, see Appendix C, *Economic Condition.*

dition, 6.3% were continually dependent on public or private aid (Appendix D, Table 4–28b). A substantially greater proportion of the women were in comfortable circumstances during the post-parole period than within a year of commitment (13.6% : 6.7%), and many fewer were dependent (14.9% : 6.3%) (Appendix E, Table 15). In this connection it should be pointed out that of those who were in comfortable economic circumstances, 78.6% were married and living with their husbands, while of those who were dependent on charity only 30.8% were married and living with their husbands.

Economic responsibility. During the post-parole period 63.2% of the women met their economic responsibilities;[34] 15.3% did not; in 19.7% of the cases self-support was not necessary, and in 1.8% more it was not possible because of chronic illness. Omitting now from consideration those women who did not have to support themselves or were unable to do so, 80.5% of the remainder carried out their economic obligations. About the same proportion of the women met their economic responsibilities during the post-parole period as either before or after (Appendix E, Table 14). It will be remembered that the substantial meeting of economic responsibilities prior to commitment is about the brightest spot in the pre-Reformatory careers of our women. As to the meeting of economic obligations during parole, the fact of supervision by the parole department undoubtedly had something to do with this.

In only 26.1% of the cases did the women themselves (if they were single or had been separated, widowed, or divorced before the beginning of the five-year post-parole period) or their husbands (if they lived together at any time during the period) have any savings during the post-parole period; 73.9% of them had no savings (Appendix D, Table 4–27). The saving habit was slightly more prevalent after parole than before commitment, when but 14.1% of the women or their husbands had any savings (Appendix E, Table 16). Whether the habit of thrift was instilled in the Reformatory can only be inferred from individual case histories.

6. Conclusion

Thus far we have seen what changes have occurred after the expiration of sentence from the Reformatory, in the environmental circumstances of our women, in their marital and family relationships, in their industrial adjustments, and in their economic life.

We now turn our attention to their recreations, habits, and delinquencies, and to the attitude of the community toward them as ex-inmates of a penal institution.

[34] For definition, see Appendix C, *Economic Responsibility.*

CHAPTER XIII

AFTER EXPIRATION OF SENTENCE (*continued*)

1. Introductory

Continuing the analysis of the careers of our women during the five years after their sentences had expired, we now examine into their recreational life, their companionships and haunts, their habits (particularly their illicit sexual activities); and consider the incidence of illegitimate pregnancies and of venereal reinfection among them; their conflicts with the law, and the attitude of the community toward them as ex-prisoners.

It will be valuable, also, to determine the extent to which the delinquency of our women during the five-year period is an index of their success or failure in their other activities.

2. Recreations and Habits

Constructive recreations and interests. During the post-parole period only 4.3% of the women spent their leisure hours in any recreations, or had any interests, which might be considered constructive, such as membership in well-supervised clubs or taking vocational courses, or studying music, and the like [1] (Appendix D, Table 4–21b). Such wholesome use of leisure during the post-parole period, rare as it was, nevertheless occurred more frequently than prior to commitment, when only .8% of the women had any constructive recreations or interests. It should be recalled, however, that during the parole period as many as 9.2% of the women spent their leisure wisely. This is no doubt due to the fact that they were under supervision and that the parole officers urged such wholesome means of expression (Appendix E, Table 41).

Companionships and haunts. The companionships of our women might be considered harmless [2] in 37.3% of the cases, and harmful in 62.7% (Appendix D, Table 4–22b). This represents a marked falling off in disreputable associations as compared to the year prior to commitment, when 97.3% of our women went about with companions whose influence could be none other than harmful. During parole, however, only 44.2% of the women had disreputable associates (Appendix E, Table 43). Here again the very fact of parole supervision and

---

[1] For definition, see Appendix C, *Constructive Recreations and Interests.*
[2] Ibid., *Companionships.*

possibly the fear of revocation of the permit to be at liberty had much to do with this decrease. The haunts or places of recreation of our women during the post-parole period might be considered harmless in 48.8% of the cases and harmful in 51.2% (Appendix D, Table 4–23).[3] There was considerably less frequenting of disreputable places, such as houses of ill fame, cheap cafés, gambling houses, than within a year of commitment, when 89.8% of our women frequented such places of recreation (Appendix E, Table 44). Thus, although our women did not utilize their leisure constructively, they at least to some extent relinquished harmful companionships and ceased to patronize disreputable places of recreation.

Bad habits. What of the habits of our women during the post-parole period? Seven tenths (71.5%) of them indulged in sex delinquency of one type or another, at least 10.2% were habitually stealing, at least 33.3% were addicted to drinking, and at least 4% of them to drugs (Appendix D, Table 4–24). Although they may have had various other bad habits, such as gambling, it was not possible to secure complete information about them (Appendix D, Table 4–24). Nevertheless, a fourth of the women (23.4%) may be said to have had no outstanding bad habits during the post-parole period, while 76.6% of them had one or more of the bad habits mentioned. But fewer of the women had such bad habits during the post-parole period than within a year of their commitment to the Reformatory (76.6% : 99.6%) (Appendix E, Table 45).

Summary of leisure and habits. Certainly definite improvement is manifest in the companionships, recreations, haunts, and habits of our women during the post-parole period. Although only 2.7% of them had no bad habits and at the same time used their leisure hours constructively,[4] almost one third of the women (30.6%), though having no bad habits, at least did not indulge in harmful recreational outlets; while two thirds of them (66.7%) had pronouncedly poor habits, associated with undesirables, and indulged in harmful recreations (Appendix D, Table 4–21a). Here again we see that there was considerably less harmful use of leisure and bad habits during the post-parole period than within a year of commitment (66.7% : 98%). During parole, however, only 51% of the women used their leisure harmfully and had bad habits (Appendix E, Table 40). This doubtless indicates a definite influence of parole oversight and the fear of return to the Reformatory.

Church attendance. Was there an increase or a falling off in church attendance during the post-parole period? Only 16% of our women attended church regularly,[5] 46.7% occasionally, 37.3% not at all (Appendix D, Table 4–22a). About the same proportion of women paid regular attention to their church duties within a year of commitment to the Reformatory. During parole, however, a greater proportion of women attended church regularly (Appendix E,

[3] For definition, see Appendix C, *Haunts.*
[4] Ibid., *Leisure and Habits.*
[5] Ibid., *Church Attendance.*

Table 42). This may also be explained by parole supervision and the fact that the parole officers at least reminded the women to attend to their church duties. Many of the Catholic women were returned to the fold during parole, but obviously did not maintain their loyalty.

3. Illicit Sex Life

Nature of sexual immorality. Recalling that all but 1.7% of our women had indulged in illicit sexual activity prior to their commitment to the Reformatory, it is of interest to find that during the post-parole period as many as 28.5% of them were not sexually immoral. During parole, however, 52.9% of the parolees apparently had no illicit sex relationships. This seeming adherence to the tenets of conventional morality during the parole period may be partly due to parole oversight and partly to the fact that the parole officers did not have full information about the sex life of their charges (Appendix E, Table 46). Considering now the character of the illicit sex activity of our women from the point of view of its seriousness,[6] we find that of all the women who committed sex offences during the post-parole period .7% (two women) were known to practise sex perversions;[7] 13.3% were professional prostitutes, 19.1% were occasional prostitutes, and 5.5% were one-man prostitutes, making a total of 37.9% who practised prostitution in some form or other during the post-parole period. A fourth of the women (24.6%) were promiscuous in their sex relationships.[8] A tenth (10.9%) of the women, although married, were promiscuously adulterous while living under the same roof with their husbands, and 2.4% more committed adultery with one man while still residing with their husbands; 14.6% of the women had illicit relations with a fiancé or lived with a man under the guise of marriage. The exact nature of the illicit sex activities of 8.9% more, though suspected, were not definitely ascertainable (Appendix D, Table 4–25).

A comparison of the nature of the most serious illicit sex practices of our women prior to commitment and during the post-parole period indicates a considerable increase in professional prostitution, and a slight increase in prostitution with one man, in promiscuous adultery, and in sex relationships with a fiancé or a lover; but a considerable decrease in occasional prostitution and in the commission of adultery with one man. An equal proportion of unattached women (single, separated, widowed, or divorced before the beginning of the post-parole period) had promiscuous sex relationships during the post-parole period as before commitment (Appendix E, Table 46). Despite the increase in professional prostitution, there is no evidence that the financial rewards were great, a woman rarely receiving more than a dollar or two each time and seldom

---

[6] See explanation on p. 89. Each woman is classified only once.

[7] For definition, see Appendix C, *Sex Irregularity, Nature of Abnormal.*

[8] These women were either single or had been widowed, separated, or divorced before the beginning of the post-parole period.

earning as much as ten dollars a night or forty dollars a week (Appendix D, Table 4–H78).

We were interested to inquire where our women, so many of whom were married and had children or lived with relatives, carried on their illicit sex practices. Such information is difficult to obtain, however. Of the seventy-two instances in which it was available, sexual irregularity took place in the homes of the women in 37.5% of the cases, in houses of ill fame in 31.9%, in hotels or hired rooms in 23.6%, in autos, coal sheds, parks, alleyways, railroad yards, in 7% (Appendix D, Table 4–H77).

Illegitimate pregnancies and children; venereal disease. A fourth (23.7%) of our women had illegitimate pregnancies during the post-parole period (Appendix D, Table 4–26a). This is a considerable decrease from the period prior to commitment, when 54.4% of the women had illegitimate pregnancies (Appendix E, Table 48). However, a part of the falling off in illegitimate pregnancies is due to the fact that some of the women, as a result of operations performed in the Reformatory, were now unable to bear children.[9] Exactly how much of this falling off is due to barrenness, however, how much to application of contraceptive practices, and how much to improved moral standards is impossible to say.

During the five-year period 25.2% of all the women bore children (Appendix D, Table 4–19b). Of these, 62.6% had legitimate children, while 37.4% gave birth to one or more illegitimate ones. This is a considerable decrease in the proportion of women having illegitimate children, for prior to commitment 70.7% of all the women bearing children gave birth to one or more illegitimate children (Appendix E, Table 47). This falling off is no doubt partly associated with increased stability in marital relationships.

Naturally it was very difficult to secure information on the extent of venereal disease among our women during the post-parole period. Statements of venereal condition could be regarded as accurate only when they were culled from official sources or derived from the women themselves. Obviously such information is not readily given. We are quite certain, therefore, that the proportion of women having venereal disease during the post-parole period is actually higher than even our substantial figures indicate. It was found that at least 23.1% of them actually had gonorrhœa or syphilis or both, and that 8.5% more probably had venereal disease, though no official proof thereof could be obtained and the persons furnishing the information could not be considered absolutely reliable (Appendix D, Table 4–5). Even without complete figures, it is obvious that venereal disease is not so widespread in our group as before commitment, when 78.4% of the women were diseased (Appendix E, Table 49). There can be little doubt, therefore, that through the treatment given at the Reformatory the attention of the women was called to the importance of preventing the recur-

[9] See p. 192.

rence of venereal infection, and that a certain proportion of them, at least, applied the knowledge thus gained of preventive measures.

4. Criminality

Frequency of arrests and convictions. We now approach what is perhaps the most important aspect of our inquiry — the delinquency and criminality of our women during the five-year period following expiration of sentence to the Reformatory as compared to the period prior to their commitment to the institution. During this five-year period 62.1% of our women were not arrested at all, while 37.9% were arrested one or more times. This is a considerable decrease in the proportion of women arrested as compared with the period preceding commitment to the Reformatory, when 66.9% of the women had been apprehended. Among the 157 women who were actually arrested, 30.6% were arrested once, 21% twice, 19.7% three or four times, 10.2% five or six times, and 18.5% seven or more times (Appendix D, Table 4–42). The average number of arrests was 3.2 ± .12, which is about the same as the average number of arrests of those arrested prior to commitment (Appendix E, Table 50).

Of those who were actually apprehended during the post-parole period 7% were never convicted, 32.5% were convicted once, 18.5% twice, 17.2% three or four times, 9.6% five or six times, and 15.2% seven or more times, the mean number of convictions being 2.85 ± .12. This becomes significant in relation to the fact that these women were arrested on the average of 3.2 ± .12 times (Appendix D, Table 4–43). It shows at least that once a woman is known to have a criminal record the proportion of convictions is higher than before,[10] for prior to commitment the women were convicted on the average of 2.64 times ± .08, though the average number of arrests was essentially the same as before (Appendix E, Table 52).

Three tenths (30.6%) of the women were arrested only once during the period following expiration of the sentence. Of those arrested two or more times, 11.9% were apprehended once in less than three months,[11] 15.6% once in three to six months, 9.2% once in six to nine months, 9.2% once in nine to twelve months, 16.5% once in twelve to eighteen months, 12.8% once in eighteen to twenty-four months, and 24.8% once in twenty-four months or more, the average frequency of arrests being one every 14.27 months ± .56 (Appendix D, Table 4–44). In comparing frequency of arrest during the post-parole period with that prior to commitment we find that arrests occurred less frequently than before, when those arrested two or more times were apprehended on the average of once in 10.06 months ± .33 (Appendix E, Table 51). This may reflect in part the deterrent effect of punishment, in part a greater facility of the women in avoiding the police, in part actual improvement in conduct.

[10] Compare the "mortality tables" in the Cleveland Survey of Criminal Justice and later surveys.   [11] For definition, see Appendix C, *Frequency of Arrests.*

Offences for which arrested. Of all the types of offences for which the 157 women were arrested at one time or another during the five-year period after expiration of sentence, 51% were arrested for offences against chastity, 45.2% for drunkenness, 37.6% for offences against the public health, safety, and policy, 18.5% for crimes against property rights, 3.2% for offences against the person, 3.2% for offences against family and children, and 1.9% for drug addiction (Appendix D, Table 4-45). As compared to the types of crimes for which the women had been apprehended prior to commitment, there is a slight decrease in the proportion of women arrested for offences against the person and property, and for juvenile offences, such as being a " stubborn child." This latter is of course fully explainable on the ground that offenders who are over seventeen years of age cannot be charged with being " stubborn " children. There is an increase in the proportion of women arrested for offences against the public health, safety, and policy and of those arrested for drunkenness. The proportions of women arrested for offences against chastity, against family and children, and for drug addiction have remained about the same (Appendix E, Table 53).

Of the 680 arrests experienced by 157 women during the post-parole period, 56.9% were for drunkenness, 19.1% were for sex offences (for example prostitution, lewd and lascivious cohabitation, fornication, frequenting houses of ill fame, adultery, common night walking, accosting or soliciting, committing bigamy); 15.7% of the arrests involved various offences against the public health, safety, and policy (for example violating a city ordinance, trespassing, violating a labour law, loitering, violating the Lord's Day, profanity, committing breach of peace, disorderly conduct, vagrancy, keeping and exposing liquor, violating the true name law, possessing a hypodermic needle); 6.2% of the arrests were for offences against property rights, mostly larceny. There were a few cases of burglary, shoplifting, robbery while armed, receiving stolen goods, and concealing leased property. One per cent of the arrests (seven) were for offences against the person, mainly assault and battery, and .5% (three) for drug addiction (Appendix D, Table 4-H56). This is indicative of a decrease in arrests for sex offences, for offences against family and children, for offences against public health, safety, and policy, and for offences against property rights. But it represents a marked increase in arrests for drunkenness. The proportion of arrests for offences against the person and for drug addiction has remained about the same (Appendix E, Table 54).

Dispositions. Of the 157 women actually arrested during the post-parole period, 48.4% were sentenced to penal institutions at one time or another during this period, 56.7% were placed on probation, 26.8% were fined, and 1.3% more were committed to jail for failure to pay a fine; 33.8% of the women had charges against them filed, 11.5% were released from jails by probation officers without trial, 5.1% had charges against them nol-prossed, and 24.8% of the women were released on a finding of no bill or not guilty (Appendix D, Table 4-46).

Of the 680 arrests, 26.2% resulted in commitment, 25.1% in probation, 13% in fines, 17.5% in filing of the case, 3.8% in release by a probation officer, 1.6% in nol-prossing, 7.5% in a finding of no bill or not guilty (Appendix D, Table 4-H57). Comparing this with the disposition of arrests occurring prior to commitment, we find that there has been an increase in the number of fines and in the number of cases filed and nol-prossed, and a decrease in the use of probation and in the finding of not guilty. The proportions of commitments and of releases by probation officers has remained about the same as in the pre-commitment period (Appendix E, Tables 55 and 56). On the whole this indicates a more lenient disposal of cases in the post-parole period than previously and their increased disposition by the prosecuting instead of the sentencing authorities.

Penal experiences. Half of the 157 women who were arrested during the post-parole period were committed to penal institutions of one type or another. Of these, 32 women were committed once, 17 twice, 14 three or four times, and 12 five to eight times (Appendix D, Table 4-6), the average number of commitments being 2.64 ± .14. It is to be noted, however, that 83.7% of all the women had no penal experiences in the five-year post-parole period, as compared to 69.5% prior to commitment to the Reformatory. However, the average number of penal experiences for those having such experiences remained about the same during the post-parole period as prior to commitment (2.64 ± .14 as compared to 2.68 ± .13) (Appendix E, Table 57).

The 76 women experienced 185 periods in penal institutions during the post-parole period. Of these, 178 resulted from commitments imposed during this period, one was the completion of a sentence imposed during the parole period, and six were the result of transfer from some other penal institution. Half (55.7%) of these 185 periods in penal institutions were spent in jails and houses of correction in Massachusetts or in other states; 33% were served at the state farm in Massachusetts, 9.7% in the Women's Reformatory in Massachusetts, 1.1% (two commitments) in reformatories in other states, and .5% (one commitment) in the Department for Defective Delinquents in Massachusetts [12] (Appendix D, Table 4-H60).

---

[12] In 1922 Massachusetts established a special institution for defective delinquents, defined in the statutes as a defendant who is "mentally defective," who "after examination into his record, character and personality . . . has shown himself to be an habitual delinquent or shows tendencies towards becoming such," provided "such delinquency is or may become a menace to the public," and who "is not a proper subject for the schools for the feebleminded or for commitment as an insane person" (*General Laws,* Chap. 333, Sec. 113). Commitment results only after the filing of an application by "a district attorney, probation officer or officer of the department of correction [under which the Massachusetts Reformatory for Women is], public welfare or mental diseases" "at any time prior to the final disposition of a case in which the court might commit an offender to the state prison, the reformatory for women, any jail or house of correction, the Massachusetts reformatory, the state farm, the industrial school for boys, the industrial school for girls, the Lyman school, any county training school, or to the custody of the department of public welfare, for any

Of the 76 women who spent time in penal institutions during the five-year span following expiration of the Reformatory sentence, 23.7% served for less than three months, 15.8% for three to six months, 22.4% for six to twelve months, 15.8% for twelve to eighteen months, 11.8% for eighteen to thirty-six months, 9.2% for thirty-six to sixty months, and 1.3% (one woman) for sixty months. The average length of time spent in penal institutions during the post-parole period was 14.66 months ± 1.01 (Appendix D, Table 4–7), as compared to 19.94 months ± .85 prior to commitment (Appendix E, Table 58). It must be remembered, however, that the pre-Reformatory period was very much longer than five years.

Official and unofficial misconduct. In the several preceding paragraphs the analysis is based on offences for which the women were actually arrested. Actual criminality cannot be determined solely by arrests, however. In addition to the 157 women who were arrested during the post-parole period there were 148 women who committed offences for which they might have been arrested, but who, for one reason or another, escaped the attention of the police. This makes a total of *76.4% of the women who were delinquent during the five-year post-parole period* [13] (Appendix D, Table 4–41a). Despite this substantial figure, there were markedly fewer delinquents in the post-parole period than prior to commitment (76.4% : 99%).[14] It will be recalled, however, that during the parole period only 55.1% of the parolees were delinquent (Appendix E, Table 61). The deterrent effect of parole supervision on certain types of offenders must be taken into account to explain this lower incidence of delinquent conduct during parole. In comparing the incidence of officially recognized and " unofficial " misconduct in the pre-commitment and post-parole periods, we find some decrease in the proportion of women who came to the official attention of the legal authorities (66.4% : 51.5%) (Appendix E, Table 60).[15]

Predominant offence. Of those women who were delinquent during the post-parole period, 51.5% were predominantly sex offenders,[16] 10.2% chiefly drunkards, .7% (two women) drug addicts; one woman (.3%) grossly neglected her family, 6.6% of the women were both sex offenders and thieves, 24.6% of them were sex offenders and drunkards, 1.9% were sex offenders and drug addicts, 1.6% committed theft, drank, were sex offenders, and possibly committed one

---

offence not punishable by death or imprisonment for life " (ibid.). Up to the present writing (1933) the special institution for defective delinquents has not evolved a program for such types based on modern educational psychology and the treatment of the feeble-minded.

[13] For definition, see Appendix C, *Principal Component of Misconduct* and also *Delinquency*.

[14] This difference cannot be accounted for entirely by the fact that the period preceding sentence was longer than the five-year post-parole period.

[15] These findings of delinquency are based on 399 of the 500 cases. A little over half the remaining 101 cases, were excluded from consideration because the women either were dead or were in institutions, penal or non-penal, for part or most of the post-parole period. In only 47 cases (9.4% of the total of 500) was the delinquent conduct of the women entirely unknown (Table 4–55).

[16] For definition, see Appendix C, *Predominant Offence*.

or two other kinds of offences; 2.3 were primarily bootleggers or were receiving stolen goods (Appendix D, Table 4–40).

In comparing the predominant offences of our women during the post-parole period and prior to commitment we find that there is a very slight decrease in sex offenders *per se,* there are fewer who commit only theft, there is a slight decrease of those who avoid their family responsibilities, of those who are both sex offenders and thieves, of those who commit sex offences in addition to two or three other types of offences, and of those who violate the liquor law or commit other kinds of offences. There is, however, a marked increase in the proportion of drunkards and of those who combine sexual offences with alcoholism or drug addiction. The proportion of drug addicts alone, however, is about the same during the post-parole period as it was prior to commitment to the Reformatory (Appendix E, Table 59).

5. Community Responsibility toward Ex-Prisoners

Social agency contacts. There can be no question that most ex-prisoners, by the very nature of the problems which brought them into a reformatory, need some assistance and oversight in making the transition from the institution and parole régimes to a life of freedom. In only 34.1% of the cases, however, were any social services rendered our women by public or private agencies during the five years following expiration of sentence. Prior to commitment, 76.6% of the women or their immediate families were dealt with by agencies. This marks a great decrease in the proportion of women assisted directly or indirectly by welfare agencies. It probably means that the problems presented by the women independently of their parental families (for most of them had long since left the parental roof and were independent or had established families), were not so acute nor of such a nature as to bring them to the attention of social service agencies, which so largely operate on a laissez-faire basis.

Number and nature of social service contacts. In 17.2% of the cases there was one contact of the woman or her immediate family with a social service agency, in 7% there were two contacts, in 7.7% three or four, and in 2.2% five or more (Appendix D, Table 4–30). Among all the women who were known to social welfare agencies during the post-parole period, the average number of contacts was 2.14 ± .09. Previous to commitment an average of 2.5 ± .07 agencies dealt with the offender or her immediate family, and during the period following parole .067 ± .04 (Appendix E, Table 18). Of 214 contacts of social agencies with these women and their families, 34.1% were concerned with problems of physical or mental health, 26.2% with matters of relief and family welfare, 29% with problems of child or adolescent welfare, and 5.6% with correctional needs (Appendix D, Table 4–31).

Nature and extent of social service needs. In view of the fact that many of our women required aid of one kind or another, it is a pity that they did not receive it. Some of them needed assistance in finding jobs, others in establishing wholesome recreational contacts, others in smoothing over critical domestic situations or in bringing up their children, and many might have benefited from little friendly services and " propping up " in general. Considering now only such needs as would be obvious to any trained social worker, we would say that at least those of our women who failed industrially needed vocational guidance (if not receiving it already); those who spent their leisure time harmfully and whose habits were bad needed to be guided into more wholesome ways of using their spare time; those whose family or marital relations were poor or who neglected their children needed friendly counsel in the solution of their difficulties; those who had venereal disease or any other physical ailment not being treated certainly needed to be taken in hand; those who were psychotic or of the type of feeble-minded who constantly create disturbance needed at least supervision if not permanent custody. In fact, in only 20.3% of the cases were there no glaring needs of the type indicated. In 7.6% of the cases all the needs were being met; in 25.4% agencies were meeting some, but not all, of the patent needs in the particular situation; while in 46.7% no such needs were being met by the constituted authorities (Appendix D, Table 4–H91).

What was the nature of these needs which did not come to the attention of social service agencies? Analysis discloses no less than 709 distinct major needs in 295 cases, and of these 37.2% had to do with absorption into more wholesome recreational activities; 28.8% involved the smoothing out of critical domestic situations, 18.6% problems relating to vocational guidance, 5.5% protection of offspring, 4.7% arranging custodial care for women who should not be at large, 2.7% problems relating to the care of health (Appendix D, Table 4–H92).

Of those women who could be deemed to need vocational guidance (those who were unsuccessful industrially), at least 59.7% did not receive it. Of the women who badly needed guidance into decent recreational channels (those who used their leisure time harmfully), at least 62.2% did not receive it. Of the ones whose family or marital relationships were poor, at least 61.5% did not even receive any friendly counsel. Of those whose illicit sexuality resulted in illegitimate children, 30% were not being dealt with by any social service agencies. Of those who were inefficient and slovenly in their housekeeping, at least 58.3% did not receive any guidance in homemaking. Of those who actually had venereal disease during the five-year follow-up period, 71.8% were not dealt with by any social agencies.

Extent of intensive rehabilitative work. An intensive case-by-case analysis of the constructive efforts in behalf of our women during the five-year post-parole period indicates that only in 34 instances was a type of supervision given to the ex-prisoners which might be truly considered rehabilitative. Interestingly enough, in four cases such oversight was rendered by some member of the Reformatory staff whose interest in the offender had continued after her release; in ten cases, by a parole agent to whom the women often turned for advice and encouragement and who took a deep interest in their most intimate problems; in four cases by an employer, in two instances by a minister, in one case by a policewoman, in five cases by probation officers under whose oversight the women happened to be placed because of conflict with the law during the post-parole period. In only eleven cases was the necessary aid given by workers of social agencies. Despite the fact that 141 of our women were known to social agencies (Appendix D, Table 4-31), in only these eleven could we, after analysis of their efforts, consider that the services rendered were really intensive and effectual. For example, a public health nurse who came into close contact with one such woman during a course of syphilitic treatments had a particularly good influence upon her and maintained a steady interest in her, helping her in her marital and vocational adjustments. An agency visitor who had taken a particular interest in her charge maintained friendly supervision of another woman for many years after the case had been "closed." In most instances the contact of the social agencies was too brief and cursory, however, and was directed toward but one phase of the ex-prisoner's problems. Often it was not even known to them that their client had a past record of delinquency and might for this reason require intensive and specialized oversight.

Who is to render such services if not the public and private social agencies? The foregoing analysis of the social services actually needed by our women and those given discloses a major breach in the dike erected by society against crime. For the community to enter elaborately upon the "reformation" of offenders by reformatory programs and brief parole oversight, only to abandon ex-prisoners to their own meagre resources thereafter, is a patently wasteful performance. The marked neglect of the problems of the ex-prisoner by social agencies may account not a little for the discouragingly high proportion who relapse into criminality when official supervision is removed. Prisoners' aid societies have on the whole failed in meeting this responsibility; some organizations must assume it if much of the good work of the better correctional institutions and parole agencies is not to be wasted.

Attitude of the community. But what of the attitude of the community in general toward delinquent women? Ex-prisoners are prone to believe that the hostile reception given them by an unsympathetic community dooms them to failure. Among our women, however, 223 of whom personally recounted their experiences in this regard, 84.3% claimed that the communities in which they have lived since their release have been quite indifferent to them; either their commitment to the Reformatory was entirely unknown or the community, though aware of the fact, made no discrimination against them because its own moral standards were so low as to accept wrongdoing with equanimity. In

9.4% of the cases our women say they were received into the community in a spirit of friendliness and were encouraged to rejoin the church or to become members of respectable clubs and in other ways to participate in community life. Only in 6.3% of the cases did the women sense a definite ostracism or experience a " hounding," sometimes on the part of the police, sometimes by employers, occasionally even by the clergy (Appendix D, Table 4–86).

When we view the growing disintegration of community life and the tenuousness of the notion of community responsibility, particularly in the light of the laissez-faire policy of the social agencies toward the problem of ex-prisoners, we realize that a more conscious and directed program is necessary for their supervision. The community cannot be charged nearly so much with hostility as with indifference to ex-prisoners.

6. Interrelationship of Major Fields of Post-Parole Activity

Introductory. In the preceding analysis the various activities of our women during a five-year period following the expiration of sentence to the Reformatory have been reviewed one by one. There remains now the question of whether there is any association between these different aspects of the individual's life. In other words, is criminality but an isolated instance of failure in social adaptation on the part of offenders or is it typically interwoven with maladjustment in other respects? [17]

Industrial stability and criminality. A marked association is found to exist between the industrial stability of our women and their conduct during the five-year post-parole period. This is shown by the following analysis: The high proportion of 64.6% of those who were industrially successful during the post-parole period were also non-delinquents; while, on the other hand, of the group who were industrial failures not a single one was non-delinquent.

Family relationships and criminality. That a high association exists between poor family relationships and delinquency is shown by the fact that of the group of women whose family relationships were good, 54% were non-delinquents, while of those whose family relationships were poor, only 2.3% were non-delinquents.

Economic responsibility and criminality. There is also considerable association between failure to meet economic obligations and delinquency, as demonstrated by the fact that of the group of women who met their economic responsibilities 22.6% were non-delinquent, while of those who failed to meet them not one woman was non-delinquent.

Environment and criminality. The marked association between environmental circumstances and crime is shown by the fact that of those whose en-

[17] In *500 Criminal Careers,* Chap. XIV, the authors have demonstrated that a high degree of association exists between failure as measured by criminal activity and failure in other fields of enterprise on the part of male graduates of a reformatory.

vironment was wholesome, the high proportion of 87% were non-delinquents, while of those whose environment was poor, 1.9% were non-delinquents.

Use of leisure and criminality. Finally, a definite association is seen to exist between poor use of leisure on the one hand and criminality on the other. This is revealed in the fact that every one of the women who used their leisure time constructively was a non-delinquent, while not one of those who used their leisure time harmfully was non-delinquent.

Criminality related to all other activities in combination. Considering now the status of our women with respect to all their activities in combination as related to their recidivism, an even greater association exists than was found between any single activity and delinquency. Thus, of the women who adjusted themselves at least fairly well in all their activities, the high proportion of 82.4% were not delinquent during the five-year post-parole period; while of those who failed in one or more respects, only 1.4% were non-delinquents.

Clearly, then, in analysing the delinquencies of female offenders, the conclusion is inescapable that we are dealing, not with the isolated phenomenon of criminal conduct, but with *general maladjustment*. There is no reliable method, moreover, of determining which arc of this vicious circle of maladjustment generally has precedence. Only occasionally is this possible, by an intensive analysis of individual cases.

7. Conclusion

In answer to the general question put at the beginning of the preceding chapter as to whether our women made any progress after their Reformatory experience it must be concluded that a definite improvement is manifest in the group during the five-year period following the expiration of sentence. Specifically, this improvement is reflected in decreased mobility, in greater household stability, in better environmental conditions, in a lesser proportion of forced marriages. It is further indicated by a greater incidence of marriages in which the conjugal relations are wholesome, in a more extensive assumption of marital responsibilities, in better homemaking practices. The general improvement among our women is also reflected in their greater affection and increased sense of responsibility toward their children, and in better family relationships as a whole. It is further shown in their better industrial adjustment, as reflected in higher earnings, in greater steadiness of employment, in holding jobs for longer periods of time; in their bettered economic condition and their greater tendency to save. We see it also in a decrease in the proportion of women who used their leisure harmfully, in a reduction in the number who had bad habits or undesirable companions. Another significant feature of the improvement of the women is a decline in illegitimate pregnancies (partially, however, attributable to sterilization) and in the incidence of venereal disease.

Finally, fewer of the women came into conflict with the law as the years went by, and those who did were arrested less frequently and imprisoned less often than before. There was in general less delinquency in the post-parole period than previously.

This comprehensive picture of improvement is not marred by the fact that on the whole our women did not do as well during the post-parole period as during parole. It must be remembered that the mere fact of surveillance had much to do with keeping certain of the ex-prisoners in line during parole. The fact that the status of the women had on the whole improved over that preceding commitment to the Reformatory would seem to indicate that several influences were operative in bringing about the result. The all-important question of whether this improvement is to be credited largely to the Reformatory or to other causes is discussed later.[18]

Of course the fact remains that three fourths of our women (76.4%) were recidivists for part or all of the five-year post-parole period. This major finding stares us in the face despite the improvement which the group made. Their conduct was still such as to call for serious reflection about the effectiveness of society's institutions for coping with delinquency, particularly in view of our finding that delinquent conduct is closely bound up with failure in other of life's activities. We have in this and the preceding chapter discovered certain suggestive correlations that should help us later to put our finger on parts of the machinery of justice and other social institutions which need special attention.

Thus far we have compared the status of our women during the five-year period after the expiration of sentence to the Reformatory with their status prior to commitment. We now turn to the question of whether a trend toward better conduct is manifest in our women despite their high incidence of delinquency. In other words, are these women developing in the general direction of reform or is the improvement during the post-parole period only temporary? It is the answer to this question that we seek in the next chapter.

[18] See Chapters XV and XVI.

CHAPTER XIV

BEHAVIOUR TRENDS

1. Introductory

In the preceding chapter we saw that an improvement had taken place in our women during the five years following the expiration of their sentences to the Reformatory. In the present chapter we examine particularly their status during the fifth year of the post-parole period, comparing it on the one hand with the five-year period as a whole and on the other with their conduct beyond the fifth year, in order to determine whether the trend is definitely upward.

2. Environmental Circumstances

During the fifth year of the post-parole period the environmental circumstances of 17.6% of the women might be considered good [1] in that their physical living-conditions, the neighbourhood influences, and the moral standards of their homes were all wholesome. The environmental circumstances of 46.3% of the women were fair and of 36.1% poor. We see, therefore, a slight increase in the proportion of women whose environmental circumstances are good in the fifth year as compared to the five-year period as a whole (17.6% : 11.6%) (Appendix D, Table 4–48). This finding, together with the fact that during the few years following the five-year post-parole period into which we were able to investigate [2] there was a still further improvement in the environmental circumstances of the women, which are now good in 19.5% of the cases, indicates a trend toward the better, which, though not marked, is persistent and progressive (Appendix D, Table 4–54). The findings are recapitulated in Table 1.

3. Family Relationships

Was there any improvement in the family relationships of our women in the fifth year? During this year 52.8% of the women maintained good family

[1] For definition, see Appendix C, *Environmental Judgment*.

[2] In most of the cases it was possible to secure information as to the status of the women during one or more years beyond the expiration of the five-year period. A period of less than one year after the end of the post-parole period was covered by our investigation in 1.3% of the cases; from one to two years in 5.2%, from two to three years in 18%, three to four years in 26.6%, four to five years in 30.1%, and five years or more in 18.8% (Appendix D, Table 4–53).

TABLE 1

TREND IN ENVIRONMENTAL CIRCUMSTANCES

(Percentages)

Class	Throughout Post-Parole Period *	During Fifth Year of Post-Parole Period †	After Fifth Year of Post-Parole Period ‡
Good.........	11.6	17.6	19.5
Fair..........	48.6	46.3	46.5
Poor..........	39.8	36.1	34.0
Total.....	100.0	100.0	100.0

* Based on 395 cases.   † Based on 363 cases.   ‡ Based on 344 cases.

relationships[3] as compared with 43.3% during the five-year period as a whole; and 47.2% of them had poor family relationships in contrast to 56.7% during the five-year period (Appendix D, Table 4–47a). Here again the improvement has been progressive (Appendix D, Table 4–52a), as is shown by Table 2:

TABLE 2

TREND IN FAMILY RELATIONSHIPS

(Percentages)

Class	Throughout Post-Parole Period *	During Fifth Year of Post-Parole Period †	After Fifth Year of Post-Parole Period ‡
Success........	43.3	52.8	56.9
Failure........	56.7	47.2	43.1
Total.....	100.0	100.0	100.0

* Based on 400 cases.   † Based on 369 cases.   ‡ Based on 350 cases.

4. Economic Responsibility

During the fifth year of the post-parole period 55.8% of our women were meeting their economic responsibilities,[4] 9.7% of them were not, 34.5% did not have to support themselves or others, and a few women were unable to support themselves because of illness. For the purposes of comparison we must omit the two latter groups. Of those who had to support themselves or any dependants, 85.1% met their economic responsibilities, while 14.9% did not. This is a slight increase over the five-year period as a whole, when 80.5% of the women fulfilled their obligations to support themselves and their dependants (Appendix D, Table 4–49a). During such time following the five-year post-parole period

[3] For definition, see Appendix C, *Family Relationships*.
[4] Ibid., *Economic Responsibility*.

as we were able to inquire into, we find that about the same proportion of women (84.3%) were still meeting their economic responsibilities as in the fifth year. Table 3 recapitulates these findings:

TABLE 3

TREND IN ASSUMPTION OF ECONOMIC RESPONSIBILITIES

(Percentages)

Class	Throughout Post-Parole Period *	During Fifth Year of Post-Parole Period †	After Fifth Year of Post-Parole Period ‡
Meeting responsibilities....	80.5	85.1	84.3
Not meeting responsibilities	19.5	14.9	15.7
Total..............	100.0	100.0	100.0

* Based on 308 cases.   † Based on 235 cases.   ‡ Based on 204 cases.

5. Industrial Adjustment

There was a definite increase in the proportion of women who were successful industrially [5] during the fifth year of the post-parole period as compared with the entire five years (26.3% : 18.6%); and an increase of those who partially succeeded (32% : 26.3%) (Appendix D, Table 4–47b). Although the improvement is not considerable, it was held during the time following the post-parole period (Appendix D, Table 4–52b), as is demonstrated in Table 4:

TABLE 4

TREND IN INDUSTRIAL ADJUSTMENT

(Percentages)

Class	Throughout Post-Parole Period *	During Fifth Year of Post-Parole Period †	After Fifth Year of Post-Parole Period ‡
Success........	18.6	26.3	27.5
Partial success.	32.0	26.3	22.5
Failure........	49.4	47.4	50.0
Total.....	100.0	100.0	100.0

* Based on 269 cases.   † Based on 213 cases.   ‡ Based on 196 cases.

6. Leisure and Habits

During the fifth year of the post-parole period there was a falling off in the harmful use of leisure [6] and in bad habits (52% : 66.7%). No greater proportion

[5] For definition, see Appendix C, *Industrial History.*

[6] Ibid., *Use of Leisure.*

of women were using their leisure constructively, however (Appendix D, Table 4–49b). But the trend is definitely away from unwholesome leisure-time outlets (Appendix D, Table 4–51b).

TABLE 5

TREND IN USE OF LEISURE AND HABITS

(Percentages)

Class	Throughout Post-Parole Period *	During Fifth Year of Post-Parole Period †	After Fifth Year of Post-Parole Period ‡
Constructive...	2.7	2.5	3.0
Negative......	30.6	45.5	50.9
Harmful.......	66.7	52.0	46.1
Total.....	100.0	100.0	100.0

* Based on 402 cases.   † Based on 358 cases.   ‡ Based on 330 cases.

7. Delinquency

Turning now to the important matter of criminality, there is a marked falling off in the proportion of delinquent women [7] in the fifth year of the period as compared with the entire five-year span (52.6% : 76.4%). (Appendix D, Table 4–50a.) Thus we see that 76.4% of our women were delinquent throughout the five-year period; 23.8%, though delinquent for part of the period, were for at

TABLE 6

DELINQUENCY TREND

(Percentages)

Class	Throughout Post-Parole Period *	During Fifth Year of Post-Parole Period †	After Fifth Year of Post-Parole Period ‡
Non-delinquent	23.6	47.4	47.4
Delinquent....	76.4	52.6	52.6
Total.....	100.0	100.0	100.0

* Based on 399 cases.   † Based on 352 cases.   ‡ Based on 333 cases.

least the last year non-delinquent; and 23.6% were non-delinquent throughout the period. This trend toward reform may be partially explained by the fact that with the passage of time some of the worst offenders have died because of alcoholism, syphilis, and the like; and some, particularly those who have developed psychoses, and the feeble-minded, have been drawn off into institutions.

[7] For definition, see Appendix C, *Delinquency*.

Other explanations of this improvement in conduct are given in Chapter XVI. There can be no doubt of a definite trend toward the better. That this trend is maintained beyond the fifth year of the five-year period is indicated by Table 6.

8. Conclusion

The foregoing analysis has revealed that there is a trend toward the better in the conduct of the women, as reflected in their environmental circumstances, in their family relationships, in the meeting of their economic responsibilities, in their industrial adjustment, in their use of leisure, in their habits, and, finally, in their criminal conduct. This improvement manifested itself at least a year before the end of the five-year post-parole period and has been maintained and even bettered in some respects during the ensuing few years about which we have data.

Only a further restudy of these women at a later time, however, will definitely establish the permanence of their improvement.

We now turn our attention to the crucial question of the extent to which the improvement or failure of the women may be attributed to the Reformatory, or to circumstances which met them after release, or to certain traits and characteristics within themselves.

PART THREE

AN AUDIT OF THE SITUATION

1. Introductory

We have seen that an appreciable proportion of our women were no longer delinquent after the expiration of their sentence to the Reformatory. To what extent may this outcome be attributed to the effect of the institutional experience? Owing to the large number of variables involved, it is admittedly difficult to isolate completely the influence of the Reformatory in curbing the delinquency of its inmates. There is an interplay of forces contributing to the good result. Many of these influences will be considered analytically in the next chapter. Meanwhile, we are concerned with the effectiveness of the Reformatory in curbing recidivism, reserving certain related matters to the latter part of the chapter.

2. Influence of the Reformatory in Curbing Recidivism

Method of determination. By a logical deduction we may arrive at a fair estimate of the part which the Reformatory itself has played in curbing recidivism.[1] The results obtained by this method, while not absolutely conclusive, are nevertheless highly suggestive. The women whose recidivism may be considered to have been curbed by the Reformatory are those who were no longer delinquent after release (whether on parole or after expiration of sentence). The women whose behaviour was not directly affected by the Reformatory experience to the extent of curbing their delinquencies are plainly those whose misconduct was resumed immediately after release, or who, though keeping within the law while under parole surveillance, recidivated thereafter. With this as a basis of differentiating between those whose delinquency was curbed essentially *by the Reformatory* and those whose delinquency was curbed as a result essentially of other influences or was not curbed at all, we made the following classification of our cases:

Group A: The women who were non-delinquent after release on parole and after expiration of sentence. About a seventh (15.2%) of our cases fall into this group. While other factors may also have contributed to the successful outcome, the influence of the Reformatory in curbing the recidivism of these women seems

[1] See 500 *Criminal Careers*, pp. 224–6, where this method was first developed.

clear, as they were delinquent upon entering the institution and no longer delinquent after leaving it.

Group B: The women who were delinquent during parole (although not necessarily thereafter) or who, though never on parole, reverted to delinquency after expiration of sentence from the Reformatory. Some two thirds of our women (65.4%) are in this group. Whatever favourable effect the Reformatory may have exerted on them, it did not translate itself immediately or at all into law-abiding conduct. If the Reformatory was the chief influence in the ultimate reform of some of these women, why did they not abandon their delinquent conduct after release therefrom? Obviously, influences other than those of the Reformatory must have entered in to produce the ultimate reformation of some women. What these possible influences are we indicate in the next chapter.

Group C: The women who behaved well while under parole supervision, but who reverted to unlawful conduct after the expiration of sentence. A fifth (19.4%) of our women belong in this group. Their antisocial reaction to a life of complete freedom would seem to indicate that whatever favourable influences the Reformatory may have exerted on their conduct, these were only temporary and partially dependent on parole oversight, including the deterrent effect of the knowledge that misbehaviour during parole might result in a return to the institution.

In comparing the background and characteristics of the women in this group with those in Group A and Group B we find that they much more resemble the latter. For in half (49.1%) of a total of 153 traits and factors in the background and make-up of our women Group C resembles Group B, in 28.8% it resembles Group A, while in 22.2% it differs from both these groups. The fact, however, that these women who behaved while on parole but recidivated later more nearly resembled the ones who were evidently uninfluenced by the Reformatory (Group B) justifies the inference that it is more the deterrent effect of parole than the influence of the Reformatory that kept these women temporarily in line; and they can hardly be considered, therefore, to have been greatly influenced by the Reformatory so far as the curbing of their delinquency is concerned.[2]

[2] A comparison of the characteristics and background of Groups A, B, and C is worth recording, as it throws some light on the type of offender who is likely to respond well to parole or similar oversight.

The women who responded to parole oversight but recidivated later (Group C) to a greater extent than the others lived with their parents at the time of their commitment to the Reformatory (42.1% as compared to 28.9% of Group A and 36.8% of Group B). A higher proportion of their parents were Catholics than in Group A (46.6% : 36.8%), but a lower than of Group B (46.6% : 59.8%). A larger proportion of them had lived in rural communities or very small towns during childhood (47.5% : 30.4% : 30.2%) and also during adolescence (31% : 23.5% : 17.3%). A higher percentage of them had poor homes in childhood than of Group A (36.2% : 25%), but a lower proportion came from such homes than those of Group B (36.2% : 48.4%); during adolescence a lower proportion had good homes than in Group A (27.5% : 32.4%) but a slightly higher than those of Group B (27.5% : 23.5%). Similarly, within a year of commitment to the Reformatory a lower percentage had good homes than those of Group A (12.3% : 25.6%), but a higher than of Group B (12.3% : 7.1%).

A smaller proportion of them were single women (39% : 54.1% : 51.2%), and of those who were

Thus we see that in only 15.2% of the cases (Group A) was the influence of the Reformatory upon the conduct of our women effective to the extent of actually curbing their delinquencies, while in 84.8% of the cases (Groups B and C) the Reformatory did not succeed in preventing recidivism. And even as

---

married, more had been married only once (91.8% : 72.7% : 89%). Fewer than of Group A assumed their marital responsibilities (19.4% : 36.4%), but more did so than of Group B (19.4% : 9.9%). More of them were poor homemakers (61.1% : 25% : 46.4%). Their attitude toward their children was poor not to as great an extent as that of Group B (27.7% : 69%), but to a greater extent than that of Group A (27.7% : 10.5%).

Among their numbers a higher percentage were Catholics than among Group A (54.1% : 41.7%), but a lower than among Group B (54.1% : 64.7%). A greater proportion than the others attended church more regularly during childhood (73.1% : 58.2% : 57%) and also during adolescence (36.8% : 19.5% : 25.2%).

Not so high a proportion drank as in Group B (37.7% : 48.3%), but more than in Group A (37.7% : 25.5%).

In a lower proportion than the others their illicit sex activities began when they were under fifteen (16.3% : 28.2% : 23.4%). Of those among them who were prostitutes, a much higher proportion were over twenty years old than the others (41.4% : 20% : 14.6%); more than of Group A had been prostitutes for more than a year prior to commitment (69% : 55%), but fewer than of Group B (69% : 78%). There were fewer professional prostitutes among them, but more occasional prostitutes (51.7% : 38.2% : 40.6%). There were more of the mistress type of sex deviate among them and fewer of the unconventional type (5.2% : 14.9% : 10.4%).

They started school later than the others, 43.5% beginning at seven or over while 34.2% and 34.7%, respectively, of the other two groups started school at that age. Far fewer went beyond grade school — 6.1% as compared to 21.5% of Group A and 8.5% of Group B. They attended school less regularly than Group A (44.4% : 57.6%), but more regularly than Group B (44.4% : 36.9%).

They earned less in their first place of employment, 57.1% receiving five dollars or less per week as compared with 27.6% and 37.8% of the others. More of them held their first job for less than a month (26.3% : 15.6% : 16.5%). On the occasion of their first conviction more of them were engaged in domestic service of one kind or another, either living out or working by the day (20.4% : 7.2% : 8.8%). They were the least regularly employed of the three groups, only 3.9% being steady workers as compared to 10.6% and 5.2%.

More of them had been arrested prior to their commitment to the Reformatory than of Group A (63.9% : 45.8%), but fewer than of Group B (63.9% : 74.3%). A lower proportion of them had first been arrested when they were eighteen years old or under (33.3% : 46.8% : 51%). Fewer of them had first been arrested for sex offences than those of Group A (44.2% : 54.1%), but more than of Group B (44.2% : 24.7%).

Fewer of them were predominantly thieves (1.7% : 2.1% : 6.3%). There was as great a proportion of chronic alcoholics among them as in Group B (5% : 5.4%). It should be mentioned that there were no drunkards or drug addicts in Group A. There were fewer predominantly sex delinquents among those who behaved well on parole but not thereafter than in Group A (65% : 81.2%), but more than in Group B (65% : 43.1%).

More of them had been in penal institutions than those in Group A (29.5% : 6.3%), but fewer than those in Group B (29.5% : 43.1%). Those in Group C who had been in penal or non-penal institutions had such experiences for eighteen months or less in a lower proportion of cases than Group A (63.6% : 73.7%), but in a higher proportion than Group B (63.6% : 47.7%).

A lower proportion were of normal mentality among those who reacted well to parole supervision and not to freedom (17.9% : 31.3% : 22.6%), and more were feeble-minded (39.3% : 20.8% : 30.8%). This gives us a clue to the fact that certain types of the feeble-minded can be allowed to return to the community provided they are kept under parole or similar oversight indefinitely.

On the basis of five or six such factors which reveal the most striking differences between those who respond to parole supervision and those who do not, a simple instrumentality could be provided either for selecting offenders for probation supervision or for an indeterminate period of parole. The predictive method described in Chapter XVII is applicable here.

to the 15.2% of the cases in Group A, we cannot say absolutely that their non-recidivism is attributable exclusively to the influence of the Reformatory. We shall hereafter refer to these two groups of cases as those *influenced* by the Reformatory (Group A) and those *uninfluenced* (Groups B and C).

Differences in characteristics of influenced and uninfluenced. Although we have objectively classified our women into those who were apparently influenced by the Reformatory and those who were not, we must recognize that their response to Reformatory treatment must have depended not only on the efforts of the institution, but also upon the previous experiences and characteristics of the inmates themselves. Owing to the many imponderables involved, it is practically impossible to determine with absolute precision how much of the good result of the Reformatory incarceration may be assigned to the institution and how much to the characteristics of the inmates. It is feasible, however, to isolate by statistical means the factors in the make-up and careers of our women which *probably assisted* the Reformatory in curbing their delinquencies, and those which evidently played little or no role therein. This is accomplished by comparing the various traits and characteristics of the women whose recidivism was apparently prevented by the Reformatory with those of the women whose subsequent behaviour indicates that they were not influenced by the Reformatory experience. The process is illustrated in Table 7:

TABLE 7

RECREATIONAL OUTLETS AND INFLUENCE OF THE REFORMATORY IN CURBING RECIDIVISM
(Percentages)

Recreational Outlets	*Influenced by Reformatory*	*Uninfluenced by Reformatory*
Constructive............	33.3	16.3
Not constructive.......	66.7	83.7
Total.............	100.0	100.0

It is clear from the table that the group of women who were influenced by the Reformatory contained a substantially larger proportion who had constructive recreational outlets prior to their commitment than those who were uninfluenced.

A total of 153 factors in the background and characteristics of our women (already described in the previous chapters, and relating to the offenders up to the time of their commitment to the Reformatory) were subjected to like analysis, with the following result:

1. In respect to 39.2% of the factors the women who were influenced by the Reformatory differed only slightly, if at all, from those who were uninfluenced.[3]

[3] The degrees of relationship were determined by the same method as that described in Chapter XVII, pp. 286-7.

It should be pointed out that the existence of only a slight relationship between these factors and the influence of the Reformatory in curbing recidivism is not tantamount to a conclusion that they played little or no part in the *origin* of the delinquency of these women. Obviously, there may be some traits and characteristics that are significant in criminogenesis which have little to do with the effectiveness of a Reformatory in curbing the recidivism of those already criminal.

The factors in this and the two succeeding footnotes are numbered as in Appendix D, "Code-Table Index," being listed in numerical rather than in any logical order of grouping, in order to make easy reference to the tables possible; anyone interested may thus readily see what the sub-categories of these factors are and how they are defined.

The factors in which the women who were influenced by the Reformatory and those who were uninfluenced practically resemble each other are:

1– 1a. Use of aliases
1– 2b. Nativity of offender
1– 3. Country of birth of offender
1– 4a. Legitimacy of offender
1– 6. Time offender in United States
1– 7. Time offender in Massachusetts
1–10b. Nature of mobility
1–11. Nature of earliest abnormal environmental experience
1–12. Age of offender at time of earliest abnormal environmental experience
1–14. Venereal disease before twenty-one years old
1–16b. Leisure and habits within year of commitment
1–18d. Kind of companions within year of commitment
1–19c. Kind of play places and haunts within year of commitment
1–20a. Regularity of church attendance in childhood
1–20b. Regularity of church attendance during adolescence
1–22. Nature of misbehaviour and habits in adolescence
1–23. Nature of misbehaviour and habits within year of commitment
1–24b. Habit of drugs prior to commitment
1–25. Age at first known delinquency
1–26. Age first left home
1–27. Reason first left home
1–29. With whom illicit sex life first began
1–30a. Rape or consent at first illicit sex experience
1–31. Age entered prostitution
1–36a. Illiteracy
1–36b. Age started school
1–37. Number of years in school
1–44. Age began work
1–47. Time held first job
1–48. Occupation at first conviction

1–49. Usual occupation
1–50. Longest period employed on any paid job
1–51. Average weekly wage prior to commitment
1–54. Last legitimate occupation before commitment
1–59b. Disposition of earnings
1–60b. Delinquency prior to offence for which committed to Reformatory
1–66. Number of penal and non-penal experiences
1–69. Time spent in foster-homes
1–70. Number of probations prior to commitment
2– 7. Birthplace of father
2– 8. Birthplace of mother
2–12. Usual occupation of father
2–17a. Has step- or foster-parents
2–17b. Has step- or half-sibs
2–18. Number of siblings in family
2–19. Rank of offender among siblings
2–20a. Number of offender's children living at time of commitment
2–21. Mental disease or defect in family
2–23a. Delinquency in family
2–24a. Nativity of parents related to offender's nativity
2–24b. Language spoken at home
2–25. Neighbourhood type in childhood
2–26. Neighbourhood type in adolescence
2–31. Household in childhood
2–32. Household stability
2–34a. Economic condition of parents in offender's childhood and adolescence
2–34b. Economic condition within year prior to commitment
2–36b. Moral standards of home in adolescence
2–39. Type of social service rendered
2–42. Age of offender at marriage

2. In respect to 38.6% of the factors the women who were influenced by the Reformatory differed appreciably from the others, but not enough to account for the variance in the effect of the Reformatory experience upon them.[4]

3. In respect to 22.2% of the factors the women who were influenced by the Reformatory and those who were uninfluenced differed markedly from each other in make-up. From this it is reasonable to infer that by reason of the presence of these traits and characteristics the Reformatory was aided (whether the officials were conscious of this or not) in favourably influencing inmates toward a law-abiding life.[5]

[4] 1–1b. Colour of offender
1– 2a. Age of offender at time of commitment to Reformatory
1– 5. Citizenship of offender
1– 8. With whom residing at time of arrest
1– 9. Type of offence for which committed to Reformatory
1–10a. Mobility prior to commitment
1–13. Reason for earliest abnormal environmental experience
1–15. Serious physical handicaps during childhood and adolescence
1–16a. Age at which menstruation established
1–18b. Nature of companions in childhood
1–18c. Nature of companions in adolescence
1–19b. Nature of play places in adolescence
1–20c. Regularity of church attendance within year of commitment
1–21. Nature of misbehaviour and habits in childhood
1–28. Age illicit sex life began
1–32. Total time a prostitute up to commitment
1–33. Total time sexually irregular up to commitment
1–34. Nature of sex life
1–38. Reason left school
1–40. Age left school
1–42c. Attendance at vocational school prior to commitment
1–43b. Assumption of economic responsibilities
1–45. First occupation
1–46. Weekly wage in first occupation
1–52. Highest legitimate weekly earnings prior to commitment
1–53. Usual reason for leaving work
1–55a. Weekly wage in last legitimate occupation
1–58. Savings
1–61. Age at first arrest

1–74. Mental condition on admission to Reformatory
1–75. Intelligence
2– 1. Cause of first arrest
2– 2. Number of arrests
2–10a. Time parents in United States
2–10b. Citizenship of father
2–11. Education of parents
2–13. Usual occupation of mother
2–14a. Industrial stability of father
2–16. Age of offender at first break in home
2–20b. Legitimacy of offender's children
2–22. Broken or poorly supervised home
2–23b. Conjugal relations of parents
2–27. Neighbourhood type within year of commitment
2–28b. Physical home during adolescence
2–29a. Physical home within year of commitment
2–29b. Neighbourhood influences in childhood
2–30a. Neighbourhood influences in adolescence
2–30b. Neighbourhood influences within year of commitment
2–34c. Family relationships within year of commitment
2–35. Parental supervision in childhood
2–36a. Moral standards of home in childhood
2–36c. Moral standards of home within year of commitment
2–37. Age of offender at first social service contact with family
2–38. Number of social service agencies dealing with family
2–40. Marital status of offender at time of commitment
2–41a. Number of marriages of offender prior to commitment
2–41b. Marital success in last marriage prior to commitment
2–46b. Number of previous sentences to Reformatory
2–47. Prior time in Reformatory

[5] The delinquency of inmates showing the characteristics which appear in parentheses after

Among these marked differences is the fact that a woman had expressed a definite vocational ambition prior to commitment to the Reformatory; that she had constructive recreations and interests prior to commitment; that her play places and haunts were not harmful during childhood; that her health during childhood had not been poor; that she did not have the drink habit; that she had attained at least the eighth grade in school; that she was not retarded in school; that she was not a failure industrially; that she was at least a fairly regular worker prior to commitment; that she was not idle when arrested; that she was arrested infrequently; that her misconduct centred in the lack of control of the sex impulse rather than other offences; the fact that she had never before been in a correctional institution.

Such findings are of great practical importance. On the basis of even a few of these characteristics, and utilizing the method of prognosis described in Chapter XVII, a simple instrumentality could be provided the Reformatory officials which would indicate to them which inmates are likely to respond to the standard reformative methods of the institution. Other methods would then have to be developed experimentally to deal with those inmates whose recidivism is not likely to be curbed readily, if at all, by treatment in a reformatory.

---

each factor, is much more likely to be curbed as a result of a reformatory experience than is the delinquency of those not having these particular characteristics.

1– 4b. Religion of offender (Protestant or Hebrew)

1–17. Vocational ambition expressed any time prior to commitment (yes)

1–18a. Constructive recreations and interests prior to commitment (yes)

1–19a. Play places and haunts in childhood (at least fair)

1–24a. Habit of drink prior to commitment (no)

1–35. Kind of school attended (public schools or schools in foreign countries)

1–39. Grade attained in school (above grade school)

1–41. Retardation in school (none)

1–42a. Scholarship (good)

1–42b. Attendance in school (regular)

1–43a. Industrial history (at least partial success)

1–55b. Employed at time of arrest for which sent to Reformatory (yes, or doing own housework)

1–56. Time since last employed prior to commitment (up to arrest)

1–57a. Steadiness of employment (at least fairly regular)

1–57b. Work habits (at least fair)

1–59a. Insurance — how paid (by self)

1–60a. Nature of delinquency (no delinquency or "unofficial" delinquency only)

1–62. Age at first commitment to peno-correctional institution (seventeen or over)

1–63. Frequency of arrests (not more than once a year)

1–64. Predominant offence (sexual)

1–65. Time served in penal institutions (none)

1–68. Number of penal experiences (none)

2– 3. Previous convictions (not more than one)

2– 6. Institutional experiences (none)

2– 9. Religion of parents (Protestant or Hebrew)

2–14b. Industrial stability of mother (regular)

2–15. Broken homes in childhood or adolescence (none)

2–28a. Physical home during offender's childhood (at least fair)

2–43a. Conjugal relations in last marriage (at least fair)

2–43b. Attitude of offender to marital responsibility (assumed responsibility)

2–44a. Competence as homemaker (at least fair)

2–44b. Attitude to children (at least fair)

Nature of Reformatory influence. It is obvious that those women upon whom the Reformatory exerted an apparently enduring influence had much in their favour to start with. However, there still remains to be determined the exact nature of the mechanisms of reformation to which they responded. With this in mind we analysed intensively those cases in which the reasons for reformation were relatively clear or could be legitimately inferred from available records and interviews. Such analysis of a considerable number of case histories from this point of view indicated that the most potent influences toward reform by the institution — granting that an offender had favourable characteristics of the kind above enumerated — resolved themselves into three general types: (1) deep attachment to some member of the Reformatory staff (most often the late superintendent, Mrs. Hodder) which of course implies a great personal interest, understanding, and handling of the offender's problems on the part of some member of the staff (see, for example, the case of Marie, pp. 142 et seq.); (2) the shock of incarceration (see the case of Louisa, pp. 182 et seq.); (3) the educational effect of the Reformatory in introducing the inmate to more desirable standards of living or equipping her for an interesting vocation (see the case of Margaret, pp. 164 et seq.). Obviously, were it not for the superiority of certain of the inmates themselves, the effort of the Reformatory to curb their delinquencies might well have been far less successful. That this is so is shown by the cases of inmates not possessing favourable traits, to whom the Reformatory staff devoted much effort with little if any permanently good result (see the cases of Alice, pp. 147 et seq., and Dora, pp. 177 et seq.).

There is much more room for research into the mechanisms of reformation and for a study of the types of offenders who respond to its different forms. Although we have made a bare beginning, it is necessary to dig more deeply beneath the surface and to study far more intensively several hundred cases of *successful* adjustment from this particular point of departure — the influence of the Reformatory in curbing recidivism. If we had a sufficiently large group of offenders who had been *reformed* by the institution, we should be able to relate their characteristics to the particular aspect of the institutional experience which facilitated their reformation. This would then serve as a guide for reformatory officials in indicating the nature of the treatment to be accorded to certain types of inmates. The goal toward which to strive is of course a defining and systematizing of the effective techniques of reformation.

It would be particularly fruitful to study the effect of the interplay of the personalities of correctional workers and offenders. Our investigation clearly shows that certain of the women were particularly attracted to the superintendent of the institution or to some other member of the staff or to the parole officers, while some women, on the other hand, were indifferent to or even repelled by these selfsame personalities.[6] It is also obvious that certain offenders

---

[6] Thus, no less than 81 of our women expressed a deep fondness for Mrs. Hodder, while 15

rather than others were particularly well liked by some of the officials while others elicited a response of dislike. This suggests the necessity of careful selection of persons to be in a supervisory capacity over offenders. It does not mean, of course, that reformation would necessarily be accomplished if the offender had a strong liking for her supervisor, who in turn, because of her affection and interest in her charge, would spend much effort on her behalf (see the case of Dora, p. 177 et seq.), as there are many reasons why this particular form of treatment is not always effectual. But it would increase the chances of reformation of those women who do respond to this type of treatment.

3. Other Beneficial Effects of Reformatory Experience

Thus far we have considered the influence of the Reformatory only in curbing delinquency. An analysis of the cases reveals, however, that many other benefits were derived by the inmates from the Reformatory experience, regardless of whether their recidivism was affected or not. These gains have to do with cure of venereal disease and improvement in general health, with inculcation of habits of industry, of better ethical standards, with educational advancement, with improvement in homemaking practices and care of children, with initiation into wholesome means of recreation, and often, for the first time in their lives, with the development of a wholesome libidinal outlet through deep affection for a fine human being. In Chapters XII and XIII we have already somewhat indicated the extent to which the Reformatory may be credited with accomplishing such results.

Interviews with the ex-prisoners themselves and occasionally with their relatives and friends, for opinions of how they believe they were benefited by the Reformatory experience, brought the response from sixty-seven of them that they had been trained in homemaking. Sixty women particularly emphasized that their health had been improved. Fifty-two were especially grateful for the vocational training which they had received. Forty women felt that they had learned better ethical standards. At least eighteen of the women claimed to have acquired wholesome ways of using their leisure, such as embroidering, knitting, and the like. Ten women claimed to have gained habits of self-control. Some women emphasized also the habits of industry which they acquired in the Reformatory; others that the institution had a " quieting effect " on them, or that they " got a start in the right direction," or that they " had a chance to think." Some mentioned the fact that they learned how to prevent illegitimate pregnancies and

---

expressed a strong dislike of her. Twenty-seven women expressed a dislike for a certain member of the staff, while only one expressed a strong fondness for her. A few women expressed a great affection for certain other officials of the institution; about 40 spoke with fondness of one or another of the parole agents, but at least as many expressed a strong dislike of them. While this information is not so complete as we should like, it is suggestive of the fact that different types of offenders are attracted or repelled by the same correctional workers.

venereal infection. Some said they learned to enjoy reading; others that they learned correct use of English. One woman said she learned " how to shoulder responsibility." Another spoke of the Reformatory with gratitude as " the only home I ever had," and a third said that " Mrs. Hodder [the superintendent] is the only mother I ever had." At least eighty-one women left the Reformatory with a deep fondness and attachment for Mrs. Hodder, twenty-six for the deputy superintendent, and a few for other members of the staff. Although their influence on the women did not always result in causing them to give up their delinquencies,[7] it gave them a warmth of affection and devotion that no other experience had been able to engender. This depth of attachment is illustrated by the case of the little Italian woman who, upon learning of the death of her beloved Mrs. Hodder, sent a wreath of flowers to the funeral with all her small savings laid by for her children's Christmas. In all the years that she has been out of the Reformatory she has carried a photograph of Mrs. Hodder in her purse and has treasured her memory in the face of many vicissitudes.

Most of the women who admitted any gain from the Reformatory experience indicated that they had benefited from it in more ways than one. For example, one woman said that she feels the Reformatory really did " save " her. She acknowledged frankly that she deserved to go there and that it was the best thing that could have happened to her. Her health was well taken care of. She learned a good deal about housekeeping, about sewing, and the like. She acquired industrious habits. She feels that she absorbed from the officers standards of life which have stood by her and helped her to establish better ethical ideals. Another woman said: " Yes, Sherborn did me good, I was pretty bad. I learned to do better." She claimed that the life there benefited her, that she learned much about housework and the care of children, sewing, and the like, and that in spite of some difficulties she believes the Reformatory officials were her friends. She thinks that the training helped to settle her down in a more conventional attitude of mind. Another woman feels that her second commitment to the Reformatory (the first was in 1909, before Mrs. Hodder became superintendent) was a blessing. The officials helped her to change her ideas of life and she made up her mind to return to her husband and give up her evil ways. She corresponded with one of the members of the staff, and this was a great help to her. She was cured of syphilis and also had a very necessary eye operation performed.

Still another claims that she was given every reasonable care and privilege, was well fed, trained in housework and in laundering and sewing, all of which has been useful to her. She looks back with gratitude to the efforts of Mrs. Hodder and the other matrons on her behalf. She feels that she was not only well treated, but that she was not exposed dangerously to the contagion of evil companionships and that she left the Reformatory with better standards of conduct. She did not care, after that, to return to the old life. Another woman counts

7 See case of Dora, pp. 177 et seq.

among the benefits gained in the Reformatory an abdominal operation and her training as a laundress. She learned this work entirely at the Reformatory and has made good use of the skill since. Another mentions the doubtful benefit of learning to conduct herself cautiously in order to keep out of the hands of the police.

Obviously, although the recidivism of some of these women may not have been entirely curbed, they gained something from the Reformatory experience which enriched and somewhat steadied them. In thus benefiting the inmates even a little, the Reformatory performs a valuable social service, for in any wholesome civilization some organ of society must be concerned with the betterment of those classes from which criminals are recruited; and if homes, schools, social agencies, and churches have failed in this responsibility toward delinquents, correctional institutions must step into the breach.

It is difficult at this point to say whether the benefits gained from the Reformatory experience will ultimately bring about an abandonment of the delinquencies of those women whose misbehaviour was not immediately curbed.[8] But even they readily acknowledged certain beneficial effects of the institutional experience.

We must face the issue, however, that, after all, either the delinquency of 84.8% of the women was not curbed at all, or its curbing cannot be credited primarily to the efforts of the Reformatory. It must be borne in mind, of course, that even under a most understanding régime, armed with full knowledge of who is reformable and how reformation can best be accomplished, there would still be a residue of inmates who could not be reformed and who would therefore need custodial care for an indeterminate period, or at least intensive supervision in the community. We have seen already, for example, that certain offenders respond well to parole surveillance, but return to their delinquent ways as soon as supervision is relaxed.[9] We know also that certain offenders respond well to institutional life, but recidivate when released. Obviously in such cases indeterminate incarceration is indicated. Much more research is needed in order to isolate such offenders by type. We already have many clues as to who they are, however.

4. Some Harmful Effects of Reformatory Experience

Under an ideal system of penal treatment offenders would not be harmed by a reformatory experience. In the present system of herding together under one roof women of various ages, of various degrees of experience in crime, of various types ranging from the young girl who is sentenced for " stubbornness " to

---

[8] See the next chapter, where the characteristics of the women who did not abandon their delinquencies until after the beginning of the post-parole period are compared with the characteristics of the non-delinquents and of those who were delinquent throughout the post-parole period.

[9] See p. 252, footnote.

the woman who has committed a murder or a hold-up — of commingling prostitutes, drunkards, drug addicts, pickpockets, the intelligent with the feebleminded — it can hardly be hoped that the more suggestible inmates will not be harmed by contact with some of the others.

At least sixty-one of our women insisted that they had been harmed in one way or another by their Reformatory experience, primarily by the acquisition of knowledge regarding illicit sex practices, perversions, methods of prostitution, techniques of abortion. Some women mentioned overhearing much vicious talk; some the forming of unwholesome companionships which were continued after release. A few vouchsafed that they had developed a feeling of inferiority which made their subsequent adjustment difficult, and some that they deeply felt the stigma of sentence and imprisonment. Some women claimed to have learned how to commit more serious crimes and how to avoid arrest.

A few illustrations may be given: One woman says she " learned a lot of bad things " in the Reformatory. She had never before heard the word " forgery," much less committed the crime. The inmates talked a great deal about methods of prostitution, abortion, and " everything imaginable." She admits she was a " pretty wise " girl before she went to the institution, but claims she was wiser when she came out. Another woman said that she acquired all sorts of sex knowledge expressed in the vilest kind of language. She claims she had heard about sex perversions practised among women, but had not theretofore actually seen anything of that kind carried out. " But there was one girl there who seemed to have a crush on me and she used to want to handle me and kiss me. I had to drive her off." Another woman said that " it's a wonder I was not ruined " at the Reformatory, as she was thrown into the company of women who talked in an indecent way about sex affairs and seemed to be desirous of instructing her in their methods.

Another woman insists that she was comparatively innocent when she went into the Reformatory, but learned all there was to know about badness from other inmates and reached the determination to try out some of their suggestions on release. Among the things which the girls discussed particularly during the recreation periods when there was no matron within earshot were methods of producing abortion, and the best technique for picking up fellows and getting as much as possible out of them. Another woman said that she heard so much about all the nastiness connected with sex that she felt " dirty through and through " when she came out. She heard of things that she never had dreamed existed, and she had a hard time getting them out of her mind. " Just think of taking a girl who has been bad once and sending her away in order to make a good girl of her, and then sticking her for a year or so among the nastiest girls you can think of, and letting them fill her mind with all this stuff."

To what extent these same women who claim to have been harmed by the Reformatory experience would have recidivated anyway can readily be inferred from the fact that those offenders whose recidivism was not curbed at all (or not until some time after the expiration of sentence) differed markedly in certain respects from those whose criminality was curbed.[10] We know definitely of only three cases in which the character of the later recidivism of the women can be largely blamed on the baneful influences exerted by companionships made in the institution, or to behaviour patterns acquired there.[11] For every inmate who insists that she was adversely influenced by more vicious inmates, there are several who assert that they paid no attention to the bad talk or suggestions for furthering acquaintanceships after release. There is no doubt that the Reformatory authorities are aware of the dangers in the free intermingling of all inmates. This is one reason why certain of the younger and less hardened offenders were placed at work in the superintendent's house,[12] where they could be better shielded from the vicious influences surrounding them.

5. Conclusion

The foregoing analysis has shown that even where the rehabilitation of our women may be credited to the efforts of the Reformatory, the peculiarly favourable make-up and background of these women largely contributed to the good result. Consequently, the rehabilitation of those offenders whose good behaviour after the expiration of sentence cannot fairly be assigned at all to the Reformatory (or to the parole system) must even more markedly be due to their advantageous background and traits. *Per contra,* recidivism for all or part of the post-parole period must be charged largely to the unfavourable characteristics of this particular group.

It is to the delineation of the traits and background of these various types of women as related to their conduct during the post-parole period that we now turn our attention. Through such analyses are reflected the major reasons for continued recidivism or for such reformation in conduct after expiration of sentence as obviously cannot be attributed to the influence of the Reformatory.

[10] See pp. 265 et seq.

[11] See the case of Margaret, pp. 164 et seq.

[12] See the cases of Marie, pp. 142 et seq., and Margaret, pp. 164 et seq. See also Chapter I, pp. 10 et seq.

CHAPTER XVI

OTHER REFORMATIVE INFLUENCES

1. Introductory

In the preceding chapter emphasis has been placed on the probable influence of the Reformatory in curbing the recidivism of our women. But, as already stressed, the successful adjustment of offenders to a law-abiding life in the community is partially dependent on factors and forces other than the Reformatory experience. For we saw, in the first place, that the Reformatory was effective largely with inmates possessing certain characteristics, and, secondly, that there were women upon whom the institution apparently made little if any impress, but who nevertheless adopted a law-abiding life some time after release.

What are these other factors and forces which make for the reformation of women delinquents? They may be classified in two groups: (a) certain factors in their background plus certain traits and activities which facilitate the reformative process,[1] and (b) certain favourable circumstances in their post-institutional careers — particularly of those women whose traits and background show them to be conducive to reform. The aim of the present chapter is to determine, as far as possible, within the limitations of the data, the probable role played by these various factors in curbing recidivism.

As the characteristics of the women are susceptible of statistical treatment, it is possible readily to determine which ones are favourable to reform. But some other circumstances operative in their post-institutional lives which favour the curbing of recidivism are, for the purposes of this research at least, not amenable to statistical treatment. It was impossible, because of their subtlety, to obtain an estimate of their incidence in the entire group. But an intensive analysis of many case histories has provided illustrations of these factors.

For the purpose of considering the part played in the reformative process by the favourable traits and background of the offenders we must first isolate the group of women who ultimately reformed and whose improvement in conduct cannot fairly be attributed to the influence of the Reformatory or the parole system. We have such a group in the women who, though continuing their misconduct for some time after sentence had expired, abandoned their

---

1 It will be noticed that this category embraces not only the characteristics favourable to the reform of the women by the *Reformatory*, but also those that facilitate reform in general, regardless of whether or not this was in a measure due to the influence of the Reformatory.

delinquencies at least a year before the end of the post-parole period. Clearly the reformation of these women, whom we shall for convenience designate as the "up-grade delinquents," cannot be attributed to the Reformatory or to parole, or it would have manifested itself during the official period of supervision rather than toward the end of the post-parole period.

By comparing the characteristics of the up-grade delinquents (a) with those of the women who *recidivated throughout* the five-year post-parole period (referred to as the "delinquents") and (b) with those who were *not delinquent throughout this period* (designated as the "non-delinquents") we should be able to ascertain the significance of the traits, background, and activities of our women in the reformative process. The up-grade delinquents comprise 23.8% of the total cases, the non-delinquents 23.6%, and the delinquents 52.6%.

2. Characteristics Favourable to Reformation as Revealed by Differences between Up-grade Delinquents, Non-Delinquents, and Delinquents

How up-grade delinquents differ from both non-delinquents and delinquents. Analysis of the traits and background of those women who, though delinquent during part of the post-parole period, abandoned their misconduct at least a year before its termination shows them to differ appreciably in the following respects from both the non-delinquents and the delinquents. The significance of these differences is discussed later:

1. Nativity. A higher proportion of the up-grade delinquents were native-born than either the non-delinquents or the delinquents (87.3% : 73.4% : 74.7%).[2] Among a higher proportion of them there was a possible reason for cultural friction between the offender and her parents by virtue of the fact that she was native-born while her parents were born abroad (56.9% : 45.6% : 45.9%).

2. Age of offender and kind of siblings. The up-grade delinquents are younger than the non-delinquents and the delinquents, particularly than the latter. At the time of their commitment to the Reformatory, a higher percentage of the up-grade delinquents were under twenty-one (58.2% : 51.1% : 34.4%); at the beginning of the post-parole period a higher proportion of them were twenty-five or younger (72.7% : 57.5% : 43.6%). A higher percentage of the up-grade delinquents had half- or step-siblings than either the non-delinquents or the delinquents (30% : 17% : 22.9%).

3. Industrial activity of parents prior to commitment. The fathers of a higher proportion of the up-grade delinquents were skilled workers than of the other two groups (40.4% : 22.5% : 24.3%).

The mothers of a higher percentage of them were gainfully employed outside the home than of the non-delinquents, but of a lower percentage than of the delinquents (42.9% : 35.2% : 51.7%)

[2] A difference of 8% or more in the incidence of the characteristics of a factor was taken to represent a significant difference.

4. Environmental conditions. (*a*) *In childhood and adolescence.* The homes of a far lower proportion of the up-grade delinquents were broken by death, separation, desertion, or divorce (3.7% : 15.7% : 10.3%), and a lower percentage of them lived elsewhere than in the parental home during their childhood (3.9% : 9.9% : 8.2%).

(*b*) *During the post-parole period.* A considerably higher percentage of the up-grade delinquents moved about excessively during the post-parole period than of the non-delinquents, but a much lower proportion than of the delinquents (45.5% : 17% : 68.6%).

A higher percentage of them resided in poor homes than of the non-delinquents, but a far lower than of the delinquents (11.1% : 5.3% : 48%).

A much higher proportion lived in poor neighbourhoods than of the non-delinquents, but a much lower percentage than of the delinquents (24% : 5.3% : 62.4%).

The general environmental circumstances of a much greater proportion of the up-grade delinquents were poor than of the non-delinquents, but of a far smaller proportion than of the delinquents (18.5% : 3.2% : 61.6%).

The moral standards of the homes of the up-grade delinquents were not so good as those of the non-delinquents, but better than of the delinquents (27.8% : 79.6% : 4.3%).

5. Education. A higher proportion of the up-grade delinquents did not go to school beyond the sixth grade than of the non-delinquents, but a lower proportion than of the delinquents (48% : 38.1% : 58.6%).

6. Industrial careers. (*a*) *In childhood and adolescence.* A smaller proportion of the up-grade delinquents began to work when they were under fourteen than of the other two groups (39.2% : 49.5% : 53.9%).

A much larger proportion of them entered factory work as their first employment rather than domestic service, restaurant or hotel work, or some other occupation (63.5% : 48.9% : 53.4%).

They held their first jobs for a shorter time than the others, 80% : 64.5% : 67.4%, respectively, holding their first jobs for less than a year.

A far lower proportion of them held any job for an appreciable time (over a year) than the other two groups (26.6% : 59.7% : 50%).

A somewhat higher proportion of up-grade delinquents lost their jobs through their own fault (90.9% : 83.3% : 83.8%).

A lower proportion met their economic responsibilities prior to commitment than of the non-delinquents, but a higher than of the delinquents (90.7%: 96.3%: 85.8%).

(*b*) *During the post-parole period.* A much lower proportion of the up-grade delinquents were occupied in doing their own housework instead of in gainful employment than of the non-delinquents, but a higher percentage than of the delinquents (28.9% : 51.9% : 14.4%).

Of all the women gainfully employed in the post-parole period, a lower proportion of the up-grade delinquents were steady workers than of the non-delinquents, but a higher proportion than of the delinquents (29.7% : 58% : 4%).

A lower proportion of the up-grade delinquents had good work habits than of the non-delinquents, but a higher percentage than of the delinquents (41.7% : 72.9% : 7.6%).

A much lower proportion of them than of the non-delinquents were able to hold a job over a year, but a substantially higher than of the delinquents (50% : 82.4% : 30.5%).

They earned less on the average than the non-delinquents, but more than the delinquents, the following proportions making as much as fifteen dollars or over per week: 72.7% : 83.3% : 62.3%.

A much lower percentage of them were industrial successes than of the non-delinquents, but a considerably higher than of the delinquents (21.6% : 66% : 5.2%).

A lower percentage of them met their economic responsibilities than of the non-delinquents, but a higher than of the delinquents (86.7% : 100% : 73.3%).

7. *Marital and family life.* (*a*) *Prior to admission to the Reformatory.* A higher proportion of the up-grade delinquents were single when committed to the Reformatory than of the other two groups (67.3% : 59.9% : 41.4%).

A lower percentage of them had children (legitimate or illegitimate) than of the other two groups (27.7% : 38.8% : 38.6%).

Of the women who had children, the up-grade delinquents were to a greater extent neglectful of them than the non-delinquents, but less so than the delinquents (46.1% : 34.4% : 60%).

Of those who were married, none assumed their marital responsibilities, as compared to 25% of the non-delinquents and 13.2% of the delinquents.

A lower percentage of them were competent homemakers than of the non-delinquents, but a higher than of the delinquents (10% : 20.8% : 3.8%).

(*b*) *During the post-parole period.* The conjugal relations of a lower proportion of the up-grade delinquents were good than of the non-delinquents, but of a far higher proportion than of the delinquents (65.2% : 84.9% : 10.7%).

A smaller percentage of the up-grade delinquents assumed their marital responsibilities than of the non-delinquents, but a much higher proportion than of the delinquents (86.7% : 100% : 16.7%).

A lower proportion of the up-grade delinquents were competent homemakers than of the non-delinquents, but a far higher proportion than of the delinquents (71.4% : 84.2% : 18.6%).

Of the women who had children, the attitude of a lower proportion of the up-grade delinquents was good toward them than of the non-delinquents, but of a much higher proportion than of the delinquents (71.1% : 89.8% : 21.6%).

Among all the women who were married and living with their husbands at any time during the five-year period, a far higher proportion of the husbands of the up-grade delinquents were themselves delinquent than of the husbands of the non-delinquents, but a lower proportion than of the husbands of the delinquents (56.5% : 17.6% : 75.9%).

8. Recreational outlets. Post-parole period. A far higher proportion of the up-grade delinquents spent their leisure time harmfully than of the non-delinquents, but a lower proportion than of the delinquents (62.3% : 0% : 94.7%).

The play places of a much higher percentage of them were unwholesome than of the non-delinquents, but of a lower proportion than of the delinquents (38.1% : 0% : 80%).

A far higher proportion of them had harmful companions than of the non-delinquents, but a much lower proportion than of the delinquents (53.8% : 0% : 90.8%).

A higher percentage of them failed to attend church at all during the post-parole period than of those who were non-delinquent, but a far lower proportion than of the delinquents (22.9% : 15.8% : 50%).

9. Physical and mental characteristics. A higher proportion of the up-grade delinquents were in good physical condition (except for venereal disease uncomplicated by other conditions) on admission to and discharge from the Reformatory than of either the non-delinquents or the delinquents (on admission: 55.2% : 44% : 49.1%; on discharge: 95.6% : 87.2% : 87.8%).

A lower percentage of the up-grade delinquents were of normal mentality than of the non-delinquents and a higher than of the delinquents (23.5% : 33% : 18.1%). As for outright feeble-mindedness the up-grade delinquents resemble the non-delinquents, but have a lesser incidence of feeble-mindedness than the delinquents (24.2% : 23.5% : 38.8%).

A higher proportion of the up-grade delinquents had some form of mental imbalance or deterioration (psychopathy, psychoneurosis, alcoholic deterioration, etc.) than of the non-delinquents, but a lower proportion than of the delinquents (65.4% : 59.6% : 71.8%).

10. Court record and penal experiences prior to admission to the Reformatory. A larger percentage of the up-grade delinquents had been previously arrested than of the non-delinquents, but a smaller than of the delinquents (61.8% : 54.3% : 72.8%).

A higher proportion of the up-grade delinquents were under twenty when first arrested than of the other two groups (72.7% : 58.7% : 56.1%).

A higher percentage were under twenty when first committed to a penal institution (65.4% : 53.3% : 47%).

So also a higher proportion had had penal experiences than of the non-delinquents, though a lower than of the delinquents (61.8% : 54.3% : 72.8%).

11. Sexual behaviour. (*a*) *Prior to admission to the Reformatory.* A higher proportion of the up-grade delinquents had their first illicit sex relations by their own consent instead of being raped than of the other two groups (91.7% : 73.7% : 76.9%).

A lower percentage of them had illegitimate pregnancies than of either the non-delinquents or the delinquents (46% : 65.5% : 55.3%).

(*b*) *During the post-parole period.* A far lower proportion of the up-grade delinquents were prostitutes within the post-parole period than of the delinquents, but a higher than of the non-delinquents (7.8% : 45.2% : 0%); and a far greater percentage were merely unconventional in their sexual relationships rather than promiscuous or prostitutes (47.1% : 8% : 0%).

Clearly there is a difference in the background and traits of those women who did not abandon their delinquencies until some time after the expiration of their sentences as compared with those who, on the one hand, did not recidivate at all and, on the other, were delinquent throughout the five-year period beyond the expiration of sentence. What is the significance of this difference? A rational answer to this question ought to bring us nearer to some explanations or hypotheses regarding the processes of rehabilitation of delinquents.

In the first place, it will be noted that with respect to most of the characteristics enumerated the up-grade delinquents fall between the two extremes — those who reformed immediately and those who continued their delinquencies throughout the post-parole period. In many ways the up-grade delinquents are not so advantageously endowed or characterized as those who abandoned their delinquencies immediately, but more so than those who continued their misconduct throughout the post-parole period. This is in general true of the physical and mental condition of the women, the solidarity of their homes during childhood and adolescence, the extent of their schooling, frequency of arrests and penal experiences, nature of their attitude toward their children, and their competence as homemakers. It also applies to their environmental circumstances after expiration of sentence, to their industrial habits, to their homemaking practices, to assumption of their marital responsibilities, and to their use of leisure.

Why, then, did they not abandon their delinquencies until several years had passed rather than immediately upon release from the Reformatory?

The up-grade delinquents are in the first place *younger* women, on the whole, than those comprising the other two groups. When released from the Reformatory, many of them were still adolescing. It was only after the passage of a few years that they began to respond to more favourable influences and more wholesome ways of living. Their advantages over the women who continued their delinquencies, in mental and physical condition, educational attainments recreational habits, home influences, industrial adjustments, and the like, were but *temporarily in abeyance;* they reasserted themselves in due course. Moreover, the passing of the years afforded an opportunity for the operation of many external influences, some of which, in combination with an advantageous and maturing endowment, ultimately brought about reform.

The non-delinquents (women who abandoned their delinquencies immediately on discharge from the Reformatory or before the end of parole), on the other hand, were not only a little more mature than the up-grade delinquents, but even more favourably equipped in personal traits and social background. Many of them were truly " accidental offenders," young women who in a more rational criminal procedure would hardly be sent to a correctional institution in the first place, and who would probably have reacted equally well to the oversight afforded by probation.

But there are a number of loose threads to be woven into this general explanation of the differences in outcome of our three groups. Let us turn aside for a moment from the main trend of this discussion to examine them. We see that as to some factors the up-grade delinquents differ from the other two groups, but these latter, in turn, *resemble each other.* The more important of these are: the greater proportion who were native-born, or native-born of foreign parentage; the lesser proportion whose homes were broken and who lived outside the parental home during childhood; the greater proportion who entered factory work as their first employment, who held their first job for less than a year, who lost their jobs by reason of their own fault; the lower proportion who began to work when under fourteen years of age, or who had children prior to admission to the Reformatory; the greater proportion whose physical condition on admission to the Reformatory was good; the greater percentage with dull mentality; the greater proportion whose first illicit sex experience occurred by consent rather than as a result of rape.

If our theory is sound, how explain the resemblance between the delinquents and the non-delinquents though they differed from the up-grade delinquents? In the first place, examination of the factors reveals that most of them deal with events of *childhood and adolescence.* While they may have played a role in the origin of the delinquencies of our women, they are not necessarily associated with continued recidivism.[3] Some criminogenic factors are of such nature as to expend their energies completely by the time offenders enter upon their adolescence, others extend their influence into the adolescent years, still others are potent beyond adolescence, and a few perpetuate their effects throughout the lives of offenders, some even into their offspring. For example, the up-grade delinquents have a higher incidence of native-born women of foreign-born parentage than either of the two extreme groups. Such a situation is likely to make for cultural friction between children and parents. But while this conflict, due to differences in language and custom, may be of considerable significance in

[3] Compare 500 *Criminal Careers,* pp. 256–7.

the onset of delinquency, it need not necessarily have anything to do with causing its continuance. The very fact that the two extreme groups — delinquents
and non-delinquents — resemble each other in the incidence of the characteristics we are now discussing is strong support for the inference that these factors
are but slightly involved, if at all, in producing recidivism. For if they are operative in perpetuating delinquency, one would reasonably expect their incidence
in these two extreme groups to be markedly dissimilar.

That the greater youthfulness of the up-grade delinquents is of real significance in accounting for the differences in outcome is also shown indirectly by an
examination of certain factors naturally related to age. In the incidence of these
factors, which we shall consider shortly, the up-grade delinquents did not greatly
differ from the delinquents upon entering the Reformatory; but after completion of the sentence they spurted ahead of them to a degree which finally resulted in their greater resemblance to the *non-delinquents* than to the delinquents. Consider, for example, their industrial history. Prior to commitment the
up-grade delinquents were characterized by industrial instability, in that they
held jobs for a shorter time than the other two groups and a higher proportion
of them lost their jobs through their own fault. In the post-parole period, however, the picture changes; then the up-grade delinquents markedly excelled
the delinquents in work habits, in steadiness of employment, and in industrial
success generally, though they still fell behind the non-delinquents. This would
seem to indicate that their earlier industrial instability and inaptitude were adolescent phenomena, cured in large measure by the passage of time and by
maturation. So also in the matter of marital and family life. Before commitment
to the Reformatory the up-grade delinquents closely resembled the delinquents
in their failure to assume marital responsibilities, in their incompetence as homemakers, in their neglect of their children. But during the post-parole period, as
the up-grade delinquents grew older and settled down, we find them markedly
outstripping the delinquents and approaching the non-delinquents in their
improved conjugal relations, their assumption of marital responsibilities, their
competence in homemaking, their more wholesome attitude toward their children, and like respects. In regard to recreation and companionships, the up-
grade delinquents resemble the delinquents more than they do the non-
delinquents even during the post-parole period, but, as will be seen below, the
passage of time has affected them for the better to a greater extent in these
respects than it has the delinquents.

Reviewing now the main trend of the discussion, we see that the differences
between the women who abandoned their delinquencies after the beginning of
the post-parole period (the up-grade delinquents) and the two extreme groups
(the non-delinquents and the delinquents) seem to be due essentially to the
following major sets of influences: (a) the fact that they are more favourably
endowed than the women who continued their delinquencies throughout the

five-year period, (b) the fact that they are on the whole less mature than the others — particularly than the delinquents — and therefore their tendency to reform does not manifest itself until later. Associated with these is (c) the fact that the passage of time affords the opportunity for the intervention of fortuitous reform-favouring situations. These favourable circumstances which may intervene between the release of offenders from a penal institution and their maturation are, as has already been pointed out, such as to render a statistical treatment of them practically impossible; but some conception of their character has been obtained from an intensive analysis of the case histories, the results of which are outlined in a later section of this chapter.

How up-grade delinquents differ from non-delinquents, but resemble delinquents. In the prior section we indicated the characteristics in which the up-grade delinquents differ from both the non-delinquents and the delinquents. It has already been revealed that in respect to certain factors the up-grade delinquents were not so favourably characterized as the non-delinquents. We now turn to a description of those factors in which there is a resemblance between the up-grade delinquents and the delinquents, but in which they both differ from the non-delinquents.[4]

1. Religion and church attendance. The up-grade delinquents (like the delinquents) contain a higher proportion of Catholics among their numbers than the non-delinquents (69.1% : 52.1%).

A lower percentage of them attended church regularly in childhood (58% : 68.3%); and a higher did not attend church at all within a year of commitment to the Reformatory (38.8% : 30.3%).

2. Industrial activity of parents. The up-grade delinquents (like the delinquents) have a lower proportion than the non-delinquents of fathers who were regular workers prior to the offenders' commitment to the Reformatory (54.5% : 73.7%).

3. Environmental circumstances. (a) *In childhood and adolescence.* The up-grade delinquents were to a greater extent than the non-delinquents reared in homes in which the physical conditions of living were poor (46.5% : 27.1%).

A lower proportion of the up-grade delinquents (and the delinquents) lived during childhood in neighbourhoods in which the influences were good (19.4% : 29.4%). The same is true regarding the neighbourhoods in which they lived during adolescence (14.6% : 25.4%). The up-grade delinquents (and the delinquents) have a higher proportion than the non-delinquents of women who lived in bad neighbourhoods within a year of commitment (70.7% : 60.3%).

They also have a somewhat higher proportion than the non-delinquents of women who moved about excessively prior to sentence to the Reformatory (68.5% : 60.6%).

They have a lower incidence than the non-delinquents of women who came

---

[4] For the purposes of this section, only the contrasting percentages — those of the up-grade delinquents and of the non-delinquents — need be given, as the delinquents closely resemble the up-grade delinquents in the factors analysed.

from homes in which the moral standards were good during their childhood (20% : 30.6%).

A somewhat higher proportion came from families in which there was delinquency on the part of one or more of the other members (79.6% : 73%).

In a far lower percentage were the conjugal relations of their parents good (47.7% : 64.9%).

A higher proportion of them came from homes in which the parental supervision was poor during their childhood (84.5% : 74.3%).

(b) *Within a year of commitment.* The up-grade delinquents (and the delinquents) lived to a larger extent in homes which were physically adequate (21.8% : 12.5%).

(c) *During post-parole period.* A considerably lower proportion of them than of the non-delinquents lived in only one or two different households throughout the post-parole period (38.2% : 84%).

4. *Education.* The up-grade delinquents (and the delinquents) have a lower proportion than the non-delinquents of women who attended the public rather than the parochial schools (53.7% : 66.3%).

They contain a far lower proportion than the others of girls who were not retarded in school (8.5% : 20.6%).

5. *Industrial and economic status.* (a) *Prior to commitment.* The up-grade delinquents (and the delinquents) have a substantially higher incidence than the non-delinquents of women who were industrial failures before entering the Reformatory (64% : 43.7%).

(b) *In the Reformatory.* A substantially lower percentage of them were found to be good workers in the Reformatory (33.3% : 53.9%).

(c) *Post-parole period.* A much lower proportion of them than of the non-delinquents were in comfortable circumstances during the post-parole period (14.6% : 31.9%).

A much higher percentage were dealt with by social service agencies during this period than of the non-delinquents (40% : 21.3%).

6. *Recreational outlets.* (a) *Prior to commitment.* The up-grade delinquents (and the delinquents) contain a larger proportion than the non-delinquents of girls who during their adolescent years frequented unwholesome play places (83.7% : 72.1%).

A higher percentage of them had undesirable companions during adolescence (92.3% : 82.7%).

A far lower proportion than of the non-delinquents had any constructive recreations or interests prior to commitment to the Reformatory (12.5% : 38.5%).

(b) *Post-parole period.* A higher percentage had no constructive recreations or interests during the post-parole period than of the non-delinquents (96.4% : 85.2%).

7. *Sex life.* The up-grade delinquents (like the delinquents) had a lower pro-

portion than the non-delinquents of women who began their illicit sex life when they were under fifteen years of age (18% : 25.8%).

8. *Behaviour in the Reformatory.* The up-grade delinquents (like the delinquents) were less well behaved in the Reformatory than the non-delinquents (42.6% : 58.5%).

A smaller proportion of them than of the non-delinquents entered the first grade of the institution's grade system after the customary five months in the second grade (83.3% : 90.4%).

9. *Time spent in the Reformatory.* The up-grade delinquents (and the delinquents) had a far higher incidence than the non-delinquents of women who spent a year and a half or longer in the Reformatory instead of a briefer period, a factor associated not only with the theoretical length of the sentence, but with misbehaviour in the institution or need of further medical care or training (50.8% : 35.1%).

How do these findings fit into the general theory suggested previously? Essentially, they lend further support to it. It will be observed that most of the above factors have in common the feature that they deal with the unfavourable environmental experiences and circumstances of *childhood and adolescence.* In this respect the up-grade delinquents closely resemble the delinquents, but differ from the *non-delinquents.* As already pointed out, some of these conditions, while probably strongly associated with the *origin* of delinquency, are not necessarily involved in its continuance. Since, moreover, the up-grade delinquents are, as already stressed, younger women than the delinquents, whatever tendency they may have had to improve did not manifest itself until later. Out of a mass of young offenders all similarly characterized with respect to such factors as the foregoing, some are destined to ultimate reform, others to recidivism.

But there must be other influences, temporarily held in abeyance, which account for the ultimate reformation of certain of the women, while others, although resembling them in so many ways during childhood and adolescence, continue to recidivate. And these factors are probably the ones in which the up-grade delinquents *differ* from the delinquents, resembling rather the non-delinquents. It is to these that we must therefore now turn our attention in order to round out or modify our original hypothesis.

How up-grade delinquents differ from delinquents, but resemble non-delinquents. With respect to the following factors the up-grade delinquents resemble the women who were continuously non-delinquent, both these groups differing (sometimes markedly) from those women who carried on their delinquencies throughout the five-year period:

1. *Mental make-up of parents.* The up-grade delinquents (as well as those non-delinquent throughout the post-parole period) have a somewhat higher

incidence of women who come from families in which there was no mental disease or defect, than the delinquents (54.8% : 47.8%).

2. Intelligence of offenders. The up-grade delinquents (as well as the non-delinquents) have a substantially lower incidence of feeble-minded among their number than the delinquents (24.2% : 38.8%).

3. Health. In childhood and adolescence. A somewhat lower proportion of the up-grade delinquents (and the non-delinquents) than of the delinquents had any marked physical handicaps during childhood or adolescence (28.3% : 35.6%).

A higher proportion of them than of the delinquents began to menstruate at thirteen or fourteen (the normal age) instead of earlier or later, usually the former (56.8% : 40.9%).

4. Environmental circumstances. (*a*) *In childhood and adolescence.* The up-grade delinquents (and the non-delinquents) have a somewhat lower incidence than the delinquents of women who had abnormal environmental experiences (foster-homes, etc.) in childhood (83.3% : 90.2%).

A lower proportion of them than of the delinquents lived in poor neighbourhoods during adolescence (36.8% : 45.6%).

A somewhat higher percentage of their families were in comfortable economic circumstances during the offender's childhood and adolescence than of the delinquents (11.1% : 7.8%).

(*b*) *Within a year of commitment.* A higher proportion of them than of the delinquents lived in only one household within the year prior to commitment to the Reformatory (42.6% : 32.9%).

5. Education. Double the proportion of them as of the delinquents remained in school until they were sixteen years or older (21.6% : 10.9%).

A lower percentage of them than of the delinquents were poor students (50% : 67.7%).

Twice as many of them entered high school as of the delinquents (14% : 6.8%).

6. Industrial and economic status. (*a*) *Prior to commitment.* To a far greater extent than the delinquents did the up-grade delinquents (like the non-delinquents) express some vocational ambition prior to commitment to the Reformatory, a factor related to intelligence and planfulness (60.5% : 37.3%).

A lower proportion of the up-grade delinquents (and the non-delinquents) than of the delinquents had poor work habits (22.2% : 33.9%).

(*b*) *During post-parole period.* A much lower proportion of them (and the non-delinquents) earned as little on an average as ten dollars or less a week during the post-parole period (14.3% : 36%).

7. Recreational outlets, etc. A lower proportion of the up-grade delinquents (and the non-delinquents) than of the delinquents played about in harmful places during childhood (21.7% : 28.1%).

A lower proportion had undesirable companions during childhood (20% : 29.6%).

A far lower proportion of them had contracted the drink habit prior to admission to the Reformatory (29.6% : 51.6%). And none had the drug habit, compared to 6.5% of the delinquents (and 2.2% of the non-delinquents).

8. Family relationships. Post-parole period. A very much higher proportion of the up-grade delinquents (and the non-delinquents) than of the delinquents maintained friendly relations with their families during the post-parole period (80.9% : 33.5%).

A very much higher proportion were married and living with their husbands at the end of the post-parole period (74.5% : 26.3%).

9. Delinquent conduct. Prior to commitment. The up-grade delinquents (like the non-delinquents) have a substantially higher incidence than the delinquents of women who did not become offenders until they were thirteen years or older, rather than earlier (50.9% : 36.7%). This should be considered in relation to the fact already stressed that a higher percentage of the up-grade delinquents were twenty-five or younger at the beginning of the post-parole period than of either the non-delinquents or the delinquents (72.7% : 57.5% : 43.6%).

The up-grade delinquents (like the non-delinquents) have a much higher proportion than the delinquents of women who were sex offenders only (uncomplicated by other offences) (69.1% : 49%).

The up-grade delinquents (like the non-delinquents) have a lower incidence of women who were prostitutes for more than a year prior to commitment (59.1% : 74.9%); and a lower proportion who were sexually irregular for two years or more prior to commitment (62% : 85%).

A smaller proportion of the up-grade delinquents (and the non-delinquents) had been predominantly prostitutes prior to commitment to the Reformatory (44.2% : 57.5%).

A much higher proportion of the up-grade delinquents (and the non-delinquents) than of the delinquents had been adulteresses (7.7% : 14.6%) and a higher percentage had been merely unconventional in their sex relationships than of the delinquents (13.5% : 8%).

10. Parole. A higher proportion of the up-grade delinquents (and the non-delinquents) than of the delinquents were released on parole instead of being kept in the Reformatory to serve the entire sentence (83.7% : 70.8%). It will be recalled that the two chief reasons for withholding parole are misbehaviour in the institution and uncured venereal disease.

Our analysis shows, then, that with respect to the following factors the up-grade delinquents resemble the non-delinquents, both differing from the women who continued to recidivate throughout the post-parole period: the lesser degree of mental defect and disease and the better economic condition of their parents; a lower proportion of mental defectiveness; the lesser extent of physical handicaps during childhood and adolescence and their more normal sexual development as reflected in the onset of menstruation between thirteen and fourteen years of age; fewer abnormal environmental experiences during childhood and adolescence; residence in better neighbourhoods during adolescence; more years in school, more education, and better scholarship; greater ambition for vocational training of one kind or another, and better work habits; more wholesome recreational outlets and companionships; less addiction to drink or drugs; and the later onset of their delinquencies. This last fact is to be particularly noted. It signifies that the antisociality of the up-grade delinquents and of the non-delinquents is not so deep-rooted as of the delinquents and is to a far greater extent an adolescent manifestation, having its beginnings principally between the ages of thirteen and seventeen rather than earlier. It should also be noted that the offences of the up-grade delinquents are more in the nature of uncomplicated sexual misconduct tending toward unconventional [5] sexual unions rather than toward adultery, great promiscuity, or prostitution. To a lesser extent than the delinquents did the up-grade delinquents commit non-sexual offences. It should be also noted that, on the whole, they responded far better to Reformatory treatment, as a higher proportion of them were released on parole than of those who continued to recidivate. And after release they maintained much more cordial relationships with their husbands and relatives.

In all these respects the up-grade delinquents closely resemble the non-delinquents; and were it not for certain differences in the characteristics of the up-grade delinquents and the non-delinquents, which have already been enumerated, they, like the non-delinquents, might have turned aside from antisocial ways immediately on discharge from the Reformatory or after parole, rather than some time later.

We must therefore reiterate the fact that in many important respects the up-grade delinquents are much more favourably circumstanced than the women who continued their delinquencies throughout the post-parole period. But since they were in some ways less advantageously endowed and nurtured than the non-delinquents, they had more handicaps to overcome. Many of these obstacles, however, such as unfavourable home conditions during childhood, while of significance in contributing to the original delinquency-creating situation, probably spent themselves with the passage of time and seemingly no longer wielded an influence on antisocial conduct. Such factors as educational equipment, on the other hand, are of a type whose influence is likely to be operative throughout life; and as to these, it will be observed, the up-grade delinquents resemble the non-delinquents rather than the delinquents.

Since the up-grade delinquents were younger than the non-delinquents at the time of expiration of sentence, their failure to abandon their delinquencies

[5] For definition, see Appendix C, *Sex Life, Nature of.*

until some time afterwards is also explainable in part on the ground that they did not mature emotionally until later.

There remains, however, a group of factors in which the up-grade delinquents resemble both the non-delinquents and the delinquents. How can this similarity between all three groups be accounted for if the theories we have suggested as to the factors contributing toward, or impeding, reformation are in general sound? To this question we turn our attention in the following section.

How up-grade delinquents resemble both non-delinquents and delinquents. There is but slight if any difference in the incidence of the following factors in the three groups under discussion:

The proportion of illiteracy among the parents.

The proportion of parental families dealt with by social service agencies (significant only as it reflects their inability to handle their own problems).

The size of the families from which offenders sprang.

The proportion of offenders who were only children or the first in rank where there was more than one child.

The proportion having step- or foster-parents.

The proportion of offenders who left the parental roof any time prior to commitment.

The moral standards of the homes during the adolescence of the offender and within a year of commitment to the Reformatory.

The proportion who contracted venereal disease before twenty-one years of age.

The proportion who had venereal disease on admission to the Reformatory.

The proportion usually engaged in factory work prior to commitment.

The proportion having no savings prior to commitment.

The economic condition of the offenders within a year of commitment.

The proportion who were using their leisure harmfully within a year of commitment.

The proportion who had harmful companions within a year of commitment.

The proportion who spent their leisure in unwholesome places of recreation within a year of commitment.

The proportion not attending church during adolescence.

The weak relationship of the offenders to their families within a year of their commitment to the Reformatory.

The few characteristics in which the up-grade delinquents, the non-delinquents, and the delinquents strongly resemble each other seem to bear out the point already made that there are a number of factors characterizing the background and the childhood and adolescence of offenders which, though possibly directly or remotely bearing some relationship to crime *causation,* apparently have little to do with determining later behaviour. Such a factor, for instance, as the illiteracy of parents may conceivably play an important role in conditioning misconduct or in preventing the parents from coping satisfactorily with the misbehaviour of their children. But once the children have embarked upon a career of delinquency or become confirmed offenders, the illiteracy of parents can hardly play a role in continued recidivism, as they usually no longer control or dominate the situation. Again, although the fact that a delinquent was the youngest and most pampered of the children, or that she had a step-parent, may very well be significant in the origin of her antisocial behaviour, it can hardly account for her recidivism after she has matured and is emancipated from familial control.

In regard to certain factors such as the acquisition of a venereal disease before admission to the Reformatory, or harmful use of leisure within a year of commitment, it must be remembered that almost all our women were, by the very nature of their delinquencies, similarly burdened. The relatively few factors in which the three groups of women resemble each other may well be the ones which were most potent in bringing about their original delinquency or were by their very nature closely associated with their delinquency; for those factors appear to be the only ones (a) which characterize all three groups, and (b) which are apparently not associated with recidivism. Before such a conclusion could stand, however, it would be necessary to study these factors microscopically in order fully to determine their implications; and to obtain, as a control, comparable statistics of the general female population of the same socio-economic level. Much more research along these lines has to be done to ascertain which of these factors (and what others) are really causative.[6]

3. Other Reform-Favouring Circumstances

Our analysis has indicated that the women who reformed in the course of the post-parole period were in many ways less favourably situated during all or most of the five years than those whose recidivism was curbed by the Reformatory and parole system, but more so than those whose delinquencies continued throughout the five-year period. This is particularly true as to their environmental circumstances, such as the physical condition of their homes, neighbourhood influences, moral standards; their industrial adjustments; the extent to which they met their economic responsibilities, their conjugal relationships, their assumption of marital responsibilities, their homemaking practices; and their use of leisure and their habits. In some few respects we found that the up-grade delinquents more nearly resembled the delinquents than the non-delinquents, particularly in their household stability, in their economic condition, in the greater extent to which they were dealt with by social service agencies, and in the dearth among them of constructive recreations and inter-

---

[6] Some comparable data have been presented in the descriptive-statistical chapters of this work.

ests during the post-parole period. In a few respects, however, the up-grade delinquents were found to resemble the non-delinquents, particularly in their friendly family relationships during the post-parole period and in the fact that, if married, they were, to as great an extent as the non-delinquents, living with their husbands.

As we have pointed out, the factors revealed by our analysis do not of course exhaust all the possible influences at work, either before or during the post-parole period, in making for reformation. There are a number of subtle influences and circumstances by which reformation is brought about which because of their nature (and perhaps rarity) do not permit of statistical treatment. Clues to these were secured by an analysis of many case records. They merely supplement our previous findings and are at least suggestive, if not absolutely conclusive:

1. Wholesome marriage and the responsibility of bringing up children. This involves also a satisfaction of the sex impulse. The case analysis shows that favourable marriage plays the largest role among these circumstantial factors of reformation, as the curbing of the delinquency of at least fifty-five women can be laid thereto.

2. Closely associated with marriage is often the supervision and protection afforded thereby to a woman who responds to rule by an " iron hand," if her husband happens to be the stronger personality of the two, which was often the case.

In the case of women who did not marry, such supervision was sometimes afforded by relatives, and even occasionally by employers.

Just as we have seen that certain women respond well to parole supervision, but recidivate when it is relaxed,[7] so we see here that some women respond to the type of oversight which can be afforded by persons not trained in parole work, but who have a sincere and personal interest in the welfare of the ex-prisoner. Case analysis shows that such influence is best exerted by an individual toward whom the offender can develop a feeling of affection and whose characteristics balance a lack in herself — as, for example, emotional stability where the offender is very unstable, or frugality where the offender is very careless with money, the combination making a whole which operates to the best interests of both. This observation bears further study and verification.

3. A weakening of the promiscuous sex urge with advancing years. (While the role of the passage of time has already been indicated, we here refer to its influence on the sex impulse, something it was impossible to study in all the cases, but which a number of the histories clearly suggest.)

4. Absorption in a satisfying vocation, and the feeling of self-respect engendered by a responsible job. (The factor of satisfactory vocational adjustment has already been taken into account in the preceding analysis; the above refers

[7] See p. 252, footnote, for characteristics of these women.

to the more subtly favourable adjustment to some particular work, such as nursing, for which a woman happens to be unusually well suited and in which she finds fulfilment.)

5. Just as assumption of family responsibilities operates in some cases toward reformation, so in other cases freedom from family responsibility tends to curb delinquency.

6. Settling in a new community where the offender does not have to over-come the handicaps of a past criminal record and is accepted in a friendly spirit seems to have been the major influence in some cases.

7. A simple routine of life in a protected environment. This is particularly applicable to certain types of feeble-minded women who, for example, can live safely in isolation on a farm, but get into difficulties in more complex sur-roundings.

8. A strong desire to reform or an honest conviction that bad conduct "doesn't pay." This was found in surprisingly few cases.

9. A religious conversion. This also is an infrequent cause of reformation.

It should not be inferred from the above that only one factor operated toward rehabilitation in each instance where reform occurred. On the contrary, intensive case-by-case analysis shows that usually two or more factors, in addition to the favourable characteristics of the ex-prisoner, brought about the good result. For example, in one instance a woman attributes her success to marriage and a fresh start in a community far away from her old associations. In another case the subsequent adjustment seems to be due to marriage to a decent man and also to the shock of sentence to the Reformatory. In another case reformation was probably due to the sexual satisfaction of marriage and to the restraints exercised by a husband whose personality is much stronger than his wife's. In still an-other instance reformation appears to be due to a happy marriage and to the satisfaction which the woman finds in practical nursing (in which she was trained at the Reformatory).

Many other illustrations can be given, but these suffice to make the point. Of course considerably more research is needed as to the type of person who re-sponds to a particular kind of reform-producing situation.

4. Circumstances Hampering Reformation

Just as certain circumstances in the post-institutional life of some types of offenders operate toward reform, so certain conditions or lacks militate against reclamation even in the case of ex-prisoners who possess the background and traits which as a rule favour the curbing of delinquent tendencies. Some recidi-vists are really the victims of lack of community understanding of their prob-lems and the absence of societal effort on their behalf. Fortune has not guided them into reform-producing situations; or the community has made little if any effort to provide the conditions favourable to a curbing of recidivism; or the community is definitely hostile or prejudiced and does not give the ex-prisoners a "fair chance" of survival by legitimate efforts. In many instances the continued tolerance in some regions of low standards of morality, as well as a general indifference to the welfare of ex-prisoners, is a major cause for the continued misbehaviour of certain women whose background and traits favour their reformation. In other instances the fact that the community does not take the trouble to enlighten ex-prisoners further as to American customs, particularly in respect to sex morality (a work which the Reformatory may have begun, but could not complete), may account for postponing or even preventing their reform.

In a community fully aroused to its responsibilities toward ex-prisoners, enforcing a sensible program for collaborating with institutional and parole officials in the work of rehabilitation, lie the now dormant conditions for the reclamation of some at least of the hordes of delinquents and criminals constantly pouring out of our correctional institutions. This conclusion is applicable to most ex-prisoners; it is particularly pertinent in respect to those offenders who, as already indicated, respond well to some kind of community oversight but not to incarceration, or to parole oversight but not to a wholly self-propelling life in freedom.

5. Conclusion

What is the significance of these findings? They reveal that the reformation of an offender is dependent upon at least two sets of variables, (a) an endowment (native and acquired) which is favourable to reform, and (b) particular treatments or conditions to which offenders having certain characteristics are most likely to respond. The fact that certain of our women and not others responded to Reformatory treatment or to parole treatment is proof of this point.

In the second place, our findings bring us closer to the intricate problem of crime-causation as contrasted with recidivism, in giving us a means of isolating, in what seems to be a logical manner, causative factors from others. We have pointed out, for example, that certain influences in the lives of offenders may be of considerable significance in criminogenesis, but probably bear only a doubtful relationship to recidivism or reform.

Thirdly, findings like the foregoing furnish an approach to a better management of the crime problem (particularly as concerns women offenders) than at present exists; for they indicate that it is possible to fit to any specific type of offender the treatment most promising to her, thereby substituting a scientific methodology for the existing practice of working more or less in the dark.

Obviously, it is not the Reformatory or the parole system or any incidental experience or treatment such as marriage, absorbing work, or "rule by an iron hand," or living in a protected environment, *alone,* that brings about the desired result of reformation, but rather the interaction of such experiences with certain characteristics found in the background and careers of certain offenders who respond to them.

Findings such as these (some of which have not been worked out in detail because further research materials are necessary) should enable the authorities to tell *in advance* of sentence or of release of prisoners, which types of offenders are likely to recidivate (under the existing régime), which are likely to respond immediately to Reformatory and parole treatment, and which may reform later, provided certain circumstances become operative in their lives. This should aid in distinguishing the offenders who require lengthy incarceration (or even lifelong isolation and control) from those who may profitably and safely be released after a brief period of supervision and instruction. Women with the characteristics of the non-delinquents, for example, might profitably be handled on probation rather than by the more stringent and expensive method of incarceration; and more thought and time might well be expended by all concerned on offenders of the type of our up-grade delinquents than upon those who are very likely to be permanent offenders.

An instrumentality which is practicable in forecasting recidivism as well as the treatment likely to be most suitable to various types of offenders is presented in the next chapter, to be used as a possible model in furthering the development of this phase of the new penology.

CHAPTER XVII

PREDICTING RECIDIVISM AND APPROPRIATE TREATMENT

1. Introductory

Prediction of recidivism. We have seen that the make-up and background of offenders is definitely related to their reformation or recidivism. A very important consequence of this finding is that it ought to be possible to utilize a sample of the characteristics of offenders for the purpose of predicting their future response to treatment. Possessed of accurate information as to such traits in any single case, courts and parole authorities ought to be able to determine beforehand what an offender's response to treatment is likely to be. The principle is the same as that by which insurance companies, knowing the facts as to the age, occupation, and health of an applicant for insurance, can predict his probable life-span and thereby determine the rate of the premium to be charged.

If the discipline of criminology ever reaches a point where it can accurately foretell the behaviour of various types of offenders, it will enter on a new and far-reaching era of development. The first steps toward such an evolution have been taken in recent years by the creation of several types of prognostic devices to be used by parole boards and, as the authors have urged, by sentencing authorities.[1] Without the employment of such devices the definite effects of treatment applied by correctional agencies can never be put to a test; the types of offenders who require prolonged or permanent custodial care cannot be differentiated; the length of extra-mural supervision needed by different classes of offenders cannot definitely be determined. Correctional and parole officials, as

[1] See H. Hart: "Predicting Parole Success," *Journal of Criminal Law and Criminology*, Vol. XIV (1923), pp. 405 et seq.; Bruce, Harno, Burgess, and Landesco: *Workings of the Indeterminate-Sentence Law and the Parole System in Illinois* (1928), Chap. XXX; and S. and E. T. Glueck: "Predictability in the Administration of Criminal Justice," *Harvard Law Review*, Vol. XLII (1929), pp. 297 et seq., reprinted in *Mental Hygiene*, Vol. XIII (1929), pp. 678 et seq.; and *500 Criminal Careers*, Chap. XVIII. See also C. Tibbits: "Success or Failure on Parole can be Predicted," *Journal of Criminal Law and Criminology*, Vol. XX (1931), pp. 11 et seq.; G. B. Vold: *Prediction Methods and Parole* (Minneapolis: Sociological Press, 1931); C. E. Gehlke: "Testing the Work of the Prison," *Annals of the American Academy of Political and Social Science*, Vol. 157 (1931), pp. 121 et seq.; and Elio G. Monachesi: *Prediction Factors in Probation* (Minneapolis: Sociological Press, 1932). For some criticisms, see W. D. Lane: "A New Day Opens for Parole," *Journal of Criminal Law and Criminology*, Vol. XXIV (1931), pp. 88 et seq.

well as judges sentencing offenders, are still working more or less in the dark.

"Common sense" methods not adequate. It is often argued that the "practical experience" and "wisdom" of the sentencing, correctional, and paroling authorities is adequate to the task of choosing the particular form of treatment required in the individual case; of determining when and if to release any offender on parole, and which offenders to incarcerate permanently. But even the most intelligent officials work blindly as long as they do not consider each case which comes before them in the light of past outcomes in hundreds of similar cases. They cannot rely on their memories of what happened to various types of offenders whom they previously sentenced, or released on parole. A systematic study of the results of different forms of penal treatment is certainly essential if the disposition of cases is to be guided scientifically on the basis of previous experience. The present research is an effort in this direction.

The staff of the Massachusetts Reformatory for Women is particularly intelligent and forward-looking. The superintendent and her aids made certain recommendations and prognoses in many of our cases. In not a few instances their prognoses were wrong and might have worked great havoc because of the very circumstance that these cases had not been considered in the light of a scientific analysis of experience with hundreds of similar cases. Actually, of seventy-eight cases in which they made a prognosis, subsequent outcomes revealed that they had grossly erred in at least two fifths of their prognoses. Consider these illustrations: In one instance the staff recommended that a woman be placed in permanent custody. Examination into the behaviour of this woman during the five-year period following the expiration of her sentence revealed that she had in fact made a very satisfactory adjustment in freedom. Had the Reformatory officials utilized predictive tables based on a study of the post-institutional adjustment of hundreds of women, they would have seen that this inmate had more than an even chance of adjustment if released on parole, a fact borne out by her subsequent reformation. The Reformatory officials prognosticated that another inmate would "revert to shiftlessness," and averred that "she is of the kind who does not profit much by experience or counsel." It happened, however, that this woman married and settled down nicely. Her home is neat and clean; she takes good care of her children and is no longer delinquent. Again, had the officials consulted prognostic tables which objectively embodied experience with similar cases, they would hardly have fallen into such a marked error of judgment, for the factors in the make-up and career of the woman indicated in advance that her rehabilitation was very probable. In still another case the Reformatory staff was of the conviction that there is "nothing about her which is at all hopeful for the future." Here again the woman in question was completely rehabilitated, and use of predictive instruments would have shown a great likelihood of this eventuality. One more case may be cited, showing that "common sense" must be supported by scientific method if true progress is to be achieved in dealing with the criminal classes.[2] In this case the Reformatory officials recommended to the parole board that the offender, who was a mental defective, be committed to a school for the feeble-minded. The family of the offender, on the other hand, urged that the authorities " give her a chance in the community first on parole." She was paroled only because there was no room for her in the school for the feeble-minded. The ultimate outcome proved that the family was far wiser in its suggestion for treatment than the Reformatory officials; for the woman, who has been watched closely by her relatives, is leading a decent life. All of which illustrates the fact that the Reformatory officials cannot really develop expertness in gauging the future conduct of inmates without checking their prognoses in numerous cases. The " common sense " approach may supplement, but it certainly cannot replace, the less impressionistic approach offered in the predictive tables to be described.

2. Construction of Prognostic Tables

Method. The first step in establishing prediction tables is to determine the relationship between the traits and characteristics of offenders and their behaviour during a reasonable period following the expiration of penal treatment (in this case, sentence to the Reformatory). In a previous work [3] these relationships (in

TABLE 8

CHURCH ATTENDANCE AND NON-RECIDIVISM
(Percentages)

Church Attendance	Rate of Non-Recidivism
Regular...............	28.4
Irregular.............	14.9
None................	40.0
Total............	23.5

the case of five hundred graduates of the Massachusetts Reformatory for men) were determined statistically by means of the somewhat involved computation of the " coefficient of mean square contingency." [4] For the purposes of this research a simpler, less time-consuming computation was found equally effective.[5] It consists in establishing the degree of association between any particular factor (such as *church attendance* in the table above) and non-recidivism, by the simple determination of the maximum percentage difference between any sub-

[2] See *500 Criminal Careers,* pp. 295–6, where the predictive method is compared with that of the typical sentencing judge.

[3] Ibid., Chaps. XVI and XVII.

[4] Ibid., footnote, p. 239.

[5] Use of this method was suggested by Professor E. A. Hooton of Harvard University, who has had wide and varied experience in the preparation of anthropologic data for statistical treatment.

class of a particular factor and the expectancy of non-recidivism for the entire group of cases involved. The method is exemplified in Table 8. It will be seen that the maximum percentage difference between a single subcategory of the factor of *church attendance* and the expectancy for the total is 16.5%, which is the difference between 40% and 23.5%.[6]

By comparing the degree of relationship to recidivism by the above method with that yielded by the more elaborate computation in the use of the mean square contingency coefficient, the following scale was established:

Maximum Difference in Percentages between Category of a Factor and Expectancy of Non-Recidivism	Degree of Relationship Indicated between the Factor and Non-Recidivism
3 and under	None
4–7	Slight
7–15	Appreciable
15–26	Considerable
26 and over	High

By relating all the pre-commitment factors in the careers of our women (family and personal history) to their conduct in the five-year period after the expiration of the Reformatory sentence, it was established that the factors listed in the footnote bear a considerable or high association to future conduct.[7]

Method of selecting factors for prediction tables. In constructing prediction tables based on the careers of offenders we may, theoretically, utilize as many factors in their lives as we wish. The fewer the factors, however, the simpler is the predictive device, the more feasible is it to apply, and the less work does it entail upon probation officers, institutional officials, and parole agents in gathering data that need to be known in the individual case. In the prognostic method developed in a previous investigation we employed the minimum number of factors which (a) reflect the major aspects of the offender's life and (b) afford a high degree of prediction.[8] This method (with modification) is further developed in the present study.

[6] Where this method yielded the same values for two different factors and it was necessary to choose between them, the *mean* difference between the percentages of all the subclasses and the expectancy of non-recidivism for the entire group of cases was computed. In the above table, for example, the mean difference is 10, obtained by averaging the difference between 23.5 and 28.4 (which is 4.9), that between 23.5 and 14.9 (8.6), and that between 23.5 and 40 (16.5).

[7] In the order of the intensity of relationship, these factors are as follows, the item in parentheses being that *subclass* of each factor which contains the lowest proportion of recidivists: delinquency (non-delinquent); leisure and habits (constructive); industrial adjustment (successful); scholarship (good); steadiness of employment (regular); mental condition (no mental disturbance); competence as homemaker (good); neighbourhood influences within a year of commitment (good); physical condition of home within a year of commitment (good); retardation in school (none); church attendance (non-attenders); household in childhood (living with relatives or foster-parents rather than with own parents); work habits (good); economic responsibility (met); neighbourhood influences during adolescence (good).

Definitions of all factors discussed in this chapter will be found in alphabetical order in Appendix C, "Definition of Terms."

[8] Since a high correlation has been proved to exist between the predictive method developed by

After reducing the 153 factors in the family and personal history of our women to the fifteen listed in footnote 7, found to bear the highest association to non-recidivism, we finally selected five of these for the construction of the prediction tables. Since each of the fifteen factors bore a high relationship to non-recidivism, *any* five might have been chosen. But certain practical considerations entered into determining the selection:

a. The feasibility of obtaining certain data. For instance, in dealing with adult offenders, it is very difficult for court and institutional officials to obtain accurate data regarding the childhood of offenders. For this reason such a factor as *church attendance in childhood* was eliminated.

b. The factor of *pre-Reformatory delinquency* was excluded because it embraced not only delinquency and criminality officially noted, but also misconduct for which the offender might have been arrested, but was not. Even official records of the prior criminality of offenders are notoriously incomplete, since offences committed in other jurisdictions (to cite but one reason for the inadequacy of official records) are often not known to local authorities. To include a factor which, in daily practice, is so inaccurately reported was not deemed wise, since more easily obtainable data accomplish the purpose of prediction just as well.

c. Of the three factors pertaining to vocation, — *industrial history, steadiness of employment,* and *work habits* — the first is a composite of the other two. *Steadiness of employment* was chosen, therefore, as it bears a higher relationship to non-recidivism than does the factor *work habits.*

d. As between *scholarship* and *school retardation,* the latter was chosen because information thereon is more readily secured by probation, parole, and institutional officials and is not so liable to variation in definition in the different schools as the factor *scholarship.*

e. Of the four factors dealing with home and neighbourhood conditions, *neighbourhood influence within a year of commitment* was selected, as it is the one on which officials can most easily secure data.

f. *Competence as homemaker* was omitted because it applies only to those women who kept house.

On the basis of the foregoing considerations, the following five pre-Reformatory factors in the careers of our women were utilized in the construction of the prognostic tables: *retardation in school, neighbourhood influences within a year of commitment, steadiness of employment, economic responsibility, mental condition.*

The actual percentage of non-recidivism ("success rate") of the different subclasses of each of these five factors is indicated below:

the authors (*500 Criminal Careers,* Chap. XVIII), in which relatively few, but *weighted,* factors were used, and that developed by Burgess, op. cit., in which numerous unweighted factors were used (see Monachesi, op. cit., and Vold, op. cit.), and since our method is more economical in its actual application, we have continued to construct predictive tables on as few factors as give the desired results.

(1) *Retardation in School* *

Subclass	Success Rate
No retardation	42.4%
Retarded one or more years	20.3%
No schooling	13.3%

* Maximum difference between percentage of any subclass and expectancy for entire group is 18.9%.

From this it is seen that of the women who were not retarded in school, 42.4% did not recidivate after the expiration of sentence to the Reformatory. Of those who were retarded a year or more, however, only half that proportion did not recidivate; while among those who had had no schooling there were still fewer who did not recidivate.

Each of the remaining factors may be similarly analysed:

(2) *Neighbourhood Influences within a Year of Commitment* *

Subclass	Success Rate
Good	45.5%
Fair	27.4%
Poor	21.3%

* Maximum difference 22.

(3) *Steadiness of Employment* *

Subclass	Success Rate
Regular	46.4%
Fairly regular	29.2%
Irregular	18.9%
Never worked	18.2%

* Maximum difference 22.9.

(4) *Economic Responsibility* *

Subclass	Success Rate
Met	27.6%
Not met	8.8%
Self-support not necessary	5.0%

* Maximum difference 18.5.

(5) *Mental Abnormality* *

Subclass	Success Rate
None	29.2%
Psychopathic, psychoneurotic, neurasthenic	22.8%
Epileptic, cong. syph., drug addict	19.2%
Alcoholic deteriorate	9.0%
Psychotic, or question of psychosis	0.0%

* Maximum difference 23.5.

Establishment of score-classes. The foregoing five factors furnished the basis for the construction of a prognostic instrument (Table 9) which judges might use in determining how any particular defendant is likely to respond to treatment (in the type of reformatory represented by the Massachusetts institution). The table was constructed as follows: (1) By adding the highest percentages in each of the five foregoing factors on the one hand, and the lowest on the other, we ascertained the upper and lower limits of the success score. The highest possible success rate on the foregoing five pre-Reformatory factors is 191.1, the lowest 57.8. (2) Between these limits we next established score-classes. (3) We then classified each of our women in the appropriate score-class according to (a) her score and (b) her recidivism.[9] Table 9, based on the five factors enumerated, illustrates the procedure:

TABLE 9

RATE OF NON-RECIDIVISM AND SUCCESS SCORE ON FIVE PRE-REFORMATORY FACTORS
(Percentages)

Success Score	Non-delin-quent	Delinquent throughout	Up-grade Delinquent	Total
Under 100.	8.0	88.0	4.0	100
100–125.	15.9	66.4	17.7	100
125–150.	31.3	54.7	14.0	100
150–175.	50.0	42.9	7.1	100
175 and over.	100.0	.0	.0	100

3. Prognostic Instrument for Courts

From the above table a judge, in determining whether to sentence a woman to a reformatory, can with considerable accuracy gauge the advisability of such a disposition of the case, providing he has reliable data on all the five factors of the defendant's history. If, for example, the offender scores less than 100 the judge can see immediately that she has less than one out of ten chances of reform (8 : 100) if sent to a reformatory or similar institution. The table further indicates to him that even some years after the completion of her sentence her chances of reforming are very low (4 : 100).[10] If the judge should have at hand similar prognostic tables for each of the other possible forms of treatment that

---

[9] It will be noted that we have distributed the delinquents into two groups: those who were delinquent to the end of the five-year period and those whose delinquency ceased at least within a year of the end of the five-year period but not before the beginning of it. An analysis of the group (see pp. 264) has already disclosed that it differs markedly enough in characteristics from the non-delinquents and the delinquents to be regarded separately.

[10] An interesting experimental application of this method to a well-known case is made by Judge Joseph N. Ulman, "The Trial Judge's Dilemma: A Judge's View," in *Probation and Criminal Justice,* edited by Sheldon Glueck (1933), note 3, p. 132.

society places at his command (probation, fine, filing the case without any super-vision, imprisonment in a jail, and the like), he could then determine which of the alternative remedies is the most likely to succeed in the particular case before him. If, for example, objectified past experience as embodied in prognostic tables were to show that a defendant of a particular type has the greatest chance of not recidivating if placed on probation, he would apply this particular form of treatment rather than some other.

4. Prognostic Instruments for Parole Authorities

Selection of parolees. The next two prognostic tables are models for the use of parole boards in determining which inmates of a reformatory to release on parole[11] and how long to keep them under parole supervision. Table 10 is based on the five factors which entered into the composition of the first prog-nostic table, plus the most significant factor in the Reformatory life of the women: namely, their work habits in the institution. Here, again, other factors in the Reformatory experience of the inmates might have been utilized in the construction of the table. But the factor chosen bears the most marked relation-ship to recidivism, and information regarding it is readily obtainable. As the inclusion of but one additional factor yields a high measure of predictability, there is little point and less economy in using more factors.

(6) *Kind of Worker in Reformatory* *

Subclass	Success Rate
Good	32.7%
Fair	18.0%
Poor	15.4%

* Maximum difference 9. No factor in the Reformatory life of the women bore more than the appreciable relationship to non-recidivism indicated by these figures. In addition to the reasons given above for choosing this particular factor instead of such others as *months spent in second grade* (of the institution's grade system), *number of previous sentences to the Reformatory, emotional stability of women in the Reformatory,* and the like, two other reasons should be given: first, we wished to avoid factors the reliability of which is partially dependent on the temperament or prejudices of institution staffs; secondly, we omitted *number of prior sentences to the Reformatory* as a factor in prognosis because there are so few women who had such prior sentences.

With the addition of the above factor to the five pre-Reformatory factors the highest possible success score becomes 223.8 and the lowest 73.2. By appro-

[11] As long as a system of completely indeterminate sentences does not exist, it is preferable that *all* prisoners, since they must be released from prison at some time, be placed under some parole su-pervision rather than belched forth into the community without any oversight during the dangerous transitional period from imprisonment to freedom. However, society may before long evolve other forms of extra-mural treatment in addition to parole or release without any supervision at all; for example, oversight by the police, or "preventive detention" as applied in continental countries, or a system analogous to the indenture practice employed in a few cases by the Reformatory for Women in Massachusetts. In such an event predictive tables based on a statistical transcription of experience with hundreds of women treated extra-murally by these various methods will be of value to the authorities charged with releasing prisoners from correctional institutions.

priately distributing the cases into their classes, we have a prognostic table (number 10) which is suitable for the use of parole boards:

TABLE 10

RATE OF NON-RECIDIVISM AND SUCCESS SCORE ON FIVE PRE-REFORMATORY AND ONE
REFORMATORY FACTORS
(Percentages)

Success Score	Non-delin-quent	Delinquent throughout	Up-grade Delinquent	Total
Under 100............	.0	100.0	.0	100
100–125..............	9.1	86.4	4.5	100
125–150..............	16.3	69.4	14.3	100
150–175..............	25.0	55.0	20.0	100
175–200..............	47.6	47.6	4.8	100
200 and over.........	100.0	.0	.0	100

From the above table parole authorities can see at a glance that an inmate of a reformatory whose score on the six factors is under 100 has no chance of making a good adjustment in the community for a reasonable period (five years) after the expiration of sentence. Such an offender requires more or less permanent incarceration or at least intensive supervision on parole for an indefinite period, if society is to be protected from her probable recidivism. It may of course be that with the passage of years and the resultant settling down she will cease to be a menace. But as long as legal authorities lack the right to hold such women for as long a time as necessary and are compelled to release prisoners either before the expiration of the maximum limit of the sentence or when the maximum is reached, parole supervision of women of this type is not likely to prevent recidivism and protect society. On the other hand, a parole board is enabled, by the use of prognostic devices like the above, to select for permanent release those inmates who are very likely not to recidivate (a woman with a success score of 200 or more is such a one). In fact, for offenders of this type, parole oversight may be altogether unnecessary. A pardoning board may also well use such a table on which to base its recommendations to the executive power. Several instances are personally known to us in which, because of political pressure or strong public sentiment, prisoners have been granted pardon who shortly reverted to criminality. If the prediction chart indicates that a prisoner has little if any chance of being a decent citizen, a pardon should not be granted; thereby society would be protected.

When to terminate parole supervision. In addition to determining whether to release a prisoner on parole, the authorities should decide, from time to time, which parolees to continue further on parole and which to discharge from supervision. At present, parole boards have to rely upon the rather meagre reports they receive from their agents regarding the conduct of parolees, whose supervision is generally terminated if they have abided by the rules of parole. Our research has shown, however, that some offenders, though good parolees, are dangerous citizens when released from oversight.[12]

A predictive instrument like Table 11 would be of practical value to parole boards in administering a completely indeterminate sentence and also (under the present upper-limit sentences) in determining which offenders could be released from a reformatory without any parole oversight or with only brief supervision. For the purpose of this predictive table we might have utilized several factors in the parole experiences of our women which were found to bear a considerable relationship to recidivism.[13] But, again, for practical considerations, and because the factor *recreations and interests during parole* was found to bear the highest association to recidivism after the expiration of sentence, it alone was embraced in the table. It is to be noted that we have not yet taken into account those women who served their full sentence in the Reformatory without parole. In order to make the prognostic table more useful, provision is made for this class of women.

(7) *Recreations and Interests during Parole* *

Subclass	Success Rate
Constructive	65.2%
Not constructive	19.7%
No parole	11.8%

* The maximum difference between the percentage of any subclass and the expectancy for the entire group is 41.7.

The score limits for Table 11 are 289 on the one hand and 85 on the other.

TABLE 11

RATE OF NON-RECIDIVISM AND SUCCESS SCORE ON FIVE PRE-REFORMATORY FACTORS, ONE REFORMATORY FACTOR, ONE PAROLE FACTOR

(Percentages)

Success Score	Non-delin-quent	Delinquent throughout	Up-grade Delinquent	Total
Under 175............	12.3	75.4	12.3	100
175–225...............	35.9	41.0	23.1	100
225 and over.........	100.0	.0	.0	100

From the above table a parole board can see that an inmate to be released at the termination of sentence, or one already on parole, whose score on the

12 See p. 252, footnote.

13 These were (in parentheses is the subclass of each factor having the lowest proportion of recidivists): recreations and interests (constructive), leisure and habits (constructive), industrial history (successful), work habits (good), economic responsibility (met), steadiness of employment (regular).

seven factors is less than 175, probably has but one chance out of ten (12.3 : 100) of making a satisfactory adjustment in freedom immediately or after a few years. On the other hand, an offender with a score of 225 or over has every chance of succeeding after the expiration of her sentence and could probably be safely returned to the community with little if any parole supervision. The problem is to protect society against certain types of offenders by keeping them on parole or under similar surveillance for adequate periods. At present parole authorities are seriously hampered by the upper limits of sentences which are fixed by the penal statutes. Even though they know or suspect that certain parolees will revert to a life of crime as soon as they are released from parole supervision, they are compelled to release them upon expiration of the upper limit of the sentence originally imposed by the court. Thoughtful penologists have long urged that sentences for the more serious or chronic types of offenders should have no upper limit, since, obviously, it is a wasteful and harmful procedure to release from supervision persons who will probably recidivate. But without the use of prognostic tables parole boards could not determine which offenders to keep under long supervision even if they had the authority to do so under a completely indeterminate sentence.

5. Prognostic Table for Courts about to Sentence Recidivists

Under the present administration of criminal justice a substantial proportion of defendants of all types appearing before our criminal courts are recidivists, many of them having already experienced probation, imprisonment, and parole. Under the proposed system of wholly indeterminate sentences it is to be hoped that many of these will be removed from the army of delinquents who today march in unbroken legions in and out of the courts.

A final prediction table is designed to aid the courts in coping with recidivists who have already been in a reformatory. Obviously, such a table should include not only the factors already embraced in the preceding prognostic tables, but one or more factors in their careers during a reasonable period beyond expiration of the reformatory sentence. As a rule, authorities are not concerned with the behaviour of offenders after the outside limits of the sentence have been completed. Such an attitude, however, while natural enough in busy officials, is short-sighted. It is an illustration of what, we venture to assert, is probably a major weakness in the process of administering criminal justice: namely, that each official, stationed at one point on the offender's journey from arrest to his ultimate return to society, regards his particular post as the all-important one, and his part in the process as an end in itself. He is all too prone to overlook the fact that his function is intimately related to those which precede and succeed his.

Of what use to society are good parolees if they relapse into delinquency and crime as soon as parole supervision is removed? Obviously, therefore, parole boards and courts should take into account the behaviour of offenders not only behind lock, bar, and wall, nor yet under parole supervision, but during a reasonable period — in this study five years — after the expiration of sentence. No less than twenty-one factors in the post-parole careers of our women were found to bear a high relationship to recidivism during this period.[14] Again proceeding on the principle of economy, we have selected for the prognostic table only four of the factors listed in footnote 14: namely: *neighbourhood influences, economic responsibility, family relationships,* and *household stability.* The practical considerations already mentioned [15] dictated the choice. The proportion of non-recidivists in each subclass of these factors is as follows:

(8) *Neighbourhood influences* *

Subclass	Success Rate
Good	73.2%
Fair	29.6%
Poor	3.1%

* Maximum difference 49.7.

(9) *Economic responsibility* *

Subclass	Success Rate
Self-support not necessary	54.3%
Responsibility met	22.6%
Responsibility not met	.0%

* Maximum difference 30.8.

(10) *Family relationships* *

Subclass	Success Rate
Success	54.0%
Failure	2.3%

* Maximum difference 30.5.

(11) *Household stability* *

Subclass	Success Rate
No change of household	49.1%
One change of household	35.2%
Two changes	12.0%
Three or more	5.8%

* Maximum difference 25.6.

[14] In the order of their degree of relationship (in parentheses the subclasses having the lowest incidence of recidivism): leisure and habits (constructive), haunts (good), environmental condition (good), sex irregularity (none), recreations and interests (constructive), moral standards (good), neighbourhood influences (good), neighourhood type (suburban), industrial history (successful), steadiness of employment (regular), physical condition of home (good), conjugal relations (good), economic condition (comfortable), marital responsibility of offender (assumed), competence as a homemaker (good), delinquency of husband (none), work habits of offender (good), family relationships (successful), economic responsibility (self-support not necessary; but where necessary, responsibility met), offender's attitude toward her children (good), household stability (no change).

[15] See p. 288.

Adding the success rates in the two extreme subclasses of each of the above factors to the score limits of the preceding prognostic table, we obtain the upper-limit score of 519.6 and the lower of 96.2. Table 12 is for use by courts in dealing with recidivists who have already experienced a reformatory sentence:

TABLE 12

RATE OF NON-RECIDIVISM AND SUCCESS SCORE ON FIVE PRE-REFORMATORY FACTORS, ONE REFORMA-
TORY FACTOR, ONE PAROLE FACTOR, AND FOUR POST-PAROLE FACTORS
(Percentages)

Success Score	Non-delinquent	Delinquent throughout	Up-grade Delinquent	Total
Under 350............	14.0	68.6	17.4	100
350–400.............	70.6	11.8	17.6	100
400 and over.........	90.9	.0	9.1	100

On the basis of this table a judge considering what the chances of permanent adjustment are for a woman recidivist if he sends her again to a reformatory can readily see that such an offender has little more than one chance in ten (14 : 100) of not recidivating if she scores less than 350; while if she scores 400 or more, she has nine out of ten chances (90.9 : 100) of permanent rehabilitation.

In a prior publication we demonstrated the feasibility of prognostic tables by applying them to a series of actual cases, which showed that the outcomes correspond to the expectancies indicated in the tables.[16]

6. Forecasting Treatment

In the foregoing analysis the point of orientation is the behaviour of the women during the post-parole period, because, as we have previously indicated, the real test of the effectiveness of the Reformatory and parole system is the ultimate behaviour of offenders who have been subjected to such treatment and not their interim conduct while under restraint. But the study of the behaviour of offenders in an institution, as contrasted with their behaviour when released, and of their conduct while under parole supervision as opposed to complete freedom, is also significant, as it affords a means of determining the particular form of treatment to be accorded different types of offenders. The criminal who responds to an institutional régime but recidivates after release (whether on parole or in complete freedom) should obviously be retained in an institution for an indefinite period.

Under the present peno-correctional system, in which there is no completely indeterminate sentence, it is difficult to say just how such offenders should be handled; for, while their retention in the institution for the entire sentence

[16] *500 Criminal Careers*, pp. 289–94.

postpones their relapse, it also deprives them of the benefit of parole oversight for a transitional period between life in an institution and complete freedom. If the time ever comes, however, when sentences are completely indeterminate, offenders of the above type will be incarcerated for many years, or at least beyond the child-bearing age, with trial periods in the community to determine when they can finally be set completely free.

There is also a type of offender who responds well to parole oversight or to something which resembles it, such as the " iron hand " of a person in authority or some relative, friend, employer, and the like. Obviously, supervision of some kind is indicated in these cases.[17]

There is yet a third group of women who respond neither to the Reformatory nor to parole oversight and who recidivate after release; and for them new forms of treatment must be experimented with. Among them, for example, are certain types of feeble-minded, psychotics, drunkards, drug addicts, psychopaths, and the like. Unfortunately, this investigation does not embrace a sufficient sample of each one of these types to permit of statistical treatment, but ample illustrations will be found in Chapters II and IX.[18]

The response of offenders to these various forms of treatment can readily be predicted by prognostic tables constructed similarly to those described in this chapter. Inasmuch, however, as the applicability of such tables is dependent upon the existence of a wholly indeterminate sentence together with a more rational system of sentencing than at present exists, we have postponed their construction.

There is still another application of the method of forecasting the results of treatment. Not only can the response of various types of offenders to the Reformatory or parole system as a whole be predicted, but also their reaction to the specific mechanisms of treatment within those institutions. A beginning in this direction has been suggested in Chapter XV.

7. Conclusion

Considerable research still remains to be done on the subject of prediction of recidivism and treatment. Meanwhile, the practical application of prediction tables would pave the way for much needed changes in the administration of criminal justice. Scientific control might thereby take the place of hunches and guess-work.

We have traced the careers of five hundred delinquent women from childhood through a substantial time beyond the completion of their sentences to the Reformatory. We have shown what relationship their characteristics bear to their ultimate rehabilitation or relapse and have indicated how feasible it is to

---

[17] For the characteristics of this group, see p. 252, footnote.
[18] See the cases of Minnie, Angelina, Dora, Florence, Alice.

employ such information in a scientific attack upon the problems involved in the sentencing, treating, paroling, and pardoning of offenders against the law. We turn, by way of conclusion, to a summary of the major issues presented by the findings of this research and to a discussion of the remedies suggested by them.

CHAPTER XVIII

SUMMARY, CONCLUSIONS, AND RECOMMENDATIONS

1. Major Findings

The soil and fruit. As we reflect on the evidence marshalled in the preceding pages, certain features of the detailed picture assume prominence. Before making suggestions toward the improvement of existing practices, it is well to summarize these outstanding features.

When we consider the family background of our women, we should rather marvel that a sizable fraction of them, by one influence or another, abandoned their misbehaviour, than that so many of them continued their delinquencies. They were born and bred in households in which poverty or near-poverty and its attendant evils and miseries were the common lot. Their fathers were inefficient, irregular workers who, even when fortunate enough to be employed, could hardly support their abnormally large families. As often as not their mothers had to neglect their household duties and responsibilities in order to supplement a meagre family income. And the homes of many of the families were unattractive, crowded, and set in unwholesome neighbourhoods, where children could hardly be happy or develop healthily.

But more serious than the physical milieu in which these girls were reared was the unfortunate psychologic atmosphere of their homes. Their parents were on the whole of low mentality and in large measure illiterate. There was misunderstanding and friction arising from the conflict of cultures between foreign-born parents and native-born children. The moral standards of a great many of these families were low, and delinquency and criminality were frequent among them. The conjugal relations of the parents were in many instances inharmonious, thus rendering the homes unfit for the proper rearing of children. To this must be added the fact that the disciplinary practices of the parents were often unintelligent or worse. As if these evils were not yet sufficient, an abnormally high proportion of the homes were early broken by the death, desertion, or divorce of the parents.

The women are themselves on the whole a sorry lot. Burdened with feeble-mindedness, psychopathic personality, and marked emotional instability, a large proportion of them found it difficult to survive by legitimate means. Many suffered from serious physical ailments or handicaps in childhood and adolescence, and the great majority were venereally diseased before they were twenty-one years old. In educational achievement they fell considerably below the average, as to both length of schooling and competence as students. Few had the advantage of vocational guidance or training. Too early in life most of them were thrown into the industrial maelstrom to sink or swim. Employed largely as factory hands or domestics, their competency as workers ranged as a rule from only fair to poor; their status was essentially that of irregular workers; their earnings were miserably low.

Most of them left their homes at an early age, and many had undesirable or abnormal environmental experiences: over a fourth of them had been in foster-homes, for example, and many had experienced commitment to institutions, often for long periods. Throughout childhood and adolescence their leisure time was largely frittered away or absorbed in harmful pursuits and endangered by companionships with the vicious and criminal with whom they frequented unwholesome places of recreation. During childhood half of our girls did not attend church regularly, and during adolescence three fourths of them were neglectful of their religious duties.

The great majority of them misbehaved in childhood or showed other evidences of abnormal development that should have been recognized as danger-signals of probable maladjustment in adult life. At least a fourth of them had "bunked out," run away from home, or truanted before they were fourteen; over a third were "stubborn children," a fourth had indulged in illicit sex practices, a seventh stole. During adolescence these misconduct trends became more widespread and marked, reaching a point where ninety-five per cent of the girls had vicious habits. Two fifths of them ran away from home or truanted from school, over four fifths indulged in illicit sex practices, a fourth had become excessive alcoholics.

Illicit sexual indulgence was the chief form of their adolescent and early-adult misbehaviour. All but two per cent of our women had been sexually irregular prior to their commitment to the Reformatory, and over seven tenths of those who were married had indulged in illicit sex acts previous to marriage. Sexual malpractices were of long duration. In fact, a fifth of the girls had their first unconventional sex experience before they were fifteen, and their average age at such time was but seventeen years. Illicit sexuality was practically simultaneous with the onset of other forms of delinquency and with unstabilizing environmental experiences (such as leaving the parental roof at an early age). Four fifths of the girls entered upon unconventional sexual practices voluntarily. In the vast majority of cases these erotic adventures were shared with casual acquaintances or "pick-ups." *Over half the entire group of five hundred women had illegitimate pregnancies, and a third gave birth to children out of wedlock.*

Over half of the women had been prostitutes before their admission to the

Reformatory. Over a fifth of these were sixteen or younger when they began to commercialize themselves. Prostitution was usually of long duration, almost four years on the average, though a fourth of the women had been prostitutes for less than a year.

The high proportion of delinquency and criminality among our women prior to their arrest and conviction for the offence which sent them to the Reformatory is evidenced in the fact that only five of them had never previously come into conflict with the law or misconducted themselves in any way which might have resulted in arrest. The predominating offence of these women was unlawful sexuality in over half the cases, immorality and stealing in a tenth, illicit sexuality and drunkenness in a sixth, and stealing (uncomplicated by other forms of misconduct) in five per cent.

Sentence to the Reformatory was not, in the vast majority of the cases, the first experience which our women had with legal authorities and institutions. Two thirds of them had been previously arrested, the average number of arrests being three and two thirds, the average frequency of arrests one in every ten months. Over a fourth of the women were first taken into custody for sex offences, a fifth for " stubbornness," a tenth for crimes against property, a tenth for drunkenness. Considering *all* their prior arrests, a third of them were for drunkenness, a fourth for offences involving chastity, a seventh for property crimes, the remainder for various other offences.

Prior to admission to the Reformatory our women had already been subjected to the entire gamut of punitive and correctional devices. Thus, seven tenths of the three hundred and thirty-three women who had been previously arrested were at one time or another placed on probation, almost half had been committed to peno-correctional institutions, a sixth had been fined, a fourth had had the charges against them placed on file. A third of all their arrests had resulted in probation, over a fourth in imprisonment, six per cent in fines, a tenth in filing, and another tenth in a finding of " not guilty."

The poor calibre of our delinquent women is further reflected in other aspects of their careers. *Thus, the women who married prior to commitment (half the group) had done so with a casualness and irresponsibility which could only end in tragedy.* Most of them married " pick-ups " — often vicious and criminal wasters and irregular, inefficient workers — with whom they had scraped acquaintance. On an average the girls were between nineteen and twenty when they married — younger than girls of the general population — an eighth of them being under fifteen, and two fifths between sixteen and eighteen. *A third of the marriages were " forced " — that is, entered into because the girls were illicitly pregnant.*

Obviously such liaisons could not work out satisfactorily. In over four fifths of the cases, the young wives neglected their family responsibilities, and in three fourths the husbands were likewise irresponsible. *Conjugal relations were poor in four fifths of the marriages; and three fourths of the unions were broken by desertion, separation, or divorce* — a much higher proportion than is found in the general population. A fifth of the marriages were disrupted within six months after they had been contracted. By a reasonable standard, only two of the three hundred and one marriages could be deemed entirely successful. The reasons for the failure of the marital ventures of our women involved not only their own shortcomings but those of their husbands. In addition to the latter's incapacity as bread-winners, the majority of them were vicious and criminal. Another reason for the early wreck of the matrimonial ship lies in the fact that in over half the cases the newly-married couples did not set up independent households, but went to live with relatives.

That the unfortunate social heritage of these families will in large measure be handed down to subsequent generations may be inferred from the fact that in at least four fifths of the cases the attitude of our women toward their children was one of indifference if not of actual hostility.

Conduct within a year of commitment. When attention is focused on the year immediately preceding the sentence of our women to the Reformatory, *the conclusion is inevitable that in most of the aspects of their lives they had become progressively worse.* Thus, in not even a tenth of the cases were husband and wife actually living together when the women were committed, and less than half of these compatibly; and a seventh of the group were living with lovers when arrested. So also the moral atmosphere of the homes within a year of commitment of the offenders was poor in three fourths of the cases; the physical condition of their homes was unwholesome in two thirds; the neighbourhood conditions were vicious in seven tenths.

The economic status of the group, if not worse than previously, had certainly not improved within a year of their commitment. Thus, seven tenths of them were unemployed when arrested for the offence which resulted in sentence to the Reformatory, three fourths were in " marginal " economic circumstances (that is, unable to save anything or hanging on the ragged edge of poverty), and one seventh were entirely dependent for support on social agencies or on relatives.

Their use of leisure time and their habits had also become definitely worse as reflected in their activities during the year preceding commitment. All but two per cent of the women were indulging in harmful spare-time pursuits, all but ten per cent were habituées of unwholesome places of recreation, and all but three per cent consorted with immoral or criminalistic persons. The proportion of those failing to attend church had also grown greater. Only two of the entire group of five hundred women had no harmful habits or did not misconduct themselves in any way. All but three per cent were carrying on illicit sexual practices, two fifths drank to excess, a fourth were runaways or truants, a fifth stole, five per cent used drugs, others expressed themselves in still different forms of antisocial behaviour. All this spells a marked rise in unwholesome and socially harmful conduct and attitude as compared with the years preceding the last year before their commitment to the Reformatory.

This swarm of defective, diseased, antisocial misfits, then, comprises the human material which a reformatory and a parole system are required by society to transform into wholesome, decent, law-abiding citizens! Is it not a miracle that a proportion of them were actually rehabilitated?

In the Reformatory. We have already stressed the abnormal mental condition and the venereal disease of many of these women — facts disclosed by their examination on admission to the Reformatory. Turning now to their status and behaviour in the institution, we may first recall that over half of them were sentenced there for sex offences, a fourth for offences against the public health, order, and the like (of which many were actually sex offences), a tenth for property crimes, the remainder for various other forms of antisocial behaviour. Over half of them were given a two-year " indeterminate " sentence, a third a five-year indeterminate, a twelfth a one-year indeterminate, the balance other forms of sentence. However, *the average time actually spent by the women in the Reformatory on these sentences was but a year and a half, while over a fourth were incarcerated for a year or less — a period hardly sufficient for rebuilding their health, giving them adequate industrial training, and developing desirable attitudes to offset the deep-rooted, asocial viewpoints and habits which characterized so many of them.*

On the whole, the women were still very young when committed. Thus, two fifths were under twenty-one, a fourth were between twenty-one and twenty-five, a sixth were twenty-six to thirty, and a fifth were over thirty. It must be remembered, however, that despite their youth, they were highly experienced in antisocial behaviour. In fact, two thirds of them had been delinquents for as long as five or more years, while the misconduct of only six per cent was of less than a year's duration.

Almost a fifth of the women entered the Reformatory either with a child (under two years of age) or in a condition of pregnancy.

How did they behave themselves in the Reformatory? The conduct of half the inmates was satisfactory, a third occasionally violated minor regulations, a fifth frequently did so or committed serious offences. Almost a third of the group were subjected to punishment by isolation at one time or another during their confinement; however, four fifths of the women were promoted to the first grade (of the institutional grade system) in the usual time. Those who were youngest when they first became delinquent — that is, the inmates whose antisocial attitudes and habits of misconduct were of longest standing and most deeply rooted — violated institution rules to a greater extent than the others.

As to their industrial training in the institution, the most significant facts are these: On the whole the women were engaged sufficiently long in the various occupations to enable them to learn at least the rudiments, though not long enough for thorough mastery. A third of them were regarded as good workers in the institution, the remainder as needing considerable if not continuous oversight.

On parole. Reviewing the parole history of these women, some three tenths of them were granted parole following their first appearance before the Board of Parole; the balance were held over in the institution, the most usual reason for postponement of parole being venereal infection. Did parole oversight help them? *While under supervision in the community, our women, as a group, behaved much better than previous to their commitment to the Reformatory.* This was reflected in their improved living-conditions, stronger family ties, higher moral standards, greater steadiness of employment, bettered work and play habits, more wholesome companionships, and the like. Obviously, then, the Reformatory experience and the oversight afforded by parole played some part in enriching and steadying the parolees.

After parole. Definite improvement during the post-parole period also occurred, as compared with the conduct of the women before their commitment. The change for the better was manifest in the greater stability of their households and in improved environmental conditions; in a lower incidence of forced marriages and in bettered conjugal relationships. It was further evidenced in a greater affection and responsibility for their children, in their more general assumption of the duties of marriage, and in more decent home-making practices. It was also reflected in a generally higher industrial standard and in less harmful use of leisure time, together with a reduction in the incidence of bad habits and objectionable companionships. Finally, the general improvement of the group was expressed in a decline in illegitimate pregnancies and in the incidence of venereal diseases; but most important of all, it was shown in a reduction in delinquency and criminality.

Trend in conduct. That the general improvement of the ex-prisoners is likely to continue is a conclusion drawn from comparisons of their behaviour during the entire five-year post-parole period with their conduct in the last year of such period, and in many instances during the course of a year or more thereafter. It should be stressed, however, that although the behaviour of the women had markedly improved over their conduct before sentence to the Reformatory, it was nevertheless not as good as it had been while they were under parole oversight.

What the Reformatory accomplished. How prominent a role did the Reformatory play in the adjustment of these women? *A small proportion of them may be deemed to have ceased their misconduct quite directly through the efforts of the institution. But even in these cases it must be concluded that the presence of a favourable background and endowment in the women themselves, plus the intervention of salutary chance factors, partially accounts for the de-*

sirable outcome. And, conversely, the persistent recidivism of most of those who failed to respond favourably to reformative treatment must be charged in a measure to their poor background and traits and to unfortunate chance circumstances. But it should be remembered that the Reformatory experience in some respects benefited many of the women even though they did not abandon their delinquencies. For their industrial and recreational habits and their home-making practices improved, they gained in health and the like — benefits which other institutions of society had theretofore failed to give them.

Treatment-types; predictive instruments. Comparison of the characteristics of those women who abandoned their delinquencies some time beyond the expiration of sentence, but at least a year before the end of the five-year post-parole period, with those who recidivated throughout the five-year period, and with those who were not at all delinquent during such period, results in these significant conclusions:

(a) *The reformation of an offender is apparently due to three sets of variables:* (1) an endowment (native and acquired) which, at least in the respects noted in Chapter XVI, is favourable to reform; (2) the provision of treatment to which an offender, with particular characteristics, is most likely to respond; (3) certain chance circumstances encountered by ex-prisoners after their return to the community. These are the keys which individually, or in varying combination, may successfully open the door to reform.

(b) *There is a variation in the potency of the many factors in the lives of offenders:* some evidently operate in criminogenesis, but not in the continuance of criminality once embarked upon; others are effective in conditioning or stimulating the original misconduct, but evidently not in inducing its continuance in later years; still others are potent in the continuation of recidivism, but appear to play only a minor role in originating the delinquent trends.

(c) *It is feasible to determine which particular forms of treatment are most likely to be efficacious with certain types of offenders,* thus furnishing the foundation for more successful sentencing practices by the courts than now exist, for more pointed efforts of correctional administrators, and more realistic action by boards of parole. We have seen, for example, that prognostic devices of the kind already developed are superior to the impressionistic forecasting of the conduct of offenders by institution officials.

By the use of predictive instruments founded on a careful analysis and synthesis of experience with hundreds of cases of different types, we may reasonably expect not only a more sensible and economical distribution of correctional effort in relation to various classes of offenders on the basis of their respective capacities for rehabilitation, but a greater protection to society; for by such a method it is possible to foretell which offenders are likely to respond to extra-mural rather than institutional treatment (probation vs. incarceration), which would do well in complete freedom (do not even require probation), which would probably benefit by incarceration, but would recidivate if left at large thereafter (parole vs. release without supervision), which could be safely released after a short period of institutional training, and which need to be incarcerated for a considerable period of time if not permanently.

These findings suggest many avenues of improvement in existing policy and practice. Were this work confined to research, it would end at this point. But the criminologist is expected to perform a dual function: not only to discover and interpret the facts about crime and correctional treatment, but to suggest ways to improve society's methods of coping with criminality; to be not only a social scientist, but also a social planner. We are therefore justified in exploring a number of possibilities for a more efficient attack upon crime which are suggested by the findings of this research.

2. Orientation of the Problem

Typicality of findings. Are our women typical of the populations of other reformatories? This question is almost impossible to answer with more than approximate accuracy, because the statistics in annual reports and special studies vary in reliability, in definition of terms, in the data included, in the legislative and institutional provisions which determine locally which types of offenders shall be sent to different institutions or placed on probation, and other such matters. These considerations affect, for example, such basic factors as age, offence, prior recidivism, and others. Bearing this qualification in mind, it is nevertheless possible to conclude that the available materials reasonably suggest, if they do not definitely prove, the frequent incidence among female offenders in other reformatories of many of the characteristics of our women, such as types of major offences, prior recidivism, culture conflict between offenders and parents, mental deficiency, poor occupational history, industrial inefficiency, low economic status, inadequate educational achievement, undesirable moral standards in the home, bad parental supervision of the children.[1]

Is the Massachusetts Reformatory and parole system typical of all such institutions? Here again the attempt to obtain absolutely conclusive data is beset by insuperable obstacles, since the personal equation is perhaps the most important element in the comparison of correctional practices. However, the opinion may justifiably be hazarded, on the basis of reports and special researches as well as a general knowledge of American correctional practices, that the local reformatory and parole régimes are superior to the average, despite the fact that today there are a number of institutions for female delinquents which are equipped more modernly than the Massachusetts Reformatory. In respect to personnel it can definitely be said that Mrs. Hodder, whose régime is reviewed in this research, was widely recognized as a leader in her field.

[1] See Eugenia C. Lekkerkerker: *Reformatories for Women in the United States* (Groningen, 1931), Chapter viii; and Sheldon and Eleanor T. Glueck: *500 Criminal Careers* (New York, 1930), pp. 8 et seq.

Thorough analysis of the actual administration of criminal justice in the more populated regions of America should convince the thoughtful student that many of the weaknesses of the Massachusetts situation are also to be found, with but minor local variations, in other jurisdictions. For they involve fundamental conceptions of the aims and administration of criminal justice and basic notions of punishment and reform. This fact justifies some generalization in making suggestions for improvement in Massachusetts practices.

Delinquency and sexual misconduct. In most efforts to improve the administration of criminal justice as it affects women, the emphasis is placed on professional prostitution.[1a] Vice is the monster that reformers seek to slay. But the background and traits of women offenders indicate first that prostitution is by no means the sum and substance of female criminality,[2] and secondly that it is a superficial social policy to stress unduly the offence of which the delinquent happens to stand charged. The biologic and social heritage of sexual offenders is essentially similar to that of other delinquents; female wrongdoers, regardless of their crimes, have much the same sordid background of unfortunate heredity, mental abnormality, ignorant and vicious parentage, underprivileged childhood, and like evils. The " treatment types " analysed in Chapter XVI do not revolve principally around the hub of prostitution or any other offence, but around certain personal and social characteristics that distinguish different classes of offenders. The fact that a woman is a professional prostitute is an important consideration in planning her particular program of treatment; but, as has been abundantly established, it is only one factor out of many, some of which are of even greater significance in understanding her needs and devising means for her rehabilitation. In brief, when it comes to a fundamental attack upon delinquency, the point of orientation should not be prostitution or any other offence, but the make-up of offenders as determined by a more scientific classification than is utilized at present in law-enforcement.[3]

Directions of improvement. Considering society's task of coping with female offenders from this point of view, the horizon of constructive effort is immediately widened. We must be more concerned with societal and community forces making for delinquency, and with agencies calculated to reduce it, than with the familiar debates about whether prostitution is best " controlled " by licensing

---

[1a] See the reports of the various commissions on the control of vice.

[2] The very fact that among our women there were but seven per cent who, on admission to the Reformatory, could be classified as habitual professional prostitutes despite the finding that the majority of the entire group had committed some sex offence tends to establish this conclusion. It is further supported by the finding that many of the prostitute group also misconducted themselves in other ways.

[3] To be sure, certain special aspects of the treatment of professional prostitution — the procurer, the " protector," segregation, licensing, repression by special police " morals squads," and the like — are not involved in considering other forms of female delinquency. But most of the fundamental issues raised by prostitution are equally presented by offences that have nothing to do with sexual licence — that is, when offenders rather than offences are recognized as basic.

professional harlots, segregating them in " red-light districts," or ruthlessly repressing them through police foot-and-club work. We must be interested less in " morals police " than in fundamental crime-preventive activities of police organizations. We must strive to improve court structure and function not by setting up special " night courts " or " morals courts " in which prostitutes are disposed of cursorily and superficially by means of fines or short-term jail sentences, but by a radical reorientation of the work of criminal courts in general so that they will scientifically adjust correctional treatment to the needs of different types of offenders. We must seek for basic improvements in rehabilitative instruments — correctional institutions, probation, parole — as they affect the different treatment types, rather than overemphasize the punishment of prostitutes. The suggestions about to be made envisage these more fundamental desiderata.

Reflection upon the facts and inferences of this research and other investigations must lead the thoughtful student to the uneasy conclusion that merely the obvious improvements in the procedures of criminal justice, though clearly called for, will probably contribute disappointingly little to a solution of the manifold problems presented by crime. For the full evidence turned up in these researches implicates the very foundations of our civilization. Let us at the outset examine some of the basic social policies and institutions involved in this problem, reserving for later discussion certain more immediate suggestions for a community attack on local crime-breeding conditions and for improvements in the processes of justice.

3. Crime and Society

The fundamental forces involved in the manifestations of human and social maladjustment that we call crime are the deeply anchored and pervasive socio-economic and biologic factors that condition all human enterprise.

Economic influences. In numerous researches it has been shown that economic insufficiency and insecurity and industrial inefficiency on the part of certain classes of the population, together with the evils they bring in their train, are among the most potent conditioning factors in the careers of offenders. True, this situation also characterizes many who never commit crimes; but the fact remains that it is exceedingly difficult to establish a milieu favourable to the prevention of delinquency and the rehabilitation of offenders so long as fundamental socio-economic forces are interfering with the process. To reduce the need of rehabilitation, we must have more widespread habilitation.

Such a conclusion is justified, as is shown by many findings in this research, some of which are particularly pertinent: that over half the mothers of our girls worked outside the home in order to supply or supplement the meagre family income; that over a fourth of the fathers were irregular workers; that three fourths of the families at one time or another during the childhood of our delinquents had to be aided by various social welfare agencies; that over two fifths of the homes were crowded and unattractive, and many were established in neighbourhoods inimical to wholesome child life; that half the girls had to leave school in order to earn a living — many of them at a tender age — only to enter upon occupations involving moral hazards. The degree of directness of the influence of poverty or near-poverty upon the misconduct of women offenders cannot be accurately determined except in certain individual instances. But that these conditions loom large in the complex of adverse factors in their careers is clear.

While such obvious reforms as slum-clearance and housing-projects can help to improve some of these adverse conditions, in the final analysis the situation calls for a more healthy and just economic planning of society as a whole.[4]

Biologic influences. Nor should we limit the deeper influences upon the delinquency problem to economic factors alone. The biologic handicaps of the parents and children involved in this study cannot be ignored, though their relative participation in the total crime-producing complex of factors is difficult to determine. It cannot be proved by even the most ardent exponent of economic determinism that these biologic weaknesses are exclusively caused or conditioned by economic factors. No one can as yet say with precision which of the handicaps of mental defect, psychopathy, neuroticism, and poor physical health found among our women and their families are innate, and how many, or which, are acquired. But unquestionably they are obstacles to a legitimate struggle for survival. However perfectly society might be organized from an economic point of view, not all crime would disappear. In the long run a fundamental attack upon the problems of antisociality depends not only on the raising of the status of the economically underprivileged, but on the elimination or better control of the biologically handicapped.

Partially in recognition of this fact, many states have enacted sterilization laws.[5] It is questionable whether the processes of human heredity are as yet sufficiently understood and prediction of the type of offspring to be expected is sufficiently reliable [6] to justify the basing of a social policy of compulsory sterili-

[4] Considering specifically commercialized vice, it is clearly the profit-making motive that is involved in its promotion. The " third party interest " exists because large sums of money are made in stimulating the demand for prostitutes and in supplying such demand. Here, then, is another potent economic factor making for delinquency.

[5] The arguments in favour of sterilization and the progress of the movement in America are set forth in *Collected Papers on Eugenic Sterilization in California.* The Human Betterment Foundation (Pasadena, 1930). A more objective appraisal will be found in J. H. Landman: *Human Sterilization, the History of the Sexual Sterilization Movement* (New York, 1932).

[6] " We assume that the Legislature would not feel justified in compelling any persons to submit to sterilisation, unless it could be shown beyond reasonable doubt that some at least of their offspring would either be mentally defective or would develop mental disorder. In the present state of knowledge no such proof can be produced. While the results of our enquiry and the other statistics we have collected may justify some prediction as to the average results in a large group of cases, it would be hazardous to attempt to forecast the genetic results of any particular union." — *Report of the Departmental Committee on Sterilisation Presented by the Minister of Health to Parliament*

zation on the ground of heredity alone.[7] On the other hand, the evidence is overwhelming that persons of the kind so largely represented in our group are unfit to care properly for children.[8] Nor can it be gainsaid that a large proportion of them are irresponsible and prolific breeders. As we have seen, they give birth to many illegitimate children, and their offspring are as a rule more numerous than in the population at large.

In determining upon a social policy to meet this serious problem, it must not be overlooked that while compulsory sterilization laws have on the whole not been abused in American jurisdictions, and while legal and administrative safeguards are thrown around such laws, they always present the danger of being transformed into instruments of oppression. Moreover, it is difficult to enforce compulsory sterilization laws.[9] Voluntary sterilization is a different matter.[10] In a field full of prejudices and queries concerning which mental abnormalities are hereditary and which acquired, what degree of mental defect or disease will be necessary in the individual case, and how and by whom the sterilization laws shall be administered, it is best to err on the side of caution. Practically, therefore, it would seem that at the present juncture voluntary sterilization laws are preferable to compulsory. Given wise social case work, in which the true implications of harmless sterilization measures will be interpreted to those who would probably benefit from such treatment, this instrumentality can be made to yield desirable societal and individual results. The adoption of voluntary sterilization measures in states which are as yet unequipped with such laws seems advisable, together with a campaign of education on the nature of sterilizing operations.[11] A less satisfactory alternative to such means of controlling irresponsible breeding by delinquents and others is to segregate them until they have passed the period of fertility.[12]

---

by Command of His Majesty, December, 1933 (London: His Majesty's Stationery Office; 1934), p. 37. This English report is admirable for its objectivity and lucidity.

[7] For a good critical analysis of the status of science in this field, see Landman, op. cit., particularly Part III. " These serious criticisms of the present status of eugenics show its great need for more science and less speculation. Any new program for social therapy must be held in abeyance until such time when an adequate scientific basis for it is established. Human sterilization, as a social program, requires more scientific evidence. In the meantime, if human sterilization must be employed, it should be employed cautiously." — Landman, op. cit., p. 197. See also the English report cited in the preceding note.

[8] " Defectives make inefficient parents; if only for social reasons they should not have children." — Report of the Departmental Committee, etc., p. 31.

[9] Ibid., pp. 37–8. Other reasons advanced against compulsory sterilization laws by the English committee are: that they prevent hopeful cases from seeking hospitalization by creating the impression that forceful sterilization is a necessary condition to release from a mental hospital; that in the United States sterilization has been most practised in jurisdictions where it is administered on a voluntary rather than a compulsory basis; that it is not practicable to define the classes to which compulsory sterilization would apply in a way " to limit its use to exceptional cases only."

[10] " By voluntary human sterilization we mean that the legal execution of the human sterilization law cannot be effected until the patient and or his legal guardian consents to the surgery." — Landman, op. cit., p. 279.   [11] In the public mind sterilization is likely to mean castration.

[12] Less satisfactory because many of them might well lead a harmless life in the community were

4. Community Responsibility for Crime Prevention

Need for prevention. This research deals with a group of women who happen to have been arrested, convicted, and sentenced to a reformatory. But is it not short-sighted for a civilized community to wait until women of the socio-economic status of our offenders have violated some provision of the penal code before giving them the aid so many need? Why should the accident of arrest and conviction for a sexual or other offence result in the belated furnishing of medical treatment, education, trade instruction, and wholesome recreational outlets to such women, when their sisters of like status who do not chance to be arrested or convicted for acts the law designates as criminal often go without these basic advantages of a civilized community? And why should children be denied the services that might help to save them from embarking on a career of delinquency and crime?

It is time for over-enthusiastic law-reformers to realize that however greatly the police, the courts, peno-correctional institutions, and parole systems are improved, only the surface is being scratched of a sickly social situation that is far deeper and more widespread than the sample of it which happens to concern the criminal law or is caught in the police net or shunted into a reformatory. We have thus far made three intensive follow-up investigations embracing a variety of offenders. A major finding in all these researches is the failure of communities actively to prevent the development of delinquent careers by controlling the milieus and processes of possible delinquency. Too often they wait until an individual is already delinquent or criminal before bringing community resources to bear upon him and his problems. This failure permeates the whole mélange of biologic abnormalities, economic underprivilege, unwholesome family life, rampant vice and crime found in families with a tendency to furnish recruits to the armies of criminals and social cripples.

Integration of community resources. As we have seen, some of the reasons for this condition have their roots deep in our entire civilization. But one more immediate reason is the lack of integration among community welfare agencies and their consequent failure to plan a continuous, realistic attack upon crime-breeding conditions. Most well-populated American cities are equipped with varied types of social agencies. Some have settlements, school centres, clubs for children; a few have child guidance clinics; others command still other facilities for the improvement of community life and the control of unwholesome conditions. But too often each such agency does not see its goals and processes as organically related to a larger whole. Even with the wealth of philanthropic

---

it not for their weakness in the above respect. This is indicated by our analysis of the factors entering into the determination of treatment types. However, certain women will have to be retained in institutions for considerable periods of time for other reasons than a tendency to unbridled and irresponsible sex expression.

organizations found in most cities, there hardly exists a single organ to integrate those aspects of the work of social welfare agencies that have a common bearing on the crime problem. In fact, most communities make no concerted effort to save themselves from disintegration or to conserve their wholesome features. A few cities, like Berkeley and Los Angeles, have begun to see the importance of a planned approach to the manifold problems of crime-prevention.[13] They have established " co-ordinating councils," calculated to focus all of the community's resources upon the common goals of making social agencies, schools, recreation centres see their functions as interrelated; salvaging the finer values of community life while stamping out the breeding-spots of delinquency; and awakening citizens to a vivid realization that the task of reducing delinquency and crime is in large measure their own responsibility.

While each community has certain problems peculiar to it, all need to integrate their facilities for the early recognition and treatment of children's problems, for the spread of mental hygiene instruction, the provision of wholesome recreational outlets, the control of commercialized recreation, the treatment of venereal diseases, and like significant projects suggested by some of the findings of this study. To meet this need of a concerted attack upon the factors which condition delinquency and criminality, it is well, therefore, in most communities, to establish a council of representatives of all the major wholesome interests, with the aim of organizing the region into a living force for conserving desirable values in community life and preventing the rise and spread of antisocial behaviour.

Some needed resources. In making an inventory of their resources for coping with forces likely to breed delinquency, many communities may find that they lack certain important facilities.

(a) One such institution, clearly suggested by some of the more essential findings of this research, is the marital- and family-guidance clinic.[14] The pressing demand for it can be inferred from such evidence as the uncommonly early age at which many of our women married; their widespread illicit sexual life both before and after marriage; the high incidence of " forced marriages "; the customary practice of " pick-up " marriages; the frequency of unhappy conjugal relations; and the considerable proportion of marriages ending in desertion, divorce, or separation — many of them within a year or less after they had been contracted. The need for some organized means of guidance in wholesome family life is further indicated by the fact that in many instances

---

13 See, for example, *Why Have Delinquents?* (Los Angeles, 1933), and H. R. Gallagher: *Crime Prevention as a Municipal Function* (Syracuse, 1930).

14 For a competent analysis of the need of instruction in marital and family life, and the various movements begun in recognition of this need, see R. P. Bridgman: " Guidance for Marriage and Family Life," and S. M. and B. C. Gruenberg: " Education of Children for Family Life," in *The Modern American Family*, The Annals of the American Academy of Political and Social Science, Philadelphia, March 1932.

there was a condition likely to make for culture conflict between parents and children; that many of our women were poor homemakers; that in a high proportion of the cases the attitude of the parents toward their children was unwholesome; that our girls came in large measure from broken homes; and that a substantial proportion of them left the family roof because of a quarrel with their parents.

To these and other serious signs of irresponsible mating, unsuccessful marital life, and unwholesome family relations must be added the fact that our women had little knowledge of legitimate methods of controlling child-birth or of the dangers of venereal infection. They were, it will be recalled, prolific breeders, and two thirds of the group had acquired one or both social diseases before they were twenty-one.

Considering the fact that existing societal institutions — the home, the school, the church, and even some child-guidance clinics — are failing in many cases to supply the needs indicated by the situation, there is justification for professionally staffed marital- and family-guidance centres. The needs involved — wholesome courtship practices, happy family relations, sound parent-child attitudes, control of the size of families, and many others — will probably become more acute as our industrial civilization continues to grow.[15]

To do effective work, the proposed marital- and family-guidance clinics will have to call into play and correlate the expert aid of social case workers, social hygienists, mental hygienists, physicians, clergymen, teachers, community health and recreation workers, character educators, and wise laymen willing to participate under professional guidance. These clinics ought not only to deal with marriage and family difficulties as they arise, but, more important, *to anticipate and try to prevent* such problems from arising by continuous educational campaigns in schools, churches, factories, and clubs.[16]

(b) In most communities an audit of resources for wholesome living and the prevention of delinquency is likely to disclose the need of additional facilities for the constructive use of spare time by both children and adults. To comprehend the significance of this need, we have but to recall that only a fifth of our women enjoyed the benefit of constructive or harmless recreations or interests in childhood; that a fourth of the group in childhood and four fifths during adolescence had harmful companions; and that similar proportions spent their

---

[15] For some indication of the influence of economic and social transformations on family life, see W. Goodsell: "The American Family in the Nineteenth Century," in *The Modern American Family*, The Annals of the American Academy of Political and Social Science, March 1932, pp. 13 et seq., and N. Carpenter: "Courtship Practices and Contemporary Social Change in America," ibid., pp. 38 et seq.

[16] Lack of space prohibits going into detail. The reader can obtain a good comprehension of various aspects of this work in *The Modern American Family*, the issue of The Annals of the American Academy of Political and Social Science cited in note 15. It will there be seen that in many communities various agencies for coping with different features of family life already exist, but there is need for an integrated attack.

spare time in unwholesome play places.[17] Each community must decide for itself the extent of its leisure-time requirements and the kinds of facilities called for. But all will probably find it necessary to make a greater effort to attract potential delinquents to wholesome ways of using their spare time, while also doing their utmost to supervise commercialized forms of recreation.

(c) Continuing their inventory, many communities will doubtless also find that church programs require modernization and expansion. The relatively low church attendance among our women and the considerable falling off in attendance during adolescence present a challenge which the clergy should not ignore. Churches can perform a great social service in developing into cultural, educational, and recreational centres that will attract, hold, and guide parishioners.

(d) Doubtless many communities, upon examination, will find that school curricula and practices require improvement. It will be recalled that a successful school career was the exception among our girls. The average length of schooling was little more than six years; over a third of the group completed their schooling in the fifth grade; three fifths attended school irregularly; a like proportion (considerably more of a percentage than in the general schoolgirl population) were poor scholars; nine tenths (again a much higher incidence than in the general population) were retarded in school achievement, most of them several years; and, finally, the education of the parents was far below the norm.

In the light of such evidence each community ought to ask itself whether its schools are taking sufficient account of children for whom the traditional courses of study are too difficult, uninteresting, or impractical. Does the community have adequate " special class " facilities? Does it have vocational training schools? Does it have good child-guidance clinics? Are its teachers trained in the principles and methods of mental hygiene? It will be recalled, for instance, that seven tenths of our girls had undesirable habits in childhood, almost a fourth of them unwholesome sexual habits. Such early tendencies toward unhealthy or antisocial behaviour ought to be noted by school-teachers, and they should be sufficiently trained in mental hygiene practices to be able to carry out the instructions of clinics.

Though all sorts of official methods of coping with delinquents and criminals had been applied to our women before they were committed to the Reformatory, very little seems to have been done by the schools to prevent their delinquency. By the time the Reformatory and parole system took hold, our women were old and wise in wrongdoing. Their illicit sexual and other habits were then of long standing; the life attitudes of many of them had been firmly fixed. Perhaps many of them were salvageable as young children, when they first began to reveal habits and traits of character that suggested the danger of future delin-

---

[17] It will be recalled that only four of our women used their leisure constructively within a year of their commitment to the Reformatory.

quency. They might then have been intelligently managed by school officials.

The above are but a few of the more important community facilities that may be found necessary in different regions, if delinquency is to be attacked realistically. Others, such as free clinics for the diagnosis and treatment of venereal diseases, nurseries where working mothers may safely leave their children at small expense, efficient bureaus and homes for aiding ex-offenders,[18] and like facilities, are also needed in many places.

In this connection it should be pointed out that in practically every substantial community there are men and women with a talent for "helping people out of trouble," whose aid could be of real value in a community program for crime-prevention. Placed under professional guidance, such citizens could furnish the personal contacts and experience in legitimate affairs of which many pre-delinquents, delinquents, and ex-prisoners are in need.

5. Crime and the Administration of Justice

Introductory. Having discussed the societal and community obligations and opportunities in the prevention of delinquency, we turn to some suggestions for improving the processes of criminal justice. Supported by organized, intelligent community resources, these processes, which too often are considered as if they functioned *in vacuo,* can become much more effective in the struggle against crime.

The chief agencies of criminal justice involved in our research are the police, the courts (and the associated indeterminate sentence), reformatories, and parole.[19] These we shall consider in order.

Police. Because of the prevailing view that the problem of female offenders is essentially one of repressing commercialized vice, the role of the police in such cases assumes great prominence. And " undoubtedly the most troublesome task of the police is the enforcement of regulations which fall within the realm of vice or public morals." [20] Law-enforcement in such cases faces numerous difficulties not encountered in ordinary police work, among which may be mentioned conflicting public attitudes toward immorality, political interference, the investment of vast sums in enterprises of commercialized vice or near-vice, the ready way in which the police can be corrupted, the difficulty of securing proper evidence, and like considerations.[21] Most of these difficulties reflect fundamental

---

[18] See pp. 237–41.

[19] There is little evidence in this particular investigation of the role of the prosecutor in the administration of justice.

[20] *Chicago Police Problems,* by the Citizens' Police Committee (Chicago, 1931), p. 27. This efficient survey was made by a committee of experts headed by Mr. Bruce Smith.

[21] See the discussions of these topics in *Chicago Police Problems,* p. 27; the *Final Report of Samuel Seabury, Referee, In the Matter of the Investigation of the Magistrates' Courts in the First Judicial Department and the Magistrates thereof, and of Attorneys-at-Law Practicing in said Courts* (New York, 1932), pp. 95 et seq.; W. C. Waterman: *Prostitution and its Repression in New York*

flaws in the attitudes and practices of modern society; and while they may be minimized by merely making changes in the organization of police departments,[22] they cannot thereby be entirely circumvented. But much can be done in reorientating the attitude of police administrators so that they will view their problems from preventive and rehabilitative as well as merely repressive angles. At best, aggressive police repression is treatment on a symptomatic rather than etiologic level. To improve their practices, police departments ought first to evolve more fundamental tests of good police work than the obvious one of the number of arrests and convictions.[23] Secondly, they must be even more ruthless in suppressing corruption among police officers than they sometimes are in repressing prostitution. This includes the correction of present practices in many cities, where arrests are selective on the basis of the friends and money the prostitute and her allies have, instead of being uniformly applied to all offenders.[24] Thirdly, police departments should place their emphasis on arresting the frequently undisclosed exploiters of commercialized vice — the white-slavers, the "protectors," the owners of brothels and other places used for immoral purposes[25] — rather than devote most of their efforts to bringing in prostitutes of long standing, for whom little can be done.

But most important of all, police departments ought to establish professionally staffed crime-prevention units, with the aim of lending the arm of the law to community efforts at curbing the development of delinquent careers and salvag-

---

City 1900–1931 (New York, 1932). For illustration of the difficulty of securing evidence in these cases, see also the story of Marie, p. 31.

[22] Students of this problem seem to overstress matters of organization rather than put emphasis on aim, policy, and personnel. See Waterman, op. cit., pp. 51–2; Chicago Police Problems, p. 27.

[23] "The diligence and efficiency of the members of the Vice Squad [in the New York Police Department] were judged by the number of arrests they made and the convictions they procured each month. The testimony shows that where the end of the month approached, and the record of arrests and convictions was low, the officers would arrest women indiscriminately, and frame up cases against them, until the number so arrested was sufficient to bring the officers' records up to the desired number." Seabury, op. cit., pp. 95–6. See also Waterman, op. cit., p. 18; and R. B. Fosdick: "Police Administration," Part I of the Cleveland Foundation Survey of Criminal Justice in Cleveland (Cleveland, 1922). Fosdick points out how difficult it is to establish fair tests of good police work.

[24] See the case of Alice pp. 147 et seq. "In all probability arrest statistics are somewhat selective in that those prostitutes who have little money and no influential friends are more liable to arrest and conviction than those in more opulent circumstances." — Waterman, op. cit., p. 126. Waterman deals with the New York situation. "Law enforcement authorities seemed to be unanimous in agreeing that the pseudo-respectable hotels and apartments were not being molested by the police. For this reason, the so-called better class of prostitutes and their customers were not passing through the machinery of the courts." — G. E. Worthington and R. Topping: Specialized Courts Dealing with Sex Delinquency (New York, 1925), p. 12. Worthington and Topping describe the Chicago situation. A similar condition on the Continent is described by A. Flexner: Prostitution in Europe (New York, 1914), pp. 146–7.

[25] Mrs. Hodder, as well as authoritative writers on the control of commercialized vice, emphasized the need of eliminating discrimination by police and courts against women and in favour of men. See p. 6, and Waterman, op. cit. "For the most part, the attitude is indulgent towards the man, severe towards the woman." — A. Flexner, op. cit., p. 104. See also ibid., p. 335.

ing such types of offenders as are represented in the upgrade-delinquent and non-delinquent graduates of the Massachusetts Reformatory.[26]

Courts. In considering court organization and function as related to a more effective coping with delinquency and criminality we are faced with the alternative of a superficial patching of the existing structure or its fundamental redesign. Thus far, specialized courts dealing with female offenders have taken the form of " morals courts " or women's courts. Their creation was due largely to the fact that sexual offences, and particularly prostitution, are the ones that receive the most emphasis in the administration of criminal justice as it affects women. By centralizing the hearing of such cases in a specialized branch of a municipal court it was hoped, as was said of the Chicago Morals Court, " to reduce commercialized prostitution by a concentration of all prostitution and allied cases in one court, which would demonstrate the tremendous volume of the business of prostitution, and thereby result in arousing the public conscience; to check up the workings of the police in this particular field; to avoid waste of judicial power, save time, promote efficiency of administration, and lastly to deal more wisely with offenders and to marshal the social agencies organized for the assistance of such cases." [27] These are desirable ends and can be attained through a *fundamental reorganization* of court systems that promises, in addition, to yield even more valuable results. To stress the " morals " feature as a basis for specializing courts is, as the evidence of the make-up and background of offenders indicates, to run the danger of taking too superficial a view of the intricate issues involved. Courts must be redesigned to improve not only trial practices, but, perhaps more important, *sentencing* practices.

One way of doing this is to extend juvenile court procedure and philosophy to adults.[28] When a realistic view is taken of the etiology of misconduct, the arguments behind the constitutionality of juvenile procedure seem equally applicable to adult offenders.[29] To be sure, they hinge on the point that in juvenile

[26] The necessity and practical value of police crime-preventive units are no longer objects of mere academic speculation. The encouraging work of the Bureaus in Berkeley, Detroit, and New York, as well as in certain foreign countries, particularly Holland, has demonstrated their importance in a general community program for coping with antisocial behaviour. See A. Vollmer: " Predelinquency," *Journal of Criminal Law and Criminology,* XIV (1923–4), pp. 279 et seq.; and " Coordinated Effort to Prevent Crime," ibid. XIX (1928–9), pp. 196 et seq.; E. L. Hutzel, M. L. Macgregor, and L. V. Harrison: *The Policewoman's Handbook* (New York, 1933); and the annual reports of the Police Department of the City of New York beginning with 1931.

[27] See Worthington and Topping, op. cit., p. 6, summarizing statements of Judge Harry M. Fisher, *Tenth and Eleventh Annual Reports, Municipal Court of Chicago, 1915–1917,* pp. 85–6.

[28] E. H. Sutherland: *Criminology* (Philadelphia, 1924), pp. 307 et seq.

[29] The arguments supporting the constitutionality of juvenile courts are clearly put in the well-known case of Commonwealth v. Fisher, 213 Penn., 48 (1905): " In pressing the objection that the appellant was not taken into custody by due process of law, the assumption, running through the entire argument of the appellant, is continued, that the proceedings of the act of 1903 are of a criminal nature for the punishment of offenders for crimes committed, and that the appellant was so punished. But he was not. . . . To save a child from becoming a criminal, or from continuing in a career of crime, to end in maturer years in public punishment and disgrace, the legislature surely

courts it is a *child* that is involved. But if one turns from the legal conception of a " child " to that held by the psychologist, psychiatrist, and social worker and reviews the evidence of the irresponsibility of women of the type described in this work, one must conclude that they need just as much protection and " salvation " as children; that many of them are, in fact, psychologically children in their incapacity for assuming social responsibilities.

But juvenile-court informality introduced into the procedure of criminal courts for adults is not without danger of abuse.[30] Adult offenders are more likely to be in jeopardy of arbitrary treatment by courts which have informal procedure, few or no rules of evidence, no jury trial, than are juvenile delinquents whose youth in a measure protects them. Therefore, without ignoring the need of improving the trial aspect of adult-court procedure, the wisdom of extending juvenile-court practices to adult tribunals so far as the method of determining guilt is concerned is still open to question.[31] This does not mean, however, that adult criminal courts cannot be radically redesigned to effectuate desirable aims and yet retain wise constitutional safeguards.

The basic direction of reform lies not in the trial procedure but in the sentencing practices of the courts. The familiar complaint against existing methods of sentencing offenders is that there is little uniformity in the punishment of offenders committing the same crimes.[32] But this problem goes deeper than non-uniform sentences; it involves the fact of *too little scientific consideration of*

---

may provide for the salvation of such a child, if its parents or guardian be unable or unwilling to do so, by bringing it into one of the courts of the state without any process at all, for the purpose of subjecting it to the state's guardianship and protection. The natural parent needs no process to temporarily deprive his child of its liberty by confining it in his own home, to save it and to shield it from the consequences of persistence in a career of waywardness, nor is the state, when compelled, as *parens patriæ,* to take the place of the father for the same purpose, required to adopt any process as a means of placing its hands upon the child to lead it into one of its courts. When the child gets there and the court, with the power to save it, determines on its salvation, and not its punishment, it is immaterial how it got there " (pp. 52–3).

As to denial of the right of trial by jury, " here again is the fallacy, that he was tried by the court for any offense. . . . There was no trial for any crime here, and the act is operative only when there is to be no trial. The very purpose of the act is to prevent a trial. . . . The act is not for the trial of a child charged with a crime, but is mercifully to save it from such an ordeal, with the prison or penitentiary in its wake, if the child's own good and the best interests of the state justify such salvation " (pp. 53–4). See also *Ex parte* Januszewski, 196 Fed. 123 (1911).

[30] See Seabury, op. cit., pp. 247, 248, 251, which illustrates the ready opportunity for abuse of power that exists in adult courts where trial procedure is too informal. It is of course not a matter exclusively of procedure, but also, and perhaps most important, of personnel; but procedural safeguards are important curbs on possible arbitrariness or corruption.

[31] As was pointed out, there is, however, a question whether certain sexual offences should be dealt with by the criminal law. See p. 98.

[32] Comparing the disposal of cases in the district and municipal courts of the Boston area, a governmental commission arrived at the conclusion that " these courts . . . exercise within their several districts the same criminal jurisdiction . . . and although the social and economic conditions of their various districts do not differ essentially, there exists a radical and multiform variation and antagonism of practice in matters essential to the enforcement of the law." — The Commonwealth of Massachusetts, House No. 1638, *Report of the Commission on the Inferior Courts of*

offenders on the part of the judges. They do not devote sufficient time and study to each offender's situation in order to determine the type of sentence best suited to his needs. And it is a serious question whether most of the judges in criminal sessions are today qualified to do so. Regardless of the excellence of their legal education, they are as a rule unequipped in such disciplines as sociology and social case-work, psychology and psychiatry, education and penology, all of which must be drawn upon if the sentencing practices of our courts are to be radically improved.

That the sentencing practices of the courts do need basic transformation is shown by much evidence in this research. In the first place it is demonstrated by the poor work of *primary classification and distribution* of offenders done by the judges in sentencing our women. This inefficiency is illustrated by these cogent findings: (a) they sentenced to the Reformatory a substantial number of irreformable prostitutes, feeble-minded and psychopathic women, including many who had previously suffered deterioration in jails and houses of correction;[33] (b) they committed many promising women — those of our non-delinquent type — to an institution, when these women might just as well have been treated in the community under probation with less expense to the state and less chance of moral contagion to themselves; (c) they frequently resorted to sentences far too brief for the objectives to be achieved; (d) they often imposed fines.[34]

Secondly, the need of improving sentencing practices can be deduced from the fact that at present the type of crime committed evidently plays too weighty a part in determining the sentence imposed. That this is unsound is shown in the following proof that the type of crime committed is frequently not a safe peg upon which to hang the sentence: (a) in analysing " treatment types " the offence committed was found to be but one element — and not always the most significant — in a complex of interrelated factors; (b) the offence committed bears but a minor relationship to future behaviour of delinquents; (c) women of all three post-parole *behaviour* types (delinquents, non-delinquents, and upgrade delinquents) are to be found within each offence group.

That it is feasible to substitute a scientific system of sentencing offenders for the existing essentially haphazard one is indicated by the findings as to the re-

---

the County of Suffolk, 1912, p. 7. See also the annual report of the City Magistrates' Courts of the City of New York (First Division), 1914, and Waterman, op. cit., p. 63.

[33] Of course not all the responsibility for this is on the judges; the fact of limited state facilities for commitment of such types is also involved.

[34] Many modern authoritative writers condemn the use of fines, particularly in cases like prostitution. See, for example, Waterman, op. cit., pp. 66, 73, 152. Fines may serve as a means of income to the state, but not infrequently they are paid by others than the one who should suffer them. Thus, either an unjust burden falls on the wrong persons, or, as in the case of a " landlady " of a house of prostitution, fines enable exploiters to further enslave their victims. That fines have very little effect in preventing repetition of offences is shown by a follow-up investigation of any series of such cases.

formability of different classes of offenders. We have shown, for example, that reformative efforts should be largely concentrated on persons of the type of the non-delinquents and up-grade delinquents. The latter group are most difficult for criminal courts to define and select from the stream of convicts to be sentenced, because they possess many of the good qualities of the non-delinquents, but also some of the characteristics of the women who continue their delinquencies unabated. They are, so to speak, " on the fence"; and the way they will jump depends on their intelligent selection by the sentencing tribunal and appropriate treatment of them thereafter.[35]

In the light of evidence like the foregoing,[36] a number of students of the sentencing practices of criminal courts have in recent years been insisting upon the importance of two elements that seem indispensable to a thorough overhauling of the existing system: (a) the sharp separation in function and personnel of the trial procedure and the sentencing procedure; (b) the establishment of one or more clearing-houses or " remand stations " in each state, to which convicted offenders would as a matter of course be committed for a period sufficient to permit of their thorough examination and study, the working-out of recommendations for sentence, and an individual plan of treatment.[37]

As to the first suggestion, it is urged that one or more sentencing bodies, staffed by trained and experienced psychiatrists, psychologists, sociologists, and educators, as well as lawyers, should be set up in each state as " treatment tribunals." [38] The second suggestion is an indispensable adjunct to the proposed division of judicial labour. Hasty judgments regarding the forces and situations involved in the criminality of the prisoner at the bar and the kind of sentence most likely to bring desired results do not usually afford a sound basis of peno-correctional treatment. This is one reason why so many of the wrong types of prisoners are sent to institutions and so many others are erroneously disposed of by probation, suspended sentence, or fine.[39] The casual impressionism of many criminal courts

---

[35] See pp. 264, 272, 278.

[36] To the above we may add two other evidences of the not altogether atypical outlook of judges of ordinary criminal courts: (1) the practice of automatic increase in punishments with repetition of crime (see Worthington and Topping, op. cit., pp. 9, 86). This simplistic solution of a complex problem rarely results as anticipated. (2) The practice of solving the problem presented by an unmarried mother, without regard to her own and her lover's make-up and background, by "blessing " the union with an enforced marriage as a condition of avoidance of punishment.

[37] See, for example, S. Glueck: "Principles of a Rational Penal Code," *Harvard Law Review,* Vol. XLI (1928), pp. 453 et seq.

[38] The implications of such a reform and the methods to be employed by the proposed sentencing tribunals are far more complex than appears. They will be fully gone into in forthcoming volumes of the Harvard Law School Crime Survey.

[39] There are other reasons for this which have largely local significance, such as, for example, the appeal and double-trial system in vogue in Massachusetts. (See Worthington and Topping, op. cit., pp. 217–20; The Commonwealth of Massachusetts, Senate No. 125, *Report of the Special Crime Commission,* Boston, 1934, pp. 67, 69, 71.) But even if the local situation were remedied by the abolition of trials *de novo* in cases appealed from the Boston Municipal Court and the district courts, the major difficulty discussed above would not be obviated. In this chapter we are largely concerned

of today ought to give way to a more thoroughgoing procedure. Adequate study of each offender at a scientifically staffed and well-equipped clearing-house and remand station should greatly improve the work of original classification and distribution of offenders by the courts.[40] In addition, courts would thereby be in a position to contribute to the fund of knowledge of the social and psychologic conditions making for delinquency, and to experiment with new forms of correctional treatment.[41] A venereal clinic and educational and vocational services attached to the clearing-house and remand station might serve not only as a place of many-sided treatment of probationers but as an important research laboratory.

Indeterminate sentence. Various portions of this study have demonstrated the desirability of either a completely indeterminate sentence or one allowing an adequate zone of discretion to institutional and parole authorities in deciding when to return prisoners to the community.[42] It has been shown further that it is possible to determine with sufficient accuracy which types of offenders require only short periods of training in an institution like the Reformatory, which need longer custodial control, which require permanent segregation,[43] which are likely to do well under a brief period of parole supervision, which will probably relapse when parole oversight is removed. We have further seen that the biologic and psychologic changes that come with the passage of time play an important role in determining at least partially whether antisocial behaviour will be continued or abandoned.[44] It would seem wise, therefore, from the standpoint of protecting society as well as rehabilitating offenders, to substitute a completely indeterminate sentence, or at least one providing a wide zone between the minimal and maximal limits, for most of the varied existing statutory punishments.[45] In Massachusetts this suggestion is particularly directed against the " two-year

---

with suggestions for improving a general situation that, with minor local differences, exists throughout the country.

[40] See pp. 15 et seq. for Mrs. Hodder's views on this subject.

We have not gone into the question whether, in Massachusetts, the proposed clearing-house and temporary detention place should be established at one of the existing penal or correctional institutions. That is a matter of local policy, and we are interested in the more general proposal described above. It may be recalled that Mrs. Hodder, the late superintendent of the Massachusetts Reformatory for Women, urged that her institution be used as the clearing-house for women offenders. A proposal has also been made that the Charlestown State Prison be utilized as a clearing-house for male offenders. Each state must decide for itself whether it can transform some existing structure into the laboratory and remand station proposed above.

[41] See p. 296.

[42] See pp. 292–3.

[43] Why are helpless derelicts, incorrigible wrongdoers, spreaders of disease, and breeders of illegitimate offspring, like Grace (pp. 152 et seq.), Florence (pp. 157 et seq.), Fleur (pp. 162 et seq.), Angelina (pp. 168 et seq.), Minnie (pp. 172 et seq.), and Dora (pp. 177 et seq.), permitted to circulate in society like bad coins, in and out of jails, farms, almshouses, hospitals?

[44] See Chapters XII to XVII inclusive, where various aspects of this important problem are analysed.

[45] What to do with the death penalty is a question to be left to local differences of policy.

indeterminate " and the " five-year indeterminate " sentences.[46] We are aware that there is one serious objection to a wholly indefinite sentence: the danger of arbitrariness in keeping imprisoned those no longer requiring incarceration. However, *periodic review* of each prisoner's record by the treatment tribunal, as a standard practice, should eliminate the possibility of any inmate being " forgotten " or dealt with unfairly by the institution authorities.[47]

It may be argued that offenders should not be subjected to the risk of protracted incarceration, perhaps lifelong imprisonment, for " a mere sex offence." Such a view ignores the true significance of the facts. We have seen that far more is involved in the careers of most of our women than an occasional lapse from moral conventions. We are dealing not only with a complicated network of biologic and socio-economic deficiencies, but with such socially dangerous consequences as the spread of venereal infection, the unrestricted birth of illegitimate, underprivileged children, and like tangible ill effects of unrestrained sexual indulgence. In effect, the majority of our women may truly be regarded as irresponsible members of society, requiring, in many cases, continuous control if not lifelong quarantine. Society has been forced to commit the mentally ill and feeble-minded to special institutions for wholly indefinite terms and to keep many of them under restraint throughout their lives; further, in a number of states, including Massachusetts, " defective delinquents " are committable to an institution for a completely indefinite period, and if need be they are kept in custody for life. From time to time numbers of the insane, feeble-minded, and defective delinquent are released from hospitals or other special institutions under conditions similar to parole. When shown to be dangerous to themselves or others, they are returned to the institutions without the expense of new trials. Persons who have violated criminal laws and who require long-time or continuous oversight ought sensibly to be dealt with likewise.

In this connection two basic principles need to be borne in mind: (a) " No one should ever be cast into [or retained within] prison so long as it is safe for himself and society that he be free." (b) " There is no rational excuse for the discharge of a criminal whom the State has at great expense once detected, arrested, tried, and convicted, so long as he continues a criminal in disposition and character, and may be expected to compel the State to incur the same expense again." [48]

---

[46] See p. 187. When the indefinite-sentence idea was first propounded, the wisdom in principle of a completely indeterminate sentence was recognized. But the idea was abandoned because its proponents feared it would fail to receive legislative support. See S. and E. T. Glueck: *500 Criminal Careers* (New York, 1930), p. 150, note 4.

[47] It will be recalled that Mrs. Hodder's plan to review each case at staff meetings every three months was not often enforced, owing to limitations of personnel and the pressure of other work (pp. 129 et seq.). But under the proposed system, review of each case at definite intervals would be an indispensable guaranty.

[48] H. M. Boies: *The Science of Penology, the Defence of Society against Crime* (New York, 1901), p. 154.

As shown by the evidence in various parts of this book, the completely indeterminate or wide-zone sentence is so indispensable an adjunct to an effective administration of criminal justice that social statesmanship requires its adoption.

Releasing authority. This brings us to the important question whether prisoners should be released by a separate parole board, as (in Massachusetts and certain other states) at present; and if so, what relation such a board should bear to the courts on the one hand, and to the correctional institutions on the other. We have already shown that lack of integration between the courts and the institutions leads to undesirable commitments of many prisoners to places where they do not belong. This is but one illustration of the general imperfect coherence in society's " system " for coping with delinquency and criminality. In fact, there is little that is systematic about the processes considered as a whole; for each institution, beginning with the police and ending with the parole board, is inclined to move in its own narrow ambit with little regard for what the others are doing.[49] But the most marked lack of integration evidently exists between the courts and the peno-correctional establishments and between the latter and the parole board.

A rational system of criminal justice would consist of an integrated series of agencies, all having the same ultimate goals and all recognizing that for their efforts to be effective they must function in the closest interrelation. As between the courts and institutions, the establishment of one or more treatment tribunals and clearing-houses should in itself bring about increased consistency of aim and method. In addition it may be necessary for the tribunals to have inspective powers over the correctional institutions.[50] As between these latter and the releasing authorities we have come to the conclusion that, since, scientifically considered, the entire process ought to be continuous, it would seem wise to turn over the work of parole boards (or parole committees of institutions) to the proposed treatment tribunals. Thereby the same experts who originally studied the offender and determined upon the best disposition of her[51] case would keep in touch with her progress in the institution (or while under probation or some other form of treatment) and would review her case at stated periods to determine how the treatment program originally planned should be modified in the light of the offender's response. Release of a prisoner from a correctional institution on parole is just as much of a modification of the treatment originally prescribed by the court as is commitment of a probationer to an institution when he

[49] See p. 294.

[50] This, in turn, would probably necessitate that the commissioner of correction or other official in charge of the correctional institutions have some close connection with, perhaps membership on, the treatment tribunal. This entire question raises a number of complex issues that have been thoroughly canvassed by the members of the Harvard Law School Crime Survey, and a detailed exposition of the implications of some of the recommended reforms may be expected in some of the forthcoming reports of that survey.

[51] These recommendations of course refer to both male and female offenders, since the issues involved are not " sex-linked."

fails to respond to oversight; yet for historical reasons the first is under direction of a separate parole board while the second remains under authority of the court which originally sentenced the offender. This disconnectedness of what ought to be a unified system is partially responsible for so much of the inefficient and contradictory treatment reflected in the case histories of offenders. If the recommended treatment tribunal were charged not only with making the original disposition of cases but with following the progress of offenders and determining when and under what conditions they could be released, the entire procedure would become more effective. Not only would a good deal of working at cross-purposes thereby be eliminated, but offenders and their families might learn to regard correctional treatment as a continuous process which, from beginning to end, is, and for successful results needs to be, under single auspices and guidance.

In the proposed system, the treatment tribunal should also have authority to transfer offenders from one institution to another. This is closely related to both the sentencing work and the parole function. Errors in primary classification could thereby readily be remedied, provided, of course, that proper institutions existed for certain offenders, such as some of the feeble-minded and psychopathic.

Not only should such a unified process make for greater efficiency, but it would also be more economical than the existing jumble of disjointed agencies and authorities. Much duplication of effort in examining offenders, determining their social background, and supervising their conduct which is carried on more or less separately in at least three different places — the court, the institution, and the parole board — would thereby be avoided. It should also be remembered in this entire connection that many offenders (such as our non-delinquents and some up-grade delinquents) would under the new system be properly disposed of through probation and would not require a later commitment to some peno-correctional institution, to be followed by oversight on parole. Women merely unconventional in their sex life, who do not present other problems requiring treatment and are not dangerous as spreaders of venereal diseases or irresponsible breeders of illegitimate children, might be summarily disposed of without any officially prescribed special control, or, at most, with only reference of their cases to appropriate social agencies for treatment of special problems. On the other hand, professional prostitutes of long standing might be placed under more or less continuous control or be entirely segregated from the community.[52] All this would mean far fewer trials for new offences committed by old offenders, and should in the long run be more economical than the existing practices.

Predictive instruments. It has been demonstrated in this and other works that it is feasible and would be valuable to implement the administration of criminal justice with prognostic devices constructed upon analyzed experience with numerous offenders of different types. The utility of such predictive in-

[52] See pp. 296–7.

struments is not confined to parole boards. They might be used effectively by the sentencing tribunals in their original work of disposing of cases;[53] by probation services, in differentiating between various forms of extra-mural treatment; by peno-correctional establishments, in determining the type of institutional régime most suited to the different classes of offenders who even under the proposed system would find their way into institutions; and, finally, by the treatment tribunals when acting as parole boards. The continual checking of actual results against the predictions made on the basis of such prognostic implements would serve to sharpen them, thereby making them ever more efficient.

Citizens' oversight of law-enforcement. The best of institutions for the administration of justice need continuous intelligent oversight if they are to function honestly and efficiently. Particularly in relation to commercialized vice and similar offences, the existence of laws is one thing, their proper enforcement quite another.[54] Recent disclosures in New York regarding the sinister partnership of politics and vice, the sordid role played by crooked bondsmen and unscrupulous lawyers in the administration of criminal "justice," the arrest and conviction of innocent women for the purpose of bribery, the evasions of responsibility for maintaining property for immoral uses, and like evils,[55] may reflect a particularly flagrant local situation. But since the New York disclosures, no large American community can afford to rest complacently and permit the processes of criminal justice to grind away without continuous oversight of its own situation. To wait until some dramatic scandal calls for a special investigation and a transient "reform movement," only to let conditions slide into an equally bad later status is to be short-sighted and uneconomical. There is therefore needed in each community a skillfully staffed citizens' organization to represent continuously the civic interest in the efficient and pure administration of criminal justice. Particularly is this true of those processes that cope with the shady zone of commercialized vice. In the past, citizens' groups have too often contented themselves with vice-repressive efforts, largely ignoring the deeper

[53] For a comparison of the efficiency of existing sentencing practices with those proposed, see S. and E. T. Glueck: *500 Criminal Careers,* pp. 295–6.

[54] In the control of commercialized vice the intelligent efforts of the American Social Hygiene Association deserve high commendation. Many states might well benefit from adoption of several or all of the model laws drafted by the Association for the more effective control of prostitution and related evils, particularly the Vice Repressive Law and the Injunction and Abatement Act. The realistic approach to law and law enforcement by the association is shown in its inclusion among its standard forms of laws of one for the removal from office of officers guilty of misfeasance or nonfeasance in office. See the *Social Hygiene Legislation Manual* (New York: The American Social Hygiene Association; 1921, revised to 1925). The association is now engaged in bringing this manual down to date.

[55] See the *Final Report of Samuel Seabury, Referee, In the Matter of the Investigation of the Magistrates' Courts in the First Judicial Department and the Magistrates thereof, and of Attorneys-at-Law Practicing in said Courts* (New York, 1932); and Waterman: *Prostitution and its Repression in New York City 1900–1931* (New York, 1932), particularly pp. 24, 29, 82–6, 144–9. See also pp. 147 et seq. of this book (case of Alice).

implications of the problems of criminal justice. They might well expand their operations to embrace a continuous watch over law administration in order to prevent the pools of justice from becoming polluted.[56]

To meet such a need in communities not yet equipped, it is suggested that a privately supported bureau of criminal justice be established to exercise a continuous, intelligent, yet discreet oversight of the processes of justice.[57]

6. The Reformatory

Structure. Turning now to the Reformatory itself, we have seen with what ingenuity and perseverance the late superintendent of the Reformatory, Mrs. Jessie D. Hodder, transformed a prison structure into a greatly improved rehabilitative establishment.[58] One of the needs she frequently alluded to was a number of cottages on the grounds of the Reformatory for the purpose of experimenting with various forms of treatment for different types of offenders. If the Massachusetts Reformatory is to continue to be housed in the present antiquated structure, the furnishing of cottages seems indispensable.[59] A similar need will be found in many other correctional establishments throughout the country. Not only are cottages useful for classification and experimental purposes, but they give an opportunity to place at least some of the younger women in a home situation much more normal than that which a large, impersonal institution can possibly supply. The annual reports of Mrs. Hodder, as well as the findings of this research,[60] also indicate that Massachusetts is further in need of special colony institutions for certain adult feeble-minded offenders, chronic alcoholics,[61] and, particularly, those " psychopathic personalities " who fail to respond to ordinary institutional care and yet cannot be allowed free circulation in society.[62] A like need, especially for institutions to house the latter group, exists in almost every other state in the Union. They are necessary not only for the long-time or permanent segregation of dangerous and irreformable offenders, but, more important, for scientific experimentation with various methods of treatment.

Régime. Structures are of course less important than what goes on within them. We must consider some of the features of the Massachusetts Reformatory for women with a view to their possible improvement as suggested by the careers of these five hundred offenders. Some of these recommendations might also be useful in other institutions, since they deal with general problems.

[56] For the difficulty of reform once corruption has spread, see Seabury, op. cit.

[57] This need is partially supplied on the Continent by Ministries of Justice.

[58] Chapter I.

[59] Since the present writing, means have been appropriated for the erection of one or two cottages on the grounds of the Reformatory.

[60] See pp. 12 et seq., p. 132.

[61] See pp. 177 et seq.

[62] See pp. 19, 45–50.

The régime envisaged by Mrs. Hodder was, as we have seen, sound and forward-looking in the main. Her efforts to counteract the routinizing influences of an institution, her realistic conception of the educative process, her handling of the prison labour problem, the adequate medical program she insisted upon,[63] her view of the value of systematic physical culture, her recognition of the fact that disciplinary problems require psychiatric attention, the controlled inmate-government system she developed, her insistence upon an experimental attitude — these and other evidences show an alertness to the major issues involved in the institutional treatment of offenders. Nevertheless, our investigation suggests the possibility of certain improvements.

Space obviously prohibits a comprehensive, detailed analysis of the foregoing and other aspects of the Reformatory régime. We therefore confine our attention to several of the more important ones, particularly those that require reconsideration by most of the peno-correctional institutions of the country; namely, (a) the role of experimentation in treatment methods, (b) means of counteracting a natural tendency in institutional life toward routine, and (c) the industrial program.

(a) One of the greatest needs disclosed by this research is that of planful experimentation with the treatment of special mental types such as psychopathic, psychoneurotic, and mentally dull offenders. Assuming these to be distributed into appropriate institutions and colonies, there remains the major work of determining what forms of treatment they will respond to most successfully. Society has for some time been segregating " defective delinquents," but, on the whole, little progress has been made in their study and treatment. Indeed, this may be said about prisoners in general. With few exceptions the prison psychiatrist has until recently approached his problems with a point of view that conceives the mental condition of offenders as something static. There has been too great a tendency to regard the make-up of offenders as more or less fixed and insulated from environmental influences rather than as a plastic, ever-changing organism in which occurs a continued interplay between the personality and its surroundings. This has led to rather superficial diagnosis and practically no attempt at therapy. In fields other than the correctional the time has long since arrived for a change of attitude and practice on the part of psychiatrists, caused not a little by the contributions of psychoanalysis. A *dynamic approach* should now be insisted upon in correctional institutions, both for therapeutic purposes and for making possible contributions to the psychology of offenders and the etiology of delinquency.[64] When it is remembered how important it is for a reformatory to teach its inmates the wholesome management

---

[63] The physical condition of almost half our women was found to be improved during their stay at the Reformatory. See p. 192.

[64] For a case of the kind that should interest psychoanalysts, see pp. 147 et seq., 157 et seq., 168 et seq. For the need of research into the mechanisms of " reformation " and into the role of personality in the reformative process, see pp. 258-9.

of the sex impulse,[65] to protect some of the more naïve young inmates against the dangers that will beset them on their return to free life,[66] to devote a good deal of time and thought to the more intimate personal problems of inmates,[67] and to understand the psychologic implications of temper outbursts and of disciplinary problems in general,[68] the need of the best possible psychiatric aid is apparent. Indeed, the entire environment of a peno-correctional institution is such as to call for placing the greatest possible emphasis upon a mental hygiene program.[69]

It is therefore suggested that various educational devices, psychoanalytic techniques, and other methods of personality study and of the control of human conduct be systematically experimented with in correctional institutions and that the results be recorded and made generally available. For this purpose the employment of experts with training in pertinent fields, constructive imagination, a love for human beings, and good judgment is indispensable.

It is further suggested that in every case a treatment diary be kept in which frequent entries are made of the methods employed, the reasons for their use, the reactions of the prisoner to them, the reasons for changes in the treatment program originally decided upon, the obstacles met with.[70] Only in some such manner will it be possible ultimately to evolve a system of therapeutic principles and practices which might be taught to workers in the field and might have wide practical application.

(b) Mrs. Hodder spoke of the need of projecting the Reformatory into the community.[71] One aspect of her efforts in that direction is the indenture system.[72] The practice of releasing prisoners on indenture deserves to be greatly extended, so that experiments may be tried with different classes of women and various types of occupation.[73] The indenture system is one of the practical means of counteracting the routinizing tendencies of an institution. Another way is to permit certain inmates to have contacts with constructive community agencies, under official oversight. Attendance at clubs, lectures, vocational schools, and settlement houses in the community surrounding a correctional institution might all be arranged for. Thereby the experience of prisoners who can safely be dealt with in this fashion would be enriched under guidance.

(c) The industrial program at the Massachusetts Reformatory seems to be

[65] See p. 100.

[66] See pp. 142 et seq.

[67] Mrs. Hodder accomplished a great deal of good in this aspect of the work, as is shown in pages 133 et seq.

[68] See pp. 11, 128 note 27, 168 et seq., 192 et seq.

[69] Compare E. C. Lekkerkerker: op. cit., p. 576.

[70] See p. 133.

[71] See p. 7.

[72] See p. 138.

[73] We are glad to learn that the present superintendent, Dr. Miriam Van Waters, is working in this direction.

somewhat better than average.[74] We have seen that on the whole our women remained in their various assignments long enough to learn the rudiments of the work.[75] It is difficult for a correctional institution to provide. Practically, penal administrators, though desiring to individualize in the assignment of inmates to various types of work and to keep them at a trade long enough to master it, are forced to modify these desiderata to meet the limitations and needs of the institution. In fact, it may be better to adopt a system of rotation whereby most inmates will receive some experience in *all* available industries than to have each spend full time on any one; for by doing the latter, the range of the offender's future employability when released is limited.[76] Nevertheless, a reformatory should from time to time modify its industries in order to take a more realistic account of the changing demands for different types of free labor. Only 16.8% of the women studied in the research used the institutional trade during the post-parole period.[77]

The industrial program of an institution is of course conditioned in large measure by the capacities of its inmates. When a better system of original classification and distribution of offenders is established, the vocational guidance and labour facilities of each institution can be made more effective. In the meantime the training in various domestic duties given many women both in reformatories and on indenture is unquestionably of value. So also is the farm work.

A practice in the Massachusetts Reformatory to be especially commended is that of devoting only half the day to industry, and at a speed and standard required of free labour. This releases the rest of the day for concern with health and educational and recreational activities. In many institutions an insufficient work-load is spread over the entire day, the inmates thereby not only lapsing into habits of laziness and inefficiency, but wasting much time that might be used for constructive purposes. The more general adoption in correctional institutions of the Massachusetts Reformatory's division of the daily program of activities should produce desirable results.

Space prevents our making detailed suggestions for possible improvements in the various other features of the institutional régime. Suffice it to say that the first requisite is *proper personnel*. Given that, the constructive ingenuity, the scientific attitude, and the love of humanity that must be blended in order to evolve a helpful correctional régime have a chance to develop;[78] without it, the best of buildings, theories, and programs will accomplish little.

[74] For a good summary of the aims and practices of institutional labour programs in women's reformatories throughout the country, see E. C. Lekkerkerker: op. cit., pp. 577–8.

[75] See pp. 197–8.

[76] The limitation of the market for goods made by prison labor must also be taken into account.

[77] See p. 212.

[78] See pp. 166, 177 et seq., 184 as to the influence of Mrs. Hodder on certain inmates of the Massachusetts Reformatory.

7. Parole

Introductory. One of the important findings of this study is that the mere fact of being " on parole " has some deterrent and settling effect on certain offenders. It will be recalled that on the whole there was a general improvement in our women during their period of parole oversight.[79] Yet the case histories show that parole supervision might be substantially bettered.

Clues to improved practices. A number of clues for more intensive case-work methods on the part of parole agents may be mentioned.

An association was found between the work habits of the women in the Reformatory and their industrial habits while on parole.[80] The fact that ordinarily parole agents can expect those who had poor work habits in the institution to have them also on parole is a challenge to the ingenuity of parole supervisors. They must devise means for accomplishing in many cases what the Reformatory evidently failed to do — the inculcation of proper industrial attitudes and habits. This is not an easy task, in view of the fact that in most instances the only alternative the parole agents can offer to a glamorous life of questionably won ease is drab and ill-paid domestic service or factory work. In this connection it should be recalled that the parolees held their first jobs on parole for very brief periods and usually left their places of employment for inadequate reasons.[81]

Another clue is the finding that there is little carry-over into free life of the constructive recreational practices taught the women in the institution.[82] In the Reformatory they are members of organized play groups; outside they tend to spend their leisure in their own way. Despite parole oversight many of the women resumed their vicious companionships when released from the Reformatory. The wholesome employment of spare time is one of the principal needs of these women, and the efforts of parole agents should therefore be directed to bringing more of them into contact with organizations for the constructive use of leisure, such as school centers, settlement houses, clubs, and the like.

Another important clue is that the conduct of the women in the institution is in general fairly predictive of the conduct to be expected from them on parole.[83] This finding is of value not only to parole boards (or treatment tribunals) in considering whom to release on parole and when to do so, but to parole agents in knowing the type of person they are to supervise. By obtaining a detailed account of the behaviour of the parolee in the institution, the parole agent can continue on parole any constructive work that may have been initiated in the Reformatory and be on her guard against antisocial tendencies of the parolee.

---

[79] The improvements occurring during parole are summarized on p. 215.
[80] See pp. 212, 227.
[81] See p. 204.   [82] See pp. 213-4.   [83] See pp. 209-10.

Still another suggestive clue in connection with parole work is the finding that the neighbourhood conditions to which the women returned after the end of parole were on the whole worse than during parole.[84] In the case of child delinquents, the frequent need of transplanting the individual to a more wholesome soil has generally been recognized and at least partially provided for by childplacing agencies. Many adult offenders are equally in need of a new start away from their old surroundings. Until agencies are created for placing certain adults in foster-homes during a period of readjustment to a life of freedom, parole agents must meet the challenge of finding permanently good homes for their charges.[85] The co-operation of informed citizens must be won in this work.

Unless one takes the narrow view of regarding parole as merely a reward for good behaviour in an institution, one must conclude that good parole work requires the preparation of the family of the offender for her return; [86] and this in turn requires a knowledge of mental hygiene and social case work. Heavy case-loads and the difficulty of keeping track of all parolees interfere with effective parole work. Yet intensive, unbroken parole supervision pays in the long run.[87] We may summarize the discussion of parole supervision by saying that, in planning the extra-mural treatment program in each case and in supervising parolees, the best family case-work practices should be followed.

While it is particularly important that ex-prisoners be intensively supervised during the transitional period from incarceration to free life,[88] parole work that aims at permanent rehabilitation of offenders rather than mere temporary deterrence through the threat of return to prison must take into account the fact that crises arise both during the parole and post-parole careers of offenders when friendly advice may mean the difference between relapse into criminal ways and continuance in law-abiding channels.[89] If the attitude and practices of the institutional and parole authorities have been such as to call forth a friendly, trusting response on the part of parolees, the latter will learn to ask their former supervisors for aid in times of crisis. But means must be provided for such assistance. In addition to privately supported agencies for aiding ex-prisoners, there might well be established equivalents in parole service to the " out-patient departments " of hospitals — places to which ex-offenders could return at any time for constructive, confidential guidance.

8. Conclusion

The suggestions made in the preceding pages may carry forward a modest distance the attack of society upon delinquency and criminality. It ought to be stressed, however, that those who harbour too great expectations from any of

---

[84] See pp. 201–2.
[85] In the case of women parolees this is frequently done through placing them as domestics.
[86] See pp. 165–6.
[87] See pp. 204–5. [88] See p. 206. [89] See pp. 143–4.

the measures proposed for coping with these great evils are doomed to disappointment. In this enterprise, as in so much of human endeavour, understanding must precede control; but unfortunately the sciences and arts upon which depend a more successful, yet civilized, attack on delinquency and criminality are as yet in a very imperfect state. We still know little about the basic problem of the relative roles of hereditary and acquired qualities in the disposition and behaviour of human beings. Psychology, psychiatry, social case work, and educational practices have as yet not reached a very high degree of effectiveness, though happily they seem ever to be improving. Wise societal planning is still in embryo. Hence it is of the utmost importance that careful biologic and sociologic research and experimentation go hand in hand with " practical programs " designed to " produce immediate results." In the last analysis, our hope lies in the methods of the scientist; that is, in disciplined intelligence conscientiously and fearlessly applied to the search for the truth wherever it may lead.

APPENDICES

APPENDIX A

METHOD OF THIS RESEARCH

1. Introductory

Research in the social sciences suffers from the lack of instruments of precision available to the pure sciences, and also from a lack of thoroughly trained investigators. The material of the social sciences is unwieldy; it cannot be forced into a laboratory mould; it is open to as many interpretations as there are special biases of the investigators. Gradually, however, as knowledge from cognate fields is woven into the fabric of the social sciences, and as greater effort is made to study and measure its content, certain principles of procedure are being built up.

Many social investigators publish "results," but very few give detailed statement of their methods or of the quality of the data on which their findings are based. It is only by a detailed presentation of procedures that any critical evaluation of their work is possible. Results, conclusions, and interpretations of studies in the social sciences are valuable only in the light of the soundness of the methodology employed, the thoroughness in the gathering of the material, and the skill and training of the investigators.

It is for this reason that the authors present, with as much detail as is feasible, a statement of the method of this research. It is hoped that it will furnish a basis for a critical evaluation of their work, and that it will serve as even a slight contribution toward a more scientific methodology in penological investigations.

2. The Background Data of this Research

In a previous work, *500 Criminal Careers,* which is a follow-up study of male offenders and of which the present book is a companion volume, we gave a detailed description of the raw materials upon which the research was based; of the methods developed for gathering, verifying, and editing the data; of the technique of locating and interviewing ex-criminals; and of the numerous problems connected with the follow-up investigations. In an appendix to the chapter on "Method" of the above cited work the schedules and questionnaires used for the work were presented.[1] Although in its essential features the method used in the present study is similar to that applied in the previous investigation,

[1] S. & E. T. Glueck: *500 Criminal Careers,* p. 343.

there are enough points of difference and a sufficient elaboration of detail in procedures to justify the writing of this appendix.

Selection of cases. For the purposes of this investigation, five hundred cases of women whose parole from the Women's Reformatory at Framingham, Massachusetts, expired between the years 1921 and 1925 were selected in consecutive order, beginning with the date of December 1924 and working backward until the required number of cases had been assembled.[2]

Contents of Reformatory records. The raw materials of this study divide themselves into two parts:

1. Those covering the time up to the end of the parole period — that is, the personal, family, Reformatory, and parole history of the individual women.

2. Those covering a five-year period after the expiration of sentence from the Reformatory (post-parole period).

These two groups are separated because the materials comprising group 1 were already available in the rough when the study was started, having been gathered by the Reformatory and parole officials; while the materials of group 2 had to be built up by the personal investigations of the authors and their assistants.

The method employed in the gathering, compiling, and analysis of the post-parole data will be described later.

Let us look into a case folder of the Women's Reformatory to see what materials are found therein. The contents of a typical *dossier* are as follows:

1. A statement of the charge for which the offender was sentenced to the Women's Reformatory, and other legal data from the complaint and mittimus.

2. The offender's own story of her life, gathered in an interview by a member of the staff of the Reformatory shortly after the woman's admission.

3. Copies of letters to and from numerous individuals and agencies with whom the research department of the Reformatory corresponded in an effort to verify and supplement the information secured directly from the offender.

4. A report of the investigation made by the field worker of the institution staff in an effort to verify the information which had been gathered in the interview with the offender.

5. Health information, including a copy of the findings of the psychometric, psychiatric, and physical examinations made by the Reformatory physician shortly after the offender's admission.

6. Institutional history, in which section are recorded various facts about

[2] Numerous index books kept at the Massachusetts Department of Correction had to be consulted before these cases could be properly segregated. The task of the research worker is made doubly difficult by the unnecessarily complicated system of recording the names, the case numbers, the dates of the original commitment, the dates of revocation, the dates and length of sentences, and courts from which convicted, and the dates of release on parole and of the expiration of the sentence. There is no particular value in a statement of how these data are kept. To find one's way through the mazes of it in order to cull out the required information is a trying task. One of the staff assistants spent four weeks at this.

the offender's work and conduct in the Reformatory, a summary of letters received by her from relatives, and a statement of visits made to the offender by relatives. There is also a summary of letters written on the offender's behalf by members of the institution staff to various persons in the community, regarding her personal affairs, such as matters of insurance, questions relating to divorce proceedings, and the like.

7. A " parole sheet," on which is entered the dates when the offender appeared before the Board of Parole, together with reasons why her parole was denied, and the date of her final release.

8. Finally, a summary of all these data prepared for the Board of Parole after the offender's story had been verified. This contains the known facts covering the same ground described in 2 above, together with corrected identifying data, criminal record, personal and family history, as well as the history of the offender in the Reformatory, the report of the physician, the offender's attitude toward her Reformatory experience, her vocational training in the institution, her plan for the future, and the addresses of her nearest relatives.

Reliability of Reformatory records. It will be seen that, with these materials on hand, a beginning of our follow-up investigations could be made. But what of the accuracy and validity of the data? Fortunately for us, ever since 1911 Mrs. Jessie Hodder, the late superintendent of the Women's Reformatory, and her research associate, Miss Barbara Sanborn, have been more conscious than is common among penal administrators of the need of thorough and carefully verified histories, and have translated their conviction into a reality. All the cases included in our study contained data uniform in detail and in the method of gathering and verifying it. Miss Sanborn, who has a particular talent for detail and accuracy, personally interviewed the offenders on their admission to the Reformatory, securing data covering place and date of birth; places of residence with definite addresses in chronological order; early and more recent home conditions; religious affiliation; schooling; ambitions; occupations and places of employment; recreational interests, companionships, delinquencies; health; dates and places of marriages, number of children, their birth-dates, and the like. Similarly, the occupations, education, character, economic condition, delinquencies, health, and mentality of parents, siblings, husbands, children, paternal and maternal relatives were carefully inquired into.

The interview with the offender usually revealed much of value. However, it served the institution officials only as a basis for further investigation and was followed by a careful and well-directed plan of verification and amplification of the statements made by the offender. Form letters were sent to city clerks for date of birth of the offender and her children, for verification of marriages, for causes of deaths of members of the family. Inquiries were forwarded to principals of the schools which the offender had attended. The family physician was communicated with as to the medical history of the offender and her family and their standards of living. The superintendents of hospitals or other institutions in which the offender or members of her family had been confined were asked for diagnoses, dates of confinement, and prognoses of the cases. The pastors of the churches which she or her family had attended were asked their opinions of the offender and the family. Employers were questioned as to the offender's ability, the exact nature of her employment, her earnings, the reasons for her discharge, and the like. The overseers of the poor of the different towns in which the family had lived were communicated with to find out if the family had been receiving relief aid. Social agencies that had dealt with the family at any time prior to the offender's admission to the Reformatory were asked to summarize their knowledge of the family and, particularly, to state their impressions of the offender. Any gaps in the court record of the offender and the members of her family were filled in by police and probation officers. A letter was also sent to the offender's family, asking for a statement of her past life.

When this information had been gathered by correspondence, the data were studied by Miss Sanborn, and supplementary facts which were needed were sought by the Reformatory field worker. As many field visits were made as were necessary to gather all the data. Then the summary statement already described was prepared, and it is now on file in each folder.

It required an examination of only fifty of the case histories to determine the validity of the data. The standard maintained by the Reformatory officials in the gathering of the materials met the requirements of this research for thoroughness and accuracy. Such of the facts as may be open to question are fully recognized by the authors and have been taken account of in this book.

One of the authors, together with a full-time assistant, spent one academic year in analysing the data covering the personal, family, Reformatory, and parole history as gleaned from the records of the institution, in accordance with the schedules and definitions set up for this purpose (see Section 3 below, and Appendices B and C).

Contents of parole records. The problem of analysing the data covering the parole period of the offenders was complicated by the fact that the records kept by the parole officers are very meagre and contain considerable unverified information. In these records, kept in the files of the Massachusetts Department of Correction, are found the following materials:

1. A brief summary from the superintendent of the Reformatory to the chairman of the Board of Parole, outlining the desirability or inadvisability of parole for the offender.

2. The certification by a prospective employer of a job to be given to the offender on release.

3. A record of the dates on which the offender reports to the parole officer during the parole period.

4. Required reports by letter from the offender to the parole agent at stated intervals, containing her address on the particular date and her place of employment.

5. Copies of letters written to the offender by the parole agent regarding such matters as permission to change her place of employment, warnings to report more regularly, et cetera.

6. "Visit slips" filled in by the parole agent after she had called on the offender or others, giving the date of visit, the offender's address, her place of employment, earnings, and remarks about her conduct. For example: "Apparently doing well. Her people report that she has no desire to do anything but what is the right thing. She has always been at home on agent's call, and is apparently doing better than she ever did before in her life." And, later: "Not at all satisfactory. Takes no interest in her work, breaks article after article with no thought of the seriousness of it. Likes her place and does not want to be changed, and promised to do better. Does not keep herself clean. She seems to feel that life should be one round of pleasure and cannot understand why she is not free to seek this whenever she wishes."

7. "Visit slips" which contain reports of interviews held by the agent with the offender whenever she comes to see the agent. These reports contain much the same data as that described above.

8. Letters from social agencies that have had any contact with the offender after the end of her parole period. Such letters are occasionally written to the parole agents in order to secure a summary of an agent's previous contacts with the offender.

9. Letters written to the parole agent by relatives of the offender and letters written by the parole agent to relatives regarding such matters as the advisability of placement of the offender as a domestic, or the need for improvement in her conduct, et cetera.

10. One-page reports of visits by relatives to the office of the parole agent regarding the offender and her problems.

11. Statements made by the parole agent to the Board of Parole regarding the offender's violation of parole rules and briefly describing the nature of her misconduct.

12. Other miscellaneous data, such as communications from employers to the agent regarding the offender's industrial problems, her misconduct, et cetera.

Reliability of parole records. It required only a cursory examination of this material to discover that it did not contain all the facts which we desired to have, and that some of the data would have to be verified and amplified. Because it was not feasible to fill in all the gaps in this material or to verify certain portions of it so many years after the event, certain facts were not pursued, either because the parole officers failed to take note of them in the course of their contacts with the offender or because such information as they did record was too scanty for our purposes—as, "venereal disease contracted during the parole period," "family relations," "conjugal relations," "competence of the offender as a homemaker," "attitude to marital responsibility," "attitude to her children," "illegitimate pregnancies during the parole period," "illegitimate occupations engaged in during the parole period," "frequency of arrests," "predominant delinquency," a summary of the types of offences which she committed during the parole period.[3] Certain other data, such as "industrial history," "economic responsibility," "work habits of the offender," "companionships," "leisure and habits," and two or three others, though included in our schedules, were known not to be thoroughly reliable and have been interpreted accordingly. Such other factors, however, as could be, were verified by us through correspondence, as, for example, date and place of marriage, birth-dates of children, court record, etc.

It is probable that the parole agents knew a great deal more about the offenders than they had recorded. But since it would be unwise to depend on their memories so many years after parole supervision was over, no attempt was made to secure information from them about the offender's history during the parole period.

Some five months' time was spent by one full-time assistant in culling out from these parole records the data covering the parole history of the offender in accordance with our schedules and definitions (see next section), with which the research assistant had to be thoroughly familiar in order to transcribe the data and to indicate which data needed verification.

It will be noted that throughout this work the authors have been careful to qualify any conclusions which they have made, on the basis of the validity of the materials and of their knowledge of how it was gathered.

Our first step, therefore, in the pursuit of this research was to become thoroughly acquainted with the background data already available.

3. Schedules, Definitions, and Codes

Before describing how the post-parole data were gathered by the authors and their staff, we need to state how the schedules, definitions, and code classifications were built up, because this process actually was begun before the post-parole studies were started, and in a sense shaped the course and detail of this portion of the study.

The factors of our research divided themselves into five parts—those covering:

1. The Personal History of the Offender.
2. The Family History.
3. The Reformatory History.

---

[3] See Appendix C for definitions of these terms, which are there arranged alphabetically.

4. The Parole History.

5. The Post-Parole History.

Preparation of statistical schedules. In building up the schedules it was necessary first to make a careful study of the materials already available (described in the previous section); secondly, to examine other studies of delinquents previously made by the authors,[4] in order not to omit any factors which might be compared with factors included in those studies; and, thirdly, to examine other descriptive studies of women delinquents in order to see what factors were emphasized in them, and not to omit from the study any factors which would be useful for purposes of comparison. One of the major difficulties in building up a science of criminology is this lack of comparable data from studies made with a like degree of thoroughness and careful definition of terminology. Therefore every contribution in this direction is important.

Once the factors to be included had been decided upon, *tentative* schedules were prepared for the reception of the data, and careful definition of terms was made. Here again we had in mind the need to collect data which would be strictly comparable with our own previous studies and with other studies of women delinquents.[5] Hence the definitions used in these other studies were adopted wherever this was possible, and factors entirely unique to the present investigation were defined, after consideration of the materials and after discussion with social workers and others as to what measuring rods to apply.

After the facts of the first fifty cases covering the personal, family, Reformatory, and parole history had been studied and entered on the schedules, the schedules and definitions were revised. As a result of this process, certain factors used in other studies were discarded because we found that the data contained in our records were insufficient and so could not feasibly be gathered in this study — as, for example, " age of parents at birth of the offender " which was used in the *Study of Women Delinquents in New York State;* and " conduct of the offender in school," which the authors used in their study of *One Thousand Juvenile Delinquents.*

About sixty or seventy factors covering the personal, family, Reformatory, and parole history were discarded at this point, because, after the materials had been subjected to a critical analysis, the deficiencies of the information were obvious. Those factors on which further data could feasibly be secured were retained, however; as, for example, vital statistics, criminal records, and any other information which could be gathered by correspondence.

At this stage the schedules covering the personal, family, Reformatory, and parole history were put into final form (see Appendix B).

[4] *500 Criminal Careers; a Study of One Thousand County-Jail Cases* (in connection with the Harvard Crime Survey); *One Thousand Juvenile Delinquents* (in connection with the Harvard Crime Survey).

[5] Notably, Mabel R. Fernald and others: *A Study of Women Delinquents in New York State* New York: Century Company; 1920).

The schedule for the post-parole period was then developed, *first*, to include certain factors which would be comparable with those in the prior and parole history of the offender — as, for example, " leisure and habits," " economic responsibility," " delinquency," et cetera — *secondly*, factors which would be comparable with our follow-up study of five hundred male delinquents;[6] and, *thirdly*, those which are entirely unique in this study, such as, " attitude of the community toward the offender," " offender's criticism of the Reformatory," " beneficial effects of the Reformatory experience," et cetera.

Defining of factors. Though the schedules were entirely ready by the time the first fifty cases had been analysed, the definitions were deliberately not crystallized until several hundred cases had been subjected to analysis; for, as exceptions to the rule presented themselves in sufficient number, they had to be provided for in the definitions. For example, the definition of " steadiness of employment " read in its final form as follows:

" *Inapplicable* — refers to women who do not work because of illness, or confinement in institutions, or lack of necessity. In the latter group is the woman who is supported at least in marginal economic circumstances (see ECONOMIC CONDITION for definition) by her husband or by a lover for whom she is keeping house; and the woman who receives compensation or insurance sufficient to maintain her in marginal economic circumstances.

" *Regular* — refers to women who are continually employed during the period judged, i.e., who have not more than an average of two months of unemployment a year.

" *Fairly regular* — refers to women who have periods of unemployment in excess of two months a year, which are compensated for by periods of sustained work.

" *Irregular* — refers to women who have frequent or long protracted unemployment, and no periods of sustained employment.

" In the case of women who had to work during only a part of the period under scrutiny their steadiness of employment for such period is to be tabulated."

When the definition was originally prepared, it did not take account of women who were supported by lovers or who received compensation or insurance, or of those women who needed to work for only a part of the period under scrutiny, because the analysis of the first fifty cases did not reveal to any great extent these particular aspects of this factor.

Those definitions, however, which had withstood the test of usage in previous studies were retained in order that the data might be comparable, though modifications or additions were made when necessary; for example, the definition of " attitude to children " was adopted from another study,[7] as follows:

---

[6] *500 Criminal Careers.*
[7] *One Thousand Juvenile Delinquents* (Harvard University Press, 1934).

"*Good* — fond of, cares for

"*Fair* — casual toward, or fond of but neglectful because of drink, absorption in a lover, etc.

"*Poor* — gives no supervision, no affection, or is abusive."

However, it was necessary to add the following to the definition, in order to provide for a considerable number of cases in which the children of the offender were not living with her:

"In the case of women whose children are not living with them for various reasons (as, for example, in custody of husband, in institutions, etc.) tabulate as

"*Good* — if she maintains an interest in them to the greatest extent possible within the limits of the particular situation.

"*Fair* — if she keeps in touch with them.

"*Poor* — if she is entirely out of touch with them."

This particular aspect of the family life of women delinquents was not clearly revealed in the study of the first fifty cases, and for this reason it was found necessary to modify the definition.

An examination of Appendix C [8] will show that the definitions of terms were exactly the same for those factors which appeared in the three periods of the study — prior to commitment, during parole, during the post-parole period.

Categorization of factors. In determining the division of each factor into appropriate categories, the comparability of the data with factors used in the previous studies of the authors and of the studies of other investigators had to be kept in mind as well as the limitations imposed by the code-machine-tabulation method, which allows for not more than twelve sub-categories of a factor. For qualitative data — as, for example, *work habits,* or *economic responsibility* — twofold or threefold classifications were used where possible in an effort to avoid error in classification. It is easy enough, for example, to differentiate the "good" from the "poor" and to determine the "fair" which falls between the two extremes. See, for example, the definition of *Leisure and habits, Conjugal relations, Home — physical.*[9] In cases in which the difference between the "good" and the "fair" group, and between the "fair" and the "poor," is not so readily determinable, a twofold classification (see *Companions,* or *Play places and haunts,* or *Economic responsibility*) was adopted. Obviously these two- and three-fold classifications of qualitative data result in rather crude measurements. It seemed to us, however, that only after great familiarity and experience with the material can measures of any greater refinement be safely applied.

In the case of quantitative data — as, for example, *Average wage* or *Longest period employed* — categories were built up from the material itself. If, let us say, it was found, after study of the first fifty cases, that the average wage of a woman was rarely over $35 a week, the classification was made in $5 intervals, ending with "$35 and over." Even though there were tables on

[8] "Definitions."   [9] Appendix C, "Definitions."

Weekly wage in other studies in which the classification continued to $100, everything over $35 was combined for purposes of comparison.

Two more illustrations of this process may be clarifying. In the tabulation of *Place of birth* a previous study had included the following countries: Austria, Hungary, Czechoslovakia, Jugoslavia, Greece, Armenia, Palestine, Syria, Turkey in Asia, Spain, Mexico, Central and South America, Scotland, and Wales. After the first fifty cases had been studied, it was found that so few cases fell into any of the above categories that they could safely be reduced to the classification " all others."

Another illustration may be given from the tabulation of *Total time a prostitute*. In the study of Fernald and others, of delinquent women,[10] the classification was made in two-year intervals through " 26 years." After our first fifty cases had been tabulated by hand and compared with the above-mentioned table, it was seen that not one woman in our group had been a prostitute for more than ten years. This was because the group we were studying was younger. Therefore the classification was changed to read " 12 years or over," and, in order to maintain the comparability of the two tables, the figures of the other study, " from 12 to 26 years," were contracted to " 12 years and over."

In making quantitative and qualitative distributions, our general principle was to set them up at first in as great detail as any other study with which we wished to make comparison, or, if there were no comparable data, in such detail as reason dictated. The first fifty cases were tabulated by hand. After seeing how the cases were distributed we made contractions to satisfy three considerations — (1) logical classification, (2) retention of comparability, (3) the limitation to twelve categories as imposed by the code-machine-tabulation method. In the case of qualitative data we adopted two- or three-fold classifications where possible for the reasons already explained. Where detail greater than that allowed for by the machine tabulation was necessary — as, for example, in *Offences committed before entrance to the Reformatory,* where there were actually different offences, hand tabulation was resorted to, but the factor of *Types of offences* (see *Summary of arrests — type*), in which there were ten categories, was tabulated by machine.

Tabulation problems. The technical difficulties involved in the machine tabulation of our data were considerable because of the large number of factors — 285 in all. Four " pre-coding " and four " punch " cards (see Appendix B for explanation and description of these) were required for machine tabulation. The first card covered the *Personal history of the offender,* the second the *Family and Reformatory history,* the third the *Parole history,* and the fourth, the *Post-parole history.* In order to make possible the correlation of certain factors appearing on different cards, a considerable number of factors — 61 in all — had to be repeated on one card or another, and the factor of *Delinquency*

[10] Op. cit.

in the post-parole period had to be repeated on all the cards in order to make possible the necessary correlations with this particular factor. For example, in the case of *Work habits prior to commitment to the Reformatory,* appearing on card 1, and *Work habits of the offender in the post-parole period,* appearing on card 4, the factor of *Work habits prior to commitment to the Reformatory* had to be repeated on card 4. The only reason why the factor *Work habits in post-parole period* was not placed on card 1 instead was because of lack of space.

All factors that were purely of descriptive interest and did not have to be correlated to any other factor were separated out before the code was made, and these were all hand-tabulated (see Appendix D — all factors the number of which is preceded by an "H"), as, for example, *Usual occupation of husband, Delinquency of husband, Vocational experiences of the offender in the Reformatory, Reasons for solitary confinement in the Reformatory, Capabilities of the offender on entrance to the Reformatory, Special attempts at rehabilitation of the offender by the parole agent, Criticisms of the Reformatory by the offender, Attitude of the community toward the offender during the post-parole period,* et cetera.

4. Follow-Up Investigations

Difference between follow-up studies of male and of female offenders. The method used in tracing and following up the group of offenders under study is much the same as that developed in the previous work of the authors.[11] Certain problems, however, are peculiar to this research because the group studied were women and because they were found to be so largely sex delinquents. In view of the fact that fifty-four per cent of the group had been committed to the Reformatory for sex offences, it was necessary to determine the character of their sex life after release, in addition to all the other facts about them. This obviously had its difficulties. Every clue had to be pursued which would lead to information regarding illicit sex activity, illegitimate children, forced marriages, or venereal disease. Where such information was officially recorded, the problem was simplified. But where no official report of sexual misconduct or of venereal disease had been made by an agency of the law or by a social agency, our search for the facts became greatly involved and it required the utmost resourcefulness and tact to secure from the offender herself or from members of her family the information desired. Much greater effort had to be directed in such cases toward gaining the confidence of the offender and her relatives than was necessary in the previous research; and many more sources of information had to be tapped, such as policewomen, probation officers, employers, neighbours, family physicians, ministers, lawyers, landlords, divorced husbands, parents-in-law, even very distant relatives, for sidelights on the offender's conduct which would reveal the character of her sex life.

---

[11] *500 Criminal Careers.*

A second difference between this and the previous research lay in the need for even greater caution in not unwittingly revealing to newly-acquired husbands and their relatives a woman's past record or the fact of her incarceration, though in a surprisingly large proportion of cases it was found that the woman had made her past known to her husband before marriage. In view of the fact that a relatively small proportion of the women had official records of arrest after release from the Reformatory, and therefore were not generally recognized as delinquents, we had to guard against the danger of any revelation to employers, and to officials of the small towns in which the woman had newly settled since release.

A third difference lay in the greater difficulty of tracing and locating a group of women than a group of men for the reason that they changed their names by marriage, or often indiscriminately adopted the names of their various lovers, and they used aliases with much less consistency than men. Because their offences were of a minor character (in the legal sense), they were rarely fingerprinted, thus seriously limiting this source of tracing, which proved so fruitful in locating male offenders.

In addition to the difficulties peculiar to the tracing of women were others which were also characteristic of the group of male offenders — great mobility, lack of knowledge by families of the whereabouts of the offender, the widespread geographical distribution of the cases, necessitating investigation by social agencies not always skilled in the art of tracing, the lack of central criminal indexes in the various states (outside of Massachusetts), lack of uniform marriage or divorce records, variation in spellings of family names, lack of social service exchanges in many large cities.

A fourth difference in our study of male and female delinquents lies in the fact that far greater detail was sought in the present than in the former work. The reader is referred to Appendix A (page 347) of 500 *Criminal Careers* for the schedule covering the five-year post-parole period used in the Men's Reformatory study and is asked to compare this with the schedule used in the present study, Appendix B (page 375). Moreover, in the present research, after securing the data covering the five-year post-parole period, the searchlight was focused on the fifth year of the period in order to ascertain the trends in the offender's environmental circumstances, her family relationships, her assumption of economic responsibilities, her industrial adjustment, the character of her leisure and habits, and her delinquencies.

All this implied a far greater preoccupation with detail by the field investigators[12] than was necessary in the first research.

These, then, are the essential points of difference in the two pieces of work. At the risk of a certain amount of repetition, a further statement is given below about the methods used in the follow-up investigations.

[12] In this investigation two field workers participated, Mr. Samuel C. Lawrence and Mrs. Mildred Cunningham.

Identifying data. The reader will recall that in the first part of this appendix we told how the data covering the personal, family, Reformatory, and parole history of the offenders had been gathered and analysed. While the records were being studied for this purpose, data were also being culled from them which would identify and locate the offender. For this purpose, as in the previous study, an *identification card* was used (see Appendix B). On this we entered the true name of the offender, the name under which she was admitted to the Reformatory, her aliases, her date and place of birth, religion, marital status, complexion, colour of her eyes and hair, her height and weight, her address at the time of her arrest for the offence for which she was sentenced to the Reformatory, the person with whom she was living at the time, the names and birth-dates of her siblings and of her husband and children, her date of commitment to the Reformatory, the court from which she was committed, the offence and the term of the sentence, her places of residence prior to her commitment and such places of residence since her release on parole as were revealed anywhere in the records, together with her last known job and her last known address.

On the reverse side of this identification card we entered any facts gleaned either from the case records of the Reformatory or from the Department of Correction, giving any clues to the whereabouts of the offender or any facts referring to the post-parole period. For example, if an ex-inmate of the Reformatory had kept in touch either with the Reformatory or with the parole officials, and a recent address or marriage name was given, this bit of information was noted. If a social agency that had contact with the offender in the post-parole period had written to either the Reformatory or parole officials for a summary of the offender's history or had in turn sent to them a statement of its dealings with her, revealing, for example, that she had been recently divorced by her husband, or that she had given birth to an illegitimate child, or that she and her husband had applied for financial assistance, such facts were noted. The names and most recently recorded addresses of parents, siblings, or other relatives were also noted. The variety of such bits of information is great and often led us to find a woman who might otherwise have disappeared into oblivion:

Case No. 1.

The whereabouts of the offender were unknown. Her parents were living in Ireland, and only one of her several siblings could be found. Her husband, from whom she was separated, was located, but did not know her whereabouts. In view of her disappearance, her finger-print record was cleared through the United States Department of Justice, without result. The brother who was located knew only that she had gone off with a lover, whose name he gave, and that she was somewhere in the East, possibly in Newark, New Jersey. The City Clerk of Newark and the police were communicated with, but no trace of her was found. On the identification card was the bit of information that the offender had a very good friend, Mrs. *X*, of whom she had seen a great deal in the past. This woman was known to live in Brockton, Massachusetts. She was traced and interviewed and was able to give a clue to the offender and her lover in Brooklyn, New York, which led to our finding and interviewing her.

Case No. 2.

This woman was traced through relatives, to New York City. It was known that she was now the wife of a man with whom she had carried on an illicit relationship even prior to her commitment to the Reformatory. Though the investigator could find no record of arrests, the fact that she had lived illicitly with her husband before marrying him kept the investigator on the alert. When her home was visited, her husband maintained that she was away for the summer, and went so far as to deny her identity, which, however, was later proved by the investigator through other sources. The investigator faced the problem of determining the nature of her activities without being able to see the offender personally. In a thickly settled suburban district of New York City this is a difficult matter. The investigator had recorded the fact from the identification card, however, that the woman had been brought up in the Presbyterian Church. Her relatives had already revealed to the investigator that she was a church worker. The investigator used this information to call on the pastor of the only Presbyterian Church in the neighbourhood and was able, through him, to get a great deal of information about the offender and her husband, both of whom had been until a short time before members of this church, but whose periodic delinquencies had created so much disturbance in the congregation that they no longer attended this particular church.

Case No. 3.

This offender had, during her parole period, been a ward maid in a hospital. The superintendent of this hospital had been very much interested in the girl, and there was a notation on the identification card that she might know something of the post-parole history of the girl. In view of the facts that the girl's parents were dead, that the siblings were widely scattered and could not be reached, and that the whereabouts of her husband was unknown, the hospital superintendent was communicated with, and, through her, trace of the girl was secured.

Case No. 4.

This woman, now almost seventy years of age, had before her commitment to the Reformatory a long record of forgeries, misappropriations of funds, prison terms in European countries and throughout the United States. Though she was located and interviewed, and though we interviewed several relatives, landlords, and one or two employers, nothing was discovered which would indicate that she had continued her criminal career. Nevertheless, in view of this long previous record, it was determined that further investigation would have to be made in order to " prove her innocence." On the identification card we had the name of the wife of a well-known physician in whose employ the offender had been just prior to her commitment. It was noted on that card that this woman had been very friendly to the offender and that she probably had kept in touch with her throughout the years. This woman was traced from Northampton, Massachusetts, where she had lived at the time of the offender's commitment, to a city in Connecticut, where she is at present living. It was revealed by an interview that she had kept steadily in touch with the offender, and that she knew her to have made a very good adjustment, with the possible exception of the fact that she had a tendency to borrow rather freely from relatives and not to pay her debts.

Routine procedures prior to field investigation. Though there is little of a routine nature in the carrying out of the follow-up investigation, there are, nevertheless, a few procedures which we always resorted to before beginning our actual field work. First of all, the cases were cleared through the Massachusetts Probation Commission, which is a central bureau of criminal records, begun in 1916, to which all the courts of Massachusetts have been reporting since July 1, 1924. This indicated to us whether a woman had a court record in the state under her maiden name or under the name by which she was sent to the Reformatory. But the absence of a record here was not taken to mean that the woman had no record in Massachusetts. Later on in the investigation, after her marriage names and aliases had been discovered, her name was again cleared through the Probation Commission, and often a record was found which had not been revealed by the first clearance.

As all the women had been fingerprinted on entrance to the Reformatory, and their finger-print records were kept in a central bureau [13] at the State House in Boston, all our cases were cleared through this file. Only rarely, however, were records from other states found in this way, mainly because women are rarely fingerprinted, and secondly because there is no uniform exchange of the finger-print records of different states — a lack which adds to the difficulty of tracing or identifying criminals.

Where records were found either through the Probation Commission or the Massachusetts Finger Print Bureau, we wrote to clerks of court or probation officers in some cases for a summary of the circumstances of the arrest and for any information which they had on file regarding the offender or her relatives. When we knew that certain courts kept very meagre or inaccurate records, or that certain probation officers preferred to give information in person rather

[13] Previously in the Department of Correction and since 1931 in the Department of Public Safety.

than in writing, inquiry was reserved for the field investigator. Where we knew from the identifying data that the women or their families had lived mainly or recently in Boston, the Social Service Exchange was consulted. This is a central clearing-house which registers contacts of most of the private and public agencies operating in Boston and sometimes in other parts of Massachusetts. Here again absence of a record was not taken to mean that the offender or her family was not known to agencies in Boston or Massachusetts — first, because she might be recorded under a name not yet determined by us, and, secondly, because cities in Massachusetts outside of Boston do not necessarily use the Boston Social Service Exchange. The cases of offenders known to be living in cities in other states in which there is a social service exchange [14] were cleared at this point. *Absence of a record was always an indication of need for further pursuit of the facts.* When social service exchanges reported that certain agencies had had dealings with the offender or her family during the five-year post-parole period, we wrote to these agencies for a summary of their dealings with them. From this source we often gleaned a recent address, a clue to the whereabouts of an offender or of members of her family, the fact of an arrest, of the birth of an illegitimate child, of a forced marriage, and data of a like nature.

Individualized field-work procedures. After this preliminary information had been collected, we reviewed each case and made a plan for tracing the offender or her relatives, depending on the amount or kind of information already available. Street and telephone directories were consulted; city and town clerks of places not having directories were written to; and, at this point or a little later, parents or siblings were asked by letter for the address of the offender. No explanation of the purpose of the investigation was made to them at this point. The letter, reading as follows, was sent on plain paper: " Would you be good enough to let me know the present or recent address of ——, or the name of her husband. I wish very much to communicate with her." This usually elicited a reply. When we got no reply, or only unsatisfactory information, a field investigator at a later time visited the relatives.

The range of information available to the field investigator at this point was great, and each case therefore had to be handled on the basis of its own particular needs.

A few illustrations of the range, kind, and amount of information available to the field investigator at this point may be helpful:

Case No. 5.

We knew from the identification card that this offender had gone to Lynn, Massachusetts, to live with her parents immediately following her release from the Reformatory; that the whereabouts of her husband was unknown; that she had apparently lived in Lynn throughout the post-parole period, and had re-

---

[14] There are 294 social service exchanges in the United States.

married; and that she had no court record. Through the street directory she and her husband, as well as her parents, were definitely located. The charitable organizations of Lynn were communicated with, but reported that they had had no contact with her or her family during the post-parole period. With this information in hand, we were able to start the field investigation.

Case No. 6.

We knew the date of this offender's marriage in the post-parole period, the name of her husband, her places of residence during the first two years of the post-parole period, and the present address of herself and her husband.

Case No. 7.

In this case we knew the address of the offender's parents, of two sisters and a brother; the address of the family physician; and the address of a previous employer.

Case No. 8.

In this case, we knew that the offender had been arrested both in Springfield, Massachusetts, and Hartford, Connecticut, during the post-parole period; that she had been an inmate of the House of the Good Shepherd in Springfield in the early part of this period; that she had a brother living in Hartford, whose exact address was known; an aunt probably living in Springfield; a friend, also a Reformatory graduate, whose exact address in Hartford was known; and that the offender herself was living either in Springfield or in Hartford, as she was known to move frequently between the two cities.

Case No. 9.

We knew that this offender in the early part of the post-parole period had been living in Haverhill, Massachusetts, with her husband and children; that she had deserted them in 1925; that one of her children was now an inmate of a state hospital, a second of a state training school, and that the third was living with her husband and her father-in-law; that she had not been in touch with her husband or children since her disappearance; that neither her husband nor her father-in-law knew of her whereabouts; that she had been in ill health during the first part of the post-parole period, while still living in Haverhill, and had been treated at the X hospital. A report of her health, revealing venereal disease, was secured from the hospital, together with a summary of a social agency in Haverhill which had had dealings with her and her family. The address of the offender's foster-father was found, and through him a recent address of the offender in New York City was secured. It has been ascertained also that she was not recorded in the finger-print files of the police in New York City.

Preparations made by investigators for field visits. Before setting out, the field workers carefully perused the material already on file covering the personal, family, Reformatory, and parole history of the offender and looked over the identification card, noting any facts which they felt would guide them in making their visits and in gaining the confidence of the offender and her relatives. These notations contained a variety of data. For example, the investigator noted that both parents of one offender were dead; that her father had been immoral and that her mother had given birth to two illegitimate children; that the offender was the fourth in rank of seven children, of whom three were dead; that one brother was a drunkard, and one sister drank and was immoral; that her parents had separated early in life; that her childhood was spent mostly with her mother and siblings; that she had left school in the seventh grade at the age of thirteen; that no misbehaviour was reported of her during childhood, but that during her adolescent period she had become a prostitute and acquired gonorrhœa; that during her adolescence she lived mostly with her father and consorted with him, with her brothers, and with several lovers; that she had been in domestic service for several years, but was discharged frequently because of her sex habits; that she had served a sentence at the Lancaster Industrial School, for fornication; that she had been twice arrested for " common night walking " and that after one arrest she received probation and after the other a commitment to a reformatory in New York State; that she was married at the age of nineteen and was divorced in Massachusetts, in 1915; that she was not fond of her children, of whom she had three, two legitimate and one illegitimate; that she was divorced from her husband, who was intemperate and a non-supporter. In addition to the above, the field worker in this case had noted down the findings of the health examination at the Reformatory, the fact that the subject's illegitimate child had died in the Reformatory; that the offender was of normal intelligence, quick-tempered, given to faultfinding, had no sense of honour; that she planned to remarry her divorced husband and be loyal to him for the sake of their children; that her husband had expressed a desire to be reunited with her; that during the parole period she lived with her husband and child and remarried him; that she kept house, and that her conduct was satisfactory in every way during this time.

Armed with such information, together with facts covering the post-parole history of the offender that had already been gathered from the case records of the Department of Correction and the Reformatory, from the Massachusetts Probation Commission, the Massachusetts Finger Print Bureau, and here and there from the Social Service Exchange, from summaries of the dealings of agencies with the families, reports of clerks of court and probation officers, from police in cities or towns in which the offender was known to have lived, and possibly with the name of a newly-acquired husband or lover, and with more or less accurate information as to the whereabouts of the offender and members of her family, the field investigators went in search of the facts covering the five-year post-parole period (see Schedule covering the Post-Parole Period, in Appendix B).[15]

Caution necessary in field investigations. The care which had to be employed by the field investigators in order not to reveal the offender's past to new husbands, employers, and others is illustrated in the following cases:

Case No. 10.

It was known that during the post-parole period the offender had been committed to a penal institution in a near-by state, from which she had been transferred to a hospital for mental diseases to be trained as a nurse. Through this penal institution it was learned that she was still connected with the hospital as a nurse. It was necessary to take every precaution in making inquiries at the hospital for the offender, in view of the fact that her past was not known to the hospital officials and that she was highly regarded in her profession. When the field investigator set out to visit the offender, he dared not telephone her to explain his purpose, for fear that she might be embarrassed; nor would he write because he was afraid that she might ignore his letter. He called personally, therefore, and without introducing himself handed her a note which he had prepared in advance and in which he explained the purpose of the inquiry. He waited while she read it so that he might have an answer, thereby avoiding both a refusal for an interview and any embarrassment to her. As the reception room at the hospital was not sufficiently private to warrant an interview, a meeting later in the day at a reputable hotel was arranged. The offender was grateful for the caution which the investigator employed, both in approaching and interviewing her and in not revealing to the hospital authorities the nature of his inquiry.

Case No. 11.

In visiting relatives it was learned that the offender, who is of French extraction, had recently married a German-American of good family; that neither he nor they knew about her Reformatory incarceration. They also stated that she had no children, and cautioned the field worker not to ask her regarding this in her husband's presence, as she was very sensitive about it and had not told her husband that she had had an operation at the Reformatory which made it impossible for her to bear children. The field worker timed her visit for a Saturday morning when the husband was likely to be out, as he proved to be. Had the field worker found the husband at home, she would have casually stated that she had dropped by in connection with the interest of some old friends of his wife's.

[15] The technique developed for establishing friendly contacts with the offenders or their families and for making the interviews have been fully described in the chapter on "Method" in *500 Criminal Careers.* The reader is referred to pages 101–8 of that work for details.

Difficulties of locating women offenders. The difficulties involved in tracing an offender because of her frequent change of names, use of aliases, or mobility are seen in the following cases:

Case No. 12.

This girl seemed to be "lost." When the field investigator started out, he knew that the offender and her husband had been living in a rural section not far from Fitchburg, Massachusetts. Visits to relatives showed that she had deserted her husband and had disappeared; that the husband was now living in a small city in Connecticut. He was visited, but could not give any definite clue except that she had gone off to Europe with a lover and had on her return settled somewhere in New York or New Jersey as his wife. He gave a clue, however, to the whereabouts of the offender's father, in northern New York State, who, in answer to an inquiry, was able to give the address of the offender and the name of the alleged husband. With this information, the offender was found and interviewed.

Case No. 13.

The offender was known to have left her husband during the early part of her post-parole period, while they were living in Pittsfield, Massachusetts. Her mother-in-law was traced to a town not far from Pittsfield, and she informed the investigator that the offender had been granted a divorce and had remarried. She did not know the new name or whereabouts of the girl, however, except that she had heard that she had gone to New Hampshire to live near her mother. An examination of the marriage records revealed the name of her husband and of his home town at the time of the marriage, which was a large manufacturing city near the New Hampshire line. Correspondence with the town clerk revealed that she and her husband were still living in this place. Personal interviews with officials of this town revealed that a few weeks previously she had divorced her second husband and had married a third. With this information, she was easily found and interviewed.

Case No. 14.

The offender was known to have been separated from her husband. Relatives insisted that she was a respectable, self-supporting woman, earning her living in a legitimate way; that she had not remarried; and that she was making her home near the city of Boston. After many visits to the relatives and the establishment of a friendly contact, her address in the city of Cambridge, Massachusetts, was finally revealed. No one of her name was found in the house, however, nor was she known to neighbours, one of whom, however, had mentioned a woman having the offender's first name as being the "wife" of a Greek, whose name they spelled out for the investigator. Because of the oddity of the offender's first name, the investigator's suspicions were aroused. However, he did not wish to call on the subject without being certain of her identity. He therefore traced through old street directories the name of the man as given by neighbours, and he found several previous addresses of this man and his supposed wife. He then consulted the police census, which gave a description of this man's wife that tallied accurately with a description of the offender. The investigator thus established her identity and was able to see her and her alleged husband personally. This led to a revelation of her illicit life during the post-parole period.

Need for establishing proof of "guilt" and "innocence." The greatest problem confronting us in the follow-up investigations was that of securing adequate data regarding the delinquent conduct of a woman in cases in which there was no police or court record or other official statement of misconduct. The offender's "innocence" as well as her "guilt" had to be established. Although a number of follow-up researches have recently appeared purporting to give reliable estimates of "successes" and "failures" of former juvenile delinquents, they are practically all open to the criticism that the search for the ex-prisoners was much too superficial. It is therefore always advisable for the reader to expect a rendering of an exact account of how the investigations in such studies were made. In the present investigation no stone was left unturned to secure the facts relating to the subject's conduct, including the nature of her sex life. The illustrations here presented are of cases in which there was no record of arrest during the five-year post-parole period and in which, therefore, the burden of proof of "guilt" or "innocence" rested on those investigating the case:

Case No. 15.
The offender, who had been married to a highly respectable man in the third year of her post-parole period, whose marriage to him was not "forced," and who was resident in a particular community only since her marriage, was definitely known through interviews with the police, a minister, and others to be a non-delinquent since living there. Because of the nature of her sex life prior to her commitment to the Reformatory, however, the investigator had to determine the nature of her activities in the early part of the post-parole period, prior to her marriage. Both the offender and her mother were interviewed and denied any immorality on her part. The investigator decided to call on a maternal aunt, whose confidence he gained and who admitted that the offender had been promiscuous before marriage and had also cohabited with her fiancé. She corroborated the fact of freedom from illicit sex activities since marriage.

Case No. 16.
Before the offender, who was located as an employee of a hospital, was seen, it was known that until recently she had been moving about in scattered sec-

tions in the East. No police or court record could be found. In view of the fact that she had been a serious sex delinquent before her commitment, and because neither her husband nor other relatives could be located, it was necessary to gain the subject's confidence in the hope that she would reveal the nature of her sex life. She acknowledged periodic sex irregularities with various lovers throughout the post-parole period. Had she not made such acknowledgment, the field investigator would have had to visit some of the cities and towns in which she was known to have lived, in order to get from others some sidelights as to her conduct and reputation.

Case No. 17.

The offender, an Italian, was located living with her husband in Philadelphia, directly over his barber-shop. She had not revealed her Reformatory history to him, and as he was practically always at home, the field investigator was forced to make his interview with her brief. According to her story, she had been a non-delinquent throughout the post-parole period. It was necessary, therefore, to seek corroboration of her statements in a way which would not arouse the suspicions of her husband. As the offender had stated in the interview that she occasionally took lodgers from a near-by university, inquiry was made at the university about her reputation; a patrolman on the beat was interviewed; and the proprietor of a near-by drug-store was seen; all on the basis of an inquiry on behalf of someone who wanted to know if Mrs. *X's* home was a thoroughly suitable one for a young student. In this way, without violating the offender's confidence or seeing her husband or her relatives, confirmation of her good conduct was obtained.

Interviewing practices. Though it may be said that no two field investigations were alike in their procedures, nevertheless certain policies, developed through experience and because of the needs of the research, were maintained. Every effort was made, for example, to see the offender personally and at least one or two of her near relatives, such as parents or siblings. The purpose of this was twofold — first, to secure the reactions of the offender and her relatives to the Reformatory experience, and, secondly, to obtain certain data regarding her places of residence and of employment, her marital history during the post-parole period, her institutional experiences, and the like, as a basis for further investigation by personal interviews, consultation of recorded material, and correspondence.

Only in instances where the offender was too remotely situated to be visited either by our own staff or by a properly qualified social worker of another agency, or had been an inmate of an institution throughout the five-year period, or was known to have a mental or physical disease of such a nature that an interview would be fruitless, was the effort to see her, personally, relaxed. In such cases near relatives were interviewed if possible.

Careful explanation was made to the offender of the reasons for the investigation, even if repeated visits had to be made to avert any possible misunderstandings. To a surprising degree, even the mentally retarded offenders could appreciate in their limited way the value of " trying to find out how you girls who have been at the Reformatory have benefited or been harmed by the experience." Very occasionally, in two or three cases in all, an offender resented the investigation and threatened to " make trouble."

Another principle guiding the investigations was that of not using pocket notes or a questionnaire in the presence of the person being interviewed.[16]

Sources of recorded data. In addition to information secured directly from interviews, many sources of already recorded information were tapped which had been, in the previous studies of the authors, found to be fruitful, as well as others which were discovered and developed in the course of this research, and were resorted to again and again:

Assessors' Books — for various clues as to property, etc.

Banks — for addresses

Bureaus of Criminal Identification, City, State, and Federal — for criminal records and other identifying data

Bureaus of Vital Statistics — for information as to marriages, births, deaths

Consulates in the United States and foreign countries — to arrange for investigations in foreign countries

Court Records, Federal, State, Municipal — for court records and disposition of cases, and for addresses

Department of Motor Vehicles — for addresses of auto owners and drivers

Employment Records — for dates and nature of employment, wages, and industrial capacity

Health Departments — for information regarding venereal diseases

Hospital Records — for medical and social data and addresses

Immigration Commission — for information regarding deportation of offenders or relatives

Index in State Department of Mental Diseases — to determine whether a person is or has been an inmate of any of the state hospitals

Industrial Accident Board — for information regarding compensation

Insurance Companies — for addresses of offenders and relatives

Labor Unions — for addresses of offenders and relatives

Licensing Bureaus — for addresses

Massachusetts Department of Correction — for institutional and parole history of offenders

Massachusetts Department of Mental Diseases, Division for the Examination of Prisoners — for social and psychiatric data

Massachusetts State Infirmary — for follow-up data on former patients

[16] This is described fully in the chapter on " Method " of *500 Criminal Careers*, p. 103.

Offices of City Clerks — for addresses and vital statistics

Parole Departments — for conduct of parolees

Penal Institutions, County, City, State — for criminal and social data regarding offenders and relatives

Police Censuses — for addresses

Police Records — for arrests and for social data where available (policewomen sometimes keep such information)

Poll-Tax Lists — for addresses

Post Offices — for identifying and other information

Probate Court Records — for verification of divorces, annulments, adoptions of children

Probation Commission of Massachusetts — for court records of offenders and relatives

Probation Records — for court data and for summary of the behaviour of the probationers

School Records — for addresses and conduct of children or siblings

Schools for Feeble-minded — for diagnoses, prognoses, dates of stay

Social Agencies, public and private, State, County, and City — for summaries of their contacts with offenders and their families

Social Service Exchanges — for list of social agencies dealing with the family

State Hospitals — for diagnoses, prognoses, dates of stay

Street Directories — for places of residence

Tax Collectors' Offices — for names and addresses of home-owners

Telephone Books — for addresses and telephone numbers

United States Army Records — for addresses

United States Coast Guard Records — for addresses

United States Merchant Marine Records — for addresses or service record of husbands or brothers

United States Navy Records — for addresses

Veterans' Bureaus — with consent of client, information regarding amount of compensation and recent addresses

Vice-Squad Records — for records of sex delinquents

Voting Lists — for addresses

As many as thirty such sources of recorded data were consulted in the course of one investigation.

Scope of field investigations. There was of course great variation in the sources of already recorded data available in the individual case and the amount and kinds of information needed or actually secured by personal examination or by correspondence. There was also great variation in the number and kind of persons interviewed in the course of each investigation. As many as fifteen people were personally seen in some cases, and as many combinations of persons interviewed as there were cases — the offender's parents (including step- and foster-parents), siblings (including step- and half-siblings), present and former husbands, other maternal and paternal relatives, employers, police, ministers, neighbours, landlords, storekeepers, proprietors of local "hang-outs," family physicians, lawyers, friends, probation officers, parole officers, social workers, and others.

Overcoming obstacles in investigations. When a follow-up investigation was begun, a "diary card" was made, on which was entered in chronological order, so that any one of the four, or sometimes five, different persons charged with any part in the follow-up investigations could see at a glance what had been accomplished up to any given point. The value of such a running record cannot be overestimated. This made possible a periodic examination of the diary cards by any of those working on a particular case, as the investigation progressed, in order to avoid duplications of effort, to determine the status of the investigation and the need for further corroboration or verification of certain facts. Whenever any one of those participating in the work "hit a snag," either in tracing an offender, in securing data, or in verifying information, the case was reviewed by one of the authors in consultation with the particular investigator, and plans for further follow-up were made. As a result of this procedure, over one hundred particularly puzzling cases out of the five hundred were rescued from temporary oblivion, after careful re-examination of all possible clues.

The following cases illustrate how certain "snags" were overcome in the course of the investigations:

Case No. 18.

It was ascertained that this offender had died in 1930, presumably in Newton, Massachusetts. We were unable to verify her death in Massachusetts, and her mother, who was interviewed, refused any information beyond the fact that the offender was "dead and buried." A brother of the offender was seen, and he stated that she had died in New York City. The Bureau of Vital Statistics in New York City was communicated with for a verification of her death, but no record was found. At this point it was decided to write again to the Bureau of Vital Statistics to search for her record under her maiden name. This second inquiry revealed the record of her death as having taken place at the *A* hospital in New York City. The hospital was written to for any information which they might have about her. The reply was made that they had never had the offender as a patient, and they referred us to the *B* hospital, which in turn replied that they had no record of the offender. Again at this point next steps had to be considered. In view of the fact that the death record definitely stated that the offender had died at the *A* hospital, it was decided to write again, and this time a reply was received with a full report on the offender, containing much information about her criminal and vocational activities as well as about her illness.

Case No. 19.

The field investigation had revealed that this offender had made a "pick-up" marriage with a soldier on leave from the United States Army, in 1925 in Lawrence, Massachusetts, which was the place of residence of herself and a sister at the time of her commitment. Her husband's home was in New York. The whereabouts of both her parents were entirely unknown at the time of her commitment, and, as she had lived with the above-mentioned sister, every effort was made to trace the sister, with the result that the sister was found to have "disappeared" from Lawrence. At this point, it seemed as though the investigation was blocked. It was then decided to examine the marriage record of the sister in order to establish the whereabouts of her husband, from whom she was known to be separated. This led to an interview with the husband, from whom it was learned that she was now divorced. He was able to give the address of the offender's father-in-law and of an aunt of hers. Interviews with them led to a visit from the offender and her sister at our office in an effort to find out "what this nosing around is all about." The offender was extremely hostile, but her sister seemed most co-operative. However, she was forced to keep silent because of the belligerent attitude of the offender. It was deemed wise at the time merely to try to explain to the offender the purposes of the investigation and to get in a very indirect way from her some inkling of her place of residence. She stated that she lived with her sister in Lawrence and that she worked in a shoe-factory; that they were both separated from their husbands. Though the offender's resistance was somewhat broken down in the course of the interview, she nevertheless was adamant in her decision to say nothing more definite as to her places of residence. City directories of Lawrence were consulted, and all the shoe-factories in Lawrence written to, in an attempt to locate the offender, without success. It was then realized that she had "covered her tracks." At this point it was necessary to consider next steps in the investigation, as a "stone wall" had been reached. In view of the fact that it was known that the sister had been divorced, her record of divorce was consulted, and the attorney in the case was located, through whom it was possible to get the sister's address, which turned out to be in Lowell, Massachusetts. The sister was then interviewed at her home at a time when the offender was not present. Her confidence was gained, and in this way the investigation was opened up and brought to a satisfactory conclusion.

The resourcefulness, skill, and patience required in the tracing of the offenders, their families, and others who might have any knowledge of them, and in verifying the information secured from them, is best illustrated by the presentation of a few complete diary cards, which are given at the close of this chapter. The many ramifications of the investigations can hardly be described in detail here.[17]

Geographic spread of investigations. Our personal field investigations carried us into 188 cities in ten different states — Massachusetts, 127; Connecticut, 17; Rhode Island, 13; New Hampshire, 10; New York, 8; New Jersey, 5; Maine, 5; Pennsylvania, 1; Delaware, 1; and Maryland, 1. In instances in which the offenders or their families were located in places too remote for personal visits by our investigators, properly qualified social workers of other agencies, or women probation or police officers, were sought to do the necessary tracing, record-searching, or interviewing. In each such case we forwarded to the agencies a statement of the history of the case to date as already known to us, together with an outline of the information desired and the need for caution in the making of the investigation.

Such investigations were made at our request throughout the New England, the Central, the Southern, the Mid-Western, and the Pacific Coast States,[18] and in Canada and European countries.[19] Sixty-seven cases in all were investigated in this way. Every one of the agencies asked to assist in making the investigations was a well-established, thoroughly reputable organization, among them being: a Charity Organization Society, a Child Guidance Clinic, a Department

[17] Something should be said of the skill and training of the two field investigators. The male investigator, Samuel C. Lawrence, is the same gentleman who participated in the study of the male offenders reported in *500 Criminal Careers.* He is a person who has had some twenty-five years of experience in social work, particularly in the interviewing of criminals, and whose knowledge of the underworld is vast. His sympathy, patience, and sense of humour can hardly be overestimated. Though at the outset of the investigations it seemed questionable whether a male investigator could get the kind of data about the personal lives of women offenders essential to the success of the work, this notion was very quickly dispelled. It was found that he was able to gain the confidence of most of the offenders and of their families.

The other investigator, Mildred C. Cunningham, a married woman with two children, has been a member of our staff since the beginning of our follow-up studies in 1925. She is a graduate of an accredited school of social work and has participated in phases of our investigations having to do with gathering data from record sources and analysing the materials for the schedules. This work required an acquaintanceship with the materials and with the definitions. In the field work she proved remarkably resourceful and patient and was assigned to investigate those cases in which, for one reason or another, a woman investigator was preferable to a man.

[18] *New England States.* Vermont: St. Johnsbury, Burlington; New Hampshire: Berlin; Maine: Harrington, Portland; Massachusetts: Holyoke, Pittsfield, Springfield.

Central States. New York: Utica, New York City, Troy, Schenectady, Pennelville, Oneonta, Lake Placid, Buffalo, Auburn, Mineola; New Jersey: Newark, Englewood, Belleville; Connecticut: Hartford; Pennsylvania: Wilkesbarre, Pittsburgh, Philadelphia, Erie.

Southern States. West Virginia: Fairmont; Maryland: Baltimore; District of Columbia: Washington; South Carolina: Greenville, Spartanburg.

Mid-Western States. Wisconsin: Racine; Ohio: Toledo, Cleveland, Akron; Michigan: Detroit; Illinois: Chicago; Indiana: Evansville; Nebraska: Omaha.

Pacific Coast States. California: Berkeley, Burbank, San Bernardino, San Francisco; Washington: Seattle.

[19] Canada: Montreal; Charlottestown, Prince Edward Island; Sidney, Nova Scotia; Halifax, Nova Scotia; Dartmouth, Nova Scotia. Europe: Portugal, Germany, England.

of Public Welfare, the S. P. C. C., a Social Service Federation, a Children's Aid Society, a Prisoners' Aid Society, a Women's Prison Association, a Girls' Service League, a Travelers' Aid Society, the American Red Cross, a Society for Mental Hygiene, a Policewomen's Bureau, a Juvenile Court Probation Department, and similarly well-qualified organizations. Because of the fact, however, that they had not necessarily had experience with this particular kind of investigation, it was not always possible to secure through them certain necessary data. In one case, for instance, the agency hesitated to visit the offender, who had recently been married, for fear of unfortunate complications in revealing to the new husband any knowledge of her past. In another case where the investigation was made, the worker was unable to secure from the husband the one fact on which the entire investigation rested — namely, the approximate date of his wife's desertion of him. In another case the executive secretary of an agency in a small Southern city personally knew the offender, who had been for many years since her release from the Reformatory a highly respected citizen of the community, and her past was not known to anyone, including this agency executive. She therefore hesitated to interview the offender.

In instances in which it was not possible to find a properly qualified person to carry on the investigation at a distant place, the offender or her family was written to directly and asked for certain information which might serve as a basis of verification by correspondence, such as places of residence throughout the five-year post-parole period, places of employment, dates and places of marriage, dates and places of birth of children, and the like. The extent and kind of information asked for depended, of course, on the needs and status of the individual case.

Analysis of follow-up investigation and supplementing of data. After all the data had been gathered and verified to the point at which it appeared as complete as possible, the case was read and analysed by one of the authors in accordance with the definitions applied (see Appendix C), and the facts entered in pencil on a paper copy of the post-parole schedule [20] (see Appendix B). In this process any missing details of pertinence were revealed, and a " second follow-up " was made to secure certain further information, either by correspondence, or by a field visit, or by direct consultation of record sources, as was necessary. For example:

Case No. 20.

The analysis revealed that one offender had syphilis. It was possible, however, that she might have contracted this from her husband. As the husband was

---

[20] It should be pointed out that, before this analysis process was undertaken, two persons analysed the same twenty-five cases to see how similar the interpretations of facts would be. It may be said that they were extremely close, and in the few instances in which there was a difference of opinion it was found to be due to the lack of clearness in the definition, which, however, could be made satisfactory by a little more detail of statement.

known to have recently been in a penal institution in Massachusetts, the institution authorities were communicated with, and it was found that the Wassermann test in this case was entirely negative, which substantiated the fact that the woman had acquired active syphilis in the post-parole period, but not from her husband.

Case No. 21.

In another case it was found that further verification of the offender's employment history was needed, and in this instance the investigator was asked to see her again to secure more specifically the names of her employers and the dates of her employment, as the verifications on the basis of the information which she had previously given were unsatisfactory.

Case No. 22.

The investigation had revealed that another offender had been a drug addict at least in the early part of her post-parole period. After the analysis of the case was made, it seemed wise to secure more details about her drug addiction. As the offender had a brother who is a registered physician, the field investigator was asked to talk with him. In this interview it was ascertained that she had continued her addiction very steadily throughout the post-parole period.

Case No. 23.

In another case a verification of a marriage of the offender was found lacking. As it was known that the marriage had taken place in Philadelphia, verification was sent for and established.

Case No. 24.

In another instance the field investigator who had interviewed the offender and her relatives in New York had neglected to ask the whereabouts of the offender's illegitimate child, born to her shortly after her entrance to the Reformatory, and whether her newly-acquired husband and his parents knew that she had been at the Reformatory. This bit of information, though not absolutely essential to the analysis, would have been of some value could it have been secured. However, the offender did not respond to the letter.

Only after this second "follow-up" was completed was it felt that any facts *unknown* at this point would have to be so classified, as search for them was futile within the limits of this investigation. Had it been possible to send our field-workers to distant places, or to make even more frequent visits than they were able to in the cases which they had personally visited, even fewer details would have had to be placed in the "unknown" category. It may be pointed out, however, that in but 21 of the 500 cases was no information whatsoever obtained, and that in the great majority of the cases the data were quite complete, as is attested by the tabulated results (see Appendix D).

Chronological summary of two follow-up investigations. Before bringing this section to a close, the diary cards kept in two cases are presented to illustrate the scope and ramifications of the follow-up investigations and how the data were verified:

Case No. 25.

Before this investigation was begun the following facts were known in addition to the usual identifying data common to all the cases:

1. Edith was supposed to have married one Charles N— shortly after her parole from the Reformatory had expired, but the place of her marriage was not known.

2. The alleged Charles N— was serving a sentence in the Massachusetts State Prison.

3. Edith's children were in the care of the Boston City Institutions Department at the time of the expiration of her sentence.

4. The whereabouts of Edith's parents as recently as 1926 were definitely known.

5. Edith had been associated in delinquency with a girl now an inmate of the State Industrial School.

6. In 1923, shortly after the expiration of her sentence, Edith had been arrested in Providence, Rhode Island. The disposition of this case was unknown, however.

7. Edith was also known to have been arrested in New York City in 1927 and to have appeared before the City Magistrates Court there.

With the above information on which to begin the investigation of the post-parole period, the following procedure was resorted to:

5- 6-31: Wrote Clerk, City Magistrates Court, New York City, for disposition of Edith's case of 1927.

5- 8-31: Wrote Providence Court for disposition of case of 1923.

5-12-31: Reply received from New York City Magistrates Court, giving cause of arrests and information that Edith had been sent to Bedford Reformatory on 3-27-27 and had been a patient at the Kingston Avenue Hospital, New York City.

5-12-31: Reply from Providence Court, which is unable to find record and suggest it may be East Providence, Seventh District Court, Rhode Island.

5-12-31: Wrote Warden of Massachusetts State Prison, asking him to obtain Edith's address from her husband, who is now an inmate.

5-14-31: Reply from Warden of Massachusetts State Prison stating that husband does not know where Edith is at present, but will let us know if he finds out.

5-19-31: Wrote Massachusetts Bureau of Vital Statistics for verification of Edith's marriage. Wrote Lancaster Industrial School for summary of their knowledge of Edith through the record of a girl friend now an inmate.

5-23-31: Wrote East Providence Court for disposition of Edith's case in 1923.

5-25-31: Reply from Lancaster Industrial School with summary of their knowledge of Edith's conduct.

5-26-31: Wrote Bedford Reformatory for Women for summary of their contact with Edith since admission in 3-27.
Wrote probation office of City Magistrates Court, New York City, for summary of dealings with Edith and for information as to her present whereabouts.

5-26-31: Wrote Superintendent, Kingston Avenue Hospital, New York City, for report on Edith's physical condition, including evidence of venereal disease.

5-26-31: Reply from Massachusetts Bureau of Vital Statistics with information that there is no record in Massachusetts of Edith's marriage.

5-26-31: Inquiry sent to the Massachusetts Board of Probation for court record of alleged husband and of Edith under her supposed husband's name.

5-28-31: Reply from East Providence Court stating that they have no record of Edith and referring to Providence Court, Sixth Judicial District.

6- 1-31: Reply from Bedford Reformatory for Women with information that Edith was released in September 1928 and sent to her mother's home, at Charlestown, Massachusetts, and that probation officer X of the Boston Municipal Court had supervised Edith until the expiration of her sentence in March 1930.
Reply from Kingston Avenue Hospital, New York City, with information that Edith had received treatment there for venereal disease and had been discharged on 3-16-27.
Reply from Probation Bureau of City Magistrates Court with copy of preliminary investigation made on Edith before she was sent to the Bedford Reformatory.
Inquiry to the Massachusetts Board of Probation returned with court record of Edith and husband.

9-30-31: Letter to Clerk, Sixth Judicial Court, Providence, for disposition of Edith's case in 1923.

10- 2-31: Reply from Sixth Judicial Court stating that there is no record there against Edith.

10-29-31: As it had been learned through the Massachusetts Probation Commission that Edith had appeared under her married name before the Boston Municipal Court, field investigator personally secured information from the court records and found that Edith's probation was to extend to 1–6–32 and that she was living at —— in Boston.

10–30–31: Edith's father was located through the Boston Street Directory at ——, South Boston.

11– 5–31: Field agent examined folder in Massachusetts State Department of Correction referring to Edith's husband, Charles N—, which revealed that he had been served with a divorce petition by Edith on 7–31–31.

11–10–31: In Suffolk Probate Court field investigator found the divorce of Edith is still pending.

11–13–31: Field investigator summarized the record of City Institutions Department on Edith's two children and found that one of them is still under care of the city.

11–16–31: Field agent called on parents of Edith at ——, South Boston, but found no one at home. Through neighbours located Edith's mother working for Volunteers of America and interviewed her. She gave Edith's present address and telephone number.

11–16–31: Field agent summarized record of Edith in Suffolk Superior Court and also ascertained that for Providence arrest of 10–19–23 Edith had been placed on probation.

11–17–31: Field agent visited Edith and had three-hour interview with her, learning that Edith's marriage had taken place in Providence.

11–30–31: Wrote to Providence for verification of Edith's marriage.

12– 2–31: Work inquiries sent to P— Restaurant, K— Knitting Co., Hotel L—, G— Hosiery Mill of New York City, N— Lunch.

12– 4–31: Wrote X Hospital for report of Edith's stay and information as to venereal disease.

12– 4–31: Field agent read old S. P. C. C. record on Edith, but found no new data.

12– 7–31: Work inquiry from K— Knitting Co. returned with notation that all employment records had been destroyed.
Work inquiry from N— Lunch returned with no information, as Edith is not known to present proprietor, who has been in charge only since October 1931.

12–28–31: Reply from X Hospital regarding Edith.

1– 3–32: Work inquiry sent again to G— Hosiery Mills, to which no reply had thus far been received.

1–11–32: Work inquiry to G— Hosiery Mills returned with no record of Edith's employment.
Reply from Providence with verification of Edith's marriage.

2– 6–32: Case analysed and found complete.

Case No. 26.

Before the investigation was started, the following facts, in addition to the usual identifying data, were available:

1. Lillian had no court record in Massachusetts.

2. She had a married daughter, Mrs. Pearl R—, presumably living in Fitchburg.

3. She had a brother, Edward G— who was said to be an employee of the Canadian Pacific Railway in Canada.

4. She had a brother, John G—, living in Chester, Pennsylvania.

5. She had a sister, Mrs. Harry G—, living in W—, Vermont.

6. She had a sister, Mrs. Lewis F—, living in Montreal.

7. At the end of her parole Lillian was living with her husband in Worcester, Massachusetts.

5-14-31: Wrote City Clerk of Worcester for address of Lillian and husband.
Wrote Mrs. Pearl R—, of Fitchburg, Lillian's daughter, for her mother's address.

5-21-31: Letter to Mrs. Pearl R— returned unopened.
Wrote City Clerk of Fitchburg for address of Mrs. Pearl R—.

5-26-31: Reply from City Clerk of Worcester with information that Lillian and husband are not listed in the latest Worcester directory.
Reply from City Clerk of Fitchburg with information that Lillian's daughter, Mrs. Pearl R—, is not listed in street directory.

6- 1-31: Wrote Lillian's sister, Mrs. Harry G—, in W—, Vermont, for her address.

6-16-31: Letter to Mrs. G— returned unopened and marked " deceased."

12-23-31: Wrote City Clerk, Montreal, for address of Lillian's sister, Mrs. Lewis F—.

12-28-31: Reply from City Clerk of Montreal with information that Mrs. Lewis F— is not listed in latest street directory.

2-17-32: Wrote Canadian Pacific Railway office at Montreal asking if Lillian's brother, Edward G—, is still working for them and requesting his address.
Wrote City Clerk, Chester, Pennsylvania, for address of Lillian's brother, John G—.

2-19-32: Reply from City Clerk of Chester, Pennsylvania, stating that Mr. John G— lives in Lennox Park, Pennsylvania (specific address given).

2-25-32: Wrote Mr. John G—, Lillian's brother, for her address.

2-27-32: Reply from Canadian Pacific Railway stating that they have no record of the employment by them of Lillian's brother, Mr. Edward G—.

3-14-32: Letter from Lillian in response to the one written on 2-25-32 to her brother, Mr. John G—, with whom she has been staying, and asking reason for our interest.

3-21-32: Reply to Lillian explaining reason for our interest and sending her a questionnaire.

3-22-32: Field agent, in Worcester, checked through old street directories for old traces of Lillian and relatives with no success.

3-23-32: Field agent, in Worcester, went to place of residence of Lillian and husband at the end of the parole period and interviewed landlord who lives at the same number and also neighbours and storekeeper, but got no information about Lillian or her husband.

Found in Worcester directory possible relatives of Lillian's husband. Field agent, in Worcester, made a call on the supposed relatives of husband, but found no one at home.

3-24-32: Field agent in City Hall, Worcester, examined old directories as far back as 1923, but found no address of Lillian or husband. Field agent examined records of the Social Service Exchange, but found that Lillian and her husband are not known to any agency in Worcester.

Field agent called at probation office of the district court in Worcester, but found no trace of Lillian or her husband.

4-11-32: Wrote to the Family Society of Philadelphia asking them to refer us to an agency in or near Lennox Park, Pennsylvania, which could discreetly interview Lillian.

4-21-32: Reply from Family Society of Philadelphia that Mrs. M— M— of X Society of Chester, Pennsylvania, has kindly offered to interview Lillian.

4-22-32: Wrote Family Society of Philadelphia thanking them for their assistance.

Wrote Mrs. M— M— of the X Society of Chester, Pennsylvania, explaining in detail the purpose of visit to Lillian, and nature of the data desired.

4-29-32: Reply from Mrs. M— M— of X Society with information obtained from Lillian's brother Mr. Edward G—. Lillian was not seen, as she has returned to her husband in Middletown, Connecticut (definite address given).

5- 9-32: Letter from Lillian, who had heard from brother that a visitor had called, and who said she would call at our office on her next visit to Boston.

Wrote Lillian thanking her for letter and asking her to let us know when she intends to visit.

5-16-32: Letter from Lillian saying she will call at office on 5-21-32.

5-17-32: Wrote Lillian thanking her for her letter and saying we would be glad to see her.

5-21-32: Lillian came to office and was interviewed.

5-27-32: As a result of interview with Lillian, wrote Family Welfare Association of Middletown, Connecticut, for summary of dealings with her. Sent work inquiry to C— P— Co., Middletown.
    "   "   "   " O— L— E— Co., Hartford.
    "   "   "   " R— F— Co., Boston.
    "   "   "   " C— C— Co., Hartford.
Sent police inquiry to Middletown, Connecticut.

5- 3-32: Reply from Family Welfare Association of Middletown, Connecticut, with summary of dealings with Lillian.
Reply from C— C— Co. with employment record.
Reply from R— F— Co. with employment record.

6- 1-32: Reply from Middletown police with information that Lillian has no police or court record there.

6- 5-32: Reply from C— P— Co. regarding Lillian's employment record.

6- 7-32: Work inquiry to O— L— E— Co. returned unclaimed.

6- 8-32: Case analysed and found complete.

5. Conclusion

A good deal of modern social research is preoccupied with the refinement of mathematical statistics. But not unless the raw materials which enter into the tables and computations are gathered, verified, and re-verified in some such manner as that illustrated in the foregoing description can sociologic inquiries stand the test of reason. Mathematico-statistical manipulations, coefficients, and Greek symbols do not assure the reliability of the original materials that enter into a piece of sociologic research. It is hoped that students not only of the crime problem but of other social problems will benefit somewhat from this detailed account of the intricate processes involved in the accumulation of the primary stuff of a sociologic inquiry.

APPENDIX B

SCHEDULES AND FORMS

Note of Explanation to Schedules

Definitions of the factors appearing on the schedules will be found alphabetically arranged in Appendix C, "Definition of Terms," and the various categories of the factors will be found in Appendix D, "Code-Table Index." The reader is asked to refer to Appendix C first in order to ascertain the numerical designation of the factor in Appendix D.

It will be noted that the format of Schedule 5, "Follow-up History," differs from the others and is altogether more satisfactory. It was set up last and reflects the experience which was gained in the preparation and utilization of the other schedules.

See Appendix A, "Method of this Research," section on *Preparation of Statistical Schedules,* pp. 341 et seq. The reader may think that the terminology used on the schedules is not always fortunate or exactly descriptive. As the terms have been defined, however, any difficulties arising from lack of linguistic clarity are resolved. The names of the factors are repeated exactly in the *definitions,* and the *code-table* appendices in order to make reference easy.

1. PERSONAL HISTORY

I. Identifying Data

Maiden name   Marriage name   No.
Committed as   Aliases   S A M W D
Color   Age   Birth date   Place   Lgtcy.
Church   Citizenship   Time in U. S.   in Mass.
Last residence   with
Accomplices   Term   Date com't.   Plea   Judge
Offense

II. Places of Residence   No. diff. cities   Mobility: in childhood   in adolescence
Earliest abn. envtl. exp.   Age   Reason

III. Developmental Physical Condition   Full-term child   Age of mother   of father
Health during infancy and childhood
      during adolescence   Menstr. est.

IV. Leisure and Habits [ ]   Childhood   Adolescence ☐   Present
Constr. recr. and intrsts.
Ambitions
Companions and lovers
Play places and haunts
Society membership
Church attendance
Habits
Misbehavior

1st known delinq.   Age   Age 1st left home   Reason
Sex life: Age began   With whom first   Rape or consent
Age entered prost.   Total time   Total time sex. irreg.   No. of men   No. illg. preg.
Prost. practiced where   Av. wkly. earnings   Only means of support

V. Education   No schooling: Illit.   Rd. and wr.   Language spoken
Kind of school attended   Age started school   No. yrs. in schl.   Rsn. left
Grade attained   Age   Grades repeated   Retardation
Scholarship   Attendance   Conduct   Age 1st truancy
Vocational school   Length of time
Subjects studied   Ability

VI. Industrial History [ ]   Economic resp. [ ]   Reason for work   necess.   satisf.
Age began work   First occup.   Wkly. wage   Time held
Occup. at 1st conv.   Usual occup.   Lgst. prd. empl.   Av. wkly. wage
Highest earnings   Usual reason for leaving
Last lgtm. occup.   Wkly. wage   Time since last empl.   Skill
Steadiness   Work habits
Savings   Insurance   How paid   Disp. of earnings

VII. Court Record [ ]   Princ. component
Cause 1st arrest   Age 1st arrest   1st conviction   1st commitment
No. arrests   of convictions   Freq. of arrests   of convictions
Seriousness of offenses   Predom. offense   Time served   No. W. R. adm.
   Summary of offenses   **Summary of dispositions**

Commitment	Restit.	Not guilty
Probation	Other conv.	Released
Fine	Rel. by P. O.	Other
Comt. non-paym.	Nol. pros.	No disp.
File	No bill	Disp. unk.

VIII. Institutional and Foster Home Experiences   Total No.   Total time
Orphanages   Juven. correctl.   F. M.   Wayward   Foster
Mental diseases   Chronic. phys.   Adult penal   Other

IX. Constructive Legal Opportunities   No.   Nature

2. FAMILY HISTORY

Schedule 2

Name   No.

I. Personal Facts	Father	Stp. father	Mother	Stp. mother	Husb.	Sibs.	Chn.
Color							
Birth place							
Religion							
Time in U. S.							
Time in Mass.							
Citizenship							
Cvl. cond.-age 0							
Education							
Usual occup.							
Indust. stab.						Own Hf	Lgt.
Number						Stp. R	Illg.
Liv. or dead-age 0							
Age							
Ct. appear.							
Ct. dk. only							
Non-ct. delinq.							
Phys. dis.							
Ment. dis.							
Ment. def.							

Broken or poorly superv. home (nature of)   Age of 0
Delinq., insanity, ment. def. in rels. or ancestors

0 only ct. delinq. in family   Only delinq. in family   Conj. rel. of parents
Nativ. of par. related to 0   Lang. spoken at home

II. Environmental Factors	Childhood	Adolescence ☐	Present
Neighborhood (Type)			
Neigh. influence			
House-type, rms.			
Home-physical			
Household-No.-who			
Sleeping arrang. of 0			
Econ. condition			
Parental superv.			
Moral stds. of home			
0's rel. to fraternity			
Affection of 0			
Affection of family			
Moral oblig. of 0 to family			

III. Social Service Agencies   Age of 0 at 1st SS contact   No. of agencies
Type of service (summary)

IV. Marital History ☐ No.	1st marr.	2nd marr.	3rd marr.	4th marr.
Age				
Date-time				
Place				
Age of husb.				
Marr. forced				
Manner of meeting				
Time known before marr.				
Conj. relations				
Reason for termination				
Att. of 0 to marr. resp.				
Att. of husb. to marr. resp.				
Compt. as hmkr.				
Household-No.-who				
Econ. status				
Rel. to fam. econ. status				
No. of pregn.-No. chn.				
Att. toward chn.				

3. REFORMATORY HISTORY

Name   Term   No.

I. Time Served   Date com't.   Transf. from   Reason

Times cont. for prle.   Reasons

Date 1st prle.   Date return   No. prev. W. R. sent.   Prior time in W. R.

Date 2nd prle.   Date return   Months to 1st prle.   to 2nd   to 3rd   to 4th

Date 3rd prle.   Date return   Total time on pres. sent.   Prle. in usual time

Date 4th prle.   Date expirn.   Transf. to   Reason

II. Physical Condition

	On adm.	Later	On disch.	Improvement
General cond.				
Nutrition				
Disease				
Weight				
Wassermann				
Vag. smear				
Illnesses in W. R.				

III. Mental Condition   Mental Disease   Traits

                                                      Intelligence

Abstract lgcl. thinking   Auditory memory   Gnrlse. moral sit'n

Abstract words   Comprehension   Imagination

Ass'n of ideas   Critical powers   Practical judgment

Ass'n of thought and words   Gen'l information

    Emotional stability   Follower or leader

    Capabilities   Chief ability

IV. Vocational Record   Training desired   Received

No. diff. occup. exp.   Kind of worker

Occup.	Time prd.	Ability and attitude	Suff. to lrn. rudiments

V. Conduct

	1st period	2nd period	3rd period
Mos. 2nd gr.			
Demotions			
No badge			
Blue badge			
Red badge			
Ever 3rd			
Solitary (where)			
Reasons			
Recog. gd. conduct			
Att. to respons.			
Conduct-summary			

    Nature of misconduct — MINOR: Pers. orderliness   Lack of self control   Other

    MAJOR: Viol. agst. person   Sex. off.   Agst. property   Agst. auth.   Escape

VI. Attitude   Social worker's impressions

To past

On adm.

To future

Later attit. in W. R.

VII. Future   O's plan

Staff recomm.

Staff disc. with prle. agent

Assets in family sit.

Liabilities in family sit.

Staff-prognosis

Schedule 4

4. PAROLE HISTORY

Name   No.

I. Reasons for Desiring Parole   Date final expir.   Agent
   1.
   2.
   3.

II. Date of Parole | To live with | Time on prle.| Date rev. | Reason | Withdrawn

	To live with	Time on prle.	Date rev.	Reason	Withdrawn
1.					
2.					
3.					

Total

III. Environmental   Mobility   Neighb. (type)   Neighb. influ.
Home (phys.)   Moral stds.

Place	With whom	Period	Reason for change

IV. Health   Illnesses   Injuries   Operations

V. Marital History [ ] Civil cond.   Change   Conj. rel.
Competence as hmkr.   Att. to marital resp.
No. children   Attit. to children

VI. Industrial History [ ]   Econ. resp. [ ]
First pd. job   By whom secured   Time held
Highest wage   Lgst prd. empl.   Av. prd. empl.   Used W. R. occup.
Difficulty sec. work
Usual occup.   Steadiness   Skill   Work habits
Usual reason left   Illeg. occup.
Savings   Disp. of earnings   Econ. cond.

Nature of work	Time	Earnings	How obtd.	Work habits	Rsn. left

VII. Leisure and Habits [ ]   Constructive
Drink   Smoking   Drugs   Theft   Street life   Other
Sex habits: Irregular   Prostit.   Others
Society membership   Church attend.   Moral oblig. to family

VIII. Court Record [ ]   Princ. component
No. arrests   Freq. arrests   Predominant off.   Seriousness of off.

Summary of offenses   Summary of dispositions

Date	Ct.	Offense	Disposition	Time served

IX. Parole Supervision   Time to 1st contact with case   with parolee
Theoret. prle. prd.   Actual prle. prd.   Rsn. for incompl. superv.
No. visits to ⊢ parolee   No. reports by ⊢ parolee   Letters to ⊢ parolee
       — relatives   — letter   — relatives
       — employers   ⊢ Total   Av.   — others
       — others   ⊢ Total   Av.
       — no one seen   **Av. of All Contacts**
       ⊢ Total   Av.

Special attempts at rehabilitation

Change in O's conduct (trend)
Attitude toward reform
Prognosis of parole officer

5. FOLLOW-UP HISTORY

Interview with:
W. R. Name
Present Name
Where (at P. P. Exp.)
Present Whereabouts

Date P. P. Exp.
Aliases

Date of Interview
Age   Number
    Pres. Age
with
with

If marr. during prle. or P. P.: Date   Term   Age of husb.   Marr. forced
Manner of meeting   Time known   Rsn. for term
Color of husb.   Birthplace   Ctzn.   Rlgn.   Time in U. S.
Industl. Stability   Education   Diseases   Defect   M. D.

I. Health (Illness, injuries, operations)

II. Inst. Exper. No. penal Non-penal Time in penal In non-penal Mos. in comm.
F. M.   M. D.   Chronic physical   Penal   Other
List

	5 yr. period	5th year		5 yr. period	5th year
III. Environmental			**IV. Economic Responsibility** ☐		
House (Type)			Savings		
Home (Physical)			Insurance		
Neighb. (Type)			Property		
Neighb. influ.			Econ. Cond.		
Mobility			Dependents		
Nature of			Disp. of earnings		
Moral standards			No. S. S. Agencies		
			Type of S. S.		
V. Family Relationships ☐		☐	**VI. Industrial History** ☐		☐
Household			Usual occup.		
Rel. to nearest rels.			Skill		
Marital status			Stead.		
Conj. rels.			Wk. Hab.		
Rsn. if poor			Av. wage		
Att. of 0 to marit. resp.			Highest wage		
Att. of husb.			Av. prd. emp.		
Compt. as homkr.			Long. prd. emp.		
No. of chn. (leg., illeg.)		Total	Used W. R. occup.		
Attit. to chn.			Why not		
Rsdnce of chn.			Illeg. occup.		
Delinq. of chn.			Diff. sec. wk.		
Delinq. of husb.			Rsns. for leaving		
VII. Leisure and Habits ☐	☐		**VIII. Delinquencies** ☐		☐
Society member.			Predom. offense		
Church attend.			Princ. comp.		
Educ'l activities			Unoff. misc.		
Companionships			No. of arrests		
Haunts			No. of conv.		
Habits			Freq. of arrests		
Street life			Freq. of conv.		
Sex irreg.			Ser. of offenses		
Sex. prac. w. whom			Summary of ct. offenses		
No. of men					
Illeg. preg.			Summary of dispositions		
Where practiced					
Earngs fr. prostit.					
Only means of support					

IX. Trend after P. P. Period (Time   )   Judgment   Trend

Family relationships
Industrial history
Economic responsibility
Leisure and Habits
Delinquency

Schedule 5 (*Continued*)

X. Reformatory & Parole Influences

Beneficial (Health, ethical ideals, vocation, homemaking, etc.)

Harmful (knowledge, companionships)

Criticisms

Constructive suggestions

Reason for improvement or failure

Effect of certain personalities on 0

XI. Attitude of Community (friendly, indiff., hostile)

Social Service needs not met

Constructive work w. girl

XII. What does Case Illustrate?

6. IDENTIFICATION CARD

(See Appendix A, "Method of Research," section on *Identifying Data*, pp. 347 et seq.)

True Name		Adm Prld Expd		R Agt No.
WR Name		Aliases		
Birth	Place	Rlgn		S ☐ M ☐ W ☐ D ☐
Compl	Eyes	Hr	Ht	Wt
Home Address		With		
Parents' Names		Addr		
Sibs				
Husband	Addr		Chn	
Offense	Date of Sentence	Ct	Term	
Prior Resid				
Residences since Release				
Last known job				
Last known Address		With		
Present Address		With		

Note of explanation to Pre-Coding and Punch Cards

We have given the designation *pre-coding card* to a form bearing the numbers from 1 through 80 (which represent the columns on the Hollerith punch card), onto which we translated the appropriate category of each factor into its " position " on the code, each " position " being designated by a number (see Appendix D, " Code-Table Index ").

Only one of the pre-coding cards is presented, as all four (see Appendix A, " Method of this Research," section on *Tabulation Problems,* pp. 344 et seq.) are alike. The * and *m* are only signs guiding the coder, the * meaning that in this column two factors are represented, and the *m* meaning that this is a " multiple " punch column (see note of explanation to " Code-Table Index," Appendix D). Our experience has shown us that such mechanical controls greatly reduce error in coding. For the further purpose of easing the coder and reducing error, the factors were arranged for coding in the order in which they appear on the schedule rather than in any alphabetical order. Occasionally the position of a factor had to be shifted on the code from its logical place in order to utilize all the available space on the punch cards.

The reader if interested is asked to consult Appendix D, pp. 491 et seq. covering the code for the post-parole (or follow-up) history (the pre-coding card for which appears below), and also to consult the schedule covering the post-parole (or follow-up) history (this Appendix).

From the pre-coding cards the data was then easily transcribed onto the punch cards by a punch operator and tabulated on the Hollerith machine which in its present stage of perfection not only sorts the cards one column at a time, but counts them three columns at a time and records the answers. The procedures necessary to check and recheck the tabulation results for the sake of accuracy need not be gone into here.

7. PUNCH CARD

LICENSED FOR USE UNDER PATENT 1,772,492

I.B.M. 5080

8. PRE–CODING CARD
FOLLOW-UP HISTORY

W. R. Name		W. R. No.	No.
1	*26	54	
2	27	55	
3	*28	56	
4	29	57	
5	30	58	
6	m31	59	
7	32	60	
8	33	61	
m9	*34	62	
10	35	63	
m11	36	64	
*12	37	65	
13	*38	66	
*14	39	67	
15	40	68	
16	*41	69	
*17	42	70	
*18	43	71	
*19	44	72	
*20	m45	73	
*21	m46	74	
*22	*47	75	
23	48	76	
m24	*49	77	
25	*50	78	
	*51	79	
	*52	80	
	53		

APPENDIX C

DEFINITION OF TERMS

Note of explanation

All the factors included in this research are listed alphabetically. The number or numbers appearing immediately below each factor are its designations in the Code-Table Index (Appendix D), in which are listed all the categories of each factor.

Where no definition or explanation of a factor or its categories appears, the factor is sufficiently explained by its title and its subclasses (Appendix D).

ACTUAL PAROLE PERIOD

    See THEORETICAL AND ACTUAL PAROLE PERIOD

AGE AT FIRST ARREST

    1–61

AGE AT FIRST COMMITMENT

    1–62

AGE AT FIRST KNOWN DELINQUENCY

    1–25

    Delinquency — any misconduct for which the person is liable to arrest, as running away from home, fornication, stealing, etc. If no delinquency prior to the first arrest was known, age at first arrest was tabulated.

AGE AT LEAVING SCHOOL

    1–40

AGE AT TIME OF COMMITMENT

    1–2a

AGE BEGAN WORK

    1–44

AGE ENTERED PROSTITUTION

    1–31

    For definition of prostitution, see SEX LIFE, NATURE OF. Prostitution as here used includes professional, occasional, and " one-man " prostitution.

AGENT, PAROLE

    3–2a

AGE FIRST LEFT HOME

1–26

AGE OF OFFENDER

1–12 — at time of earliest abnormal environmental experience

2–16 — at first break in home

2–37 — at first social service contact with offender's family

4–2 — at end of post-parole

AGE STARTED SCHOOL

1–36b

ALIASES

1–1a

The purpose of this is to indicate not only what aliases offender used, but whether she used any.

AMBITION, VOCATIONAL

1–17 — expressed at any time prior to commitment

ATTENDANCE IN SCHOOL

1–42b

Regular — only occasional absence.

Irregular — absences so frequent as to interfere with the continuity of schooling (an average of one absence weekly).

ATTITUDE OF COMMUNITY TO OFFENDER

4–H86 — during post-parole

Friendly — community knows she is an ex-prisoner, yet accepts her into its activities, as church, club, etc.

Indifferent — community does not know that offender is an ex-prisoner, or, though aware of this fact, makes no discrimination against her as its own moral standards are low.

Hostile — community, as police, church, club, neighbours, know offender is an ex-prisoner and discriminate against her because of it.

ATTITUDE OF HUSBAND TO MARITAL RESPONSIBILITY

2–H69 — on all marriages prior to commitment

4–H73 — on all marriages contracted between offender's release on parole and end of post-parole period

Assumes — does not neglect or desert wife or children; not unfaithful; not abusive to wife or children. Assumes his economic responsibility toward them. See definition of ECONOMIC RESPONSIBILITY.

Neglects — fails to meet the above standards.

Inapplicable — if husband separated, divorced, or dead before beginning of particular period under scrutiny.

ATTITUDE OF OFFENDER TO MARITAL RESPONSIBILITY

2–43b — on last marriage prior to commitment

2–H68 — on all marriages contracted prior to commitment

4–18b — during post-parole

4–H72 — on all marriages contracted between release on parole and end of post-parole

Assumes — does not neglect or desert husband or children; not unfaithful; not physically or mentally abusive to mate or children. Assumes household duties and economic responsibilities (see definition of ECONOMIC RESPONSIBILITY).

Neglects — fails to meet the above standard.

Not applicable — if offender was single or if separated or divorced from husband prior to beginning of period judged.

ATTITUDE TO CHILDREN

2–44b — prior to commitment

4–20a — during post-parole

This includes illegitimate children.

Good — fond of, cares for.

Fair — casual toward; or fond of, but neglectful because of drink, absorption in a lover, etc.

Poor — gives no supervision, no affection, or is abusive.

In the case of women whose children are not living with them for various reasons (as, for example, because children are in custody of husband, in institutions, etc.) tabulate as

Good — if she maintains an interest in them to the greatest extent possible within the limits of the particular situation.

Fair — if she keeps in touch with them.

Poor — if she is entirely out of touch with them.

ATTITUDE TOWARD REFORM

3–31a — during parole

Good — shows eagerness to reform.

Poor — indifferent to any idea of reform.

This information was gleaned from parole officers' reports of personal contacts with the women.

AVERAGE NUMBER OF VISITS TO PAROLEE

3–29 — during parole

This means the average number of times per month that the parolee was seen personally by the parole agent. The calculation is based on the " actual " parole period if the woman had been excused from reporting, or if she was in another state or in a foreign country by permission and not required to make reports to the parole agent. If, however, the parolee had disappeared during the parole period, the calculation is based on the " theoretical " parole period, as the parole officer is required to search for the parolee. See THEORETICAL AND ACTUAL PAROLE PERIOD for definition of these terms.

AVERAGE VISITS TO CASE BY PAROLE AGENT

3-30

This includes visits not only to offender, but to relatives, employers, and others.

AVERAGE WEEKLY WAGE

1-51 — prior to commitment

4-35 — during post-parole

If woman is engaged in any job which includes maintenance, five dollars is added to the weekly salary to cover this.

BENEFICIAL EFFECTS OF STAY AT REFORMATORY

4-H81

This information was secured from the offenders or their families. It is incomplete and only suggestive.

BIRTHPLACE

1-3   — of offender

2-7   — of father

2-8   — of mother

2-H75 — of last legal husband before commitment

4-H67 — of last husband married between release of offender on parole and end of post-parole period

BIRTHPLACE — NATIVITY OF OFFENDER

1-2b

BROKEN HOMES

2-15

A broken home is one from which one or both parents are removed by death, separation, desertion, divorce, imprisonment, illness (in hospital), or commitment to a hospital for mental diseases, being absent from the home for a year or more, or for frequent brief intervals.

BROKEN OR POORLY SUPERVISED HOMES

2-22

If no break in the home has occurred before offender was twenty-one years old, any evidence of poor parental supervision was noted. Where more than one break in the home has occurred, or there is more than one evidence of poor supervision, only *one* is tabulated in the order indicated by the code.

BY WHOM FIRST PAROLE JOB SECURED

3-12

CAPABILITIES OF OFFENDER

2-H90 — on entrance to Reformatory

This refers to the type of work or special abilities of the offenders as reported by them on entrance. It is therefore incomplete information.

CAUSE OF FIRST ARREST

2-1

CHILD OR PREGNANCY ON ADMISSION

    2–57a

CHILDREN, NUMBER LIVING

    2–20a — at time of commitment

      Refers to legitimate and illegitimate children.

CHURCH ATTENDANCE

    1–20 — prior to commitment

    3–24b — during parole

    4–22a — during post-parole

      Regular — every Sunday.

      Irregular — only occasionally.

      Inapplicable — unable to attend, as ill, in institution where attendance is required.

CHURCH — RELIGION

    1–4b — of offender

    2–9 — of parents

CITIZENSHIP

    1–5 — of offender

    2–10b — of father

    2–H76 — of husband (last legal marriage before offender committed)

    4–H68 — of husband (last marriage contracted between release on parole and end of post-parole)

CIVIL CONDITION

    3–8a — at beginning of parole period

      See MARITAL STATUS.

COLOUR — MIXED MARRIAGES

    2–H74 — refers to last marriage before commitment

    4–H66 — refers to last marriage between release on parole and end of post-parole

COLOUR OF OFFENDER

    1–1b

      Negro — full-blooded Negro or mulatto.

      Negroid — offspring of one white parent and one coloured parent.

COMPANIONS

COMPANIONSHIPS

    1–18b — in childhood

    1–18c — in adolescence

    1–18d — within year of commitment

    3–24a — during parole

    4–22b — during post-parole

      Harmful — any with whom association might lead to delinquency, as thieves, streetwalkers, pickpockets, drunks, pick-ups, idlers, bootleggers, drug-pedlars, etc.

Harmless — those whose influence, though not necessarily wholesome, is at least not harmful.

Inapplicable — is in institution during the particular period studied or is chronically ill.

COMPETENCE AS HOMEMAKER

2–44a — on last marriage prior to commitment

2–H70 — on all marriages prior to commitment

4–19a — during post-parole

4–H74 — on all marriages made between release on parole and end of post-parole

Good — systematic, economical, clean, neat.

Fair — some of the qualifications of the good homemaker, but, because of low mentality or temperamental difficulties or other reasons, at times a poor homemaker.

Poor — wasteful, indifferent, careless.

Applies also to women who, though not keeping house for their husbands, are acting as homemakers for relatives.

CONDUCT IN WOMEN'S REFORMATORY

2–54b

Good — a non-offender.

Fair — commits occasional minor offences.

Poor — commits frequent minor offences or occasional serious offences.

Inapplicable — transferred to other institution, or died within first five months of incarceration, or ill.

Major offences — violence against person, including fighting, quarrelling, assault; rebellion against authority, including crookedness, possessing anything brought in from outside, insolence, defiance, disobedience of orders, refusal to work, malicious mischief, vile language, attempt to escape, lying.

Minor offences — personal disorderliness, including such offences as bed not properly made, clothing not in proper order, coat not buttoned, etc.; lack of self-control, including offences such as inattention, idleness, laziness, laughing, fooling, talking out of turn, shirking.

CONJUGAL RELATIONS

2–23b — of parents

2–43a — on last marriage prior to commitment

2–H67 — on all marriages prior to commitment

4–18a — on last marriage during post-parole

4–H71 — on all marriages made between release on parole and end of post-parole

Good — living together, compatible, no undue quarrelling.

Fair — living together, but gross incompatibility, i.e. undue quarrelling; indifference to each other, yet no open breach.

Poor — separated, deserted, divorced, or occasional desertion or separation.

Note: In 2–23b CONJUGAL RELATIONS OF PARENTS refers to own parents if both living. If one or both not living, refers to their last known relationship unless one parent died before offender was five years old. In such cases it refers to the relationship of one own parent to a step-parent or to foster-parents.

CONSTRUCTIVE RECREATIONS AND INTERESTS

1–18a — prior to commitment

3–20b — during parole

4–21b — during post-parole

Yes — purposeful use of leisure time for self-development, as vocational courses, studying music, member of well-supervised club, etc.

No — not a member of a well-supervised club, not using leisure to further self vocationally, etc.

CONSTRUCTIVE SUGGESTIONS

4–H83 — for Women's Reformatory

These refer to suggestions for improving régime at the Women's Reformatory, made by the offender or near relatives. Incomplete, but suggestive.

CONSTRUCTIVE WORK WITH OFFENDER

4–H89 — during post parole

This refers to any work of supervision, rehabilitation, readjustment, carried on during the post-parole period by the Women's Reformatory staff, parole agents, social agencies, etc. The purpose of the table is to indicate to what extent planned aid or supervision is rendered during the post-parole period.

CRITICISMS OF REFORMATORY

4–H84

These were made by the offenders or their near relatives. Incomplete, but suggestive.

DATE OF COMMITMENT TO REFORMATORY

2–56

DATE OF EXPIRATION OF SENTENCE

2–59a

DATE OF POST-PAROLE EXPIRATION

4–1

DELINQUENCY

1–60b — of offender prior to commitment

2–23a — of family

2–25b — of offender during parole

2–H81 — of last husband prior to commitment

4–20b — of husband with whom offender lived in post-parole

4–41b — of offender in post-parole

4–50a — of offender during fifth year of post-parole

4–50b — of offender after post-parole

4–55 — of offender in five-year post-parole period and fifth year in combination

Non-delinquent — no police or court record and no misconduct for which might be arrested, as drinking, abuse of family, stealing, etc. — i.e. no " unofficial " misconduct (see PRINCIPAL COMPONENT OF MISCONDUCT for definition of " unofficial " misconduct).

Delinquent — " official " or " unofficial " misconduct.

Inapplicable — person is in institution or chronically ill during particular period studied. In the case of delinquency of husband *inapplicable* means that offender was not living with him during the period judged and his delinquency therefore is not to be noted by us.

DEVELOPMENTAL PHYSICAL CONDITION

1–15 — serious handicaps during childhood and adolescence

This takes account only of chronic physical conditions or such handicaps as partially or totally incapacitate the individual for normal recreational outlets during childhood or adolescence and which might therefore be contributory to a personality maladjustment.

DIFFICULTY SECURING WORK

4–H80 — in post-parole

Very incomplete. Information is therefore used for illustrative purposes only.

DISPOSITION OF EARNINGS

1–59b — prior to commitment

3–21a — during parole

4–29 — during post-parole

Offender's dependents may be parents or other relatives who for various reasons need assistance from her. Husband and children are not regarded as dependents unless husband is for legitimate reasons unable to work, or the woman is widowed, divorced, or separated and the support of the children therefore devolves upon her.

EARLIEST ABNORMAL ENVIRONMENTAL EXPERIENCE

1–11 — nature of

This refers to the nature of the first departure of the offender from the home or environment in which she was reared, a departure caused by a situation sufficiently serious, unusual, or marked in character to denote a breach in the family and/or community ties.

See REASON FOR EARLIEST ABNORMAL ENVIRONMENTAL EXPERIENCE, table 1–13.

ECONOMIC CONDITION

> 2–34a — of parents
> 2–34b — of offender within year of commitment
> 3–21b — of offender during parole
> 4–28b — of offender during post-parole

If the offender is single, widowed, separated, or divorced, this refers to her own economic status. If she is married and living with her husband, it refers to their joint status.

Dependent — receives aid continually from public funds or persons outside the immediate family. This means chronic dependency. Aid may be given in the form of money, clothing, food, coal, or medical assistance, etc.

Marginal — lives on daily earnings and accumulates little or nothing; is on the margin between self-support and dependency. Here are included instances in which temporary aid is resorted to once or twice in order to tide over a critical situation — for example, in case of illness of breadwinner or desertion by husband. Aid may be given for a few days or even a month, and with this little assistance the person or family is able to manage its own problem.

Comfortable — sufficient funds accumulated to maintain self and/or family for at least four months during periods of illness or unemployment of breadwinner.

ECONOMIC RESPONSIBILITY

> 1–43b — prior to commitment
> 3–10b — during parole
> 4–26b — during post-parole
> 4–49a — during fifth year of post-parole
> 4–51 — after post-parole

Self-support not necessary — if, during particular period studied, offender does not work and is supported at least in marginal economic circumstances by her husband or a lover for whom she is keeping house, or receives compensation or insurance sufficient to keep her in marginal economic circumstances.

Meets responsibility — this refers to the offender who, if single, or separated, widowed, or divorced, and without dependents, supports herself or makes earnest effort to do so (except if ill or otherwise incapacitated), even if by illegitimate employment; or, if she has dependents, aids or makes every effort to aid in their support; or, if she is married and lives with her husband, or if she lives with married children who assume the responsibility for her support, and husband or other breadwinner is in-capacitated, or the income of husband or other breadwinner keeps the family on the borderline of dependency (see definition of ECONOMIC CONDITION), she contributes toward or makes every effort to contribute toward support of the family.

Fails to meet responsibility — does not meet the above standard.

EDUCATION OF HUSBAND

   2–H77 — of last husband to whom married before commitment

   4–H69 — of last husband to whom married between release on parole and
          end of post-parole

EDUCATION OF PARENTS

   2–11

   This refers to offender's own parents if offender was over five years of age when the first break in the home occurred, and to step- or foster-parents (as the case may be) if offender was under five years of age when the first break in the home occurred. It indicates the highest educational achievement of either parent. For definition of *broken home* see AGE OF OFFENDER AT FIRST BREAK IN HOME.

EFFECT OF CERTAIN PERSONALITIES ON OFFENDER

   4–85

   This refers to strong attraction to or great dislike of certain members of the Reformatory staff or parole agents, and indicates how various of-fenders are attracted or repelled by the same personality. Information only illustrative.

EMOTIONAL STABILITY OF OFFENDER

   2–60a

   This refers to normality of emotional control. Though there was no way of accurately gauging this, some information on this point was gleaned from diagnoses made of offender's mental condition while she was at the Women's Reformatory or from recorded misbehaviour manifestations.

   The data is very incomplete.

EMPLOYED AT TIME OF ARREST FOR WHICH SENT TO WOMEN'S REFORMATORY

   1–55b

ENVIRONMENTAL JUDGMENT

   4–15 — during post-parole

   4–48 — in fifth year of post-parole

   4–54 — after post-parole

   This is a composite picture of neighbourhood influences (see NEIGHBOUR-HOOD INFLUENCE for definition), physical aspects of the home (see HOME — PHYSICAL for definition), and moral standards (see MORAL STAND-ARDS for definition). If a person has been assigned to the " good " class in all three of these factors, she is here assigned to the *good* class.

If fair — *fair*.
If poor — *poor*.
If two good, one fair or poor — *fair* (except if neighbourhood influence fair — *good*).
Two fair, one good — *fair*.
Two fair, one poor — *fair*.
Two poor, one fair — *poor*.
Two poor, one good — *fair*.
One good, one fair, one poor — *fair*.

FAMILY RELATIONSHIPS

Or MORAL OBLIGATIONS TOWARD FAMILY

2–34c — within year of commitment
3–19b — during parole
4–14b — during post-parole
4–47a — during fifth year of post-parole
4–52a — after end of post-parole

The purpose of this is to roughly gauge the strength of offender's ties to her family.

Success — if offender is single, separated, divorced, or widowed before beginning of particular period studied and has no children, and she lives in her parental home, considers it more than merely a place to eat and sleep in (i.e., does not live at home only when or because she is in need of funds); if she lives away from home, keeps in touch with parents or closest relatives, but not only when in need of funds. If offender has children, however, her relationship to them only is considered, and must be *good* or *fair* (see ATTITUDE TO CHILDREN). If offender is married and living with her husband at beginning of period judged, her conjugal relations must be *good* or *fair* (see CONJUGAL RELATIONS), and her attitude to her children, if she has any, must be *good* or *fair* (see ATTITUDE TO CHILDREN). If offender is divorced or separated or widowed before beginning of period judged and has no children, considered as though single (see above).

Failure — does not meet the above standard.

FIRST JOB DURING PAROLE, NATURE OF LEGITIMATE

3–11

See OCCUPATIONS.

FIRST OCCUPATION

1–45

See OCCUPATIONS.

FOSTER-HOMES, TIME SPENT IN

1–69

FREQUENCY OF ARRESTS

    1–63 — prior to commitment

    4–44 — during post-parole

Frequency of arrests prior to commitment to the Reformatory on the sentence studied is calculated as follows: from the period covering the first arrest to the date of the arrest for the offence on which committed to the Reformatory is subtracted the total period of the time spent in penal or non-penal institutions. Into the remaining period of time is divided the number of arrests which occurred during this period (not including the arrest for which the offender was committed to the Reformatory on the sentence studied). Frequency of arrests during the five-year post-parole period is calculated on the basis of sixty months, from which is subtracted the length of time the offender spent in penal or non-penal institutions during this period. Into the time remaining is divided the number of arrests occurring in the sixty-month period.

Incalculable — if only one arrest occurred in the period under scrutiny.

GENERAL CONDITION ON ADMISSION TO THE REFORMATORY

    2–50b

Classification used by Reformatory physician:

Good — no physical disorder (except for uncomplicated venereal disease).

Fair — mild physical disorder as anæmia, gonorrhœa, or acute secondary syphilis with pelvic pain, sore throat and lesions, etc.

Poor — serious physical disorder, as heart trouble complicated by other conditions.

GRADE ATTAINED IN SCHOOL

    1–39

HABITS

    1–21 — during childhood

    1–22 — during adolescence

    1–23 — within year of commitment

    1–24a — habit of drink prior to commitment

    1–24b — habit of drugs prior to commitment

    4–24 — during post-parole

This refers to any habits which may lead to conflict with the law (except smoking).

HARMFUL EFFECTS OF WOMEN'S REFORMATORY

    4–H82

This information was secured from the offenders and their families. It is incomplete, but suggestive.

HAUNTS

(See PLAY PLACES AND HAUNTS for definition.)

    1–19a — in childhood

1–19b — in adolescence
1–19c — within year of commitment
4–23 — during post-parole

HEALTH — VENEREAL DISEASE

1–14 — before twenty-one years old
2–50a — on admission to Reformatory
4–5   — during post-parole

This means gonorrhœa and/or syphilis

If offender was said to have venereal disease but no official proof thereof could be found and the sources of the information could not be accepted as absolutely reliable, she was categorized as *doubtful*. This term has a different meaning, however, in 2–50a — VENEREAL DISEASE ON ADMISSION TO REFORMATORY, where it means that the results of tests made on admission are uncertain for the presence of venereal disease.

HIGHEST WAGE

1–52 — prior to commitment
3–15 — during parole
4–36 — during post-parole

HOME — PHYSICAL

2–28a — during childhood
2–28b — during adolescence
2–29a — within year of commitment
3–5a — first home during parole
4–10 — during post-parole

Good — adequate space (not more than two people, excluding infant, to a bedroom), light, ventilation, cleanliness, sufficient furniture.

Fair — more than one of the above advantages plus one unfavourable factor.

Poor — overcrowding, dirt, shabby furnishing, lack of ventilation, etc. One or more of these factors and no advantages to offset them. Cases of extreme overcrowding belong in this class even if the home is good or fair in other respects.

Varied — here are included those the character of whose physical home changes from one type to another during the particular period studied, as described above. The predominant type is indicated, however.

HOUSEHOLD IN CHILDHOOD

2–31

This refers to the make-up of the household in which offender was resident for more than half the time until she was fourteen years old. If she was shifted about among parents, relatives, foster-parents, so that she was for less than half the time in any one home, tabulated as *various*.

HOUSEHOLD STABILITY

2–32 — prior to commitment

3–7 — during parole

4–16 — during post-parole

This refers to the number of changes in household that offender experiences during the particular period studied. For example, if offender lives for a time with her parents and then goes away to work and lives alone, this is counted as one change; if she then marries and lives with husband, this is two changes; if she leaves her husband to go to a lover, this is three changes; if she leaves a lover and returns to the parental home, this is four changes.

Where offender has been living with her parents and marries and the husband comes to live with her in her parental home, this is not tabulated as a change. Additions to the household are not changes in the sense in which the term is used here.

HOUSEHOLD

2–H71 — with whom living during all marriages prior to commitment

ILLEGITIMATE OCCUPATION

4–38b

This refers to any occupation engagement in which is against the law and from which income is derived, as prostitution, bootlegging, deriving profits from prostitution, drug-selling, disposing of stolen goods.

See also USUAL OCCUPATION.

ILLEGITIMATE PREGNANCIES

1–30b — prior to commitment

4–26a — during post-parole

ILLITERACY

1–36a

INDUSTRIAL HISTORY

1–43a — prior to commitment

3–10a — during parole

4–32 — during post-parole

4–47b — during fifth year of post-parole

4–52b — after post-parole

This is a composite of WORK HABITS (see definition) and STEADINESS OF EMPLOYMENT (see definition).

Success — work habits *good*, and offender a *regular* worker.

Partial success — work habits *good*, and offender either a *fairly regular* or *irregular* worker; or work habits *fair* or *poor*, but offender works *regularly*.

Failure — work habits *poor*, and offender is a *fairly regular* or *irregular*

worker or is engaged in illicit occupations to the exclusion of all, or almost all, legitimate work.

Inapplicable — those who during the particular period studied are unable to work because of illness; or who are confined in institutions; those who do not work because of lack of necessity (see ECONOMIC RESPONSIBILITY — *Self-support not necessary*). If such women work occasionally to supplement their income or because they enjoy working, the determination of their industrial success is based on their *work habits* and not on the *steadiness* of their employment.

INDUSTRIAL STABILITY

2–14a — of father

2–14b — of mother

2–H78 — of last husband before offender's commitment

4–H70 — of last husband married between release on parole and end of post-parole

Regular — with very few breaks in employment and these not the fault of worker.

Fairly regular — some unemployment, largely the fault of worker, but compensated for by some periods of continuous work.

Irregular — frequent breaks in employment due to loafing, laziness, drunkenness, dishonesty, etc.

INSTITUTIONAL EXPERIENCES, NATURE OF

2–6 — prior to commitment

4–9 — during post-parole

INSTITUTIONAL EXPERIENCES — TOTAL NUMBER

1–66

See 2–6 INSTITUTIONAL EXPERIENCES, NATURE OF.

INSURANCE

1–59a — prior to commitment

4–28a — during post-parole

INTELLIGENCE

2–51a

As measured by psychometric examination given at Reformatory shortly after entrance of offender.

INTERVIEW — WITH WHOM HELD

4–H58

This is not a statement of all persons interviewed in connection with the investigation of the post-parole history of the offender. It is meant only to indicate whether the offender herself was seen; and if not, whether any members of her immediate family were seen; and if no relatives, others, etc.

KIND OF SCHOOL ATTENDED

    1–35

KIND OF WORKER IN REFORMATORY

    2–54a

    Good — reliable, industrious, capable, efficient. Does not need supervision.

    Fair — effort and willingness are great, but ineffective unless under some supervision.

    Poor — unreliable, lazy, dishonest, and needing constant supervision.

LANGUAGE SPOKEN AT HOME

    2–24b

LAST LEGITIMATE OCCUPATION BEFORE COMMITMENT

    1–54

    See OCCUPATIONS.

LAST RESIDENCE WITH WHOM

    1–8 — at time of commitment

    3–6 — at beginning of parole

    3–37 — at end of parole

    4–3 — at end of post-parole

LATER ATTITUDE AT WOMEN'S REFORMATORY

    2–61b

    This refers to the offender's attitude toward her commitment and to the Reformatory after she has been there for some months, as a contrast to her attitude on admission.

LEGITIMACY

    1–4a — of offender

    2–20b — of offender's children born prior to commitment

    3–9 — of offender's children born during parole

    4–19b — of offender's children born during post-parole

    Legitimate — child conceived in wedlock, or conceived out of wedlock, but whose parents married before his birth.

    Illegitimate — child whose parents never were married, or who married after his birth.

LEISURE AND HABITS

    1–16b — within year of commitment

    3–20a — during parole

    4–21a — during post-parole

    4–49b — in fifth year of post-parole

    4–51b — after post-parole

    Constructive — is a member of well-supervised recreational groups, such as Y. W. C. A.; or is utilizing leisure time to further self educationally or vocationally; and has no bad habits.

Negative — is at least not engaged in harmful activities, though not using leisure time constructively. No pronounced bad habits. If *unconventional sex* is the only bad habit, offender is included in this group. See SEX LIFE, NATURE OF, for definition.

Harmful — pronounced bad habits, associations, recreations, which may lead to criminal conduct, such as immoral companions, gangs, drug addiction, excessive drinking, gambling. The presence of any one or combinations of these factors places the offender in this group.

LIVING OR DEAD — HUSBAND

2–H80 — at time offender sent to Reformatory

LONGEST PERIOD EMPLOYED

1–50 — prior to commitment

3–16a — during parole

4–37 — during post-parole

MANNER OF MEETING HUSBAND

2–H65 — all husbands prior to commitment

4–H63 — all husbands married between release on parole and end of post-parole

MARITAL HISTORY JUDGMENT

2–41b — on last marriage prior to commitment

2–H62 — on all marriages prior to commitment

4–H75 — on all marriages contracted between release on parole and end of post-parole

Good — husband and wife living together and both assuming their marital responsibilities (see ATTITUDE OF OFFENDER TO MARITAL RESPONSIBILITY and ATTITUDE OF HUSBAND TO MARITAL RESPONSIBILITY).

Fair — husband and wife living together, but one or both not assuming their marital responsibilities.

Poor — husband and wife not living together during particular period studied, or living together but separating frequently. Both neglecting their marital responsibilities.

MARITAL — LENGTH OF TIME ALL MARRIAGES LASTED

2–H63 — all marriages prior to commitment

4–H61 — all marriages contracted between release on parole and end of parole

This means to date of separation or desertion (whether followed by divorce or not).

MARITAL — NUMBER OF MARRIAGES

2–41a — prior to commitment

4–4   — between release on parole and end of post-parole

MARITAL STATUS

Or CIVIL CONDITION

2–40   — at time of commitment

3–8a — at beginning of parole
3–8b — at end of parole
4–17b — at end of post-parole
4–H93 — at beginning of post-parole
    In 3–8b and 4–17b, if offender died during the period but before the end
of it, her marital status at time of her death is tabulated.

MARRIAGE

    2–41a — prior to commitment
    4–4   — between release on parole and end of post-parole

MARRIAGES FORCED

    2–H64 — all marriages prior to commitment
    4–H62 — all marriages between release on parole and end of post-parole
    Forced — if offender pregnant at time of marriage, or, though not preg-
nant, cohabits before marriage and parent, priest, or court urges marriage.

MENSTRUATION ESTABLISHED, AGE AT WHICH

    1–16a

MENTAL CONDITION ON ADMISSION TO REFORMATORY

    2–52
    This refers to mental balance or mental abnormalities. Although two or
more of the conditions listed may be present in one person, she is classified in the order of precedence indicated in the code.
    Neurotic traits — includes egocentricity, seclusiveness, hypochondria, im-
pulsiveness, jealousy, self-pity, untruthfulness, grudgefulness, stubbornness, obscenity.

MENTAL DISEASE OR DEFECT IN FAMILY

    2–21
    The family (meaning immediate blood relatives — i.e., parents and sib-
lings) is assigned to one category only, in the order of precedence indicated in the code.

MISBEHAVIOUR AND BAD HABITS

    1–21 — in childhood
    1–22 — in adolescence
    1–23 — within year of commitment

MOBILITY

    1–10a — prior to commitment
    3–2b — during parole
    4–12b — during post-parole
    Mobility — changes in environment which indicate that the offender does
not take root and establish close associations in any one community. This
is indicated by excessive moving within a city (more than once a year);
or from city to city on the average of once in two years; or by coming
from or going to a foreign country.

MONTHS IN COMMUNITY DURING POST-PAROLE PERIOD

   4–8

   This means the number of months, out of the sixty-month period studied, that the individual is not under institutional care of one kind or another (including hospitals for physical conditions).

MONTHS IN " SECOND GRADE " AT REFORMATORY

   2–61a

   This has reference to the system of promotions of an inmate at the Women's Reformatory from the " second grade," which the offender enters on admission, to the " first grade," to which she is normally promoted in five months if her behaviour is satisfactory.

MONTHS TO FIRST PAROLE

   2–48

   No parole — includes not only those offenders who served the maximum sentence in the institution, but those who were transferred from the Women's Reformatory to another institution and were or were not paroled from there.

MORAL OBLIGATIONS OF OFFENDER TO FAMILY

   OR FAMILY RELATIONSHIPS.

   2–34c — prior to commitment
   3–19b — during parole
   4–14b — during post-parole
   4–47a — during fifth year of post-parole
   4–52a — after post-parole

MORAL STANDARDS OF HOME

   2–36a — during childhood
   2–36b — during adolescence
   2–36c — within year of commitment
   3–5b — of first home during parole
   4–14a — during post-parole

   This refers to the atmosphere of the home in which offender lives during the particular period studied. If she is living alone, the standards of her immediate physical environment are considered. The conduct and moral attitudes of the offender herself are here excluded from consideration.

   Good — wholesome ideals, and no delinquency except for slight violation of automobile regulations or violation of licence laws.

   Fair — no delinquency except for slight violation of auto or licence laws, but an absence of wholesome ideals.

   Poor — homes in which there is immorality, alcoholism, or other delinquency, or where such conduct is lightly regarded.

   If offender is married and living with her husband during period studied and their conduct and ideals are good, but their children are delinquent, classified as *fair* and not *poor*.

Varied — during period studied, offender lives in several homes of different moral standards. The predominating standards are indicated, however.

This last refinement of category applies only to the post-parole period. In the prior and parole periods, the offender was classified on the basis of the standards predominating in the majority of homes in which she lived during the period judged.

NATURE OF MISCONDUCT IN REFORMATORY

2–55

Personal orderliness — refers to such offences as bed not properly made, clothing not in proper order, coat not buttoned, etc.

Lack of self-control — inattention, laughing or talking out of turn, fooling.

Violence against person — fighting, quarrelling, assault.

Sex offences — of any kind (attempted or accomplished).

Against property — destroying or injuring property, stealing.

Against authority — any indication of rebellion against authority, as insolence, defiance, disobedience of orders, refusal to work, attempt to escape, etc.

NATURE OF MOBILITY

1–10b — prior to commitment

3–2b — during parole

4–13 — during post-parole

Excessive moving within a city — on an average of more than once a year.

Excessive moving from city to city — on an average of more than once in two years.

NATIVITY OF PARENTS RELATED TO OFFENDER'S NATIVITY

2–24a

NEIGHBOURHOOD INFLUENCES

2–29b — during childhood

2–30a — during adolescence

2–30b — within year of commitment

3–4 — of first home on parole

4–12a — during post-parole

Good — no street gangs, no centres of vice or crime within a radius of two square blocks in the city or a mile in the country; opportunity for constructive recreation (see CONSTRUCTIVE RECREATIONS for definition) within easy walking-distance, as public playgrounds, school or community centres, parks, etc.

Fair — no street gangs, no centres of vice or crime within a radius of two square blocks in the city or a mile in the country, but no opportunities for constructive recreation within walking-distance.

Poor — corner gangs, centres of vice or crime within a radius of two square blocks in the city or a mile in the country regardless of whether facilities for constructive recreations exist within walking-distance or not.

Varied — during period under study offender lives in different kinds of neighbourhoods.

NEIGHBOURHOOD — TYPE

    2–25 — during childhood

    2–26 — during adolescence

    2–27 — within year of commitment

    3–3 — of first home on parole

    4–11 — during post-parole

A radius of two square blocks in urban districts, and of one mile in rural, from the particular place of residence of the offender during the period studied characterized as:

Urban, partly residential — if it is a business, factory, or lodging-house area.

Urban, residential — if it is an area of tenements or private houses used mainly as permanent residences and not to house transients and from which business or factory areas are more than two blocks distant.

Suburban — if it is an outlying residential district of a city in which there are mainly detached houses with considerable open space.

Rural or small town — if the area is open country, or the town has a population of five thousand or under.

Varied — if the offender has shifted during the period studied from a neighbourhood of one type to another type, she is classified in this group, but the type of neighbourhood in which she lived for the longest time during the period studied is indicated.

NUMBER OF ARRESTS

    2–2 — prior to commitment

    4–42 — during post-parole

NUMBER OF CONVICTIONS

    2–3 — prior to commitment

    4–43 — during post-parole

NUMBER OF DIFFERENT OCCUPATIONAL EXPERIENCES AT WOMEN'S REFORMATORY

    2–53

NUMBER OF PENAL EXPERIENCES

    1–68 — prior to commitment

    4–6 — during post-parole

NUMBER OF PREVIOUS SENTENCES TO WOMEN'S REFORMATORY

    2–46b

NUMBER OF REPORTS BY PAROLEE, FREQUENCY OF

3-33

This includes personal visits made by the parolee to the parole officer as well as reports by letter.

NUMBER OF SOCIAL SERVICE AGENCIES

2-38 — prior to commitment

4-30 — during post-parole

See TYPE OF SOCIAL SERVICE RENDERED for definition.

NUMBER OF YEARS IN SCHOOL

1-37

OCCUPATION AT FIRST CONVICTION

1-48

OCCUPATIONS

1-45   — first occupation

1-48   — occupation at first conviction

1-49   — usual occupation

2-12   — usual occupation of father

2-13   — usual occupation of mother

2-H79 — usual occupation of husband

3-11   — first occupation during parole

3-17   — usual occupation during parole

3-36   — types of occupational experiences during parole

4-33   — usual occupation during post-parole

The classification of occupations of women utilized in this study has been adapted from that used by Mabel R. Fernald and others, in *A Study of Delinquent Women in New York State,* so that the findings of the two studies might be comparable.

Domestic service — includes women working at general housework, or as nurse-girls, waitresses, cooks, ladies' maids, or housekeepers, all in private homes. This group refers to all cases in which living is in addition to wage.

Factory work — includes women working in a factory where there is a group of people. *Laundry workers in a laundry* are also included in this group, as the general conditions of work are similar to those in factories. *Home work* — includes women who are able to earn their living by remaining in their own homes and who for the most part work alone. This is a somewhat heterogeneous group of dressmakers at home, lodging-house keepers, janitresses, and those who bring work home from a factory. This class is intended to show especially the contrast in conditions of work from those of the previous group. *Restaurant and hotel work* — includes waitresses in restaurants and hotels or rooming-houses, chambermaids in hotels, laundry workers in hotels, restaurant-keepers, and even managers of small hotels.

Work in stores — includes clerks, saleswomen, models, cash-girls, messengers, errand-girls, demonstrators, milliners, and women who themselves keep small stores.

Clerical work — includes bookkeepers, cashiers, stenographers, typists, shipping clerks, and other office girls.

Day work — includes women engaged in any kind of domestic service (see above), but living out; or women who clean offices and factories.

Other — includes vaudeville performers, hairdressers, practical nurses, midwives, attendants, ward maids.

Illegitimate occupation — includes women engaged in any occupation which is against the law, as prostitution, drug-selling, etc.

Own housework — includes those who keep house for their husbands or children, or for their parents or other relatives, or for a lover.

For classification of occupations of father, mother, husband, see 2–12, 2–13, 2–H79.

OFFENCE

    1–9   — for which committed to Reformatory

    1–H71   - summary of all offences prior to commitment

    2–1   — cause of first arrest

    2–5   — types of offences prior to commitment

    4–45   — types of offences during post-parole

    4–H56 — summary of all offences committed during post-parole

PARENTAL SUPERVISION

    2–35

Good — wholesome, intelligent control, but not so rigid as to arouse fear or hatred in the child.

Fair — erratic control, at times lax, at times rigid.

Poor — very lax or extremely rigid.

PAROLE DELINQUENCY UNKNOWN TO PAROLE OFFICER

    3–H38

This is a very meagre statement of delinquency occurring during the parole period which was not known by the parole agent. It is a reflection of the superficiality of parole supervision.

PAROLE FROM WOMEN'S REFORMATORY

    2–59b

PAROLE SUPERVISION — TOTAL VISITS MADE BY PAROLE AGENTS

    3–H41

PENAL EXPERIENCES, NATURE OF

4–H60 — during post-parole

This includes transfers from one institution to another as well as direct commitments.

PENAL EXPERIENCES, NUMBER OF

1–68 — prior to commitment

4–6 — during post-parole

PERIOD OF TIME REMAINED IN FIRST PAROLE HOME

3–34

This does not pertain to the physical home, but to the family with whom offender lived. Even though the family may have moved about a great deal, the length of time that the offender remained with them is here referred to.

PHYSICAL CONDITION

2–51b — on discharge from Reformatory

Improved — *poor* on admission and *fair* or *good* on discharge; *fair* on admission and *good* on discharge (see GENERAL CONDITION ON ADMISSION for definition).

Same — no change.

Worse — *good* on admission and *fair* or *poor* on discharge; *fair* on admission and *poor* on discharge.

PLAY PLACES AND HAUNTS

1–19a — during childhood

1–19b — during adolescence

1–19c — within year of commitment

4–23 — during post-parole

Good — play places that are under constructive supervision, as public playgrounds, community centres, school recreation centres.

Fair — places in which there is no constructive supervision, but where the influences are not necessarily harmful, as public dance-halls, skating-rinks, beaches, since the great majority of patrons are not there for illicit purposes.

Poor — play places that are distinctly harmful in character in that most of those who frequent them have an illicit purpose as their objective, as houses of ill fame, gambling-dens, bootlegging joints, etc.

PRACTICAL JUDGMENT

2–60b

This is a personal estimate of the offender's judgment made by the Reformatory psychologist. It was not possible to secure a definition of the terms used in the classification. Of little value, as data meagre.

PREDOMINANT OFFENCE
>1–64 — prior to commitment
>4–40 — during post-parole
>>This is a social category of offences which not only is based on official (see PRINCIPAL COMPONENT OF MISCONDUCT for definition) criminal records, but includes offences for which the person may, but has not, come into conflict with the law.
>>As the group of women studied are largely sex offenders, a differentiation is made between those whose only offences are sexual in character and those who committed some other type of offence in addition.

PRINCIPAL COMPONENT OF MISCONDUCT
>1–60a — prior to commitment
>3–25b — during parole
>4–41a — during post-parole
>>*Official* — based on police or court records
>>*Unofficial* — delinquency for which the person has not come to the attention of official agencies of the law.

PRIOR TIME IN WOMEN'S REFORMATORY
>2–47

PROBATIONS
>1–70 — number prior to Reformatory

PROGNOSIS REGARDING MISCONDUCT AFTER RELEASE
>2–54c — by members of Women's Reformatory staff
>3–31b — by parole officers
>>*Good* — will succeed (see DELINQUENCY for definition).
>>*Fair* — chances of failure or success are about even.
>>*Poor* — will fail.

RAPE OR CONSENT AT FIRST ILLICIT SEX EXPERIENCE
>1–30a

REASON FIRST LEFT HOME
>1–27
>>This refers to the reason for the first departure of offender from the parental home and parental supervision.

REASON FOR CHANGE FROM FIRST PLACE OF RESIDENCE
>3–35 — during parole
>>*Fault of offender* — disappeared, was arrested, left for illicit purposes, quarrelled, etc.
>>*Not fault of offender* — married, moved to be nearer her work, etc.

REASON FOR EARLIEST ABNORMAL ENVIRONMENTAL EXPERIENCE
>1–13
>>See EARLIEST ABNORMAL ENVIRONMENTAL EXPERIENCE for definition.

REASON FOR TERMINATION OF MARRIAGE

2–H73 — all marriages prior to commitment

4–H65 — all marriages occurring between release on parole and end of post-parole

REASON LEFT FIRST PAROLE JOB

3–14

See REASONS FOR LEAVING WORK.

REASON LEFT SCHOOL

1–38

REASON LEFT WORK

3–19a — during parole

See REASONS FOR LEAVING WORK.

REASONS CONTINUED FOR PAROLE

2–H83

This refers to reasons why the offender was not paroled in the usual time.

REASONS FOR FAILURE

4–H88 — after release

This is sometimes the reason stated by offender or relatives and sometimes the opinion of the field investigator or case analyst.

REASONS FOR IMPROVEMENT IN CONDUCT

4–H87 — after release

This is sometimes the reason stated by offender or relatives and sometimes the opinion of the field investigator or case analyst.

REASONS FOR INCOMPLETE OR BROKEN PAROLE SUPERVISION

3–28

This refers to the reasons why offender is not technically or actually under supervision of the parole agent for part or all of the parole period. See 3–27.

REASONS FOR LEAVING WORK

1–53 — usual reason prior to commitment

3–14 — reason for leaving first job on parole

3–19a — usual reason during parole

4–39 — usual reason during post-parole

See USUAL REASONS FOR LEAVING WORK.

Fault of worker — arrested, discharged for inefficiency, dishonest, drunk, etc.

Not fault of worker — laid off because of slack work, left to marry, left because needed to help at home, left as ill.

REASONS FOR SOLITARY CONFINEMENT

2–H88 — during stay at Reformatory

RELATION TO FAMILY ECONOMIC STATUS (all marriages)

2–H72

This is a comparison of the economic condition (see ECONOMIC CONDITION) of offender and her husband with the economic condition of offender's family.

RELATION TO NEAREST RELATIVES

4–17a

This refers to the strength of the family ties existing between the offender and her nearest blood relatives; i.e., to one or both parents if they are living, or to her siblings if one or both parents are not living. If the offender has no parents or siblings, she is classified with the *inapplicable* group.

RELIGION

1–4b — of offender

2–9 — of parents

RESIDENCE OF CHILDREN

4–H76

RETARDATION IN SCHOOL

1–41

This is measured on the basis of the following scale:

Age	Grade
6	I
7	II
8	III
9	IV
10	V
11	VI
12	VII
13	VIII
14	IX
15	X
16	XI
17	XII

RETURNS TO REFORMATORY

2–46a

This means either on revocation or on " in-between " sentence.

REVOCATION TO WOMEN'S REFORMATORY

3–25a

This applies to the fact of revocation of parole, regardless of whether offender was actually returned to the Reformatory.

REVOCATIONS AND NEW SENTENCES

    3–H40 — occurring during parole period

In-between sentence means a sentence imposed before the expiration of the parole period.

SAVINGS

    1–58 — prior to commitment

    4–27 — during post-parole

If offender is single or widowed, separated, or divorced before the beginning of the period judged, this refers to savings made by her personally. If offender is married and living with her husband or living with a lover as his wife, his savings or their joint savings are considered.

SCHOLARSHIP

    1–42a

Good — above average.

Fair — average.

Poor — below average.

SEX IRREGULARITY — EARNINGS FROM PROSTITUTION

    4–H78

This is for illustrative purposes only, and the information is **very incomplete.**

SEX IRREGULARITY, NATURE OF ABNORMAL

    4–25

See SEX LIFE, NATURE OF.

SEX IRREGULARITY — WHERE PRACTISED

    4–H77

This is for illustrative purposes only, and the information is very incomplete.

SEX LIFE — AGE ILLICIT BEGAN

    1–28

For definition of types of illicit sex life see SEX LIFE, NATURE OF.

SEX LIFE, NATURE OF

    1–34 — prior to commitment

    3–23 — during parole

    4–25 — during post-parole

Some, or portions, of these definitions were borrowed from Abraham Flexner: *Prostitution in Europe.*

Even though a person may be engaging in illicit sex life of various kinds during the period studied, she is classified only under one type, in the order indicated below. Thus, *sex perversion* takes precedence over *prosti-*

tution in any form, *prostitution* over *adultery, adultery with several* over *promiscuity,* etc.

Sex pervert — refers to the woman who practises any form of abnormal sex expression, such as exhibitionism, has relations with other women, etc.

Professional prostitute — refers to the woman who earns her livelihood entirely by prostitution and has no legitimate employment. She has sex relations habitually and promiscuously, for money or other mercenary consideration.

Occasional prostitute — refers to the woman who either alternately emerges from or relapses into promiscuous prostitution between periods of legitimate employment, or who carries on prostitution without interrupting some legitimate employment.

One-man prostitute — refers to the woman of the mistress type who gives herself to one man only for a period of time in return for money or other mercenary consideration.

Adulteress, promiscuous — refers to the woman who lives for all or part of the time under the same roof with her husband and yet indulges in promiscuous sex relations (see below for definition of *promiscuous*). It is to be noted that the term *adultery* is not here used in the strictly legal sense.

Promiscuous, unattached — refers to the woman who has sex relations with several men because of either strong sex urge, or desire for excitement, adventure, or affection. No mercenary considerations are involved. This applies not only to single women, but to women who are widowed, separated, or divorced before beginning of the particular period under study.

Adulteress with one — refers to the woman who, though living with her husband during all or part of the particular period under study, is having an illicit alliance with one man, but not for mercenary considerations.

Unconventional — refers to the woman who enters an informal union which serves as a substitute for marriage, or until a child is born, or who has sex relationships with her fiancé before marriage, or with a lover regardless of marital intentions. She is neither a prostitute, nor promiscuous, nor adulterous.

Doubtful — in view of the fact that it is not always possible to ascertain the nature of the sex life of a woman, particularly if she does not make herself a public nuisance or is not known to the police, this category includes those women who, though not prostitutes, adulterous, or very promiscuous, are probably unconventional or slightly promiscuous in their sex relationships, though the suspicion thereof is not substantiated by proof. This categorization is based on rumour and hearsay sufficient to raise a question about her sex morality, however.

SEX LIFE — WITH WHOM ILLICIT FIRST BEGAN
1–29

SIBLINGS — NUMBER IN FAMILY
2–18

This refers to the number of offender's siblings that were born alive, including half-siblings but excluding step-siblings. Offender is included in the number of siblings.

SIBLINGS — NUMBER OF OFFENDERS HAVING STEP- OR HALF-SIBLINGS
2–17b

SIBLINGS — RANK OF OFFENDER AMONG
2–19

This refers to offender's age rank among her siblings and half-siblings who were born alive (including her step-siblings).

SLEEPING-ARRANGEMENTS OF OFFENDER IN CHILDHOOD
2–33

SOCIAL SERVICE AGENCIES INTERESTED IN FAMILY — BY TYPES
See TYPE OF SOCIAL SERVICE RENDERED.

SOCIAL SERVICE NEEDS NOT MET DURING POST-PAROLE PERIOD
4–H90 — glaring needs only
4–H91 — by cases
4–H92 — by needs

This refers to the nature of only the most glaring needs.

SOLITARY CONFINEMENT AT WOMEN'S REFORMATORY
2–H86

SOLITARY CONFINEMENT — PLACES PROVIDED FOR AT REFORMATORY
2–H87

SPECIAL ATTEMPTS AT REHABILITATION BY PAROLE AGENTS
3–H39

This includes matters like marital adjustment, arrangements for recreation, arousing of educational interests, vocational adjustment, giving of advice and encouragement.

STAFF PROGNOSIS
2–54c

See PROGNOSIS REGARDING MISCONDUCT.

STAFF RECOMMENDATIONS
2–H85

This refers either to recommendations made by the members of the staff at the Reformatory for the care and training of the girl in the institution, or to any recommendations made by them to the parole agents in regard to the supervision of the offender on parole.

STEADINESS OF EMPLOYMENT

1–57a — of offender prior to commitment

3–18a — of offender during parole

4–34a — of offender during post-parole

Inapplicable — refers to women who do not work because of illness, or confinement in institutions, or lack of necessity.

In the last group is the woman who is supported in at least marginal economic circumstances (see ECONOMIC CONDITION for definition) by her husband or by a lover for whom she is keeping house; and the woman who receives compensation or insurance sufficient to maintain her in marginal economic circumstances.

Regular — refers to women who are continually employed during the period judged — i.e., who have not more than an average of two months of unemployment a year.

Fairly regular — refers to women who have periods of unemployment in excess of two months a year, which are compensated for by periods of sustained work.

Irregular — refers to women who have frequent or long-protracted periods of unemployment, and none of sustained employment.

In the case of women who had to work for only a part of the particular period under study (until marriage, for example) their steadiness of employment for such time is referred to.

STEP- AND FOSTER-PARENTS

2–17a

SUMMARY OF ARRESTS

See SUMMARY OF OFFENCES.

SUMMARY OF DISPOSITIONS

1–H72 — all dispositions prior to commitment

2–4   — types of dispositions prior to commitment

4–46   — types of dispositions during post-parole

4–H57 — all dispositions during post-parole

SUMMARY OF OFFENCES

1–H71 — all offences prior to commitment

2–5   — types of offences prior to commitment

4–45   — types of offences during post-parole

4–H56 — all offences during post-parole

TERM OF SENTENCE

2–45

THEORETICAL AND ACTUAL PAROLE PERIOD

3–1   — theoretical parole period

3–27 — time difference between theoretical and actual parole period

Theoretical parole period — the time from the date of release on parole to the official date of expiration of parole.

Actual parole period — theoretical parole period minus the portions thereof during which the offender is not technically under the supervision of the parole officer, as, for instance: offender is deported or is outside of Massachusetts by permission of the parole department and is not required to make reports; offender is committed to a state hospital or a penal institution and therefore, according to the rules of Massachusetts parole department, is no longer supervised by the parole agent.

If, however, offender disappeared while on parole, or was excused from reporting because of good behaviour, or, though in another state or country, was required to report by letter, she is in all such instances considered to be technically under parole supervision.

TIME COVERED BY PERIOD FOLLOWING POST-PAROLE PERIOD

    4–53

This means the length of time between the expiration of the five-year post-parole and the date on which the investigation of the case was completed by us.

TIME HELD FIRST OCCUPATION

    1–47

TIME HELD FIRST PAROLE JOB

    3–13

TIME IN PENAL INSTITUTIONS

    1–65 — prior to commitment

    4–7 — during post-parole

TIME KNOWN HUSBAND BEFORE MARRIAGE

    2–H66 — all marriages prior to commitment

    4–H64 — all marriages between release on parole and end of post-parole

TIME OFFENDER IN MASSACHUSETTS

    1–7

TIME OFFENDER IN UNITED STATES

    1–6 — offender

    2–10a — parents

TIME PARENTS IN UNITED STATES

    2–10a

Means longest period either parent in United States.

TIMES CONTINUED FOR PAROLE AT WOMEN'S REFORMATORY

    2–H89

Continuance — a holding over of the offender in the Reformatory beyond the time at which she would normally be entitled to release on parole.

TIME SERVED IN PENAL INSTITUTION

    1–65 — prior to commitment

    4–7 — during post-parole

TIME SINCE LAST EMPLOYED

    1–56 — prior to commitment

TIME TO FIRST CONTACT WITH CASE BY AGENT

    3–26

> *Case* as used here does not necessarily mean the offender herself, but may mean her employer, or her parents, or her husband, etc. — i.e., anyone immediately concerned in her welfare.

TIME TO FIRST CONTACT WITH PAROLEE

    3–32

> This refers to visit or communication with the parolee herself by the parole agent.

TO LIVE WITH WHOM

    1–8 — with whom living at time of commitment

    3–6 — with whom living at release on parole

    3–37 — with whom living at end of parole

    4–3 — with whom living at end of post-parole

TOTAL TIME A PROSTITUTE

    1–32

> See SEX LIFE, NATURE OF, for definition of *prostitute*.

TOTAL TIME IN PENAL AND NON-PENAL INSTITUTIONS

    1–67

TOTAL TIME IN WOMEN'S REFORMATORY ON PRESENT SENTENCE

    2–49

> This refers to the actual length of time that offender was at the Reformatory and therefore excludes any time which she spent in other institutions during this sentence by transfer (either from or to the Reformatory) except brief periods in hospitals for confinement or other illness, or time on indenture.

TOTAL TIME SEXUALLY IRREGULAR UP TO COMMITMENT

    1–33

> See SEX LIFE, NATURE OF.

TRAINING DESIRED — RECEIVED

    2–60c

> This refers to the vocational training for which the offender expressed preference on entrance to the Reformatory.

TRANSFER TO WOMEN'S REFORMATORY FROM OTHER INSTITUTION

    2–57b

TRANSFER FROM WOMEN'S REFORMATORY TO OTHER INSTITUTION

    2–58

TYPE OF SOCIAL SERVICE RENDERED

2–39 — prior to commitment

4–31 — during post-parole

This refers in 2–39 to offender's parents and in 4–31 to offender herself if she is single, separated, widowed, or divorced; and to herself, her husband, and children if she is married and living with them.

Health, physical — includes free hospital care, free clinic attendance, supervision by a hospital social service department or department of health.

Health, mental — includes free mental hospital or out-patient treatment, and schools for feeble-minded.

Relief and family welfare agencies — includes all public and private agencies giving relief, or any service that has to do with problems of family adjustment, as domestic relations and unemployment.

Child or adolescent welfare — includes all agencies of the non-punitive type dealing specifically with problems of childhood and adolescence, as the Society for the Prevention of Cruelty to Children.

Correctional — any agencies dealing with delinquent children or adolescents, as state industrial schools, truant schools.

USED WOMEN'S REFORMATORY OCCUPATION

3–16b — during parole

4–38a — during post-parole

This refers to the utilization of the occupational training received at the Reformatory, either directly by engaging in the selfsame occupation, or indirectly by using a technique learned at the Reformatory.

USUAL OCCUPATION

1–49 — of offender prior to commitment

2–12 — of father prior to offender's commitment

2–13 — of mother prior to offender's commitment

2–H79 — of husband prior to offender's commitment

3–17 — of offender during parole

4–33 — of offender during post-parole

See OCCUPATIONS for definition of categories.

The *usual occupation* is the type in which the worker is longest engaged during the period under scrutiny, or the type to which he most often returns.

Because of paucity of information the *usual occupation of father* was judged by his occupation at the time of offender's commitment, or by his most recent occupation. If the offender had a step- or a foster-father before she was five years of age, his occupation rather than that of her own father is referred to.

The *usual occupation of mother* from the birth of the offender until she was twenty-one years old is referred to. If, however, the offender had a step- or foster-mother before she was five years of age, her occupation, rather than that of the actual mother, is referred to.

USUAL REASON FOR LEAVING WORK

    1–53 — prior to commitment

    3–19a — during parole

    4–39 — during post-parole

    Usual reason if possible; otherwise, last known reason.

    See REASONS FOR LEAVING WORK.

VENEREAL DISEASE

    1–14 — before twenty-one years of age

    2–50a — on admission to Reformatory

    4–5 — during post-parole

    See HEALTH — VENEREAL DISEASE.

VOCATIONAL EXPERIENCES AT WOMEN'S REFORMATORY [1]

    2–H84

    Wherever possible the classification is made under type of work carried on rather than department in which the work was done:

A. Industries

1. *Shirt room:* The various processes in the manufacture of shirts and many other articles for state use are taught, including the operation of single-needle and double-needle power sewing-machines and buttonhole machines. Interest in the work is increased through the study of the manufacture of textiles from the raw cotton, wool, and flax. Some years a few plants of cotton have been grown in the room for demonstration purposes. The women who have the ability to advance are able to work up to positions as forewomen in the department.

2. *Flag room:* In this department, also, single-needle and double-needle power machine operation is taught, as well as the various processes in the making of flags and pennants. Stenciling and painting of the state flag requires painstaking skill and technique. Study of the historical significance and development of the national flag leads to interest in further study of history.

3. *Knitting room:* The machines in this department consist of winders, ribbers, merrow machines, and loopers. The various processes in the manufacture of stockings are taught, including winding, knitting, topping, looping, welting, pressing, inspecting, and mending. Friendly rivalry in the development of technique and speed in production make this a popular department. Women who will return to knitting-mill communities find here an opportunity to learn a trade which they may follow upon returning to their homes.

---

[1] Prepared by Miss Barbara Sanborn.

4. *Cannery:* This department, developing from a feature of the general house-keeping in which surplus of garden truck was preserved for winter use, has grown to be one of the basic industries of the institution. Although only a seasonal occupation, the women assigned to this department gain experience in canning vegetables and fruit, which they utilize later in their own homes.

B. Farm Work

1. *Gardens:* Training consists of planting, weeding, hoeing, transplanting, berry picking, and harvesting of vegetables and fruit.

2. *Dairy:* These helpers care for and feed the cows and young stock, assist in the pasteurization of milk and cream, and in the buttermaking.

3. *Poultry plant:* Training includes care and raising of poultry, care of poultry products, planning and care of poultry houses.

C. General Institution Activities

1. *General cleaning:* This training includes sweeping, dusting, scrubbing, making beds, washing windows, whitewashing, painting, and minor repairs such as setting window glass, screening windows, etc.

2. *Clothes and linen rooms:* This includes such duties as collecting and marking soiled articles for the laundry, sorting and distributing articles returned from the laundry, mending garments and household linens.

3. *Laundry:* Hand washing and machine washing, mangle-tending, plain and fancy hand ironing, checking and sorting of laundry, are among the processes taught here. Both steam dryers and open-air drying are used.

4. *Kitchen:* From the simple processes of cleaning and caring for floors, sinks, and tables, washing kitchen utensils, cleaning and paring vegetables, cleaning and preparing meats, fowl, and fish, advancement is possible through the various forms of simple cooking to assisting or cooking meats and pastries. Electrically operated bread-mixers afford experience in large-quantity bread-making.

5. *Dining-rooms:* These departments furnish training in general care of dining-rooms, hand and machine dish-washing, polishing of silver, table-setting, serving of food, waiting on tables, with possible promotion to the position of head waitress.

6. *Store-room:* All requisitions for supplies of every type are filled and delivered through this department. Women employed here learn to keep careful accounts, attend to the storage of foods, vegetables, and other supplies, handle freight, do some meat-cutting, sort and candle eggs, fit inmates with shoes, and perform miscellaneous tasks such as picking and sorting fruit and other farm products.

7. *Receiving and discharging department:* New inmates are assisted to bathe,

wash their hair, and dress in institution garments. Clothing and other personal effects brought into the institution are fumigated, listed, bundled, marked, and stored. Inmates about to be released are fitted to suitable clothing, and their garments are pressed and altered as necessary by helpers in this department.

8. *Rug room:* To this department kitchen, dining-room, and other helpers are assigned when not otherwise occupied. Hooked rugs, woven rugs, braided rugs, and many other useful articles are made from the waste pieces left from the cutting of garments, from spool-knitted ropes of unravelled threads of burlap bags which have been dyed, from pieces of twine and tape dyed, etc. This department has for years taken upon itself, as a spare-time activity, the task of making Christmas gifts for each inmate, baby, and officer of the institution. Ingenuity has been shown in utilizing waste of various descriptions in the making of gifts, ranging from the knitting of socks and booties for the babies to the making of intricate embroidered articles.

9. *Sewing class:* This class affords practice in hand sewing, the work ranging from the simplest stitches to the more involved garment-making. Many of the babies' garments are made in this class.

10. *Gymnasium:* Assistants in this department, in addition to general cleaning, have practice in the checking and care of the athletic togs and equipment, assist in the set-up of equipment, and otherwise assist the physical education teacher both in the gymnasium and on the athletic field.

11. *Library and chapel:* Assistants in this combined department have the general cleaning and care of their department, collect and carry library books, assist in the record-keeping in the library, assist the chaplain in preparations for chapel services, aid other inmates during Sunday letter-writing periods. They, with the gymnasium helpers, have responsible duties in the preparations and rehearsals for dramas, which are frequently given by the inmates.

12. *Front office:* This helper acts as messenger throughout the institution and holds a much coveted position of responsibility. She escorts new inmates to their first assignments, goes to departments for inmates who are desired elsewhere, assists in filling the weekly requisitions made by inmates for goods purchased outside the institution (i.e., toilet and dental supplies, fruit, sewing-materials, etc.), daily raises and lowers the national and state flags, rings the institution bell.

13. *Teachers:* Under supervision, certain inmates who are equipped to do so teach classes in Americanization and other elementary studies.

D. Hospital Work

1. *Hospital* helpers receive instruction in bedside care of the acute and chronic sick and are given practice in bathing and simple massage, taking temperatures and pulse, carrying trays, and otherwise waiting upon sick patients. They are

taught measures of precaution against transmission of infectious diseases, the technique of sterilization of instruments and supplies, preparation of bandages and other hospital supplies.

2. *Dental room:* The dentist's helper takes care of the cleaning of the room, is taught sterilization of instruments, and acts as an unprofessional general helper to the dentist.

3. *Diet kitchen:* Helpers in this department are taught the preparation of special diets, the filling of babies' feeding formulas, the setting up of trays.

4. *Day nursery:* The physical care of the babies is taught, including teaching the child habits of eating, bodily function, and rest.

E. Indenture

By careful selection, certain inmates are permitted to leave the institution upon indenture,[2] to work in a local hospital as ward maids, kitchen helpers, and laundresses. These women are earning while serving their sentences, and are by this method able to prove their ability to return to life outside the institution.

VOCATIONAL SCHOOL

1-42c

This refers to attendance at any vocational training school prior to admission to Reformatory, excluding, however, vocational training received in peno-correctional institutions.

WEEKLY WAGE

1-46 — at first occupation
1-51 — average weekly wage prior to commitment
1-52 — highest weekly wage prior to commitment
1-55a — in last legitimate occupation prior to commitment
3-15 — highest weekly wage during parole
4-35 — average weekly wage during post-parole
4-36 — highest wage during post-parole

If worker gets board and room, five dollars a week is added to wages.

WEIGHT — IMPROVEMENT IN, AT WOMEN'S REFORMATORY

2-H82

WHEREABOUTS OF OFFENDER AT POST-PAROLE EXPIRATION

4-H59

WHY DID NOT USE WOMEN'S REFORMATORY OCCUPATION

4-H79

Information is very incomplete and is used for illustrative purposes only.

WITH WHOM LIVING

1-8 — at time of commitment

[2] Gen. Laws of Mass., Tercentenary Edition, 1932, Chap. 127, Secs. 85, 86. The law was originally passed in 1879, though the practice of indenture goes back to colonial times.

3-6　— at release on parole
3-37 — at end of parole
4-3　— at end of post-parole

WORK HABITS

1-57b — prior to commitment
3-18b — during parole
4-34b — during post-parole

Inapplicable — see STEADINESS OF EMPLOYMENT for definition.

Good — refers to the woman who by her reliability, industriousness, and capacity is an asset to her employer.

Fair — refers to the woman who has the capacity for being a *good* worker, but who interrupts her employment by drinking, drug addiction, prostitution, etc. Refers also to the woman whose effort is great, but who is inefficient.

Poor — refers to the woman who by her unreliability, laziness, dishonesty, is a liability to her employer.

Illegal — is classed here if engaged in illegitimate employment throughout particular period under study.

APPENDIX D

CODE-TABLE INDEX

Note of explanation.

This study was tabulated on the Hollerith machine. In order to prepare the data for tabulation it was necessary to assign to each factor a column number (the Hollerith tabulation card has eighty columns, each providing for twelve positions or categories of a factor). If it was not necessary to use a whole column for a factor, as, for example *aliases,* which required only three positions or categories — " used aliases," " no aliases," " unknown " — it was possible, in order to save space, to " split " a column and use it for a second and even a third factor. Each column is assigned a number ranging from 1 to 80, and where more than one factor appears in a column, we for convenience differentiated these by " a ", " b ", " c ", etc. Table numbers preceded by an " H " designate those factors which were for one reason or another tabulated by hand.

Each category of a factor is assigned a number or " position " in a column. Thus, for example, the factor *citizenship of offender* (in Code 1) is in column 5 (designated 1–5) and one of its categories " citizen by naturalization " is assigned to position 2 (figure directly to left).

It will be noted by the reader that occasionally categories do not appear in their logical order, as, in Table 2–11, *Education of Parents,* " one illiterate, one reads and writes," which should have been assigned to position 3 instead of to position 11. Such occasional irregularities in the position of the categories are due to the impossibility of determining in advance all the categories of a factor. We have always left two or three positions vacant in each column in order to allow for additional categories as the work proceeded.

The figures appearing to the left of the category numbers indicate the incidence of each category. It was deemed wise to publish these in order that anyone interested may have the figures readily available. Percentages have also been included, usually on the basis of the total of known cases and occasionally on the basis of such totals as most readily express the meaning of the particular table. Unless otherwise indicated (as in a " multiple punch " table) the tables total to 500 and the percentages to 100. Any omissions from inclusion in the percentages are designated by a dash. The reader is invited to make any other combinations of categories or to work out percentages on any basis more suitable to his own purposes.

Wherever a line appears beneath a category (as in Table 1-21, *Misbehaviour and Bad Habits in Childhood,* under category 2 — "unknown") it means that in the categories appearing below the line, each case may be recorded more than once. This is what we have designated a "multiple punch" column and totals to more than 500 (the number of cases studied in this research), but it represents the findings on the 500 cases. The sum of the incidence of the categories "none" and "unknown," if subtracted from 500, gives the number of cases actually represented by the remaining categories or subclasses of the factor.

For definitions of the factors, see Appendix C, "Definition of Terms," where they are arranged alphabetically.

CODE I. PERSONAL HISTORY OF OFFENDER BEFORE COMMITMENT TO REFORMATORY

1–1a. ALIASES

%	No.	
52.5	260	1. Used aliases
47.5	236	2. No aliases
—	4	3. Unknown

1–1b. COLOUR OF OFFENDER

93.6	468	4. White
5.2	26	5. Negro
0	0	6. Negroid
1.2	6	7. Other
—	0	8. Unknown

1–2a. AGE AT TIME OF COMMITMENT TO REFORMATORY

41.2	206	1. 20 and under
22.6	113	2. 21–25
16.4	82	3. 26–30
9.8	49	4. 31–35
5.0	25	5. 36–40
2.2	11	6. 41–45
1.8	9	7. 46–50
.8	4	8. 51–55
.2	1	9. 56 and over

1–2b. BIRTHPLACE — NATIVITY OF OFFENDER

75.7	377	10. Native-born
24.3	121	11. Foreign-born
—	2	12. Unknown

1–3. Birthplace of Offender — Country of Birth of Foreign-born

%	No.	
—	262	1. Massachusetts
—	115	2. Other places in the United States
13.2	16	3. Canada — French
24.8	30	4. Canada — other
9.9	12	5. Great Britain
10.8	13	6. Ireland
7.4	9	7. Italy
4.1	5	8. Portugal and Atlantic islands
10.8	13	9. Poland and Lithuania
11.6	14	10. Russia and Finland
7.4	9	11. Other
—	2	12. Unknown

1–4a. Legitimacy of Offender

%	No.	
92.0	426	1. Legitimate
3.2	15	2. Conceived or born out of wedlock — parents never married
2.4	11	3. Conceived or born out of wedlock — parents married later
2.4	11	4. Question of legitimacy
—	37	5. Unknown

1–4b. Church — Religion of Offender

%	No.	
58.7	290	6. Catholic
39.3	194	7. Protestant
2.0	10	8. Hebrew
.0	0	9. Other
—	6	10. Unknown

1–5. Citizenship of Offender

%	No.	
86.5	377	1. Citizen by birth
1.8	8	2. Citizen by naturalization
.2	1	3. Has first papers
2.3	10	4. Citizen by marriage
9.2	40	5. Alien
—	64	6. Unknown

1–6. Time Offender in United States

%	No.	
—	377	1. Life
3.3	4	2. Less than 2 years
4.1	5	3. 2–3 years
6.5	8	4. 4–5 years
16.3	20	5. 6–9 years
13.0	16	6. 10–13 years
23.6	29	7. 14–17 years
33.2	41	8. 18 years and over
—	0	9. Unknown

1–7. Time Offender in Massachusetts

54.2	265	1. Life
1.0	5	2. Never
8.0	39	3. Less than 2 years
5.5	27	4. 2–3 years
3.5	17	5. 4–5 years
6.3	31	6. 6–9 years
5.5	27	7. 10–13 years
7.2	35	8. 14–17 years
8.8	43	9. 18 and over
—	11	10. Unknown

1–8. Last Residence with Whom (at time of arrest)

29.7	148	1. Parents (one or both)
3.8	19	2. Sib or sibs (no parents)
2.2	11	3. Other relatives
8.8	44	4. Husband
2.0	10	5. Children
13.7	68	6. Lover
5.2	26	7. Employer
22.3	111	8. Alone
12.3	61	9. Other
—	2	10. Unknown

1–9. Offence for which Committed to Reformatory (by type)

%	No.	
.8	4	1. Against person
12.6	63	2. Against chastity — adultery
6.8	34	3. ” ” — common night walking
4.4	22	4. ” ” — fornication
1.0	5	5. ” ” — keeping house of ill fame
24.4	122	6. ” ” — lewd and lascivious person
4.8	24	7. ” ” — other
3.4	17	8. Against family and children
23.8	119	9. Against public health, safety, and policy (except drink or drugs)
6.6	33	10. Drink
.2	1	11. Drugs
11.2	56	12. Against property rights

1–10a. Mobility Prior to Commitment (after five years of age)

66.2	329	1. Yes
33.8	168	2. No
—	3	3. Unknown

1–10b. Mobility, Nature of

—	168	4. No mobility
15.7	45	5. Excessive moving within a city
46.5	133	6. Moving from city to city
37.8	108	7. From foreign country to United States
—	27	8. Unknown
—	19	9. Other

1–11. Earliest Abnormal Environmental Experience, Nature of

11.0	54	1. None
18.4	90	2. Ran away or left
13.1	64	3. To live with relatives
10.0	49	4. To foster-home (not relatives)
14.0	68	5. To non-penal institution
4.3	21	6. To correctional institution
4.5	22	7. Excessive moving
20.2	99	9. Immigration or long period in foreign country with parents
4.5	22	10. Other
—	11	11. Unknown

1–12. Age of Offender at Time of Earliest Abnormal Environmental Experience

%	No.	
—	54	1. No abnormal environmental experience
25.3	109	2. Under 7 years
13.4	58	3. 7–10 years
17.1	74	4. 11–14 years
30.8	133	5. 15–18 years
8.1	35	6. 19–22 years
5.3	23	7. 23 years and over
—	14	8. Unknown

1–13. Reason for Earliest Abnormal Environmental Experience

—	54	1. No abnormal environmental experience
12.5	54	2. Death of one or both parents
4.6	20	3. Separation, desertion, divorce of parents
.7	3	4. Illness of parents (mental or physical)
23.0	99	5. Migration
15.7	68	6. Delinquency of offender
12.5	54	7. Neglect of offender, or home for other reasons unsuitable
17.1	74	8. Ran away from home
6.0	26	9. To seek employment
7.9	34	10. Other reasons
—	14	11. Unknown

1–14. Health — Venereal Disease Before 21 Years Old

67.8	227	1. Yes
30.1	101	2. No
2.1	7	3. Doubtful
—	165	4. Unknown

1–15. DEVELOPMENTAL PHYSICAL CONDITION — SERIOUS HANDICAP DURING CHILDHOOD AND ADOLESCENCE

%	No.	
—	92	1. Unknown
65.7	268	2. None
1.2	5	3. Deafness
3.2	13	4. Defective vision (partial or total blindness)
2.2	9	5. Paralysis of limb or deformity or serious injuries
.5	2	6. Violent headaches, dizziness, etc.
.5	2	7. Tuberculosis
.3	1	8. Asthma
10.8	44	9. Fits, convulsions, hysterics, fainting-spells
1.2	5	10. Epilepsy
1.2	5	11. Rheumatism
13.2	54	12. Other

1–16a. MENSTRUATION ESTABLISHED, AGE AT WHICH

.9	3	1. 10 years or earlier
18.0	63	2. 11–12 years
45.0	157	3. 13–14 years
31.0	108	4. 15–16 years
4.6	16	5. 17–18 years
.5	2	6. 19–20 years
.0	0	7. Over 20 years
—	151	8. Unknown

1–16b. LEISURE AND HABITS WITHIN YEAR PRIOR TO COMMITMENT

.8	4	9. Constructive
1.2	6	10. Negative
98.0	485	11. Harmful
—	5	12. Unknown

1–17. AMBITION, VOCATIONAL, EXPRESSED AT ANY TIME PRIOR TO COMMITMENT

%	No.	
51.5	182	1. None
15.8	56	2. Nurse
4.0	14	3. Teacher
5.4	19	4. Nun
7.1	25	5. Business position requiring training as clerk, bookkeeper, stenographer
4.8	17	6. Actress
5.7	20	7. Dressmaker or milliner
5.7	20	9. Other
—	147	10. Unknown

1–18a. CONSTRUCTIVE RECREATIONS AND INTERESTS ANY TIME PRIOR TO COMMITMENT

19.7	80	1. Yes
80.3	327	2. No
—	93	9. Unknown

1–18b. COMPANIONS AND LOVERS — IN CHILDHOOD

73.9	184	4. Harmless
26.1	65	5. Harmful
—	251	6. Unknown

1–18c. COMPANIONS AND LOVERS — IN ADOLESCENCE

13.0	52	7. Harmless
87.0	356	8. Harmful
—	92	9. Unknown

1–18d. COMPANIONS AND LOVERS — WITHIN YEAR OF COMMITMENT

2.7	13	10. Harmless
97.3	467	11. Harmful
—	20	12. Unknown

1–19a. Play Places and Haunts — in Childhood

%	No.	
3.8	7	1. Good
72.3	133	2. Fair
23.9	44	3. Poor
—	316	4. Unknown

1–19b. Play Places and Haunts — in Adolescence

	0	5. Good
18.9	63	6. Fair
81.1	270	7. Poor
—	167	8. Unknown

1–19c. Play Places and Haunts — Within Year of Commitment

0	0	9. Good
10.2	43	10. Fair
89.8	377	11. Poor
—	80	12. Unknown

1–20a. Church Attendance — in Childhood

55.4	233	1. Regular
38.7	163	2. Irregular
5.9	25	3. None
—	79	4. Unknown

1–20b. Church Attendance — in Adolescence

24.1	101	5. Regular
62.8	264	6. Irregular
13.1	55	7. None
—	80	8. Unknown

1–20c. Church Attendance — Within Year of Commitment

13.5	56	9. Regular
50.0	207	10. Irregular
36.5	151	11. None
—	86	12. Unknown

I-21. Misbehaviour and Habits — in Childhood
[multiple punch]

%	No.	
31.0	110	1. None
—	145	2. Unknown
25.6	91	3. Bunking out, runaway, truancy
38.6	137	4. Stubbornness (unmanageable, disobedient, defiant, quarrelsome, temper tantrums, lazy)
11.5	41	5. Lying
23.9	85	6. Heterosexual habits
2.3	8	7. Other sex habits (as masturbation)
14.1	50	8. Stealing
1.7	6	9. Drink
0	0	10. Drugs
1.1	4	11. Smoking (any)
5.9	21	12. Other

Note: Percentages on the basis of known total of cases having the habits or misconduct indicated.

I-22. Misbehaviour and Habits — in Adolescence
[multiple punch]

%	No.	
5.3	24	1. None
—	48	2. Unknown
42.3	191	3. Bunking out, runaway, truancy
15.7	71	4. Stubbornness (unmanageable, disobedient, defiant, quarrelsome, temper tantrums, lazy)
7.7	35	5. Lying
86.9	393	6. Heterosexual habits
2.7	12	7. Other sex habits (as masturbation)
18.6	84	8. Stealing
25.4	115	9. Drink
2.7	12	10. Drugs
11.7	53	11. Excessive smoking
6.2	28	12. Other

Note: See note for I-21.

1–23. MISBEHAVIOUR AND HABITS — WITHIN YEAR OF COMMITMENT
[multiple punch]

%	No.	
0.4	2	1. None
—	1	2. Unknown
23.8	119	3. Bunking out, runaway, truancy
7.6	38	4. Stubbornness (unmanageable, disobedient, defiant, quarrelsome, temper tantrums, lazy)
5.6	28	5. Lying
94.0	469	6. Heterosexual habits
2.8	14	7. Other sex habits (as masturbation)
20.6	103	8. Stealing
41.4	207	9. Drink
4.8	24	10. Drugs
15.4	77	11. Excessive smoking
7.4	37	12. Other

Note: See note for 1–21.

1–24a. HABIT OF DRINK PRIOR TO COMMITMENT

42.0	207	1. Yes
58.0	286	2. No
—	7	3. Unknown

1–24b. HABIT OF DRUGS PRIOR TO COMMITMENT

4.9	24	4. Yes
95.1	470	5. No
—	6	6. Unknown

1–25. AGE AT FIRST KNOWN DELINQUENCY

2.3	11	1. Under 7 years
2.9	14	2. 7–8 years
4.9	23	3. 9–10 years
9.9	47	4. 11–12 years
20.5	97	5. 13–14 years
22.8	108	6. 15–16 years
17.1	81	7. 17–18 years
8.2	39	8. 19–20 years
11.4	54	9. 21 years or over
—	26	10. Unknown

1–26. Age First Left Home

%	No.	
—	47	1. Never left home (before marriage or present commitment)
—	0	2. Unknown if left home
8.9	38	3. 4 years or under
9.6	41	4. 5–8 years
10.1	43	5. 9–12 years
14.8	63	6. 13–14 years
23.1	99	7. 15–16 years
15.9	68	8. 17–18 years
8.9	38	9. 19–20 years
8.7	37	10. 21 years and over
—	26	11. Age unknown

1–27. Reason First Left Home

—	47	1. Did not leave home
—	0	2. Unknown if left home
5.9	25	3. Sentenced to penal or correctional institution
22.5	96	4. Break-up of household
10.6	45	5. To go to or seek employment
8.2	35	6. To migrate to United States
10.1	43	7. Committed to non-penal institution
26.1	111	8. Ran away for 6 months or more or for frequent brief periods (for any reason except quarrel)
2.6	11	9. Committed to care of state
5.1	22	10. Quarrel with family
8.9	38	11. Other
—	27	12. Reason unknown

1–28. Sex Life — Age Illicit Began

1.8	8	1. Never
1.9	9	2. 6–9 years
18.2	83	3. 11–14 years
56.2	256	4. 15–18 years
14.1	64	5. 19–22 years
3.8	17	6. 23–26 years
3.0	14	7. 27–30 years
.8	4	8. 31–34 years
.2	1	9. 35 years and over
—	44	10. Unknown whether irregular, and age unknown

1–29. Sex Life — With Whom Illicit First Began

%	No.	
—	8	1. None
16.5	54	2. Pick-up
20.2	66	3. Casual acquaintance (as neighbour, client in restaurant)
32.3	106	4. Friend
15.0	49	5. Fiancé
.6	2	6. Own father
2.1	7	7. Step- or foster-father
3.0	10	8. Other relative
5.5	18	9. Schoolmate
4.8	16	10. Fellow employee
—	164	11. Unknown or other

1–30a. Rape or Consent at First Illicit Sex Experience

—	8	1. No illicit sex life
79.5	210	2. Consent
20.5	54	3. Rape
—	228	4. Unknown

1–30b. Illegitimate Pregnancies

45.6	201	6. No
54.4	240	7. Yes
—	59	8. Unknown

1–31. Age Entered Prostitution

—	158	1. Not a prostitute
—	99	2. Unknown if a prostitute
.9	2	3. Less than 13 years old
3.2	7	4. 13–14 years
18.5	41	5. 15–16 years
30.2	67	6. 17–18 years
19.8	44	7. 19–20 years
11.7	26	8. 21–22 years
15.7	35	9. 23 years, and over
—	21	10. Age unknown

I–32. TOTAL TIME A PROSTITUTE UP TO COMMITMENT

%	No.	
—	158	1. Not a prostitute
—	99	2. Unknown if prostitute
16.2	35	3. Less than 6 months
11.1	24	4. 6–11 months
21.7	47	5. 12–23 months
20.0	43	6. 2 and 3 years
8.3	18	7. 4 and 5 years
6.5	14	8. 6 and 7 years
6.5	14	9. 8 and 9 years
3.7	8	10. 10 and 11 years
6.0	13	11. 12 years and over
—	27	12. Time unknown

I–33. TOTAL TIME SEXUALLY IRREGULAR UP TO COMMITMENT

1.6	8	1. Never
3.2	15	2. Less than 6 months
4.2	20	3. 6–11 months
10.3	50	4. 12–23 months
19.6	96	5. 2 and 3 years
16.3	79	6. 4 and 5 years
7.8	38	7. 6 and 7 years
8.4	41	8. 8 and 9 years
19.6	96	9. 10 years and over
9.0	44	10. Time unknown
—	13	11. Unknown whether irregular

I–34. SEX LIFE, NATURE OF ILLICIT

—	8	1. None
7.1	33	2. Professional prostitute
42.7	196	3. Occasional prostitute
3.1	14	4. One-man prostitute
22.4	103	5. Promiscuous — unattached
6.8	31	6. Adulteress — promiscuous
6.8	31	7. Adulteress — with one
8.7	40	8. Unconventional
2.4	11	9. Doubtful
0	0	10. Pervert
—	33	11. Unknown

1-35. Kind of School Attended

%	No.	
4.5	22	1. None
56.7	276	2. Public in United States
8.6	42	3. Parochial in United States
.4	2	4. Private in United States
2.8	13	5. Orphanage in United States
16.4	80	6. Public and parochial in United States
2.0	10	7. Public and private in United States
8.2	40	8. Schools in foreign countries
.4	2	9. Schools in foreign countries and in United States
—	13	10. Unknown

1-36a. Illiteracy

93.5	460	1. Literate
6.5	32	2. Illiterate
—	8	3. Unknown

1-36b. Age Started School

5.1	18	4. 4 years
29.5	104	5. 5 years
27.7	98	6. 6 years
25.0	88	7. 7 years
7.1	25	8. 8 years
5.6	20	9. 9 years and over
—	22	10. Never attended school
—	125	11. Unknown

1-37. Number of Years in School

—	155	1. Unknown
—	22	2. No schooling
6.8	22	3. 3 years or less
4.0	13	4. 4 years
4.0	13	5. 5 years
7.1	23	6. 6 years
15.8	51	7. 7 years
22.3	72	8. 8 years
21.7	70	9. 9 years
18.3	59	10. 10 years and over

1–38. Reason Left School

%	No.	
—	22	1. Did not attend school
51.7	208	2. Economic reasons
8.2	33	3. Inability to do school work
3.7	15	4. Physical disability
9.5	38	5. Dissatisfaction or lack of interest
5.7	23	6. Graduated
1.8	7	7. Expelled
5.2	21	8. Committed to correctional or other institution
14.2	57	9. Other
—	76	10. Unknown

1–39. Grade Attained in School

—	22	1. Never attended school
33.3	135	2. 5th grade or lower
16.8	68	3. 6th grade
17.5	71	4. 7th grade
21.7	88	5. 8th and 9th grades
2.5	10	6. Special or ungraded class
7.2	29	7. Began but did not complete high school
1.0	4	8. Graduated from high school
0	0	9. Entered college
—	73	10. Unknown

1–40. Age at Leaving School

—	22	1. No schooling
3.2	14	2. 10 years and under
1.6	7	3. 11 years
4.5	20	4. 12 years
17.0	75	5. 13 years
40.4	178	6. 14 years
20.0	88	7. 15 years
9.0	40	8. 16 years
4.3	19	9. 17 years
—	37	10. Unknown

1-41. Retardation in School

%	No.	
—	22	1. No schooling
10.7	39	2. Retarded one year
23.8	87	3. Retarded two years
24.7	90	4. Retarded three years
29.9	109	5. Retarded four or more years
.5	2	6. Special or ungraded class
0	0	7. Advanced one year
0	0	8. Advanced two or more years
10.4	38	9. Normal grade for age
—	113	10. Unknown

1-42a. Scholarship

—	22	1. No schooling
11.8	29	2. Good
27.7	68	3. Fair
60.5	149	4. Poor
—	232	5. Unknown

1-42b. Attendance in School

—	22	6. No schooling
40.7	108	7. Regular
59.3	158	8. Irregular
—	212	9. Unknown

1-42c. Vocational School of Any Kind Prior to Commitment

94.3	462	10. No
5.7	28	11. Yes
—	10	12. Unknown

1-43a. Industrial History

2.9	13	1. Success
38.8	175	2. Partial success
58.3	263	3. Failure
—	15	4. Inapplicable (in institution mostly; unable to work as ill; no need to work)
—	34	5. Unknown

1–43b. Economic Responsibility

%	No.	
—	79	6. Unknown
41.1	173	7. Met in legitimate employment
10.9	46	8. Met in illegitimate employment
9.5	40	9. Not met
6.2	26	10. Self-support not necessary
.5	2	11. Chronic illness, or for other good reasons dependent
31.8	134	12. Met — means unknown

1–44. Age Began Work

—	15	1. Not employed up to commitment
14.2	66	2. Under 14 years
37.4	174	3. At 14 years
33.6	156	4. 15–16 years
8.4	39	5. 17–18 years
4.3	20	6. 19–20 years
2.1	10	7. 21 years and over
—	20	8. Unknown

1–45. First Occupation

—	28	1. Unknown or never worked
22.5	106	2. Domestic service
53.4	252	3. Factory work
1.5	7	4. Home work
4.4	21	5. Restaurant and hotel work
4.9	23	6. Work in stores
2.9	14	7. Clerical work
8.9	42	8. Day work
1.5	7	9. Other

1–46. Weekly Wage at First Occupation

—	15	1. Never worked
39.7	112	2. $5 and under
51.0	144	3. $6–$10
8.9	25	4. $11–$15
.4	1	5. $16–$20
0	0	6. $21–$25
0	0	7. $26 and over
—	203	8. Unknown

1-47. Time Held First Occupation

%	No.	
—	15	1. Never worked
19.0	54	2. Less than 1 month
31.3	88	3. 1–3 months
8.0	23	4. 4–6 months
8.8	25	5. 7–9 months
0	0	6. 10–11 months
23.5	67	7. 1–2 years
6.6	19	8. 3–4 years
2.8	8	9. 5 years and over
—	201	10. Unknown

1-48. Occupation at First Conviction

%	No.	
—	118	1. Unknown or never worked
6.0	23	2. Domestic service
14.7	56	3. Factory work
1.3	5	4. Home work
1.3	5	5. Restaurant and hotel work
.8	3	6. Work in stores
1.3	5	7. Clerical work
4.7	18	8. Day work
1.8	7	9. Other
13.9	53	10. Illegitimate occupation
10.0	38	11. Own housework
44.2	169	12. Idle

1-49. Usual Occupation

%	No.	
—	26	1. Unknown or never worked
13.4	62	2. Domestic service
47.7	221	3. Factory work
1.5	7	4. Home work
6.5	30	5. Restaurant and hotel work
1.7	8	6. Work in stores
1.7	8	7. Clerical work
7.0	32	8. Day work
2.1	10	9. Other
8.4	39	10. Illegitimate occupation
10.0	46	11. Own housework
—	11	12. Idle

1–50. Longest Period Employed on Any Paid Job

%	No.	
—	11	1. Never worked
15.2	42	2. Less than 3 months
13.7	38	3. 3–6 months
14.1	39	4. 6–9 months
6.9	19	5. 9–12 months
18.1	50	6. 12–24 months
14.4	40	7. 2–3 years
8.3	23	8. 3–4 years
3.2	9	9. 4–5 years
6.1	17	10. 5 years and over
—	212	11. Unknown

1–51. Average Weekly Wage Prior to Commitment

—	11	1. Never worked
1.9	6	2. Less than $5
44.9	142	3. $5–$10
40.8	129	4. $10–$15
11.1	35	5. $15–$20
1.0	3	6. $20–$25
.3	1	7. $25–$30
0	0	8. $30–$35
0	0	9. $35 and over
—	173	10. Unknown

1–52. Highest Legitimate Weekly Earnings Prior to Commitment

—	11	1. Never worked
.9	3	2. Less than $5
17.3	59	3. $5–$10
39.4	134	4. $10–$15
26.8	91	5. $15–$20
8.8	30	6. $20–$25
5.0	17	7. $25–$30
0	0	8. $30–$35
1.8	6	9. $35 and over
—	149	10. Unknown

1–53. Usual Reason for Leaving Work

%	No.	
—	16	1. Inapplicable (as never worked)
5.1	18	2. Steady worker, seldom changes
75.2	264	3. Fault of worker
5.7	20	4. Not fault of worker
3.7	13	5. To better self
10.3	36	6. Other
—	133	7. Unknown

1–54. Last Legitimate Occupation Before Commitment

%	No.	
—	40	1. Unknown or never worked
19.4	85	2. Domestic service
44.4	194	3. Factory work
1.6	7	4. Home work
14.2	62	5. Restaurant and hotel work
3.4	15	6. Work in store
2.1	9	7. Clerical work
10.3	45	8. Day work
4.6	20	9. Other
—	20	11. Own housework
—	3	12. Idle

1–55a. Weekly Wage in Last Legitimate Occupation

%	No.	
—	15	1. Never worked
3.8	11	2. $5 and under
44.8	130	3. $6–$10
35.8	104	4. $10–$15
12.8	37	5. $15–$20
2.8	8	6. $20–$25
0	0	7. $25 and over
—	195	8. Unknown

1–55b. Employed at Time of Arrest for which Sent to Reformatory

%	No.	
—	85	9. Unknown
71.6	297	10. Idle
23.6	98	11. Working
4.8	20	12. Own housework

1-56. TIME SINCE LAST EMPLOYED PRIOR TO COMMITMENT

%	No.	
—	15	1. Never worked
—	98	2. To arrest
49.0	148	3. Less than 3 months
16.2	49	4. 3–5 months
10.6	32	5. 6–8 months
4.3	13	6. 9–11 months
7.3	22	7. 12–23 months
6.3	19	8. 2 and 3 years
6.3	19	9. Over 3 years
—	85	10. Unknown

1-57a. STEADINESS OF EMPLOYMENT

—	15	1. Never worked
7.5	34	2. Regular
32.8	149	3. Fairly regular
59.7	271	4. Irregular
—	31	5. Unknown

1-57b. WORK HABITS

—	15	6. Never worked
16.2	60	7. Good
55.4	205	8. Fair
28.4	105	9. Poor
—	115	10. Unknown

1-58. SAVINGS

—	4	1. Inapplicable
14.1	42	2. Yes
85.9	256	3. No
—	198	4. Unknown

1-59a. INSURANCE — HOW PAID

25.2	27	1. No insurance
21.5	23	2. Paid by self
47.7	51	3. Paid by relatives or others
5.6	6	4. Insurance — unknown how paid
—	393	5. Unknown

1–59b. DISPOSITION OF EARNINGS

%	No.	
72.2	260	6. Self, or husband and children, has no other dependents
4.2	15	7. Self, has dependents
23.6	85	8. Contributes to support of others
—	21	9. No earnings
—	119	10. Unknown

1–60a. PRINCIPAL COMPONENT OF MISCONDUCT

	0	1. Inapplicable
—	0	1. Inapplicable
—	5	2. No delinquency
66.4	328	3. Based on official record
33.6	166	4. On unofficial only
—	1	5. Unknown

1–60b. DELINQUENCY

1.0	5	6. Non-delinquent
99.0	491	7. Delinquent
—	3	8. Unknown
—	1	10. Inapplicable

1–61. AGE AT FIRST ARREST

7.9	39	1. Under 15 years
11.9	59	2. 15–16 years
22.5	111	3. 17–18 years
16.0	79	4. 19–20 years
18.2	90	5. 21–24 years
8.5	42	6. 25–28 years
15.0	74	7. 29 years and over
—	6	8. Unknown

1–62. AGE AT FIRST COMMITMENT TO PENO-CORRECTIONAL INSTITUTION

4.9	24	1. Under 15 years
7.3	36	2. 15–16 years
21.5	106	3. 17–18 years
16.9	83	4. 19–20 years
18.9	93	5. 21–24 years
11.0	54	6. 25–28 years
19.5	96	7. 29 years and over
—	8	8. Unknown

1–63. Frequency of Arrests

%	No.	
—	164	1. Never arrested
—	109	2. Incalculable (as only one arrest)
17.8	39	3. 1 arrest in less than 3 months
20.6	45	4. 3–5 months
19.6	43	5. 6–8 months
12.3	27	6. 9–11 months
4.1	9	7. 12–14 months
8.2	18	8. 15–17 months
3.7	8	9. 18–20 months
1.8	4	10. 21–23 months
11.9	26	11. 24 months and over
—	8	12. Unknown

1–64. Predominant Offence

%	No.	
—	5	1. None
56.1	275	2. Sex
4.7	23	3. Stealing
3.9	19	4. Alcoholism
.8	4	5. Drug addiction
.8	4	6. Avoidance of family responsibility
9.2	45	7. Sex and stealing
15.7	77	8. Sex and alcoholism
.8	4	9. Sex and drug addiction
3.9	19	10. Sex and two or three others
4.1	20	11. Other (stubborn child)
—	5	12. Unknown or inapplicable

1–65. Time Served in Penal Institutions (Peno-Correctional)

%	No.	
—	340	1. None
—	3	2. Unknown if any
26.5	39	3. Less than 6 months
18.4	27	4. 6–12 months
12.2	18	5. 12–18 months
9.5	14	6. 18–24 months
13.0	19	7. 24–30 months
4.7	7	8. 30–36 months
7.5	11	9. 36–48 months
8.2	12	10. 48 months and over
—	10	11. Time unknown

1–66. Institutional Experiences — Total Number of Penal and Non-Penal

%	No.	
22.6	112	1. One
10.1	50	2. Two
6.5	32	3. Three
4.3	21	4. Four
3.2	16	5. Five
1.6	8	6. Six
.8	4	7. Seven
4.3	21	8. Eight and over
1.4	7	9. Number unknown
45.2	224	10. None
—	5	11. Unknown if any

1–67. Total Time in Penal and Non-Penal Institutions

—	224	1. No institutional experience
—	5	2. Unknown if any institutional experience
23.5	61	3. Less than 6 months
17.8	46	4. 6–12 months
15.1	39	5. 12–18 months
5.4	14	6. 18–24 months
7.7	20	7. 24–30 months
3.1	8	8. 30–36 months
7.7	20	9. 36–48 months
19.7	51	10. 48 months and over
—	12	11. Time unknown

1–68. Penal Experiences, Number of (including correctional)

68.4	340	1. None
—	3	2. Unknown if any
14.5	72	3. One
6.8	34	4. Two
3.8	19	5. Three, four
2.6	13	6. Five, six
0.8	4	7. Seven, eight
0.8	4	8. Nine, ten
0.6	3	9. Eleven and more
1.7	8	10. Number unknown

1–69. FOSTER-HOMES, TIME SPENT IN

%	No.	
70.9	346	1. No foster-home experience
—	12	2. Unknown if any foster-home experience
3.1	15	3. Less than 6 months
1.2	6	4. 6–12 months
2.7	13	5. 12–18 months
1.0	5	6. 18–24 months
1.4	7	7. 24–30 months
0	0	8. 30–36 months
1.8	9	9. 36–48 months
15.2	74	10. 48 months and over
2.7	13	11. Time unknown

1–70. PROBATIONS, NUMBER OF, PRIOR TO COMMITMENT TO REFORMATORY

30.2	150	1. One
9.3	46	2. Two
4.2	21	3. Three
1.8	9	4. Four
1.0	5	5. Five
0.4	2	6. Six
1.0	5	7. Seven and over
33.0	164	8. No prior arrest; no probation
19.1	95	9. Arrest, but no probation
—	3	10. Unknown

1–H71. SUMMARY OF OFFENCES COMMITTED PRIOR TO OFFENCE FOR WHICH SENT TO REFORMATORY (1261)

1.4	18	Against person
23.9	301	Against chastity
1.1	14	Against family and children
20.1	253	Against public health, safety, and policy
35.1	443	Drink
.62	8	Drugs
14.4	181	Property rights
3.3	42	Violation of probation or default
.08	1	Escape

1–H72. SUMMARY OF DISPOSITIONS OF OFFENCES (1261)

%	No.	
28.4	352	Commitment
34.6	430	Probation
6.0	74	Fine
1.7	21	Commitment for non-payment of fine
11.9	148	File
.08	1	Restitution
4.0	50	Released by probation officer
.6	8	Nol-pros
.16	2	No bill
9.7	120	Not guilty or released
2.3	28	Other
—	20	Disposition unknown
.56	7	No disposition

CODE II. PERSONAL HISTORY OF OFFENDER BEFORE COMMITMENT TO REFORMATORY (continued), 2–1 to 2–7

2–1. CAUSE OF FIRST KNOWN ARREST

1.8	9	1. Offence against person
7.6	38	2. Offence against chastity — adultery, polygamy
5.8	29	3. Offence against chastity — common night walking or frequenting house of ill fame
5.2	26	4. Offence against chastity — fornication
1.0	5	5. Offence against chastity — keeping house of ill fame or sharing proceeds of prostitution
18.0	90	6. Offence against chastity — lewd and lascivious person
20.2	101	7. Stubborn child (runaway, truancy, waywardness, breaking glass, unnatural act)
2.4	12	8. Against family and children
16.2	81	9. Against public health, safety, and policy (except drink and drugs)
9.0	45	10. Drink
.4	2	11. Drugs
12.4	62	12. Against property

2-2. NUMBER OF ARRESTS

%	No.	
20.1	100	1. One
15.7	78	2. Two
14.3	71	3. Three, four
7.6	38	4. Five, six
3.2	16	5. Seven, eight
.8	4	6. Nine, ten
1.4	7	7. Eleven, twelve
3.8	19	8. Over twelve
—	3	9. Unknown
33.1	164	10. None

2-3. NUMBER OF CONVICTIONS

36.6	122	1. One
22.5	75	2. Two
10.0	33	3. Three
6.9	23	4. Four
6.0	20	5. Five
3.3	11	6. Six
1.5	5	7. Seven
8.1	27	8. Eight and over
—	3	9. Unknown if arrested
5.1	17	10. None
—	164	11. No arrests

2-4. SUMMARY OF DISPOSITIONS (by type)
[multiple punch]

33.4	167	1. No prior arrests or unknown if arrested
45.6	152	2. Commitment
70.9	236	3. Probation
17.1	57	4. Fine
3.3	11	5. Commitment for non-payment of fine
23.7	79	6. File
0	0	7. Restitution
7.8	26	8. Released by probation officer
2.1	7	9. Nol-pros
.6	2	10. No bill
26.1	87	11. Not guilty or released
—	54	12. Disposition unknown or other

Note: Percentages are based on total of 333 women arrested, to indicate what proportion of those arrested experienced each type of disposition.

2–5. SUMMARY OF OFFENCES (by type)
[multiple punch]

%	No.	
6.6	22	1. Against person
52.0	173	2. Against chastity
3.6	12	3. Against family and children
30.0	100	4. Against public health, safety, and policy (except drink and drugs, but including violation of liquor laws)
29.7	99	5. Drink
1.5	5	6. Drugs
23.7	79	7. Against property rights
—	167	8. No arrests or unknown if arrested
27.0	90	9. Stubborn child, runaway, wayward, truancy.

Note: Percentages are based on 333 women arrested.

2–6. INSTITUTIONAL EXPERIENCES, NATURE OF (668)
[multiple punch]

%	No.	
45.2	224	1. None
—	5	2. Unknown if any
9.1	40	3. Juvenile correctional schools
13.2	58	4. Orphanages, convents, private schools
1.4	6	5. Schools for feeble-minded
29.2	128	6. House of Good Shepherd, maternity homes, etc.
8.7	38	7. Hospitals for mental diseases
5.4	24	8. Hospitals for chronic physical diseases
27.1	119	9. Adult penal institutions
5.9	26	10. Other (almshouses, town farms)

CODE II. FAMILY HISTORY OF OFFENDER BEFORE COMMITMENT TO REFORMATORY, 2–7 to 2–44, and 2–H62 to 2–H82

2–7. BIRTHPLACE OF FATHER

%	No.	
18.6	90	1. Massachusetts
21.2	103	2. Other places in United States
13.6	66	3. Canada — French
8.5	41	4. Canada — other
6.8	33	5. Great Britain
12.6	61	6. Ireland
3.7	18	7. Italy
2.3	11	8. Portugal and Atlantic islands
5.2	25	9. Poland and Lithuania
3.0	15	10. Russia and Finland
4.5	22	11. Other
—	15	12. Unknown

2–8. BIRTHPLACE OF MOTHER

18.4	90	1. Massachusetts
23.1	113	2. Other places in United States
13.1	64	3. Canada — French
10.2	50	4. Canada — other
5.7	28	5. Great Britain
12.9	63	6. Ireland
3.5	17	7. Italy
2.2	11	8. Portugal and Atlantic islands
5.1	25	9. Poland and Lithuania
3.1	15	10. Russia and Finland
2.7	13	11. Other
—	11	12. Unknown

2–9. RELIGION OF PARENTS

%	No.	
54.5	253	1. Both Catholic
34.7	161	2. Both Protestant
2.2	10	3. Both Hebrew
—	12	4. Both unknown
8.4	39	5. Catholic — Protestant
0.2	1	6. Christian — Hebrew
—	10	7. One Catholic, other unknown
—	14	8. One Protestant, other unknown
—	0	9. One Hebrew, other unknown
—	0	10. Other

2–10a. TIME PARENTS IN UNITED STATES

%	No.	
51.1	243	1. Life
.8	4	2. Five years or less
2.1	10	3. Six through ten years
2.7	13	4. Eleven through fifteen years
33.0	157	5. Sixteen years and over
10.3	49	6. Never
—	24	7. Unknown

2–10b. CITIZENSHIP OF FATHER

%	No.	
—	193	8. Citizen by birth
37.4	67	9. Naturalized
4.5	8	10. First papers
58.1	104	11. Alien
—	128	12. Unknown

2–11. EDUCATION OF PARENTS

%	No.	
—	39	1. Unknown
20.2	93	2. Both illiterate or known parent illiterate
9.1	42	3. One reads or writes, other unknown
33.4	154	4. Both read and write
10.6	49	5. One attended common school
7.4	34	6. Both attended common school
3.9	18	7. One attended high school
.4	2	8. Both attended high school
.4	2	9. One attended college
0	0	10. Both attended college
14.6	67	11. One illiterate, one reads and writes

2–12. Usual Occupation of Father

%	No.	
—	28	1. Unknown
25.6	121	2. Skilled trade (plumber, cabinet-maker, machinist, electrician, mechanic, carpenter, bricklayer, stone-cutter, painter, tin-smith, mason, ironworker, tailor, barber, cobbler, baker, chef, cook)
1.5	7	3. Public service (policeman, fireman, postman, motorman, conductor)
3.4	16	4. Small shopkeeper or contractor
19.9	94	5. Factory worker
27.3	129	6. Day labourer (rough work as longshoreman, fisherman, ditch-digger, teamster)
1.1	5	7. Profession
1.7	8	8. Clerical occupation (white-collar worker in business, sales-man, insurance broker, foreman)
1.3	6	9. Pedlar
10.0	47	10. Farmer
7.0	33	11. Porter, waiter, janitor, watchman, etc.
1.2	6	12. Other

2–13. Usual Occupation of Mother

—	35	1. Unknown
44.3	206	2. Housewife
19.6	91	3. Work in factory
18.5	86	4. Domestic work
3.9	18	5. Farm work
.4	2	6. Unspecified
6.9	32	7. Home work (except running lodging-house or store)
1.1	5	8. Runs lodging-house
.4	2	9. Runs store
4.9	23	10. Other

2–14a. Industrial Stability of Father

56.7	216	1. Regular
18.4	70	2. Fairly regular
24.9	95	3. Irregular
—	119	4. Unknown

2–14b. Industrial Stability of Mother

%	No.	
—	194	5. No Work
54.1	106	6. Regular
21.9	43	7. Fairly regular
24.0	47	8. Irregular
—	110	9. Unknown

2–15. Broken Homes — Reasons for All Breaks in Childhood or Adolescence [multiple punch]

%	No.	
38.2	183	1. No break of this kind in childhood or adolescence
—	21	2. Unknown
19.2	92	3. Death of mother in childhood
6.9	33	4. Death of mother in adolescence
18.2	87	5. Death of father in childhood
9.8	47	6. Death of father in adolescence
20.3	97	7. Separation or desertion or divorce of parents in childhood
2.3	11	8. Separation or desertion or divorce of parents in adolescence
10.0	48	9. Remarriage of mother in childhood
2.7	13	10. Remarriage of mother in adolescence
7.1	34	11. Remarriage of father in childhood
1.3	6	12. Remarriage of father in adolescence

Note: Percentages are on basis of 479 (500—21).

2–16. Age of Offender at First Break in Home

%	No.	
—	179	1. No break
47.6	141	2. Under 7 years
16.2	48	3. 7–10 years
17.2	51	4. 11–14 years
12.9	38	5. 15–18 years
5.4	16	6. 19–22 years
.7	2	7. 23 years and over
—	25	8. Unknown

2–17a. Step- and Foster-parents

%	No.	
76.7	379	1. Own parents only
15.6	77	2. Step-parent
7.7	38	3. Foster-parents
—	6	4. Unknown

2–17b. SIBLINGS — NUMBER OF OFFENDERS HAVING STEP- OR HALF-SIBLINGS

%	No.	
3.1	15	5. No sibs
75.4	368	6. Own sibs only
16.0	78	7. Own and half-sibs
2.7	13	8. Own and step-sibs
1.8	9	9. Own, step-, and half-sibs
.2	1	10. Step-sibs only
.8	4	11. Half-sibs only
—	12	12. Unknown

2–18. SIBLINGS — NUMBER OF IN FAMILY

3.1	15	1. Only child
4.7	23	2. Two sibs
10.5	51	3. Three sibs
9.7	47	4. Four sibs
11.5	56	5. Five sibs
10.1	49	6. Six sibs
11.9	58	7. Seven sibs
8.6	42	8. Eight sibs
9.3	45	9. Nine sibs
20.6	100	10. Ten or more sibs
—	14	11. Unknown or inapplicable

2–19. SIBLINGS — RANK OF OFFENDER AMONG

3.2	15	1. Only child
22.7	108	2. First
18.9	90	3. Second
20.4	97	4. Third
11.9	57	5. Fourth
8.6	41	6. Fifth
6.1	29	7. Sixth
4.4	21	8. Seventh
3.8	18	9. Eighth or over
—	24	10. Unknown

2–20a. Children — Number Living at Time of Commitment
(offender's children)

%	No.	
21.9	109	1. One
10.5	52	2. Two
5.8	29	3. Three
3.0	15	4. Four
4.4	22	5. Five or more
—	3	6. Unknown
54.4	270	7. None

2–20b. Legitimacy of Offender's Children

—	247	8. No children
29.3	73	9. Legitimate children only
22.5	56	10. Legitimate and illegitimate children
48.2	120	11. Illegitimate children only
—	4	12. Unknown

2–21. Mental Disease or Defect in Family

41.4	137	1. None noted
10.9	36	2. Mental disease in immediate family
17.8	59	3. Mental defect in immediate family
3.6	12	4. Mental disease and mental defect in immediate family
9.1	30	5. Mental disease in blood relatives (not in immediate family)
.6	2	6. Mental defect in blood relatives (not in immediate family)
1.8	6	7. Mental disease and mental defect in relatives (not in immediate family)
—	169	8. Unknown
14.8	49	9. No known mental disease, but "peculiarity" in immediate family

2–22. BROKEN OR POORLY SUPERVISED HOMES

%	No.	
9.8	46	1. None
37.6	177	2. Broken by death
20.8	98	3. Broken by sporadic or permanent desertion or separation or by divorce
4.0	19	4. Broken by prolonged absence of one or both parents because of illness or imprisonment
5.1	24	5. Poor supervision as evidenced by delinquency of one or both parents
1.5	7	6. Poor supervision as evidenced by incompatibility of parents
7.6	36	7. Poor supervision as evidenced by poor discipline by both parents
8.5	40	8. Poor supervision as evidenced by fact that mother works out and no substitute in home
4.0	19	9. Poor supervision as evidenced by fact that child welfare agencies had to intervene
—	29	10. Unknown
1.1	5	11. Poor supervision as evidenced by fact that father is intemperate, parents constantly quarrelling

2–23a. DELINQUENCY IN FAMILY

%	No.	
45.5	194	1. Court record in immediate family
31.0	132	2. No court record in immediate family, but unofficial delinquency
4.2	18	3. No official or unofficial delinquency in immediate family, but among relatives or foster-families
19.3	82	4. No delinquency in immediate family or among relatives
—	74	5. Unknown

2–23b. CONJUGAL RELATIONS OF PARENTS

%	No.	
48.4	192	7. Good
24.2	96	8. Fair
27.4	109	9. Poor
—	103	10. Unknown

2–24a. Nativity of Parents Related to Nativity of Offender

%	No.	
23.7	115	1. All foreign
31.3	152	2. All native
24.9	121	3. Parents same foreign; offender native
1.9	9	4. Parents mixed foreign; offender native
17.8	86	5. One parent native; one foreign; offender native
.4	2	6. One parent native; one foreign; offender foreign
—	15	7. Unknown

2–24b. Language Spoken at Home

67.3	317	8. English only
17.8	84	9. Other language only
14.9	70	10. English and other
—	29	11. Unknown

2–25. Neighbourhood Type in Childhood

—	4	1. Inapplicable (in institutions mostly)
20.4	98	2. Urban, partly residential
13.6	65	3. Urban, residential
25.1	120	4. Urban, unspecified
3.8	18	5. Suburban
34.0	163	6. Rural, or small town
3.1	15	7. Varied
—	17	8. Unknown

2–26. Neighbourhood Type in Adolescence

—	10	1. Inapplicable (in institutions mostly)
26.0	122	2. Urban, partly residential
12.8	60	3. Urban, residential
34.0	160	4. Urban, unspecified
5.1	24	5. Suburban
18.3	86	6. Rural, or small town
3.8	18	7. Varied
—	20	8. Unknown

2-27. Neighbourhood Type Within Year of Commitment

%	No.	
—	7	1. Inapplicable (in institutions mostly)
33.4	162	2. Urban, partly residential
13.0	63	3. Urban, residential
41.6	202	4. Urban, unspecified
2.7	13	5. Suburban
7.4	36	6. Rural, or small town
1.9	9	7. Varied
—	8	8. Unknown

2-28a. Home, Physical, During Offender's Childhood

24.0	88	1. Good
31.6	116	2. Fair
43.3	159	3. Poor
1.1	4	4. Varied
—	133	5. Unknown

2-28b. Home, Physical, During Offender's Adolescence

24.1	81	6. Good
31.2	105	7. Fair
42.9	144	8. Poor
1.8	6	9. Varied
—	164	10. Unknown

2-29a. Home, Physical, Within Year of Commitment

11.1	44	1. Good
21.9	87	2. Fair
65.7	261	3. Poor
1.3	5	4. Varied
—	103	5. Unknown

2-29b. Neighbourhood Influences in Childhood

17.6	62	6. Good
49.7	175	7. Fair
32.1	113	8. Poor
0.6	2	9. Varied
—	148	10. Unknown

2–30a. Neighbourhood Influences in Adolescence

%	No.	
14·7	50	1. Good
41.1	140	2. Fair
41.9	143	3. Poor
2.3	8	4. Varied
—	159	5. Unknown

2–30b. Neighbourhood Influences Within Year of Commitment

5.9	25	6. Good
23.2	99	7. Fair
69.3	296	8. Poor
1.6	7	9. Varied
—	73	10. Unknown

2–31. Household in Childhood

68.7	334	1. Lived with both parents and sibs, with or without relatives
12.6	61	2. With one parent, and sibs (if any)
9.1	44	3. With one parent and one step-parent
0	0	4. With two step-parents or one step-parent and no own parent in home
4.5	22	5. With relatives
3.5	17	6. With foster-parents
1.2	6	7. Alone or in institution
0.4	2	10. Various (shifting about)
—	14	11. Unknown

2–32. Household Stability Prior to Commitment

20.2	97	1. One change
24.5	118	2. Two
8.3	40	3. Three
2.9	14	4. Four
1.0	5	5. Five
.6	3	6. Six
1.0	5	7. More than six
14.5	70	8. No change
—	18	9. Unknown
27.0	130	11. Several, but exact number unknown

2–33. Sleeping-Arrangements of Offender in Childhood

%	No.	
	423	1. Unknown
	17	2. Own room
	33	3. Shares room with one or two sisters
	15	4. Other normal arrangements
	8	5. Abnormal arrangements
	4	6. All in one room, but separate beds

Note: Percentages are not indicated, as "unknown" group is so large.

2–34a. Economic Condition of Parents in Offender's Childhood and Adolescence

8.7	42	1. Comfortable
78.0	376	2. Marginal
13.3	64	3. Dependent
—	18	4. Unknown

2–34b. Economic Condition of Offender Within Year Prior to Commitment

6.7	33	5. Comfortable
78.4	384	6. Marginal
14.9	73	7. Dependent
—	10	8. Unknown

2–34c. Moral Obligations of Offender to Family (within year of commitment)

12.6	56	9. Succeed
87.4	390	10. Fail
—	48	11. Unknown
—	6	12. Inapplicable (no family)

2-35. PARENTAL SUPERVISION IN CHILDHOOD

%	No.	
8.2	26	1. Both parents good
16.6	53	2. Both parents fair
64.3	205	3. Both parents poor
1.2	4	4. One parent good, one parent fair
1.2	4	5. One parent good, one parent poor
8.5	27	6. One parent fair, one parent poor
—	5	7. One parent good, one parent unknown
—	10	8. One parent fair, one parent unknown
—	50	9. One parent poor, one parent unknown
—	116	10. Both parents unknown

2-36a. MORAL STANDARDS OF HOME IN CHILDHOOD

%	No.	
20.9	91	1. Good
30.9	134	2. Fair
48.2	209	3. Poor
—	66	4. Unknown

2-36b. MORAL STANDARDS OF HOME IN ADOLESCENCE

%	No.	
20.5	89	5. Good
24.4	106	6. Fair
55.1	239	7. Poor
—	66	8. Unknown

2-36c. MORAL STANDARDS OF HOME WITHIN YEAR OF COMMITMENT

%	No.	
10.4	49	9. Good
14.9	70	10. Fair
74.7	352	11. Poor
—	29	12. Unknown

2-37. AGE OF OFFENDER AT FIRST SOCIAL SERVICE AGENCY CONTACT WITH FAMILY

%	No.	
—	110	1. No contact
—	23	2. Unknown if contact
18.4	65	3. 5 years of age or less
13.6	48	4. 6–10 years
21.8	77	5. 11–15 years
27.2	96	6. 16–20 years
7.1	25	7. 21–25 years
7.9	28	8. 26–30 years
4.0	14	9. 31 years and over
—	14	10. Age unknown

2-38. NUMBER OF SOCIAL SERVICE AGENCIES

18.6	87	1. One
18.6	87	2. Two
11.5	54	3. Three
7.0	33	4. Four
5.3	25	5. Five
4.5	21	6. Six
11.1	52	7. Seven or more
23.4	110	8. None
—	23	9. Unknown if any
—	8	10. Number unknown

2-39. TYPE OF SOCIAL SERVICES RENDERED (by 697 agencies)
[multiple punch]

—	110	1. Not known to any agencies
—	23	2. Unknown whether dealt with by agencies
18.7	130	3. Health, physical
7.5	52	4. Health, mental
28.1	196	5. Relief and family welfare agencies
35.6	248	6. Child or adolescent welfare
5.4	38	7. Correctional
4.7	33	8. Other

2-40. MARITAL STATUS OF OFFENDER AT TIME OF COMMITMENT

%	No.	
—	4	1. Unknown if married or single
48.7	242	2. Single
8.9	44	3. Living with husband
36.6	181	4. Separated
3.2	16	5. Divorced
2.4	12	6. Widowed
.2	1	7. Married, but status unknown

2-41a. MARITAL — NUMBER OF MARRIAGES OF OFFENDER PRIOR TO COMMITMENT

84.6	215	1. One
12.2	31	2. Two
3.2	8	3. Three
0	0	4. Four or more
—	242	5. None
—	4	6. Unknown whether married

2-41b. MARITAL HISTORY JUDGMENT (on last marriage prior to commitment)

—	4	7. Unknown if married
—	242	8. Single
0	0	9. Good
15.7	38	10. Fair
84.3	206	11. Poor
—	10	12. Unknown

2-42. AGE OF OFFENDER AT FIRST MARRIAGE

—	246	1. Single or unknown if married
12.3	31	2. Under 16 years
37.9	96	3. 16–18 years
26.5	67	4. 19–21 years
11.9	30	5. 22–24 years
4.7	12	6. 25–27 years
4.3	11	7. 28–30 years
.8	2	8. 31–33 years
1.2	3	9. 34–36 years
.4	1	10. 37 years and over
—	1	11. Age unknown

2-43a. CONJUGAL RELATIONS ON LAST MARRIAGE

%	No.	
—	4	1. Unknown if married
—	242	2. Single
7.8	19	3. Good
11.5	28	4. Fair
80.7	197	5. Poor
—	10	6. Unknown

2-43b. ATTITUDE OF OFFENDER TO MARITAL RESPONSIBILITY ON LAST MARRIAGE

—	242	7. Single
—	4	8. Unknown if married
15.1	33	9. Assumes
84.9	186	10. Neglects
—	35	11. Unknown

2-44a. COMPETENCE AS HOMEMAKER

—	246	1. Single, or unknown if married
6.8	9	2. Good
45.5	60	3. Fair
47.7	63	4. Poor
—	122	5. Unknown

2-44b. ATTITUDE TO CHILDREN

—	270	6. No children
14.2	22	7. Good
36.1	56	8. Fair
49.7	77	9. Poor
—	70	10. Attitude unknown
—	5	11. Unknown if children

CODE II. REFORMATORY HISTORY, 2–45 to 2–61b, 2–H82
through 2–H90

2–45. TERM OF SENTENCE

%	No.	
0	0	1. Indeterminate
8.2	41	2. One-year indeterminate
53.6	268	3. Two-year indeterminate
2.4	12	4. Minority sentence
1.0	5	5. Four-year indeterminate
34.0	170	6. Five-year indeterminate
.2	1	7. Determinate, for less than three years
.2	1	8. Determinate, for three, four, or five years
.4	2	9. Determinate, for seven, eight, nine, or ten years

2–46a. RETURNS TO REFORMATORY (of those paroled)

86.5	326	1. Not returned
11.1	42	2. Returned once
1.9	7	3. Returned twice
0.5	2	4. Returned three times
0	0	5. Returned four times

2–46b. NUMBER OF PREVIOUS SENTENCES TO REFORMATORY

92.0	460	6. None
7.0	35	7. One
.4	2	8. Two
.6	3	9. Three
0	0	10. Four or more

2–47. PRIOR TIME IN REFORMATORY

—	460	1. None
7.5	3	2. Less than 6 months
32.5	13	3. 6–12 months
12.5	5	4. 12–18 months
10.0	4	5. 18–24 months
27.5	11	6. 24–30 months
2.5	1	7. 30–36 months
7.5	3	8. 3 years and over

2–48. Months to First Parole

%	No.	
1.6	6	1. 4 months or less
3.6	14	2. 5–8 months
31.1	120	3. 9–12 months
23.1	89	4. 13–16 months
19.4	75	5. 17–20 months
15.3	59	6. 21–24 months
5.9	23	7. 25 months and over
—	114	8. No parole

2–49. Total Time in Reformatory on Present Sentence

5.0	25	1. Less than 3 months
1.6	8	2. 3–6 months
3.2	16	3. 6–9 months
14.0	70	4. 9–12 months
18.8	94	5. 12–15 months
13.4	67	6. 15–18 months
10.0	50	7. 18–21 months
10.6	53	8. 21–24 months
16.0	80	9. 24–30 months
1.8	9	10. 30–36 months
5.6	28	11. 36 months and over

2–50a. Venereal Disease on Admission to Reformatory

21.5	103	1. None
6.9	33	2. Syphilis
45.4	218	3. Gonorrhœa
25.4	122	4. Syphilis and gonorrhœa
.8	4	5. Probably
—	20	6. Unknown

2–50b. General Condition on Admission

44.9	205	7. Good
43.1	197	8. Fair
12.0	55	9. Poor
—	43	10. Unknown

2–51a. INTELLIGENCE

%	No.	
0	0	1. Supernormal — I.Q. 111 and **over**
21.8	103	2. Normal — I.Q. 91–110
28.0	132	3. Dull — I.Q. 81–90
16.1	76	4. Borderline — I.Q. 71–80
31.8	150	5. Feeble-minded — I.Q. 50–70
2.3	11	6. Imbecile — I.Q. below 50
—	28	7. Unknown

2–51b. PHYSICAL CONDITION ON DISCHARGE FROM REFORMATORY

45.4	177	8. Good on admission and remained good
43.3	169	9. Improved
9.5	37	10. Same
1.8	7	11. Worse
—	110	12. Not stated

2–52. MENTAL CONDITION ON ADMISSION TO REFORMATORY

2.0	10	1. Psychosis
6.4	32	2. Constitutional psychopathic inferiority
4.8	24	3. Psychopathic personality or traits
4.2	21	4. Epilepsy (or probably epileptic, or epileptic characteristics)
2.6	13	5. Alcoholism or delirium tremens
2.0	10	6. Drug addiction
2.4	12	7. Psychoneurosis, neurasthenia
.4	2	8. Congenital syphilis
2.4	12	9. Question of mental disease
14.8	74	10. Emotional instability
25.0	125	11. Neurotic traits
33.0	165	12. None noted

2–53. Number of Different Occupational Experiences at Reformatory

%	No.	
31.4	156	1. One
31.8	158	2. Two
18.1	90	3. Three
10.9	54	4. Four
4.2	21	5. Five
.6	3	6. Six
.2	1	7. Seven
—	3	8. Unknown or inapplicable (as ill)
2.8	14	10. None

2–54a. Kind of Worker in Reformatory

38.1	177	1. Good
54.6	254	2. Fair
7.3	34	3. Poor
—	35	4. Unknown or inapplicable (as ill)

2–54b. Conduct in Women's Reformatory up to First Parole

49.0	235	5. Good
31.9	153	6. Fair
19.1	92	7. Poor
—	20	8. Unknown or inapplicable (as ill)

2–54c. Staff Prognosis

403	9. None recorded
14	10. Good
13	11. Fair
70	12. Poor

Note: Percentages are not given, as the " none " group is so large.

2-55. NATURE OF MISCONDUCT IN REFORMATORY
[multiple punch]

%	No.	
49.0	235	1. None
—	20	2. Unknown or inapplicable (as ill)
2.9	14	3. Personal disorderliness
37.9	182	4. Lack of self-control
0	0	5. Other minor offences
2.9	14	6. Violence against person
2.5	12	7. Sex offences
7.5	36	8. Offences against property
34.2	164	9. Offences against authority
1.2	6	10. Other major offences
1.7	8	11. Vile language or notes

Note: Percentages are on basis of 480 (500—20).

2-56. DATES OF COMMITMENT TO REFORMATORY

%	No.	
1.4	7	1. 1914 or before
.8	4	2. 1915
5.4	27	3. 1916
11.2	56	4. 1917
12.4	62	5. 1918
18.2	91	6. 1919
14.6	73	7. 1920
16.0	80	8. 1921
16.2	81	9. 1922
3.8	19	10. 1923

2-57a. CHILD OR PREGNANCY ON ADMISSION TO REFORMATORY

%	No.	
6.4	32	1. Admitted with a child
8.8	44	2. Pregnant—child born in Reformatory, lived
2.6	13	3. Pregnant—child born in Reformatory, died; or pregnant, followed by miscarriage or curettage
82.2	411	4. Not accompanied by a child and not pregnant

2–57b. Transfer to Reformatory from Other Institution

%	No.	
78.6	393	6. Sentenced directly to Reformatory
16.8	84	7. Transferred from probation or parole
.8	4	8. Transferred from a jail or house of correction
1.0	5	9. Transferred from a reformatory or prison in another state
2.2	11	10. Transferred from Lancaster Industrial School
.6	3	11. Transferred from House of the Good Shepherd

2–58. Transfers from Reformatory to Other Institution

75.4	377	1. Not transferred
11.4	57	2. Temporary transfer to hospital for confinement or other illness
.4	2	3. Transferred by reason of illness and not returned
4.2	21	4. Indentured at Framingham Hospital or elsewhere
3.6	18	5. Transferred to another penal institution and not returned to Reformatory
.8	4	6. Transferred to a school for feeble-minded
2.4	12	7. Transferred to a hospital for mental diseases
1.8	9	8. Transferred to a penal institution, but returned to Reformatory

2–59a. Date of Expiration of Sentence

18.6	93	1. 1921
27.0	135	2. 1922
28.6	143	3. 1923
25.8	129	4. 1924

2–59b. Parole from Reformatory

75.4	377	6. Paroled
15.8	79	7. Not paroled; served entire sentence in Reformatory
4.6	23	8. Not paroled; transferred to other institution and remained there at least to expiration of Reformatory sentence
1.8	9	9. Not paroled, as died in Reformatory
0	0	10. Not paroled, as escaped from Reformatory
.6	3	11. Not paroled, as remained on indenture to expiration of sentence
1.8	9	12. Paroled, but from another institution to which transferred

2–60a. Emotional Stability as Manifested by Conduct or Diagnosis at Reformatory

%	No.	
49.6	248	1. Unstable
—	21	2. Unemotional
—	50	3. Very suggestible
—	181	4. Not stated

Note: Percentage is on basis of 500.

2–60b. Practical Judgment

31	5. Good
26	6. Fair
92	7. Poor
351	8. Not stated

Note: Percentages not worked out, as " not stated " group is so large.

2–60c. Training Desired Received at Reformatory

93	9. Yes
72	10. No
335	11. Not stated

Note: Percentages not worked out, as " not stated " group is so large.

2–61a. Months in Second Grade

81.8	400	1. Five
6.1	30	2. Six
1.0	5	3. Seven
4.5	22	4. More than seven, or returned to second grade
6.6	32	5. Less than five because transferred, died, paroled early, etc.
—	11	6. Not stated

2–61b. Later Attitude in Reformatory

35.2	144	7. No change
63.3	259	8. Improved
1.5	6	9. Worse
—	91	10. Not stated

CODE II. FAMILY HISTORY (continued), H62 to H82

2–H62. MARITAL HISTORY JUDGMENT (all marriages prior to commitment)

%	No.	
.7	2	Good
16.4	47	Fair
82.9	238	Poor
—	14	Unknown

Note: 301 marriages.

2–H63. MARITAL — LENGTH OF TIME MARRIAGE LASTED (all marriages prior to commitment)

19.5	56	Less than six months
11.9	34	6–12 months
4.2	12	12–18 months
3.1	9	18–24 months
8.0	23	2–3 years
6.3	18	3–4 years
7.3	21	4–5 years
3.1	9	5–6 years
4.5	13	6–7 years
11.5	33	7 years and over
15.3	44	Still living together
5.3	15	Off and on
—	14	Unknown

2–H64. MARRIAGE — FORCED (all marriages prior to commitment)

34.1	88	Forced
65.9	170	Not forced
—	43	Unknown if forced

2–H65. MANNER OF MEETING HUSBAND (all husbands prior to commitment)

31.2	58	Pick-up
29.0	54	Casual acquaintance
39.8	74	By proper introduction through parents, relatives, friends
—	115	Unknown

2–H66. TIME KNOWN HUSBAND BEFORE MARRIAGE
(all husbands prior to commitment)

%	No.	
13.6	29	Less than one month
14.0	30	1–2 months
8.4	18	3–4 months
8.9	19	5–6 months
2.3	5	7–8 months
.9	2	9–10 months
16.4	35	11–12 months
26.6	57	Over one year
8.9	19	Brief
—	87	Unknown

2–H67. CONJUGAL RELATIONS (on all marriages prior to commitment)

8.3	24	Good
10.0	29	Fair
81.7	236	Poor
—	12	Unknown

2–H68. ATTITUDE OF OFFENDER TO MARITAL RESPONSIBILITY
(on all marriages prior to commitment)

16.2	41	Assumes
83.8	212	Neglects
—	48	Unknown

2–H69. ATTITUDE OF HUSBAND TO MARITAL RESPONSIBILITY
(all husbands prior to commitment)

26.4	68	Assumes
73.6	190	Neglects
—	43	Unknown

2–H70. COMPETENCE AS HOMEMAKER (on all marriages prior to commitment)

8.0	12	Good
44.7	67	Fair
47.3	71	Poor
—	151	Unknown

2–H71. Household — With Whom Living (during all marriages prior to commitment)

%	No.	
48.2	134	Alone with husband
33.5	93	Husband and parents or in-laws
6.1	17	Husband and other relatives
10.1	28	Husband and boarders
2.1	6	Other
—	23	Unknown

2–H72. Relation to Family Economic Status (during all marriages prior to commitment)

20.9	56	Lower
71.6	192	Same
7.5	20	Better
—	33	Unknown

2–H73. Reason for Termination of Marriage Before Commitment to Reformatory (all marriages)

89.5	230	Desertion, separation, divorce
10.5	27	Death
—	44	Not broken

2–H74. Colour — Mixed Marriage (last marriage before commitment)

96.1	244	Same
3.9	10	Mixed
0	0	Unknown

Note: 254 women were married.

2–H75. BIRTHPLACE OF HUSBAND (last husband before commitment)

%	No.	
32.6	77	Massachusetts
34.7	82	Other places in United States
2.5	6	Canada — French
4.7	11	Canada — other
2.1	5	Great Britain
1.3	3	Ireland
.4	1	Germany
6.0	14	Italy
2.1	5	Portugal and Atlantic islands
5.1	12	Poland and Lithuania
2.1	5	Russia
.4	1	Finland
6.0	14	Other
—	18	Unknown

2–H76. CITIZENSHIP OF HUSBAND (last husband before commitment)

82.4	159	Citizen by birth
3.6	7	Citizen by naturalization
2.6	5	Has first papers
11.4	22	Alien
—	61	Unknown

2–H77. EDUCATION OF HUSBAND (last husband before commitment)

14.8	28	Illiterate
52.4	99	Reads and writes
23.3	44	Attended common school
9.0	17	Attended high school
.5	1	Attended college
—	65	Unknown

2–H78. INDUSTRIAL STABILITY OF HUSBAND (last husband before commitment)

%	No.	
34.7	67	Regular
16.6	32	Fairly regular
48.7	94	Irregular
—	61	Unknown

2–H79. Usual Occupation of Husband (last husband before commitment)

%	No.	
20.8	50	Trade (skilled)
5.0	12	Policeman, fireman, postman, motorman, conductor, sailor
.8	2	Baker, chef, cook
.4	1	Pedlar
1.2	3	Small shopkeeper
27.4	66	Factory hand
6.6	16	Teamster, truck-driver, chauffeur
24.1	58	Day labourer, longshoreman, fisherman
6.6	16	Porter, waiter, janitor, watchman, restaurant hand
.8	2	Profession
6.3	15	Clerk, salesman, insurance broker, bondsman
—	13	Unknown or other

2–H80. Husband Living or Dead at Time Offender Sent to Reformatory

93.2	218	Living
6.8	16	Dead
—	20	Unknown

2–H81. Delinquency of Husband (last husband before commitment)

41.5	97	Court record (exclusive of drink)
6.8	16	Court record for drink only
32.5	76	Unofficial delinquency
19.2	45	No delinquency
—	20	Unknown

2–H82. Weight — Improvement in at Reformatory

3.5	13	Same
12.6	47	Loss
83.9	312	Gain
—	128	Unknown

2-H83. REASONS CONTINUED FOR PAROLE

%	No.	
60.6	117	Health needs further attention
8.3	16	Further training (of emotions or personality)
16.5	32	Custodial type
3.1	6	Pending arrangement in community (as marriage or deportation)
8.3	16	Misbehaviour
1.6	3	Does not desire parole
1.6	3	Prefers to remain on indenture

2-H84. VOCATIONAL EXPERIENCES AT WOMEN'S REFORMATORY (1048)

42.0	203	General cleaning
14.3	69	Dining-room
21.5	104	Kitchen
23.4	113	Laundry
2.5	12	Clothes room
12.4	60	Nursery
2.9	14	Storeroom
14.5	70	Farm work
2.1	10	Office work
2.1	10	Receiving-room
8.7	42	Hospital work
4.3	21	Indenture
10.8	52	Sewing
11.2	54	Flag room
29.4	142	Shirt room
9.7	47	Stocking room
5.2	25	State use room

Note: Percentage is based on 483 (500—17), as 17 inmates had no vocational experience in the Reformatory.

2-H85. STAFF RECOMMENDATIONS

11	Regarding care in Women's Reformatory
45	Regarding care in other institution
68	Regarding parole supervision

Note: No percentages made, as the numbers are so small.

2–H86. Solitary Confinement at Women's Reformatory

%	No.	
68.8	344	No
31.2	156	Yes

2–H87. Solitary Confinement — Places Provided for at Reformatory

.7	2	Reception room
19.6	58	Solitary work-room
64.1	189	Own room
4.1	12	Punishment cell
11.5	34	Dungeon

Note: 295 confinements (of 156 offenders).

2–H88. Reasons for Solitary Confinement

58.3	172	Offence against authority
3.7	11	Offence against property
1.4	4	Offence against chastity
3.0	9	Offence against person
1.4	4	Lack of self-control
29.8	88	Personal disorderliness
2.4	7	Miscellaneous

Note: 295 confinements (of 156 offenders).

2–H89. Times Continued for Parole at Women's Reformatory

29.0	145	No continuance
42.0	210	One continuance
15.2	76	Two continuances
6.8	34	Three continuances
1.0	5	Four continuances
0.2	1	Five continuances
5.8	29	Not brought up for parole

2-H90. Capabilities of Offender on Entrance to Women's Reformatory

%	No.	
65.6	328	Cooking
6.2	31	General housework
36.8	184	Waitress
32.2	161	Chamber work
68.6	343	Laundry
40.8	204	Embroidery
37.6	188	Knitting
34.8	174	Crocheting
67.8	339	Sewing
16.4	82	Singing
11.8	59	Playing piano or other musical instrument
5.8	29	Other (pottery-making, tatting, basketry, millinery, drawing, designing, dressmaking, hairdressing, dancing, typing, tennis)

Note: Percentages are based on 500.

CODE III. PAROLE HISTORY (of 377 offenders on parole)

3-1. Theoretical Parole Period

%	No.	
4.2	16	1. One month or less
9.0	34	2. 1–3 months
12.2	46	3. 3–6 months
10.1	38	4. 6–9 months
8.0	30	5. 9–12 months
13.3	50	6. 12–18 months
3.4	13	7. 18–24 months
2.9	11	8. 24–30 months
3.7	14	9. 30–36 months
5.6	21	10. 36–42 months
17.0	64	11. 42–48 months
10.6	40	12. 48 months and over

3-2a. AGENT — PAROLE

%	No.	
44.2	165	1. Officer A
38.1	142	2. Officer B
7.2	27	3. Both
—	4	4. Unknown
3.2	12	5. Other (under supervision of parole or probation officer in other state or of member of Reformatory staff)
7.3	27	6. Out of state (no parole supervision)

3-2b. MOBILITY AND NATURE OF

14.7	42	8. In one city
41.1	117	9. City to city
44.2	126	10. No mobility
—	14	11. Unknown
—	78	12. Inapplicable (on parole less than 6 months)

3-3. NEIGHBOURHOOD TYPE — FIRST HOME ON PAROLE

25.6	91	2. Urban, partly residential
33.8	120	3. Urban, residential
5.4	19	4. Urban, unspecified
17.2	61	5. Suburban
18.0	64	6. Rural, or small town
—	22	8. Unknown

3-4. NEIGHBOURHOOD INFLUENCES OF FIRST HOME ON PAROLE

49.7	157	2. Good
27.8	88	3. Fair
22.5	71	4. Poor
—	61	6. Unknown

3-5a. HOME, PHYSICAL — FIRST HOME ON PAROLE

66.7	186	1. Good
19.3	54	2. Fair
14.0	39	3. Poor
—	98	6. Unknown

3–5b. MORAL STANDARDS OF FIRST HOME ON PAROLE

%	No.	
63.3	183	7. Good
18.0	52	8. Fair
18.7	54	9. Poor
—	88	12. Unknown

3–6. TO LIVE WITH WHOM ON PAROLE

%	No.	
36.3	136	1. One or both parents
.3	1	4. Two step-parents or one step-parent and no own parent
11.3	42	5. Relatives, without parents (usually sisters)
.3	1	6. Foster-parents
1.9	7	7. Alone
12.7	48	8. With husband or/and children
35.3	132	9. Employer
1.9	7	10. Other
—	3	11. Unknown

3–7. HOUSEHOLD STABILITY

%	No.	
34.6	114	1. No change
19.1	63	2. One
7.0	23	3. Two
5.2	17	4. Three
4.6	15	5. Four
1.2	4	6. Five
15.2	50	7. More than five
—	6	9. Unknown
13.1	43	10. Several, but exact number unknown
—	42	11. Too brief to judge (on parole for less than three months)

3–8a. CIVIL CONDITION AT BEGINNING OF PAROLE PERIOD

%	No.	
47.8	180	1. Single
14.3	54	2. Married, living with husband
28.9	109	3. Separated
6.1	23	4. Divorced
2.9	11	5. Widowed

3–8b. Marital Status at End of Parole Period

%	No.	
—	31	6. Unknown, or unknown if married or single
36.4	126	7. Single
26.3	91	8. Married, living with husband
27.5	95	9. Separated
6.6	23	10. Divorced, or marriage annulled
2.6	9	11. Widowed
.6	2	12. Married illegally

3–9. Legitimacy of Children Born during Parole

92.3	324	1. No children born during parole period
6.3	21	2. Legitimate children born during parole period (including illegitimate pregnancies, with marriage before birth of the child)
.8	3	3. Unmarried — having illegitimate children
.6	2	4. Married — having illegitimate children only
—	26	6. Unknown if children
.3	1	8. Children, but legitimacy unknown

3–10a. Industrial History Judgment

22.7	45	2. Success
54.6	108	3. Partial success
22.7	45	4. Failure
—	108	5. Inapplicable (no need to work, illness, or on parole less than three months)
—	71	6. Unknown

3–10b. Economic Responsibility

—	75	7. Unknown or inapplicable (on parole less than three months)
58.6	177	8. Met legitimately
6.0	18	9. Met illegitimately
4.6	14	10. Not met
29.8	90	11. Self-support not necessary, or cannot be judged, as parole of less than three months
1.0	3	12. Self-support not possible because of chronic illness or other legitimate reasons

3-11. First Job during Parole, Nature of Legitimate

%	No.	
—	95	1. Inapplicable (never worked, or did not go to work at once)
49.4	135	2. Domestic service
27.5	75	3. Factory work (including laundry work)
1.5	4	4. Home work
3.7	10	5. Restaurant and hotel work
1.5	4	6. Work in stores
2.6	7	7. Clerical work
7.6	21	8. Day work
6.2	17	9. Other
—	9	10. Unknown

3-12. By Whom First Parole Job Secured (on first parole only)

%	No.	
—	13	1. Unknown by whom secured
30.8	83	2. Offender
12.3	33	3. Offender's family
52.8	142	4. Parole agent
1.1	3	5. Reformatory official
.4	1	6. Friend
0	0	7. Minister
1.9	5	8. Former employer
.7	2	9. Other
—	95	10. Inapplicable (did not go to work immediately; or did own housework, or housework for relatives)

3-13. Time Held First Parole Job (on first parole only)

%	No.	
31.1	67	1. Less than 1 month
20.5	44	2. 1–2 months
12.6	27	3. 2–3 months
7.4	16	4. 3–4 months
5.6	12	5. 4–5 months
4.2	9	6. 5–6 months
12.6	27	7. 6–12 months
5.1	11	8. 12–24 months
0.9	2	9. 24 months and over
—	19	10. Unknown
—	95	11. Inapplicable (did not work; or did not work immediately after parole)
—	48	12. Throughout parole

3–14. Reason Left First Parole Job

%	No.	
—	48	1. Did not leave
42.7	84	2. Fault of worker
49.2	97	3. Not fault of worker
8.1	16	4. To better self
0	0	5. Other
—	37	6. Unknown
—	95	7. Inapplicable (did not work at all, or did not work immediately after release on parole)

3–15. Highest Wage Received during Parole

%	No.	
2.2	6	2. Less than $5
36.0	95	3. $5–$10
40.0	105	4. $10–$15
17.4	46	5. $15–$20
3.7	10	6. $20–$25
.7	2	7. $25–$30
0	0	8. $30–$35
0	0	9. $35 and over
—	51	10. Unknown
—	62	11. Inapplicable (did not work)

3–16a. Longest Period Employed during Parole

%	No.	
37.4	76	1. 3 months or less
23.7	48	2. 3–6 months
13.3	27	3. 6–9 months
8.9	18	4. 9–12 months
11.3	23	5. 1–2 years
5.4	11	6. 2–3 years and over
—	126	7. Inapplicable (did not work, or unknown, or on parole less than three months)
—	48	8. Held throughout

3–16b. Used Reformatory Occupation

%	No.	
10.5	37	9. Yes, and had been occupied in it prior to commitment
77.6	274	10. Did not use any occupation learned at Reformatory
—	24	11. Unknown or inapplicable
11.9	42	12. Used occupation learned at Reformatory and had not been previously employed therein

3–17. Usual Occupation

%	No.	
—	41	1. Unknown, or never worked
30.6	103	2. Domestic work
28.0	94	3. Factory work
.6	2	4. Home work
3.3	11	5. Restaurant and hotel work
1.2	4	6. Work in stores
2.1	7	7. Clerical work
4.8	16	8. Day work
5.6	19	9. Other
2.1	7	10. Illegitimate
21.7	73	11. Own housework

3–18a. Steadiness of Employment

%	No.	
37.5	83	1. Regular
38.5	85	2. Fairly regular
24.0	53	3. Irregular
—	48	4. Unknown
—	108	5. Inapplicable (never worked; or less than 3 months on parole, period too brief to judge)

3–18b. Work Habits

%	No.	
26.5	52	6. Good
52.6	103	7. Fair
20.9	41	8. Poor
—	73	9. Unknown
—	46	10. Inapplicable (as less than 3 months on parole, period too brief to judge; or worked once for less than 3 months)
—	62	11. Never worked

3–19a. Reason Left Work (Usual)

%	No.	
—	108	1. Inapplicable (never worked, or engaged in illegitimate occupation, or on parole less than 3 months)
19.1	39	2. Steady worker, seldom changes
43.1	88	3. Fault of worker
36.8	75	4. Not fault of worker
1.0	2	5. To better self
0	0	6. Other
—	65	7. Unknown

3-19b. MORAL OBLIGATION TO FAMILY

%	No.	
59.6	137	8. Succeed
40.4	93	9. Fail
—	97	10. Unknown
—	4	11. Inapplicable (no family)
—	46	12. Period too brief to judge (less than 3 months)

3-20a. LEISURE AND HABITS

6.7	16	1. Constructive
42.3	101	2. Negative
51.0	122	3. Harmful
—	138	4. Unknown (mostly because period too brief)

3-20b. CONSTRUCTIVE RECREATIONS AND INTERESTS

9.2	27	6. Yes
90.8	268	7. No
—	82	8. Unknown or inapplicable (period too brief to judge)

3-21a. DISPOSITION OF EARNINGS

—	1	1. Inapplicable (ill)
39.2	74	2. Self only. Has no dependents
49.2	93	3. Helps support husband and/or children
5.8	11	4. Contributes to support of others (i.e., outside of her immediate home)
—	55	5. No earnings
—	132	6. Unknown, or period too brief to judge (less than 3 months on parole)
5.8	11	7. Self only, but has dependents, or allows self to be supported by relatives

3-21b. ECONOMIC CONDITION

3.1	10	8. Comfortable
93.5	304	9. Marginal
3.4	11	10. Dependent
—	52	11. Unknown

3–22. Habits
[multiple punch]

%	No.	
	113	1. Sex
	35	2. Stealing
	51	3. Drink
	5	4. Drugs
	7	8. Other

46.5	117	9. None
—	124	10. Unknown
—	1	11. Inapplicable (ill)

Note: Percentage based on 252 (377—125).

3–23. Sex Life, Nature of Abnormal

52.9	127	1. None
.8	2	2. Professional prostitute
10.8	26	3. Occasional prostitute
.4	1	4. One-man prostitute
16.7	40	5. Promiscuous, unattached
2.2	5	6. Adulteress, promiscuous
.4	1	7. Adulteress, with one
3.3	8	8. Unconventional
12.5	30	9. Doubtful
0	0	10. Pervert
—	136	11. Unknown
—	1	12. Inapplicable (ill)

3–24a. Companionships

55.8	121	1. Harmless
44.2	96	2. Harmful
—	159	3. Unknown
—	1	4. Inapplicable (ill)

3–24b. Church Attendance

40.3	48	6. Regular
58.0	69	7. Irregular
1.7	2	8. None
—	257	9. Unknown
—	1	10. Inapplicable (ill)

3-25a. Revocation

%	No.	
79.3	299	1. Not revoked
20.7	78	2. Revoked

3-25b. Principal Component of Misconduct

%	No.	
14.3	54	4. Unknown, even though in Massachusetts
3.4	13	5. Disappeared and conduct entirely unknown
.3	1	6. Inapplicable (as invalid)
30.5	115	7. No delinquency
15.6	59	8. Based on official record of arrests
21.8	82	9. Based on unofficial misconduct, no arrests
14.1	53	10. Unknown, out of state

3-26. Time to First Contact with Case by Agent

%	No.	
46.9	175	1. Less than 1 month
18.5	69	2. 1-2 months
13.9	52	3. 2-4 months
2.1	8	4. 4-6 months
0.8	3	5. 6-8 months
0.8	3	6. 8-10 months
0.3	1	7. 10-12 months
1.6	6	8. Year or more
—	4	9. Unknown
15.1	56	11. Never

3-27. Theoretical and Actual Parole Period, Time Difference Between

%	No.	
53.6	202	1. No difference
5.0	19	2. Briefer by less than 1 month
5.8	22	3. 1-2 months
4.5	17	4. 3-4 months
3.2	12	5. 5-6 months
3.5	13	6. 7-8 months
1.1	4	7. 9-10 months
2.1	8	8. 11-12 months
6.6	25	9. 13-24 months
14.6	55	10. 25 months and over

3–28. Reason for Incomplete or Broken Parole Supervision

%	No.	
—	202	1. Not broken or incomplete
7.4	13	2. Parolee is in other state or foreign country without supervision and is not required to report (i.e., given permission to leave state)
21.7	38	3. Disappeared and not found
6.3	11	4. Excused from reporting because of good behaviour
0	0	5. At Reformatory on in-between sentence
.6	1	6. Dropped (after futile attempt to locate)
40.0	70	7. In other state or country, but reports by letter
19.4	34	8. Sporadic disappearances
1.7	3	9. Death of offender
1.7	3	10. Sentenced to non-penal institution
1.2	2	11. Sentenced to a penal institution (not Women's Reformatory)

3–29. Average Number of Visits to Parolee

%	No.	
18.1	56	1. One visit in a month or less
27.5	85	2. Over 1–2 months
29.1	90	3. 2–4 months
11.7	36	4. 4–6 months
2.9	9	5. 6–8 months
2.0	6	6. 8–10 months
1.6	5	7. 10–12 months
7.1	22	8. 12 months and over
—	68	11. Parolee not seen by Massachusetts parole authorities

3–30. Average Visits to Case

%	No.	
31.4	100	1. One visit in a month or less
33.3	106	2. In over 1–2 months
23.6	75	3. 2–4 months
5.4	17	4. 4–6 months
1.6	5	5. 6–8 months
0.9	3	6. 8–10 months
0.3	1	7. 10–12 months
3.5	11	8. 12 months and over
—	3	9. Unknown
—	56	11. No one in case seen

3–31a. Attitude toward Reform during Parole

%	No.	
	280	1. None stated
	59	2. Good
	28	3. Poor

Note: Percentages not given, as known group is so small.

3–31b. Prognosis of Parole Officer

	371	6. None made
	5	7. Good
	1	8. Fair
	0	9. Poor

Note: Percentages not given, as known group is so small.

3–32. Time to First Contact with Parolee Personally by Parole Officer

43.0	161	1. Less than 1 month
16.6	62	2. 1–2 months
14.4	54	3. 2–4 months
2.7	10	4. 4–6 months
1.6	6	5. 6–8 months
.8	3	6. 8–10 months
.3	1	7. 10–12 months
2.4	9	8. Year or more
—	3	9. Unknown
18.2	68	11. Never

3–33. Number of Reports by Parolee to Parole Agent, Frequency of

74.5	278	1. Average of one a month or more
9.7	36	2. Average of one in over 1–2 months
5.4	20	3. Average of one in 2–4 months
2.9	11	4. Average of one in 4–6 months
.8	3	5. Average of one in 6–8 months
.5	2	6. Average of one in 8–10 months
1.1	4	7. Average of one in 10–12 months
1.9	7	8. Average of one in 12 months and over
2.1	8	9. Inapplicable (did not have to report)
—	4	10. Unknown
1.1	4	11. Failed to report

3-34. Period of Time Remained in First Parole Home

%	No.	
15.6	59	1. One month or less
20.1	76	2. 1–3 months
12.5	47	3. 3–6 months
5.0	19	4. 6–9 months
4.0	15	5. 9–12 months
2.7	10	6. 12–18 months
1.6	6	7. 18–24 months
.5	2	8. 24–30 months
.8	3	9. 30–36 months
0	0	10. 36–42 months
.3	1	11. 42 months and over
36.9	139	12. Throughout parole period

3-35. Reason for Change from First Place of Residence

%	No.	
31.6	116	1. Fault of offender
30.5	112	2. Not fault of offender
37.9	139	3. Did not leave
—	10	4. Unknown or other

3-36. Occupational Experiences during Parole, Types of
[multiple punch]

%	No.	
—	33	1. Unknown or idle
46.5	160	2. Domestic service (including housework and institutional work)
39.2	135	3. Factory work
3.8	13	4. Home work
11.0	38	5 Restaurant and hotel work
5.2	18	6. Work in stores
4.4	15	7. Clerical work
13.7	47	8. Day work
9.0	31	9. Other
4.1	14	10. Illegitimate occupation
30.8	106	11. Own housework or for relatives (as parents)

Note: Percentages on basis of 344 (377—33).

3-37. With Whom Living at End of Parole

%	No.	
24.1	91	1. In parental home
6.6	25	2. With relatives
.3	1	3. With foster-parents
1.9	7	4. Alone
24.5	91	5. With husband
18.3	69	6. With employer
.3	1	7. With lover
12.9	50	8. Unknown to parole officer
.5	2	9. Other
1.3	5	10. Institution (other than the Reformatory)
8.0	30	11. Reformatory
1.3	5	12. Dead

3-H38. Parole — Delinquency Unknown to Parole Officer

9	Arrest in Massachusetts
7	Arrest in other states
16	Unofficial delinquency

Note: Percentages not given, as numbers are so small.

3-H39. Special Attempts at Rehabilitation by Parole Agents

57.6	217	No attempts
42.4	160	Attempts

3-H40. Revocations and New Sentences during Parole (by incidence and not by case)

65	Revocation followed by return to Reformatory
25	Revocation but no return to Reformatory
23	Revocation but warrant withdrawn
3	In-between sentence to Reformatory
18	In-between sentence to another penal institution

Note: Percentages not given, as numbers are so small.

3-H41. Parole Supervision — Total Visits Made by Parole Agents (3740)

65.3	2444	Visits to parolees
13.5	503	Visits to relatives
3.1	117	Visits to employers
15.1	563	Visits to others
3.0	113	Visits, but no one seen

CODE IV. FIVE-YEAR POST-PAROLE PERIOD

Note: Unless otherwise stated, the category "Inapplicable" includes those who died before the beginning of the post-parole period or shortly thereafter, and those who were in institutions for all or most of the period.

4-1. DATE OF POST-PAROLE EXPIRATION

%	No.	
0	0	1. 1925
18.4	92	2. 1926
27.6	138	3. 1927
28.6	143	4. 1928
25.4	127	5. 1929

4-2. AGE OF OFFENDER AT END OF POST-PAROLE PERIOD

15.7	76	1. 21–25 years
35.5	172	2. 26–30 years
18.5	90	3. 31–35 years
14.7	71	4. 36–40 years
8.1	39	5. 41–45 years
4.8	23	6. 46–50 years
0.8	4	7. 51–55 years
1.9	9	8. 56 years and over
—	16	9. Died before beginning of period

4-3. WITH WHOM LIVING AT END OF FIVE-YEAR POST-PAROLE PERIOD

8.9	41	1. Parents (one or both)
2.0	9	2. Sib or sibs (no parents)
0.4	2	3. Other relatives
41.7	192	4. Husband and/or children
2.1	10	5. Children (no husband)
8.3	38	6. Lover
5.9	27	7. Employer
12.2	56	8. Alone
11.1	51	9. Institution
0	0	10. Other
7.4	34	11. Dead
—	40	12. Unknown

4-4. Marriage during Parole or Post-Parole Period

%	No.	
50.6	225	1. No marriage
46.7	208	2. Married once
2.5	11	3. Married twice
0.2	1	4. Married three times
—	39	5. Unknown if married during this period
—	16	6. Died before beginning of period

4-5. Health — Venereal Disease

23.1	71	1. Yes
68.4	210	2. No
8.5	26	3. Doubtful
—	159	4. Unknown
—	34	5. Died before beginning of period, or in institutions throughout

4-6. Number of Penal Experiences

83.7	385	2. None, or inapplicable (as dead or in institutions)
—	39	3. Unknown if any
7.0	32	4. One
3.7	17	5. Two
3.0	14	6. Three, four
1.5	7	7. Five, six
1.1	5	8. Seven, eight
0	0	9. Nine, ten
0	0	10. Eleven or more
—	1	11. Number unknown

4-7. Time in Penal Institution

—	39	1. Unknown if any
—	385	2. None, or inapplicable (as dead or in non-penal institution)
23.7	18	3. Less than 3 months
15.8	12	4. 3–6 months
22.4	17	5. 6–12 months
15.8	12	6. 12–18 months
6.6	5	7. 18–24 months
3.9	3	8. 24–30 months
1.3	1	9. 30–36 months
6.6	5	10. 36–48 months
2.6	2	11. 48–60 months
1.3	1	12. 60 months

4-8. Months in Community

%	No.	
—	40	1. Unknown
7.4	34	2. None
0.2	1	3. Less than 3 months
0.7	3	4. 3–6 months
0.7	3	5. 6–12 months
0.9	4	6. 12–18 months
1.5	7	7. 18–24 months
1.3	6	8. 24–30 months
1.5	7	9. 30–36 months
6.1	28	10. 36–48 months
9.3	43	11. 48–60 months
70.4	324	12. 60 months

4-9. Institutional Experiences, Nature of
[multiple punch]

—	39	2. Unknown if any
73.3	348	3. None
3.7	17	4. School for feeble-minded
2.6	12	5. House of the Good Shepherd
4.1	19	6. Hospital for mental diseases
2.0	9	7. Hospital for chronic physical diseases
16.5	76	8. Penal institutions
0.2	1	9. Other

Note: Percentages are on basis of 461 (500—39).

4-10. Home, Physical

—	38	1. Inapplicable
21.4	85	2. Good
37.5	149	3. Fair
27.7	110	4. Poor
3.5	14	5. Varied — good
6.6	26	6. Varied — fair
3.3	13	7. Varied — poor
—	65	8. Unknown

4–11. NEIGHBOURHOOD, TYPE

%	No.	
—	38	1. Inapplicable
42.0	174	2. Urban, partly residential
21.0	87	3. Urban, residential
5.1	21	4. Urban, unspecified
4.6	19	5. Suburban
8.2	34	6. Rural, or small town
19.1	79	7. Varied
—	48	8. Unknown

4–12a. NEIGHBOURHOOD INFLUENCES

—	38	1. Inapplicable
21.4	48	2. Good
37.5	149	3. Fair
27.7	148	4. Poor
3.5	10	5. Varied — good
6.6	26	6. Varied — fair
3.3	20	7. Varied — poor
—	61	8. Unknown

4–12b. MOBILITY

52.8	219	9. Yes
47.2	196	10. No
—	47	11. Unknown
—	38	12. Inapplicable

4–13. MOBILITY, NATURE OF

—	38	1. Inapplicable
—	196	2. No mobility
45.2	99	3. Excessive moving in one city
54.8	120	4. Excessive moving to other cities, states, and countries
—	47	5. Unknown

4–14a. MORAL STANDARDS

%	No.	
—	38	1. Inapplicable
23.1	91	2. Good
23.1	91	3. Fair
44.4	175	4. Poor
2.5	10	5. Varied — good
3.1	12	6. Varied — fair
3.8	15	7. Varied — poor
—	68	8. Unknown

4–14b. FAMILY RELATIONSHIPS

43.3	173	9. Succeed
56.7	227	10. Fail
—	61	11. Unknown or no family *
—	38	12. Inapplicable

* Two have no family.

4–15. ENVIRONMENTAL JUDGMENT

11.6	46	1. Good
48.6	192	2. Fair
39.8	157	3. Poor
—	19	4. Inapplicable (in institution all or most of period)
—	65	5. Unknown
—	16	6. Died before beginning of post-parole period
—	3	7. Died during early post-parole period and too little known to make any judgment
—	2	8. In foreign country. Investigation not practicable

4–16. HOUSEHOLD STABILITY

28.3	116	1. One
19.0	78	2. Two
12.7	52	3. Three
6.6	27	4. Four
3.4	14	5. Five
1.2	5	6. Six
19.0	78	7. More than six
0.5	2	8. No change
—	52	9. Unknown
—	38	10. Inapplicable
9.3	38	11. Several, but exact number unknown

4–17a. Relation to Nearest Relatives

%	No.	
—	114	1. Unknown or inapplicable (dead, in institution throughout or most of time, or died early in period, or no family)
53.9	208	2. Friendly
21.2	82	3. In touch only when in need
24.9	96	4. Entirely out of touch or very seldom in touch

4–17b. Marital Status at End of Five-Year Period

—	38	5. Inapplicable
—	37	6. Unknown, or unknown whether married or single
16.2	69	7. Single
43.5	185	8. Married, living with husband
28.5	121	10. Separated
8.0	34	11. Divorced
3.8	16	12. Widowed

4–18a. Conjugal Relations

—	121	1. Inapplicable (as separated, divorced, or widowed before beginning of post-parole period; in institution; dead)
—	6	2. Unknown whether married or single
—	69	3. Single
41.0	107	4. Good
24.9	65	5. Fair
34.1	89	6. Poor
—	43	7. Unknown, or married too brief a time to judge

4–18b. Attitude of Offender to Marital Responsibility

—	75	8. Single, or unknown whether married or single
54.2	137	9. Assume
45.8	116	10. Neglect
—	51	11. Unknown
—	121	12. Inapplicable (as separated, divorced, or widowed before beginning of post-parole period; in institution; dead)

4–19a. Competence as Homemaker

%	No.	
—	104	1. Inapplicable (as separated, divorced, or widowed before beginning of post-parole period and not keeping house for children, relatives, or lovers; in institution; dead)
—	75	2. Single, or unknown whether married or single
48.1	116	3. Good
36.1	87	4. Fair
15.8	38	5. Poor
—	80	6. Unknown

4–19b. Legitimacy of Children Born during Post-Parole Period

—	317	7. No children born during period
62.6	67	8. Legitimate children born during period
15.9	17	9. Illegitimate children only — offender unmarried
10.3	11	10. Illegitimate children — offender married
11.2	12	11. Legitimate and illegitimate children
—	76	12. Unknown or inapplicable

4–20a. Attitude to Children

—	50	1. Inapplicable (dead, in institution, or children adopted before offender came out of Reformatory)
—	175	2. No children
47.8	107	3. Good
21.9	49	4. Fair
30.3	68	5. Poor
—	51	6. Unknown

4–20b. Delinquency of Husband (during post-parole period)

—	69	7. Single
45.3	111	8. No delinquency
29.8	73	9. Court record (except if only for drink)
6.9	17	10. Drunkenness only (official or unofficial)
18.0	44	11. Unofficial misconduct (except drunkenness)
—	186	12. Unknown or inapplicable (as separated, divorced, or widowed before beginning of period)

4-21a. Leisure and Habits Judgment

%	No.	
—	38	1. Inapplicable
2.7	11	2. Constructive
30.6	123	3. Negative
66.7	268	4. Harmful
—	60	5. Unknown

4-21b. Constructive Recreations and Interests

%	No.	
—	38	6. Inapplicable
4.3	17	7. Yes
95.7	383	8. No
—	62	9. Unknown

4-22a. Church Attendance

%	No.	
—	38	1. Inapplicable
16.0	53	2. Regular
46.7	154	3. Irregular
37.3	123	4. None
—	132	5. Unknown

4-22b. Companionships

%	No.	
—	38	6. Inapplicable
37.3	148	7. Harmless
62.7	249	8. Harmful
—	65	9. Unknown

4-23. Haunts

%	No.	
—	38	1. Inapplicable
2.3	8	2. Good
46.5	160	3. Fair
51.2	176	4. Poor
—	118	5. Unknown

4–24. HABITS
[multiple punch]

%	No.	
10.2	41	2. Stealing
33.3	134	3. Drink
4.0	16	4. Drugs
1.0	4	5. Gambling
23.4	94	9. None
—	60	10. Unknown
—	38	11. Inapplicable

Note: Percentages are on basis of 402 (500—60—38).

4–25. SEX IRREGULARITY, NATURE OF ABNORMAL

%	No.	
28.5	117	1. None
9.5	39	2. Professional prostitute
13.7	56	3. Occasional prostitute
3.9	16	4. One-man prostitute
17.6	72	5. Promiscuous, unattached
7.8	32	6. Adulteress, promiscuous
1.7	7	7. Adulteress, with one
10.5	43	8. Unconventional
6.3	26	9. Doubtful
0.5	2	10. Pervert
—	52	11. Unknown
—	38	12. Inapplicable

4–26a. ILLEGITIMATE PREGNANCIES

%	No.	
—	38	1. Inapplicable
76.3	200	2. None
23.7	62	3. Yes
—	200	4. Unknown

4–26b. ECONOMIC RESPONSIBILITY

%	No.	
—	38	5. Inapplicable
41.3	162	6. Met legitimately
21.9	86	7. Met illegitimately
15.3	60	8. Not met
19.7	77	9. Self-support not necessary
1.8	7	10. Self-support not possible because of chronic illness or other legitimate reason
—	70	11. Unknown

4–27. Savings

%	No.	
—	38	1. Inapplicable
26.1	93	2. Yes
73.9	263	3. No
—	106	4. Unknown

4–28a. Insurance

—	38	1. Inapplicable
59.1	169	2. No insurance
40.9	117	3. Insurance
—	176	4. Unknown

4–28b. Economic Condition

—	38	5. Inapplicable
13.6	56	6. Comfortable
80.1	330	7. Marginal
6.3	26	8. Dependent
—	50	9. Unknown

4–29. Disposition of Earnings

—	38	1. Inapplicable
59.1	240	2. Self, or husband and children
10.8	44	3. Self, has dependents
5.2	21	4. Contributes to support of others
24.9	101	5. No earnings
—	56	6. Unknown

4–30. Number of Social Service Agencies

—	38	1. Inapplicable
65.9	272	2. None
—	49	3. Unknown if any
17.2	71	4. One
7.0	29	5. Two
5.8	24	6. Three
1.9	8	7. Four
1.2	5	8. Five
0.3	1	9. Six
0.7	3	10. Seven or over
—	0	11. Number unknown

4-31. TYPE OF SOCIAL SERVICE
[multiple punch]

%	No.	
—	38	1. Inapplicable
—	272	2. Not known to any agencies
—	49	3. Unknown whether dealt with by agencies
26.2	56	4. Health, physical
7.9	17	5. Health, mental
26.2	56	6. Relief or family welfare
29.0	62	7. Child or adolescent welfare
5.6	12	8. Correctional
5.1	11	9. Other

4-32. INDUSTRIAL HISTORY JUDGMENT

—	38	1. Inapplicable
18.6	50	2. Success
32.0	86	3. Partial success
49.4	133	4. Failure
—	97	5. Never worked (as no need, or illness, or in and out of institutions)
—	96	6. Unknown

4-33. USUAL OCCUPATION

—	87	1. Unknown or inapplicable
9.9	41	2. Domestic service
22.3	92	3. Factory work
0.3	1	4. Home work
10.2	42	5. Restaurant and hotel work
2.9	12	6. Work in stores
0.7	3	7. Clerical work
8.2	34	8. Day work
4.8	20	9. Other
14.8	61	10. Illegitimate
22.5	93	11. Own housework
3.4	14	12. Idle

4-34a. Steadiness of Employment

%	No.	
—	141	1. Inapplicable (own housework throughout, or dead, or in institution throughout or most of time, or died early in period)
18.2	50	2. Regular
31.8	87	3. Fairly regular
27.7	76	4. Irregular
22.3	61	5. Illegitimate occupation
—	85	6. Unknown

4-34b. Work Habits

—	141	7. Inapplicable (as in 34a)
25.4	67	8. Good
33.0	87	9. Fair
18.5	49	10. Poor
23.1	61	11. Illegitimate occupation
—	95	12. Unknown

4-35. Average Wage

—	141	1. Inapplicable (as in 34a)
—	61	2. Illegitimate occupation
2.9	5	3. Less than $5
22.4	38	4. $5-$10
51.8	88	5. $10-$15
15.9	27	6. $15-$20
6.4	11	7. $20-$25
0.6	1	8. $25-$30
0	0	9. $30-$35
0	0	10. $35 and over
—	128	11. Unknown

4-36. HIGHEST WAGE

%	No.	
—	141	1. Inapplicable (as in 34a)
—	61	2. Illegitimate occupation
0.6	1	3. Less than $5
6.4	10	4. $5–$10
23.7	37	5. $10–$15
37.2	58	6. $15–$20
17.3	27	7. $20–$25
8.3	13	8. $25–$30
2.6	4	9. $30–$35
3.9	6	10. $35 and over
—	142	11. Unknown

4-37. LONGEST PERIOD EMPLOYED

—	141	1. Inapplicable (as in 34a)
—	75	2. Incalculable (on and off in one place; illegitimate occupation)
17.8	23	3. Less than 3 months
11.6	15	4. 3–6 months
9.3	12	5. 6–9 months
10.9	14	6. 9–12 months
15.5	20	7. 1–2 years
16.3	21	8. 2–3 years
10.1	13	9. 3–4 years
4.7	6	10. 4–5 years
3.8	5	11. 5 years and over
—	155	12. Unknown

4-38a. USED WOMEN'S REFORMATORY OCCUPATION

—	38	1. Inapplicable
16.8	69	2. Yes
83.2	342	3. No
—	51	4. Unknown

4-38b. ILLEGITIMATE OCCUPATION

—	38	5. Inapplicable
15.6	61	6. As usual occupation
18.3	71	7. Any illegitimate occupation
66.1	257	8. No illegitimate occupation
—	73	9. Unknown

4–39. USUAL REASON FOR LEAVING WORK

%	No.	
—	202	1. Inapplicable (did not work, illegitimate occupation, dead, in institution)
11.5	20	2. Steady worker, seldom changes
41.4	72	3. Fault of worker
40.2	70	4. Not fault of worker
6.9	12	5. To better self
0	0	6. Other
—	124	7. Unknown

4–40. PREDOMINANT OFFENCE

—	94	1. None
51.5	157	2. Sex
0.3	1	3. Stealing
10.2	31	4. Alcoholism
0.7	2	5. Drug addiction
0.3	1	6. Avoidance of family responsibility
6.6	20	7. Sex and stealing
24.6	75	8. Sex and alcoholism
1.9	6	9. Sex and drug addiction
1.6	5	10. Sex and two or more others
2.3	7	11. Other (bootlegging, selling liquor, receiving stolen goods, etc.)
—	101	12. Unknown or inapplicable

4–41a. PRINCIPAL COMPONENT OF MISCONDUCT

—	38	1. Inapplicable
23.6	94	2. No delinquency
39.3	157	3. Based on official record
37.1	148	4. On unofficial only
—	63	5. Unknown

4–41b. DELINQUENCY

23.6	94	6. Non-delinquent
76.4	305	7. Delinquent
—	47	8. Unknown
—	54	9. Inapplicable

4-42. Number of Arrests

%	No.	
11.6	48	1. One
8.0	33	2. Two
4.3	18	3. Three
3.1	13	4. Four
2.7	11	5. Five
1.2	5	6. Six
7.0	29	7. Seven and over
—	38	8. Inapplicable
—	11	10. Unknown if arrested
62.1	257	11. None
—	37	12. Unknown

4-43. Number of Convictions

12.3	51	1. One
7.0	29	2. Two
3.9	16	3. Three
2.7	11	4. Four
2.7	11	5. Five
0.9	4	6. Six
5.8	24	7. Seven and over
—	38	8. Inapplicable
—	11	10. Unknown if arrested
64.7	268	11. No arrests, and no convictions if arrested
—	37	12. Unknown

4-44. Frequency of Arrests

—	86	1. Unknown, unknown if arrested, inapplicable
—	257	2. Never arrested
—	48	3. Incalculable (as only one arrest)
11.9	13	4. One arrest in less than 3 months
15.6	17	5. In 3–6 months
9.2	10	6. In 6–9 months
9.2	10	7. In 9–12 months
11.0	12	8. In 12–15 months
5.5	6	9. In 15–18 months
11.9	13	10. In 18–21 months
0.9	1	11. In 21–24 months
24.8	27	12. In 24 months and over

4–45. SUMMARY OF ARRESTS — TYPES
[multiple punch]

%	No.	
3.2	5	1. Against person
51.0	80	2. Against chastity
3.2	5	3. Against family and children
37.6	59	4. Against public health, safety, and policy (except drink or drugs)
45.2	71	5. Drink
1.9	3	6. Drugs
18.5	29	7. Against property rights
—	257	8. No arrests
—	48	9. Unknown if arrested
—	38	10. Inapplicable

Note: Percentages are on basis of 157 women arrested.

4–46. SUMMARY OF DISPOSITIONS — TYPES
[multiple punch]

%	No.	
—	343	1. No arrests, unknown if arrested, inapplicable
48.4	76	2. Commitment
56.7	89	3. Probation
26.8	42	4. Fine
1.3	2	5. Commitment for non-payment of fine
33.8	53	6. File
0	0	7. Restitution
11.5	18	8. Released by probation officer
5.1	8	9. Nol-prossed
1.9	3	10. No bill
22.9	36	11. Not guilty or released
8.3	13	12. Disposition unknown or other, or awaiting disposition.

Note: Percentages on basis of 157 women arrested.

4–47a. FAMILY RELATIONS IN FIFTH YEAR

%	No.	
52.8	195	1. Success
47.2	174	2. Failure
—	61	3. Unknown
—	70	4. Inapplicable (no family, in institution, dead, or for other reasons)

4-47b. Industrial History in Fifth Year

%	No.	
26.3	56	5. Success
26.3	56	6. Partial success
47.4	101	7. Failure
—	89	8. Unknown
—	198	9. Inapplicable (in institution, dead, too ill to work, no need to work)

4-48. Environmental Judgment in Fifth Year

17.6	64	1. Good
46.3	168	2. Fair
36.1	131	3. Poor
—	70	4. Unknown
—	33	5. Dead
—	16	6. Institution
—	18	7. For other reasons inapplicable

4-49a. Economic Responsibility in Fifth Year

34.6	124	1. Met legitimately
21.2	76	2. Met illegitimately
9.7	35	3. Not met
33.4	120	4. Self-support not necessary
1.1	4	5. Self-support not possible because of chronic illness or other legitimate reasons
—	74	6. Unknown
—	67	7. Inapplicable (dead, in institution throughout, or for other reasons)

4-49b. Leisure and Habits in Fifth Year

2.5	9	8. Constructive
45.5	163	9. Negative
52.0	186	10. Harmful
—	75	11. Unknown
—	67	12. Inapplicable (dead, in institution throughout, or for other reasons)

4–50a. Delinquency in Fifth Year

%	No.	
52.6	203	1. Delinquent
47.4	149	2. Non-delinquent
—	81	3. Unknown
—	67	4. Inapplicable (dead, in institution throughout, or for other reasons)

4–50b. Delinquency after Post-Parole Period

%	No.	
52.6	175	5. Delinquent
47.4	158	6. Non-delinquent
—	98	7. Unknown
—	69	8. Inapplicable (dead, in institution throughout, and for other reasons inapplicable)

4–51a. Economic Responsibility after Post-Parole Period

%	No.	
31.3	105	1. Met legitimately
20.0	67	2. Met illegitimately
9.6	32	3. Not met
37.3	125	4. Self-support not necessary or possible
1.8	6	5. Chronic illness, or for other legitimate reason dependent
—	96	6. Unknown
—	69	7. Inapplicable (dead, in institution throughout, or for other reasons)

4–51b. Leisure and Habits after Post-Parole Period

%	No.	
3.0	10	8. Constructive
50.9	168	9. Negative
46.1	152	10. Harmful
—	101	11. Unknown
—	69	12. Inapplicable (dead, in institution throughout, or for other reasons)

4–52a. Family Relations after Post-Parole Period

%	No.	
56.9	199	1. Succeed
43.1	151	2. Fail
—	78	3. Unknown
—	72	4. Innapplicable (no family, dead, in institution throughout, or for other reasons)

4–52b. Industrial History after Post-Parole Period

%	No.	
27.5	54	5. Success
22.5	44	6. Partial success
50.0	98	7. Failure
—	101	8. Unknown
—	203	9. Inapplicable (in institution, dead, too ill to work, no need to work)

4–53. Time Covered by Period Following Five-Year Post-Parole Period

1.3	6	1. Less than 1 year
5.2	24	2. 1–2 years
18.0	83	3. 2–3 years
26.6	123	4. 3–4 years
30.1	139	5. 4–5 years
18.8	87	6. 5 years and over
—	38	7. Dead

4–54. Environmental Condition after Post-Parole Period

19.5	67	1. Good
46.5	160	2. Fair
34.0	117	3. Poor
—	88	4. Unknown
—	38	5. Dead
—	29	6. In institution throughout
—	1	7. For other reasons inapplicable

4–55. Delinquency in Five-Year Period and Fifth Year in Combination

%	No.	
20.8	94	1. Non-delinquent
55.2	250	2. Delinquent throughout (including unknown in 5th year and 5th year inapplicable; dead in fifth year, but delinquent before)
12.1	55	3. Delinquent up-grade
2.7	12	4. School for feeble-minded throughout
1.5	7	5. Hospital for mental diseases throughout
0	0	6. Penal institutions throughout
2.7	12	7. Doubtful delinquency
—	47	8. Unknown
4.4	20	9. Dead (including a few who died after beginning of post-parole period, but information lacking)
0.4	2	10. In hospital for chronic physical disease large part of time, and during time out unknown whether delinquent or non-delinquent; or chronic illness at home
0.2	1	11. Hospital for mental diseases large part of time, and conduct outside unknown

4–H56. Summary of Offences (all offences)

%	No.	
1.0	7	Against person
19.1	130	Against chastity
0.6	4	Against family and children
15.7	107	Against public health, safety, and policy (except drink and drugs)
56.9	387	Drink
0.5	3	Drugs
6.2	42	Against property rights

Note: Percentages based on 680 arrests.

4–H57. Summary of Dispositions (all dispositions)

%	No.	
26.2	178	Commitment
25.1	171	Probation
12.4	84	Fine
.6	4	Commitment for non-payment of fine
17.5	119	File
3.8	26	Released by probation officer
1.6	11	Nol-prossed
0.1	1	No bill
7.4	50	Not guilty or released
5.3	36	Disposition unknown, or other, or awaiting disposition

Note: Percentages based on 680 arrests.

4–H58. Interview — With Whom Held

%	No.	
44.6	223	Offender
35.4	117	Near relatives
4.6	23	Others (police, probation officer, employer, social agencies)
15.4	77	Record data or correspondence only

4–H59. Whereabouts of Offender at Post-Parole Expiration

%	No.	
4.8	24	Penal institution
5.4	27	Non-penal institution
19.2	96	Boston and vicinity
28.2	141	Other cities in Massachusetts
24.8	124	Other states
2.6	13	Foreign countries
0.8	4	Fugitive from justice
1.6	8	Drifting around
6.8	34	Dead
1.6	8	Unknown, but known for part of period
4.2	21	Completely unknown

4–H60. Penal Experiences, Nature of, During Post-Parole Period

%	No.	
9.7	18	Women's Reformatory in Massachusetts
.5	1	Department for Defective Delinquents in Massachusetts
33.0	61	State farm in Massachusetts
55.7	103	Jails and houses of correction in Massachusetts and elsewhere
1.1	2	Reformatories in other states

Note: Percentages based on 185 penal experiences.

4-H61. Marital—Length of Time All Marriages Lasted (all marriages occurring between release on parole and end of post-parole period)

%	No.	
4.4	10	Less than six months
6.2	14	6–12 months
3.5	8	12–18 months
3.5	8	18–24 months
5.7	13	2–3 years
4.9	11	3–4 years
2.2	5	4–5 years
3.1	7	5–6 years
2.2	5	6–7 years
0.9	2	7 years and over
59.9	136	Still living together
3.5	8	Off and on
—	6	Unknown

Note: In this table and in the succeeding ones through 4–H65, and in tables 4–H71 through 4–H76, percentages are based on 233 marriages.

4-H62. Marital—Forced Marriages (all marriages occurring between release on parole and end of post-parole period)

%	No.	
24.1	51	Forced
75.9	161	Not forced
—	21	Unknown if forced

4-H63. Manner of Meeting Husband (all marriages occurring between release on parole and end of post-parole period)

%	No.	
33.8	46	Pick-up
39.0	53	Casual acquaintance
17.6	24	By proper introduction through parents, relatives, friends
9.6	13	Knew him before committed to Reformatory
—	97	Unknown

4-H64. TIME HUSBAND KNOWN BEFORE MARRIAGE (all marriages occurring between release on parole and end of post-parole period)

%	No.	
2.1	3	Less than one month
7.5	11	1–2 months
6.8	10	3–4 months
4.8	7	5–6 months
2.1	3	7–8 months
0.7	1	9–10 months
13.7	20	11–12 months
43.2	63	Over one year
19.1	28	Brief, but exact time unknown
—	87	Unknown

4-H65. REASON FOR TERMINATION OF MARRIAGE (all marriages occurring between release on parole and end of post-parole period)

%	No.	
87.5	77	Desertion, separation, divorce
12.5	11	Death
—	136	Not broken
—	9	Unknown

4-H66. COLOUR — MIXED MARRIAGE (last marriage which occurred between release on parole and end of post-parole period)

%	No.	
99.1	220	Same
0.9	2	Mixed

Note: In this table and succeeding ones through 4–H68, the percentages are based on 222 husbands.

4-H67. BIRTHPLACE OF HUSBAND (last marriage which occurred between release on parole and end of post-parole period)

%	No.	
77.5	158	United States
2.0	4	Canada — French
3.4	7	Canada — other
0.5	1	Great Britain
0.5	1	Ireland
0	0	Germany
3.9	8	Italy
2.5	5	Portugal and Atlantic islands
4.4	9	Poland, Lithuania, and Russia
0.9	2	Finland
4.4	9	Other
—	18	Unknown

4–H68. Citizenship of Husband (last marriage which occurred between release on parole and end of post-parole period)

%	No.	
92.4	158	Citizen by birth
4.7	8	Citizen by naturalization
0.6	1	Has first papers
2.3	4	Alien
—	51	Unknown

4–H69. Education of Husband (last marriage which occurred between release on parole and end of post-parole period)

Illiterate
Reads and writes
Attended common school
Attended high school
Attended college
Unknown

Note: Data insufficient for tabulation.

4–H70. Industrial Stability of Husband (last marriage which occurred between release on parole and end of post-parole period)

48.6	88	Regular
24.9	45	Fairly regular
26.5	48	Irregular
—	41	Unknown

4–H71. Conjugal Relations (in all marriages made between release on parole and end of post-parole period)

40.3	89	Good
24.0	53	Fair
35.7	79	Poor
—	12	Unknown

4–H72. Attitude of Offender to Marital Responsibility (in all marriages made between release on parole and end of post-parole period)

56.1	119	Assumes
43.9	93	Neglects
—	21	Unknown

4-H73. ATTITUDE OF HUSBAND TO MARITAL RESPONSIBILITY (in all marriages made between release on parole and end of post-parole period)

%	No.	
62.1	121	Assumes
37.9	74	Neglects
—	38	Unknown

4-H74. COMPETENCE AS HOMEMAKER (in all marriages made between release on parole and end of post-parole period)

49.2	93	Good
37.6	71	Fair
13.2	25	Poor
—	44	Unknown

4-H75. MARITAL HISTORY JUDGMENT (in all marriages made between release on parole and end of post-parole period)

50.0	107	Success
50.0	107	Failure
—	19	Unknown

4-H76. RESIDENCE OF CHILDREN (of all marriages occurring between release on parole and end of post-parole period)

—	90	No children
55.9	76	With offender and husband
9.5	13	With relatives
9.5	13	In institution
5.8	8	With offender
2.9	4	With husband
9.5	13	Scattered
6.9	9	Foster-home
—	7	Unknown

4-H77. SEX IRREGULARITY — WHERE PRACTISED

One home
Hotels or hired rooms
Houses of ill fame
Outdoors (coal-sheds, parks, alleyways, railroad yards, etc.)
Automobiles

Note: Data insufficient for tabulation.

4–H78. Sex Irregularity — Earnings from Prostitution

Less than $5 a week
$5–$10
$10–$15
$15–$20
$20–$25
$25–$50
$50 and over

Note: Data insufficient for tabulation.

4–H79. Why Did Not Use Women's Reformatory Occupation in Post-Parole Period

Methods outside of Reformatory different
Preferred other kind of work
No opportunity for employment in which trained at Reformatory
Seasonality of employment

Note: Data insufficient for tabulation.

4–H80. Difficulty Securing Work in Post-Parole Period

No
Yes
Unknown

Note: Data insufficient for tabulation.

4–H81. Beneficial Effects of Women's Reformatory

%	No.	
77.6	388	None, or inapplicable
22.4	112	Yes

4–H82. Harmful Effects of Women's Reformatory

87.8	439	None, or inapplicable
12.2	61	Yes

4–H83. Constructive Suggestions for Women's Reformatory

92.4	462	None, or inapplicable
7.6	38	Yes

4-H84. Criticisms of Women's Reformatory

%	No.	
84.0	420	None made
16.0	80	Yes

4-H85. Effect of Certain Personalities on Offender

81	Fond of superintendent of Reformatory
15	Disliked superintendent of Reformatory
26	Fond of deputy superintendent
1	Disliked deputy superintendent

Note: Percentages not given, as numbers are so small.

4-H86. Attitude of Community to Offender during Post-Parole Period

—	277	Not stated, or inapplicable
9.4	21	Friendly
84.3	188	Indifferent
6.3	14	Hostile

4-H87. Reasons for Improvement in Conduct after Release

62	Marriage or other satisfactory outlet of desire for affection
9	Maturity
6	Vocational adjustment
20	Reformatory experience
6	Close supervision
2	Fear of return to Reformatory
1	Separation from husband
2	Wholesome environment
3	Good material to start with
1	Freedom from responsibility

Note: Percentages not given, as numbers are so small.

4–H88. Reasons for Failure in Conduct after Release

%   No.

9	Alcoholism
9	Mental disease
5	Habit of delinquency
1	Sex perversion
5	Unfortunate marriage
1	Drug addiction
2	Psychopathy
1	Inadequate supervision
3	Feeble-minded needing custodial care
2	Excessive sex urge
4	Emotional instability
1	Reformatory experience

Note: Percentages not given, as numbers are so small.

4–H89. Constructive Work with Offender during Post-Parole Period

4	By Reformatory official
10	By parole agent
11	By social worker
4	By employer
5	By probation officer
1	By policewoman
2	By minister

Note: Percentages not given, as numbers are so small.

4–H90. Social Service Needs of Offender Not Met
(most glaring needs only)

%	No.	
25.4	30	Vocational
35.6	42	Recreational
16.9	20	Family rehabilitation
0.9	1	Relief
1.7	2	Health, physical
0.9	1	Health, mental
14.4	17	Friendly supervision
0.9	1	Americanization
3.3	4	Custodial care

Note: Percentages on basis of 118 glaring needs.

4–H91. Social Service Needs Not Met (by cases)

%	No.	
20.3	83	No needs
7.6	31	All known needs met by social agencies
25.4	104	Some needs met and some not met
46.7	191	No known needs met
—	18	In institution throughout
—	16	Dead
—	57	Unknown

4–H92. Social Service Needs Not Met (by needs)

18.6	132	Vocational
37.2	264	Recreational
28.8	204	Family rehabilitation
5.5	39	Child welfare
0	0	Relief
0.6	4	Health, physical
2.1	15	Health, mental
2.2	16	Friendly supervision
0.3	2	Americanization
4.7	33	Custodial care

Note: Percentages on basis of 709 needs.

4–H93. Marital Status at Beginning of Post-Parole Period

—	16	Inapplicable (died before beginning of period)
—	33	Unknown, or unknown whether married or single
39.9	180	Single
21.7	98	Married, living with husband
30.2	136	Separated
5.5	25	Divorced
2.7	12	Widowed

PERIOD COMPARISONS

Note of Explanation.

In the following tables are presented the status of our cases during the period before commitment to the Reformatory, in juxtaposition with their status during the parole period (where such data was available), and during the five-year post-parole period. The value of this comparison lies in determining mass changes or trends in the group. The definitions of the factors may be found in Appendix C, "Definition of Terms." "Unknown" and "inapplicable" categories have been omitted in setting up the comparisons, and occasionally other categories.

Only percentages are given, but the total number of cases on which the percentages are based is indicated in each table. Percentages total to 100 unless otherwise indicated.

The tables have been grouped by subject.

In comparing the status of the women during parole with their status as to certain factors prior to commitment, we would have utilized the same 377 cases if not for the fact that the comparisons between the 377 parolees and the entire 500 women involved in the study resulted in essentially the same way. We preferred, therefore, for the sake of ease in comparisons between the pre-Reformatory, parole, and post-parole period, to retain the total of 500.

Environmental Factors

1. HOME, PHYSICAL

	Within year of commitment %	First home during parole %	During post-parole period %
Good	11.1	66.7	24.9
Fair	21.9	19.3	44.1
Poor	67.0	14.0	31.0
Total Cases	397	279	397

2. NEIGHBOURHOOD, TYPE

	Within year of commitment %	First home during parole %	During post-parole period %
Urban	90.7	82.0	72.7
Rural, or small town	7.4	18.0	8.2
Varied	1.9	0	19.1
Total Cases	485	355	414

3. NEIGHBOURHOOD INFLUENCES

	Within year of commitment %	First home during parole %	During post-parole period %
Good	6.2	49.7	24.9
Fair	23.6	27.8	44.1
Poor	70.2	22.5	31.0
Total Cases	420	316	401

4. MORAL STANDARDS OF HOME

	Within year of commitment %	First home during parole %	During post-parole period %
Good	10.4	63.3	25.6
Fair	14.9	18.0	26.2
Poor	74.7	18.7	48.2
Total Cases	471	289	394

5. MOBILITY

	Prior to commitment %	During parole %	During post-parole %
Yes	66.2	55.8	52.8
No	33.8	44.2	47.2
Total Cases	497	285	415

6. NATURE OF MOBILITY

	Prior to commitment %	During parole %	During post-parole %
Excessive moving in one city	15.7	26.4	45.2
Excessive moving to other cities, states, or countries	84.3	73.6	54.8
Total Cases	286	159	219

7. INSTITUTIONAL EXPERIENCES (penal and non-penal)

	Prior to commitment %	During post-parole %
No	45.3	74.6
Yes	54.7	25.4
Total Cases	495	445

Family Relationships

8. WITH WHOM LIVING
(see *To Live with Whom*)

	At time of commitment %	At release on parole %	At end of parole %	At end of post-parole %
Parents (one or both)	29.7	37.0	29.4	9.6
Sibs or other relatives	6.0	11.3	8.0	2.6
Husband	10.2	12.8	26.1	45.1
Children (no husband)	2.0	0	0	2.4
Lover	13.7	0	.3	8.9
Employer	5.2	35.0	22.2	6.3
Alone	22.3	1.9	2.2	13.1
In institution	0	.3	11.2	12.0
Other	10.9	1.9	.6	0
Total Cases	498	374	313	426

9. Household Stability

	Prior to commitment %	During parole %	During post-parole %
One	34.7	34.6	28.8
Two	24.5	19.1	19.0
Three	8.3	7.0	12.7
Four and more	32.5	39.3	39.5
Total Cases	482	329	410
	Av. $1.87 \pm .04$	Av. $2.89 \pm .09$	Av. $3.19 \pm .08$

10. Marital Status

	At time of commitment %	At beginning of post-parole %	At end of post-parole %
Single	48.8	39.7	16.2
Married, living with husband	8.9	21.7	43.5
Separated	36.7	30.2	28.5
Divorced	3.2	5.5	8.0
Widowed	2.4	2.7	3.8
Total Cases	494	451	423

11. Attitude to Children

	Prior to commitment %	During post-parole %
Good	14.2	47.8
Fair	36.1	21.9
Poor	49.7	30.3
Total Cases	155	224

12. Family Relationships

	Within year of commitment %	During parole %	During post-parole %
Succeed	12.6	59.6	43.3
Fail	87.4	40.4	56.7
Total Cases	446	230	400

Economic Responsibility

13. DISPOSITION OF EARNINGS

	Prior to commitment %	During parole %	During post-parole %
Self, or husband and children.			
Has no other dependents	72.2	88.4	78.7
Has other dependents, but does not contribute to their support	4.2	5.8	14.4
Contributes to support of others	23.6	5.8	6.9
Total Cases	360	189	305

14. ECONOMIC RESPONSIBILITY

	Prior to commitment %	During parole %	During post-parole %
Met	89.8	93.3	80.5
Not met	10.2	6.7	19.5
Total Cases	393	209	308

Note: It must be remembered that the proportion of cases in which self-support was not necessary because of marriage greatly increased during the parole and post-parole period. This group is omitted from the comparison, however.

Economic Condition

15. ECONOMIC CONDITION

	Within year of commitment %	During parole %	During post-parole %
Comfortable	6.7	3.1	13.6
Marginal	78.4	93.5	80.1
Dependent	14.9	3.4	6.3
Total Cases	490	325	412

16. Savings

	Prior to commitment %	During post-parole %
Yes	14.1	26.1
No	85.9	73.9
Total Cases	298	356

17. Insurance

	Prior to commitment	During post-parole
No	25.2	59.1
Yes	74.8	40.9
Total Cases	107	286

18. Number of Social Service Agencies

	Prior to commitment %	During post-parole %
None	23.4	65.9
One	18.6	17.2
Two	18.6	7.0
Three	11.5	5.8
Four	7.0	1.9
Five	5.3	1.2
Six	4.5	0.3
Seven or over	11.1	0.7
Total Cases	469	413
	Av. 2.5 ± .07	Av. .067 ± .04

19. Type of Social Service Rendered

	Prior to commitment %	During post-parole %
Health, physical	18.7	26.2
Health, mental	7.5	7.9
Relief or family welfare	28.1	26.2
Child or adolescent welfare	35.6	29.0
Correctional	5.4	5.6
Other	4.7	5.1
Total Social Agencies	697	214

Marital History

20. MARITAL — NUMBER OF MARRIAGES

	Prior to commitment %	Between release on parole and end of post-parole period %
None	48.8	50.6
One	43.4	46.7
Two	6.2	2.5
Three	1.6	0.2
Total Cases	496	445

21. MANNER OF MEETING HUSBAND

	Marriages contracted prior to commitment %	Marriages contracted between release on parole and end of post-parole period %
Pick-up	31.2	33.8
Casual acquaintance	29.0	39.0
By proper introduction through parents, relatives, or friends	39.8	27.2
Total Marriages	186	136

22. TIME HUSBAND KNOWN BEFORE MARRIAGE

	Marriages contracted prior to commitment %	Marriages contracted between release on parole and end of post-parole %
Less than 3 months	27.6	9.6
3–6 months	26.2	30.7
7–12 months	19.6	16.5
Over 12 months	26.6	43.2
Total Marriages	214	146

23. MARRIAGES FORCED

	Marriages contracted prior to commitment %	Marriages contracted between release on parole and end of post-parole %
Forced	34.1	24.1
Not forced	65.9	75.9
Total Marriages	258	212

24. MARITAL — LENGTH OF TIME ALL MARRIAGES LASTED

	Marriages contracted prior to commitment %	Marriages contracted between release on parole and end of post-parole %
Less than 6 months	19.5	4.4
6–12 months	11.9	6.2
1–2 years	7.3	7.0
2–3 years	8.0	5.7
3–4 years	6.3	4.9
4–5 years	7.3	2.2
5–6 years	3.1	3.1
6–7 years	4.5	2.2
7 years and over	11.5	0.9
Still living together	15.4	59.9
Living together on and off	5.2	3.5
Total Marriages	287	227
	Av. 35.9 months ± 1.4	Av. 31.7 months ± 1.94

25. CONJUGAL RELATIONS

	Marriages contracted prior to commitment %	Marriages contracted between release on parole and end of post-parole %
Good	8.3	40.3
Fair	10.0	24.0
Poor	81.7	35.7
Total Marriages	289	221

26. COMPETENCE AS HOMEMAKER

	Marriages contracted prior to commitment %	Marriages contracted between release on parole and end of post-parole %
Good	8.0	49.2
Fair	44.7	37.6
Poor	47.3	13.2
Total Marriages	150	189

27. Reason for Termination of Marriage

	Marriages terminated prior to commitment %	Marriages terminated between release on parole and end of post-parole period %
Desertion, separation, or divorce	89.5	87.5
Death	10.5	12.5
Total Marriages Broken	257	88

28. Attitude of Offender to Marital Responsibility

	All marriages prior to commitment %	All marriages between release on parole and end of post-parole period %
Assumes	16.2	56.1
Neglects	83.8	43.9
Total Marriages	253	212

29. Attitude of Husband to Marital Responsibility

	All marriages prior to commitment %	All marriages between release on parole and end of post-parole period %
Assumes	26.4	62.1
Neglects	73.6	37.9
Total Marriages	301	195

30. Marital History Judgment

	All marriages prior to commitment %	All marriages between release on parole and end of post-parole period %
Success	17.1	50.0
Failure	82.9	50.0
Total Marriages	287	214

Industrial History

31. Usual Occupation

	Prior to commitment %	During parole %	During post-parole %
Factory work	46.6	27.3	22.3
Domestic service	13.1	30.0	9.9
Home work	1.5	.6	0.3
Restaurant and hotel work	6.3	3.2	10.2
Work in stores	1.7	1.2	2.9
Clerical work	1.7	2.0	0.7
Day work	6.8	4.7	8.2
Other	2.1	5.5	4.8
Illegitimate occupation	8.2	2.0	14.8
Own housework	9.7	21.2	22.5
Idle	2.3	2.3	3.4
Total Cases	474	344	413

32. Longest Period Employed

	Prior to commitment %	During post-parole %
Less than 3 months	15.2	17.8
3–6 months	13.7	11.6
6–9 months	14.1	9.3
9–12 months	6.9	10.9
1–2 years	18.1	15.5
2–3 years	14.4	16.3
3–4 years	8.3	10.1
4–5 years	3.2	4.7
5 years and over	6.1	3.8
Total Cases	277	129
	Av. 19.4 months ± .72	Av. 20.02 months ± 1.03

33. HIGHEST WEEKLY WAGE
(in legitimate occupation)

	Prior to commitment %	During parole %	During post-parole %
Less than $5	.9	2.2	0.6
$5–10	17.3	36.0	6.4
$10–15	39.4	40.0	23.7
$15–20	26.8	17.4	37.2
$20–25	8.8	3.7	17.3
$25–30	5.0	.7	8.3
$30 and over	1.8	0	6.5
Total Cases	340	264	156
	Av. $15.45 ± .22	Av. $12.35 ± .19	Av. $18.95 ± .37

34. AVERAGE WEEKLY WAGE
(in legitimate occupation)

	Prior to commitment %	During post-parole %
Less than $5	1.9	2.9
$5–10	44.9	22.4
$10–15	40.8	51.8
$15–20	11.1	15.9
$20–25	1.0	6.4
$25–30	.3	0.6
Total Cases	316	170
	Av. $11.25 ± .14	Av. $13.10 ± .23

35. USUAL REASONS FOR LEAVING WORK

	Prior to commitment %	During parole %	During post-parole %
Fault of worker	83.8	43.1	41.4
Not fault of worker	16.0	56.9	58.6
Total Cases	315	204	174

36. Used Women's Reformatory Occupation

	During parole %	During post-parole %
Yes	22.4	16.8
No	77.6	83.2
Total Cases	353	411

37. Steadiness of Employment

	Prior to commitment %	During parole %	During post-parole %
Regular	7.5	37.5	18.2
Fairly regular	32.8	38.5	31.8
Irregular	59.7	24.0	50.0
Total Cases	454	221	274

38. Work Habits

	Prior to commitment %	During parole %	During post-parole %
Good	16.2	26.5	25.4
Fair	55.4	52.6	33.0
Poor	28.4	20.9	41.6
Total Cases	370	196	264

39. Industrial History Judgment

	Prior to commitment %	During parole %	During post-parole %
Success	2.9	22.7	18.6
Partial success	38.8	54.6	32.0
Failure	58.3	22.7	49.4
Total Cases	451	198	269

Leisure and Habits

40. Leisure and Habits Judgment

	Within year of commitment %	During parole %	During post-parole %
Constructive	.8	6.7	2.7
Negative	1.2	42.3	30.6
Harmful	98.0	51.0	66.7
Total Cases	495	239	402

41. Constructive Recreations and Interests

	Within year of commitment %	During parole %	During post-parole %
Yes	.8	9.2	4.3
No	99.2	90.8	95.7
Total Cases	495	295	400

42. Church Attendance

	Within year of commitment %	During parole %	During post-parole %
Regular	13.5	40.3	16.0
Irregular	50.0	58.0	46.7
None	36.5	1.7	37.3
Total Cases	414	119	330

43. Companions

	Within year of commitment %	During parole %	During post-parole %
Harmless	2.7	55.8	37.3
Harmful	97.3	44.2	62.7
Total Cases	480	217	397

44. Haunts
(see *Play Places and Haunts*)

	Within year of commitment %	During post-parole %
Harmless	10.2	48.8
Harmful	89.8	51.2
Total Cases	420	344

45. Habits

	Within year of commitment %	During post-parole %
No bad habits	.4	23.4
Bad habits	99.6	76.6
Total Cases	499	402

Illicit Sex Life

46. Sex Life, Nature of Illicit

	Prior to commitment %	During parole %	During post-parole %
No	1.7	52.9	28.5
Yes	98.3	47.1	71.5
Total Cases	467	240	410
Professional prostitute	7.2	1.8	13.3
Occasional prostitute	42.7	23.0	19.1
One-man prostitute	3.0	.9	5.5
Promiscuous, unattached	22.4	35.4	24.6
Adulteress, promiscuous	6.8	4.4	10.9
Adulteress, with one	6.8	.9	2.4
Unconventional	8.7	7.0	14.6
Doubtful	2.4	26.6	8.9
Pervert	0	0	0.7
Total Cases	459	113	293

47. LEGITIMACY OF CHILDREN

	Born prior to commitment %	Born during post-parole %
All legitimate	29.3	62.6
All or some illegitimate	70.7	37.4
Total Cases	249	107

48. ILLEGITIMATE PREGNANCIES

	Prior to commitment %	During post-parole %
No	45.6	76.3
Yes	54.4	23.7
Total Cases	441	262

49. VENEREAL DISEASE

	Before 21 years old %	On admission to Reformatory %	During post-parole %
Yes (or probably)	69.2	78.4	31.6
No	30.8	21.6	68.4
Total Cases	328	476	307

Criminal Record

50. NUMBER OF ARRESTS

	Prior to commitment %	During post-parole %
None	33.1	62.1
One	20.1	11.6
Two	15.7	8.0
Three, four	14.3	7.5
Five and over	16.8	10.8
Total Cases	497	414
	Av. 3.66 ± .12 (of those arrested)	Av. 3.2 ± .12 (of those arrested)

51. Frequency of Arrests

	Prior to commitment %	During post-parole %
Incalculable (as only one arrest)	33.3	30.6
One arrest in less than 3 months	12.0	8.3
In 3–6 months	13.7	10.8
6–9 months	13.1	6.4
9–12 months	8.2	6.4
12–15 months	2.7	7.6
15–18 months	5.5	3.8
18–21 months	2.4	8.3
21–24 months	1.2	0.6
24 months and over	7.9	17.2
Total Cases	328	157
	Av. one arrest in 10.06 months ± .33	Av. one arrest in 14.27 months ± .56

52. Number of Convictions

	Prior to commitment %	During post-parole %
None	5.1	7.0
One	36.6	32.5
Two	22.5	18.5
Three	10.0	10.2
Four	6.9	7.0
Five	6.0	7.0
Six	3.3	2.5
Seven and over	9.6	15.3
Total Cases	333	157
	Av. (of those arrested) 2.64 ± .08	Av. (of those arrested) 2.85 ± .12

53. SUMMARY OF ARRESTS (by type)

	Prior to commitment %	During post-parole %
Against person	6.6	3.2
Against chastity	52.0	51.0
Against family and children	3.6	3.2
Against public health, safety, and policy (except drink and drugs)	30.0	37.6
Drink	29.7	45.2
Drugs	1.5	1.9
Against property	23.7	18.5
Stubborn child	27.0	0
Total Women Arrested	333	157

Note: Percentages are on basis of women arrested.

54. SUMMARY OF OFFENCES

	Prior to commitment %	During post-parole %
Against person	1.5	1.0
Against chastity	24.7	19.1
Against family and children	1.1	0.6
Against public health, safety, and policy (except drink and drugs)	20.8	15.7
Drink	36.4	56.9
Drugs	.7	.5
Against property rights	14.8	6.2
Total Offences	1218	680

55. SUMMARY OF DISPOSITIONS (by type)

	Prior to commitment %	During post-parole %
Commitment	45.6	48.4
Probation	70.9	56.7
Fine	17.1	26.8
Commitment for non-payment of fine	3.3	1.3
Filed	23.7	33.8
Restitution	0	0
Released by probation officer	7.8	11.5
Nol-prossed	2.1	5.1
No bill	0.6	1.9
Not guilty or released	26.1	22.9
Number of Women Arrested	333	157

Note: Percentages are on basis of number of women arrested.

56. SUMMARY OF DISPOSITIONS

	Prior to commitment %	During post-parole %
Commitment	29.2	27.6
Probation	35.6	26.6
Fine	6.1	13.0
Commitment for non-payment of fine	1.7	.6
Filed	12.3	18.5
Restitution	.1	0
Released by probation officer	4.2	4.0
Nol-prossed	.6	1.7
No bill	.2	.2
Not guilty or released	10.0	7.8
Total Dispositions	1206	644

57. Number of Penal Experiences

	Prior to commitment %	During post-parole %
None	69.5	83.7
One	14.7	7.0
Two	7.0	3.7
Three, four	3.9	3.0
Five and more	4.9	2.6
Total Cases	489	460

Av. (of those having penal experiences) 2.68 ± .13

Av. (of those having penal experiences) 2.64 ± .14

58. Time in Penal Institutions

	Prior to commitment %	During post-parole %
Less than 6 months	26.5	39.5
6–12 months	18.4	22.4
12–18 months	12.2	15.8
18–24 months	9.5	6.6
24–30 months	13.0	3.9
30–36 months	4.7	1.3
36–48 months	7.5	6.6
48 months and over	8.2	3.9
Total Cases	147	76

Av. 19.94 months ± .85

Av. 14.66 months ± 1.01

59. PREDOMINANT OFFENCE

	Prior to commitment %	During post-parole %
Sex	56.1	51.5
Stealing	4.7	.3
Alcoholism	3.9	10.2
Drug addiction	.8	.7
Avoidance of family responsibility	.8	.3
Sex and stealing	9.2	6.6
Sex and alcoholism	15.7	24.6
Sex and drug addiction	.8	2.0
Sex and two or more other	3.9	1.6
Other	4.1	2.3
Total Cases	490	305

60. PRINCIPAL COMPONENT OF MISCONDUCT

	Prior to commitment %	During parole %	During post-parole %
Official record of delinquency	66.4	41.8	51.5
Unofficial misconduct	33.6	58.2	48.5
Total Delinquents	494	141	305

61. DELINQUENCY

	Prior to commitment %	During parole %	During post-parole %
Non-delinquent	1.0	44.9	23.6
Delinquent	99.0	55.1	76.4
Total Cases	496	256	399

INDEX

A NOTE ON THE TYPE
IN WHICH THIS BOOK IS SET

This book is set in Granjon, a type named in compliment to ROBERT GRANJON, *but neither a copy of a classic face nor an entirely original creation. George W. Jones drew the basic design for this type from classic sources, but deviated from his model to profit by the intervening centuries of experience and progress. This type is based primarily upon the type used by Claude Garamond (1510–61) in his beautiful French books, and more closely resembles Garamond's own than do any of the various modern types that bear his name.*

Of Robert Granjon nothing is known before 1545, except that he had begun his career as type-cutter in 1523. The boldest and most original designer of his time, he was one of the first to practise the trade of type-founder apart from that of printer. Between 1549 and 1551 he printed a number of books in Paris, also continuing as type-cutter. By 1557 he was settled in Lyons and had married Antoinette Salamon, whose father, Bernard, was an artist associated with Jean de Tournes. Between 1557 and 1562 Granjon printed about twenty books in types designed by himself, following, after the fashion of the day, the cursive handwriting of the time. These types, usually known as " caractères de civilité," he himself called " lettres françaises," as especially appropriate to his own country. He was granted a monopoly of these types for ten years, but they were soon copied. Granjon appears to have lived in Antwerp for a time, but was at Lyons in 1575 and 1577, and for the next decade at Rome, working for the Vatican and Medici presses, his work consisting largely in cutting exotic types. Towards the end of his life he may have returned to live in Paris, where he died in 1590.

This book was composed, printed, and bound by The Plimpton Press, Norwood, Mass. The paper was manufactured by S. D. Warren Co., Boston.

Date Due

RY

364.97 FORSYTH LIBRARY
main

Five hundred

2 1765 0007 4275 2

PENOLOGY

By Sheldon and Eleanor T. Glueck

FIVE HUNDRED CRIMINAL CAREERS

" I have no hesitation in saying that this is a great contribution to the science of penology. In fact, it may be said to open up a new era in which scientific research will precede action along penological lines." — Sanford Bates, Federal Superintendent of Prisons.

" A book whose conclusions are so sensational that they may radically affect the thought of our time on methods of dealing with the criminal." — *The New York Times.*

By Samuel W. Hartwell

FIFTY–FIVE "BAD" BOYS

" The description Dr. Hartwell gives of the principles, plan and technique he has worked out, his discussion of the fundamental problem and his attitude toward it are so full and frank, so fresh and original, and his account of each case so complete, honest and interested that psychiatrists will find his book stimulating and helpful. To parents and teachers of problem children it ought to bring much illumination of their difficulties." — *The New York Times.*

These are Borzoi Books, published by
ALFRED A. KNOPF

FIVE HUNDRED DELINQUENT WOMEN